SECOND EDITION

THE WESTERN HUMANITIES

Roy T. Matthews & F. DeWitt Platt

MICHIGAN STATE UNIVERSITY

MAYFIELD PUBLISHING COMPANY

MOUNTAIN VIEW, CALIFORNIA
LONDON • TORONTO

Library of Congress Cataloging-in-Publication Data

Matthews, Roy T.
   The western humanities/Roy T. Matthews &
   F. DeWitt Platt—2nd ed.
      p.   cm.
   Includes bibliographical references and index.
   ISBN 1-55934-412-1
   1. Civilization, Western—History.   I. Platt,
   F. DeWitt
II. Title
CB245.M375   1994
909'.09812—dc20

94-16373
CIP

International Standard Book Number information:

The Western Humanities, 2/e	1-55934-412-1
The Western Humanities, 2/e, Volume 1	1-55934-418-0
The Western Humanities, 2/e, Volume 2	1-55934-421-0
Readings in the Western Humanities, Volume 1	1-55934-456-3
Readings in the Western Humanities, Volume 2	1-55934-457-1
The Western Humanities, 2/e (#412-1) with *Readings* Volume 1 and *Readings* Volume 2	1-55934-463-6
The Western Humanities, 2/e (#412-1) with *Readings* Volume 1 (#456-3)	1-55934-464-4
The Western Humanities, 2/e (#412-1) with *Readings* Volume 2 (#457-1)	1-55934-465-2
The Western Humanities, 2/e, Volume 1 (#418-0) with *Readings* Volume 1 (#456-3)	1-55934-466-0
The Western Humanities, 2/e, Volume 2 (#421-0) with *Readings* Volume 2 (#457-1)	1-55934-467-9

Please call Mayfield Publishing Company at (800) 433-1279 to inquire about
additional packaging options.

Manufactured in the United States of America

10 9 8 7 6 5 4 3 2 1

Mayfield Publishing Company
1280 Villa Street
Mountain View, California 94041

Sponsoring editor, Holly J. Allen; developmental editor, Kathleen En-
gelberg; production editors, Carol Zafiropoulos and April Wells-Hayes;
manuscript editor, Beverley DeWitt; art director, Jeanne M. Schreiber; art
manager, Jean Mailander; illustrators, Joan Carol, Judith Ogus, Robin
Mouat, and Jean Mailander; photo editor, Melissa Kreischer; text designer,
Anna Post George; cover designer, Jeanne M. Schreiber; manufacturing
manager, Martha Branch. The text was set in 9½/12 Palatino by
CRWaldman Graphic Communications and printed on 60# Sterling Web
Gloss by the Banta Company.

To Lee Ann and Dixie

There is nothing nobler or more
admirable than when two people
who see eye to eye keep house as
man and wife, confounding their
enemies and delighting their
friends, as they themselves know
better than anyone.

—Homer, *The Odyssey*

PREFACE

Anyone teaching the Western humanities today faces an imposing challenge: overcoming the present-mindedness of the contemporary world. Most students, mirroring society at large, demonstrate little knowledge or even concern about the great artistic and literary monuments and movements of the Western tradition or about the political, economic, and social milestones of Western history. They seem caught up in the popular culture of the moment, forgetful of even the recent past. Very often, when they do recognize a work of art or literature, they still cannot relate it to a specific time or place or to other artistic works. In *The Western Humanities,* we address this problem by placing the cultural achievements of the Western tradition in their historical context. We discuss not only the works that were produced in successive periods but the prevailing historical and material conditions that so powerfully influenced their form and content. Our intention is to demystify the cultural record by showing that literature and the arts do not spring forth spontaneously and independently of each other but reflect a set of specific historical circumstances. By providing this substantial context, out of which both ideas and artifacts emerge, we hope to give students a deeper understanding of the meaning of cultural works and a broader basis for appreciating the humanities.

At the same time that we point out the linkages between cultural expression and historical conditions, we also emphasize the universal aspects of creativity and expression. People everywhere have the impulse to seek answers to the mysteries of human existence; to discover or invent order in the universe; to respond creatively to nature, both inner and outer; to delight the senses and the mind with beauty and truth; to communicate their thoughts and share their visions with others. Thus, another of our intentions is to demonstrate that the desire to express oneself and to create lasting monuments has been a compelling drive in human beings since before the dawn of civilized life. We believe that this emphasis will help students see that they, along with their ideas, questions, and aspirations, are not isolated from the past but belong to a tradition that began thousands of years ago.

Our third aim is to help young people prepare themselves for the uncertainties of the future. When students examine the past and learn how earlier generations confronted and overcame crises—and managed to leave enduring legacies—they will discover that the human spirit is irrepressible. In the humanities—in philosophy, religion, art, music, literature—human beings have found answers to their deepest needs and most perplexing questions. We hope that students will be encouraged by this record as they begin to shape the world of the twenty-first century.

The first edition of *The Western Humanities* was an outgrowth of more than twenty-five years of university teaching for each of us. Instructing thousands of undergraduate students through the years had left us dissatisfied with available textbooks. In our eyes the existing books failed in one of two ways: They either ignored material developments and focused exclusively on cultural artifacts without context or perspective, or they stressed political, social, and economic changes with too little or too disjointed a discussion of literature and the arts. Our goal in writing this book was to balance and integrate these two elements—that is, to provide an analysis and an appreciation of cultural expression and artifacts within an interpretive historical framework. We have been pleasantly surprised by the success of our textbook's first edition. Its adoption at numerous colleges and universities nationwide and in Canada has confirmed the correctness of our initial vision and validated the six seemingly interminable years of work invested in it. With the publication of this second edition, we welcome the opportunity to revise and expand some chapters, thereby strengthening the quality of the book. It is our hope that this new edition of *The Western Humanities* will continue to assist instructors in meeting today's teaching challenges as well as help the next generation of students to understand and claim their cultural heritage.

ORGANIZATION AND CONTENT

The Western Humanities is organized chronologically, in twenty-one chapters, around successive historical periods, from prehistory to the present. In our introduction for students we distinguish three sweeping historical periods—ancient, medieval, and modern—although we do not formally divide our study into parts. We explain that the first of these periods extends from about 3000 B.C. to A.D. 500 and includes the civilizations of Mesopotamia, Egypt, Greece, and Rome (covered in Chapters 1–7). The second period extends from about 500 to 1500, when Western civilization became centered in Europe and was largely dominated by the Christian church (Chapters 8–10). The third period, beginning in about 1400 and extending to the present, witnessed the gradual birth of the modern world (Chapters 11–21). Timelines are provided in the introduction to support these distinctions and to give students a basic framework for the study of the humanities.

In the body of the book, the first part of every chapter, approximately one-third by length, covers the material conditions of the era—the historical, political, economic, and social developments. From the mass of available historical information we have distilled what we consider the crucial points, always aiming to capture the essence of complex periods and to fashion a coherent narrative framework for the story of Western culture. In this discussion many of the major themes, issues, and problems of the period come into view. The remaining part of each chapter is devoted to cultural expression, both in the realm of attitude and idea—philosophy, history, religion, science—and in the realm of cultural artifact—art, music, drama, literature, and film. In this part we describe and analyze the significant cultural achievements of the age, focusing on pervasive themes, choices, and elements of style. We examine how intellectuals, artists, writers, and other creative individuals responded to the challenges presented to them by their society and how they chose values and forms by which to live. Included among these individuals are those whom the Western tradition has often neglected or discounted, namely, women and members of racial and ethnic minorities. Their experiences, roles, and rich contributions are given their rightful place alongside those of the more conventionally favored artists, thinkers, and writers. Expanded culture sections in this second edition reflect even more fully the diverse nature of Western civilization. Beginning with the Early Middle Ages, several women artists, writers, and intellectuals have been added—in sum, eight authors, five painters, and one performance artist, including the writers Christine de Pizan and Aphra Behn and the painters Artemisia Gentileschi and Frida Kahlo. The works of these writers cover a range of literary genres, from histories to plays and novels, and the artists' contributions influenced two major movements in European painting.

The coverage of music has also been expanded in the second edition through inclusion of additional composers who, from the Late Renaissance to Late Modernism, enriched the choices in Western music through their innovative contributions.

As the integrated study of all forms of creative human expression, a survey of the humanities can be unwieldy and confusing for the beginning student. We believe that the clearest and most effective way to present this closely woven web of experience and expression is to untangle the various realms and discuss them separately. Thus, our treatment of cultural achievements is broken down into sections on art, architecture, music, literature, and so on. These sections vary in length, order, and focus from chapter to chapter, just as preferred or more developed forms of expression vary from one period to another. This approach gives students an unobstructed view of each form and reveals the continuities—as well as the strains and disruptions—in that form from one period to the next.

At the same time, we work from a unified perspective and stress the integrated nature of the humanities. We emphasize that the creative works of a particular period represent a coherent response to the unique character and deepest urges of that period. By pointing out linkages and reverberations, we show that the various areas of expression are tied together by shared stylistic elements and by the themes and issues that inform and shape the era. Rather than weave our own synthesis so tightly into this discussion that instructors would have to spend their class time sorting out our point of view from the true subject of the book, we prefer to present the material in as direct a way as possible. We believe this approach gives instructors the flexibility to teach from their own strengths and perspectives, and we invite them to do so. We have paid special attention to sorting out and explaining complex ideas and sequences of events carefully and clearly, to make the study of the humanities accessible to a broad range of students.

Each chapter ends with a brief section describing the cultural legacy of that era. Here we show what achievements proved to be of lasting value and endured into succeeding periods, even to the present day. Students will find that some ideas, movements, or artistic methods with which they are familiar have a very long history indeed. They will also discover that the meaning and ascribed value of cultural objects and texts can change from one time and place to another. Our goal here is not only to help students establish a context for their culture but to show that the humanities have developed as a dynamic series of choices made by individuals in one era and transformed by individuals in other eras. We hope to convey both the richness and the energy of the Western tradition, to which so many have contributed and from which so many have drawn.

SPECIAL FEATURES
AND LEARNING AIDS

In addition to the overall distinctive qualities of *The Western Humanities*—its interpretive context for the humanities, its balanced treatment of history and culture, its focus on the cultural legacy of each period—the book has several specific features that we believe contribute to its usefulness and appeal. Chapter 8 includes an extended discussion and analysis of Islamic history and culture, broadening the horizons of the Western tradition to cover this important area. Chapter 15, another unique chapter, presents a concise discussion of the seventeenth-century revolutions in science and political philosophy that laid the foundations for what we consider modern thinking. In the second edition, in response

to reviewers' suggestions, the history sections in Chapters 19–21 have been reduced in length and the culture sections expanded—without, we believe, harming the proportion of material events to cultural artifacts. The historical narrative in Chapter 21 has been extended to the present day with an analysis of the events of the early 1990s and an expanded discussion of the diverse artists and writers who express themselves in the global style known as Post-Modernism. Throughout the book we consider not just art, literature, and music but also less commonly covered topics such as history, theology, and technology.

The Western Humanities is abundantly illustrated with high-quality photographs—more than 450 in all, over 300 of them in color. Accompanying the illustrations are extended captions that provide information not found in the text about the work, its meaning, its creator, or its linkages with other works. Each chapter opens with a full-page color photograph representative of the period. This photograph is reproduced again in the body of the chapter with an accompanying caption.

Several types of learning aids are incorporated in the text to help students grasp and remember information. Maps appear in every chapter, providing visual orientation, and numerous timelines graphically represent the progression of events and their relation to each other. The judicious use of color in both maps and timelines increases their usefulness. Diagrams and line drawings are provided where careful visual explication is necessary, as in identifying the elements of an architectural style. Tables throughout the text organize historical and cultural information in a succinct and memorable way. The study of the humanities entails the use of many concepts and terms that may be unfamiliar to students. Key terms appear in bold type when they are introduced in the text; they are also defined at the end of the book in an extensive Glossary, which has been expanded in the second edition to include a wider selection of words associated with music and musical instruments, literary terms and forms, and architectural features. Pronunciation guidelines are given in the Glossary where necessary. New terms are listed at the end of each chapter as a review and study aid. In-text pronunciation guides for difficult names of artists and humanists are a new feature of the second edition. In each case, the pronunciation is placed at the point in the text where the individual's contribution is discussed in full, rather than merely mentioned. The Index identifies the page locations for these pronunciations.

The domains of the humanities are so vast that no book can pretend to hold them all. To extend the boundaries of the book we provide annotated suggestions for further reading at the ends of all the chapters. Here we identify and briefly discuss recommended editions or translations of all the primary materials mentioned in the text. Beginning in Chapter 11 we also include annotated suggestions for listening. These sections direct students who are interested in broadening their musical experience to the major or representative works of the composers treated in the text.

A growing concern today is how to help college students become more skillful writers. In response to this need, we have included an appendix on writing research papers and examination essays in the humanities. Here we give general guidelines on writing and more specific suggestions about choosing and researching a topic in the humanities, writing an acceptable college paper, and preparing for exams.

The Western Humanities is also published in an alternative two-volume version. Chapters 1 to 12 are included in Volume I, *Beginnings Through the Renaissance,* and Chapters 11 to 21 are included in Volume II, *The Renaissance to the Present.* For instructors who teach only one part of the course, this version offers flexibility and convenience. Since some schools with two-term courses include the Renaissance in the first term and others in the second, we have included coverage of the Renaissance period in both volumes.

ANCILLARY PACKAGE

As instructors, we are keenly aware of the problems encountered in teaching the humanities, especially to large, diverse classes. We have therefore created an Instructor's Manual, as well as a comprehensive package of ancillary resource materials, designed to help solve those problems.

We believe these supplementary materials will be particularly useful to instructors who must manage large classes. Our Instructor's Manual identifies both general teaching strategies and specific lecture suggestions that can be used to present the humanities and create a lively classroom environment. Each chapter of the manual includes the following sections: teaching strategies and suggestions; a detailed lecture outline accompanied by a listing of historical and cultural developments in non-western cultures (expanded in the second edition); highlighted learning objectives for each chapter; listings of additional resources (film and music suggestions); further suggested readings. We have thoroughly revised and expanded the test items provided at the end of each chapter. The test items are broken down into identification, discussion/essay, and multiple choice questions, with answers keyed to the appropriate pages in the text.

The Instructor's Manual concludes with a section containing forty-five Listening Guides written by Jack Boyd of Abilene Christian College. These guides offer students an introduction to the listening experience by discussing and interpreting specific musical selections, which are available on accompanying compact disks to instructors who have adopted the text. The Listening Guides may be photocopied and distributed to students.

Also available with *The Western Humanities* is an expanded set of slides of art and architecture, along with slides of the maps and timelines from the text. Instructors without access to extensive art and music libraries may find the slides, Listening Guides, and compact disks especially useful. All are designed to help instructors provide their students with an experience of Western art and music that is as direct as possible.

ACKNOWLEDGMENTS

Preparing the second edition of this text has been a rewarding experience for us. The task has been made more enjoyable by the participation and support of many people, whom we want to single out and thank. First, we acknowledge and express gratitude for the help of former students over the years. Their questions and insights have affected the way we address certain issues and frame particular arguments. DeWitt Platt would like especially to thank students from his Artistic and Cultural Traditions of Europe course, who have read their way through the first edition of this text and provided helpful suggestions for this revision. Second, our heartfelt gratitude to Pat Thompson, head of the MSU Art Library, who, as always, has willingly and with a smile aided us with the art and architecture, answering questions, locating relevant materials, and consulting other art librarians around the country via e-mail.

Beyond the confines of MSU, we have also been fortunate in the people who have worked closely with us at Mayfield Publishing Company over the past several months. Though most of those named below only joined this project for the second edition, they have shared our vision and for this we are most appreciative. First and foremost we wish to thank Holly Allen, the sponsoring editor, who has been patient and supportive all the way; her cooperative spirit has made this revision less onerous than we feared. Beverley DeWitt, the copyeditor, is awesome; her eagle eye led to considerable improvements in this revision. Special thanks to April Wells-Hayes, production editor, for her unflappability, good humor, and, most of all, excellent advice about new art in the last two chapters. Also thanks to Carol Zafiropoulos, who guided so professionally the early stages of the production process. Jeanne Schreiber, art director, Melissa Kreischer, photo editor, Jean Mailander, art manager, and Susan Breitbard and Robin Mouat, production artists, have worked to transform our manuscript into this beautiful book; we thank you.

We offer our thanks to the following academic reviewers for their criticism and their encouragement:

First edition reviewers: Lawrence Bryant, California State University, Chico; Charles H. Cutter, San Diego State University; David H. Darst, Florida State University; Sterling Eisiminger, Clemson University; Ann W. Engar, University of Utah; Jon D. Green, Brigham Young University; Fred W. Hallberg, University of Northern Iowa; Stephen L. Harris, California State University, Sacramento; Mark Hawkins, Foothill College; Robert E. Lynch, New Jersey Institute of Technology; Frederic H. Miller, California State University, Fullerton; George E. Moore, San Jose State University; Christine Oravec, University of Utah; Don Porter, College of San Mateo; Irvin M. Roth, Foothill College; Stanley J. Underdal, San Jose State University; and Audrey V. Wilson, Florida State University.

Second edition reviewers: Jan Allen, Seminole Community College; Lynn Bartholome, Ferris State University; Camille Caruso, West Virginia University; Judith Chambers, Hillsboro Community College, Dale Mabry Campus; Eugene A. Greco, Miami-Dade Community College, South Campus; Laurie Holton, St. Petersburg Junior College; Stephen C. Law, University of Central Oklahoma; Paul Satzman, Suffolk Community College; Robert Turley, University of Toledo; Judy Wagner, St. Johns River Community College; and Sheila D. Willard, Middlesex Community College.

CONTENTS

1
PREHISTORY AND NEAR EASTERN CIVILIZATIONS   *1*

2
AEGEAN CIVILIZATION:
The Minoans, the Mycenaeans, and the Greeks of the Archaic Age   *27*

6
JUDAISM AND THE RISE OF CHRISTIANITY   135

7
LATE ROMAN CIVILIZATION   159

8
THE SUCCESSORS OF ROME: Byzantium, Islam, and the Early Medieval West   181

9
THE HIGH MIDDLE AGES: The Christian Centuries   209

10
THE LATE MIDDLE AGES:
1300–1500   243

11
THE EARLY
RENAISSANCE: Return
to Classical Roots,
1400–1494   273

12
THE HIGH RENAISSANCE
AND EARLY MANNERISM:
1494–1564   299

18
**THE TRIUMPH OF
THE BOURGEOISIE:
1830–1871**   *461*

19
**THE AGE OF EARLY
MODERNISM:
1871–1914**   *489*

20
**THE AGE OF THE MASSES
AND THE ZENITH
OF MODERNISM:
1914–1945**   *523*

21
THE AGE OF ANXIETY AND BEYOND: 1945–   *553*

INTRODUCTION
Why Study Cultural History?

To be ignorant of what occurred before you were born is to remain always a child.
— CICERO, FIRST CENTURY B.C.

Anyone who cannot give an account to oneself of the past three thousand years remains in darkness, without experience, living from day to day.
— GOETHE, NINETEENTH CENTURY A.D.

The underlying premise of this book is that some basic knowledge of the Western cultural heritage is necessary for those who want to become educated human beings in charge of their own destinies. If people are not educated into their place in human history—five thousand years of relatively uninterrupted though sometimes topsy-turvy developments—then they are rendered powerless, subject to passing fads and outlandish beliefs. They become vulnerable to the flattery of demagogues who promise heaven on earth, or they fall prey to the misconception that present-day events are unique, without precedent in history, or superior to everything that has gone before.

Perhaps the worst that can happen is to exist in a limbo of ignorance—in Goethe's words, "living from day to day." Without knowledge of the past and the perspective it brings, people may come to believe that their contemporary world will last forever, when in reality much of it is doomed to be forgotten. In contrast to the instant obsolescence of popular culture, the study of Western culture offers an alternative that has passed the unforgiving test of time. Long after today's heroes and celebrities have fallen into oblivion, the achievements of our artistic

and literary ancestors—those who have forged the Western tradition—will remain. Their works echo down the ages and seem fresh in every period. The ancient Roman writer Seneca put it well when he wrote, in the first century A.D., "Life is short but art is long."

When people realize that the rich legacy of Western culture is their own, their view of themselves and the times they live in can expand beyond the present moment. They find that they need not be confined by the limits of today but can draw on the creative insights of people who lived hundreds and even thousands of years ago. They discover that their own culture has a history and a context that give it meaning and shape. Studying and experiencing their cultural legacy can help them understand their place in today's world.

THE BOUNDARIES OF THE WEST

The subject of this volume is Western culture, but what exactly do we mean, first, by "culture," and second, by the "West"? *Culture* is a term with several meanings, but we use it here to mean the artistic and intellectual expressions of a people, their creative achievements. By the *West* we mean that part of the globe that lies west of Asia and Asia Minor and north of Africa, especially Europe—the geographical framework for much of this study.

The Western tradition is not confined exclusively to Europe as defined today, however. The contributions of peoples who lived beyond the boundaries of present-day Europe are also included in Western culture, either because they were forerunners of the West, such as those who created the first civilizations in Mesopotamia and Egypt, or because they were part of the West for periods of time, such as those who lived in the North African and Near Eastern lands bordering the Mediterranean Sea during the Roman and early Christian eras. Regardless of geography, Western culture draws deeply from ideals forged in these lands.

When areas that had been part of the Western tradition at one time were absorbed into other cultural traditions, as happened in Mesopotamia, Egypt, and North Africa in the seventh century when the people embraced the Muslim faith, then they are generally no longer included in Western cultural history. Because of the enormous influence of Islamic civilization on Western civilization, however, we do include in this volume both an account of Islamic history and a description and appreciation of Islamic culture. Different in many ways from our own, the rich tradition of Islam has an important place in today's world.

After about 1500, with voyages and explorations reaching the farthest parts of the globe, the European focus of Western culture that had held for centuries began to dissolve. Starting from this time, the almost exclusive European mold was broken and Western values and ideals began to be exported throughout the world, largely through the efforts of missionaries, soldiers, colonists, and merchants. Coinciding with this development and further complicating the pattern of change were the actions of those who imported and enslaved countless numbers of black Africans to work on plantations in North and South America. The interplay of Western culture with many previously isolated cultures, whether desired or not, forever changed all who were touched by the process.

The Westernization of the globe that has been going on ever since 1500 is perhaps the dominant theme of the twentieth century. What human greed, missionary zeal, and dreams of empire failed to accomplish prior to 1900 has been achieved in this century by modern technology, the media, and popular culture. The world today is a global village, much of it dominated by Western values and styles of life. In our time, Westernization has become a two-way interchange. When artists and writers from other cultures adopt Western forms or ideas, they are not only Westernizing their own traditions but also injecting fresh sensibilities and habits of thought into the Western tradition. The globalization of culture means that a South American novel or a Japanese film can be as accessible to Western audiences as a European painting and yet carry with it an intriguingly new vocabulary of cultural symbols and meanings.

HISTORICAL PERIODS AND CULTURAL STYLES

In cultural history the past is often divided into historical periods and cultural styles. A historical period is an interval of time that has a certain unity because it is characterized by the prevalence of a unique culture, ideology, or technology or because it is bounded by defining historical events, such as the death of a military leader like Alexander the Great or a political upheaval like the fall of Rome. A cultural style is a combination of features of artistic or literary expression, execution, or performance that define a particular school or era. A historical period may have the identical time frame as a cultural style, or it may embrace more than one style simultaneously or two styles successively. Each chapter of this survey focuses on a historical period and includes significant aspects of culture—usually the arts, architecture, literature, religion, music, and philosophy—organized around a discussion of the relevant style or styles appropriate to that time.

The survey begins with prehistory, the era before writing was invented, setting forth the emergence of human beings from an obscure past. After the appearance of writing in about 3000 B.C., the Western cultural heritage is divided into three sweeping historical periods: ancient, medieval, and modern.

The ancient period dates from 3000 B.C. to A.D. 500 (Time Line 1). During these thirty-five hundred years the light of Western civilization begins to shine in Mesopotamia and Egypt, shines more brightly still in eighth-century B.C. Greece and Rome, loses some of its luster when Greece succumbs to Rome in 146 B.C., and finally is snuffed out when the Roman empire collapses in the fifth century A.D. Coinciding with these historical periods are the cultural styles of Mesopotamia; Egypt; Greece, including Archaic, Classical (or Hellenic), and Hellenistic styles; and Rome, including Republican and Imperial styles.

The medieval period, or the Middle Ages, covers events between A.D. 500 and 1500, a one-thousand-year span that is further divided into three subperiods (Time Line 2). The Early Middle Ages (500–1000) is typified by frequent barbarian invasions and political chaos so that civilization itself is threatened

TIME LINE 1   **THE ANCIENT WORLD**

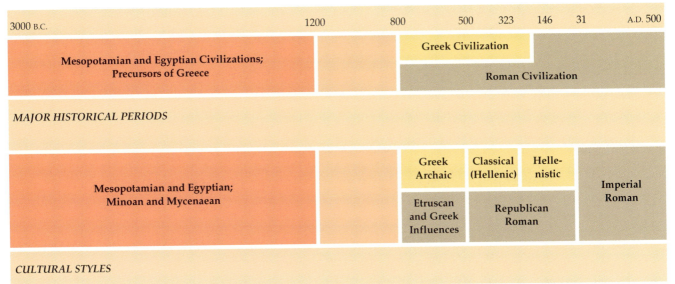

and barely survives. No single international style characterizes this turbulent period, though several regional styles flourish. The High Middle Ages (1000–1300) is a period of stability and the zenith of medieval culture. Two successive styles appear, the Romanesque and the Gothic, with the latter dominating culture for the rest of the medieval period. The Late Middle Ages (1300–1500) is a transitional period in which the medieval age is dying and the modern age is struggling to be born.

The modern period begins in about 1400 (there is often overlap between historical periods) and continues today (Time Line 3). With the advent of the modern period a new way of defining historical changes starts to make more sense—the division of history into movements, the activities of large groups of people united to achieve a common goal.

The modern period consists of waves of movements that aim to change the world in some specific way.

The first modern movement is the Renaissance (1400–1600), or "rebirth," which attempts to revive the cultural values of ancient Greece and Rome. It is accompanied by two successive styles, Renaissance style and Mannerism. The next significant movement is the Reformation (1500–1600), which is dedicated to restoring Christianity to the ideals of the early church set forth in the Bible. Although it does not spawn a specific style, this religious upheaval does have a profound impact on the subjects of the arts and literature and the way they are expressed, especially in the Mannerist style.

The Reformation is followed by the Scientific Revolution (1600–1700), a movement that results in the abandonment of ancient science and the birth of

TIME LINE 2   **THE MEDIEVAL WORLD**

TIME LINE 3   THE MODERN WORLD

modern science. Radical in its conclusions, the Scientific Revolution is somewhat out of touch with the style of its age, which is known as the Baroque. This magnificent style is devoted to overwhelming the senses through theatrical and sensuous effects and is associated with the attempts of the Roman Catholic church to reassert its authority in the world.

The Scientific Revolution gives impetus to the Enlightenment (1700–1800), a movement that pledges to reform politics and society according to the principles of the new science. In stylistic terms the eighteenth century is schizophrenic, dominated first by the Rococo, an extravagant and fanciful style that represents the last phase of the Baroque, and then by the Neoclassical, a style inspired by the works of ancient Greece and Rome and reflective of the principles of the Scientific Revolution. Before the eighteenth century is over the Enlightenment calls forth its antithesis, Romanticism (1770–1870), a movement centered on feeling, fantasy, and everything that cannot be proven scientifically. The Romantic style, marked by a revived taste for the Gothic and a love of nature, is the perfect accompaniment to this movement.

Toward the end of the nineteenth century Modernism (1870–1970) arises, bent on destroying every vestige of both the Greco-Roman tradition and the Christian faith and on fashioning new ways of understanding that are independent of the past. Since 1970 Post-Modernism has emerged, a movement that tries to make peace with the past by embracing old forms of expression while at the same time adopting a global and multivoiced perspective.

Although every cultural period is marked by innovation and creativity, our treatment of them in this book varies somewhat, with more space and greater weight given to the achievements of certain times. We make these adjustments because some periods

or styles are more significant than others, especially in the defining influence that their achievements have had on our own era. For example, some styles seem to tower over the rest, such as Classicism in fifth-century-B.C. Greece, the High Renaissance of sixteenth-century Italy, and Modernism in the mid–twentieth century, as compared to other styles, such as that of the Early Middle Ages or the seventeenth-century Baroque.

AN INTEGRATED APPROACH TO CULTURAL HISTORY

Our approach to the Western heritage in this book is to root cultural achievements in their historical settings, showing how the material conditions—the political, social, and economic events of each period—influenced their creation. About one-third of each chapter is devoted to an interpretive discussion of material history, and the remaining two-thirds are devoted to the arts, architecture, philosophy, religion, literature, and music of the period. These two aspects of history do not occur separately, of course, and one of our aims is to show how they are intertwined.

As just one example of this integrated approach, consider the Gothic cathedral, that lofty, light-filled house of worship marked by pointed arches, towering spires, and radiant stained glass windows. Gothic cathedrals were erected during the High Middle Ages, following a bleak period when urban life had virtually ceased. Although religion was still the dominant force in European life, trade was starting to flourish once again, town life was reviving, and urban dwellers were beginning to prosper. In part as testimonials to their new wealth, cities and towns commissioned architects and hired workers to erect these soaring churches, which dominated the landscape for miles around and proclaimed the economic well-being of their makers.

We adopt an integrated approach to Western culture not just in considering how the arts are related to material conditions but also in looking for the common themes, aspirations, and ideas that permeate the artistic and literary expressions of every individual era. The creative accomplishments of an age tend to reflect a shared perspective, even when this perspective is not explicitly recognized at the time. Thus, each period possesses a unique outlook that can be analyzed in the cultural record. A good example of this phenomenon is Classical Greece in the fifth century B.C., when the ideal of moderation, or balance in all things, played a major role in sculpture, architecture, philosophy, religion, and tragic drama. The cultural record in other periods is not always as clear as that in ancient Greece, but shared qualities can often be uncovered that distinguish the varied aspects of culture in an era to form a unifying thread.

A corollary of this idea is that creative individuals and their works are very much influenced by the times in which they live. This is not to say that incomparable geniuses—like Shakespeare in Renaissance England—do not appear and rise above their own ages, speaking directly to the human mind and heart in every age that follows. Yet even Shakespeare reflected the political attitudes and social patterns of his time. Though a man for the ages, he still regarded monarchy as the correct form of government and women as the inferiors of men.

THE SELECTION OF CULTURAL WORKS

The Western cultural heritage is vast, and any selection of works for a survey text reflects choices made by the authors. All of the works we chose to include have had a significant impact on Western culture, but for different reasons. We chose some because

they blazed a new trail, such as Picasso's *Demoiselles d'Avignon* (see Figure 19.19), which marked the advent of Cubism in painting, or Fielding's *Tom Jones*, one of the earliest novels. Other works were included because they seemed to embody a style to perfection, such as the regal statue called *Poseidon* (or *Zeus*) (see Figure 3.20), executed in the Classical style of fifth-century Athens, or Dante's *Divine Comedy*, which epitomized the ideals of the High Middle Ages. Still other works caught our attention because they served as links between successive styles, as is the case with Giotto's frescoes (see Figure 10.18), or because they represented the end of an age or an artistic style, as in the haunting sculpture called *The Last Pagan* (see Figure 7.15). Finally, we included some works, especially paintings, simply because of their great beauty, such as Chardin's *Little Girl Playing Shuttlecock* (see Figure 16.1) or Roberts's *The Conversation* (see Figure 21.25).

Through all the ages of Western cultural history, through all the shifting styles and tastes embodied in painting, sculpture, architecture, poetry, and song, there glows a creative spark that can be found in human beings in every period. This diversity is a hallmark of the Western experience, and we celebrate it in this book.

A CHALLENGE TO THE READER

The purpose of all education is and should be self-knowledge. This goal was first established by the ancient Greeks in their injunction to "Know thyself," the inscription carved above the entrance to Apollo's temple at Delphi. Self-knowledge means awareness of oneself and one's place in society and the world. Reaching this goal is not easy, because becoming an educated human being is a lifelong process, requiring time, energy, and commitment. But all journeys begin with a single step, and we intend this volume as a first step toward understanding and defining oneself in terms of one's historical and cultural heritage. Our challenge to the reader is to use this book to begin the long journey to self-knowledge.

PREHISTORY
AND NEAR EASTERN
CIVILIZATIONS

A man or woman born in the West in the earlier part of this century and still living today has seen more change in a lifetime than previous generations experienced for hundreds of years. Yet despite the rapid rate of change in modern times, Western civilization stands firmly on a foundation that is almost five thousand years old, and people in the West often turn back to this foundation to discover their heritage and to cast new light on their values. As the clock seems to speed up, the past becomes increasingly important as a guide to the future.

Before we begin to explore this heritage and what it means today, we need to discuss two important terms—*culture* and *civilization*. **Culture** usually refers to the sum of human endeavors: methods and practices for survival; political, economic, and social institutions; and values, beliefs, and the arts. ***Civilization***, on the other hand, refers to the way people live in a complex political, economic, and social structure, usually in an urban setting and usually after making certain technological and artistic advances. Culture is passed from one generation to another by human behavior, speech, and artifacts; civilization is transmitted primarily by writing (Figure 1.1). The term *culture* can also be used to refer to the creative, artistic, and intellectual expressions of a civilization. We will use the term in both these senses. In the words of Matthew Arnold, the nineteenth-century English poet and critic, culture is

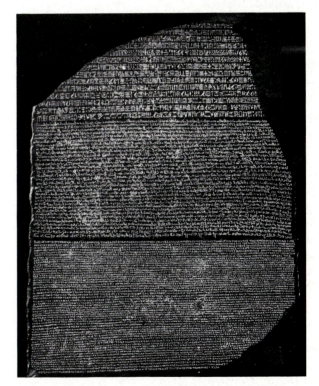

FIGURE 1.1   Rosetta Stone. Ca. 197–196 B.C. British Museum. *Although scholars knew that Egypt had a writing system, they were unable to solve the mystery of hieroglyphics until the nineteenth century. The key was provided by the Rosetta Stone, discovered by members of Napoleon's expedition when he invaded Egypt in 1799. On the stone the same event is described in hieroglyphics, in Egyptian cursive script, and in Greek. By comparing the Greek text with the other two, scholars were able to decipher both Egyptian scripts. This discovery marks the origin of modern Egyptology.*

◀   *Nefertiti*: Ca. 1350 B.C. Agyptisches Museum, Berlin.

"the best that has been thought and said." To this we would add, "and done."

PREHISTORY AND EARLY CULTURES

Where and when does the story of human culture begin? The latest evidence from paleoanthropology, the study of early human life, indicates that human beings originated in the distant past in lands far from western Europe. Human development thus begins during prehistory, long before our predecessors compiled—or could compile—written records of their cultures. The first ancestors of human beings probably appeared about four to five million years ago. Although this seems ancient, it's recent compared to the appearance of life forms on earth, estimated at two to three billion years ago, and to the formation of the planet itself, believed to have occurred some four to six billion years ago.

The periods of time involved in these processes are so vast that only metaphors can make them comprehensible. If we take the seven-day week, made familiar by the biblical account of creation, and combine it with recent scientific estimates about when the earth and life began, then the following analogy may be made. The earth was created just after midnight on Monday morning, the first life appeared about Thursday noon, and the early ancestors of human beings didn't show up until about eleven o'clock on Sunday night. To complete the analogy, the birth of civilization occurred almost an hour

later, in the last tenth of a second before midnight on the last day of the week.

Although the record of human evolution is incomplete and obscured by time, sufficient evidence exists to show that hominids, the earliest primate ancestors of modern humans, probably originated in eastern Africa. From among them, about two million years ago, the genus *Homo* evolved, a form marked by a larger brain and the ability to adapt somewhat to the environment. Hominids of the *Homo* genus made and used tools and developed rudimentary cultures. Anthropologists designate this earliest cultural period as the *Paleolithic*, or Old Stone Age. It corresponds to the geological period known as the Pleistocene epoch, or Ice Age, the time of extensive climate changes caused by the advance and retreat of massive glaciers (Time Line 1.1).

Stone Age culture spread widely over a vast area, but remains of hominid life are scarce and incomplete. Evidence indicates that hominids lived in packs, followed herds of wandering animals, and ate wild seasonal fruits and vegetables. Anthropologists believe that duties and work divided along sex lines as all-male teams hunted game for meat and fur while females and children gathered plant foods, prepared meals, and tended the young. During the night, all sought shelter together in caves for safety and refuge against the elements. This way of life hinged on cooperation and food sharing among small social groups.

In the early Old Stone Age, or Lower Paleolithic, hominids invented crude stone tools, used fire, and probably developed speech—a major breakthrough that allowed them to communicate in ways denied

TIME LINE 1.1   GEOLOGICAL TIME AND PREHISTORIC CULTURAL PERIODS   All dates approximate and B.C.

FIGURE 1.2 Bison Cave Painting. Ca. 14,000–12,000 B.C. Altamira, Spain. *This polychrome bison, one of several on the cave's ceiling, is outlined in black and colored in red. These bison varied in size from 4 to 6 feet long. Whether the animals were painted separately or as part of a total design is unknown, but the artist has succeeded in capturing the strength and power of the beasts.*

other animals. Their first tools were simple choppers and, somewhat later, hand axes. In the Middle Paleolithic, more advanced hominids developed pointed tools and scrapers, which they chiseled with precision and care. In the Upper Paleolithic, double-faced blades became common.

By about 200,000 B.C. the species *Homo sapiens* had evolved from earlier hominids, and between 50,000 and 30,000 B.C. this species apparently displaced other, less advanced hominids. More fully developed physically and mentally, they slowly spread throughout the Eastern Hemisphere and eventually migrated into the Western Hemisphere over the land bridge between Siberia and Alaska. Their tools were more sophisticated and included bows and arrows, fishhooks, and needles. By this time, they were living together cooperatively, burying their dead with rit-

uals, and beginning to paint and sculpt. Especially through their cave paintings and carved figurines, these ancestors of ours made a breakthrough to symbolic thought.

Paintings of reindeer, bison, and horses in caves in Altamira, Spain, and Lascaux, France, dating from the Upper Paleolithic, are the earliest examples of human art. Many of these paintings, located deep in caves, were probably used as part of ceremonies and rituals prior to a hunting expedition. By painting numerous wild animals pierced with arrows, the artists were attempting to ensure a successful hunt that would supply the tribe with food (Figure 1.2). The ritual participants were, in effect, practicing magic.

Another type of Upper Paleolithic art was the carved female figurine, found at Willendorf, Austria (Figure 1.3). Made of limestone, the statue is faceless

FIGURE 1.3 Figurine from Willendorf. Ca. 25,000 B.C. Museum Naturhistorisches, Vienna. *Discovered around A.D. 1908, this female statuette measures just under 5 inches high. Carved from limestone, it still shows evidence of having been painted red. Many other statues like it have been discovered, but this one remains the most famous because of the unusual balance it strikes between symbolism and realism.*

and rotund. The distended stomach and full breasts suggest that the figurine was used as a fertility symbol and image of a mother goddess, representing the creative power of nature. As a mythological figure, the mother goddess appeared in many ancient cultures, beginning in Paleolithic times. This figurine may have been used in religious ceremonies to ensure the propagation of the tribe, or, as Earth goddess, to guarantee a bountiful supply of food. The statue also reveals the aesthetic interests of the sculptor, who took care to depict the figure's hands resting on her breasts and the rows of tightly knit hair.

As the last glaciers retreated from Europe, as tundra and steppes gave way to forests and herds of reindeer and elephants were replaced by elk and deer, human beings were forced to adapt to new living conditions. Their stone tools became more advanced and included knives and hammers. Following a transitional period known as the Mesolithic (about 10,000–8000 B.C.), a transformation occurred that has been called the most important event in human history: Hunters and gatherers became farmers and herders. Thus began the *Neolithic* period, or New Stone Age (about 8000 B.C.). At various places all over the world—in southeast Asia, in Central America, in parts of South America, and in the Near East—human beings ceased their nomadic existence and learned to domesticate wild animals by herding them together, breeding them, and using them as beasts of burden and sources of food and hides. They learned to plow the earth and sow the seeds of wild grains and grasses, providing themselves with a much more reliable food supply. This in turn encouraged the development of permanent settlements and eventually the rise of urban centers. The agrarian pattern of life begun at this time dominated the West until about two hundred years ago.

Precisely why and how the agrarian revolution came at this time is a hotly debated topic among anthropologists. Nonetheless, most agree that with the retreat of the last glaciers from Europe, methods of food gathering changed dramatically, causing either surpluses or shortages. In some areas, grain surpluses allowed populations to grow, and this led to forced migrations as the number of humans outstripped the available food. In less productive lands, the people began to experiment with domesticating animals and planting grains. These innovations in marginal lands caused food production to rise, soon matching that found in more fertile areas, so that eventually a uniform agricultural economy spread to many parts of the globe. Thus, economic causes accounted for the transformation from food-gathering to food-producing cultures.

The agricultural revolution expanded across the Near East and probably into Europe and Africa. Between 6000 and 3000 B.C. human beings also learned to mine and use copper, ending the Neolithic Period and ushering in the Age of Metals. In about 3000 B.C., artisans combined copper and tin to produce bronze, a strong alloy, which they used in their tools, weapons, and jewelry.

The Bronze Age, which extended from about 3000 to about 1200 B.C., gave rise to two major civilizations in the Near East. The earlier developed in Mesopotamia, the land between the Tigris and Euphrates rivers (in present-day Iraq), and the other, probably emerging just slightly later, originated along the Nile River in Egypt. Mesopotamian and Egyptian civilizations shared certain characteristics: Both were ruled by kings who were in turn supported by a priestly caste; their economies were slave-based; their societies were stratified, with class privileges at the upper end; small, educated elites shared power with the rulers; and palaces and religious edifices were built for ceremonial and governmental purposes. These early civilizations made deep and lasting impressions on their neighbors and successors that helped shape life in the Western world.

THE CIVILIZATIONS OF THE TIGRIS AND EUPHRATES RIVER VALLEY: MESOPOTAMIA

The Tigris-Euphrates river valley forms part of what is known as the Fertile Crescent, which starts at the Persian Gulf, runs slightly northwestward through the Tigris-Euphrates valley, and then turns westerly to the Mediterranean Sea and curves south along the shoreline toward Egypt (Map 1.1). This arc of land contained some of the most arable soil in the Near East, many of the heavily traveled trade routes, and most of the early centers of civilization.

Mesopotamia is a Greek word meaning "land between the two rivers." The hill country and Zagros Mountains rise to the east of the Tigris-Euphrates valley, and the vast Arabian desert stretches to the west. The twin rivers course down to the Persian Gulf, draining an area approximately 600 miles long and 250 miles wide. Near the mouth of the gulf, on the river delta, human wanderers settled down in about 6000 B.C., founding villages and tilling the land. Despite the heat, the marshes, the unpredictable, violent floods that swept down the river valleys, and the invaders who came from both the mountains and the desert, some of these communities prospered and grew.

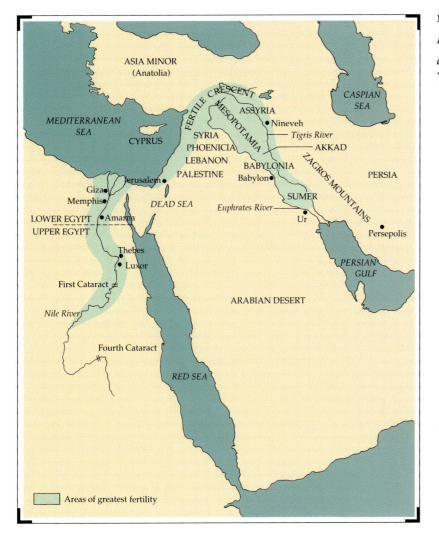

MAP 1.1

Mesopotamia and Ancient Egypt: The Fertile Crescent

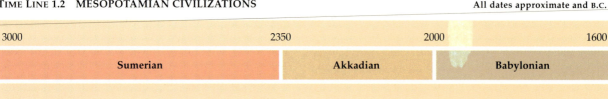

The Sumerian, Akkadian, and Babylonian Kingdoms

Three successive civilizations—Sumerian, Akkadian, and Babylonian—flourished in Mesopotamia over a period of nearly 1500 years (Time Line 1.2). The Sumerians established the first of these, and, indeed, as historian Samuel Kramer asserts, "History began at Sumer." The rulers of Sumer created an exalted image of a just and stable society with a rich cultural life, a standard that captured the imagination of their people and was adopted eventually by friend and foe alike.

Sumer's most inspirational king, Gilgamesh [GILL-guh-mesh], ruled during the first Dynasty of Ur (about 2700 B.C.), a state centered between the rivers. Because of his adventures and exploits, this king was later immortalized as a hero in the poem *The Epic of Gilgamesh*. A second ruler, Urukagina, reformed the law codes and sponsored public works projects near the end of the Sumerian period, about 2350 B.C. His reforms, following years of harsh and unfair rule, restored the rights of his subjects and revitalized the economy. Yet Urukagina's vision failed in its goal. The despotic policies and domestic squabbles of his successors weakened Sumer and made the cities an easy prey for the Akkadians of northern Mesopotamia.

The Akkadian dynasties, lasting from about 2350 to about 2000 B.C., incorporated the Sumerian way of life into their own society and carried this hybrid civilization far beyond the Tigris-Euphrates valley. According to legends—which are similar to the later story of the Hebrew leader, Moses—Sargon, the first and greatest Akkadian ruler, was born of lowly origins and abandoned at birth in the reed marshes; yet Sargon survived and rose to prominence at the Sumerian court. Excavated inscriptions reveal that Sargon conquered the Sumerians and founded a far-flung empire to the east and northeast. At its height, Sargon's power was felt from Egypt to India, but his successors, lacking his intelligence and skill, could not hold the Akkadian empire together. The incursions of the Guti tribes from the Zagros Mountains brought about the final collapse of the weakened Akkadian empire and the division of southern Mesopotamia into petty kingdoms.

Babylonia was the third civilization in Mesopotamia. From northern Mesopotamia, their power base, the Babylonians governed the entire valley from about 2000 to 1600 B.C. Under their most successful military leader and renowned law giver, Hammurabi [ham-uh-RAHB-e] (1792–1750 B.C.), the Babylonians reached their political and cultural ascendancy. However, the ruler of the Old Hittite Kingdom, a state centered in Asia Minor, invaded Babylon in about 1600 B.C. and toppled the dynasty of Hammurabi.

Agriculture dominated the economy of Mesopotamia throughout its long history. Harsh living conditions and unpredictable floods forced the inhabitants to learn to control the rivers through irrigation systems and cooperative tilling of the soil. In the earlier years, the farmers planted small scattered holdings beside the river's banks, using crude tools to direct the sluggish water onto their crops through short channels. Later, they dug a complex canal system to irrigate their cultivated plots, which might lie some distance from the river. As production increased, prosperity allowed larger populations to thrive. Villages soon grew into small cities—with populations ranging from 10,000 to 50,000—surrounded by hamlets and tilled fields. Trade developed with nearby areas, and wheeled vehicles—perfected by the Sumerians—and sailboats carried goods up and down Mesopotamia and eventually throughout the Fertile Crescent.

By the beginning of the Bronze Age, the family had replaced the tribe or clan as the basic unit in society. Families now owned their lands outright. In cooperation with and under the general direction of the religious and secular authorities, families worked their fields and maintained the irrigation ditches. Marriages were arranged by parents, who always made economics an essential consideration in such matters. According to the law codes, women possessed some rights, such as holding property; but a wife was clearly under her husband's power. Divorce was easier for men than for women, and women were punished more severely than men for breaking moral and marital laws. Recent scholarship has suggested that women's status and roles became more limited as the state apparatus in Mesopotamia became more complex. In sum, from being able to participate actively in economic, religious, and political life so long as their dependence on and obligation to male kin and husbands were observed, women in Mesopotamian culture progressively lost their relative independence because rulers extended the concept of patriarchy (rule by the fathers) from family practice into public law.

The political structure reflected the order and functions of the social system. At the top stood the ruler who, depending on the time and circumstances, might be a powerful king or merely a local lord. He was supported by an army, bureaucracy, judicial system, and priesthood. The king usually obtained advice from prominent leaders, meeting in council, who constituted the next layer of the social order: rich landowners, wealthy merchants, priests, and military chiefs. The next group consisted of artisans, craftspeople, and petty businesspeople and traders. Below them were small landowners and tenant farmers. At the bottom of the social scale were serfs and slaves, who had either been captured in war or had fallen into debt.

The Cradle of Civilization

The three Mesopotamian civilizations responded to the same geography, climate, and natural resources, and their cultures reflected this shared background. The Sumerians were probably the most influential: From Sumer came writing, the lunar calendar, a mathematical computation system, medical and scientific discoveries, and architectural innovations. However, each civilization, through its religion, literature, law, and art, deeply affected other Near Eastern people.

Writing Thousands of clay tablets inscribed with the wedge-shaped symbols of Sumerian script have been uncovered in Mesopotamia, indicating that the Sumerians had developed a form of writing by 3000 B.C. With the invention of writing, new roads opened up for human cultures. Now, people no longer had to rely on memory, speech, and person-to-person interactions to communicate and transmit information. Instead, they could create a permanent body of knowledge that could accumulate and be passed on from one generation to the next. With writing came the possibility of civilization.

At first, the Sumerians needed a simple way to keep agricultural and business records and to record the deeds and sayings of their rulers. Their earliest symbols are *pictograms*, or pictures, carefully drawn to represent particular objects. To these they added *ideograms*, pictures drawn to represent ideas or concepts. A simple drawing of a bowl, for example, could be used to mean "food." As these pictures became more and more stylized, meaning began to be transferred from the represented object to the sign itself; that is, the sign began to stand for a word rather than an object.

Later, Sumerian scribes and writers identified the syllabic sounds of spoken words and created *phonograms*, symbols for separate speech sounds, borrowing from and building on the earlier pictograms and ideograms. The written symbols now represented sounds rather than objects or ideas. These simplified and standardized symbols eventually resulted in a phonetic writing system of syllable-based sounds that, when combined, produced words (Figure 1.4). (It was left to later civilizations to separate vowel sounds from syllables and thus create a true alphabet, based on individual speech sounds.)

	1	2	3	4	5
Man					
Ox					
To Eat					

FIGURE 1.4 Sumerian Cuneiform Writing. Ca. 3000–1000 B.C. *The columns illustrate the evolution of Sumerian writing from pictograms to script. Column one shows the pictogram: a man, an ox, and the verb "to eat" (represented by the mouth and a bowl). In column two, the pictographic symbols have been turned 90 degrees, as the Sumerians did in their first writing. Columns three and four show how the script changed between 2500 and 1800 B.C. Column five is an Assyrian adaptation of the Sumerian cuneiform script.*

The Sumerians could now express complex, abstract concepts, and their system could be used to write other languages. The Akkadians and Babylonians adopted and modified the Sumerian script to keep records and preserve their literature, including *The Epic of Gilgamesh* and the Code of Hammurabi. By the end of the Bronze Age (about 1200 B.C.), other written languages existed, but Akkadian-Sumerian was the language of diplomacy and trade in the Near East.

The Sumerian writing system has been labeled *cuneiform*, a term derived from the Latin word *cuneus*, which means "wedge." Using wedge-shaped reeds or styluses, scribes pressed the symbols into wet clay tablets, and artists and craftspeople, wielding metal tools, incised the script into stone monuments or cylindrical pillars. Preserved for thousands of years in hardened clay and stone, cuneiform writing has provided invaluable insight into the life and culture of ancient Mesopotamia.

Religion   Sumerian, Akkadian, and Babylonian religions, despite individual differences, shared many basic attitudes and concepts that became the foundation for other Near Eastern belief systems. The underlying beliefs of Mesopotamian religion were that the gods had created human beings to serve them, that the gods were in complete control, and that powerless mortals had no choice but to obey and worship these deities. The hostile climate and unpredictable rivers made life precarious, and the gods appeared capricious. The Mesopotamians held a vague notion of a shadowy netherworld where the dead rested, but they did not believe in an afterlife as such or any rewards or punishments upon death. Happiness seldom was an earthly goal; pessimism ran as a constant theme throughout their religion and literature.

Mesopotamian religion had three important characteristics. It was *polytheistic*—many gods and goddesses existed and often competed with one another; it was *anthropomorphic*—the deities possessed human form and had their own personalities and unique traits; and it was *pantheistic*—hundreds of divinities were found everywhere, in nature and the universe. Since Mesopotamians thought of their gods in human form with all the strengths and weaknesses of mortals, they believed their deities lived in the same way as people, and they were pragmatic in approaching the supernatural powers. For example, they believed that their deities held council, made decisions, and ordered the forces of nature to wreak havoc or to bestow plenty on mortals.

Mesopotamians divided the deities into two basic groups, the sky gods and the earth gods. In these two categories were the four major deities: Anu, the heaven god; Enlil, the air god; Enki, the water god; and Ninhursag, the mother goddess. Enlil emerged as the most powerful god for the Sumerians. He gave mortals the plough and the pickaxe, and he brought forth for humanity all the productive forces of the universe, such as trees, grains, and "whatever was needful." Although Enlil had to carry out the orders of the other gods, who often set off waves of destruction, he was not a god of misdeeds.

Rituals, ceremonies, and the priesthood were absolutely essential to Mesopotamian religion. Although the average Mesopotamian might participate in worship services, the priests played the central role in all religious functions. They also controlled and administered large parcels of land, which enhanced their power in religious as well as economic and political matters. Priests carefully formulated and consciously followed the procedures for rites and rituals, which were written down and stored in their temples. This cultic literature not only told the Mesopotamians how to worship but also informed them about their deities' origins, characteristics, and deeds. Religious myths and instructions constituted a major part of Mesopotamian literature and made writing an essential component of the culture.

Literature   Of the surviving epics, tales, and legends that offer glimpses into the Mesopotamian mind, the most famous is *The Epic of Gilgamesh*. King Gilgamesh, whose reign in about 2700 B.C. is well documented, became a larger-than-life hero in Sumerian folk tales (Figure 1.5). In all probability the Gilgamesh epic began as an oral poem and was not put in writing on clay tablets for hundreds of years. The most complete surviving version, from 600 B.C., was based on a Babylonian copy written in Akkadian and dating from about 1600 B.C. Although this poem influenced other Near Eastern writings with its characters, plot, and themes, *The Epic of Gilgamesh* stands on its own as a poetic utterance worthy of being favorably compared with the Greek and Roman epics of later times.

Through its royal hero, *The Epic of Gilgamesh* focuses on fundamental themes that concern warriors in an aristocratic society: the need to be brave in the face of danger, the choice of death before dishonor, the conflict between companionship and sexual pleasure, the power of the gods over weak mortals, and the finality of death. Above all, it deals with human beings' vain quest for immortality. As the tale begins, the extravagant and despotic policies of Gilgamesh have led his subjects to pray for relief. In response, a goddess creates from clay a "wild man" of tremendous physical strength and sends him to kill Gilgamesh. But Enkidu, as he is called, is instead tamed by the love of a prostitute, loses his innocence, wrestles Gilgamesh to a draw, and becomes his boon companion.

FIGURE 1.5 Gilgamesh Fighting a Lion. Ca. 2500–2000 B.C. Impression of cylinder seal. British Museum. *Superhuman feats were attributed to the Sumerian king as he was transformed into a legendary figure. The scene depicted on this small agate seal is probably the earliest artistic representation of a literary scene in the Western tradition.*

As the epic unfolds, Gilgamesh chooses friendship with Enkidu rather than the love offered by the goddess Ishtar. Gilgamesh is punished for this choice by being made to watch helplessly as Enkidu dies from an illness sent by the gods. Forced to confront the fate awaiting all mortals, a grieving Gilgamesh begins a search for immortality.

The next section of the epic, which details Gilgamesh's search, includes the Sumerian tale of the great flood, which parallels the later Hebrew story of Noah and the ark. Although the Sumerian account of the flood was probably a later addition to the original story of Gilgamesh, the episode does fit into the narrative and reinforces one of the epic's major themes: the inescapable mortality of human beings. Gilgamesh hears the story of the flood from its sole survivor, Utnapishtim. Utnapishtim tells Gilgamesh how he built an ark and loaded it with animals and his family, how the waters rose, and how he released birds from the ark to discover if the waters were receding. The old man then explains how the gods, feeling sorry for the last remaining human, granted him immortality. Utnapishtim refuses to divulge the secret of eternal life to Gilgamesh, but the old man's wife blurts out where a plant may be found that will renew youth but not give immortality. Although Gilgamesh locates the plant, he loses it on his journey home. Gilgamesh, seeing the city of Uruk which he had built, realizes that the deeds humans do on earth are the measure of their immortality and that death is inevitable.

The Epic of Gilgamesh is essentially a secular morality tale. Gilgamesh's triumphs and failures mirror the lives of all mortals, and the Sumerians saw themselves in Gilgamesh's change from an overly confident and powerful hero to a doubting and fearful human being. Those who, like Gilgamesh, ignore the power of the deities have to pay a heavy price for their pride.

Law The Mesopotamians produced the fairest and most humane law codes prior to the Hebrews. The central theme of Sumerian law, whose first extant records date from about 2050 B.C., was justice. From the earliest times, the Sumerian kings understood justice to mean "the straight thing," that is, dealing fairly with all of their subjects and prohibiting the exploitation of the weak by the strong. This concept of equity applied especially to economic matters, such as debts, contracts, and titles to land.

The most famous set of laws from Mesopotamian civilization is that of the Babylonian king Hammurabi. Dating from about 1700 B.C., the Code of Hammurabi has been found preserved on a seven-foot-high black stone *stele*, or pillar. At the top, Hammurabi is depicted standing in front of Shamash, the Babylonian and Sumerian god of justice. Like other ancient lawgivers (Moses, for example),

FIGURE 1.6 Code of Hammurabi. Ca. 1790–1750 B.C. Louvre, Paris. *Hammurabi stands on the left while the god Shamash, with flames shooting out of his shoulders and holding the symbols of power in his hands, sits on the right. The relief, with its details and folds of cloth, is carved deep enough into the hard stone stele to suggest a three-dimensional sculpture.*

Hammurabi receives the legal code from a deity. Below the two figures are carved the prologue, the collection of laws, and an epilogue (Figure 1.6).

The prologue lists Hammurabi's accomplishments and sings his praises, while making it clear that the gods were the source of his power to establish "law and justice." The epilogue warns future rulers to carry out these laws or else be subject to defeat and ruin.

The laws concerning punishment for crimes are based on the judicial principle of *lex talionis*, or re-

taliation, which demands an "eye for an eye," although Hammurabi's code often substitutes payments in kind for damages done. Every major area of civil and criminal law was covered in the code, including property rights, sales, contracts, inheritance, adoption, prices and wages, and personal rights for women, children, and slaves. Hammurabi's code, like other Mesopotamian laws, was only one part of a complex judicial system that encompassed judges, courts, trials, legal proceedings, and contracts.

Art and Architecture   The art of Mesopotamia, like the rest of its culture, evolved from Sumerian styles to the Akkadian and Babylonian schools. Artisans worked in many forms—small seals, pottery, jewelry, vases, reliefs, and statues—and in many media—clay, stone, precious gems, gold, silver, leather, and ivory. Artifacts and crafted works from all three civilizations recorded the changing techniques of the producers as well as the shifting tastes of the consumers, whether they were rich individuals decorating their homes or officials issuing commissions for statues to adorn their temples. The temples, usually the center of the city and set on high mounds above the other structures, were often splendidly ornamented and housed exquisitely carved statues of gods and goddesses.

A fine example of Sumerian artistry is a bull's head carved on the sound box of a lyre (Figure 1.7). Working in gold leaf and semiprecious gems, the unknown artist has captured the vigor and power of the animal in a bold and simple style. Such elegant musical instruments were played in homes and in palaces to accompany the poets and storytellers as they sang of the heroes' adventures and the deities' powers.

Mesopotamian artists carved thousands of figures, many on the walls of temples and palaces and others as free-standing statues. A notable early type of free-standing statue that became standard in Sumerian temples depicts a figure in a contemplative, worshiping pose, his hands folded and clasped in front of him. Many of these are likenesses of Gudea, a ruler who flourished in about 2250 B.C. (Figure 1.8).

In contrast to the finely crafted sculpture, Mesopotamian architecture often seems uninspired, particularly the domestic architecture. Most Mesopotamian houses were square or rectangular, showing little variety. Even though the Mesopotamians knew about the arch, the vault, and the column, they did not employ them widely; they used primarily the basic *post-and-lintel construction* of two vertical posts capped by a horizontal lintel, or beam, for entranceways. The clay bricks used in construction limited the builders in styles and decorations, notably on the gurat resembled a hill or a stairway to the sky from which the deities could descend; or perhaps the structure was conceived as the gods' cosmic mountain. A temple of welcome for the gods stood on the top of the ziggurat, approached by sets of steps. Below, a complex of shrines, storehouses, and administrative offices were constructed around the base or on the several levels of the massive hill. In the low plain of the Tigris-Euphrates valley, the ziggurat literally and figuratively dominated the landscape. The Tower of Babel, described in the Jewish scriptures as reaching to the sky, may have been suggested by the Sumerian ziggurats.

FIGURE 1.8 *Gudea. Ca. 2150 B.C. Louvre, Paris. Little is known of Gudea, but over thirty small statues have been found of this Guti ruler. The body and head of this statuette, which measures 17¾ inches high, were discovered separately and later joined together.*

FIGURE 1.7 Bull's Head on Lyre. Ca. 3000–1500 B.C. Baghdad Museum, Baghdad. *The lyre's sound box, on which the bull's head is carved, is a hollow chamber that increases the resonance of the sound. Music played an important role in Mesopotamian life, and patrons often commissioned the construction of elegant instruments. Thus, even at this early stage of civilization, those with wealth influenced the arts.*

exterior. If private homes of clay bricks looked drab from the street, however, they were often attractive inside, built around an open courtyard with decorated rooms. The exteriors of temples and palaces were sometimes adorned with colored glazed bricks, mosaics, and painted cones arranged in patterns, or, more rarely, imported stone and marble.

Archeologists have not yet determined exactly how Mesopotamian cities were laid out. Urban centers were protected by walls, whose imposing and elaborately decorated gates proclaimed the city's wealth and power to inhabitants and visitors alike. The most prominent structure in each Sumerian city was the **ziggurat**, a terraced brick and mudbrick pyramid that served as the center of worship. The zig-

FIGURE 1.9   Ziggurat of Ur. Ca. 2100 B.C. Ur (Muqaiyir, Iraq). *A temple to Nanna, the moon god, stood on the top of the ziggurat, which was terraced on three different levels. On the first level was an entranceway approached by two sets of steps on each side and one in the front. The base measured 200 by 150 feet and stood 70 feet high.*

Of the numerous ziggurats and temples that have survived, the best preserved one is at Ur in southern Mesopotamia (modern Iraq) (Figure 1.9). Built around 2100 B.C., this ziggurat was laid out to the four points of the compass. A central stairway led up to the highest platform, on which the major temple rested. The citizens of Ur built this ziggurat to the moon god Nanna. Other cities constructed similar massive podiums in the hopes that they would please the gods and goddesses, that the rivers would be kind to them, and that life would continue. Thus the central themes of Mesopotamian civilization manifested themselves in the ziggurats.

THE CIVILIZATION OF THE NILE RIVER VALLEY: EGYPT

Another great river, the Nile, provided the setting for Egyptian civilization. Unlike the culture of the Mesopotamian valley, however, Nilotic culture evolved continuously, responding mainly to internal changes rather than to external influences. It thus achieved a unified character that lasted for about three thousand years. Isolated by deserts on either side, Egypt developed an introspective attitude that was little influenced by neighboring cultures and led

to a sense of cultural superiority. Subjected to the annual floodings of the Nile and aware of the revolutions of the sun, Egypt saw itself as part of a cyclical pattern in a timeless world.

The periodic overflowings of the Nile made civilized life possible in Egypt. Red sandy deserts stretched east and west of the waterway. Beside the Nile's banks, however, the black alluvial soil of the narrow floodplain offered rich land for planting, although the river's gifts of water and arable land were limited. Irrigation canals and ditches plus patient, backbreaking labor were required to deliver the life-giving liquid into the desert.

Because the survival and prosperity of the people depended on the Nile, the river dominated and shaped the Egyptian experience. About 95 percent of the people lived on the less than 5 percent of Egyptian land that was arable. The resulting concentration of people led to the emergence of the agricultural village, the fundamental unit of Egyptian civilization. The reward for farm labor tended to be subsistence living, yet the perennial hope that next year's flood would bring a more bountiful harvest created an optimistic outlook that contrasted with the darker Mesopotamian view.

The Nile linked the "Two Lands," Upper and Lower Egypt, two regions whose differing geography made for two distinct ways of life. Since the Nile flows northward, Lower Egypt referred to the northern lands fed by the river's spreading delta, a region made wealthy by its fertile soil. In contrast, Upper Egypt, or the southern lands, was an area of near subsistence living due to the harsh topography and poor farming conditions. In addition, Lower Egypt, because of its proximity to both Mediterranean and Near Eastern cultures, tended to be more cosmopolitan than the provincial, isolated lands of Upper Egypt.

The earliest Neolithic settlers in the Nile valley probably arrived about 6000 B.C. These earliest Egyptians took up an agricultural life, wresting control of the surrounding lands, taming the river, and domesticating animals. In the rich alluvial soil they cultivated barley, wheat, and vegetables for themselves and fodder for their animals. They hunted with bows and arrows and fished with nets, thereby supplementing their simple fare. They also planted flax from which thread was woven into linen on primitive looms. Most tools and weapons were made of stone or flint, but copper, which had to be imported, became more important after 3500 B.C. The early Egyptians lived in simply furnished, flat-topped houses built of sun-dried bricks. These basic patterns characterized peasant life throughout much of Egypt's history.

Continuity and Change over Three Thousand Years

Egypt stepped from the shadows of its illiterate past in about 3100 B.C., when Menes [MEE-neez] proclaimed himself king and united the upper and lower lands. His power reached from the Mediterranean to the first cataract, or waterfall, of the Nile, making Egypt a state to be reckoned with in the Near East. Egypt's lengthy, complex history is conventionally divided into twenty-six dynasties, which are in turn classified into groups. The three major groups of dynasties are known as the Old Kingdom, the Middle Kingdom, and the New Kingdom. They are preceded and followed, respectively, by two dynastic groups known as the Early Dynastic Period

and the Late Dynastic Period. In addition, two intermediate dynastic groupings (the First and the Second) precede and follow the Middle Kingdom (see Time Line 1.3).

In the Early Dynastic Period (about 3100–2700 B.C.), the kings brought prosperity through their control of the economy and fostered political harmony through diplomacy and dynastic marriages. These rulers, claiming to be gods on earth, adopted the trappings of divinity and built royal tombs to ensure their immortality.

With the Old Kingdom (about 2700–2185 B.C.) Egypt entered a five-hundred-year period of peace and prosperity. Isolated from major civilizations, Egypt rose to greatness as its political institutions matured and its language was adapted to literary uses. The most enduring accomplishment of the Old Kingdom became the pyramid—the royal tomb devised by the Fourth Dynasty kings (Figure 1.10). Massive in size and awesome as the visible symbol of the kings' power, the pyramids served to link the rulers with the gods and the cosmos. Yet, although the kings could impress their people with divine claims, they could neither subdue the forces of nature nor make their power last forever. For reasons not fully understood, these rulers loosened their control over the state and thus ushered in an age of political fragmentation called the First Intermediate Period.

In the First Intermediate Period (about 2185–2050 B.C.), civil war raged sporadically and starvation wiped out much of the populace. Eventually, a family from Thebes in Upper Egypt reunited the state and initiated the Middle Kingdom (about 2050–1800 B.C.). The new dynasty, the twelfth, extended Egypt's southern boundary and helped bring about a cultural renaissance, especially in literature, but unity was short-lived.

The Second Intermediate Period (about 1800–1552 B.C.) was an age of chaos provoked both by repeated failures of the Nile to flood and by a resurgence of local warlords. A weakened Lower Egypt succumbed to the Hyksos, Semitic-speaking invaders from Palestine. Backed by warriors in horse-drawn

TIME LINE 1.3   EGYPTIAN CIVILIZATION   All dates approximate and B.C.

6000	3100	2700	2185	2050	1800	1552	1079	525
Neolithic and Predynastic Periods	Early Dynastic Period	Old Kingdom	First Intermediate Period	Middle Kingdom	Second Intermediate Period	New Kingdom	Late Dynastic Period	Persian Conquest

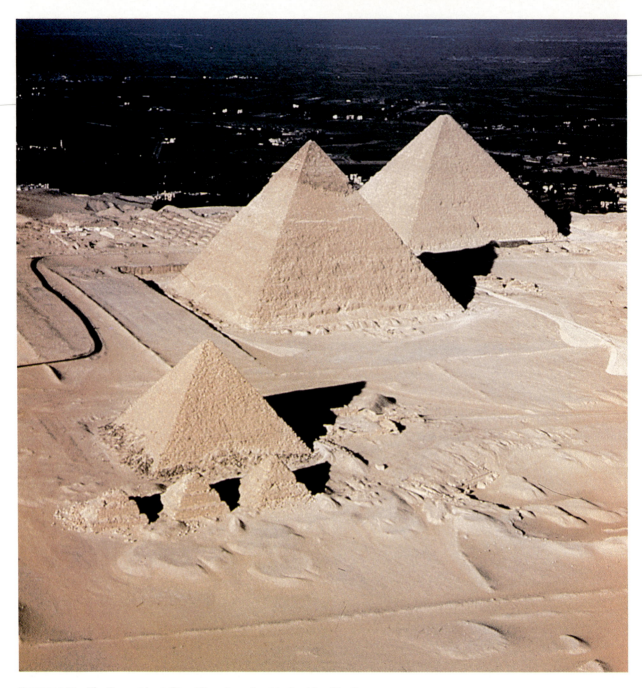

FIGURE 1.10 The Pyramids at Giza. View from the Air, Looking Northeast.
Pyramid of Mykerinus (foreground), ca. 2525 B.C.; Pyramid of Kheops (center), ca.
2590 B.C.; Pyramid of Khephren (rear), ca. 2560 B.C. *The Fourth Dynasty was the Age
of Pyramids, when this characteristic shape was standardized and became a symbol of
Egyptian civilization. The Great Pyramid, in the center, was the first structure at Giza.*

chariots, the Hyksos with their bronze weapons easily defeated the copper-armed Egyptians. The Hyksos era constituted a watershed in Egypt's history because it ended the isolation that had fed the feelings of cultural superiority. Egyptian nobility now joined aristocracies everywhere in employing the horse for war and sport, and Egyptian artisans fully entered the Bronze Age.

Ahmose I [AHM-os], a Theban king, drove out the Hyksos and inaugurated the New Kingdom (1552–1079 B.C.), the most cosmopolitan era in Egyptian history. Pursuing the Hyksos into Palestine, Ahmose conquered the foreign peoples along the way, creating the first Egyptian empire. To the northeast, Egypt's kings, now called pharaohs, pursued imperial ambitions against the cities in Palestine, Phoenicia, and Syria, a move that provoked deadly warfare with the Hittites of Anatolia. Egypt finally secured its possessions by peacefully dividing up the Near East with the Hittites and the Assyrians. To the south, the pharaohs pushed Egypt's frontiers to the Nile's fourth cataract. As the empire grew, Egypt's society underwent the greatest changes of its entire history, including religious innovation by a ruling family, widespread material affluence, extravagant temple building, and artistic and literary experimentation.

But imperial success gave way to decline after 1200 B.C., signaled by the pharaoh's growing dependence on unreliable foreign troops. Bands of homeless wanderers, called Sea Peoples by the Egyptians, began to disrupt trade and normal social life. Over the course of a century, the marauding invaders forced Egypt to withdraw behind its historic borders and thus brought the empire to an end. The success of the Sea People's challenge, despite their small numbers, lay in their new weapons, for these destructive migrants were the leading edge of the Age of Iron. Egypt's lack of iron ore probably contributed fatally to its military decline.

During the Late Period (about 1079–525 B.C.), Egypt slipped into senility. Ignoring their kingdom's weak condition, the pharaohs continued to meddle, albeit unsuccessfully, in the affairs of the Near East until Egypt fell to Assyria. When Assyrian power declined, a Libyan dynasty ruled Egypt until the Persians subdued them in 525 B.C. Egypt, now part of the Persian Empire, ceased to exist as an independent state.

Just as the pharaoh dominated the state, so the rulers controlled the predominantly agrarian economy. Although in theory all land belonged to the pharaoh, in practice departments of government or the priesthood of a temple exploited the land and the king's serfs. Upper Egypt provided the bulk of farm produce that Lower Egypt exported to Mediterranean neighbors. In prosperous years the pharaohs claimed up to half of the farm crops to support their building programs, especially funerary monuments. But in years of famine dynasties fell and the state splintered into separate units.

Foreign trade was also a royal monopoly. The government obtained cedar from Lebanon, olive oil from Palestine, and myrrh from Punt, probably on the Somali coast. Since Egypt never developed a coinage, the pharaohs bartered for these imports with papyrus rolls (for writing), linen, weapons, and furniture. The pharaohs also exported gold from the eastern desert and copper from the Sinai peninsula. In addition, Egypt served as the carrier of tropical African goods—ebony, ivory, and animal skins—to the eastern Mediterranean.

Egyptian society was hierarchical, and at the top stood the pharaoh—the king and god incarnate. Because divine blood coursed through the ruler's veins, he could marry only within his own family. Tradition decreed that the Chief Queen, who was identified with the goddess Hathor, the mother of the god Horus, would produce the royal heir. If she failed to produce offspring, the successor pharaoh was selected from sons of the ruler's other wives or royal cousins. On rare occasions, when there was no suitable heir, the Chief Queen became the pharaoh, as did Hatshepsut [hat-SHEP-soot] in the New Kingdom.

Ranked below the ruling family were the royal officials, nobles, large landowners, and priests. The pharaoh's word was law, but these groups were delegated powers for executing his will. Early in the Old Kingdom, many opportunities existed for commoners to rise in the royal service, but the priests and bureaucrats gradually closed off avenues for social mobility by making their offices hereditary. On a lower level, artists and artisans worked for the pharaonic court and the nobility. Although their status was low, those who headed their professions were accorded inflated titles and positions. At the bottom of the social pyramid peasants and a small number of slaves formed the bulk of Egypt's population. Personal liberty took second place to the general welfare, and peasants were pressed into forced labor during natural disasters such as floods and at harvest time.

A Quest for Eternal Cultural Values

Until the invasion of the Hyksos, Egypt, in its splendid isolation, forged a civilization whose serene values and timeless forms deeply mirrored the religious beliefs of the rulers and the stability of the state. But as contact with other cultures and civilizations grew, Egyptian culture changed to reflect new influences. Writers borrowed words from other languages, for example, and sculptors displayed the human figure in more natural settings and poses. Still, Egyptian culture retained its distinctive qualities, and innovations continued to express traditional ideals.

Religion   Egypt was a *theocracy*, or a state ruled by a god. Believing that the deities had planned their country's future from the beginning, the Egyptians thought of their society as sacred. From the time that Menes first united Egypt, religious dogma taught that the king, as god on earth, embodied the state. Egyptian rulers also identified themselves with the deities. For example, Menes claimed to be the "two ladies," the goddesses who stood for Upper and Lower Egypt. Other rulers identified themselves with Ra, the sun god, and with Ra's son, Horus, the sky god who was always depicted as having the head of a falcon. Because of the king's divinity, the resources of the state were concentrated on giving the ruler proper homage, as in the Old Kingdom's massive tombs, designed on a superhuman scale to ensure his safe passage to the next life.

Egyptian subjects worshiped the pharaoh, but the pharaoh could venerate any deity he pleased. Hence, the shifting fortunes of Egypt's many cults depended on the ruler's preference. For example, Ptah (who, like the Hebrew God in Genesis, created through speech) became the god of Memphis, which was the capital of the Old Kingdom. The kings of the Fifth Dynasty, on the other hand, called themselves sons of Ra, the sun god, and they honored this celestial deity by building him temples more impressive than their own royal tombs. Later, the Twelfth Dynasty brought Amen (a word meaning "hidden one") to the fore, and a series of rulers adopted his name, as in Amenemhat [AH-men-EM-het]. Royal favor to a god generally increased the wealth and influence of the god's cult and priests. Consequently, by the time of the New Kingdom, society had become top-heavy with priests and their privileged religious properties.

Egypt came close to having a national deity during the New Kingdom when Akhenaten [ahk-NAHT-uhn] (about 1369–1353 B.C.) reshaped the royal religion at his capital, Amarna. Elevating Aten, the god of the sun's disk, to supremacy above the other gods, Akhenaten systematically disavowed the older divinities—a heretical view in tolerant, polytheistic Egypt. This innovation aroused the opposition of conservative nobles who supported the powerful priests of the Theban god, Amen. Akhenaten ultimately failed, and later pharaohs tried to erase his name and memory from history. The Amarna revolution, however, like the religious choices of the

pharaohs generally, had little effect on the ordinary Egyptian, who continued to believe that the pharaoh could intervene with the other gods for the benefit of all.

The foremost distinguishing mark of Egyptian religion was its promise of immortality—a belief that generated a more optimistic attitude toward human existence than that found in Mesopotamia. At first, in the Old Kingdom, only the kings were accorded this reward. Eventually, nobles and royal officials were buried in the vicinity of the rulers' tombs, thereby ensuring their immortality as assistants to the risen god in the afterlife. By the First Intermediate Period, the nobles had claimed their own right to immortality by erecting tombs on which the royal funerary texts were copied. Later, immortality apparently was opened to all Egyptians, although only the wealthy minority could afford the cost of a proper burial.

Writing and Literature   Late predynastic Egypt learned the idea of writing, but not foreign words, from Mesopotamia. The Egyptians initially drew pictographs, called **hieroglyphs**, for such words as "hoe," "arrowhead," and "plow." This early hieroglyphic script could also depict abstract words for which no adequate picture was available, but because such picture writing was time-consuming and clumsy to execute, the scribes soon made the pictographs function as signs, or clusters of consonants, for other words (Figure 1.11).

Egyptian literature produced no single great work that rivals *Gilgamesh,* but the Egyptian experience was rich in its variety of literary **genres**, or types of literature. For example, Pyramid Texts, the writings inscribed in burial chambers, formed the chief literary genre in the Old Kingdom. As this era gave way to the First Intermediate Period, new prose genres, like prophecies and pessimistic writings,

FIGURE 1.11 Egyptian Writing. *From the Old Kingdom onward, the hieroglyphs (in the top line) constituted the style of formal writing that appeared on tomb walls and in monuments. Religious and governmental scribes soon devised two distinct types of cursive script, a careful manuscript hand (in the middle line) and a more rapid hand (in the bottom line) for administrative documents and letters.*

	Hieroglyphics	Literary hieratic	Swift hieratic	Translation
				Amon
				rôemt / mankind
				per-'o / Pharaoh
				hru / day

FIGURE 1.12 IMHOTEP. Step Pyramid of King Djoser. Ca. 2680 B.C. Sakkareh, Egypt. *Though isolated from its neighbors until about 1730 B.C., Egypt was influenced by surrounding cultures, as the design for the step pyramid at Sakkareh shows. Resting on a rectangular base and rising in six progressively smaller stages, this pyramid was modeled on Mesopotamia's ziggurat. But unlike the ziggurats, which were made of dried clay bricks, it was built of cut stone, the first building to be so constructed in the world.*

arose that addressed the prevalent political disintegration and social upheaval. Such was the tenor of the times that writers expressed views contradicting Egypt's otherwise optimistic attitudes to death and life. *An Argument between a Man Contemplating Suicide and His Soul* describes a desperate mortal finally choosing the emptiness of death rather than life in a materialistic and violent world.

The prophecies, *hymns* (songs of praise to the gods), and prose narratives of the Middle Kingdom constitute the classical period of Egyptian letters. The most famous work of the Middle Kingdom, as well as of all Egyptian literature, is the *Story of Sinuhe,* a prose tale that celebrates the ruler Senusert I and his subject, the hero named in the title. Fleeing Egypt, Sinuhe earns fame and fortune in Lebanon yet yearns for his beloved homeland. Sinuhe's exploits smack of the folk tale, for in one episode he subdues a taunting giant of a man, much as David defeated Goliath in the Old Testament story. Eventually, a gracious Senusert writes Sinuhe, forgiving his wandering subject's unnamed crime and inviting him to return home. The travel yarn concludes with a homecoming scene in which a joyful Sinuhe is reintegrated into Egyptian court society.

The richest period in Egyptian letters occurred during the New Kingdom. In addition to songs praising the pharaoh, poets now composed lyrics telling of the pain of parted lovers, and new genres included model letters, wisdom literature, and fairy tales. Akhenaten's revolution led to unique forms of literary expression, as in the *Hymn to Aten,* which praised this universal god. While the hymn has similarities to Psalm 104 of the Old Testament, Akhenaten's text, unlike the Jewish scriptures, was not a declaration of **monotheism**, the belief that there is only one god. Instead, the *Hymn to Aten* recognized a special link between Akhenaten and his family and the god of the solar disk but without keeping the ruling dynasty from worshiping other deities.

Architecture   The classic Egyptian building was the pyramid, whose shape seemed to embody a constant and eternal order. During the Old Kingdom, the pyramid became the only building deemed suitable for a ruler-god's resting place preparatory to the afterlife. A modified version of the pyramid appeared first in about 2680 B.C. in the step pyramid of King Djoser [ZHO-ser] at Sakkareh, opposite Memphis (Figure 1.12). Later Egyptian rulers preferred the true pyramid form, and this design did not develop further.

The true pyramid appeared in the Old Kingdom when the Fourth Dynasty ruler Kheops [KEE-ahps] erected the Great Pyramid at Giza, across the Nile from Cairo (see Figure 1.10). The anonymous architect executed this largest stone building in the world—

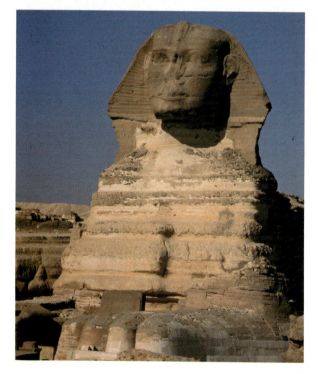

FIGURE 1.13 Hatshepsut's Temple. Ca. 1490 B.C. Deir el Bahri, across from Luxor, Egypt. *Hatshepsut's temple was planned for the same purpose as the pyramids—to serve as a shrine for the royal remains. In actuality an ascending series of three colonnaded courtyards, this temple provided a spectacular approach to a hidden sanctuary carved in the steep cliffs.*

FIGURE 1.14 The Great Sphinx. Ca. 2560 B.C. Giza, Egypt. *Sphinxes, creatures part lion and part human, were often depicted in Egyptian art. The most famous sphinx was the one at Giza, carved from the rock on the site. The sphinx's colossal size prevented the anonymous sculptor from rendering it with any subtle facial expressions. More significant as a monument than as a great work of art, the Great Sphinx had a practical purpose—to guard the nearby pyramid tombs.*

6.25 million tons—with mathematical precision. Many of the tomb's two million stones were quarried on the site, although most were obtained farther upstream and ferried to Giza during the flooding of the Nile. The infinitesimally small deviation between the two sets of opposing base sides of the pyramid showed the scientific spirit already at work in this early stage of Egypt's history. Later, two of Kheops's successors, Khephren [KEF-ren] and Mykerinus [MIK-uh-REE-nus], added their pyramids to make the complex at Giza the symbol of the Old Kingdom and one of the wonders of the ancient world.

The fascination with majestic pyramids ended with the Old Kingdom, and the pyramids eventually gave way to funerary temples when the New Kingdom pharaohs began to construct splendid monuments for themselves that reflected Egypt's new imperial status. The temple of Queen Hatshepsut is perhaps the most beautiful example of this architectural development (Figure 1.13). Designed by the royal architect Senmut, the temple of Hatshepsut was carved into the face of the mountain at Deir el Bahri, across the Nile from Luxor. Senmut, adopting the post-and-lintel style of construction, gave the queen's temple two levels of pillared colonnades, each accessible by long sloping ramps. The most arresting features of Hatshepsut's temple are its round columns, which are used alongside rectangular pillars in the *porticoes*, or covered entrances. These columns—with their plain tops and grooved surfaces—suggest the graceful columns of later Greek architecture, although some scholars dismiss this similarity as coincidental. Be that as it may, this Egyptian monument, like the later Greek temples, shows a harmonious sense of proportion throughout its impressive colonnades.

Sculpture, Painting, and Minor Arts   In the royal graveyard at Giza, artisans of the Old Kingdom carved from the living rock a mythical creature that stirred the imagination of most peoples in the ancient world—a sphinx, half-lion and half-man (Figure 1.14). Although this creature often inspired feelings of dread, in actuality there was little mystery to the sphinx, since its original purpose was to guard the royal tombs, perhaps to frighten away grave robbers. Indeed, this first sphinx's face was that of Khephren, the Fourth Dynasty king whose pyramid stood nearby. Today, this crumbling relic stands as a reminder of the claims to immortality of the Old Kingdom rulers.

The sheer size and mythical character of the Great Sphinx set it apart from Old Kingdom sculptures in the round, which favored human-scaled figures and realistic images. The life-size statue of King Mykerinus and his Chief Queen, found beneath the ruler's pyramid at Giza, showed this art's brilliant realism (Figure 1.15). The sculpture embodies the characteristics of what became the standard, or classical, Egyptian style: their left legs forward, the king's clenched fists, their headdresses (sacred regalia for him and wig for her), their rigid poses, their serene countenances, and the figures' angularity. Although sculpted in the round, the couple was intended to be viewed from the front, so the work has a two-dimensional quality.

In contrast to practices in the Old Kingdom, the wives of rulers in the New Kingdom acquired claims to divinity in their own right. A statue of Hatshepsut represents her in the clothing and with the sacred pose of pharaoh (Figure 1.16). Having first been Chief Queen to Thutmose III [thoot-MOH-suh] in the New Kingdom, after his death she seized leadership, probably with the cooperation of the powerful Theban priesthood of Amen. Although more than a thousand years separated this sculpture from that of Mykerinus (see Figure 1.15), in its expression of dignity and authority the statue of Hatshepsut bears a strong resemblance to the earlier work, thus demonstrating the continuity of the Egyptian style.

FIGURE 1.15 *King Mykerinus and His Chief Queen.* Ca. 2525 B.C. Museum of Fine Arts, Boston. *This life-sized slate sculpture of Mykerinus, a Fourth Dynasty ruler, and his Chief Queen was removed from its resting place beneath the king's pyramid at Giza (see Figure 1.10). In addition to such sculptures, the royal tombs contained furniture, including beds, chairs, and tables, and funerary equipment, such as vessels, figurines of attendants, and ornaments.*

FIGURE 1.16   *Hatshepsut.* Ca. 1460 B.C. Metropolitan Museum of Art. *This sculpture is one of over two hundred statues of Hatshepsut intended to adorn her massive and elegant funeral temple at Deir el Bahri in the western hills of Thebes. Despite the authoritative pose and regalia that convey her Pharaonic status, she is subtly represented as a woman.*

A major challenge to Egypt's traditional, austere forms occurred in Akhenaten's revolutionary reign. A low-relief sculpture of the royal family exemplifies the naturalism and fluid lines that this artistic rebellion favored (Figure 1.17). Akhenaten nuzzles one of his daughters in an intimate pose, while his wife dandles another daughter on her knees and allows a third to stand on her right arm. The domesticity of this scene is quite unlike the sacred gestures of traditional Egyptian sculpture, but the religious subject of this relief remains true to that tradition, as the rays streaming from the disk of Aten onto the royal family indicate.

The most extraordinary artistic achievement of the Amarna period is the carved portrait head of Queen Nefertiti (Figure 1.18), a life-size sculpture discovered in 1912 by a team of German archeologists in the desert sands near the long-lost city founded by Akhenaten for the god Aten. This statue-head with its unfinished left eye, deliberate or accidental, is one of the most arresting images of world art. Painted in flesh tones and natural colors and imbued with the naturalism of the Amarna style, the Queen has a fascinating vitality that is unsurpassed. A modern critic has called her the eternal female, ceaselessly watching.

Nefertiti's unusual headdress signifies her status as a potent force in this culture. Rising straight up from her forehead, this crown is decorated with the *uraeus,* the image of a cobra ready to strike. By custom, this powerful and protective symbol was part

FIGURE 1.17   *Family Scene: Pharaoh Akhenaten, Queen Nefertiti, and Their Three Daughters.* Ca. 1350 B.C. Agyptisches Museum, Berlin. *The religious ideas associated with Akhenaten's reforms are expressed in the lines streaming from the sun's disk above the royal couple. Each ray of the sun ends in a tiny hand that offers a blessing to the royal family.*

FIGURE 1.18 *Nefertiti. Ca. 1350 B.C. Agyptisches Museum, Berlin. This portrait head of Nefertiti is characterized by sleekness and seductive charm, a look achieved through the sculptor's fusing of the fluid Amarna style with the formality of Egypt's traditional art. To create the image of sleekness, the sculptor has pushed Nefertiti's face forward like the prow of a ship cutting through the wind. And the figure's erotic charm emerges from the ironic tension between the Queen's dreamy, deeply hooded eye and the lively, arched eyebrows. The artistic result is a woman of mystery, supremely sexual yet as unapproachable as a goddess.*

of the kingly *regalia* (tokens of royal authority) and could only be worn by rulers and their Great (principal) Queens. Modern scholars have proved that Nefertiti was the only Great Queen in Egypt's long history to actually share power with her husband. (Another exception, Queen Hatshepsut, actually ruled alone as pharaoh.) The prevalence of images of Nefertiti in so much of the art that remains from Amarna confirms this Queen's importance on the political level and thus underscores her central role in the Amarna revolution.

Just as Egypt's sculpture in the round developed a rigid *canon*, or set of rules, so did two-dimensional representations acquire a fixed formula, whether in relief sculptures or in wall paintings. The Egyptians never discovered the principles of perspective. On a flat surface, the human figures were depicted in profile, with both feet pointing sideways, as in the low-relief sculpture from an Old Kingdom tomb shown in Figure 1.19. However, the artistic canon required that the eye and the shoulders be shown frontally, and both arms had to be visible along with all of the fingers. The craftsman determined the human proportions exactly, by the use of a grid. Throughout most Egyptian art history, the human figure was conceived as being 18 squares high standing and 14 squares high seated, with each unit equivalent to the width of one "fist"; anatomical parts were made accordingly proportional. The canon of proportions was established by the time of the Old Kingdom, and its continued use, with slight variations, helped Egyptian art retain its unmistakable style. Wall paintings, in contrast to relief sculptures, permitted a greater sense of space to be created, but the rules regarding the human figure still had to be observed

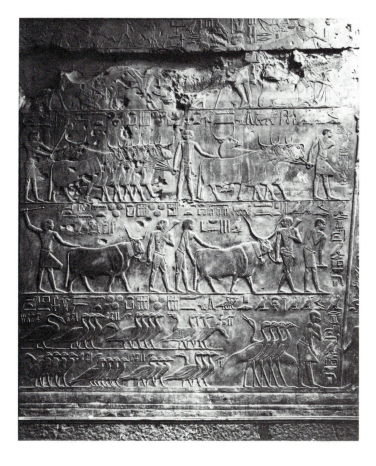

FIGURE 1.19 Herdsmen and Cattle. Ca. 2563–2423 B.C. Tomb of Ptahhopep, Sakkareh, Egypt. *In this relief sculpture, the cattle as well as the human figures are depicted with feet sideways. Though failing to show perspective, the Egyptian artist nevertheless has created a realistic scene. The cattle move in the casual way of domesticated animals, with the odd one here and there turning away from the forward motion. Near the top two herdsmen lead the cattle while a third one prods them along with a rod.*

FIGURE 1.20 Banqueting Scene. Ca. 1567–1320 B.C. British Museum. *In a small space, the Egyptian painter has created a delightful banqueting scene, a favorite subject in tomb decoration. The scene depicts nearly nude dancers accompanied by extravagantly dressed musicians, whose braided hair cascades around their faces.*

FIGURE 1.21 Ceremonial Chair for King Tutankhamen. Ca. 1334–1323 B.C. Cairo Museum, Egypt. *This elegantly decorated chair was intended for the ruler's use in a religious ceremony, probably at his coronation. As such, it is the ancestor of all royal thrones in the West. Its lion-paw legs became a favorite motif in Western-style furniture.*

Time Line 1.4   HEIRS TO THE MESOPOTAMIAN AND EGYPTIAN CULTURES   All dates approximate and B.C.

(Figure 1.20). Given these stringent conventions, the Egyptian artists who worked in two dimensions were amazingly successful in creating the image of a carefree society bubbling with life.

Besides their excellence in sculpture and painting, the Egyptians set an incomparable standard in the minor arts, examples of which have been found in royal tombs. Discovered in 1922, the burial chamber of the New Kingdom pharaoh Tutankhamen [too-tahn-KAHM-en] has yielded up the richest domestic treasures. Of the thirty-four excavated royal tombs, only that of King Tut—as he is popularly known—escaped relatively free from violation by thieves in ancient times. A decorated chair may be taken as representative of the elegant craftsmanship of the hundreds of objects found in Tutankhamen's tomb. His ceremonial cedar chair, faced with gold, ivory, and bronze, has exquisite carved figures in the back (Figure 1.21). These carvings include the god of eternity, with his arms outstretched, and hieroglyphs that honor and praise the dead ruler.

HEIRS TO THE MESOPOTAMIAN AND EGYPTIAN EMPIRES

With the decline of Mesopotamian and Egyptian empires after 1000 B.C., successor kingdoms arose in the eastern Mediterranean, notably those of the Hittites, the Assyrians, the Medes, and the Persians. If the length of their rule and the richness of their achievements failed to measure up to Mesopotamian and Egyptian civilizations, they nevertheless brought law and order to numerous peoples over vast territories and offered a convincing model of what civilized life ought to be.

The Hittites and Assyrians were rival empires whose fortunes ebbed and flowed, although Assyrian power lasted longer than Hittite (see Time Line 1.4). In 612 B.C., Nineveh, the Assyrian capital city, was sacked by the Medes, an Indo-European people from the southwest Iranian plateau, and the Assyrian empire passed under their control. Medean rule, however, was shortly supplanted when their empire fell to the Persians, another nomadic Indo-European tribe, in about 550 B.C. With masterly skill, successive Persian rulers forged the strongest and largest empire that the eastern Mediterranean had seen until this time. At its height, Persian rule extended from Egypt in the south to central Russia in the north, and from Cyprus in the west to the Indus River in the east. Only Greece eluded Persia's grasp. In 327 B.C. Alexander the Great defeated the last Persian king, thus allowing the Greeks to assimilate the Persian lands.

Persian culture followed in the footsteps of Assyria, but Persian art lacked the savagery associated with the Assyrian style. Instead, Persian art emphasized contemplative themes with less action (Figure 1.22). Persian culture's most original and enduring contribution was the religion of Zoroaster [ZOHR-uh-was-ter] or Zarathustra [zah-ra-THUSH-trah], a

FIGURE 1.22 Nobles Marching up the Stairs. Ca. 512–494 B.C. Persepolis, Iran. *This charming relief sculpture, carved on the side of a stairway at the Persian capital, Persepolis, depicts aristocrats mounting the stairs to greet their king on New Year's Day, a sacred festival celebrated on the summer solstice. Each noble bears a flower offering to the monarch as a sign of his devotion.*

prophet who lived in about 600 B.C. Rejecting polytheism, Zoroaster taught a dualistic religion in which the god of light, Ahuramazda, engaged in a universal struggle with the god of darkness, Ahriman. According to Zoroaster, those who lead puritanical lives not only gain favorable treatment in the afterlife but also ensure the triumph of the forces of good. Key ideas of Zoroastrianism influenced other religions: Zoroaster's martyrdom, the prophet's life filled with miracles, the evil spirit as the Prince of Darkness, and the notion of a Last Judgment.

The Legacy of Early Near Eastern Civilizations

Mesopotamia and Egypt provided the earliest models of civilization in the West. In both, large numbers of people were organized into societies characterized by class stratification, a division of labor, complex political, economic, and religious forms, technological advances, and cultural achievements. They weren't the only ancient civilizations—others developed in China, India, South America, and elsewhere—but they are the ones to which Westerners most directly trace their cultural roots.

Mesopotamia's gifts to Western civilization are impressive. In addition to writing, they established urbanism as a way of life in contrast to agrarian or village existence. In more practical matters, they created a mathematical system based on 60 that gave the world the 60-minute hour and the 360-degree circle. They also divided the seasons and devised a lunar calendar to mark off periods of days to aid them in their planting. Trade and commerce forced them to come up with ways of counting, of measuring, and of weighing that became the standard procedures for other Near Eastern peoples for centuries. Mesopotamian myths, legends, and epics found their way into the folk tales and literature of other cultures.

Egypt made equally impressive contributions to the West. Egyptian bureaucrats, who wanted to predict the correct date for the rising of the Nile's waters, originated a solar calendar that is the basis of the Western calendar. The Egyptian model, which divided the year into twelve months of thirty days each with five days of holiday at the end, was conveyed to Western culture by the Romans. In architecture, Egyptian builders devised the column with a decorated capital, which later Greek architects probably adopted. The Greek builders also borrowed the Egyptian tradition of sound engineering principles rooted in mathematics. Similarly, Greek sculptors owed a debt to Egyptian forms and poses. Indeed, the Egyptian idea of an aesthetic canon influenced both sculptors and artists in Greece.

In literature, the Egyptians explored a variety of genres—such as wisdom writing—and folk tales that influenced the Hebrews and Greeks. In science, Egyptian physicians became renowned throughout the Near East for their medical learning and knowledge of drugs. Finally, with its priceless treasures, its mysterious pyramids, and its cult of the dead, Egypt inspired curiosity and excitement in foreigners from ancient times onward. One of the first Western tourists to visit Egypt was the Greek historian Herodotus, whose writings in the fifth century B.C. helped to create the Egyptian mystique. The world's fascination with the culture of ancient Egypt has not abated today.

KEY CULTURAL TERMS

culture

civilization

Paleolithic

Neolithic

pictogram

ideogram

phonogram

cuneiform

polytheism

anthropomorphism

pantheism

stele

post-and-lintel
  construction

ziggurat

hieroglyphs

theocracy

genre

hymn

monotheism

portico

regalia

canon

SUGGESTIONS FOR FURTHER READING

PRIMARY SOURCES

KASTER, J., ed. and trans. *The Literature and Mythology of Ancient Egypt.* London: Allen Lane, 1970. An up-to-date anthology that includes creation myths, rituals, stories, songs, proverbs, and prayers.

KRAMER, S. N. *History Begins at Sumer.* Philadelphia: University of Pennsylvania Press, 1981. A standard collection of original Sumerian sources by one of the most renowned modern Sumerian scholars.

PRITCHARD, J. B. *Ancient Near Eastern Texts Relating to the Old Testament.* Princeton: Princeton University Press, 1969. For the serious student, a collection of the most important non-biblical texts, including myths, histories, prayers, and other types of writing.

SANDARS, N. K., ed. *The Epic of Gilgamesh.* New York: Penguin, 1972. The editor's informative introduction sets the tone for this famous ancient epic.

AEGEAN CIVILIZATION

The Minoans, the Mycenaeans, and the Greeks of the Archaic Age

Although Mesopotamia and Egypt offer successful models of civilization, the tradition of Greece is often the first in which Westerners feel they can recognize themselves. What ties us moderns to ancient Greece is their vision of humanity, for they were the first to place human beings at the center of the universe. The Near Eastern cultures focused on deities and godlike rulers, paying little attention to the strivings of humanity. The Greeks, on the other hand, no longer saw mortals as the inconsequential objects of divine whim. Instead, men and women assumed some importance in the scheme of things; they were seen as having some control over their destinies and some moral responsibility for their actions. By the fifth century B.C., the Greek philosopher Protagoras could proclaim, ''Man is the measure of all things.''

With their new way of thinking, the Greeks surged forward in all areas of creativity, ultimately reaching heights that some think have never been equaled. Because of their grandeur and noble appeal, Greek poetry, sculpture, and architecture became the standard against which later works were frequently judged. From the Greeks the Western tradition has inherited many of its political forms and practices, its views on human behavior, its insistence on philosophical rigor, and its approach to scientific inquiry. In essence, through their human-centered consciousness and their cultural achievements, the Greeks laid the foundation of Western civilization.

◀ *Bull Leaping.* Ca. 1500 B.C. Archaeological Museum, Heraklion, Crete.

Greek culture developed in the basin of the Aegean Sea (Map 2.1). On rocky coasts and rugged islands and peninsulas, the people coaxed a subsistence living from the thin, stony soil and turned to the sea for trade, conquest, and expansion. During the Bronze Age, the inhabitants of the island of Crete and the Greek peninsula traded with the Egyptians and the Hittites of Anatolia. The early Greeks borrowed and adapted a writing system from the Phoenicians. They were indebted to the Egyptians for sculptural techniques and to other Near Eastern civilizations for techniques in working with metal and clay, for music and mathematics, and for elements of their religious system.

The people we now know as the Greeks were not the first to thrive in the Aegean basin (Time Line 2.1). Before their story begins, in the period known as the Archaic Age and dating from about 800 B.C., two other distinctive civilizations—the Minoan and the Mycenaean—established centers of culture in the area and left their mark on those who followed.

PRELUDE: MINOAN CIVILIZATION, 3000–1300 B.C.

During the same time that civilizations were flourishing in Egypt and Mesopotamia, another culture was developing among the Neolithic settlements on the island of Crete. By about 2000 B.C. a prosperous

MAP 2.1

The Aegean World

TIME LINE 2.1   MINOAN AND MYCENAEAN CIVILIZATIONS

All dates approximate and B.C.

FIGURE 2.1   The Central Court at Knossos. Ca. 1750–1650 B.C. *The central court, measuring about 164 feet by 82 feet, was an open space surrounded by rooms and passageways to other parts of the palace. When British archeologist Sir Arthur Evans uncovered these ruins in 1902, he became convinced that he had discovered the palace of the legendary King Minos and labeled the civilization Minoan—a descriptive term used interchangeably with Cretan.*

and stable mercantile civilization had emerged, and between 1700 and 1400 B.C. it reached its high point in wealth, power, and sophistication. This society, labeled Minoan after King Minos, a legendary Cretan ruler, apparently was organized into a complex class system that included nobles, merchants, artisans, bureaucrats, and laborers. Noble life was based in palaces, and twentieth-century archeological excavations of several palace sites indicate that communities were linked in a loose political federation, with the major center at Knossos on the north coast. Remarkably, no fortified walls protected the Minoan palaces, suggesting that the cities remained at peace with one another and that the island itself afforded adequate protection against invading sea raiders. Crete's tranquil image is further supported by the absence of weapons in excavated remains.

The palace at Knossos has revealed more about Cretan life than any other cultural artifact. The palace's central court, though no longer paved or walled, still provides a sense of the grandeur and expanse of this once-magnificent site (Figure 2.1). An impressive plumbing and drainage system brought

running water to and from the palace, and a complex layout of rooms and passageways on several levels turned the interior into a maze. Below ground, a storage area contained huge earthenware pots that held grains, oils, and wines, probably collected as taxes from the populace and serving as the basis of trade and wealth. Beautiful *friezes* (bands of designs and figures) decorated the walls of rooms and hallways. *Frescoes*—paint applied directly on wet plaster—of dolphins, octopuses, and other ocean creatures enlivened the palace walls.

Although archeologists have discovered two written Cretan scripts, which they have labeled Linear A and Linear B, neither of these scripts has revealed anything about Minoan political, social, or philosophical systems. Minoan religion appears to have been matriarchal, centering on the worship of a mother goddess, or great goddess, creator of the universe and source of all life. Statues of a bare-breasted goddess with snakes in her hands show how the deity was portrayed, but the precise purpose of these statues is unknown (Figure 2.2). Minoans also honored numerous minor household goddesses and

30

FIGURE 2.2 Earth Goddess with Snakes. Ca. 1600–1580 B.C. Archaeological Museum, Heraklion, Crete. *This cult figure, about 11 inches high, was discovered in the Treasury of the Knossos Palace. Her triangular dress, with its apron and flounced skirt, is similar to those of Cretan youths in surviving frescoes.*

venerated trees and stone pillars, to which they probably attributed supernatural powers. Near the end of their era, the Minoans began to bury their dead in underground tombs and chambers, but neither the reason for the new burial practice nor its ritualistic meaning has been discovered.

What has been uncovered on the palace walls, and which apparently had deep religious significance, is a fresco depicting bull leaping—a sport or ritual activity perhaps associated with a bull cult (Figure 2.3). Regardless of its meaning, this daring act is probably more fiction than fact: The maidens (painted white) stand at either end of the bull while a male athlete (painted red) somersaults over the beast's back, a feat that is virtually impossible to accomplish.

Minoan trade dominated the eastern Mediterranean until about 1380 B.C., when the island was dev-

FIGURE 2.3 *Bull Leaping.* Ca. 1500 B.C. Archaeological Museum, Heraklion, Crete. *This fresco (approximately 32 inches high) from the east wing of the palace at Knossos is one of the largest paintings recovered from Crete. The association of young men and women with bulls in this scene brings to mind the legend of the Minotaur, in which seven youths and seven maidens were periodically sacrificed to a monster, half man and half bull, who lived in an underground labyrinth, supposedly on Crete.*

astated by a natural catastrophe—perhaps a volcanic eruption on a nearby island, an earthquake, a tidal wave, or a combination of these disasters. Weakened by Mycenaean incursions over the preceding centuries, Minoan civilization quickly fell to these raiders from the Greek mainland or to other invading seafarers. Whatever the whole story, the Minoans disappeared suddenly and mysteriously, leaving few remnants of their peaceful civilization.

The Greeks of the Archaic Age had no direct knowledge of Minoan civilization. What shaped the Greek attitude towards the Minoans was information conveyed through mythology. Myths are usually considered fiction, but buried within them are often actual folk memories or deep psychological truths.

For example, Crete is traditionally the birthplace of the god Zeus. The Minoans worshiped a Zeus who was born in a cave, grew to manhood, and died. They venerated the site of his birth and honored him as a child. The later Greeks, however, believed Zeus to be the immortal father and ruler of the Olympian deities, and they were incensed by the Minoan belief that the god died. The grain of truth in this story may be that although the Greeks eventually dominated Crete in physical terms, elements of Minoan religion found their way into later Greek beliefs; thus, in a sense, the Olympian gods *were* born in Crete.

Mythology created the image of Minoan civilization as sophisticated, materialistic, and pleasure-loving by later Greek standards. Significantly, modern excavations have borne out this impression. The Archaic Greeks, despite the allure of Crete, did not see the Minoan past as part of their heritage. Nonetheless, Cretan influences on Greece may be detected in language, religion, social organization, and economic pursuits.

BEGINNINGS: MYCENAEAN CIVILIZATION, 1900–1100 B.C.

Unlike the Minoans, the Mycenaeans continued to live for the Greeks of the Archaic Age through the *Iliad* and the *Odyssey*. The events related in these two epic poems occur during the Mycenaean Age, and the stories furnished the Greeks with many of their heroes—Achilles, the doomed warrior, for example, and Odysseus, the tough and wily wandering sailor. Eventually, the Greeks traced their tradition to Mycenae, honoring its warriors as their ancestors and as models of ideal noble behavior and values.

Mycenaean civilization, named by archeologists for Mycenae, one of its most prominent fortress cities, developed on the rugged lower Greek peninsula known as the Peloponnesus. An aggressive, warrior people perhaps from the plains of southern Russia or from the Tigris-Euphrates valley, the Mycenaeans arrived on the peninsula in about 1900 B.C., and by about 1500 B.C., they ruled the entire Peloponnesus.

A feudal order similar to that found later in medieval Europe characterized the Mycenaean political system. Family ties and marriages, tentative alliances, and uneasy truces bound the local rulers in a confederation of petty kingdoms. The kings of these fortress states and their warriors controlled the surrounding countryside. A staunch loyalty developed between the kings and their noble allies, generating a rigid class structure that exploited those who were not warriors.

A royal tax system created a need for a large bureaucracy of collectors and civil employees who ranked just below the ruling elite. Paralleling the bureaucracy were the retainers, military providers, and servants who supported the kings and nobles. At the low end of the social scale stood the merchants, traders, artisans, small landowners, peasants, and slaves—the last, like the royal servants, probably captured in wars or raids.

The ruins of the Mycenaean fortress-palaces, with their massive double walls, narrow escape passages, and wide gateways, stand as mute testimony to the harshness of the militaristic life and the power of the local king. The best known palace ruin, at Mycenae, contains the famous Lion Gate, constructed from four massive hewn stones, or **ashlars** (Figure 2.4). On one of these stones two carved lions, separated by a column, face each other and stretch out their long, muscular bodies. Placed there to watch over the fortress and to remind the populace of the ruler's power, the beasts must have intimidated all visitors who entered or left the citadel.

Within the fortresses and across the eastern Mediterranean archeologists have found jars, containers, vessels, and terra cotta figurines, revealing the high level of the Mycenaeans' artistic skill with clay and their wide-ranging trade and travel. The weapons and personal items crafted for the warriors show especially impressive artistic skills. A decorated sword blade of a lion hunt, inlaid in gold and silver, exemplifies the attention to delicate detail that the artisan brought to this art (Figure 2.5).

Mycenaean religion appears to have been a fusion of Minoan and local deities. Like the Minoans, the Mycenaeans venerated numerous household goddesses and worshiped aspects of nature in caves and natural shrines. Local deities seem to have been of two kinds: Some were predecessors of the Olympian gods and goddesses worshiped by the later Greeks and had the same names; others were nature divinities and spirits. Two sets of **shaft graves** have been

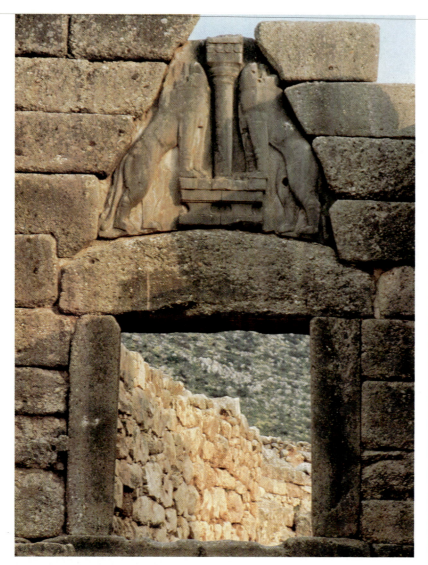

FIGURE 2.4   The Lion Gate at Mycenae. Ca. 1300 B.C. *The Lion Gate is a massive structure of four gigantic blocks—two posts and a beam forming the entrance and a triangular block on which are carved the two 9-foot-high lions and the central column. So impressive were the megalithic fortresses of the Mycenaeans to the later Greeks that they called them cyclopean, convinced that only a race of giants, the Cyclopes, could have built them.*

FIGURE 2.5   *Lion Hunt.* Ca. Sixteenth Century B.C. National Museum, Athens. *An anonymous artisan has decorated every part of this 9-inch dagger. Whether or not the weapon was ever actually used in battle is not clear, but its fine details and realistic figures must have made it a prized possession of a Mycenaean warrior. This dagger survived because it was buried alongside its owner in a funeral mound.*

FIGURE 2.6 Mycenaean Shaft Grave Circle. Ca. 1600–1500 B.C. *About 92 feet in diameter, the circle contained six graves that, upon excavation, yielded well-preserved skeletons along with jewelry, ornaments, weapons, and vases. The positioning of the bodies in the graves is thought to indicate Egyptian influences.*

excavated at Mycenae, yielding fabulous gold treasures and indicating that the Mycenaeans buried their dead with honor (Figure 2.6). Perhaps influenced by the Egyptians, they wrapped the bodies and surrounded them with precious objects and pottery. From such practices and attitudes evolved the worship of heroes, a central aspect of Greek culture.

The Mycenaean feudal system flourished for several centuries, and after 1380 B.C., when Crete fell, the Mycenaeans extended their raiding and trading activities throughout the eastern Mediterranean. In about 1250 B.C. they attacked the wealthy and strategic city of Troy, on the western coast of present-day Turkey, near the Dardanelles (see Map 2.1). Although similar expeditions had brought booty to the Mycenaeans on earlier occasions, this long, exhausting foray weakened them, leaving them open to conquest by more vigorous tribes. Ironically, this siege of the Trojan citadel probably inspired the *Iliad* and the *Odyssey*, Homer's enduring epics. Overwhelmed by the Dorians from the north, Mycenaean civili-

zation faded, and by about 1100 B.C. the Age of the Mycenaeans closed. The three-century hiatus in Greek history that followed, when writing disappeared and cultural activities virtually ceased, served to heighten the fascinating image of the Mycenaeans for the Greeks of later times.

The Mycenaeans, as presented to them by Homer, gave the Greeks many of their ideals. Heir to three centuries of oral traditions about the Mycenaeans, Homer invented the Age of Heroes. He sang to the Greeks of a glittering past that both inspired and sobered them. In the *Iliad* and the *Odyssey* the Greeks found a universe with a basic moral order and a people with a distinct ethos, or ethical code. The pursuit of excellence that Homer attributed to his heroes became an ideal of historical Greece. Many aristocrats even traced their ancestry back to Homer's warriors and, through them, to the gods and goddesses. So rich was Homer's world that art and literature drew on it for subjects and incentive throughout Greek history. Through him the Mycenaeans gave the

Greeks their myths, their religion, their ethics, their perception of the universe, and their insight into human character.

INTERLUDE: THE DARK AGES, 1100–800 B.C.

With the fall of the Mycenaean citadels, a period known as the Dark Ages began, and life reverted to simpler patterns. People now lived in isolated farming communities and produced only essential tools and domestic objects. Commercial and social interchange among communities, already made hazardous by the mountainous terrain, became even more dangerous, and communication with the eastern Mediterranean kingdoms nearly ceased.

Yet some fundamental changes were slowly occurring even during this era. Political power was gradually shifting from kings to the heads of powerful families, laying the foundation for a new form of government, and iron gradually replaced bronze in tools, weapons, and other crafted objects—thus ending the Bronze Age and beginning the Iron Age in Greece. Many Mycenaeans fled to the coast of Asia Minor, which later came to be called Ionia, thus paving the way for the formation of an extended Greek community around the Aegean and Mediterranean seas.

THE ARCHAIC AGE, 800–479 B.C.

In about 800 B.C. the Greeks emerged from their long years of stagnation and moved into an era of political innovation and cultural experimentation. Although scattered and isolated, they shared a sense of identity based on their common language, their heroic stories and folk tales, their myths and religious practices, and their commercial and trading interests. They claimed a common mythical parent, Hellen, who fathered three sons—the ancestors of the three major Greek tribes, the Ionians, the Aeolians, and the Dorians—and thus they called themselves Hellenes and their land Hellas. In the next three centuries the Greeks would reconstruct their political and social systems, develop new styles of art and architecture, invent new literary genres, and make the first formal philosophical inquiries into the nature of human behavior and the universe. By the end of this period, they would have laid the foundations for a new world.

Political, Economic, and Social Structures

By the beginning of the Archaic Age, the isolated farming community had evolved into the *polis* (plural, *poleis*), a small, well-defined city-state. Several hundred of these poleis lay scattered over the Greek mainland and abroad. Although each polis had its own separate history and unique traits, they all shared certain features. An *acropolis*, or fortified hilltop, served as a citadel where the rulers usually resided (Figure 2.7). Temples and holy shrines stood on the acropolis or below in an *agora*. The agora, an open area where political leaders held forth, citizens assembled, and the populace congregated to conduct business and socialize, was the center of a polis. The pursuit of both public and private matters in an agora served to bind the citizens of a polis together in their daily lives and to foster civic pride and loyalty. In effect, a polis, through its control of the religious, cultural, and psychological components of its relatively closed community, molded the citizenry into an organic body with a collective identity.

Simultaneously with the emergence of the polis in about 800 B.C., the political system underwent a basic change. The kings had been deposed by the leaders of noble families who owned most of the land and possessed the weapons and horses. These wealthy warriors established *oligarchies*, or government by the few. The kingships, once abolished, faded into memories and myths used by the nobles to inspire and guide future generations. Although the oligarchies worked to benefit the aristocrats, they were also characterized by exemplary leadership, civic idealism, and cultural and artistic patronage. However, most oligarchies eventually failed because of unforeseen and far-reaching military and economic changes.

New military tactics now made obsolete the aristocrats who had distinguished themselves in battle as sword-wielding warriors in horse-drawn chariots. Foot soldiers—armed with long spears, protected by shields and personal armor, and grouped in closed ranks called phalanxes—were proving more effective in battles than individual warriors. These foot soldiers, or hoplites, were recruited from among independent farmers, merchants, traders, and artisans, who were also profiting from an expanding economy. As their military value became evident, these commoners soon demanded a voice in political decisions.

At the same time, a growing population, beginning to strain the limited agricultural resources, led to an era of overseas expansion and colonization. The Hellenes sent citizens to join their earlier Ionian

FIGURE 2.7   Acropolis, Athens. View from the West. *The acropolis dominates Athens in the twentieth century just as it did in ancient times when it was the center of Athenian ceremonial and religious life. Today it is the towering symbol of Athens' cultural heritage as well as the center of the local tourist industry. A landmark in the history of town planning, the acropolis is the ancestor of all carefully laid out urban environments from ancient Rome to Renaissance Florence to modern Brasilia.*

settlements and to establish new colonies along the coasts of Spain, North Africa, the Black Sea and southern Russia, and Sicily and southern Italy, which became known as *Magna Graecia*, or Greater Greece.

Foreign ventures and expanded trade increased the wealth of the new middle class and reinforced their desires for more economic opportunities and political influence, but the entrenched aristocracy blocked their way to power. Frustrated by the inability of reform efforts to solve deep-seated problems, in the sixth century B.C. many poleis turned to rulers whom they entrusted with extraordinary powers to make sweeping economic and political changes. Many of these tyrants, as the Greeks called them, restructured their societies to allow more citizens to benefit from the growing economy, to move up the social scale, and to participate in the political process. However, some tyrants perpetuated their

rule through heirs or political alliances and governed harshly for years, thus giving the word *tyrant* its modern meaning.

Regardless of the different results of the tyrants' reigns, by about 500 B.C. life in the poleis was similar in many ways. Citizens—freeborn males who could claim the right to enter into politics by virtue of family and wealth—voiced their opinions in a widening democratic process. They sat on juries, debated in the assemblies, and defended their polis in time of war. Civic responsibility, recognized as a central element in everyday life, was now passed on by the aristocrats to this new band of citizens.

Although horizons were expanding for the male citizens, other members of this predominantly middle-class society were severely restricted in political and economic matters. Women—except for priestesses and a rare literary figure like Sappho—were subservient to men. In Athens, for example, women possessed no legal or economic status, for they were by law under the control of the males in the household. Typically, women remained secluded at home, tending to the children and waiting on their husbands. Families often married off their daughters for economic gain; and, once married, the daughters were expected to be hardworking, loyal, and obedient.

Foreigners, with a few exceptions, were placed in special categories that restricted their personal rights and limited their economic opportunities. Some poleis, like Sparta, simply barred most foreigners, whereas Athens was more tolerant. Slaves, on the other hand, had no rights and were treated as property. Some ambitious and bright slaves did improve their plight and even won their freedom, but for every ex-slave, thousands of unfree men and women toiled and suffered in mines, on farms, and in houses without any legal protection or hope of future improvement.

Case Studies of the Greek Polis: Sparta and Athens

Of the hundreds of poleis that evolved during the Archaic Age, Sparta and Athens stand out for their vividly contrasting styles of life and their roles in subsequent Greek history. As case studies, the two poleis represent almost opposite ways of solving problems common to any organized society.

Sparta, the principal symbol of Dorian civilization, chose to guarantee its integrity and future through stringent and uncompromising policies. The earliest Spartans forcibly subjugated the original inhabitants of the lower Peloponnesus and ruthlessly enslaved them. To prevent rebellions and to control this population of *Helots,* as they were called, a vigilant Sparta was forced to keep its military always on the alert. (The Helots outnumbered the free Spartans by ten to one.) Thus, Sparta created a rigid hierarchical society of well-trained, tough, and athletic men, women, and children. The Spartans also estab-

lished a genuine oligarchy: a constitutional government operated by five officials elected annually by a small body of citizens. The ruling class, obsessed with keeping order in the society, passed laws forbidding immigration, limiting material possessions, and restricting creativity. Sparta was admired for its loyal, brave soldiers and for its stable social order; but Sparta never contributed to the artistic and intellectual enrichment of Greece.

By contrast, Athens, the symbol of Ionian civilization, reached greater artistic, intellectual, and literary heights than any other polis. The city of Athens, which allowed the surrounding countryside to go its own way, was a much more open society than Sparta; as a result, the clans in Attica, as the area was known, shared a sense of community with the Athenians and supported them in wartime.

The history of Athens echoes the general pattern of change in the poleis during the Archaic Age (Time Line 2.2). At the beginning of this era, aristocrats ruled Athens through councils and assemblies. As long as farming and trading sustained an expanding population, the nobles ruled without challenge. But at the beginning of the sixth century B.C., many peasant farmers found themselves burdened with mounting financial problems and threatened with prison or slavery for debts they could not pay. Saddled with these debts and having no voice in the government, the farmers began to protest what they perceived as unfair and arbitrary laws.

In about 590 B.C. the Athenians granted an aristocrat named Solon special political powers to reform the economy and make other changes. He abolished debts and guaranteed a free peasantry, overhauled the judicial system, and set down the laws in writing. Solon also restructured the Athenian constitution by giving the lower ranks of free men— those without great name or noble family but with some property or wealth—the right to participate in government.

Solon's principal successor was Cleisthenes [KLICE-thu-neez], who established democracy in Athens. He came to power in 508 B.C. and broadened

TIME LINE 2.2   THE ARCHAIC AGE IN GREECE   All dates B.C.

ca. 800		600	590		508	490	479
Dark Ages	Expansion and Colonization	Solon in Athens 600–590	Political, Social, Economic Reforms		Cleisthenes in Athens 508–490	Persian Wars	Golden Age
Political and cultural activity revives							

TIME LINE 2.3   EVENTS OF THE PERSIAN WARS   **All dates B.C.**

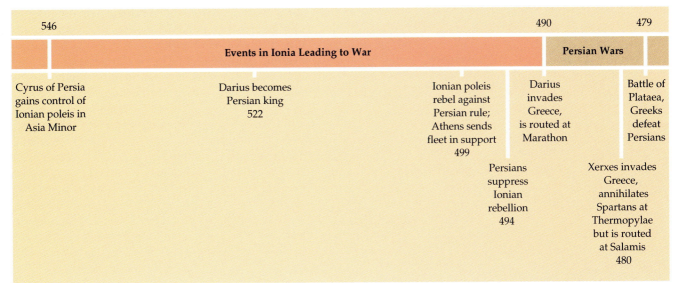

the governmental base by opening it to all free male citizens (called the *demos*) regardless of their property or bloodlines. Cleisthenes also expanded the ruling executive body and made its membership chosen by lot. At the same time, he placed final authority in the *ecclesia*, the assembly composed of the demos. Cleisthenes reorganized the society into geographical rather than clan units, thus tying together regional and economic interests. His democratic reforms, which lasted for almost two centuries, created an atmosphere in which civic pride and artistic energy were unleashed, inaugurating the Golden Age that made Athens both the pride and the envy of all the other Greek city-states.

The Persian Wars

Cleisthenes' domestic reforms were one of the two major events that heralded the end of the Archaic Age and the coming of Greece's Golden Age. The other event, the Persian Wars, proved to be pivotal not only for Greece but for Western civilization as well. If the autocratic Persians had won these wars, the democratic institutions, the humanistic values, and the cultural landmarks that the Greeks were just then establishing would have been lost.

By the mid–sixth century B.C., the Persians ruled a huge empire in the Near East encompassing most of the ancient world and including the Greek poleis in Ionia. When Darius [duh-RYE-us], king of the Persians at the end of the sixth century, demanded taxes and tribute from the Ionian Greeks, they revolted and looked to their homeland for support. A few poleis, including Athens, sent an expedition that

Darius eventually defeated. To prevent future uprisings and to punish the Greek mainlanders, Darius invaded the Greek peninsula. When the Persians landed near Athens at Marathon in 490 B.C., they faced a greatly outnumbered Athenian army, but the Athenians fought brilliantly, routing the invaders and destroying many of their ships. The victorious Greeks immediately marched westward to Athens and arrived just before the second Persian army, which, after assessing their situation, sailed home. At the battle of Marathon, a small band of Athenians had turned back the powerful Persian Empire (Time Line 2.3).

However, the Persians soon found a new and determined ruler in Xerxes [ZIRK-seez], son of Darius, who led an army of 180,000 soldiers into northern Greece and overran much of the area. Under Spartan leadership, the Greeks planned to trap the Persians at Thermopylae, a mountain pass in the north, and they put together a navy to fight the Persians at Artemisium, off the eastern coast. The Greeks held their own at Artemisium, but at Thermopylae they were annihilated, even though they fought to the last soldier.

Xerxes raced southward and sacked Athens, whose inhabitants had barely escaped across the Saronic Gulf to the island of Salamis. Through clever Athenian leadership the Persian navy was tricked and drawn onto the narrows of the gulf, where the swifter Greek ships outmaneuvered the cumbersome Persian craft. After witnessing the humiliating destruction of his fleet with most of his troops aboard, Xerxes returned to Persia. The remains of the Persian army left in Greece were routed at Plataea in 479 B.C., thus ending this major threat to the Greek

TABLE 2.1   THE NINE MUSES AND
            THEIR AREAS OF CREATIVITY

NAME	ART OR SCIENCE
Calliope	Epic poetry
Clio	History
Erato	Erotic poetry and mime
Euterpe	Lyric poetry and music
Melpomene	Tragedy
Polyhymnia	Sacred hymn
Terpsichore	Dance and song
Thalia	Comedy
Urania	Astronomy

way of life. This final victory over the mighty Persians created a euphoric mood in Athens and set the stage for the ensuing Golden Age.

The Emergence of Greek Genius: The Mastery of Form

During the Archaic Age, the Greeks developed a variety of literary, philosophical, and artistic forms that they used to probe the meaning of the universe and of human existence as well as to celebrate their joyous sense of life. These cultural accomplishments, like those of the older Near Eastern civilizations, were associated with the religious beliefs and practices that played a central role in Greek life and history. In fact, the Greeks believed that creativity itself was a divine gift from the *muses*, the nine goddesses of artistic inspiration (Table 2.1). Guided by their muses, they created enduring works of art with a universal appeal.

Religion   The Greeks made religion an ongoing part of their private and public affairs. Indeed, the polis and religion could not be separated, for in the eyes of the Greeks the fate of each community depended on the civic deity. Public rituals and festivals drew together the citizens, infused them with civic pride, and reminded them of their common heritage. During the Archaic Age, Greek religion—an amalgam of deities derived from the original settlers as well as invaders and foreigners—evolved into two major categories: the Olympian and the chthonian. The *Olympian deities* dwelled in the sky or on mountain tops and were associated with the Homeric heroes and the aristocracy. The *chthonian deities* (from the Greek *chthon*, meaning "the earth") lived underground and were associated with the peasants and lower social orders.

The Olympian religion shared some traits with the polytheistic cults of the ancient Near East, including the notion that the deities intervene in daily affairs, the belief that they are like humans in many respects, and the idea of a pantheon of gods and goddesses. The Greeks endowed their deities with physical bodies and individual personalities, creating a fascinating blend of charm and cruelty, beauty and childishness, love of justice and caprice. This family of unruly and willful deities quarreled with each other and played favorites with their mortal worshipers as they pleased. Faced with such favoritism among the deities, the Greeks themselves developed a strong moral sense. The Greeks came to believe that as long as they recognized the divinities' power and did not challenge them—and thus become victims of *hubris*, or pride—they would survive and often prosper.

Homer's poems lay out the complex relations and kinships in the Olympic pantheon and explain the functions and roles of the twelve principal deities, but Homer by no means invented these supernatural beings; they had been around long before his time. Indeed, their confusing traits and characters are probably the result of a fusion of numerous gods and goddesses whose origins predate the Greeks. Notwithstanding the deities' erratic characteristics, however, the Greeks never forgot that the Olympian system reflects a moral order and sense of justice.

Zeus, a sky god and first among the immortals, reigned as king on Mount Olympus, hurling thunderbolts and presiding over the divine councils. He sired both immortals and mortals, for his sexual appetite knew no bounds. Hera, probably the great goddess of earlier cultures, was the sister and wife of Zeus. She watched over the women who appealed to her for help and kept a close eye on her wandering husband. Zeus' two brothers controlled the rest of the universe, Poseidon ruling the seas, all waters, and earthquakes, and Hades guarding the underworld. Zeus' twin offspring, Apollo and Artemis, symbolized the sun and the moon, respectively. Apollo, Zeus' favorite son, personified the voice of reason. Artemis, in contrast, watched over childbirth and guarded wild creatures. Zeus' lying son Ares delighted in fierce battles, and, as the war god, he possessed a quick temper and few morals. He and Aphrodite—Zeus' daughter and the goddess of love and beauty—were adulterous lovers. Ironically, Homer has Aphrodite married to Hephaestus, the ugly and lame son of Zeus who was a master smith and the patron of craftspeople.

Three other children of Zeus rounded out the Olympic roster. Athena, the goddess of wisdom and patron goddess of Athens, combined varied duties, including warfare, the arts, and handicrafts. Having sprung full-blown from the head of Zeus, Athena was worshiped as a virgin goddess. Hermes, the god of trade and good fortune, was also the patron of thieves, although he was best known as a messenger for his fellow deities. Hestia, a relatively minor goddess, protected the hearth (Table 2.2).

The chthonian gods and goddesses were probably derived from ancient earth and harvest deities. At first they were worshiped only by the lower orders, but as the demos grew in influence, chthonian rituals spread and were soon integrated into the civic calendar. Nevertheless, these cults were open only to initiates who were sworn to silence; hence, they were called mystery cults from the Greek word *mystos*, keeping silent.

The chthonian practices originally invoked the powers of the earth to ensure a successful planting and a bountiful harvest. The two most important crops in Greece—grains and grapes, the sources of bread and wine, respectively—led to two major cults, those of Demeter and Dionysus. Demeter, a sister of Zeus, was a harvest goddess. She, in turn, had a daughter, Persephone, whom Hades abducted to his kingdom below ground. According to her cult legend, Demeter finally rescued Persephone but not before Hades had tricked Persephone into eating a fruit that made her return to the underworld for part of each year. Thus, during the winter months the earth is bare, but when Persephone and Demeter are together, the earth is fecund and the grains grow. At Eleusis, a small village in Attica, Demeter was the focus of a mystery cult. Prospective initiates from all over Greece traveled there, apparently to receive her promise of immortal life.

TABLE 2.2   THE OLYMPIAN DEITIES AND THE AREAS THEY RULED

GOD OR GODDESS	DUTIES AND RESPONSIBILITIES
Zeus	Chief deity and keeper of order on Olympus
Hera	Mother goddess, protector of women
Poseidon	Ruler of waters
Hades	Keeper of the Underworld
Apollo	God of wisdom and moderation
Artemis	Virgin goddess who aided women
Ares	Amoral god of violence and warfare
Aphrodite	Goddess of passion, love, and beauty
Hephaestus	Patron of craftspeople
Athena	Goddess of wisdom and warfare
Hermes	God of merchants and thieves; messenger for the deities
Hestia	Protector of the hearth

Whereas Demeter's followers honored her in a dignified manner, Dionysus's worshipers, through wild dancing and wine drinking, hoped to be reinvigorated by their god and born again. Such irrational behavior stands in opposition to the usual image of the rational Greek character. Eventually, a Dionysus cult arose in Athens, where his followers annually held ceremonies honoring his power as god of the vine (Figure 2.8). Over the years these rituals became civic festivals that, in turn, spawned the competitive performances of tragic drama in Athens in the sixth century B.C.

FIGURE 2.8 EXEKIAS. *Dionysus Crossing the Sea.* Ca. 535 B.C. Staatliche Antikensammlungen, Munich. *Painted in the basin of a circular drinking bowl, Dionysus, the god of wine, is depicted sailing alone in a fish-nosed boat. This work by Exekias, one of the most admired artists of the Archaic Age, illustrates the beautiful mastery of space that characterized the best vase painting of the time. Dionysus reclines under a billowing sail, surrounded by gamboling dolphins. Sprouting from the boat is a vine carrying bunches of grapes—the symbol of the wine god. Exekias' simple design is typical of Archaic painting.*

FIGURE 2.9 EUPHRONIOS. *The Death of Sarpedon.* Ca. 520 B.C. Metropolitan Museum of Art. *This vase painting illustrates a famous scene from Book 16 of the* Iliad. *Following Homer, the painter has depicted the fallen warrior Sarpedon, the son of Zeus and a mortal woman, being carried to his rest by winged figures representing Death and Sleep. Euphronios uses bold colors to dramatize the scene, such as bright red for the gushing blood from Sarpedon's wounds and the device carried by Hermes, the bearded god with curly hair portrayed in the center. Though he is not mentioned in Homer, Hermes' presence is appropriate, since, among his other duties, he guided dead souls into the underworld.*

Epic Poetry   The originator of the major traditions of *epic poetry* is traditionally believed to be Homer (about 800 B.C.), a *bard*, or poet who sang his verses while accompanying himself on a stringed instrument. In the *Iliad* and the *Odyssey*, Homer sang of the events before, during, and after the Trojan War, stories that had circulated among the Greeks since the fall of Mycenae. Homer entertained an aristocratic audience eager to claim kinship with the Mycenaean past. For many years his poems were transmitted orally by other bards and probably did not exist in written versions until the seventh century B.C. Homer's authorship and, indeed, even his very existence are established solely by tradition; nothing is actually known about him. Nevertheless, by the end of the Archaic Age the appeal of Homer's poetry had embraced all social levels, and his authority approached that of a modern combination of television, Shakespeare, and the Bible.

The basic appeal of the Homeric epics lies in their well-crafted plots, filled with dramatic episodes and finely drawn characters. Set against the backdrop of the Trojan War, the *Iliad* describes the battle of Ilium, another name for Troy, and the *Odyssey* recounts events after the Greeks defeat the Trojans (Figure 2.9). The earlier of the epics, the *Iliad*, focuses on Achilles, the epitome of heroic Greek manhood. In contrast to the battlefield heroics of the *Iliad*, the *Odyssey* narrates the wanderings of the Greek warrior Odysseus after the fall of Troy. Moreover, the *Odyssey* celebrates marriage, for Odysseus, despite some amorous adventures, remains fixed on thoughts of his wife Penelope, who waits for him in Ithaca.

In both poems, the deities merrily intrude into the lives of mortals, changing and postponing the fate of friend and enemy alike. So great was Homer's authority that his works made him the theologian of Greek religion. His stories of the gods and goddesses, while not completely replacing other versions of their lives, became the standard that circulated wherever Greek was spoken. Homer presented Zeus, the nominal protector of the moral order, as forever under siege by other gods seeking help for their favorite mortals. Although some later Greeks deplored Homer's inattention to moral issues, his roguish portraits of the deities remained indelibly imprinted in the minds of the general populace.

Homer's poetic expression also gave texture to the Greek language. Similes, figures of speech in which two unlike things are compared, help bring the dramatic, exotic events of the stories down to earth. For example, Homer creates a vivid image of Odysseus as a ferocious killer when he compares him to a lion ''covered with blood, all his chest and his flanks on either side bloody. . . .'' In a less violent simile, Homer has Achilles compare his fellow Greeks to ''unwinged'' baby birds and himself to their nurturing mother. Homer's images also provide a rich repertory of ready phrases and metaphors, known as **Homeric epithets**, such as ''the wily Odysseus,'' ''the swift-footed Achilles,'' and ''rosy-fingered dawn.''

Besides shaping the language, Homer served as a guide to behavior for the Archaic Greeks. Because they became part of the Greek educational curriculum, his poems acquired an ethical function. A young man who took Achilles or Odysseus for a model would learn to maintain his well-being, to speak eloquently in company with other men, to give and receive hospitality, to shed tears in public over the death of his closest friend, to admire the beauty of women, to esteem the material wealth of other nobles, to appreciate songs of bravery, and, above all, to protect his reputation as a man and warrior. On the other hand, a young woman who imitated Penelope, the patient and faithful wife of Odysseus, would inhabit a more circumscribed world, as she learned to weave at the loom, to manage a household, to cultivate her physical beauty, and to resist the advances of other men.

Lyric Poetry   Verses sung to the music of the **lyre** (a stringed instrument), or **lyric poetry**, became the dominant literary expression in the late Archaic Age, and lyric verses have dominated Western poetry ever since. Lyric poetry, which originated later than the epic, expressed an author's personal, private thoughts, though the muse Euterpe was credited with the inspiration. The shift from epic to lyric poetry in the sixth century B.C. coincided with changes in the polis, where the rising democratic spirit encouraged a variety of voices to be heard.

Of the several types of lyric poetry, monody, or the solo lyric, became the most influential in Archaic Greece. Poets of monody achieved relative simplicity by using a single line of verse or by repeating a short stanza pattern. These solo lyricists did not hesitate to reveal their most intimate thoughts or details of their private lives.

Unlike the Homeric epics, which survive relatively whole, the solo lyrics are mutilated in the extreme. For example, the bulk of what remains of Sappho's [SAF-oh] verses consists of random lines and references gleaned from later commentators and only one or two entire lyrics. And of the music, the whole has been lost. The ancients, however, regarded Sappho (about 600 B.C.) as the greatest of the writers of solo lyrics. The philosopher Plato hailed her as the tenth muse in a short lyric he dedicated to her. A truly original writer, Sappho apparently owed no debt to Homer or any other poet. Her work is addressed to a small circle of aristocratic women friends on her native island of Lesbos in the Aegean. She was deeply personal in her interests, writing chiefly about herself, her friends, and their feelings for one another. In her elegant but restrained verses, Sappho sang mostly about moods of romantic passion: of longing, unrequited love, absence, regret, dead feelings, jealousy, and fulfillment. Sappho's willing vulnerability and her love of truth made the solo lyric the perfect vehicle for confessional writing (Table 2.3).

TABLE 2.3   LITERARY FIGURES OF THE ARCHAIC AGE

WRITER	WHEN FLOURISHED	ACHIEVEMENT
Homer	About 800 B.C.	Author of the *Iliad*, the first epic, and the *Odyssey*; both works focus on the aristocratic world
Hesiod	Late eighth to early seventh centuries B.C.	Author of *Works and Days*, first poetic work celebrating peasant life
Archilochus of Paros	Seventh century B.C.	First known lyric poet
Sappho of Lesbos	About 600 B.C.	Epitome of lyric poetry

Natural Philosophy   The mental attitudes that partly accounted for the democratic challenge to established authority in the Archaic Age also brought forth thinkers who questioned the power and, ultimately, the existence of the gods. Just as the democrats constructed a human-centered state, so did the philosophers conceive of a world where natural causes and effects operated. These Greek thinkers invented what the Romans later called natural philosophy, a term that includes both what we would call "science" and what we would call "philosophy." The close connection between science and philosophy persisted for twenty-three centuries, until the eighteenth century A.D., when they came to a parting of the ways, largely because of the Newtonian revolution. From that point on, science simply demonstrated what happened in nature without speculating about its purpose.

The origins of natural philosophy, like those of lyric poetry, are hidden in the incomplete historical record and distorted by the fragmented extant writings, but we can nevertheless say that formal Western philosophy began on the Ionian coast in the sixth

TABLE 2.4   PHILOSOPHERS OF THE ARCHAIC AGE

PHILOSOPHER	TIME	ACHIEVEMENT
Thales	About 585 B.C.	First philosopher and founder of philosophic materialism
Pythagoras	About 580–about 507 B.C.	Founder of philosophic idealism
Heraclitus	About 545–about 485 B.C.	First dialectical reasoning; belief in continual flux

century B.C. There, in the polis of Miletus, a set of thinkers known as the Milesian school speculated that beneath the ever-changing natural world was an unchanging matter (Table 2.4).

Thales [THAY-leez] (flourished 585 B.C.), the founder of the Milesian school, reasoned that the fundamental substance was water. From the standpoint of modern science, Thales was wrong and so were the rest of his circle who proposed other elements—air and "the infinite"—as the underlying essence. But more important than their conclusions regarding matter was their conviction that there is regularity in the universe and that human reason can ultimately understand the natural order. Their belief in rationality not only determined the direction of speculative thought but initiated the steps that led to the invention of physics, chemistry, botany, and other sciences. Proposing that the universe was governed by natural laws, these first philosophers questioned divine explanations for natural events, a development deplored by those who found the key to life in a divine spirit.

When the Persians conquered Asia Minor near the end of the sixth century B.C., the center of intellectual thought shifted to Athens and to southern Italy and Sicily, where a tradition had emerged that challenged the Milesian School. Pythagoras [puh-THAG-uh-ruhs] (about 580–about 507 B.C.), the leader of the Sicilian school, rejected the concept of an underlying substance. Instead, he proclaimed, "Everything is made of numbers," by which he meant that mathematical relationships explained the basic order in nature. His musical studies probably led Pythagoras to this conclusion. He may have observed that a plucked string vibrated, making a certain sound; if the string were cut in half and plucked again, then a new note an octave higher than the first, with twice as many vibrations per second, would be heard. Hence, mathematical ratios determined musical sounds. Pythagoras then concluded that "numbers" explained everything in the "cosmos," his term for the orderly system embracing the earth and the heavens. Later, ancient astronomers building on Pythagorean beliefs claimed that the planets, in moving through their orbits, made music—the "music of the spheres."

A third philosopher, Heraclitus [her-uh-KLITE-uhs] (about 545–about 485 B.C.), appeals more to the modern age than any other thinker in Archaic Greece. Rejecting the materialism of Thales and the idealism of Pythagoras, Heraclitus pioneered a philosophic tradition that found truth in constant change, as in his well-known idea that a person cannot step twice into the same flowing river. In addition, Heraclitus devised the earliest dialectical form of reasoning when he speculated that growth arises

TIME LINE 2.4   LANDMARKS IN ARCHITECTURE AND SCULPTURE, ARCHAIC AGE

All dates B.C.

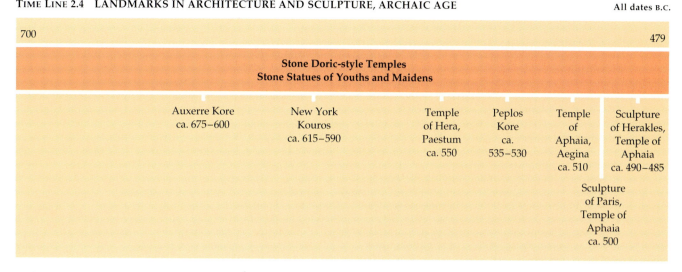

out of opposites, a fundamental tenet of dialectic thought. This original idea led him to argue that ''strife is justice'' and that struggle is necessary for progress. Heraclitus's dialectical reasoning anticipated certain nineteenth-century thinkers, and his notion of continual flux has attracted modern physicists.

Architecture   The supreme architectural achievement of the Greeks, the temple, became the fountainhead of the building components, decorative details, and aesthetic principles that together have largely shaped Western architecture down to Post-Modernism in the late twentieth century. In its origins during the Archaic Age, the temple was a sacred structure designed to house the cult statues of the civic deities. The early houses of worship were probably made of wood, which explains why no remains of these Greek temples have been discovered. However, as the Archaic Age gathered economic momentum and wealth accumulated, each polis rebuilt its wooden sanctuaries in stone (Time Line 2.4).

A diagram of a typical temple illustrates how much the building has influenced Western architecture (Figure 2.10). Generic Greek architecture is called *post-beam-triangle construction* (also known as post-and-lintel construction). *Post* refers to the columns; *beam* indicates the horizontal members, or *architraves*, resting on the columns; and *triangle* denotes the triangular area, called a *pediment*, at either end of the upper building. Other common features include the *entablature*, which is the name for all of the building between the columns and the pediment; the *cornice*, the horizontal piece that crowns the entablature; and the *stylobate*, the upper step of the base on which the columns stand. A typical temple had columns on four sides which, in turn, enclosed

a walled room, called a *cella*, that housed the cult image. Each temple faced east, with the doors to the cella placed so that, when opened, they allowed the sunrise to illuminate the statue of the deity.

The earliest temple style in Greece was called *Doric*, both because it originated in the Dorian poleis and because the style's simplicity of design and scarcity of decorative detail reflected the severe Dorian taste (Figure 2.11). The Doric columns have plain tops, or *capitals*, and the columns rest directly on the stylobate without an intervening footing. On the entablature of each Doric temple is a sculptural band, called a *frieze*, which alternates three-grooved panels, called *triglyphs*, with blank panels, called *metopes*, that could be left plain or filled with *relief* sculptures. The triglyphs are reminders of the temple's origin as a wooden building when logs, faced with bronze, served as overhead beams.

An excellent example of the Doric style in the Archaic Age is the Temple of Hera in Poseidonia, now called Paestum, in southern Italy (Figure 2.12). The Temple of Hera is the oldest (about 550 B.C.) and best-preserved of three cult sanctuaries on this site. Constructed from coarse local limestone, this large temple has a somewhat ungainly appearance, due in part to the massive architrave and the small spaces between the columns. The builders attempted to remedy this defect (without total success) by introducing refinements into the temple's design. The columns were made to appear strong and solid enough to support the entablature by enlarging the middles of the shafts, a technique known as *entasis*. The artisans also carved vertical grooves, called *fluting*, along the shafts to give the columns a graceful, delicate surface and enhance their visual three-dimensionality.

Eventually, after much experimentation, Greek

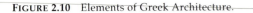

FIGURE 2.10 Elements of Greek Architecture.

FIGURE 2.11 Greek Architecture of the Doric Order.

architects overcame the awkwardness of the early Doric style by deciding that a temple's beauty was a function of mathematical proportions. The Temple of Aphaia—erected in 510 B.C. by the citizens of Aegina, Athens' neighbor and perennial enemy— seemed to embody this principle (Figure 2.13). The architect of this temple achieved its pleasing dimensions by using the ratio 1:2, placing six columns on the ends and twelve columns on the sides. The Temple of Aphaia, with its harmonious proportions and graceful columns, became the widely imitated standard for the Doric style over the next half century.

Sculpture Like the art of Mesopotamia and Egypt, Greek sculpture was rooted in religious practices and beliefs. The Greek sculptors fashioned images of the gods and goddesses to be used in temples either as objects of worship or as decorations for the pediments and friezes. Of greater importance for the development of Greek sculpture were the *kouros* (plural, kourai) and the *kore* (plural, korai), free-standing statues of

FIGURE 2.12   Temple of Hera at Paestum. Ca. 560–550 B.C.
*This temple stands not only as a model of Archaic Greek
architecture but as a reminder of Greek wealth and expansion.
Colonists from mainland Greece settled southern Italy, the land
they thought of as "greater Greece," in the seventh and sixth
centuries B.C., bringing with them the Olympian gods and
goddesses and their ideas of how to build temples in their honor.*

FIGURE 2.13   Temple of Aphaia, Aegina. View from the
Southeast. 510 B.C. *The Temple of Aphaia in Aegina became the
standard for the Doric Temple style from its creation until it was
superseded by the Athenian Parthenon in the 440s. Built of local
limestone and covered in stucco and painted, the Temple of
Aphaia gleamed like a jewel in its carefully planned site
overlooking the Saronic Gulf. Constructed and decorated with
strict attention to artistic refinements, such as the slender
columns and the lifelike sculptures, this temple represents the
climax of Archaic architecture.*

youths and maidens, respectively. Before 600 B.C. these
sculptures had evolved from images of gods, to statues
of dead heroes, and finally into memorials that might
not even be directly related to the dead person to
whom they were dedicated.

What made the *Archaic* statues of youths and
maidens so different from Egyptian and Mesopotamian art was the Greek delight in the splendor of the
human body. In their representations of the human
form, the Greeks rejected the sacred approach of the
Egyptians and Mesopotamians, which stressed conventional poses and formal gestures. Instead, Greek
sculptors created athletic, muscular males and robust maidens filled with life. For the Greeks, the
health and beauty of the subjects was as important
as the statues' religious purpose.

The first Archaic statues of youths owed much to
the Egyptian tradition, but gradually Greek sculpture broke free of its origins. An early example of the
kourai type of sculpture is the New York Kouros
(Figure 2.14), named for its present location in New

FIGURE 2.14 New York Kouros. Ca. 615–590 B.C.
Metropolitan Museum of Art. *The New York Kouros is one of
many similar statues dating from about the beginning of the sixth
century B.C. During that century the male and female statues
evolved from stiff and stereotyped models to natural and
anatomically correct forms.*

York City's Metropolitan Museum of Art. Artisti-
cally, this marble statue of a youth with the left foot
forward, the clenched fists, the arms held rigidly at
the sides, the stylized hair, and the frontality, that is,
the quality of being designed for viewing from the
front, shows the Egyptian influence (see Figure 1.15).
The Greek sculptor has moved beyond Egyptian
techniques, however, by incorporating changes that
make the figure more lifelike, such as by attempting
to show the correct shape of the knees and suggesting an actual person's mouth. That the result is not
a realistic or an idealized human figure is less important than that the sculptor has studied the human
body with fresh eyes and endeavored to represent it
accurately. With such ground-breaking works as the
New York Kouros, the Greeks launched a dynamic
tradition that later artists continually reshaped.

A generation after the New York Kouros, new
sculptors expressed their changed notion of a beautiful living male body in such works as the Ptoon
Kouros (Figure 2.15). This sculpture, which was
probably a dedicatory offering to a god or goddess,
still shows a powerful Egyptian influence, but it
takes a giant step forward to a greater sense of life.
The taut body and massive torso convincingly reproduce the athletic qualities of an Olympic competitor, and the curious facial expression, known as
the "archaic smile," gives an enigmatic quality to the
marble figure.

The korai sculptures, like the statues of youths,
evolved from a frozen, lifeless style toward a greater
realism, although women were never depicted in the
nude at this stage in Greek sculpture. The earliest
draped korai sculptures mixed Mesopotamian and
Egyptian traditions with Greek ideas, sometimes
producing an interesting but awkward effect. Such
an early work is the Auxerre Kore (Figure 2.16)—
named for the museum in Auxerre, France—whose
cylindrical shape is copied from Mesopotamian
models and whose stiff pose, wiglike hair, and thin
waist are borrowed from Egypt. The Greek sculptor
added the broad mouth and the Greek peplos (a
loose-fitting outer robe) decorated with a meander
pattern, but the Auxerre Kore, despite its charming
details, is rigid and inert.

The Peplos Kore (Figure 2.17), dating about a century later, expresses beautifully the exciting changes
that were taking place in late Archaic sculpture. The
statue wears a chiton, or tunic, over her upper torso,
and a belted peplos. The sculptor has replaced the
rigidity of the Egyptian pose with a more graceful
one, as shown, for example, by the way the figure
holds her right arm. Traces of a painted necklace
may be seen, for the Peplos Kore, like all Greek
sculpture, was painted to make the figure as true to

FIGURE 2.15   Ptoon Kouros. Ca. 540–520 B.C. National Museum, Athens. *The Ptoon Kouros possesses the distinguishing characteristics of all kourai: frontality, attention to bodily details, and a general formality. However, the subtle innovations in the Ptoon Kouros foreshadow the Hellenic sculpture style.*

FIGURE 2.16 Auxerre Kore. Ca. 675–600 B.C. Louvre, Paris. *The Auxerre Kore represents a fairly early stage in the development of this female form. The small size of the sculpture (about 29½ inches high) suggests that it may have been part of a burial rite.*

FIGURE 2.17 Peplos Kore. Ca. 535–530 B.C. Acropolis Museum, Athens. *The Peplos Kore represents the highest achievement in the art of the kore. The beauty of the face, the elegance of the dress, and the expectancy of the countenance—this maiden could have been one of those who inspired Sappho's love lyrics.*

FIGURE 2.18 *Paris.* West Pediment, Temple of Aphaia, Aegina. Ca. 500 B.C. Staatliche Antikensammlungen, Munich. *The pedimental sculptures on the Temple of Aphaia illustrate the rapid changes that were occurring in artistic ideals and techniques in the period just preceding the Golden Age of Athens. The sculpture of Paris from the earlier west pediment is formal and stylized in comparison with its counterpart on the east pediment.*

FIGURE 2.19 *Herakles.* East Pediment, Temple of Aphaia, Aegina. Ca. 490–485 B.C. Staatliche Antikensammlungen, Munich. *The statue of Herakles from the east pediment of the Temple of Aphaia shows the advances made in sculpture in the ten to fifteen years since the figure of Paris was crafted for the west pediment. More realistic, detailed, and lifelike than Paris, Herakles is emotionally charged and tense yet composed and restrained—a state admired and often depicted by Hellenic artists. Both archers were sculpted in marble.*

life as possible. The often awkward archaic smile is here rendered to perfection, giving this lovely maiden an aristocratic demeanor.

The Greek tradition of representing males nude and females clothed persisted throughout the Archaic Age and well into the succeeding Classical Age. The Greeks readily accepted male nudity, witnessing it in the army on campaigns, in the gymnasium during exercises, and in the games at Olympia and elsewhere, and this acceptance is reflected in their art. But they were much less comfortable with female nudity (except in Sparta, where women exercised in the nude), so women were usually depicted draped or robed.

The political turmoil brought on by the Persian Wars occurred simultaneously with the revolutionary changes in sculpture that were leading to a new style of art. The Temple of Aphaia at Aegina provides a laboratory setting for the transition from the Archaic to the Hellenic Style (480–323 B.C.) because

of the different ages of the building's statues: The sculptures for the west pediment (about 500 B.C.) were made some fifteen years earlier than those on the east pediment (about 490–485 B.C.). Their stylistic differences demonstrate the changes that were underway.

An earlier statue (from the west pediment) depicts the Trojan hero Paris as a nude, somewhat sensual bowman, poised, ready to release an arrow (Figure 2.18). Paris, his body and face revealing very little tension, might have been posing, rather than preparing for action. A later sculpture (from the east pediment) portrays the legendary hero Herakles as a clothed archer, in a stance copied from the *Paris* figure (Figure 2.19). But what a contrast! Herakles' more muscular body is tensed and ready for action. While neither face registers emotion, Herakles' gaze and set jawline convey a more lifelike image of a warrior. The *Herakles* figure is a transitional work to the next style—the Hellenic.

The Legacy of Archaic Greek Civilization

The Archaic Age in Greece was a precious moment in the story of the arts and humanities. Inheriting survival techniques from Neolithic cultures, continuing the urban ways of Mesopotamia and Egypt, and, more importantly, drawing spiritual and psychological sustenance from the Minoans and Mycenaeans, the Archaic Greeks developed a unique consciousness that expressed, through original artistic and literary forms, their views about the deities and themselves and how they both interacted. A mark of the creative power of the Archaic Greeks is that at the same time that they were inventing epic poetry, lyric poetry, the post-beam-triangle temple, the kore and kouros sculptures, and natural philosophy, they were involved in founding a new and better way to live in the polis.

The new way of life devised by the Archaic Greeks gave rise to what we call, in retrospect, the *humanities*—those original artistic and literary forms that made Greek civilization unique. But the cultural explosion of this brilliant age is inseparable from the Greeks' restless drive to experience life to the fullest and their deep regard for human powers. Having devised their cultural forms, the Archaic Greeks believed passionately that by simply employing these models, either through studying them or by creating new works, the individual became a better human being. In this way, the Archaic Greeks' arts and humanities were imbued with an ethical content, thus suggesting for some—notably philosophers—an alternative way of life to that offered by religion.

Wherever we look in this age, we see creative energy, a trait that has characterized Western civilization through the ages. Even though the different cultural forms did not develop at the same pace during the Archaic Age—sculpture, for example, was not as expressive as lyric poetry—still, these early aesthetic efforts were fundamentally different from those of the earlier Near Eastern civilizations. The touchstone of the humanistic style developed by the Archaic Greeks was their belief in human powers, both intellectual and physical. Indeed, the most powerful literary voice of this age, Homer, was quoted over and over for his claim that mortals and divinities are part of the same family. Less confident people, hearing this assertion, might have reasoned that human beings are limited in their earthly hopes. But, for the Greeks of this period, Homer meant that humans are capable of godlike actions. The reverence that the Archaic Greeks expressed for all noteworthy deeds, whether in poetry, in warfare, or in the Olympic games, attested to their belief in the basic value of human achievement.

KEY CULTURAL TERMS

frieze	*pediment*
fresco	*entablature*
ashlar	*cornice*
shaft graves	*stylobate*
oligarchy	*cella*
muse	*Doric*
Olympian deities	*capital*
chthonian deities	*triglyph*
hubris	*metope*
epic poetry	*relief*
bard	*entasis*
Homeric epithet	*fluting*
lyre	*kouros*
lyric poetry	*kore*
post-beam-triangle	*Archaic*
construction	*humanities*
architrave	

SUGGESTIONS FOR FURTHER READING

PRIMARY SOURCES

BARNSTONE, W., ed. and trans. *Greek Lyric Poetry.* New York: Bantam Books, 1962. Selections from literary fragments dating from the seventh century B.C. to the sixth century A.D.; includes helpful biographical notes.

HOMER. *Iliad.* Translated by R. Lattimore. Chicago: University of Chicago Press, 1962. An excellent modern translation of the story of the Trojan War.

———. *Odyssey.* Translated by R. Lattimore. New York: Harper & Row, 1968. The epic of Odysseus's adventures after the fall of Troy, again in Lattimore's lively translation.

WHEELWRIGHT, P., ed. *The Presocratics.* New York: Bobbs-Merrill, 1966. A nearly complete collection of quotations from early philosophers that captures the flavor of sixth-century Greek thought.

Of all the many translations of Greek literature, the Loeb Classical Library, published by Harvard University Press, is probably the best.

3

CLASSICAL GREEK CIVILIZATION
The Hellenic Age

With the defeat of the Persians at Plataea in 479 B.C., the Greeks entered the *Hellenic* Age, a period that lasted until the death of Alexander the Great of Macedon in 323 B.C. During the more than 150 years of the Hellenic Age, the Greek world was buffeted by military explosions. The Greeks defeated the Persians for a second time and survived a century of destructive civil war, only to succumb ultimately to the Macedonians. But throughout these turbulent times the Greeks never wavered in their supreme confidence in the superiority of their way of life.

The Greek world consisted of several hundred poleis (city-states), located on the mainland, on the Aegean Islands and the coast of Asia Minor, and in the lands bordering the Mediterranean and Black Seas (Map 3.1). Athens was the cultural center of Greece, but many poleis contributed both materially and intellectually to Hellenic civilization. Corinth, for example, located on the isthmus between Athens and the Peloponnesus, dominated the economy of the Ionian Sea west of Greece, and the poleis of southern Italy (*Magna Graecia*) nurtured important schools of philosophy.

◀ *Orestes Slaying Aegisthus*. Ca. Late Sixth Century B.C. Kunsthistorisches Museum, Vienna.

GENERAL CHARACTERISTICS OF HELLENIC CIVILIZATION

Despite diversity among the poleis, the Greeks of the Hellenic Age shared certain characteristics. Competitiveness and rivalry were certainly dominant features, as was an increasingly urban style of life (Figure 3.1). Most Greeks still lived in the countryside, but the city now dominated politics, society, and the economy because, regardless of where citizens lived, they had to travel to the city to discharge their civic obligations.

Popular attitudes toward the Olympian deities were also changing, and public worship began to be assimilated into civic festivals. The great art of the age reflected this fusion in such works as the Parthenon, the temple to the goddess Athena, who was the protector of Athens (Figure 3.2). With gods and goddesses playing increasingly ceremonial rather than personal roles, religion became demystified and lost some of its value in the lives of the citizens. Religious dissatisfaction was also triggered by expanded political rights: The more democratic poleis raised the collective hopes of their citizens without being able to satisfy all of their personal longings.

Another feature of Hellenic civilization was a high regard for the balanced life and for moderation as the way to achieve it. In Athenian tragedy a recurrent theme is the danger of great wealth and high position. The playwrights preached that riches and

MAP 3.1

The Athenian Empire, 431 B.C.

FIGURE 3.1 *Athletes Playing Ball.* Second Quarter of the Fifth Century B.C. National Museum, Athens. *From the dawn of the Archaic period in about 800 B.C., sports, especially competitive sports, were integral to Greek life. In the* Iliad, *which appeared at about that time, Homer describes the athletic games that were played at the funeral of the warrior Patroclus. Later, in Hellenic times, artists used sports contests as subjects, as in this low-relief sculpture depicting a ball game played with curved sticks. The athletes' superbly muscled bodies and the overall sense of calm seriousness are typical of the art of the Hellenic period.*

FIGURE 3.2 *Athena.* Roman Copy Based on Fifth-Century Statue by Phidias. Staatliche Museen, Berlin. *The stern features of Athena corresponded well with her function as a war goddess and the patron of Athens. Phidias's sculpture disappeared in ancient times, but numerous copies such as this one have survived. The original sculpture was larger than life and dominated the inner sanctum of the Parthenon.*

FIGURE 3.3 *Apollo.* West Pediment, Temple at Olympia. Ca. 460 B.C. Olympia Museum. *Apollo's serene countenance in this splendidly crafted head reflects his image as the god of moderation. As the deity who counseled "Nothing in excess," Apollo was a potent force in combating the destructive urges that assailed the Greeks.*

status bred pride and led to envy by other citizens or, worse, envy by the gods. A modest life was the safest way to avoid personal calamity.

The Greeks also sought a balance between the opposite extremes that they recognized in human nature, symbolized by Apollo, god of moderation, and Dionysus, god of excess. As the god of light, Apollo embodied rational thought, ethical ideals, and aesthetic balance. Apollo's temple with its oracle at Delphi was one of the holiest shrines in Greece, second only to the island of Delos, his birthplace (Figure 3.3).

Dionysus, on the other hand, was the god of wine, of drunken revelry, of sexual excess, and of madness. Women known as **maenads** followed and worshiped him, sometimes tearing apart beasts in their blind frenzy. By the Hellenic Age, these excesses were confined to rural areas, for the Dionysiac impulse was constantly being tamed by the Apollonian spirit and the urban way of life. In Athens, the drunken worship of Dionysus was transformed into a civic festival, the Dionysia, from which tragedy, perhaps the highest expression of the Greek ethical genius, was born (Figure 3.4).

Greek citizens of Hellenic times, then, were proud of their own polis and competitive in their approach to life. They typically lived in a city, where they participated in civic functions and religious rites. They were skeptical about the gods and goddesses but believed strongly in a life of moderation. However,

FIGURE 3.4 *Dionysus and His Followers.* Ca. 430 B.C. Staatliche Museen, Berlin. *Scrolling around a perfume vase, this painting depicts a bearded Dionysus seated on the right with his followers. Of his twelve devotees, eleven are maenads, young female revelers; the last is the bearded Silenus, the foster father and former schoolmaster of Dionysus. Silenus is depicted on the lower left in his usual drunken, disorderly state.*

despite the many basic things that they shared with their fellow Greek citizens in the other poleis—a common land, common language, common ancestry, common history, and Homer—they were never to be citizens of a politically united Greek world.

DOMESTIC AND FOREIGN AFFAIRS: WAR, PEACE, AND THE TRIUMPH OF MACEDONIA

On the eve of the Hellenic Age, the Greeks, having defeated the Persians, were united in only two senses: in their continuing opposition to Persia and in their hostility to any polis that tried to control the others. Although they cooperated on short-term goals that served their common interests, goodwill among the poleis usually evaporated once specific ends were met.

Despite rivalries, the Greek economy expanded. A rising tide of middle-class citizens took advantage of the economic opportunities created by the fluctuations of war and politics, causing manufacturing to grow and commerce to flourish. Speculators amassed huge fortunes by supplying ships or insuring cargoes, and entrepreneurs enriched themselves by buying and selling arms. Although the economic base remained agricultural, people increasingly flocked to the polis to make their fortunes, to participate in government, and to discover a more stimulating life.

The Hellenic Age can be divided into four distinct phases: (1) the Delian League; (2) wars in Greece and with Persia and the Thirty Years' Peace; (3) the Peloponnesian War; (4) Spartan and Theban hegemony and the triumph of Macedonia (Time Line 3.1). While these conflicts raged, life within the polis went on; and in some poleis, notably Athens, extraordinary political, cultural, and intellectual changes were occurring.

After defeating the Persians, the Greeks realized that a mutual defense organization was the key to freedom from further Persian attack. In 478 B.C., a

TIME LINE 3.1   PHASES OF HELLENIC HISTORY

All dates B.C.

479	460		431	404			323
Delian League	Wars in Greece and with Persia	Thirty Years' Peace	Peloponnesian War	Spartan and Theban Hegemony		Triumph of Macedonia	

number of poleis met on Delos, Apollo's sacred island, and formed the Delian League, a defensive alliance, with Athens at its head. But within a short time, Athens began to transform the league into an instrument of imperialism. Flush with military successes and arrogant about the superiority of democracy, Athens intervened in the domestic affairs of other poleis and imposed its form of government on them. When a league member refused to pay the tribute to the Delian treasury or tried to withdraw, for example, Athens sent soldiers to force the rebellious polis to submit. As the oppressive nature of Athenian policies emerged, Athens' independent neighbors became alarmed.

Athenian power, however, was restricted by strained relations with Sparta, by the continuing menace of Persia, and by the highly unstable Delian alliance. When a negotiated settlement finally resolved Persian claims, the Delian League fell apart, leaving Athens vulnerable to her enemies on the Greek mainland. Led first by Thebes and later by Sparta, the Greek poleis launched attacks on Athens. The war dragged on as both sides sparred for position and shifted their alliances. Then, in 445 B.C., when Sparta unexpectedly withdrew, Athens won a quick victory that forced her enemies to negotiate.

The ensuing period of time, known as the Thirty Years' Peace (which in fact lasted only fourteen years), brought the Golden Age of Athens to its zenith. Athenian democracy expanded so that even the poorest citizens were empowered with full rights. Artists and sculptors beautified the Acropolis, and the three great Athenian tragedians—Aeschylus, Sophocles, and Euripides—were active in the drama festivals. Drawing on the Delian treasury, Pericles [PER-uh-kleez], the popular leader and general, launched a glorious building program that was essentially a massive public works project (Figure 3.5).

The most eloquent summation of Athenian democracy was offered by Pericles in a speech over the Athenian war dead. Claiming that the soldiers had not died in vain, he defended Athens' open way of life, its tolerance of diverse beliefs, and the versatility of its citizens. With a glance toward hated Sparta, Pericles praised the Athenian ability to love beauty without sacrificing military strength. He concluded with the boast that Athens was the model for Greece.

Pericles' eloquence, however, looked like a cloak for imperialism to most of Greece, and those poleis that were not enamored of Athens became convinced that war was the only way to restrain Athenian aggression. Athens' foreign policy and its expansionism had given rise to an alliance system so delicately balanced that neither side could allow the other to gain the slightest advantage. When Athens' neighbor Corinth went to war with Corcyra (present-day Corfu) in western Greece over a disputed colony, Corcyra appealed to Athens for aid. The Athenians seized the opportunity to gain influence for the first time in the west and sent troops to Corcyra. Athens' initial victories, however, frightened Corinth, which convinced the Spartans to join it and form the Peloponnesian League. The Peloponnesian War (431–404 B.C.) had begun.

Knowing the Peloponnesian League to be superior on land, Pericles abandoned offensive strategy and withdrew to a defensive position in Athens. He believed that the Athenians could hold out indefinitely within their own walls and win in a war of attrition. But like so many generals before and since, Pericles could not anticipate or control everything.

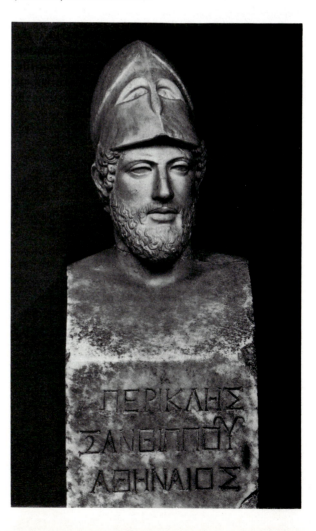

FIGURE 3.5 *Pericles.* Ca. 440 B.C. Vatican Museum. *Pericles possessed a vision of Athens as the political, economic, and cultural center of the Greek world. This portrait bust, even though it is a Roman copy of the Greek original, conveys his strong sense of leadership and determination.*

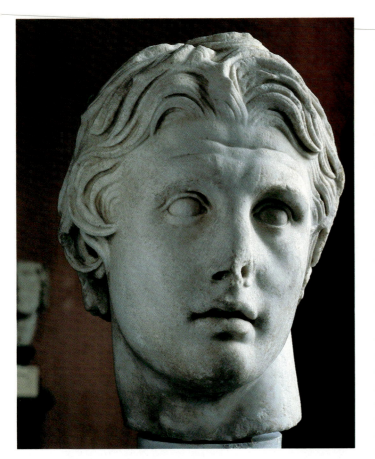

FIGURE 3.6 *Alexander the Great.* Ca. 200 B.C. Istanbul Museum. *Alexander's youth and fine features, idealized perhaps in this portrait bust, add to the legends that have accumulated around one of the most famous conquerors in history. Later rulers measured themselves against Alexander, whose dream of a united world was cut short by his early death.*

A plague broke out in Athens in 430 B.C., killing off many citizens, including Pericles himself. The first phase of the war ended in 421 B.C., when a demoralized and repeatedly defeated Athens sued for peace.

The second half of the Peloponnesian War shifted from the Greek peninsula to distant Sicily and the west—a move that sealed Athens' fate. In 416 B.C., Segesta, a Sicilian polis, begged Athens for military assistance. After a long and heated debate, the Athenians decided to send help. The Sicilian expedition proved to be a disaster, because the Athenians, trying to conduct a war so far from home, were soundly defeated on land and sea and never recovered from their losses. Athens' enemies slowly destroyed what was left of the Athenian fleet, and the once-great polis, stripped of its last line of defense and under

seige, capitulated. Athens never recovered its lost military and economic power.

In the early decades of the fourth century B.C., the various poleis scrambled for power. First Sparta and then Thebes emerged as the preeminent city-state, but the ultimate result of these power struggles was only to weaken further the poleis and make them easy prey for an invader.

At the northern edge of the civilized Greek world, that invader was gathering its forces. Macedonia was a primitive Greek state, governed by kings and populated with a people speaking a rough dialect of the Greek language, unintelligible to Athenians. Their king, Philip, having been a hostage in Thebes when young, had become a *philhellene*—a lover of Greek civilization. A brilliant soldier, Philip subdued neighboring barbarians and warlords and expanded Macedonia to the east as far as the Black Sea. He then moved southward, conquering the poleis of central Greece. Reacting with alarm, Athens, Thebes, Corinth, and other poleis hastily raised an army, but Philip's well-disciplined troops crushed them at Chaeronea in 338 B.C. After establishing a league between Macedonia and the poleis, he granted the Greeks autonomy in everything except military affairs. Philip now announced an all-out war against Persia but was assassinated before he could launch his first campaign.

Philip's nineteen-year-old son, Alexander, succeeded to the throne. Tutored in philosophy by the famous thinker Aristotle, Alexander nevertheless had the heart of a warrior. When Thebes and other poleis attempted to take advantage of the unsettled situation at Philip's death, Alexander swiftly put down the uprising and burned Thebes to the ground, sparing only the house of the poet Pindar. Placing a general in command of Greece, Alexander turned his sights to the east (Figure 3.6).

Alexander dreamed of a world united under his name and a culture fused from Hellenic and Persian roots. His armies marched into Asia Minor, Egypt, and Mesopotamia, absorbing the great Persian Empire; then they swept through Asia all the way to the banks of the Indus River in India. Along the way, Alexander destroyed and looted the great centers of eastern civilization, but he also founded new cities and spread Greek culture everywhere he went.

Alexander's dream ended abruptly with his death in 323 B.C. at the age of thirty-two. Seizing the opportunity presented by his sudden death, the Greeks revolted against the Macedonian oppressors, but they were quickly overwhelmed. The Macedonians then occupied Athens and installed an aristocratic government. Thus ended democracy and Hellenic civilization—in Greece.

FIGURE 3.7 *Athletes in the Palaestra.* Second Quarter of the Fifth Century B.C. National Museum, Athens. *This low-relief sculpture depicts athletes warming up in the open-air exercise area where spectators would congregate to urge on their favorites. The youth on the left is preparing for a foot race, and the one on the right tests his javelin. The pair in the center has just begun to wrestle. This relief and the relief shown in Figure 3.1 were originally two sides of a sculptured base built into a wall that the Athenians constructed after the Persian Wars.*

THE PERFECTION OF THE TRADITION: THE GLORY OF HELLENIC GREECE

Throughout this era of shifting political fortunes, artistic and intellectual life flourished. Athens—bursting with creative energy—was the jewel of the Greek world. Atop her Acropolis, perfectly proportioned marble temples gleamed in the brilliant Aegean sun. Below, in the agora, philosophers debated the most profound questions of human nature. Hundreds of citizens congregated outdoors daily to serve in the assembly, where they passed laws or sat on juries that made legal rulings. Other citizens who were at leisure cheered on the athletes exercising in the open-air gymnasium (Figure 3.7). During drama festivals, the whole city turned out to share the gripping tragedy or to laugh uproariously at the latest comedy.

The culture that flourished in Greece at this time is known as *Classic*, or *Classical*, a term with varied meanings. *Classic* means, first of all, "best" or "preeminent," and the judgment of the Western tradition is that Greek culture was in fact the highest moment in the entire history of the humanities. *Classic* also means having permanent and recognized significance; a classic work establishes a standard against which other efforts are measured. In this second sense, the aesthetic values and forms of Greek cul-

ture have been studied and imitated in all later stages of Western history. By extension, "the Classics" are the works that have survived from Greece and Rome.

Classic also refers to the body of specific aesthetic principles expressed through the art and literature of Greece and Rome, a system known as *Classicism*. The first stage of Classicism, which originated in the Hellenic Age, emphasized simplicity over complexity, balance, or symmetry, over asymmetry, and restraint over excess. At the heart of Classicism was the search for perfection, for the ideal form— whether expressed in the proportions of a temple constructed in marble or in the canon of the human anatomy molded in bronze or in a philosophical conclusion reached through logic. Hellenic Classicism found expression in many areas: theater, music, history, natural philosophy, architecture, and sculpture.

Theater: Tragedy

One of the most prominent institutions of Greek civilization was the theater, in which the dramatic form known as *tragedy* reached a state of perfection. Greek theater originally arose in connection with the worship of Dionysus. The word *tragedy* in Greek means "goat song," and this word may refer to a prehistoric religious ceremony in which competing

FIGURE 3.8   Theater at Epidauros. Ca. 300 B.C. *The best-preserved theater in Greece is the one at Epidauros. Although tragedy was created only in Athens, the popularity of the art form led to the construction of theaters all over Greece—a telling index of Athens' cultural imperialism. The acoustics in this ancient auditorium were remarkable. Performers' voices could clearly be heard throughout the theater even though it is in the open with fifty-four rows of seats accommodating 14,000 spectators.*

male *choruses*—groups of singers—sang and danced, while intoxicated, in homage to the god of wine; the victory prize may have been a sacrificial goat. Whatever its precise origins, by the Archaic Age theater in Athens had taken the form of a series of competitive performances presented annually during the Great Dionysia, celebrated in March.

Features of the Tragic Theater   At first, the chorus served as both the collective actor and the commentator on the events of the drama. Then, in the late sixth century B.C., according to tradition, the poet Thespis—from whose name comes the word *thespian,* or "actor"—introduced an actor with whom the chorus could interact. The theater was born. Initially, the main function of the actor was simply to ask questions of the chorus. During the Hellenic Age the number of actors was increased to three, and occasionally, late in the fifth century B.C., a fourth was added. Any number of actors who did not speak might be on the stage, but only the three leading actors engaged in dialogue. In the fifth century B.C., the chorus achieved its classic function as mediator between actors and audience. As time went on, however, the role of the chorus declined, and the importance of the actors increased. By the fourth century B.C., the actor had become the focus of the drama.

Because the focus of tragedy was originally the chorus, the need for a space to accommodate their dancing and singing determined the theater's shape. The chorus performed in a circular area called an *orchestra,* or "dancing place," in the center of which was a functioning altar, serving as a reminder that tragedy was a religious rite. The audience sat around two-thirds of the orchestra on wooden bleachers or stone seats under the open sky. The other third of the orchestra was backed by a building called the *skene,* which could be painted to suggest a scene and through which entrances and exits could be made (Figure 3.8).

Such simple set decorations may have provided a slight bit of realism, but Greek theater was not concerned with either realism or the expressiveness of individual actors. Ideas and language were what counted. The actors—all men, even in the female roles—wore elaborate masks designed to project their voices, platform shoes, and long robes, which helped give the dramas a timeless, otherworldly quality.

Plays were performed in tetralogies (sets of four) on successive days of the Great Dionysia. Each competing playwright offered three tragedies, not necessarily related in theme or subject, that were performed during the day, and a satyr-play that was performed later. A *satyr-play* usually featured the indecent behavior and ribald speech of the satyrs—sexually insatiable half-men, half-goats—who followed Dionysus. That the Greeks liked to watch three deeply serious dramas followed by a play full of obscene highjinks demonstrates the breadth of their sensibility.

Tragic Drama The essence of Greek tragedy is the deeply felt belief that mortals cannot escape pain and sorrow. The dramatists shared with Homer the insight that "we men are wretched things, and the gods . . . have woven sorrow into the very pattern of our lives." Although terrible things happened in the tragedies—murder, incest, suicide, rape, mutilation—the attitude of the play toward these events was deeply moral. Violence for its own sake was not the concern of the playwright, and violence was never depicted on stage.

The tragedies were primarily based on the legends of royal families—usually the dynasties of Thebes, Sparta, and Argos—dating from the Age of Heroes of which Homer sang in his epics (Figure 3.9). Since the audience already knew these stories, their interest focused on how the playwright treated a familiar tale, what his ideas were about its moral significance, and how his language shaped those ideas.

The plots dealt with fundamental human issues that did not admit of easy solutions, such as the decrees of the state versus the conscience of the individual or divine law versus human law, to name two recurring topics. Humans were forced to make hard choices without being able to foresee the consequences of their decisions. Nonetheless, the dramatists affirmed that a basic moral order existed underneath the shifting tide of human affairs. The

political leaders of Athens recognized and accepted tragedy's ethical significance and educative function and thus made the plays a central part of their civic calendar.

According to the Greek philosopher Aristotle, whose immensely influential theory of tragedy, the *Poetics*, was based on his study of the dramas of the Hellenic Age, the purpose of tragedy was to work a cathartic, or purging, effect on the audience, to "arouse pity and terror" so that these negative emotions could be drained from the soul. The tragic heroes were warnings, not models; the spectators were instructed to seek modest lives and not aim too high. Many tragedians pursued these themes and competed in the Dionysia, but the works of only three still survive—Aeschylus, Sophocles, and Euripides.

Aeschylus Aeschylus [ES-kuh-luhs] (about 525–about 456 B.C.), the earliest of the three dramatists, won first prize in the Great Dionysia thirteen times. He composed about ninety plays, but only seven are extant. His masterpiece, the *Oresteia*, is the only trilogy that has come down intact, and even here the satyr-play is missing. The framing plot for the trilogy was the homecoming from Troy of the Greek king Agamemnon, who had sinned by sacrificing his daughter to gain military success; his murder by his vengeful and adulterous wife, Clytemnestra; and the dire consequences of this killing.

Aeschylus's treatment of these terrible events in the *Oresteia* embodies some of the principles of Classicism. In the first place, Aeschylus shows great

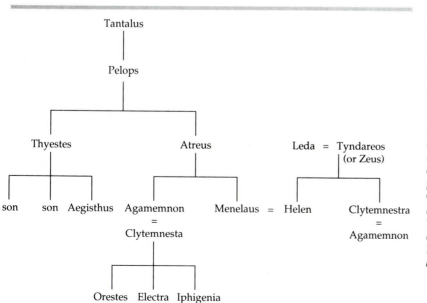

FIGURE 3.9 Genealogy of the House of Argos. *The tragic fate of the House of Argos (or the family of Atreus) was well under way before the opening scene of Aeschylus's tragedy* Agamemnon. *Thyestes seduced the wife of his brother Atreus; in retaliation, Atreus killed Thyestes' two sons and served them to him in a stew. Thyestes then cursed the line of Atreus, and dire consequences followed. Most importantly, Agamemnon, the son of Atreus, sacrificed his own daughter in order to gain favorable weather for his planned invasion of Troy. Besides the Oresteia, three more tragedies survive that have plots based on the House of Argos. Those other plays—which have no inner connection like Aeschylus's trilogy—are* Iphigenia in Taurus, Iphigenia in Aulis, *and* Electra, *all by Euripides.*

FIGURE 3.10 *Orestes Slaying Aegisthus.* Ca. Late Sixth Century B.C. Kunsthistorisches Museum, Vienna. *This vase painting presents a different version of events in Argos from those given by Aeschylus in the* Libation Bearers, *the second play of the* Oresteia. *The vase painter portrays Clytemnestra bearing an axe (left), a detail Aeschylus omitted, and the sister between Orestes and his mother is not named Electra as she is in the* Oresteia. *However, painter and playwright agree that Orestes killed Aegisthus, his mother's lover.*

simplicity by avoiding distracting subplots: The first play, *Agamemnon,* tells the story of the king's death and Clytemnestra's triumph; the second, the *Libation Bearers,* relates the vengeance murder of Clytemnestra by her son, Orestes; and the third, *Eumenides,* halts—with the help of the Olympians Athena and Apollo—the cycle of revenge by instituting an Athenian court to try such cases. The trilogy is symmetrical in that Agamemnon is killed in the first play as punishment for the murder of his daughter, Clytemnestra's death in the second avenges her slaying of Agamemnon, and the courtroom drama of the third absolves Orestes of the crime of matricide.

Finally, Aeschylus shows great restraint inasmuch as all deaths occur offstage, and the chorus or messengers only describe them. However, for the Athenian audience, the *Oresteia* had moral significance as well as stylistic power. By transforming the Furies, the blind champions of vengeance killing, into the "Kindly Ones" (*Eumenides*), Aeschylus, in effect, affirmed the ethical superiority of the rational Olympians over the earthbound chthonian divinities (see Chapter 2). In the *Oresteia* Aeschylus confronts and resolves the opposition between several seemingly irreconcilable polarities—Olympian and chthonian gods, divine and human justice, religious cult and civic ritual, and fate and free will (Figure 3.10).

Sophocles Sophocles [SOF-uh-kleez] (about 496–406 B.C.), the most prolific of the great tragedians, wrote about 125 plays, but only seven survive. He was popular among the Athenians, who awarded him first prize twenty-four times. Sophocles' *Antigone* (442 B.C.) expresses beautifully the principles of Classical tragedy. The simple plot treats the conflicts between King Creon and his niece Antigone. The principal, although not the sole, philosophical issue explored by the play is whether human or divine law should take precedence. Antigone's two brothers have killed each other in a dispute over the Theban crown. Creon decrees that Eteocles, who died defending the city, be buried with honor but that the body of the rebel Polyneices be left as carrion for wild beasts. Antigone, whose name in Greek means "born to oppose," defies his order and buries her brother in compliance with religious teachings. Arrested and imprisoned, Antigone hangs herself, and Creon's son and wife kill themselves. Too late, King Creon sees the light; he gives up his throne saying, "There is no man can bear this guilt but I."

More tensions than that between state and divine law are at issue here. Creon represents the typical tyrant, concerned only with "law and order." His son, Haemon, is the voice of democracy, opposing the tyrannical will of his father. Creon believes in the superiority of public power over domestic life, in the necessity of the state to seek power for its own sake, in the priority of war over the commands of love, and in the right of men to control women. When the king tries to persuade his son to renounce his love for the disobedient Antigone, they argue about all four of these issues. Whether the Athenian citizens sided with Creon or Haemon is unknown, but *Antigone* has become the classic example of a tragic dilemma where two rights confront one another. In his desire for balance, Sophocles gives equally powerful arguments to the play's opposing characters.

Sophocles returned to the history of the Theban dynasty in later plays about Antigone's ill-fated father, Oedipus. In *Oedipus the King* he tells how the Theban ruler unwittingly kills his father and marries his mother and later blinds himself to atone for his guilt. Aristotle held up this play as a model in his analysis of Greek tragedy. In *Oedipus at Colonus,* his last play, Sophocles portrays the former king at peace with himself and his destiny.

Euripides   By the time Euripides [yu-RIP-uh-deez] (about 480–406 B.C.) was writing for the stage, Athens was fighting for its existence in the Peloponnesian War, and with him, the creative phase of Classical theater came to an end. Euripides was in tune with the skeptical mood of the later years of this struggle, and by presenting unorthodox versions of myths and legends, he exposed the foolishness of some popular beliefs and, sometimes, the emptiness of contemporary values. When he staged *The Trojan Women* in 415 B.C., the Athenians could not have missed the parallel between the cruel enslavement of the women of Troy after the Greeks destroyed their city and the fate of the women of Melos, which Athens had just subjugated.

For his ninety or more tragedies (of which eighteen survive), the Athenians awarded the first prize to Euripides only five times, perhaps because his unorthodox plays angered the audience. But later ages, far removed from the stresses of Hellenic times, found his dramas more to their liking. Among the extant works, *The Bacchae* is his masterpiece, a gruesome tale about the introduction of the worship of Dionysus into Thebes. In this play the bacchae, or bacchantes (another name for the followers of Dionysus), blinded by religious frenzy, kill the king of Thebes under the delusion that he is a wild animal. Euripides' dark tragedy may have been a warning to the citizens of Athens about the dangers of both excess and repression in religion and politics.

Euripides followed Classical principles in *The Bacchae,* using a single plot, offstage violence, and well-defined conflict, but he also extended the range of Classical drama with his unorthodox, even romantic language, and his skeptical treatment of familiar themes. Moreover, Euripides pointed the way toward a different sort of theater by having the severed head of the hero brought on stage at the end of the tragedy.

With Euripides the creative phase of Classical theater came to an end. The playwrights who followed him seem to have read their works aloud rather than staging them with actors and choruses. The plays of all the Greek dramatists were presented frequently throughout Greece, however, as well as later in the Macedonian and Roman Empires.

Theater: Comedy

Comedies were performed in the Great Dionysia just as the tragedies were, and they were also entered in contests in another festival known as the Lesser Dionysia, celebrated in late winter. The comedies refused to take anyone or anything seriously. They featured burlesque actions, buffoonery, slapstick, obscenity, and horseplay, and actors wore grotesque costumes with padded bellies or rumps to give a ridiculous effect. Comic playwrights invented their own plots and focused on contemporary matters: politics, philosophies, the new social classes, and well-known personalities. Even the deities were ridiculed and portrayed in embarrassing situations.

The freedom of the comic playwrights could exist only in a democracy. And yet the freedom was limited to a highly ritualized setting—the drama festivals—that allowed, even encouraged, the overturning of rules and the burlesquing of traditions. This controlled expression of the unspeakable provided a catharsis that strengthened communal bonds in the polis. At the same time, the authors demonstrated their faith in the basic good sense of the average citizen.

The comedies of Aristophanes [air-uh-STOF-uh-neez] (about 445–about 388 B.C.) are the primary source for what is known as **Old Comedy**, comic Greek plays with a strong element of political criticism. Aristophanes composed forty-four works in all, of which eleven are extant. Like Euripides, he wrote his plays for war-torn Athens, and he satirized famous contemporaries such as the thinker Socrates, depicting him as a hopeless dreamer. Aristophanes must have stepped on many toes, for the Athenians awarded him first prize only four times.

In *Lysistrata*, Aristophanes transcended the limitations of the comedic form and approached the timeless quality of the tragedies. A sexually explicit and hilarious comedy, *Lysistrata* points out the absurdity of the prolonged Peloponnesian War, and,

FIGURE 3.11 Detail, Scene from a Comedy. Mid–Fourth Century B.C. British Museum. *This scene, painted on a mixing bowl, portrays a situation from a Greek comedy. The actors on the right and left are outfitted in the grotesque costume of comedy with padded rumps and genitals. That these characters are on stage is indicated by the decorations at the bottom of the frame.*

by implication, of all war. In the play, Lysistrata, an Athenian matron, persuades the women of Athens and Sparta to withhold sex from their husbands until they sign a peace treaty. Filled with sexual innuendos, obscenities, and ridiculous allusions to tragic dramas, the play ends with stirring reminders to the Greeks of their common ancestry, their joint victory over the Persians earlier in the century, and their reverence for the same gods. First staged in 411 B.C., seven years before Sparta won the Peloponnesian War, this play commented on but failed to derail Athens' headlong rush to disaster (Figure 3.11).

After the Peloponnesian War and the restoration of a harsher democracy in 403 B.C., free speech was severely repressed in Athens. Comedies still relied on burlesque and slapstick, but their political edge was blunted. For all practical purposes, the great creative age of Greek theater was now over.

Music

Like other peoples of the ancient Near East, the Greeks used music both in civic and religious events and in private entertainment. But the Greeks also gave music a new importance, making it one of the humanities along with art, literature, theater, and philosophy. Music became a form of expression subject to rules, styles, and rational analysis. One reason for this was that the Greeks believed music fulfilled an ethical function in the training of young citizens. They also believed that music had divine origins and was inspired by Euterpe, one of the nine muses (thus the word "music").

Nevertheless, the vast library of Greek music has vanished, scattered by time's indifferent wind. What knowledge there is of that lost heritage, which can only be partially reconstructed from surviving treatises on musical theory and references in other writings, shows a tradition which, despite some differences, became the foundation of Western music. Greek music apparently followed the diatonic system, which had been invented by Pythagoras, using a scale of eight notes, each of which was determined by its numerical ratio to the lowest tone. The Greek composers also devised a series of scales, called *modes,* which functioned roughly like major and minor keys in later Western music. The modes, however, were not interchangeable the way keys are, because the Greeks believed that each mode produced a different emotional and ethical effect on the listener. Thus, the Dorian mode, martial and grave in its emotional impact, was thought by the Greeks to make hearers brave and dignified; the tender and sorrowing Lydian mode, to make them sentimental and weak; and the passionate and wild Phrygian mode, to make them excited and headstrong. Believing that such emotional manipulation made free citizens difficult to govern, Plato banished virtually all music from his ideal republic. Modern research has been able to reproduce all of the Greek modes, but otherwise this music remains a mystery.

Despite music's high ethical status in Greece, it had no independent role in Hellenic culture. Instead, music was integrated with verse, notably in epic and lyric poetry and in tragedy and comedy, with either the lyre (a stringed instrument) or the aulos (a wind instrument) providing accompaniment.

History

The study of history began in the fifth century B.C., when inquisitive and articulate Greeks started to analyze the meaning of their immediate past and to write down in prose the results of their research, or *historia*—the Greek word for inquiry. The Greeks before the Classical period had only a dim sense of their past; what they knew came from Homer, random artifacts, and the ruins of Mycenaean grandeur. Herodotus [he-ROD-uh-tuhs] (about 484 B.C.–about 430 B.C.) was the first to approach history as a separate study and the first to practice historical writing in anything like the modern sense. He was motivated by the belief that the present had its causes in the past and could be a guide for the future. His *Histories* presented an account and an analysis of the Persian Wars, which Herodotus interpreted in terms of Europe versus Asia, or West versus East. In his desire to be fair to both sides, he traveled to Persia and recorded what he learned there.

The *Histories* have been criticized for implausible and inaccurate information, but Herodotus's clear prose style, his concern for research, his efforts to be impartial, his belief in historical cause and effect, and his desire to leave a record of the past as a legacy to future generations have justly earned him the title "Father of History."

Yet, for all his excellence, Herodotus pales in comparison with Thucydides [thew-SID-uh-deez] (died about 401 B.C.). His subject was the Peloponnesian War, to some of whose events he was an eyewitness. Thucydides was much more skeptical and inquiring than Herodotus, and although he was an avid demo-ocrat and an admirer of Pericles, he strove to be completely fair in his account of Periclean Athens. He saw the weaknesses of his beloved polis and realized the baleful effects of imperialism. In his *History of the Peloponnesian War* he even wrote objectively of his own role as the losing admiral in a naval battle.

Thucydides was also able to use ordinary events to illuminate human motives and fundamental causes and effects in history. Like the dramatists writing at the same time, he showed that human weaknesses and flaws created the real-life tragedies he observed around him. His insight into human nature was penetrating as he chronicled how individuals shift loyalties and redefine their values to justify their actions.

This masterful writer rose above his narrative to give lessons to future generations, arguing that events that happened in the past would, at some time and in similar ways, recur. Yet he denied that history repeats itself simplistically, and he warned that his book must be read closely and thoughtfully if it were to be understood wisely.

Natural Philosophy

When the Hellenic Age opened, natural philosophy remained divided into two major camps: the materialists and the idealists (see Chapter 2). The materialists, who perpetuated the inquiries of Thales and the Milesian school, believed that the world was made of some basic physical thing. The idealists, in contrast, who stemmed from Pythagoras and the Sicilian school, were nonmaterialists, reasoning that the physical world was illusory and that behind it was a spiritual force or a metaphysical power.

By the mid–fifth century B.C., this simple pattern was being challenged by new philosophies, and by 400 B.C. a revolution in thought had occurred that overshadowed everything that had gone before. The first assault came from Elea in Sicily, where a new school of thinkers proposed to reconcile materialism and idealism. Then, in Athens the Sophists questioned philosophical inquiry itself and the notion of absolute truth. These corrosive figures provoked Socrates, the most revolutionary thinker of the entire ancient world, to respond to their claims. Socrates' life is regarded as a watershed in Greek thought. All Greek thinkers before him are now known as Pre-Socratics, and those who came after him—chiefly Plato and Aristotle in Hellenic Greece—followed his lead in studying the human experience.

The Pre-Socratics The major pre-Socratic thinkers were concerned with determining the nature of the physical world. For Parmenides [par-MEN-uh-deez]

FIGURE 3.12 *Socrates.* Fourth Century B.C. British Museum. *This Roman marble copy of the original Greek statue supports the unflattering descriptions of Socrates by his contemporaries. By portraying the philosopher with a receding hairline and a dumpy body, the anonymous sculptor has made one of the world's most extraordinary human beings look very ordinary and human.*

(about 515–? B.C.) and his followers in Elea, for example, the world was a single, unchanging, unmoving object whose order could be known through human reason. This attempt to reconcile materialism and idealism was modified by Parmenides' student Empedocles [em-PED-uh-kleez] (about 484–about 424 B.C.), who claimed that everything, animate or inanimate, originated in the four elements of earth, water, fire, and air. These elements were unchanging, but the opposing forces of Love and Strife could combine them in different ways, to the detriment or benefit of humans. This essentially metaphysical explanation of change later influenced Aristotle.

Another school of pre-Socratic thinkers was the Atomists, who believed that everything was made up of atoms—eternal, invisible bodies of varying size that, by definition, could not be divided into smaller units—and the void, the empty space between the atoms. Atomic theory was developed most fully by Democritus [de-MOK-ruht-us] of Thrace (about 460 B.C.–?). The movement and shape of the atoms were sufficient to explain not only physical objects but feelings, tastes, sight, ideas—in short, every aspect of the physical world.

Anaxagoras [an-ak-SAG-uh-ruhs] (about 500–428 B.C.), although not an Atomist, also explained the world in terms of small particles. His unique contribution was the idea that the combinations and divisions of these particles were controlled by a nonphysical agency he called *nous* (reason or mind). Socrates praised him for the originality of this conception, and then faulted him for seeing *nous* only as a mechanical force without religious significance.

The Sophists   The Sophists—from the Greek word *sophia*, or "wisdom"—scorned pre-Socratic speculation about atoms and elements as irrelevant and useless. These traveling teachers claimed to offer their students (for a fee) knowledge that guaranteed success in life. Their emphasis on the development of practical skills, such as effective public speaking, led their critics to accuse them of cynicism and a lack of interest in higher ethical values, but the Sophists were deeply serious and committed to humanistic values. Protagoras [pro-TAG-uh-ruhs] (481–411 B.C.), the most renowned of the Sophists, proclaimed in a dictum that "Man is the measure of all things." This summed up the Sophists' argument that human beings, as the center of the universe, have the power to make judgments about themselves and their world. The Sophists helped free the human spirit to be critical and creative. If there was a danger in their teaching, it was a tendency toward unrestrained skepticism.

The Socratic Revolution   Socrates [SAH-kruh-teez] (about 470–399 B.C.), the thinker who launched a new era in philosophy, did not hesitate to condemn the Sophists. He claimed to oppose everything they stood for, especially their tendency to undermine values without offering new ones in their place. But Socrates shared certain traits with the Sophists, such as his rejection of philosophizing about nature, his focus on human problems, and his desire to empower individuals to make their own moral choices. What basically separated Socrates from the Sophists was his passionate conviction that an enduring moral and intellectual order existed in the universe.

Socrates' method for arriving at true moral and intellectual values was deceptively simple yet maddeningly elusive. At the heart of his thinking was the *psyche* (mind, or soul); being immortal, the psyche was deemed more important than the mortal and doomed body. Those who want wisdom must protect, nourish, and expand their psyches by giving their minds the maximum amount of knowledge, but not just any knowledge. The knowledge the psyche acquired had to be won through stimulating conversations and debates as well as by contemplation of abstract virtues and moral values. Only then could the psyche approach its highest potential.

"Virtue is Knowledge," claimed Socrates; he meant that a person who knows the truth, acquired through personal struggle to self-enlightenment, will not commit evil deeds. And this moral dictum may be reversed: Those who do wrong do so out of ignorance. If people used their psyches to think more deeply and clearly, they would lead virtuous lives. His belief in the essential goodness of human nature and the necessity of well-defined knowledge became a central tenet of Western thought.

After having pointed out the proper path to wisdom, Socrates left the rest up to his students. Bombarding inquiring youths with questions on such topics as the meaning of justice, he used rigorous logic to refute all of the squirming students' attempts at precise definition. Then—as shown by Plato's dialogues, the principal source for Socrates' life—the students, collapsing into confusion, admitted the serious gaps in their knowledge. Socrates' step-by-step questions, interspersed with gentle humor and ironic jabs, honed his students' logical skills and compelled them to begin a quest for knowledge in light of their self-confessed ignorance. The Socratic method was adopted by many teachers in Greece and Rome and remains an honored pedagogical device.

The Athenians of this era began to perceive Socrates as a threat to their way of life. This short, homely and rather insignificant looking man—as surviving statues reveal—aroused suspicion in the polis by his public arguments (Figure 3.12). When Athens fell to the Spartans in 404 B.C., opposition to Socrates began to swell. Many citizens now found subversion or even blasphemy in his words and in the behavior of his followers. Five years after the end of the Peloponnesian War, Socrates was accused of impiety and of corrupting the Athenian youth, and a jury declared him guilty and sentenced him to die. Plato, a former student, was so moved by Socrates' eloquent, though ineffective, defense and by the injustice of his death that the younger man dedicated the remainder of his life to righting the wrong and explaining the Socratic philosophy.

Plato   The spirit of Socrates hovers over the rest of Greek philosophy, especially in the accomplishments of his most famous student, Plato (about 427–347 B.C.). Plato's philosophy is the fountainhead of Western *idealism,* a thought system that emphasizes spiritual values and makes ideas, rather than matter, the basis of everything that exists. *Platonism* arose out of certain premises that were Socratic in origin—the concept of the psyche and the theory of remembrance. Like Socrates, Plato emphasized the immortal and immutable psyche over the mortal and changeful body. But Plato advanced a new polarity, favoring the invisible world of the Forms, or Ideas, in opposition to the physical world. The psyche's true home was the world of the Forms, which it inhabited prior to birth and after death—the time when the psyche was lost in wonder among the eternal Ideas. In contrast, the body lived exclusively in the material world, completely absorbed by the life of the senses. Once trapped inside the body, the psyche could glimpse the higher reality, or Forms, only through remembrance.

Nonetheless, Plato thought that through a set of mental exercises the psyche would be able to recall the Ideas to which it had once been exposed. The best training for the psyche was the study of mathematics, since mathematics required signs and symbols to represent other things. After the mastery of mathematics, the student proceeded, with the help of logic, to higher stages of abstract learning, such as defining the Forms of Justice, Beauty, and Love. By showing that wisdom came only after an intellectual progression that culminated in an understanding of the absolute Ideas, Plato silenced the Sophists, who claimed that knowledge was relative.

A major implication of Plato's idealism is that the psyche and the body are constantly at war. The psyche's attempts to remember the lost Ideas met resistance from the body's pursuit of power, fame, and physical comforts. This dualism especially plagued the philosopher, the lover of wisdom; but the true philosopher took comfort in recognizing that at death the psyche would return freely to the world of the Forms.

Plato identified the Form of the Good, the ultimate Idea, with God. Yet the Platonic deity was neither the creator of the world nor the absolute and final power. Instead, Plato's deity was necessary for his idealism to function; in his thought, God was the source from which descended the imperfect objects of the natural world. In a related theological notion, he, like Socrates, attributed the presence of evil to ignorance; but Plato added the psyche's misdirected judgment and insatiable bodily appetites as other causes of evil.

Socrates' death provoked Plato to envision a perfect state where justice flourished. The book that resulted from Plato's speculations—the *Republic*—sets forth his model state and, incidentally, launched the study of political philosophy in the West. Plato thought that a just state could only be realized when all social classes worked together for the good of the whole, each class performing its assigned tasks. Because of the importance of the psyche, social status was determined by the ability to reason and not by wealth or inheritance. A tiny elite of philosopher kings and queens, who were the best qualified to run the state, reigned. Possessing wisdom as a result of their education in the Platonic system, they lived simply, shunning the creature comforts that corrupted weaker rulers.

The two lower ranks were similarly equipped for their roles in society by their intellects and their training: A middle group provided police and military protection, and the third and largest segment operated the economy. In Plato's dream world both the individual and the society aimed for virtue, and the laws and the institutions ensured that the ideal would be achieved.

Aristotle   Socrates may have been revolutionary; Plato was certainly poetic; but Aristotle [AIR-uh-stot-uhl] (384–322 B.C.) had the most comprehensive mind of the ancient world. His curiosity and vast intellect led him into every major field of inquiry of his time, except mathematics and music. Born in Macedonia, he was connected to some of the most glittering personalities of his day. He first studied philosophy under Plato in Athens, then tutored the future Alexander the Great back at Philip's court. After Philip's conquest of Greece, Aristotle settled in Athens and opened a school, the Lyceum, that quickly rivaled the Academy, the school Plato had established.

Although his philosophy owed much to Platonism, Aristotle emphasized the role of the human senses. To Aristotle, the natural world was the only world; no separate, invisible realm of Ideas existed. Nature could be studied and understood by observation, classification, and comparison of data from the physical world, that is, through the empirical method.

Aristotle rejected the world of the Forms because he believed that Form and Matter were inseparable, both rooted in nature. Each material object contained a predetermined Form that, with proper training or nourishment, would evolve into its final Form and ultimate purpose. This growth process, in his view, was potentiality evolving into actuality, as when an embryo becomes a human or a seed matures into a plant. Thus, the philosopher could conclude that everything had a purpose or end.

Aristotle's thought rested on the concept of God, which he equated with the First Cause. Aristotle's God was a philosopher's deity, purely rational, self-absorbed, and uncaring about the world or its inhabitants. Had this deity been anything else, Aristotle's God would not have been the supreme power or First Cause.

Rejecting Platonic dualism and its exclusive regard for the psyche, Aristotle devised a down-to-earth ethical goal—a sound mind in a healthy body—that he called happiness. To achieve happiness, he advised striking a mean, or a balance, between extremes of behavior. For example, courage is the mean between the excess of foolhardiness and the deficiency of cowardice. Noting that actions like murder and adultery are vicious by their very nature, he condemned them as being unable to be moderated. Although Aristotle disavowed many of Plato's ideas, he agreed with his former mentor that the cultivation of the higher intellect was more important than that of the body.

Aristotle's ethics are related to his politics, for he taught that happiness finally depended on the type of government under which an individual lived. Unlike Plato, who based his politics on speculative thinking, Aristotle reached his political views after careful research. First collecting over 150 state constitutions, Aristotle then classified and compared them, concluding that the best form of government was a constitutional regime ruled by the middle class. His preference for the middle class stemmed from his belief that they, exciting neither envy from the poor nor contempt from the wealthy, would honor and work for the good of all.

Aristotle's influence on Western civilization is immeasurable. His writings formed the core of knowledge that Christian scholars later studied as they struggled to keep the light of civilization burning after the collapse of the Roman Empire. Likewise, Jewish and Moslem thinkers ranked his books just below

FIGURE 3.13   The Delphic Sanctuary. Aerial View. Late Sixth Century–Late Fourth Century B.C. *The ruins of Apollo's temple—this is an active earthquake zone—are in the center of the illustration, marked by a rectangular foundation and a few standing columns. A Sacred Way, or road, zigzagged up the mountain to the temple's entrance. During the fourth century B.C., a gymnasium for boys and a theater were established in the sanctuary, and a stadium was constructed for athletic contests.*

their own religious scriptures. Today, Aristotelianism is embedded in the official theology of the Roman Catholic Church, and Aristotle's logic continues to be taught in college philosophy courses.

Architecture

Of all the Greek art forms, architecture most powerfully embodied the Classical ideals of the Hellenic Age. The stone temple, the supreme expression of the Hellenic building genius, now received its definitive shape. Ironically, the Doric temple, which had originated in the Archaic Age, reached perfection in Ionian Athens. The versatile Athenians also perfected a new architectural order, the **Ionic,** which reflected more clearly their cultural tradition.

Sanctuaries   Before there were temples, however, Greece had sanctuaries, places considered sacred to a god or goddess. Of these sacred places, Apollo's shrine at Delphi was the oldest and the most famous (Figure 3.13). Delphi, thought to be the center of the earth, was hallowed ground to the entire Greek world, and the major poleis supported the god's priesthood there.

Apollo's temple was the most splendid building on the site. Inside was Apollo's oracle—the only woman permitted at Delphi—to whom people journeyed from all over Greece with their questions.

With the rise of the poleis, the concept of a holy place set aside from the business of everyday life was adapted to the religious needs of each community. By the Hellenic Age, each polis had its own sacred area, usually built on a hill or protected by walls, which contained buildings and altars. Although each polis worshiped the entire pantheon of deities, one god or goddess was gradually singled out as a patron, and a temple was erected to house the statue of this particular divinity.

The Temple: The Perfection of the Form   By Hellenic times, the Greek world was polarized between eastern (the mainland and the Aegean Islands) and western (Magna Graecia) styles of temple design, although in both styles the temples were rectilinear and of post-beam-triangle construction. Influenced by the Pythagorean quest for harmony through mathematical rules, the eastern builders had standardized six as the perfect number of columns for the ends of temples and thirteen, or twice the number of end columns plus one, as

FIGURE 3.14 Second Temple of Hera at Poseidonia. Ca. 450 B.C. *This temple of Hera is among the best preserved structures from the ancient world. Since Hera may have been a chthonian goddess prior to becoming consort to Olympian Zeus, it is appropriate that this Doric temple, with its ground-hugging appearance, be her monument.*

the perfect number of columns for the sides. These balanced proportions, along with simple designs and restrained decorative schemes, made the eastern temples majestically expressive of Classical ideals.

Architects in western Greece, somewhat removed from the centers of Classical culture, were more experimental. Their buildings deviated from the eastern ideals, as can be seen in the Second Temple of Hera at Poseidonia, built of limestone in about 450 B.C. (Figure 3.14). The best-preserved of all Greek temples, this Doric structure does not have the harmonious proportions of the eastern version of this style. Although the Second Temple of Hera owed much to eastern influences, including the six columns at the ends and the porches, it had too many (fourteen) columns on the sides, its columns were too thick, and the low-pitched roof made the building seem squat.

Between 447 and 438 B.C., the architects Ictinus [ik-TIE-nuhs] and Callicrates [kuh-LICK-ruh-teez] perfected the eastern-style Doric temple in the Parthenon, a temple on Athens' Acropolis dedicated to Athena (Figure 3.15). When completed, this temple established a new standard of Classicism, with eight columns on the ends and seventeen on the sides and with the numerical ratio of 9:4 used throughout, expressed, for example, in the relation of a column's height to its diameter. Inside, the builders designed two chambers, an east room for a 40-foot-high statue of Athena and a smaller room housing the Delian League treasury. The rest of the Acropolis project, finally finished in 405 B.C., included the Propylaea, the gate leading to the sanctuary; the temple of Athena Nike, a gift to Athens' patron goddess thanking her for a military victory; and the Erechtheum, a temple dedicated to three deities.

Ictinus and Callicrates introduced many subtle variations, called refinements, in their designs, so that no line is exactly straight, horizontal, or perpendicular. For example, the stepped base of the temple forms a gentle arc so that the ends are lower than the middle; the floor slopes slightly to the edges; and the columns tilt inward away from the ends. These and other refinements were no accidents but were intended to be corrections for real and imaginary optical illusions. The Parthenon's fame exerted such authority that these refinements, along with harmonious proportions, became standardized as the essence of Greek architecture.

The second order of Greek architecture, the Ionic, originated in the late Archaic Age and, like the Doric, came to flower in Hellenic times. The Ionic style, freer than the Doric and more graceful, reflected its origins in the Ionian world; traditionally,

FIGURE 3.15 ICTINUS AND CALLICRATES. The Parthenon. Close-up View from the East. Third Quarter of the Fifth Century B.C. Athens. *A great humanistic icon, the Parthenon has had a long history since its days as a Greek temple. It served successively as a Christian church, a mosque, and an ammunitions depot, until it was accidentally blown up at the end of the seventeenth century A.D. Today, concerned nations through UNESCO are cooperating with the Greek government to preserve this noble ruin.*

the Ionians contrasted their opulence with the simplicity of the Dorians. In place of the alternating metopes and triglyphs of Doric buildings, the Ionic temple had a running frieze to which sculpted figures might be added. More decorated than the plain Doric, the Ionic columns had elegant bases, and their tops were crowned with capitals that suggested either a scroll's ends or a ram's horns. What solidified the Ionic temple's impression of elegance were its slender and delicate columns.

The Athenians chose the Ionic style for the exquisite, though eccentric, Erechtheum, the last of the great buildings erected on the Acropolis (Figure 3.16). The artistic freedom associated with the Ionic style may have led the architect, Mnesicles [NES-uh-kleez], to make the floor plan asymmetrical and to introduce so many design variations, but a more likely explanation was Mnesicles' need to integrate three existing shrines into a single building—those of the Olympians Athena and Poseidon and that of the legendary King Erechtheus, who introduced the

FIGURE 3.16 MNESICLES. The Erechtheum. View from the West. Ca. 410 B.C. Athens. *The Erechtheum was probably built to quiet conservatives who rejected Athena's new temple, the Parthenon, as a symbol of Athenian imperialism. Reflecting its ties with the past, the Erechtheum housed the ancient wooden cult statue of Athena, which pious Athenians believed had fallen from the sky. Its Ionic porches set the standard for the graceful Ionic order.*

FIGURE 3.17 MNESICLES. The Erechtheum. View from the South. Ca. 410 B.C. Athens. *The Erechtheum presented a unique and charming exterior with each wall offering a different perspective. Two Ionic porches of differing dimensions faced the northern and eastern sides; this Porch of the Maidens, which was inaccessible from the outside, fronted the southern wall; and the western exposure was a blank wall.*

horse to Athens. Mnesicles took the unusual step of stressing the site's unbalanced nature by adding two Ionic porches and the temple's crowning feature, the Porch of the Maidens (Figure 3.17). By his bold design, Mnesicles created a marvelous illusion of harmony that was in keeping with the age's Classical ideals.

Sculpture

Equally impressive is the Greek achievement in sculpture. Believing that the task of sculpture was to imitate nature, the Greeks created images of gods and goddesses as well as of men and women that have haunted the Western imagination ever since. They not only forged a canon of idealized human proportions that later sculptors followed, but also developed a repertoire of postures, gestures, and subjects that have become embedded in Western art.

During the Hellenic Age, Classical sculpture moved through three separate phases: The *Severe style*, which ushered in the period and lasted until 450 B.C.; the *High Classical style*, which coincided

with the zenith of Athenian imperial greatness; and the *Fourth Century style*, which concluded with the death of Alexander the Great in 323 B.C.

Sculpture in the Severe style, inspired perhaps by its association with funeral customs, was characterized by a feeling of dignified nobility. The *Kritios Boy*—showing a figure fully at rest—is an elegant expression of this first phase of Classicism (Figure 3.18). Kritios [KRIT-ee-uhs], the supposed sculptor, fixed the mouth severely and altered the frontality, a feature of the Archaic style, by tilting the head subtly to the right and slightly twisting the upper torso. The flat-footed stance of the Archaic kourai has given way to a posture that places the body's weight on one leg and uses the other leg as a support. This stance is called *contrapposto* (counterpoise), and its invention helped to make the Classical revolution; thereafter, sculptors were able to render the human figure in freer and more relaxed poses.

Mourning Athena, another sculpture from the same period, conveys an air of gentle sorrow (Figure 3.19). Athena stands, with her left foot resting on the toes, while she reads the names of the dead incised into a monument—the source of the sculpture's

FIGURE 3.19 *Mourning Athena.* Ca. 460 B.C. Acropolis Museum, Athens. *This low-relief sculpture was carved into a stele, or standing stone, to serve as a votive offering to the goddess Athena. The work was found on the Athenian Acropolis, but the accompanying inscription has been lost. The sense of melancholy surrounding the attentive goddess makes this one of the most arresting sculptures in Greek art.*

FIGURE 3.18 *Kritios Boy.* Ca. 480 B.C. Acropolis Museum, Athens. *This statue is carved from marble probably mined at Mt. Pentelicus in Attica. Two features—the treatment of the eyes, which were originally set with semiprecious stones, and the roll of hair—show that the Kritios sculptor was accustomed to working in bronze. The figure's beautifully rendered muscles and sense of inner life announce the arrival of the Hellenic style.*

name. The Severe style is expressed in Athena's strongly masculine profile, her firmly set mouth and bowed head, and her contrapposto stance (the weight distributed between her staff and her right leg). The goddess's draperies fail to hang straight down—an unnatural touch that sculptors corrected in works done in the High Classical style. Overall, *Mourning Athena* affirms quiet reflection in the midst of human calamity, a mood that epitomizes the Severe style.

In contrast to the Severe style, which accepted repose as normal, the High Classical style was fascinated with the aesthetic problem of showing motion in a static medium. The sculptors' solution, which became central to High Classicism, was to freeze the action, resisting the impulse to depict agitated movement, in much the same way that the tragic playwrights banished violence from the stage. In effect, the High Classical sculptors stopped time, allowing an ideal world to emerge in which serene gods and mortals showed grace under pressure. A striking representation of this aspect of High Classicism is the bronze statue of *Poseidon*, or *Zeus*, found in the Aegean Sea off Cape Artemision. It captures to perfection High Classicism's ideal of virile grace (Figure 3.20). The mature god, signified by the beard and fully-developed body, is shown poised, ready to hurl some object. In such sculptures as this, the Greeks found visual metaphors for their notion that deities and mortals are kin.

High Classical sculptors wanted to do more than portray figures in motion; some, most especially Polykleitos of Argos, continued to be obsessed with presenting the ideal human form at rest. In his search for perfection, Polykleitos [pol-e-KLITE-uhs] sculpted a bronze male figure of such strength and beauty—the *Doryphoros*, or *Spearbearer*—that its proportions came to be regarded as a canon, or set of rules, to be imitated by other artists (Figure 3.21). In the *Doryphoros* canon, each of the limbs bears a numerical relation to the body's overall measurements; for example, the length of the foot is one-tenth of the

FIGURE 3.20 *Poseidon* (or *Zeus*). Ca. 460–450 B.C. Bronze, height 6'10". National Museum, Athens. *The nobility of the Greek conception of their gods is nowhere better revealed than in this magnificent bronze sculpture of Poseidon (or Zeus). Grace, strength, and intellect are united in this majestic image of a mature deity. Poseidon's eyes originally would have been semiprecious stones, and the statue would have been painted to create a more realistic effect.*

FIGURE 3.22 The Location of the Sculptures on the Parthenon. *This cutaway view shows the metopes, Ionic frieze, and pediments of the Parthenon, which were covered with sculptures celebrating the glory of Athens.*

FIGURE 3.21 *Doryphoros.* Marble copy of a bronze original by Polykleitos. Ca. 440 B.C. Museo Nazionale Archeologico, Naples. *The Doryphoros expresses the classical ideal of balanced repose. The nude figure rests his weight upon the right leg. The left arm, extended to hold the now missing spear, balances with the right leg. The left foot, barely touching the ground, balances with the relaxed right arm. Besides representing idealized repose, the Doryphoros was also recognized as the embodiment of human beauty with its ordered proportions, well-toned musculature, and rugged features.*

figure's height. Other principles of High Classicism embodied in the *Doryphoros* include the slightly brutal facial features, which were typical of this style's masculine ideal, the relaxed contrapposto, and the controlled muscles.

Greek architecture reached its zenith in the Parthenon, and, similarly, Classical Greek sculpture attained its height in the reliefs and sculptures of this celebrated temple. Under the disciplined eye of the sculptor Phidias [FIHD-e-uhs], craftspeople carved patriotic and mythological subjects destined for various parts of the building. Taken as a whole, the sculptures revealed the Parthenon to be a tribute to Athenian imperialism as much as to the goddess Athena (Figure 3.22).

On the Parthenon's metopes—the rectangular spaces on the Doric frieze—sculptors portrayed scenes in the prevailing High Classical style. In panel after panel, the metope sculptors depicted perfect human forms showing restraint in the midst of

FIGURE 3.23 *Centaur versus Lapith. Metope XXX, South Face of the Parthenon. Ca. 448–442 B.C. British Museum. This struggling pair was designed to fit comfortably into the metope frame, and thus the proportions of the figures in relation to each other and to the small space were worked out with precision. The intertwined limbs of the warrior and the centaur visibly demonstrated the new freedom of High Classicism. The anguished countenance of the Lapith, however, is almost unique in High Classicism and is a portent of the more emotional faces of the Hellenistic style, the next major artistic development.*

FIGURE 3.24 *Poseidon, Apollo, and Artemis. Parthenon frieze. Ca. 448–442 B.C. Acropolis Museum, Athens. The Hellenic style always stressed the human dimension of the Greek gods and goddesses, embodying Homer's claim that gods and humans are of the same race. In this section of the Parthenon frieze, the Homeric deities spring to life, resplendent in their beautiful bodies and handsome faces.*

struggle, such as Amazons against men, Greeks against Trojans, and gods against giants. The south metopes portrayed the battle between the legendary Lapiths and the half-men, half-horse Centaurs (Figure 3.23). For the Greeks, the struggle between the human Lapiths and the bestial Centaurs symbolized the contest between civilization and barbarism, or, possibly, between the Greeks and the Persians.

Inside the columns, running around the perimeter of the upper *cella* walls in a continuous band, was a low-relief frieze. Borrowed from the Ionic order, this running frieze introduced greater liveliness into High Classicism. The 525-foot-long band is filled with hundreds of men and women, walking and riding horses, along with sacrificial animals for Athena and the rest of the Olympians. The subject of this vivid scene is the procession of the Great Panathenaea festival, Athens' most important civic and religious ritual, which was held every four years. This panoramic view of the thrilling procession concluded with a stunning group portrait of the twelve gods and goddesses, seated in casual majesty, awaiting their human worshipers. In one scene, a bearded Poseidon talks quietly with Apollo, while Artemis at the right absentmindedly adjusts her robe (Figure 3.24). Their tranquil faces, their sense of inner life, and the prevailing calm are the marks of mature Classicism. The entire Parthenon frieze was the most ambitious work of sculpture in the Greek tradition.

The transition to Fourth Century style coincided with the end of the creative phase of tragedy and the disintegration of the Greek world as it passed into the Macedonian political orbit. Sculpture remained innovative, since each generation seemed to produce a master who challenged the prevailing aesthetic rules, and free expression continued as a leading principle of Fourth Century style. But sculptors now expressed such new ideas as beauty for its own sake and a delight in sensuality. Earlier Classicism had stressed the notion that humans could become godlike, but the last phase concluded that gods and mortals alike reveled in human joys.

This new focus is apparent in Praxiteles' [prax-SIT-uhl-eez] *Hermes with the Infant Dionysus.* This sculpture, perhaps the only original work by a known sculptor that survives from ancient Greece, portrays two gods blissfully at play (Figure 3.25). Hermes, lounging in a casual yet dignified pose, probably dangled grapes before the attentive baby god. The contrapposto posture, beautifully defined in Hermes' stance, became widely imitated as the **''Praxitelean curve.''** Hermes' sensuous body, his intent gaze, and his delicate features are hallmarks of Fourth Century Classicism; by the next generation Praxiteles' treatment of the male figure had superseded the more rugged *Doryphoros* canon.

FIGURE 3.25   PRAXITELES. *Hermes with the Infant Dionysus.* Ca. 350–340 B.C. Olympia Museum. *In this statue of Hermes, Praxiteles changed the look of Classical art with his rendering of the god's body. For example, Hermes' small head and long legs contributed to the Praxitelean canon for the male figure. The sculptor has also created a dramatic contrast between Hermes' well-muscled body and his soft face. As a direct result of Praxiteles' new vision, sculptors in the Hellenistic Age became interested in more frankly sensual portrayals of the human figure, both male and female.*

The Legacy of Hellenic Civilization

Although Athens failed in its dream of political mastery of Greece, the Athenian miracle so impressed its contemporaries that Attic culture dominated the Hellenic Age. Tragic poets, comic playwrights, and natural philosophers made the Attic dialect the medium of expression for poetry and prose. The buildings on the Athenian Acropolis expressed visually the purity and restraint of the Attic style. And Athenian democracy, which served as the exciting teacher of its citizens, was the envy of most of the other Greek poleis. After the fall of Greece to Macedonia, however, the idea of democracy fell into disrepute. Almost 2000 years passed before some in Europe were ready to give democracy a second chance.

But *humanism,* the other great creation of Athens, survived as a guide to refined living for the cultivated classes in the West. Athenian culture became the heart of the educational curriculum that was followed in Hellenistic civilization; that model was adopted by Rome and transmitted in the humanistic tradition to Europe. In time, the study and the practice of humanistic learning—literature, philosophy, theater, music, and the arts and architecture—became the crowning glory of Western civilization, affecting private individuals and entire societies.

Moreover, Classicism—the style of humanistic achievements in the Hellenic Age—had three great effects on the Western tradition. First, the principles of Greek Classicism—balance, simplicity, and restraint—set the standard by which the styles of other times are often measured. Second, the actual works of Classicism became basic building blocks of Western culture. In the realm of thought, the works of Plato and Aristotle quickly acquired a luster of authority and re-

tained it until the seventeenth century A.D. Aristotle's literary criticism created a new writing genre, and his analysis of tragedy made this type of play the ultimate challenge to ambitious writers. The Greek tragedies themselves—of Aeschylus, Sophocles, and Euripides—are thought by many to be unsurpassed.

The comic plays of Aristophanes are less well known today, but their spirit still lives in period comedies and contemporary political satire. The histories of Herodotus and Thucydides retain their vitality as important sources for their respective eras, although modern research has cast doubt on some of their conclusions. Architecture has had the most potent effect of Greece's accomplishments; the ruins on the Athenian Acropolis and elsewhere are eternal reminders of this Greek heritage. Finally, the idealized statues of men and women, such as the *Doryphoros,* have inspired Western artists with their vision of noble beings alert to the rich possibilities of human life.

The third and perhaps most important contribution of Classicism to the Western tradition was a skeptical spirit that was rooted in democracy. By asserting that the purpose of human life can best be realized in cities that are shaped by the citizens' needs, as Athenian humanism claimed, the humanists declared war on all tyrants, hierarchical societies, and divinely ordered states—in other words, the prevailing order of the ancient world. Because of this critical aspect of humanism, the Greek heritage has sometimes been called into question and, during repressive periods, been subjected to attack. On the contrary, however, the passion for questioning, for inquiry, which characterizes the skeptical spirit, is at the core of Western consciousness.

KEY CULTURAL TERMS

Hellenic   *modes*
maenad   *idealism*
Classic (Classical) *Platonism*
Classicism   *Ionic*
tragedy   *Severe style*
chorus   *High Classical style*
orchestra   *Fourth Century style*
skene   *contrapposto*
satyr-play   *Praxitelean curve*
Old Comedy   *humanism*

SUGGESTIONS FOR FURTHER READING

PRIMARY SOURCES

AESCHYLUS. *Oresteia.* Translated by R. Fagles. New York: Penguin, 1986. A good modern version of the only dramatic trilogy that survives from ancient Greece.

ARISTOPHANES. *Lysistrata.* Translated by J. Henderson. New York: Oxford University Press, 1987. This modern version captures the antiwar spirit and bawdy humor of the original comedy.

EURIPIDES. *The Bacchae and Other Plays.* Translated by P. Vellacott. New York: Penguin, 1972. An excellent collection of Euripides' dramas, in each of which strong-minded women play major roles.

HERODOTUS. *The Histories.* Translated by A. de Sélincourt. New York: Penguin, 1972. Prefaced with an informative introduction, this translation captures both the language and the narrative of the first history book in Western literature.

KAPLAN, J., ed. *The Pocket Aristotle.* New York: Washington Square Press, 1966. Edited selections from the *Physics,* the *Nicomachean Ethics, Politics,* and *Poetics* give a sense of Aristotle's method of inquiry.

ROUSE, W. H. D., trans. *Great Dialogues of Plato.* New York: New American Library, 1963. Includes the full text of the *Republic,* the *Apology, Phaedo,* and *Symposium.*

SOPHOCLES. *The Theban Plays.* Translated by E. F. Watling. New York: Penguin, 1974. The three plays about the misfortunes of King Oedipus and his family; includes *Oedipus Rex* and *Antigone.*

THUCYDIDES. *The Peloponnesian War.* Translated by R. Warner. New York: Penguin, 1970. An updated translation that captures the sweep and drama of the original.

4

CLASSICAL
GREEK CIVILIZATION
The Hellenistic Age

The Hellenistic Age covers the relatively brief period from the death of Alexander the Great in 323 B.C. to the triumph of Rome over Macedonian Greece in 146 B.C. During this time a new urban civilization sprang up in the eastern Mediterranean basin across most of Alexander's old empire. In contrast to Hellenic civilization, this new civilization was dominated by large metropolitan centers tied together by trade and commerce. More racially mixed and ethnically varied than Hellenic Greece, this civilization has come to be called *Hellenistic* because of the preeminent role Greece played in its development. Greece, for example, furnished the Hellenistic world with its diplomatic and commercial language, its bureaucrats, and most of its cultural forms. And yet Hellenistic culture was eclectic, for the subjects of the various states made their presence known (Figure 4.1). From Oriental roots came such key motifs of Hellenistic society as the concept of a ruler who

◀ *Nike of Samothrace* (side view).
Ca. 190 B.C. Louvre, Paris.

FIGURE 4.1 Black Youth Singing. Second Century B.C. Bibliothèque Nationale, Paris. *Since the Archaic Age, Greek artists had occasionally depicted black Africans in their works. During the Hellenistic Age, with the migration of peoples and the increased use of slaves, sculptors frequently chose black figures as subjects. This small bronze statue of a young African is an illustration of the racial diversity of the Hellenistic Age. Originally, the figure held a small musical instrument—now lost—which accounts for its exaggerated pose.*

is also divine, the aesthetic ideal that identifies grandiosity with earthly majesty, and new religious cults that promised immortality.

Because the accomplishments of Hellenic Greece loom so large in Western history, the Hellenistic Age is sometimes belittled or even ignored. This neglect is misguided, however. Alexander's dream of a peaceful world community united by a common leader and his role as the leader of such a world-state had an impact that has lasted into modern times. The multiracial states of the Hellenistic period are the first examples of a type whose modern versions include the United States and the former Soviet Union. And, not least, Hellenistic achievements in philosophy, art, and architecture are considerable.

The fusion of Mediterranean civilizations that characterized Hellenistic society destroyed the Hellenic political order in which poleis were guided by their citizens. In its stead arose the large Hellenistic kingdoms, ruled by men who declared themselves deities. The Hellenistic economic order rested on specialized luxury crafts and professionalized occupations, international trade and banking, and an abundant and cheap supply of slaves. The large ports exported and imported basic agricultural commodities such as grain, olive oil, wine, and timber, exchanging them for expensive handmade consumer products like pottery, silks, and jewelry, as well as luxury items like spices. Shipping firms, insurance companies, and banks watched over the transfer of these goods and enriched themselves in the process.

Class divisions in Hellenistic society were pronounced. In the larger cities and port towns, especially, the discrepancies in the social order were strikingly apparent and clearly entrenched. For the rich, urban life was often luxurious and cosmopolitan, but the bulk of society remained provincial, untouched by the glamour of Hellenistic high life. Those in the middle social ranks, primarily small tradespeople and skilled artisans, struggled to keep ahead and hoped to improve their plight. However, for the poorest free classes—laborers, unskilled workers, and small landowners—life offered little hope on this earth. At the bottom of society, slaves, whose numbers mounted during the wars of this period, were expected to toil and bear the brunt of all backbreaking labor.

THE STAGES OF HELLENISTIC HISTORY

The shadow of Rome hung over the Hellenistic world, although the kingdoms were unaware that their fate depended on the rising western Mediterranean power. While Rome watched, the Hellenistic states quarreled and jockeyed for power. The events of this age fall into two stages: (1) the disintegration of Alexander's empire and the rise of the successor states; and (2) the arrival and triumph of Rome (Time Line 4.1).

The End of the Empire and the Rise of the States

The years from 323 to 307 B.C. saw the shattering of Alexander's dream of a united Greek and Persian civilization. Alexander left no designated successor. After his death, his chief generals divided his empire, carving out three dynastic kingdoms that, along with a few minor states and leagues of Greek city-states, survived until Rome began to move into the area. The era of the successor states (307 to 215 B.C.) was the zenith of Hellenistic culture. Politically, the states were hardly ever at peace, but culturally they were united. Greeks and barbarians mingled freely, and a civilization began to emerge that was not unlike what Alexander had imagined. This period saw the growth and spread of the *koine*, a form of col-

TIME LINE 4.1   THE HELLENISTIC AGE   All dates B.C.

323	307		215		148	133		31
	Disintegration of Alexander's Empire	Founding and Rise of Successor States		Macedonian Wars		Rome Conquers Greek Peninsula	Roman Incursion into Hellenistic States	
Death of Alexander 323						Pergamum ceded to Rome 133	Rome conquers Seleucid empire 65	Rome defeats Cleopatra 31

MAP 4.1

The Successor States and the Hellenistic World

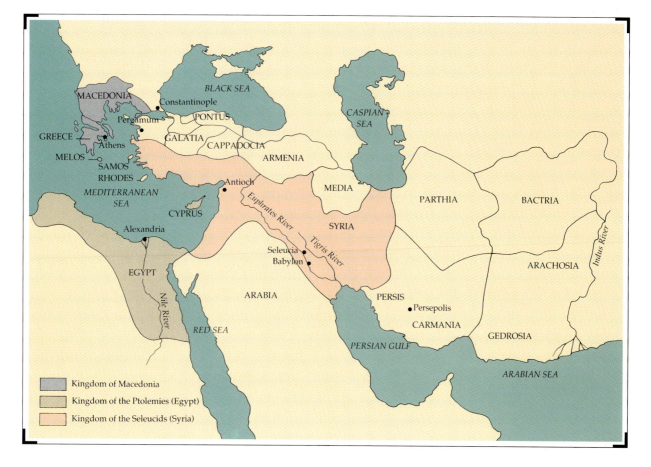

Kingdom of Macedonia

Kingdom of the Ptolemies (Egypt)

Kingdom of the Seleucids (Syria)

loquial Greek that was spoken throughout the Hellenistic world, from Gaul to Syria.

The three successor states were based in Macedonia, in the former Persian empire, and in Egypt. Alexander's general Antigonus [an-TIG-uh-nuhs] founded the kingdom of Macedonia, which controlled Greece until two leagues of poleis challenged Macedonian hegemony. The ensuing warfare with the Greek leagues wore down Antigonus's heirs and ultimately weakened this state.

A second general, Seleucus [suh-LEW-kuhs], established a dynasty in Asia Minor, building his government on the ruins of the old Persian empire. At its height, Seleucid power extended as far east as present-day Iraq. In about the middle of the third century B.C., however, the eastern region of the Seleucid kingdom broke away and formed the two smaller states of Parthia and Bactria, who would later prove to be prickly adversaries of Rome. In time, the Seleucid rulers, distracted by the invading Gauls, a wandering tribe of Celtic peoples from central and eastern Europe, lost control of their kingdom and had to relinquish their northwestern lands

in Asia Minor to a new kingdom known as Pergamum, named after an old Greek city.

To a third general, Ptolemy [TAHL-uh-me], fell the richest prize of all, Egypt, the oldest civilization surviving in the ancient world. Although the Ptolemaic dynasty included weak and corrupt rulers, Egypt enjoyed a resurgence as a unified and independent state. The Ptolemies made Alexandria their capital, and eventually this city became the greatest urban center of the Hellenistic Age, enriched by the grains harvested in the Nile River valley and the goods and traffic that passed through its port (Map 4.1).

The Arrival and Triumph of Rome

The second phase of Hellenistic Civilization began in the late third century B.C. when Macedonia joined Carthage, a Phoenician state in North Africa opposite Sicily, in its struggle against Rome. Thereafter, the unforgiving Romans used every opportunity to

FIGURE 4.2 Acropolis at Pergamum. Second Century B.C. Reconstruction by H. Schlief. Staatliche Museen, Berlin. *The architecture of Pergamum was in the Hellenic style, but the city's mixed population and economy made it the commercial and political hub of a Hellenistic kingdom. Under Eumenes II the capital and the country reached its height of power around 160 B.C.*

humiliate their enemy on the Greek peninsula. Between 215 and 148 B.C., Rome fought four wars with Macedonia, thus becoming entangled in Greek political and military squabbles. Finally, in 146 B.C. Rome, after conquering and subduing northern Greece, brought the entire peninsula under its control. The other Hellenistic kingdoms soon submitted. In 133 B.C. the ruler of Pergamum willed his state to Rome, hoping thereby to give an advantage to his subjects, who now passed under Roman rule. The Seleucid kingdom was conquered by the Romans in 65 B.C., after three different wars in Asia Minor. Egypt maintained its freedom longer than any other Hellenistic state, until 31 B.C., when Cleopatra and her forces were defeated by Octavian and the Roman navy.

THE CITIES OF HELLENISTIC CIVILIZATION

Alexander's most enduring legacy to the Hellenistic world was his new image of the city. The city is as old as civilization itself, since urban life is by definition a component of civilized existence. But in the vision of Alexander the Great, cities became keystones holding together his diverse and vast empire and serving as centers of government, trade, and culture. Alexander thought that each metropolitan area would radiate Greco-Oriental civilization, bringing urban culture to the hinterland. During his conquests, Alexander is reputed to have founded over seventy cities, many of which were named for him.

Pergamum

During the Hellenistic era, Alexander's successors emulated him, establishing urban centers such as Antioch on the Orontes River in southern Asia Minor and Seleucia, the new capital of the Seleucid kingdom, near Babylon, almost at the junction of the Tigris and Euphrates rivers. Antioch and Seleucia, however, were provincial capitals in comparison to the new city of Pergamum in western Asia Minor, which now emerged as a brilliant center of art and thought, bringing together Greek and Persian civilizations. The Attalids, the ruling dynasty of Pergamum, decorated their city's acropolis with a splendid palace, a library second in the number of volumes only to the one in Alexandria, and a marble temple to Athena. Scattered on the hillside beneath the acropolis were shrines, markets, and private dwellings of the more prosperous citizens. At the base of the hill the tradespeople, artisans, and slaves lived crowded together (Figure 4.2).

Alexandria in Egypt

For all its claims to grandeur, however, Pergamum could not surpass the size, wealth, beauty, or culture of the premier Hellenistic city, Alexandria in Egypt. Founded by Alexander, this Egyptian center was the most famous and enduring of the conqueror's namesake towns (Figure 4.3). Under the Ptolemies, Alexandria grew to be a world city that attracted both the ambitious who came seeking opportunities and the apathetic who wanted to be left alone. Every attraction known to human desires is said to have existed here, just as in the teeming cities of the twentieth century. By the end of the first century B.C., Alexandria's population had climbed to almost one million, and the city was divided into five sections, including one reserved for royalty and separate residential quarters for the Egyptians and the Jews.

Unlike a self-contained Hellenic Age polis with a relatively homogeneous population, Alexandria resembled a modern metropolis in which activity revolves around the pursuit of wealth. With busy harbors, bustling markets, and international banks, Alexandria became a hub of commercial and financial enterprises. Economic interests held together Alexandria's population of mixed racial and ethnic groups.

Alexandria's economic vitality was matched by the splendor of its cultural achievements. The world's first museum—a temple to the muses—was built here as a place for scholars to study and to exchange ideas. For the convenience of these thinkers, there was erected nearby the famed library, whose staff collected the classics of Greek civilization, including the works of Plato and Aristotle, the tragedies of Aeschylus, Sophocles, and Euripides, the comedies of Aristophanes, and the scientific treatises of many Hellenistic philosophers. At the time of the Roman conquest in the late first century B.C., the library contained nearly 700,000 volumes, the largest collection in the ancient world. By then, Al-

exandria had become a beacon for great minds who were attracted by the city's rich intellectual life and cosmopolitan atmosphere.

THE ELABORATION OF THE GREEK TRADITION: THE SPREAD OF CLASSICISM TO THE HELLENISTIC WORLD

The Hellenistic world to some extent rejected the simplicity, balance, and restraint that had characterized Hellenism and embraced a more emotional, theatrical view of culture (Figures 4.4 and 4.5). The expansiveness of Alexander's territorial conquests found an echo in the expansion of emotional and expressive content in the arts. As new energies, languages, and traditions were poured into old artistic and literary forms, the seriousness of Hellenism began to give way to a Hellenistic love of playfulness along with an interest in ordinary, everyday subjects.

Hellenistic culture also reflected the tastes and needs of the period's diverse states. Greek tragedy lost its vitality when separated from its roots in the independent polis, but comedy appealed to sophisticated urban audiences who were seeking diversion. Nondramatic literature became rather artificial as authors concentrated on perfecting their style or

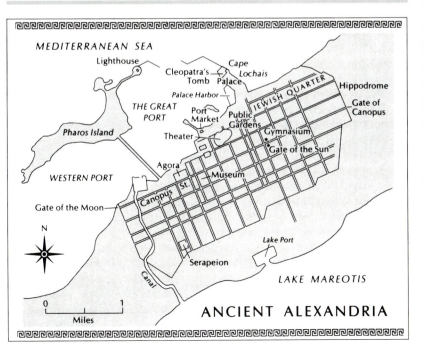

FIGURE 4.3 Plan of Ancient Alexandria. Third Century B.C. *Designed by Deinocrates of Rhodes, Alexander's personal architect, Alexandria was laid out in a grid formed by intersecting avenues and streets. The entire city was enclosed by a wall, accessible by four massive gates at the ends of the major avenues. To the north lay two harbors that made the city the most vital port in the Mediterranean. The harbors were protected by an outer island at the point of which stood the lighthouse of Pharos—now lost. Remarkable for its colossal size, the lighthouse was considered one of the wonders of the ancient world.*

FIGURE 4.4   *Nike of Samothrace. Ca. 190* B.C. *Louvre, Paris. The* Nike of Samothrace—*commonly called the "Winged Victory" because Nike was the Greek goddess of victory—is a perfect symbol of the war-dominated Hellenistic Age. Carved to appear to be striding into the wind, with wildly agitated draperies and soaring wings, this sculpture embodies exuberant action, a defining feature of this turbulent age in which the successors of Alexander fought among themselves, only to succumb to Rome in the end. In the depiction of Nike's costume, ranging from the transparent band of "fabric" around the navel to the draperies swathing the thighs and legs, this work also illustrates this age's superb virtuosity. Originally part of a sculptural group on the island of Samothrace, which included a war galley, a fountain, and a reflecting pool (now lost), the Nike still gives the impression of standing on the prow of a swiftly moving ship.*

FIGURE 4.5   *Nike of Samothrace (side view).*

pursuing exotic scholarship. New philosophies and religions arose in response to the isolation and loneliness that many people experienced in the overcrowded cities. And, finally, grandiose architecture addressed the propaganda needs of autocratic rulers, and realistic sculpture reflected the tastes of an increasingly urban, secular culture.

Nevertheless, the values of Hellenistic culture did not so much replace the standards of Hellenic Classicism as they enriched and elaborated the older ideals. Like Hellenism, the Hellenistic style depicted the realities of the physical world rather than finding truth in fantasy or abstraction. And Hellenistic artists and authors agreed with their Hellenic forebears that art must serve moral purposes that are revealed through content as well as through formal order.

Drama and Literature

In the Hellenistic Age, Greek comedy began to resemble modern productions. The grotesque padding worn by the actors gave way to realistic costumes; masks were redesigned to be representative of the portrayed characters; and the actors assumed a dominant status over the chorus. Comedies became a form of popular amusement in most of the major cities, and Hellenistic playwrights developed a genre known as *New Comedy* to appeal to the pleasure-seeking audiences who were flocking to the theaters. Avoiding political criticism and casual obscenity, New Comedy presented gently satirical scenes from middle-class life.

The plays were generally comic romances on such themes as frustrated first love or marital misunderstandings, and although the endings were inevitably happy and there was much formula writing—somewhat like today's situation comedies on television—the plays reflected the comprehensive range of the Hellenistic style. The characters, for example, were familiar types drawn from the rich diversity of Hellenistic society—the courtesan, the slave, the fawning parasite. New Comedy remained steadfastly middle-class, however, for the traditional social order always prevailed in the end. For example, a favorite plot device of New Comedy hinged on discovering that a seemingly lowborn character was actually from a respected—and often wealthy—family.

Both ancient and modern critics tend to regard Menander [muh-NAN-duhr] (about 343–about 291 B.C.) as the leading author of New Comedy. He wrote more than one hundred plays for the Dionysus festival in Athens, winning first prize for comedy eight times, and is credited with perfecting the *comedy of manners*, a humorous play that focuses on the way people interact in society.

The Girl from Samos is a robust example of his work. Dating from around 321 B.C., this comedy concerns the identity of an orphaned baby and features a cast of stock characters: a courtesan, a young lover, an old lover, a humorous neighbor, and two comic slaves. In the play Menander first presents a household in which the father believes that he and his son are wooing the same woman, when, in actuality, the son is involved with the girl next door. Then, when a foundling appears, absurd misunderstandings arise and false accusations are made. The play ends happily with all characters reconciled, the son wed to his true love, and the father and mistress married in a joyous ceremony—a typical New Comedy resolution. Western comedy would be inconceivable without Menander. His style was assimilated into Roman comedy, which passed the spirit of his work into the dramas of the Italian Renaissance and from there into the comedies of Shakespeare and Molière.

In nondramatic literature, the Hellenistic Age produced a style known as *Alexandrianism*. The Ptolemaic rulers who built the library and museum in Alexandria used state subsidies to lure scholars and poets to the city to study the works that were, by purchase or plunder, finding their way into the library's vast collections. The writers produced works of many types—poetry, history, biography, literary criticism, and essays on geography and mathematics—but their work is generally of historical interest only. Alexandrian literature is often obscure and ornate, derivative, and scholarly in an arid way.

A writer who stands apart in the Alexandrian school is the poet Theocritus [the-OCK-ruht-us] (about 310–250 B.C.), who worked within the confines of the style but achieved genuine literary distinction. He created a new poetic form, the *pastoral*, which was to have a long and influential history in later Classical and modern European literature. These poems describe the lives of shepherds and farmers in a somewhat artificial, idealized way. Theocritus drew his images from his memory of his earlier years in rural Sicily, and his charming, nostalgic verses appealed to many who had also left the quiet rustic life for the excitement of the Hellenistic cities.

Theocritus also wrote what he called *idylls* (from the Greek meaning "little picture"), which were verses offering small portraits or vignettes of Hellenistic life. Some of these poems reveal a great deal about everyday affairs, noting the common concerns and aspirations of all generations—love, family, religion, and wealth.

FIGURE 4.6   A Religious Ceremony. A.D. 159. Yale University Art Gallery, New Haven. *Although this relief is dated from the 2nd century A.D., it is characteristic of Hellenistic religious practices that continued into Roman times. In the center is depicted Zeus Olympius-Baalshamin, a combination of Greek and Semitic deities. On the left is a priest burning an offering on an altar and dressed in Near Eastern garb; on the right is a priest wearing Greek clothing.*

Philosophy and Religion

For many people, everyday life changed drastically during the Hellenistic Age. The sense of belonging that had characterized life in the Hellenic poleis was replaced by a feeling of isolation, of loneliness, even of helplessness, particularly in the urban centers. As a consequence, two seemingly contradictory points of view grew up: individualism *and* internationalism. Those who held these attitudes were searching for continuity in a rapidly changing world, were seeking identity for the individual through common interests, values, and hopes, and were striving to understand events that seemed unpredictable and beyond human control.

Philosophies and religions arose with answers that seemed as contradictory as the problems themselves. One philosophy urged a universal brotherhood of all human beings, united regardless of race or status of birth; another, despairing of the world, excluded most people from its ranks and appealed to a chosen few. Religions, similarly, provided a multitude of answers. One faith preached salvation in a life after death, while another turned to magic to escape Fate—that blind force that controlled human life.

In the long run, such diversity of choice tended to foster tolerance, since no single set of beliefs prevailed or satisfied everyone (Figure 4.6). Having many alternatives spared society the anguish and bigotry that would have arisen if only two or three points of view had been competing. Because of the

ease of communication and travel in the Hellenistic period, these new philosophies and religions quickly gained converts everywhere, regardless of class or geographic location.

The most enduring of this period's philosophies, Cynicism, Skepticism, Epicureanism, and Stoicism, attracted the better-educated and more influential groups in Hellenistic society. Of these four theories, Cynicism and Skepticism appealed to only a few, while Epicureanism and Stoicism had a much larger following.

Cynicism   Of the four schools, *Cynicism* had the least impact on Hellenistic civilization. The Cynics, believing that society diverted the individual from the more important goals of personal independence and freedom, denounced all religions and governments, shunned physical comfort, and advocated the avoidance of personal pleasure. In the Cynics' logic, true freedom came with the realization that if one wanted nothing, one could not lack anything. By isolating themselves from society, they gained a type of self-sufficiency the Greeks called *autarky.*

The first and most famous Cynic, Diogenes [die-AHJ-uh-neez] (about 412–about 323 B.C.), openly scorned the ordinary values and crass materialism of his society. His contrary personality so fascinated Alexander the Great that the ruler, upon being insulted by the Cynic, is reported to have said that if he were not Alexander, he would prefer to be Diogenes! (Figure 4.7). A few Cynics earned the respect of some thinkers, but the principles of Cynicism offended the educated, and its pessimism offered no hope to the masses.

Skepticism The proponents of *Skepticism* argued that nothing could be known for certain, an extreme conclusion they were led to by their belief that the senses were unreliable sources of knowledge. Thinking that everything was relative, the Skeptics maintained that all ideas must be questioned and that no single philosophy was true. When their critics pointed out that such unrelenting questioning was clearly not a practical answer to life's uncertainties, the Skeptics replied that certainty could be achieved only by admitting that truth was unknowable—a circular response. The Skeptics thought that if they recognized that intellectual inquiry was fruitless, then they could avoid frustration and achieve *autarky*, or self-sufficiency—the same goal as that of the Cynics and the Stoics.

The Skeptics, even though they attracted a smaller audience than the Cynics, had a greater impact on Western reasoning. Pyrrho [PEER-oh] of Elis founded Skepticism and pursued the native strain of Greek thinking to its logical conclusion, but he never wrote anything. Skepticism had some appeal for the early Romans, who brought the Greek philosopher and teacher Carneades [kar-NEE-uh-deez] (about 214–129 B.C.) to Rome in 155 B.C. Carneades, one of the first Greek thinkers to make this journey, shocked his Roman audience. The pious Romans took Carneades' universal doubt as a denial of the stability and permanence of their state and its values. Although Skepticism faded after Carneades' death, the movement was revived during the Roman Empire and eventually passed into the mainstream of Western thought.

Epicureanism The strict and quiet way of life advocated by *Epicureanism* appealed to aristocrats who were more interested in learning than in politics. It began as the philosophy of the Greek thinker Epicurus

FIGURE 4.7 *Diogenes and Alexander the Great*. First Century A.D. Villa Albani, Rome. *This Roman relief shows that Diogenes and Alexander the Great, two figures of the Hellenistic Age, were living presences for the Romans. The philosopher Diogenes is carved sitting in his famous tub, a symbol of his contempt for creature comforts. The world conqueror Alexander is on the right, pointing his finger at the Greek thinker. The dog portrayed on top of the tub is a reference to Cynicism (the word* cynic *is from the Greek word for "dog"). Diogenes asserted that humans should live simply—like dogs.*

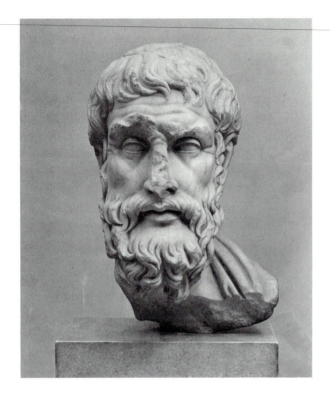

FIGURE 4.8 *Epicurus.* Ca. 290–280 B.C. Metropolitan Museum of Art. *This marble bust of Epicurus, discovered in southern Italy and inscribed with his name, is a copy of the original bronze sculpture. Many busts and likenesses of Epicurus have been found, indicating the popularity of his philosophy in Hellenistic times and especially during the Roman era.*

[ep-uh-KYUR-uhs] (about 342–270 B.C.), who founded a school in Athens where pupils, including slaves and women, gathered to discuss ideas (Figure 4.8). Epicurus based his ethical philosophy on the Atomic theory of those Greek thinkers who saw the universe as completely determined by the behavior of atoms moving in empty space (see Chapter 3). Epicurus accepted this picture, but with one significant modification: He argued that because atoms on occasion swerved from their set paths and made unpredictable deviations, it was possible, even in a deterministic universe, for humans to make free choices. Like the Atomists, Epicurus also believed that the senses presented an accurate view of the physical world. Thus, by using the mind as a storehouse for sense impressions and by exercising free will in their choices, individuals could reach moral judgments and ultimately form an ethical code.

For Epicurus, the correct ethical code led to happiness, which was realized in a life of quiet, separated and withdrawn from the trying cares of the world. Furthermore, those who would be happy should keep their wants simple, not indulge excessive desires, and resist fame, power, and wealth, which only brought misery and disappointment.

Another characteristic of Epicurean happiness was freedom from fear—fear of the gods, of death, and of the hereafter. Although Epicurus believed that the gods existed, he also believed that they cared nothing about human beings, and therefore no one need be afraid of what the gods might or might not do. As for death, there was, again, nothing to agonize over because when it did occur, the atoms that made up the soul simply separated from the body's atoms and united with other particles to create new forms. With death came the end of the human capacity to feel pleasure or pain and thus the end of suffering. Consequently, death, rather than being feared, should be welcomed as a release from misfortune and trouble. Pleasure, in the Epicurean view, is the absence of pain. The happy Epicurean, standing above the cares of the world, had reached *ataraxia*, the desireless state that the Hellenistic Age deemed so precious.

Stoicism   Both Epicureanism and *Stoicism* claimed that happiness was the final goal of the individual, and both were essentially materialistic, stressing the importance of sense impressions and the natural world. The Stoics, however, identified the supreme deity with nature, thus making the natural world divine and inseparable from the deity. The supreme being was also another name for reason, or *logos*, and hence nature was also rational. Since the Stoics' God was law and the author of law, this led to the notion that the workings of nature were expressed in divine laws.

The Stoics likewise discovered God in humanity. The Stoics' God, being identical with reason, gave a spark to each mortal's soul, conferring the twin gifts of rationality and kinship with divinity. The Stoics thus believed that reason and the senses could be used jointly to uncover the underlying moral law as well as God's design in the world, proving God's wisdom and power over human life and nature.

There was in Stoicism a tendency to leave everything up to God. Stoics came to accept their roles in life, whether rich or poor, master or slave, healthy or afflicted, and such a resigned and deterministic outlook could (and did) lead to apathy or unconcern. However, the ideal Stoic, the Wise Man, never became apathetic. He overcame Stoicism's fatalistic tendency by stressing his own sense of and dedication to duty. Doing one's duty was part of following the deity's plan, and the Stoic willingly performed his tasks, no matter how onerous or laborious. The reward for living a life of duty was Virtue. Having achieved Virtue, the Stoics were freed from their emotions, which they thought only corrupted them.

The Stoics had thus achieved *autarky,* the state of existence sought by many Hellenistic philosophers.

Stoicism was unique among the Hellenistic philosophies in holding out the promise of membership in a worldwide brotherhood. Perhaps inspired by Alexander the Great's dream, the Stoics advocated an ideal state, guided by God and law, that encompassed all of humanity of whatever race, sex, social status, or nationality in a common bond of reason. As humans carried out their duties in this larger community, they would rise above local and national limitations and create a better world.

Because of their practical optimism, the Stoics drew the largest number of followers among political leaders and intellectuals, who found the Cynics, the Skeptics, and the Epicureans too pessimistic. In the end, however, all four philosophies satisfied only a small portion of the vast Hellenistic population. They failed to appeal to persons who were confused by the intellectual theories or who derived no personal satisfaction from the teachings. Instead, the bulk of the people, spurred on by a growing sense of helplessness, began to believe that Fate ruled their lives.

Fate and the Mystery Cults   The belief in Fate, a concept borrowed from Babylonia, gripped the lives of many in the Hellenistic world. To them, Fate ruled the universe, controlled the heavens, and determined the course of life. Although no one could change the path of this nonmoral, predestined force, individuals could try to avoid the cruel consequences of Fate by various methods. The pseudoscience of astrology, also from Babylonia, offered one alternative. Magic was now revived, and many people used sacred objects to conjure up good spirits or to ward off evil ones. Nevertheless, it was the mystery cults—springing from the primitive chthonian religions of Greece (see Chapters 2 and 3) and elsewhere—that eventually emerged as the most popular and effective response to Fate (Figure 4.9).

During the Hellenistic Age numerous chthonian cults spread from the Seleucid kingdom and Egypt to the Greek mainland, where they were combined with local beliefs and rituals to create religions that fused different beliefs and practices. By the second century B.C., converts were being attracted from all over the Hellenistic world to the well-established mystery cults of Orpheus and Dionysus in Greece and to the new religions coming out of Egypt and the old Persian lands. The growth of these cults, in turn, sparked an increase in religious zeal after about 100 B.C. The result was more ceremonies and public festivals and the revival of older faiths.

The Egyptian mystery cults grew and became quite popular across the Hellenistic world. Ptol-

FIGURE 4.9   *Tyche, or "Good Fortune."* Early Third Century B.C. Vatican Museum. *During the Hellenistic Age the personal fears that many people experienced led to the popularity of Tyche, the goddess of good fortune. At the same time, however, the older forms of worship persisted. For instance, the people of the new city of Antioch claimed Tyche as their patroness, much as the earlier Greeks had worshiped particular Olympian deities.*

emy I, the Macedonian founder of the Ptolemaic dynasty in 323 B.C., invented a new god, Serapis, in an effort to unite the Egyptians and Greeks. Serapis became a favorite deity of the masses outside of Egypt, and this god's followers built shrines everywhere.

But the goddess Isis, already well-known to the Egyptians, overshadowed the newly minted Serapis. According to her cult legend, Isis rescued her husband-brother, Osiris, from his enemies and brought him back to life with her unwavering love. This resurrection symbolized to the faithful the new life awaiting them at death. In time, Isis became associated with many foreign goddesses, fusing with them to become the most honored goddess of the ancient world.

From the Seleucid kingdom, the remnants of Babylonian and Persian cultures offered two radically different cults to the Hellenistic Age, the brutal religion of Cybele and the philosophical religion founded by Zoroaster (see Chapter 1). Cybele, the Great Mother goddess, appealed to many women and even a few men, despite the self-mutilation that male believers had to undergo in order to gain the promise of a new life. Under different names, the Great Mother goddess was worshiped throughout the Hellenistic world and in Rome. Later, Mithraism, an offshoot of Zoroastrianism, with its emphasis on duty and loyalty, caught the attention of Rome's soldiers, thereby assuring the spread of this belief wherever Roman legions were stationed.

The secret rites of the mystery cults, which communicated the thrill of initiation and the satisfaction of belonging, answered deep psychological needs in their Hellenistic converts. This universal appeal cut across class and racial lines and attracted an ever-widening segment of the populace. With their promise of immortality, these rituals contributed to the atmosphere of the Roman world in which Christianity would later be born.

Architecture

As in Hellenic times, architecture in the Hellenistic Age reflected the central role that religion played in the life of the people. Public buildings served religious, ceremonial, and governmental purposes, and the temple continued as the leading type of structure. The altar, which had originated in Archaic Greece as a simple structure where holy sacrifices or offerings were made, now became a major structural form, second in importance only to the temple, because of its use in state rituals.

Hellenistic architecture modified the basic temple and altar forms inherited from Hellenic models to express the grandeur demanded by the age's rulers. These monarchs, having carved up the empire of Alexander the Great, were mesmerized by his manner of rule. To these power-hungry men, Alexander's claim to divinity had opened up a new vision of statecraft. As a result, Alexander's successors built temples and altars whose massive size and elaborate decoration manifested both their own earthly majesty and the divine authority of whatever deity with whom they claimed kinship.

The Corinthian Temple   The *Corinthian* temple came to embody Hellenistic splendor. The Corinthian col-

umn had first appeared in the Hellenic Period, when it was probably used as a decorative feature. Because it was taller, more slender, and more ornamented than either the Doric or the Ionic column, the Corinthian column was now used on the exterior of temples built by Hellenistic builders for their kings. In time, Hellenistic taste decreed that the Corinthian column was appropriate for massive buildings. After the Hellenistic Age, the Corinthian order became the favorite of the Roman emperors, and it was revived in the Renaissance and diffused throughout the Western world, where it survives today as the most visible sign of Hellenistic influence.

The most outstanding Corinthian temples combined grandeur with grace, as in the Olympieum in Athens, now a ruin (Figure 4.10). Commissioned by the Seleucid king Antiochus IV [an-TIE-uh-kuhs], the Olympieum expressed his notion of a diverse, international culture united under Zeus, his divine counterpart and the lord of Mount Olympus. The temple, the first to use Corinthian columns, was constructed during three different and distinct historical eras. The stylobate, or base, was laid in the late Archaic Age, the Corinthian columns were raised by a Hellenistic king in about 175 B.C., and the temple was finally completed in A.D. 130 under the Roman emperor Hadrian, a great admirer of Greek culture. The temple is stylistically unified, however, because it was finished according to the surviving plans of its second century B.C. architect. Despite its massive size and its lack of mathematical refinements, the Olympieum presented an extremely graceful appearance with its forest of delicate Corinthian columns, consisting of double rows of twenty columns each on the sides and triple rows of eight on the ends.

The Altar   Before there were temples, there were altars, the oldest religious structure in the Greek world. The earliest altars were simple slabs, made wide enough to allow sacrificial animals to be slaughtered. During the Hellenistic Age the altars were substantially enlarged. The biggest appears to have been the 650-foot-long altar, permitting the sacrifice of more than one hundred cattle at one time, funded by the tyrant of Syracuse in the third century B.C.

Although the Syracusan altar has disappeared, the dismantled altar of Zeus at Pergamum has recently been discovered and reassembled. It is easy to see why ancient travelers called it one of the wonders of the world (Figure 4.11). The actual altar, not visible in the photograph, stands lengthwise in a magnificent Ionic colonnaded courtyard. The courtyard itself is raised on a *podium*, or platform; below the courtyard, the sides of the structure are decorated with a sculpted frieze depicting the deities at

FIGURE 4.10 The Olympieum. Various dates: Late Sixth Century B.C.; Second Quarter of Second Century B.C.; Completed, Second Quarter of Second Century A.D. Athens, Greece. *The thirteen standing Corinthian columns were part of the original plan of the Olympieum's architect. After the temporary cessation of building in 164 B.C., some of this temple's unfinished columns were transported to Rome and reused in a building there. Their use in Rome helped to popularize the Corinthian style among political leaders and wealthy tastemakers.*

FIGURE 4.11 Altar of Zeus at Pergamum. (Reconstruction.) Third and Second Quarters of the Second Century B.C. Pergamum Museum, Berlin. *This masterpiece of Hellenistic architecture was erected in the 170s B.C. by Eumenes II, the king of Pergamum, to commemorate his victories over various barbarian states in Asia Minor. Eumenes believed himself to be the savior and disseminator of Greek culture, and this altar with its giant frieze was meant to suggest Hellenic monuments, such as the Athenian Parthenon.*

FIGURE 4.12 *Gaul and Wife.* Roman copy of a bronze original. Ca. 230–220 B.C. Terme Museum, Rome. *The rulers of the Hellenistic kingdom of Pergamum preferred art that was showy and overwrought, a taste that perhaps stemmed from their insecurity at being a new dynasty. A Pergamene style of sculpture developed under these kings in which gestures were theatrical and anatomical features were portrayed in exaggerated depth. Gaul and Wife is a superb example of this style.*

FIGURE 4.13 Old Market Woman. Roman copy of a Hellenistic bronze. Third or Second Century B.C. Metropolitan Museum of Art. *Many Hellenistic sculptors depicted old women in pathetic situations, tired, drunk, or begging. Scholars are divided as to whether these statues were meant to be admired for their truthfulness or represented aristocratic contempt for an ugly social phenomenon.*

war. The overall design—with the frieze below the columns—appears to be an inversion of the usual temple plan. Constructed by Eumenes II [YOU-muh-neez] of the Attalid dynasty, this altar was but one part of a concerted effort to transform Pergamum into another Athens. Thus, the idea of a "new" Athens—a recurrent motif in the humanistic tradition—had already been formulated by the Hellenistic Age.

Sculpture

Like Hellenistic architects, Hellenistic sculptors adapted many of the basic forms and ideas of the Hellenic style to meet the tastes of their day. The Hellenistic sculptors perpetuated such Hellenic principles as contrapposto and proportion as well as the

Hellenic emphasis on religious and moral themes. But Hellenistic art increasingly expressed a secular, urban viewpoint, and Hellenic restraint often gave way to realism, eroticism, and violence, expressed and enjoyed for their own sake.

Between 230 and 220 B.C., King Attalos I [AT-uh-luhs] of Pergamum dedicated in Athens a group of bronze sculptures that celebrated his recent victory over the barbaric Gauls. By donating these bronzes to Athens, which was outside of Pergamum's political orbit, the Attalid ruler hoped to establish his cultural credentials as a defender of Greek culture and thus further his claims to rule over the entire Hellenistic world.

One of these pieces, *Gaul and Wife* (which survives only in a Roman marble copy), shows a barbarian chief killing his spouse and fatally wounding himself rather than be enslaved (Figure 4.12). The sculptor demonstrates his keen eye for realistic details in the collapsed body of the woman and the man's open wound oozing with blood. The Hellenistic style's appreciation of the melodramatic is evident in the anguish of the defiant Gaul as his attention is divided between stabbing himself and supporting his fallen wife. But by treating a foreign enemy with such nobility, the anonymous sculptor perpetuates the deep moral sense that was central to Hellenic art.

A radically different subject is expressed in the *Old Market Woman*, which, like a stock character from New Comedy, depicted a well-known social type (Figure 4.13). The old woman, who might have strolled out of the market place of any Hellenistic city, represented a **genre subject**, or a scene taken from everyday life. The original third-century B.C. bronze portrayed a stooped figure, straining under the combined weight of her groceries and her advancing years. In this Roman marble copy, the left arm is missing, but she carries in her right a fowl and a brimming bucket. Her deeply lined and wrinkled face and her sagging breasts express the realism of Hellenistic style.

Among the masterpieces of Hellenistic art are the sculptures of the Pergamum altar frieze, which can be seen in Figure 4.11. The subject is a battle between the Olympian deities and the Giants, the monstrous race of pre-Greek gods and goddesses who were the offspring of Gaea (Earth) and Uranus (Sky, or the Heavens)—the first rulers of the universe. The Giants, having overturned their parents, are then defeated by *their* own children, the Olympian deities. To the Greeks, the final triumph of the Olympian gods and goddesses symbolized the coming of a just and moral order both in the universe and in their own society. Hence, when the Attalid rulers chose this subject for the altar frieze, they affirmed that they were continuing the values of Greek civilization. With the exception of the frieze on the Parthenon, the figures on this altar represent the most ambitious sculptural project in the ancient world.

Filled with high-powered energy, the Pergamum frieze displays figures that threaten to explode from the space in which they are barely contained. In one celebrated panel, Athena grasps the dying Giant Alkyoneus while her sacred snake bites him on the chest (Figure 4.14). Her agitated draperies appear to

FIGURE 4.14 *Athena Battling with Alkyoneus.* From the Great Frieze of the Pergamum Altar, East Section. Second Quarter of Second Century B.C. Pergamum Museum, Berlin. *An unusual aspect of the sculptor's rendering of the Giants was the diversity of their bodily forms. In the illustration, Alkyoneus' outspread wings identify him as a Giant and an offspring of Gaea, the goddess of the Earth, who is shown on the bottom right.*

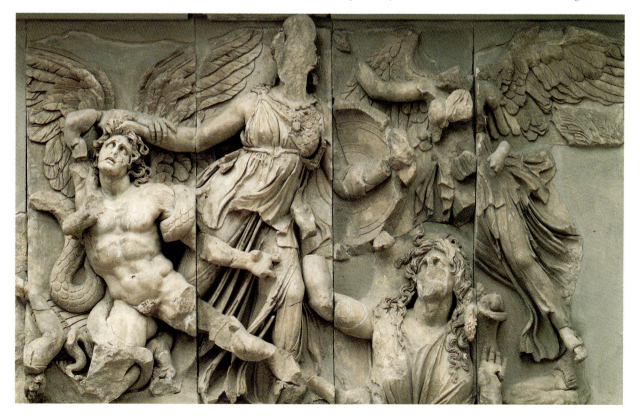

be billowing in a strong wind, so that the folds hang expressively rather than simply disclosing her body, as in the Hellenic style. The expression of pain on Alkyoneus' face—deeply furrowed brow and bulging eyeballs—and the straining muscles with prominent veins reflect the Pergamum school's taste for exaggeration.

The sculpture of the Hellenistic Age is also characterized by a frank appreciation of female beauty, a famous example of which is the *Aphrodite of Melos,* perhaps better known as the Venus de Milo (Figure 4.15). This original sculpture, carved from Parian marble, shows many borrowings from the tradition of Praxiteles, as shown in his *Hermes with the Infant Dionysus* (see Figure 3.25). Both Aphrodite and Hermes exhibit exaggerated contrapposto, a sensuous, even erotic, modeling of the body, and a serene countenance with an unmistakable gaze. However, the Hellenistic sculptor, demonstrating a playful flair, teases the viewer with the rolled down draperies that call attention to Aphrodite's exposed lower torso.

The *Horse and Jockey,* original bronzes that were retrieved in this century from a sunken ship in the Aegean Sea off Artemision, show Hellenistic fluidity rather than the frozen style of Hellenic art (Figure 4.16). Whether the two figures are a true ensemble is a subject of scholarly debate. Arguing against their unity is the size disparity between the small jockey and the enormous horse. But the balance seems in favor of treating them as a group, especially when the jockey is seated on the horse. In this juxtaposition, the horse's forward motion seems to cause the jockey's cloak to blow behind him. The boy, contorting his face with the strain of the race, stretches out his left hand, as if to urge his mount on to victory. This sculpted pair shows other innovations in Hellenistic art. The boy athlete, who looks rather like a ragged street urchin, represents the new interest in children that arose in Hellenistic art. And the straining horse contrasts dramatically with the serene, well-proportioned horses on the Parthenon frieze.

FIGURE 4.15 *Aphrodite of Melos (Venus de Milo). Ca. 160–150* B.C. Louvre, Paris. *This celebrated statue represents the classicizing tendency in Hellenistic art. The head is executed in the pure Hellenic style, as seen in the serene countenance, the exquisitely detailed hair, and the finely chiseled features. However, the body with its frank sensuality and its coy draperies is clearly in the Hellenistic style.*

FIGURE 4.16 *Horse and Jockey of Artemision.* Mid–Second Century B.C. National Museum, Athens. *The jockey and horse may have been intended by an athlete as a votive offering to a deity for victory in a competition. Such statues had been erected in Greece from the Archaic Age onward.*

FIGURE 4.17 *Crouching Aphrodite.* Ca. 100 B.C. Rhodes Museum. *This era frankly enjoyed wine, women, and song, and the many sculptures of Aphrodite, such as this famous one, are visual reminders of this aspect of Hellenistic life.*

Rhodes: Late Hellenistic Style

Although much of the Hellenistic world, including Greece, fell into Roman hands in 146 B.C., the Aegean island of Rhodes remained free for over sixty more years (see Map 4.1). During this period, independent Rhodes became a cultural center that rivaled the older cities of Pergamum, Alexandria, and Athens in terms of concentration of scientists, artists, and humanists. The Rhodian style, which was influenced by the Pergamene school, was the final stage of Hellenistic art. This style alternated between lighthearted and gay on the one hand and colossal and theatrical on the other.

In response to their patrons, Rhodian sculptors developed the specialty of depicting scenes from the life of Aphrodite. Because the bath provided an opportunity for portraying her body nude at a realistic moment, this setting became the one preferred by these artists. The *Crouching Aphrodite* is an exquisite example of this Rhodian type (Figure 4.17). Fresh from her bath, Aphrodite casually fluffs her wet hair in order to dry it. Her crouching position provides a measure of modesty, but, otherwise, this is a sensual rendition of the goddess in all her nude glory.

The school of sculpture on Rhodes, even after the island's absorption into Rome, was still able to produce the sublime masterpiece of Rhodian and Hellenistic art, *The Laocoön Group* (Figure 4.18). The sculptors of this famous group, probably Hagesandros [haj-uh-SAN-drohs], Polydoros [pol-e-DOOR-uhs], and Athanadoros [ah-thay-nuh-DOOR-uhs], were all members of a local dynasty of sculptors. Their sculpture depicts the priest Laocoön and his sons. According to Vergil's *Aeneid*, the Roman epic, the story recounts that Laocoön, a priest of Neptune, warned the Trojans not to bring the wooden horse—which, unknown to him, concealed a party of Greek warriors—into their city. (Laocoön's admonition to beware Greeks bearing gifts has become proverbial.) As Laocoön finished his speech, sea serpents, sent by the gods, raced out of the sea and crushed him and his two sons to death. The Trojans interpreted Laocoön's speech as an impious act against the gods, and they hauled the horse into Troy.

FIGURE 4.18   HAGESANDROS, POLYDOROS, AND ATHANADOROS. *The Laocoön Group. Ca. A.D. 50. Vatican Museum. Parallels are frequently made between the distorted features of the dying Laocoön and the mortally wounded Alkyoneus from the Pergamum altar (see Figure 4.14). This similarity points to some connection between the Rhodian and Pergamene schools of sculpture, though the exact relationship is a matter of controversy.*

In the *Laocoön* sculptural group, the snakes, which grasp and bite the priest and his sons, serve to integrate the three figures into an image of unrelieved horror: Laocoön's face is contorted in anguish as the serpent bites him; on the left, one of his sons is already dead; and the other son seems to be disentangling himself from the serpentine coils. This cele-brated work, with its technical virtuosity and its rhetorical violence, is a fitting climax to almost four hundred years of Hellenistic art. The *Laocoön* sculptural group vanished after the fall of Rome only to be rediscovered in the early sixteenth century A.D., when it influenced the sculptor Michelangelo and the subsequent rise of Baroque art.

The Legacy of the Hellenistic World

In the Hellenistic Age, Athens and its culture achieved the status of an inspiring model to be honored and emulated. But the Hellenistic rulers had no interest in democracy; indeed, their larger political interests often conflicted with the needs of local subjects. Nor did these kings want to further humanism, which they regarded as either irrelevant to imperial goals or subversive of them. What appealed to the Hellenistic kings was a narrow, lifeless humanism, as exemplified by the dynasties of the Attalids in Pergamum and the Ptolemies in Egypt. The Hellenistic monarchs wanted to do no more than create new cultural centers that rivaled the fame of the old Athens. The great Hellenistic centers of Pergamum and Alexandria—with their libraries, poets, scientists, artists, schools of philosophy, marble buildings, and monuments—were per-ceived as politically useful to these ambitious rulers. In other words, they wanted to harness art to politics for propaganda purposes.

The Hellenistic world bequeathed the idea of a "new Athens" to Rome, which further diffused the Greek heritage to the major cities of the entire Mediterranean area. After the fall of Rome, the medieval rulers adopted this tradition, making their governments responsive to the religious and, to a lesser extent, the cultural needs of their citizens. With the rise of the secular state in the eighteenth century A.D., governments began to dissociate themselves from the religious lives of their people. But state support of the arts and humanities increased and remains today a legacy of the Hellenistic Age to the modern world.

KEY CULTURAL TERMS

Hellenistic
koine
New Comedy
comedy of manners
Alexandrianism
pastoral
idyll
Cynicism
autarky

Skepticism
Epicureanism
ataraxia
Stoicism
logos
Corinthian
podium
genre subject

SUGGESTIONS FOR FURTHER READING

PRIMARY SOURCES

AUSTIN, M. M., ed. *The Hellenistic World from Alexander to the Roman Conquest: A Selection of Ancient Sources in Translation.* Cambridge: Cambridge University Press, 1981. Letters, decrees, and official pronouncements from the Hellenistic period; provides a real sense of the time.

SHAPIRO, H., and CURLEY, E., eds. *Hellenistic Philosophy: Selected Readings.* New York: Modern Library, 1965. Selections from writings on Epicureanism, Stoicism, Skepticism, and Neo-Platonism, with short introductions.

5

ROMAN CIVILIZATION
The Pre-Christian Centuries

Roman civilization is as ancient as the Greek civilization discussed in the preceding two chapters. From its legendary founding in 753 B.C., Rome grew steadily from a tiny city-state ruled by kings to a powerful republic, constantly adjusting to internal and external forces, and ultimately to a vast empire that controlled the known Western world. This chapter surveys the history and culture of Rome from its founding to the time when the empire teetered on the brink of collapse in A.D. 284. Chapter 7 picks up the story of Rome and follows it through its rejuvenated and Christian period to the last days of the empire. Before that, Chapter 6 examines the Judeo-Christian tradition that wove itself inextricably into the Western heritage during the first centuries of imperial Rome.

THE COLOSSUS OF THE MEDITERRANEAN WORLD

In A.D. 248 the Romans celebrated the one-thousandth anniversary of the founding of their city. By this date, the Roman way of life had engulfed not only the peoples and cultures of the ancient Near East and the eastern Mediterranean but had also brought the light of civilized existence to the primitive tribes living in North Africa, in western Europe

◄ *Flagellation Scene*. Villa of Mysteries. Ca. 60–40 B.C. Pompeii, Italy.

to the Rhine River, in central Europe to the Danube River, and in England (Map 5.1). So vast was Rome's dominion and so powerful its influence that until the eighteenth century Rome was the exemplar of power and wealth, one that the nations of Europe could only dream of equaling. Roman civilization had a profound and lasting impact on life in the West (Figure 5.1).

General Characteristics of Roman Civilization

Who were the Romans, and how did they create such a successful civilization? The Romans were and remained, above all, a practical people, interested chiefly in what was useful. Possessed of a virile moral sense, they were inclined to view intellectual brilliance with suspicion. Furthermore, Roman authority figures, such as political leaders and fathers, cultivated the virtue known in Latin as *gravitas*, or gravity, meaning a deep-seated seriousness (Figure 5.2). By Greek standards, the Romans were a dull lot, too self-controlled and afraid of the imagination. But the Romans made up for their absence of intellectual fire by their ingenious adaptations of borrowed cultural forms, and they compensated for their lack of originality through a gift for governing.

Early Rome was a minor city-state founded by herdsmen and farmers on seven low hills beside the Tiber River in central Italy. Over their long rise to world leadership, the Romans changed radically, but

MAP 5.1

The Roman Empire under Augustus

they never ceased to honor their agrarian roots. Roman morality and Roman law both echoed a rural ethic by stressing the need to submit to the order of nature and to live within one's means. Roman literary culture was also deeply imbued with a reverence for a rustic past. When Rome became prosperous and powerful, many writers bemoaned the corrupting power of luxury and appealed to the homespun values of Rome's founders. Rome's agrarian tradition also contributed the ideal of the patriotic farmer-soldier. Early leaders of the republican period who never strayed far from their farming heritage became national idols, celebrated in biographies and held up to school boys as models.

Another important Roman value was the sanctity of the family. Divorce was unheard of until the late republican era, and even then family values continued to be eulogized by moralists and honored by political leaders. Within the Roman family the roles of the father and the mother were strictly defined. The family was guided by the father, the *paterfamilias*, who exercised legal power of life and death over his entire household, including his spouse, children,

and other relatives as well as servants and slaves (Figure 5.3). The paterfamilias wielded greater authority than his Greek counterpart, but, in contrast, the Roman matron was freer and had more practical influence than the secluded wives of Greece. In general, the Roman matron was conspicuously present in society, attending and presiding at gatherings along with her mate and supervising the education of both her male and female offspring (Figure 5.4).

In Rome as elsewhere in the ancient world, religion permeated the life of the family. Each Roman household kept an undying fire burning on its hearth, symbolic of the goddess Vesta, to ensure the family's continuity. Above each hearth stood statuettes of Lares, the outdoor spirits guarding fields and buildings, and Penates, the interior protectors of cupboards and barns (Figure 5.5). Beyond the living, the family revered the deceased male ancestors, whose funeral masks adorned the walls and were regularly used in domestic rituals.

In sum, the Roman citizen was secure in the knowledge of both Rome's and his place in the world and in the cosmos. And the Roman matron, though

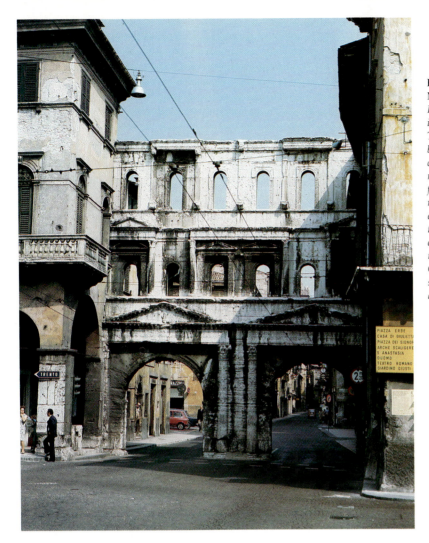

FIGURE 5.1 Porta Borsari at Verona. Mid–First Century A.D. Verona, Italy. *Roman architectural innovations strongly influenced the architecture of later periods. This structure was originally attached to a building that served as a gate to the Roman city of Verona. The building itself was razed during the Renaissance, but the facade was left standing and served as a model for palaces of that era. The wall, composed of stacked, rounded arches, is a typical Roman design. Most of the wall openings are beautifully framed with triangular pediments overhead and Corinthian columns or pilasters on the sides, resulting in a visual effect of ordered diversity.*

FIGURE 5.2 Statue of a Republican General. 75–50 B.C. Museo Nazionale, Rome. *This statue portrays an unknown military leader from the Late Republic. The deeply serious though realistic face is typical of the Roman style. By this time Roman generals were imitating the custom of Hellenistic leaders of having themselves depicted as nude or seminude figures. This fashion ended abruptly with the reign of Augustus, when rulers began to be represented wearing a cuirass, or breastplate (see Figure 5.23).*

FIGURE 5.3 Portrait Head of the Banker Lucius Caecilius Jucundus. Mid–First Century A.D. Museo Nazionale, Naples. *The stern gaze and sagging features of Lucius Caecilius Jucundus convey the quiet dignity and authority of a typical* paterfamilias. *This realistic portrait (note the large mole on his cheek) may have been based on a death mask.*

FIGURE 5.5   Statuettes of Lares. First Century B.C. Museo Nazionale, Naples. *These statuettes portray the Lares, the deities who guarded each Roman home. At first, images of the Lares were painted inside small family shrines, but wealthy citizens began to commission statuettes of these household deities. The posture of the bronze Lares—dancing on the balls of their feet and pouring wine from a drinking horn into a libation bowl—was also typical of the painted figures. The swinging skirts reflect a stylistic current that began in Hellenic art.*

FIGURE 5.4   *Eumachia.* Mid–First Century A.D. Museo Nazionale, Naples. *This statue of Eumachia, which was found at Pompeii, shows that Roman matrons were involved in public life. The inscription on the statue's base praises her for having donated a building in the town's forum for the use of the fullers—workers involved in the making of woolen cloth. Her statue was paid for by the fullers' association in gratitude for her gift. Her idealized face reflects the Hellenic ideal preferred during the reign of Augustus in the first century A.D.*

lacking the voting rights citizenship gave to her spouse, played many roles that society and tradition demanded of her. Like her husband, she understood the social rules and what her culture had called her to do.

The Etruscan and Greek Connections

Although the Romans took great pride in their native tradition, they were receptive to change and able to assimilate the contributions of superior cultures, as their experience with the Etruscans and Greeks demonstrates. In the late seventh century B.C., Rome, still

a small city-state, was subjugated by the Etruscans, a sophisticated urban people of obscure origins in northern Italy. The Etruscans excelled at commerce and conducted a brisk maritime trade with the advanced cultures of the eastern Mediterranean (Figure 5.6). Under Etruscan domination, Rome prospered and became a hub of commerce and transportation. And under Etruscan tutelage the Romans began to put their spoken language into writing, using the Etruscan alphabet. Even what are called Roman numerals were invented by the Etruscans.

But despite the obvious advantages that contact with a higher culture had given them, the Romans rankled under Etruscan rule, and in 509 B.C. they expelled Tarquin the Proud, the last Etruscan king, and

FIGURE 5.6 *Apollo of Veii.* Early Fifth Century B.C. Museo Nazionale di Villa Guilia, Rome. *This magnificent striding statue of Apollo shows strong influences from the art of Archaic Greece, such as the proportion of the torso to the limbs and the enigmatic smile. But the superb mastery of movement achieved by the Etruscan artist is well in advance of the Greek style.*

TIME LINE 5.1   THE ROMAN MILLENNIUM, 753 B.C.–A.D. 248

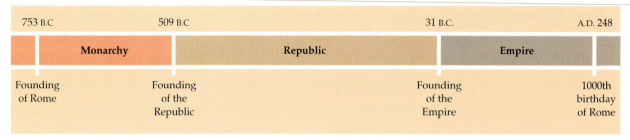

converted Rome into an independent republic. The Etruscan experience made the Romans intense foes of kings and monarchies, a dislike that was to play a central role in Roman history.

Whereas the Etruscans had conquered the Romans, it was the Romans who made the opening move in conquering the Greeks, absorbing the Greek colonies in southern Italy in 275 B.C. and later vanquishing the Greek mainland and Aegean Islands in 146 B.C. Between 146 and 31 B.C., Rome assimilated the separate Hellenistic kingdoms and made them part of a growing overseas empire. Styling themselves after the defeated rulers, the Roman emperors eventually claimed to be immortal gods, turning the state into a divine monarchy. The emperors also adopted the civilizing mission of the Hellenistic kingdoms, thus giving Rome's domestic and foreign policies a new moral dimension, if not a new direction.

The effect of the conquest of these kingdoms was to propel Rome to the world's center stage, making Roman civilization the climax of ancient developments. However, in the end Greek civilization conquered the conquerors, for when the Greek cultural forms (lyric and epic poetry, the arts, and architecture, among others) were imported into Rome, the Romans were forced out of their exclusively practical ways. The Romans coined the term *humanities* to refer to the artistic, literary, and philosophical activities the Greeks considered basic to civilized life. But the humanities themselves were Greek inventions, as was the belief that the study and practice of the humanities is stimulating to the soul (mind). Thus the humanities, which originated among the intellectuals and artists of Archaic and Hellenic Greece, were preserved and transmitted by the Romans, an achievement that some historians regard as Rome's finest.

The Roman empire, which was centuries in the making, is best understood in the context of its origins and of the subsequent historical events that helped shape its final form. Pre-Christian Roman history can be conveniently divided into three periods on the basis of the prevailing type of government—monarchy

(753–509 B.C.), republic (509–31 B.C.), and empire (31 B.C.–A.D. 284) (Time Line 5.1). In each period, elements of earlier times and Roman traits and values endured.

Rome in the Age of Kings, 753–509 B.C.

During the Age of Kings, some basic components of Roman political, social, and economic structures were established. For example, the Romans introduced the earliest version of their mixed constitution. Rome *was* ruled by kings, but royal authority was hedged in by other forms of power. The kings had to receive advice from a council of landowners who also helped to select the ruler. The aristocratic council nominated someone to be king, and the entire people ratified its choice. This balanced system ended in about 600 B.C. when the Etruscans imposed their rulers on Rome.

Another major component of Roman history— class struggle—appeared at the end of the Etruscan monarchy. Some urban dwellers, debarred by poverty and birth from the aristocracy, took advantage of the commercial opportunities now presented by Rome's expansion and began to engage in trade. The plebeians, as this class was called, accumulated wealth and began to challenge the social power of the landed aristocrats. Although class tensions did not lead to war in this instance, the meaning of the encounter was not lost on the Roman landowners. When the aristocrats abolished the monarchy and set up the Roman republic, they denied citizenship to poor farmers and to urban dwellers, a policy of exclusion that laid the groundwork for centuries of class conflict.

The Roman Republic, 509–31 B.C.

In 509 B.C., the Roman aristocrats threw off their Etruscan overlords and founded a republic. Unlike the Greeks, who never made a larger and more lasting political order than short-lived leagues of city-states, the Romans established a republic whose provinces eventually embraced the shores of the eastern Mediterranean and lasted almost five hundred years. This achievement in self-government—in terms of both duration and vastness of geographical area—by the citizens of the Roman republic has not been surpassed in Western history.

Rome's republic falls into three principal divisions of early, middle, and late. During these tumultuous periods, Rome became a world power, eventually dominating the entire Mediterranean basin. And, at the same time, great political and cultural changes were transforming all of Roman civilization (Time Line 5.2).

The Early Republic, 509–264 B.C. Two major crises, one domestic and one foreign, faced the Early Republic and threatened to overwhelm the fledgling state. The domestic issue stemmed from the division of society into two classes—the landed, aristocratic patricians and the unorganized, disenfranchised plebeians. As the patricians dismantled the monarchy and set up a republic, they gave themselves free rein over the state and continued to exclude the plebeians from political life. The patrician objective was to create a system that would prevent a single man from gaining control of the government—the return of a king. They placed the executive power in the hands of two consuls, each with veto power over the other. They gave legal, fiscal, and other power to magistracies—public offices—and legislative and judicial powers to an assembly.

But the real center of power was the Senate, the successor to the old council of landowners that had existed under the kings. Senators, who served for life, were usually elected late in their careers after having moved through the ranks of the magistracies.

Eventually, senatorial judgments achieved the force of law, and in the end, the glory and future of the Roman republic depended on able and patriotic Senators.

All of these reforms were watched jealously by the plebeians, who had no part in them. Gradually class hatred turned into sometimes violent class struggle between the two orders. Over the next two centuries, the plebeians steadily won concessions, until finally, by 287 B.C., they had gained all the rights of citizenship enjoyed by the patricians.

The foreign issue faced by Rome during this period was the military conquest of the various peoples inhabiting the Italian peninsula. During these first foreign wars, the Romans originated the brilliant strategy that became the key to their military success, a policy that allowed some freedom to the conquered and yet subtly tied them to Rome. Instead of burdening defeated people with heavy taxes, the Romans demanded that they supply fresh troops for her armies. The Romans also treated each tribe separately, giving them greater or lesser rights as the specific situation allowed. To all of their former foes the Romans showed great tolerance, allowing them to remain self-governing and to practice their own religions.

The Middle Republic, 264–133 B.C. Challenging hurdles to growth made the Middle Republic an exhilarating time. Roman armies had conquered Italy, but up and down the peninsula restless tribes were not yet securely in Rome's orbit. The task now was to tie them to Rome and convert them to the Roman way of life. In comparison to later problems, this proved to be fairly easy—the Romans simply made the peninsula the cornerstone of their state. They founded municipalities and colonies throughout Italy and enticed new settlers with offers of free land and full Roman citizenship. Those

TIME LINE 5.2 THE ROMAN REPUBLIC, 509–31 B.C.

All dates B.C.

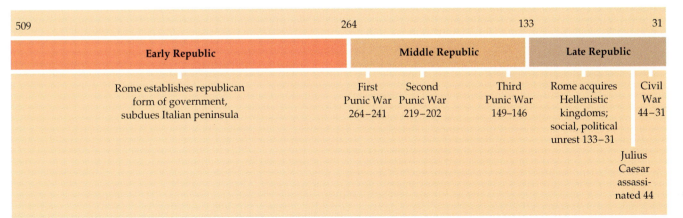

509		264		133		31
Early Republic		**Middle Republic**		**Late Republic**		
Rome establishes republican form of government, subdues Italian peninsula		First Punic War 264–241	Second Punic War 219–202	Third Punic War 149–146	Rome acquires Hellenistic kingdoms; social, political unrest 133–31	Civil War 44–31
					Julius Caesar assassinated 44	

eager to partake of this generous plan were chiefly land-hungry plebeians and ambitious newcomers. At first these settlements were Roman islands in a foreign sea, but over time Rome's irresistible pull attracted the remaining population. Before the Middle Republic ended, Roman law and the Latin language were triumphant in the Italian peninsula.

Beyond the peninsula, Rome faced the challenge of Carthage, a Phoenician state in North Africa that dominated the western Mediterranean and blocked Rome's expansion into that area. Rome's interest in taking over the wealthy island of Sicily, which was controlled by Carthage, led to the Punic Wars (from the Latin *poeni* for ''Phoenician'') (264–146 B.C.), a series of three separate but related conflicts whose objective was control of the western Mediterranean.

Rome was the ultimate victor in each of these wars. At the end of the Third Punic War in 146 B.C., Rome laid siege to Carthage, eventually razing the capital city and killing or enslaving the inhabitants. The once insignificant city-state now controlled Sicily, Corsica, Sardinia, and North Africa as well as the Italian peninsula.

Supremacy was not without its price, however, for the wars engendered basic transformations in both the Roman state and its character. The republic's imperialistic ambitions were whetted by the acquisition of Sicily, Rome's first overseas property, and the seizure of Corsica and Sardinia that followed. And during the Second Punic War, Italy was invaded by the Carthaginian general Hannibal, whose forces ravaged the countryside for fourteen years. His scorched-earth policy devastated Italy's farm country, and small farms began to be replaced by huge ranches worked by slaves. Italy's social fabric was permanently changed.

Having made themselves masters in the west, the Romans moved quickly to conquer the east. The lessons that they had learned from their earlier wars were now put into practice in their struggles with the Hellenistic states, and within a short time, Roman tactics had brought the Hellenistic world to its knees (Table 5.1). Some kingdoms became Roman provinces; others were left in an enfeebled condition to be taken over later.

The republic practiced the same tolerant policies abroad that had worked so well in Italy, although Rome made one major distinction among her new subjects. In the east, the Romans granted greater freedom to the older Hellenistic cultures, but in the west, Rome forcefully organized and civilized the provinces. Everywhere, though, the republic installed Roman governors to keep public order and to collect state taxes. At the end of the Middle Republic, Romans could justly call the Mediterranean *Mare Nostrum*—''Our Sea.''

The Late Republic, 133–31 B.C. Rome in the Late Republic was ruled by an oligarchy of patrician families who dominated the Senate and clung stubbornly to their rights and privileges. During this time, Roman power continued to spread throughout the Mediterranean basin. In the east, Rome annexed Pontus (the south shores of the Black Sea), Judea (modern Israel), and Syria, and in the west the wild tribes of Gaul were brought to heel. But the economic and social problems born in the Punic Wars now multiplied and shook the republic to its roots. While reformers had some success in addressing these dilemmas, the issues proved intractable, and by 31 B.C. the republic lay in shambles.

One problem was generated by the rise of the equestrian order (*equites* in Latin), a social class that was grouped with the patricians for tax purposes but that lacked their political power. During the Punic Wars the equites began to amass huge fortunes, and in the Late Republic they strengthened their economic position even further by taking advantage of the business opportunities in Rome's imperial do-

TABLE 5.1   ROME'S CONQUEST OF THE HELLENISTIC WORLD, 146–31 B.C.

STATE	DATE OF CONQUEST/ ACQUISITION	ROMAN PROVINCE
Macedonia and Greece	146 B.C.	Macedon
Pergamum	133 B.C.	Asia
Bithynia	74 B.C.	Bithynia-Pontus
Seleucid Kingdom	63 B.C.	Syria
Judea	63 B.C.	Judea
Egypt	31 B.C.	Egypt

mains. In their quest for political power, they backed the reformers who were pressing for greater plebeian rights. By the middle of the first century B.C., open warfare had broken out between the equites and the Senators, thus contributing to the anarchy of the period.

At the same time, the nature of the masses was changing. Class divisions deepened in the Late Republic as increasing numbers of independent farmers were pushed off the land by the large estate owners. Many of these landless citizens found their way to Rome, where they became part of a permanent underclass who lived in perpetual poverty and sold their votes to the highest bidders. In an effort to keep them quiet, the last governments of the republic instituted free bread and public amusements, scornfully referred to by critics as "bread and circuses." The popularity of gaudy entertainments in Rome and other cities showed that the farmer-soldier ideal had given way to a different mentality. The new Romans were more excited over bloody sporting events like gladiatorial contests than they were concerned about political rights and duties.

The republic's last and best hope for substantive reform came in the person of Gaius Julius Caesar, who played a major role in Roman politics from 60 to 44 B.C. In the public's eyes Caesar had emerged as a great hero by pacifying Gaul (modern France). He was also the commander of a formidable army, whose personal devotion to him made Caesar a very powerful man. By 48 B.C. he had defeated rival generals to become Rome's sole ruler, taking his authority from the many titles and powers he held, including dictator for life, consul, tribune, censor, and head of the armies. Later, the Roman emperors recognized him as their predecessor by calling themselves Caesar, or ruler. With the possible exception of Alexander the Great, no other Western ruler has generated such praise or blame from philosophers, poets, and artists. And even in his death Julius Caesar became the archetype of destiny's hero cut down in his prime.

What made Caesar's life so memorable was that he was more than the representative of equestrian interests; a lofty vision seemed to animate his reforms. He initiated building projects that gave work to the urban poor, allowed the Italians outside Rome more self-rule, and demonstrated his appreciation of higher culture by founding Rome's first public library. But Caesar's enemies in the Senate believed that the dictator wanted to be king—the dreaded fear dating back to Etruscan Rome. On the Ides of March (March 15) in 44 B.C. a band of senatorial assassins murdered Caesar and once again plunged Rome into chaos.

In the years of unrest that followed Caesar's assassination, two rival leaders emerged: Marc Antony, one of Caesar's lieutenants, and Octavian, Caesar's great-nephew and adopted son. Octavian defeated Antony in the Battle of Actium in 31 B.C. and became the leader of the Roman world. His accession to power marks the beginning of the *Pax Romana* (Roman peace), a two-hundred year period of unprecedented tranquility and economic growth. But if Rome had at last found a savior in Octavian, the price was high: the gradual dismantling of the republic and the establishment of an autocratic empire.

Growing Autocracy: Imperial Rome, 31 B.C.–A.D. 284

When Octavian returned peace and order to Rome, he pledged to restore the republic. He maintained the government offices, the Senate, and the political machinery, but beneath the calm surface, in the depths of the Roman state, a basic shift was taking place. All power was being transferred from the republic's multifaceted system to one man in the city of Rome, the emperor. With no legal safeguards against the emperor's will, the citizens, in effect, became subjects of his personal whim. This autocratic trend meant the gradual strangling of political liberty in Rome, the very trait that had made the republic great.

The emperors of Rome enhanced their power both by stifling dissent and by encouraging praise for themselves. Their greatness was stressed during public events by cheering crowds, while officials ensured that the applause was sufficiently loud. These spectacles had the aim of attaching the populace more firmly to the regime. When the rulers adopted the Hellenistic practice of emperor worship, the emperor's public appearances became increasingly filled with pomp and ceremony.

The political structure forged by Octavian remained intact for about three centuries, from 31 B.C. to A.D. 284. This span of years may be broken into two parts: the two-hundred-year *Pax Romana*, or Roman Peace (31 B.C.–A.D. 193), and nearly a century of civil wars (A.D. 193–284) (Time Line 5.3).

Pax Romana, *31 B.C.–A.D. 193*   Octavian, who became known as Augustus Caesar, or "revered ruler," established his power by converting Egypt—Rome's wealthiest province—into his personal property and by bringing the military to heel, making it the loyal mainstay of his rule. He then used the military to push back Rome's frontiers, stopping at what he considered

TIME LINE 5.3   THE ROMAN EMPIRE, 31 B.C.–A.D. 284

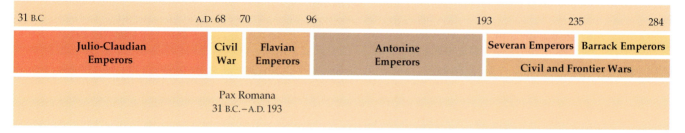

| 31 B.C | | A.D. 68   70 | | 96 | | 193 | 235 | 284 |

Julio-Claudian Emperors | Civil War | Flavian Emperors | Antonine Emperors | Severan Emperors | Barrack Emperors

Civil and Frontier Wars

Pax Romana
31 B.C.–A.D. 193

FIGURE 5.7   Timgad. Ca. A.D. 100. Timgad, Algeria. *Timgad, strategically located at the intersection of six Roman roads in north Africa, was typical of the towns built from scratch by the Romans during the* Pax Romana *and populated by ex-soldiers and their families. The town was planned as a square with two main avenues crossing in the middle where the forum stood and all other streets intersecting at right angles. The so-called Arch of Trajan in the foreground marked one of the main thoroughfares, which was lined with columns. Temples, baths, fountains, markets, a theater, and private homes gave the city the reputation of being a pleasant place to live.*

its natural northern borders, the Rhine and Danube rivers. Most of his successors recognized and honored the wisdom of this defensible line.

Augustus extended the celebrated *Pax Romana* to the people that he conquered. Governors were dispatched to rule and collect taxes, army camps were created to keep law and order, and colonies and municipalities were founded to relieve the land hunger in Rome. At the same time, the amenities of urban life arrived: temples, altars, schools, arenas, libraries, market places, aqueducts, fountains, baths, and paved roads connecting each far-flung outpost to the highway system that culminated in Rome (Figure 5.7).

The rule of Augustus (31 B.C.–A.D. 14) ushered in one of the longest running economic booms in Western history, which finally ended in about A.D. 193. Like politics under Augustus, economic life now became centralized. Guided by a burgeoning imperial bureaucracy, agriculture, industry, and trade flourished. With inflation under control and taxes light, most classes prospered from this growth. At the same time, Rome became a true melting pot. Except for the Greek-speaking East, the empire blended peoples who spoke Latin and followed Roman customs. The social and ethnic issues that had sparked civil wars under the republic had faded from memory. Patrician power was waning, and the equestrians were coming into their own. Both Senators and emperors now came from the equestrian order as well as from the provinces of Greece and Spain.

Civil Wars, A.D. 193–284 Despite its economic successes, however, the empire was profoundly hampered by a major problem: how to select a new emperor. Adoption and inheritance were both tried, but either practice could—and did—result in disaster. In the final years of the *Pax Romana*, the emperor Marcus Aurelius [ah-REE-lee-us] (A.D. 161–180) named his son Commodus [KOHM-uh-duhs] to succeed him. So unworthy was Commodus of the office bestowed on him that some historians have singled out his reign as marking the beginning of Rome's "fall." Commodus was murdered in A.D. 193, and his death ushered in decades of civil wars, military rule, violence, and chaos. Renegade armies propped up rulers who were invariably killed either by rival conspirators or disappointed supporters. Of the twenty-seven so-called Barrack Emperors in the third century, only four died natural deaths.

The empire was beset by problems from both within and without. Searching for loot, implacable Germanic tribes began crossing the northern frontiers. Runaway inflation and a debased coinage wiped out fortunes and caused a return to barter exchange. The army worsened the situation by forc-

ibly requisitioning food and supplies. In addition, a plague ravaged Rome and many of the provinces, killing perhaps hundreds of thousands.

In A.D. 284, Diocletian, a general from Illyria (former Yugoslavia) seized power by killing his rival. In time, his reforms would snatch Rome from the brink of destruction and disaster, as described in Chapter 7.

THE STYLE OF PRE-CHRISTIAN ROME: FROM GREEK IMITATION TO ROMAN GRANDEUR

Hellenistic culture became the foundation of Roman civilization. Often, Rome simply expanded on Hellenistic ideas, but in areas for which the Romans had a special gift, as in lyric poetry and comedy, they created works that rivaled the Greek originals. And in architecture, the Romans made their greatest mark, because this art form naturally blends the utilitarian with the aesthetic.

As in any civilization, Roman cultural achievements were shaped by their political and social contexts. Especially notable in the long evolution of Roman culture is the shift in style that occurred as the republic gave way to the empire, a shift that can be seen in every area of cultural expression.

Under the republic, artistic achievements were inspired by the Greek model and appealed to the privileged few. Under the empire, a distinctive Roman style began to emerge in response to the tastes of the masses, and spectacle became important in Roman culture. In this atmosphere, philosophy survived mainly as an antidote to the restrictions of the imperial regime. Literature flourished among an educated elite, but flattery and propaganda crept into the works of even the greatest writers. And architecture and sculpture became increasingly monumental and theatrical.

Roman Religion

The native Roman religion was deeply affected by the cults of neighboring and conquered peoples. The *syncretism*, as this blending of religion is called, began in earliest times. After their initial contacts with the Greeks in southern Italy, the Romans started to intermingle their divinities with those of the Greek religious system, who seemed to be always either making mischief or making love (Table 5.2). Thereafter, the Greek deities enlivened Rome's religion and inspired her writers, musicians, and artists with thrilling stories. And even after the fall of Rome, the

TABLE 5.2   THE CHIEF ROMAN GODS AND GODDESSES AND THEIR GREEK COUNTERPARTS

ROMAN	GREEK
Jupiter	Zeus
Juno	Hera
Neptune	Poseidon
Pluto	Hades
Apollo	Apollo
Diana	Artemis
Mars	Ares
Venus	Aphrodite
Vulcan	Hephaestus
Minerva	Athena
Mercury	Hermes
Vesta	Hestia

FIGURE 5.8 *Elagabalus.* (Marcus Aurelius Antoninus Heliogabalus). First Quarter of Third Century A.D. Museo Capitolino, Rome. *This youth ruled Rome from A.D. 218 until 222, when he was assassinated at the age of eighteen. A fanatic devotee of the sun god, he introduced the worship and the trappings of this Syrian cult into imperial circles. The face in this imperial portrait conveys a curious mix of weakness and determination.*

Greco-Roman gods and goddesses continued to live in the art, music, and literature of Europe.

From the Punic Wars onward innovative cults sprang up in Rome. From Egypt came the worship of Isis, a religion that promised immortality, and from Asia Minor the cult of Cybele, a mother goddess. Army veterans returning from Persia brought back Mithra, the mortal son of the sun god, whose cult excluded women (Figure 5.8). Mithra's followers observed each seventh day as Sun Day and December 25 as the god's birthday; the faithful also underwent a baptism in the blood of a sacred bull.

Religious innovation was perpetuated in imperial Rome until Greek and oriental cults finally submerged the old Roman beliefs. Most of all, the emperor cult provided unity amid religious diversity. Emperor worship succeeded admirably, except among two groups of Roman subjects who refused to recognize the ruler's divinity—the Jews and the Christians, whose story of resistance and rebellion is told in Chapter 6.

Language, Literature, and Drama

Latin, the Roman language, was at first an unimaginative, functional language, suited only to legal documents, financial records, and military commands. But with the growth of law and oratory in the Early Republic, grammar was standardized, vocabulary was increased, and word meanings were clarified. As the Romans conquered, they made Latin the language of state, except in the Greek-speaking East. By the late empire, Latin had spread throughout the civilized world and was the common tongue for the vast majority of Roman citizens.

Latin literature began to flourish in the Middle Republic (264–133 B.C.) with lyric and epic poetry, comedy, and tragedy, all in the Greek style, although writers were beginning to develop a distinctive Roman style. Over the centuries, Roman literature changed with the changing times, evolving through several quite distinct periods.

The First Literary Period, 250–31 B.C. The writing of the first literary period was noteworthy for its strongly Greek flavor and, in some writers, its grave moral tone. This period also saw the rise of a Roman theatrical tradition influenced both by roots reaching back to boisterous Etruscan religious celebrations and by contact with the Greek theater. Many educated Romans in this period could speak Greek, and many had seen performances of tragedies and comedies during their travels.

Plautus [PLAW-tuhs] (about 254–184 B.C.), a plebeian from Italy, launched Rome's great age of comic theater with his almost 130 plays. His genius lay in breathing fresh life into the stale plots and stock characters borrowed from Menander and other Hellenistic, New Comedy playwrights. In his hands, the mistaken identities, verbal misunderstandings, and bungled schemes seemed brand new. Rome's other significant comic playwright was Terence [TAIR-ents] (about 195–159 B.C.), a Carthaginian slave who was brought to Rome, educated, and set free. Although he wrote only six plays, he won the acclaim of Rome's educated elite, perhaps because of the pure Greek tone and themes of his works. Terence's highly polished style later inspired the magisterial Cicero. When the theater revived in Renaissance Europe, playwrights first turned to Plautus and Terence for characters and plots.

As Roman comedy began to decline, superseded by the vast spectacles that the masses demanded, two major poets with distinctively different personalities and talents appeared: Lucretius and Catullus. Both were heavily influenced by Greece. Lucretius [lew-KRE-shuhs] (about 94–about 55 B.C.) stands in the long line of instructive literary figures dating from Homer. A gifted poet, Lucretius wrote *De Rerum Natura (On the Nature of Things)* to persuade the reader of the truth of Epicureanism, the philosophy based on scientific atomism that denied divine intervention in human affairs (see Chapter 4). As literature, *On the Nature of Things* ranks as one of the poetic masterpieces of the ancient world with its well-turned Latin phrases and its imaginative and vivid language.

In contrast to Lucretius's lengthy poem, the verses of Catullus [kuh-TUHL-uhs] (about 84–about 57 B.C.) are characterized by brevity, one of the hallmarks of the Alexandrian school of the Hellenistic Age. Catullus's "small" epics, epigrams, and love poems also closely imitate the scholarly and romantic qualities of Alexandrianism. Catullus is best remembered for his racy love poems, reflecting the lives of his highborn circle in Rome. These poems dwell on his long and often heartbreaking affair with his mistress, Clodia, whom he called Lesbia, in honor of the willful Sappho. Catullus's carefully honed lyrics express his innermost feelings of desire, disappointment, and jealousy.

The efforts of Lucretius and Catullus pale, however, when placed beside those of their contemporary Cicero (106–43 B.C.). An equestrian from Italy, he dominated Roman letters in his own day so much that his era is often labeled the Age of Cicero. By translating Greek treatises into Latin, he created a philosophical vocabulary for the Latin language where none had existed before. Between the fall of Rome and A.D. 1900, Cicero's fame among educated Europeans was such that he was regarded as an au-

FIGURE 5.9 *Cicero.* First Century B.C. Museo Capitolino, Rome. *The anonymous sculptor of this bust of Cicero has caught the character of the man as recalled in literary sources. Honored as one of Rome's finest intellectuals and a patriot devoted to rescuing the state from chaos, he is depicted deep in thought with stern and resolute features. This idealized portrait contributed to the mystique of Cicero as a hero of the Roman republic.*

thority on the order of Plato and Aristotle. For centuries his collected speeches served as models both of public oratory and of written argument. Similarly, his philosophical tracts set the agenda for generations of thinkers and reformers. Today's readers rank Cicero's personal letters as his masterpiece. These nearly eight hundred letters, frank in style and language, offer an honest, unique self-portrait of a major public figure in ancient times (Figure 5.9).

The Second Literary Period: The Golden Age,* 31 *B.C.–* A.D. *14 The second period of Roman literature coincided with the personal reign of Augustus and is considered the Golden Age of Roman letters. This period's three greatest writers, Vergil, Horace, and Ovid, captured the age's euphoric mood as peace and stability once more returned to Rome. Of the three writers, Vergil best represented the times through his vision of Rome and his stirring verses.

The works of Vergil [VUR-jill] (70–19 B.C.), an Italian plebeian, were inspired by Greek literary forms—idylls (or vignettes), didactic (instructive) poems, and epics—yet his use of native themes and his focus on the best traits in the Roman people give an authentic Roman voice to his work. Deeply moved by Augustus's reforms, he put his art in the service of the state. Vergil's pastoral poetry, the *Eclogues* and *Georgics*, celebrated rural life and urged readers to seek harmony with nature in order to find peace—advice that became a significant moral theme of the Western heritage. But Vergil is best known for the *Aeneid*, an epic poem in twelve books that he wrote in imitation of the Homeric epics. In this work, infused with Roman values and ideals, Vergil gave full voice to his love of country, his respect for Augustus, and his faith in Rome's destiny.

The *Aeneid* tells of Aeneas, the legendary Trojan hero who wandered the Mediterranean before founding Rome. In the first six books, Vergil models his tale on the *Odyssey*, writing of travel and love. The second half is modeled on the *Iliad*, stressing fighting and intrigue. The *Aeneid* became Rome's bible and its literary masterpiece. Children were often required to memorize passages from the poem to instill in them the values that had made Rome great. Aeneas served as the prototype of the faithful leader who would not be diverted from his destined path. The work's rich language led later poets to mine the *Aeneid* for expressions and images. As Homer inspired Vergil, so Vergil became the model for Western poets when imaginative literature was revived in late medieval Europe.

The second major poet of the Golden Age was Horace (65–8 B.C.), another Italian plebeian who also welcomed Augustus as Rome's savior and offered patriotic sentiments in his verses. His poems, which were written to be read aloud, use Alexandrian forms such as odes and letters in verse. He helped to create a new poetic genre, the *satire*, which rebuked the manners of the age. Horace was at his best in addressing the heartbreaking brevity of life: ''. . . what has been, has been, and I have had my hour.''

Ovid [AHV-uhd] (43 B.C.–about A.D. 17), the third voice of the Golden Age, was a wealthy Italian equestrian who did not devote his verses to patriotic themes or pay lip service to conventional morality. Ovid's love poems speak of the purely sensual and fleeting quality of sex and ignore the enduring value of committed love. His *Art of Love* offers advice, in a manner bordering on the scientific, on how to seduce women, whether willing or not. Such advice contrasted with Vergil's and Horace's attempts to raise the moral level of the Romans.

Ovid's masterpiece was the *Metamorphoses,* or *Transformations*. Somewhat irreverently, he breathed new life into more than two hundred Greek and Roman myths and legends that centered on the transformation of people into other forms. This work is the source of our knowledge of many Classical myths, and medieval and Renaissance poets turned to it continually for inspiration.

The Third Literary Period: The Silver Age, A.D. 14– 200 In the third literary period, the patriotic style of the previous era was replaced by the critical views of writers who often satirized the Roman society and state. Lacking the originality of the Golden Age, the writers of this era looked to their predecessors for models, while they polished their phrases and reworked earlier themes. This shift in literary taste reflected a new educational ideal that stressed skills in debate and oratory. As a result, moral considerations became secondary to aesthetic effects, with writers using rhetorical flourishes and exaggerated literary conceits.

One of Rome's outstanding Silver Age talents was Seneca [SEN-e-kuh] (4 B.C.–A.D. 65). Born into a wealthy equestrian family in Spain, Seneca became a powerful senator and one of the age's chief thinkers. He is best remembered as a dramatist, though his works failed to measure up to the Greek heritage. His ten extant plays relied on emotionalism, rhetorical excess, and stage violence—the perennial traits of Roman tragedy. After his day the staging of tragedies ceased, not to be revived for more than fifteen hundred years.

The Silver Age produced Rome's last great Latin poet, Juvenal [JOO-vuh-nuhl] (about A.D. 60–about 140), who trained his censorious gaze on the follies of the empire. Juvenal expressed his outraged observations in sixteen satires, the literary form originated by Horace and others. The voice that speaks in Juvenal's satires is embittered, perhaps a reflection of his obscure social origins. But the carefully crafted language—obscene, bilious, and evocative but always just right—made him the master of this genre in Rome if not in world letters.

The leading historian of the Silver Age was Tacitus [TASS-i-tus] (A.D. 55?–117). He honored the Greek tradition of historical writing which dictated that history must be written according to literary rules, that the proper study of history is contemporary events, and that effects in history have human, not supernatural, causes.

Tacitus acquired his knowledge of statecraft as the governor of the province of Asia (modern southwest Turkey). Among his works are two that have earned him the front rank among Roman historians. The *Annals* focus on the rulers after the death of Augustus in A.D. 14 until the murder of Nero in 68. The *Histories* then pick up the story of Rome and carry it through 96, when the tyrannical Domitian was assassinated.

Tacitus was a master of the Latin language and had a flair for dramatic narrative. Like other Roman historians, he wrote history with a moral purpose, but his critical spirit set him apart from those who had nothing but glowing praise for Rome. Instead, Tacitus's perspective is that of a proud senator who cannot conceal his distaste for Rome's loss of political freedom. In his works he sought to uncover the origins of the misrule that had almost destroyed Rome in his day, and he ended by concluding that tyranny was an innate flaw in the imperial office.

Philosophy

The Romans adopted the ethical aspects of Greek thought, but they rejected systematic philosophy as dangerous, fearing that the study of philosophy would draw their young men away from the military to lives of dreamy speculation. As a result, Roman thought stressed rules of behavior with little regard for metaphysics.

In time, Roman versions of Epicureanism and Stoicism reached a wide audience, notably among influential aristocrats. Although Epicureanism had little impact, mainly because its focus on withdrawal from worldly cares contradicted the Roman sense of duty, Stoicism's effect was potent and lasting. Stoic values seemed to confirm the farmer-soldier ideal, suggesting that the early Romans were unintentional Stoics. In addition, Stoicism under the empire caused a few aristocrats to resist, if passively, the growing menace of autocracy; these hardy Stoics, some of whom, like Seneca, lost their lives for their ideas, believed that the natural law was superior to the earthbound justice of the rulers.

Stoicism   Although Stoicism was introduced to Rome in the Late Republic, its greatest influence was achieved in the empire through the writings and teaching of Seneca, Epictetus, and the emperor Marcus Aurelius.

Seneca's fame as a dramatist has been noted above. His fame as a philosopher rests on his *Letters on Morality*. These letters, which were usually written in response to pressing ethical problems, are filled with good advice, even though they break no new philosophical ground. Thus, for example, Seneca counseled a grieving acquaintance to maintain dignity and inner strength in the face of a loved one's death.

Seneca's *Letters* survived the fall of Rome, while the works of most other thinkers temporarily disappeared. Consequently, he became one of the great guides for Western thought when philosophy was revived in the Middle Ages. In the modern world, however, his reputation has suffered because of his closeness to Nero, an emperor of legendary cruelty. Despite Seneca's noble philosophy, doubt has been cast on his personal morality.

No such cloud hovers over Epictetus [ep-ik-TEET-uhs] (about A.D. 55–115) who not only preached but lived his Stoic creed. According to tradition, Epictetus, though a slave in Rome, won his freedom because of his teachings. He subsequently founded a school in Asia Minor and attracted enthusiastic converts. He did not write anything, but Arrian, a pupil, composed the *Discourses* and the *Handbook,* both in Greek, which together preserved the essence of his master's ideas.

Epictetus's philosophy reflected his own victory over personal misfortune. He advised patience in the face of trouble, indifference to material things, and acceptance of one's destiny. While these ideas represented a rehash of basic Stoic beliefs, his moral wholeness gave them a special appeal.

Stoicism's finest hour arrived in A.D. 161 when Marcus Aurelius became emperor (Figure 5.10). Converted to Stoicism in his youth, the emperor wrote an account (in Greek) of his daily musings—called *Meditations*—while he was engaged in almost continual warfare against Germanic invaders along the Danube. His journal came to light after his death and was soon recognized as a masterpiece of Stoicism.

Like all Stoics, the emperor admonished himself to play with dignity the role that providence had assigned. If a divine plan guides the universe, then he must accept it; if, however, the world is ruled by chance, then a well-regulated mind is the best defense. Such reasoning enabled Marcus Aurelius to avoid moral confusion. Although the *Meditations* are Stoic in tone, a careful reading reveals their author to be a hard-headed Roman who was somewhat lacking in intellectual rigor. Marcus Aurelius's death in A.D. 180 signaled the end of Stoicism. The next century witnessed the swamping of all philosophies in the military anarchy and oriental cults of the times.

Neo-Platonism   Some Roman thinkers adopted Greek Stoicism; others were interested in blending the various Greek schools—Platonic, Aristotelean, Stoic,

FIGURE 5.10 *Marcus Aurelius.* Ca. A.D. 173. Bronze, height 16′8″. Piazza del Campidoglio, Rome. *The unknown artist has represented Marcus Aurelius as a warrior emperor, but the militaristic image is offset somewhat by the Stoic ruler's face. Here we see revealed a human being lost in thought and far removed from pomp and power. This magnificent equestrian statue marked the climax of sculpture in the Roman empire.*

among others—into a philosophic synthesis. The outstanding example of this latter trend was **Neo-Platonism,** a school of thought founded primarily by Plotinus [plo-TIE-nuhs] (A.D. 205–270) in the third century A.D. Neo-Platonism was the last major school of philosophy in the ancient world. The movement began as an attempt to correct the problem at the heart of Plato's system—the seemingly irreconcilable split between the absolute world of Ideas and the perishable material world. This Platonic dualism could and did lead to the notion that the everyday world has little purpose in the overall scheme of things. Plotinus now succeeded in bridging the two worlds with his theories, and his writings later influenced Christian thinkers in the Middle Ages and the Italian humanists of the Renaissance.

Plotinus resolved Platonic dualism not with logical analysis but with mystical insight, claiming that the union of the physical and spiritual worlds could be grasped only through an ecstatic vision. His retreat from philosophy into mysticism occurred during the turbulent era of the Barrack Emperors and the flight of many people from the cities to country villas and estates.

Law

The most original contribution of the Roman mind was law. Rome's law created a notion of justice founded on such ideals as fairness and equity for both citizens and subjects, as well as the presumption of innocence in criminal cases. These principles later became central to the Western legal tradition. But the most important facet of Roman law was born in Stoicism: the idea of **natural law,** or a higher justice than that made by human forces. This doctrine of natural law is the basis of the American Declaration of Independence.

Rome's law evolved over many centuries, starting in 450 B.C. with the first written code, the Twelve Tables. The Twelve Tables, which represented a plebeian victory over the patricians, treated basic aspects of civil life such as personal and property rights, religious practices, and moral behavior. But this milestone did not rid Rome of class distinctions; it merely recognized conflicting rights and thus necessitated a judge above both parties. In later times class divisions continued to affect the way the law was applied, since the dispensing of justice always favored the rich.

The branch of Roman law dealing with property rights was called civil law and developed through the office of the *praetor.* Each praetor, at the beginning of his term, issued an edict describing the legal procedures and precedents he would follow. The body of decisions handed down by the praetors eventually came to constitute Rome's system of civil law.

By the Late Republic, the development of law was enhanced by the advice of legal experts, called *jurisconsults* or *jurisprudentes.* They tended to broaden Roman justice with their Stoic views. The most creative phase of Roman law occurred in the second and third centuries A.D., when eminent jurisconsults helped to codify the law and extend its principles to cover all the citizens of the empire.

The Visual Arts

Architecture and sculpture dominated Rome's visual arts, but they were pressed into the service of practical needs. The Romans commissioned buildings and statues to serve the state, religion, or society, but they recognized that the practical did not have to forgo beauty, and many of Rome's engineering feats were beautiful in their functional elegance.

The early Romans learned lessons in architecture from the Etruscans, but after encountering the Greeks of Magna Graecia, they rebuilt Rome along Greek lines. By the second century B.C., wealthy Romans were collecting Greek statues in all styles— Archaic, Hellenic, and Hellenistic. Under Augustus, the Hellenic style in both sculpture and architecture became supreme, inching its way across the empire over the next two centuries. By the third century A.D. a new architectural style had arisen, blending Greek and Roman. This Greco-Roman blend is the style that passed into medieval civilization after the collapse of the Western Empire.

Architecture   Over the years the Romans used many types of materials in their public and private buildings. The architects of the Early Republic built with sun-dried bricks and used terra cotta, a fired clay, for roofs and decorations. As Rome's wealth grew and new materials were imported, the bricks retained an important though less visible role in buildings, chiefly in foundations and walls. By the Late Republic two new products were adapted from the Greeks, mortar and ashlars (massive hewn stones), which, in time, revolutionized the face of Rome.

Much of the impetus for the building revolution sprang from the Romans' improvement of the recipe for mortar. They produced a moldable concrete by mixing lime, sand, small rocks, and rubble, but because the concrete was visually unappealing, the builders began to cover it with slabs of expensive and highly polished marble and granite imported from Greece or quarried in Italy.

The temple became one of Rome's chief architectural forms. The basic source for the Roman temple was the Greek model with its post-beam-triangle construction, although Etruscan influence was also significant. The Romans adapted the Greek column as either support or decoration, preferring the ornamented Corinthian order to the plainer Doric and Ionic.

The Romans' most significant innovations in architecture were made with the rounded arch, which already had a long history by the time that they began to experiment with it. The Mesopotamians probably invented this arch, the Greeks knew about it,

(a)

(b)

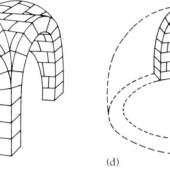

(c)

(d)

FIGURE 5.11 Structures Used in Roman Architecture. *Beginning with the basic arch (a), the Romans created the barrel vault (b) and the cross vault (c). These structural elements, along with the dome (d), which they formed by rotating a series of arches around a central axis, gave the Romans the architectural elements they needed to construct their innovative temples and monuments.*

FIGURE 5.12 Maison Carrée. Ca. 16 B.C. Nîmes, France. *This temple was probably modeled on temples in Rome, since buildings with Corinthian columns and similar overall designs were being constructed in the capital at this time. Reproducing architecture in the provincial cities was another way in which the Romans spread civilization throughout their conquered lands.*

and the Etruscans used it in their drainage systems. The arch's basic round form is created with wedge-shaped stones called *voussoirs*. A *keystone* at the center of the semicircle locks the arch in place. The installed arch is amazingly strong, diverting the weight of the upper walls both outward and downward onto columns or other supports (Figure 5.11).

The Romans demonstrated their inventive genius by creating ceilings, or *vaults*, from arches—by transforming the simple rounded arch into barrel vaults, groined vaults, and domes. They created the *barrel vault*—named because it looks like a barrel divided lengthwise—by building a series of contiguous arches. They intersected two barrel vaults at right angles in order to produce a *groined* or *cross vault*. Finally, the dome, the crown jewel of Rome's architectural vocabulary, was created by, in effect, turning an arch in a full circle (see Figure 5.11). The Romans were also able to build arches more safely after they discovered the correct mathematical ratio (1:2) between the height of an arch and the width of its base.

The prototype of imperial temples is the well-preserved Maison Carrée in Nîmes, France, a major provincial city under Augustus. Built about 16 B.C., the Maison Carrée incorporated Etruscan and Greek ideas (Figure 5.12). Raised on a platform in the Etruscan manner, this temple shows other Etruscan borrowings in the central stairway, the deep porch, and the engaged columns, that is, the columns built into the walls of the *cella*, the inner sanctum housing the cult statue. Greek influences are visible in the low gable—the triangular end of the building's roof—and the Corinthian columns. The Greek notion that beauty lies in mathematical harmony is also expressed in the predetermined ratio of the area of the cella to the area of the temple's porch. The aesthetic appeal of the Maison Carrée has made it one of the most famous buildings of Roman culture. In the eighteenth century Thomas Jefferson modeled the Statehouse in Richmond, Virginia, on this Roman temple.

Besides perfecting their version of the rectilinear temple, the Romans also invented the round temple, as seen in the Pantheon, a sanctuary dedicated to all of their deities. The Pantheon consists of three different units: the entrance porch, or portico, with its supporting columns; the huge drum, housing the sanctuary proper, which is attached to the porch; and the dome set on top of the drum (Figure 5.13). This design showed the Romans' reliance on a native heritage, because the rounded shape was probably inspired by the circular religious shrines of the pre-Romans, as modern archeology has shown. The Pantheon also combined a religious with a secular image: The dome symbolized both the heaven of the deities and the vastness of the empire.

But the Pantheon did more than to reflect the deep longings of the Roman people; its rich interior illustrated the Roman genius for decoration (Figure 5.14). A polychrome marble floor and a dome with recessed panels created a dazzling interior, and statues,

FIGURE 5.13 Pantheon Exterior. A.D. 126. Rome. *In modern Rome the Pantheon is crowded into a piazza where it faces a monument topped by an Egyptian obelisk. However, when built under the Emperor Hadrian, the Pantheon was part of a complex of structures that complemented each other, and the temple's facade faced a set of columns in an open forecourt. Its original setting reflected the Roman sense that urban space should be organized harmoniously.*

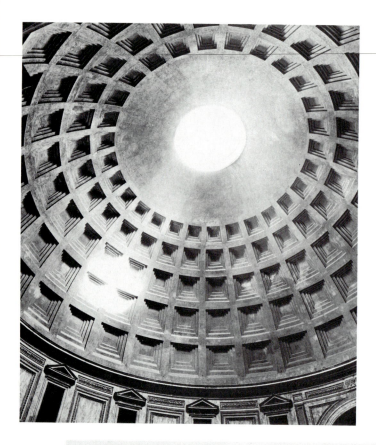

FIGURE 5.14 Pantheon Interior. A.D. 126. Rome. *The inner diameter of the dome is 144 feet. The height of the dome is 72 feet, or one half of the total height (144 feet) of the building. The sunlight sweeps around the interior and plays on the dome's decorations as the earth turns, creating constantly changing patterns of light and design.*

decorative columns, triangular pediments, niches, and other architectural details alternated around the circular room. The most unusual effect of all was the round hole, thirty feet in diameter, called the *oculus*, or eye, which opened the dome to the sunlight and the elements. As the oldest standing domed structure in the world, the Pantheon is the direct ancestor of St. Peter's Basilica in Rome and St. Paul's Cathedral in London.

Rome's architecture consisted of more than beautiful temples. The city of Rome was the center of gov-

FIGURE 5.15 Roman Forum. Ca. 100 B.C. to ca. A.D. 400. *The forum was literally the center of the Roman world, for here the Romans erected the Golden Milestone from which all roads led out across the empire. The temples and public buildings, crowded together in a relatively small area, were rebuilt over several centuries as rulers added to Rome's architectural legacy.*

ernment for the Mediterranean world, the nucleus of the state's religious system, and the hub of an international economy. And at the heart of the city was its *forum*, which functioned like the agora of Greek city-states. In the forum citizens conducted business, ran the government, and socialized among the complex of public buildings, temples, sacred sites, and monuments (Figure 5.15). The high priest of Roman religion, the Pontifex Maximus, lived in the forum, and nearby stood the curia, or senate house. Under the empire the forum became a symbol of Roman power and civilization; the leading cities in each province had forums.

As part of his reforms, Augustus rebuilt and beautified much of the republican forum. Later emperors, like Trajan (A.D. 98–117), constructed their own forums, which not only served as new centers for trade and government but also perpetuated their names. Today, Trajan's forum, which originally included a library, law courts, and plazas for strolling, has vanished except for one of the most significant monuments of the Roman Empire, a column commemorating Trajan's conquest of Dacia (modern Romania) (Figure 5.16).

Another symbol of empire, the triumphal arch, originated in the republic in the second century B.C. The Romans used both single and triple arches to celebrate military victories and erected them across the empire. The style of these memorials varied until the Arch of Titus, constructed in A.D. 81, became the accepted model. This arch, which commemorated the capture of Jerusalem by the then general Titus in A.D. 70, stood at the entrance to the Via Sacra, the thoroughfare of the Roman Forum (Figure 5.17). Inscribed on the attic, or top story, of the arch is the dedication, and decorating the sides are composite columns, a Roman innovation that intertwined flowers in the capitals of Ionic columns. Inside the arch are reliefs of Titus's victorious march into Rome after subduing the Jews.

In addition to forums, columns, and arches, the emperors also commissioned amphitheaters as monuments to themselves and as gifts to the citizens. The amphitheaters were the sites of the gladiatorial contests and other blood sports that were the cornerstone of popular culture in the empire. The most famous of these structures was called the Colosseum, although it was actually named the Flavian amphitheater, in honor of the dynasty who built it (Figure 5.18). The name Colosseum, dating from a later time, referred to a large statue of the emperor Nero that stood nearby.

The exterior of the Colosseum was formed by stacking three tiers of rounded arches on top of one another; Greek columns were then inserted between

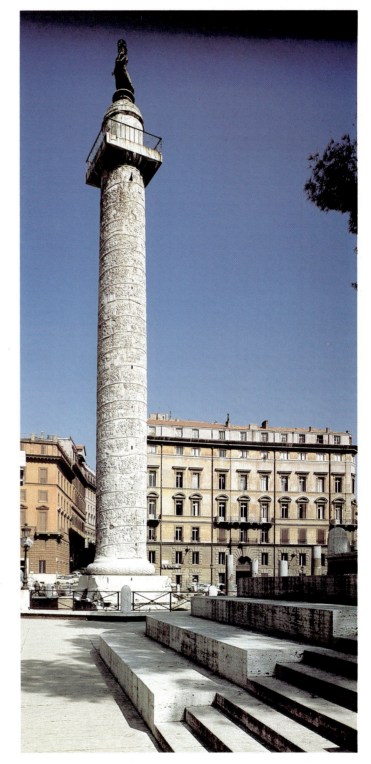

FIGURE 5.16   Trajan's Victory Column. A.D. 106–113. Rome. *Borrowing the idea of a victory column from Mesopotamia, the pragmatic Trajan used art to enhance his power in the eyes of the citizens. This work commemorated his conquest of Dacia— present-day Romania. The marble column, set on a foundation, enclosed a winding stairway that led to an observation platform and a statue of Trajan. Spiraling around the column's shaft was a stone relief sculpture that told the story of Trajan's victory in lively and painstaking detail.*

◄ **FIGURE 5.17** Arch of Titus. Ca. A.D. 81. Rome. *The Arch of Titus, like so many structures in Rome, was eventually incorporated into other buildings. Only in the early nineteenth century A.D. was the arch restored to its original splendor. Inspired by this arch, modern architects have designed similar structures throughout the Western world.*

the arches as decorations—Doric columns on the first level, Ionic on the second, and Corinthian on the third. A concrete and marble block foundation supported this immense amphitheater. The playing area, or arena (Latin for "sand"), was made of wood and usually covered with sand. A honeycomb of rooms, corridors, and cages ran underneath the wooden floor. The Colosseum's vast size and unusual features, like its retractable overhead awning,

made it one of the triumphs of Roman engineering, but the spectacular and brutal contests between men and wild beasts, in varied combinations, symbolized the sordid side of Rome.

Up and down the Italian peninsula and across the ancient world, the urban governments built forums, temples, and amphitheaters, laid roads, and engineered aqueducts in emulation of Rome. Sometimes old towns were made to conform to imperial standards. Pompeii, founded by the Greeks in southern Italy, was typical of the older provincial towns that the Romans remodeled to suit their needs. The Romans left Pompeii's temples and public buildings standing, but a new forum gave the old city a modern look, with municipal offices, a business center, temples to the emperors and to Apollo, and a shrine

FIGURE 5.18 Colosseum. Ca. A.D. 80–100. Rome. *Although the Flavians were a short-lived dynasty, starting with Vespasian in A.D. 69 and ending with Domitian in 96, they left Rome this structure, one of its most enduring landmarks. The Romans created the oval amphitheater (literally "theater on both sides") by joining two semicircular Greek theaters, another example of their ingenuity and practicality.*

FIGURE 5.19 The Forum at Pompeii. Ca. 150–120 B.C. Pompeii, Italy. *This forum served as the civic center of this provincial town of 15,000 to 20,000 inhabitants. Four streets, from the north, south, east, and west, converged here, but no traffic was allowed in the central area.*

honoring the civic deities. On the edge of town were such amenities as a palaestra—an exercise yard with swimming pool—and several markets (Figure 5.19). But disaster abruptly ended the urban renewal of Pompeii. In A.D. 79 nearby Mount Vesuvius, an active volcano, erupted and buried the city and most of its people—a horrible fate for the city, but one that produced a rich treasure for archeologists, who began excavations in the 1700s.

Like modern urban centers, Roman towns needed a continuous supply of water. In meeting the water demands of the cities, the Romans displayed their talent for organization and their preference for the practical by creating an elaborate network of aqueducts, sluices, and syphons that ran by gravity from a water source in nearby hills and culminated in a town's reservoirs and fountains.

The Romans started building underground aqueducts about 300 B.C. and constructed the first elevated aqueduct in 144 B.C. Under Augustus, they completed an aqueduct across the Gard River near

FIGURE 5.20 Pont du Gard. Ca. Late First Century A.D. Gard River, near Nîmes, France. *This aqueduct spanning the river was only one segment of the thirty-one-mile system that supplied water to Nîmes. Between 8,000 and 12,000 gallons of water were delivered daily, or about 100 gallons per inhabitant.*

Nîmes in southern France (Figure 5.20). Known as the Pont du Gard, this aqueduct had a beautiful functional design. Six large arches form the base, and above them are eleven smaller ones supporting a third tier of thirty-five even smaller arches. Atop the third tier is the sluice through which the water flowed, by gravity, to Nîmes. This graceful structure stands today as a reminder of how the Romans transformed an ordinary object into a work of art.

Sculpture Unlike Roman architecture, Roman sculpture was deeply affected by the tastes of artists and patrons as well as by class interests. For example, certain trends in the republic ran along class lines: The patricians gravitated to the Greek styles and the plebeians favored the local art, which is called Italo-Roman. Under the empire the same needs that gave rise to temples and amphitheaters were at work in changing the look of imperial sculpture.

Although Roman portrait sculpture never broke through to a distinct style during this period, it

FIGURE 5.21 *Head of Brutus.* Ca. 350–50 B.C. Palazzo dei Conservatori, Rome. *The finely detailed hair, beard, and facial lines are the work of a skilled sculptor, perhaps a Greek from southern Italy. The broad range of possible dates for this bronze head (ca. 350–50 B.C.) indicates that scholars still disagree over when it was cast.*

FIGURE 5.22 *Anonymous Youth.* 40–30 B.C. Cleveland Museum of Art, Cleveland, Ohio. *This bronze head measures 15 inches and is scaled closely to human dimensions. It is unknown whether the head was to be attached to a body or to be placed on a* herm, *a square stone pillar.*

nevertheless passed through three definite phases. The first phase, lasting from the third to the first centuries B.C., can be seen in the *Head of Brutus* (Figure 5.21). Brutus, one of the great heroes who helped to turn out the last Etruscan king, is shown as a stern and resolute leader. In contrast, the artist who cast the *Anonymous Youth* (Figure 5.22) captured the characteristic realism of sculpture in the Late Republic. The *Anonymous Youth,* clearly worried and uncertain, was intended as a warning rather than as an inspiration to the viewer. This type of realistic sculpture, with its sense of unease, represents the second phase of Roman sculpture.

The third phase was shaped by the reign of Augustus. According to his biographer Suetonius, the emperor boasted that he found Rome a city of brick and left it a city of marble, and Augustus certainly did influence the direction of sculpture and architecture. Under his rule imperial portraiture reverted to the idealism of Hellenic Greece, displacing the realistic art of the Late Republic. But Augustus's pure idealism did not prevail for long, for under his suc-

cessors sculpture became more propagandistic, that is, more symbolic of imperial power. This move to symbolic idealism reflected the later emperors' need to find a highly visible way in which to overawe, and thus draw together, Rome's increasingly diversified masses.

Two major sculptural works associated with Augustus, the Prima Porta portrait and the Ara Pacis, or the Altar of Peace, helped to popularize the idealistic style. Augustus's statue, commissioned after his death, stood in a garden on his widow's estate, Prima Porta, just outside Rome (Figure 5.23). The pure Hellenic style is evident in Augustus's relaxed stance and idealized face, both of which were

FIGURE 5.23 *Augustus,* from Prima Porta. Ca. A.D. 14. ▶
Marble, height 6′7½″. Vatican Collection. *This larger than life statue still bears traces of bright colors. Found in Prima Porta, the villa of Augustus's wife, Livia, the statue resembled Augustus closely yet presented him as godlike. Augustus's successors commissioned similar sculptures to convey a sense of their dignity and power.*

◀ **FIGURE 5.24** Ara Pacis. 9 B.C. Rome. *Like the Prima Porta statue, the Ara Pacis became a model for later emperors, who emulated its decorations, symbols, and size. The altar was rediscovered in the sixteenth century, excavated in the nineteenth and early twentieth centuries, and restored in 1938.*

modeled on the *Doryphoros* by Polykleitos (see Figure 3.21). However, the accompanying symbols reveal the propagandistic intent of the sculpture and are portents of the path that imperial portraits will take. For example, the cupid represents Venus, who was the mother of Aeneas, and thus Augustus is symbolically connected to the legendary origins of Rome.

The second idealistic sculpture, the marble Ara Pacis, was funded by the Senate as an offering of thanks to Augustus for his peacekeeping missions. The entire structure was set on a platform and enclosed by three walls. On the fourth side, an entrance with steps led up to the altar (Figure 5.24). Relief sculptures decorated the exterior walls, some in an idealized style and others in a realistic style (Figure 5.25). The resulting tension between realism and idealism marked this altar as an early work in the imperial style.

This type of sculpture reached its highest potential as a propaganda tool on triumphal arches and victory columns, such as the Arch of Titus and Trajan's Column. One of the reliefs from the Arch of Titus, the *March of the Legions,* portrayed the army's victory march into Rome after the destruction of the Temple in Jerusalem in A.D. 70 (Figure 5.26).

The continuous frieze from Trajan's Victory Column is one of the sculptural marvels of the Roman world (Figure 5.27). This low-relief sculpture winds around the column like a long comic strip, telling the story of Trajan's campaign against Dacia. The emperor, always made slightly larger than his soldiers, looms over them in several scenes, his likeness serving as a visual reminder of his presence and his power. Scholars still study the carvings of campsites and fortifications on this relief, finding them a rich source for Roman military history.

The last great sculpture from this period is the equestrian statue of Marcus Aurelius (see Figure 5.10). This work reveals a falling away from Augustan idealism to a rugged, individualized style, although one that was still highly propagandistic in its use of symbols. In the Prima Porta statue Augustus had been portrayed as a military leader; his gesture

◀ **FIGURE 5.25** *Family of Augustus,* Ara Pacis Relief. 9 B.C. Rome. *The figures in low relief, moving from right to left, are separated yet linked by their placement and clothing. The child to the right of center is given great prominence: He faces right while all the adults in the foreground are looking left and a man places his hand on the child's head. This singling out of the child may be an act of endearment or of recognition that he is to be the emperor.*

FIGURE 5.26 *March of the Legions,* from the Arch of Titus. Ca. A.D. 80. Marble relief, approx. 6′ × 12½′. Rome. *This rectangular marble relief occupies the south side of the Arch of Titus. It commemorates the Roman victory in the Jewish War of A.D. 66–70, when the Romans put down a rebellion by the Jews in Judea and subsequently dispersed them across the Roman world. In the relief, the Roman soldiers hold aloft the Jewish holy relics from the Temple as they seem to press forward and pass under the arch on the right.*

◀ **FIGURE 5.27** Detail of Trajan's Victory Column. A.D. 113. Rome. *Wrapped around the 100-foot-high column is the 645-foot relief carving with 2,500 figures depicting Trajan's two campaigns against the Dacians. Color was applied to heighten the realistic effect of the work which, in its original setting, could be viewed from nearby buildings.*

showed that he was addressing his troops. But the rest of the symbols surrounding Augustus suggested that he ruled from his capital in Rome. The symbols in the Marcus Aurelius statue, on the other hand, stress that he was a warrior emperor, even though the gesturing motion of Augustus is repeated.

Painting and Mosaics Murals, or wall paintings, the most popular type of painting in Rome, have been found in private dwellings, public buildings, and tem-

FIGURE 5.28 *Flagellation Scene.* Villa of Mysteries. Ca. 60–40 B.C. Pompeii, Italy. *The figures in this brilliantly colored wall frieze seem almost to be present in the room, partly because they are just under full life size and partly because the artist has placed them on a narrow painted ledge as if on a stage. The lack of depth in the mysterious scene adds to the illusion.*

ples. Surviving works hint at a highly decorative and brightly colored art. Originally the Romans applied tempera or paint set in a binding solution directly onto a dry wall. However, this quick and easy method produced a painting that soon faded and peeled. Later they adapted fresco painting as the most practical and lasting technique. Paints were mixed and worked into a freshly plastered wall. The colors dried into the wall, resulting in a nearly indestructible painting. The Romans were inspired by many subjects: landscapes, Greek and Roman myths, architectural vistas, religious scenes, and genre scenes, or "slices of life."

Of the many paintings scattered around the Roman world, the murals in the Villa of the Mysteries at Pompeii are the most famous. These intriguing and controversial scenes, which fill the walls in several rooms, portray twenty-nine nearly life-size figures engaged in some mystery cult rite (Figure 5.28). The grouped figures—well balanced and separated—create tension among the participants, and the varied expressions on the faces of the women,

FIGURE 5.29 *Scene from an Amphitheater.* Third Century A.D. Villa at Nenning, Trier, Germany. *This detail from a large, complex mosaic depicts a gladiatorial contest. The rendering of the athletes—the muscular bodies and the shadows they cast on the ground—was part of the artistic tradition that went back to Greek mosaics. This pavement mosaic from a villa in Trier, a city in Gaul, shows that the popular tastes in the provinces were the same as those in Rome.*

FIGURE 5.30 *The Street Musicians.* Ca. 100 B.C. Museo Nazionale, Naples. *This mosaic may portray a scene from a comic play. Two masked figures dance and play the tambourine and the finger cymbals while a masked female figure plays the tibia, or double flute. This mosaic was found in the so-called Villa of Cicero at Pompeii.*

which are impossible to decipher, heighten the sense of theater.

The Romans learned to make *mosaics* from the Hellenistic Greeks in the third century B.C. But by the third century A.D. several local Roman mosaic styles had sprung up across the empire. Although subjects varied, certain ones seemed always to be in vogue, such as still lifes, landscapes, Greek and Roman myths, philosophers and orators, and scenes from the circus and amphitheaters. A pavement mosaic from the third century A.D. shows the intricacy of design and variety of color that artisans achieved even in the Roman provinces (Figure 5.29).

Music

The absorption of the Greek tradition in music was so complete that later Roman music, in effect, simply perpetuated Greek forms and ideas. And yet the Romans used music only for practical purposes and rejected the Greek notion that music performed an ethical role in educating the soul or mind.

Not until imperial times did music come to play an important role in Roman life. Under the emperors music became wildly popular, as all classes succumbed to its seductive charms. *Pantomimes*—dramatic productions with instrumental music and dances—became the spectacle favored by the Roman masses. In the long run the pantomimes became a symbol of music's decadent trend under the empire. The largest of these productions featured 3,000 instrumentalists and 3,000 dancers, but the more common size was 300 performers in each category. A more serious sort of music was kept alive by the wealthy classes, who maintained household orchestras and choruses for their private amusement. An even more cultivated audience encouraged poets like Horace to set their verses to music, thus continuing the Greek tradition of lyric poetry.

Although what Roman music actually sounded like remains a subject of conjecture, their musical instruments, borrowed from across the Mediterranean world, can be identified with some certainty. From Greece came the stringed instruments, the lyre and the kithara, along with such woodwinds as the single *aulos,* or oboe, and the double aulos—called by the Romans the tibia (Figure 5.30). From the Etruscans came the brasses. The Romans delighted in the harsh sounds made by these instruments, incorporating them into their military music just as the Etruscans did. The hydraulic organ, or water organ, was probably perfected in Hellenistic Alexandria, but in imperial Rome it became a crowd pleaser, adding deep, voluminous sounds to the pantomimes. The taste of the imperial Roman audience is evident in the water organ, which was impressive not for its musical qualities but as a feat of engineering expertise.

The Legacy of Pre-Christian Rome

Western civilization is built on the ruins of Rome. While no pre-Christian institutions survived to form a basis of European organization, other tangibles persisted in abundance, so that the mark of Rome may still be seen and heard in countless ways. The very languages of western Europe bear the stamp of Rome, and Roman law forms the basis of the legal codes of many Western countries. Until the beginning of the twentieth century, the European educational ideal was based on the Roman curriculum, in which students studied the *trivium*—the three arts of grammar, logic, and rhetoric—and the *quadrivium*—the four sciences of arithmetic, geometry, music, and astronomy. Even today, this ideal persists at the heart of Western education.

Rome's greatest legacy to the Western world was its shining image of a healthy civilization: a just and well-regulated society of multiethnic, multiracial citizens. The Idea of Rome, as we may call this achievement, was adapted from the Hellenistic rulers. However, the Hellenistic cities lacked the cohesiveness and longevity—and, most important, the vision—of the Roman creation. When the ancient world was swept away, the Idea of Rome remained a beacon in the darkness that descended over Europe.

KEY CULTURAL TERMS

syncretism   *groined vault (cross vault)*
satire   *oculus*
Neo-Platonism   *forum*
natural law   *mural*
voussoir   *mosaic*
keystone   *pantomime*
vault   *aulos*
barrel vault

SUGGESTIONS FOR FURTHER READING

PRIMARY SOURCES

APULEIUS. *The Golden Ass.* Translated by R. Graves. New York: Farrar, Straus & Giroux, 1951. A sound translation of one of the most lively and entertaining tales in ancient literature.

HORACE. *The Complete Works of Horace.* Introduction by C. Kraemer. New York: Modern Library, 1936. Masterly translations of the works that made Horace Rome's outstanding lyric poet.

JUVENAL. *The Sixteen Satires.* Translated by P. Green. New York: Penguin, 1970. Superb vernacular versions of Juvenal's bitter works.

VERGIL. *The Aeneid.* Translated by W. F. J. Knight. New York: Penguin, 1964. A sound English prose version of Vergil's poetic epic about Aeneas, the Trojan warrior whose conquests made possible the future supremacy of Rome.

6

JUDAISM AND THE RISE OF CHRISTIANITY

The great civilizations discussed so far—Mesopotamian, Egyptian, Greek, and Roman—were all wealthy, powerful, and culturally dynamic, and they contributed enormously to the Western heritage. Yet an even greater contribution, one that cannot be measured in terms of buildings, governments, or monuments, came from a politically insignificant people who lived in a tiny corner of the eastern Mediterranean during ancient times—the Jews. This people created a religion that helped to shape the character of the civilizations of the Western world. Through the Hebrew Bible—the Old Testament to Christians—Judaic beliefs were passed on into both Christianity and Islam and were spread around the world. In addition, the fruitful interaction of the Judeo-Christian heritage with the Greco-Roman Classical ideals enriched and transformed the Western humanities.

JUDAISM

Judaism is one of the oldest living religions in the world. It originated in the third millennium B.C. among a tribal Middle Eastern people who placed themselves at the center of world history and created sacred texts for passing on their heritage. Unlike the

history and religion of other ancient peoples, the history and religion of the Jews are so inextricably connected that they cannot be separated.

The People and Their Religion

In about 2000 B.C. many tribes were wandering throughout the Middle East. They had been displaced from their homeland in the Mesopotamian river basin by the political upheavals that accompanied the collapse of the Akkadian kingdom and the coming of the Babylonians. Some of these nomads eventually settled in the stretch of arable land along the eastern coast of the Mediterranean Sea that is part of the Fertile Crescent. Sometimes forcefully, sometimes peacefully, these patriarchal tribes, under the guidance of the oldest and most respected male members, founded communities united by blood lines, economic interests, and folk traditions. One of these tribes, led by the patriarch Abraham, occupied territory called Canaan (Time Line 6.1). The Hebrews, as Abraham's tribe was known, settled not among the Canaanites in the thriving towns along the coast and trade routes but in the hill country to the east, where they tended their flocks and practiced their crafts (Map 6.1).

Although they had many similarities with other Middle Eastern tribal peoples, the Hebrews considered themselves unique. This belief was based on the relationship between Abraham and a great supernatural being who spoke to him and whom he obeyed. This deity made a *covenant*, or solemn

◀ *The Good Shepherd*. Mid–Third Century A.D. Fresco, Crypts of Lucina, Catacomb of Callixtus, Rome.

TIME LINE 6.1   JEWISH CIVILIZATION

2000 B.C	1500	1250	1020	926	586	538	168	63	A.D. 70
Hebrews in Canaan	Hebrews in Egypt	Hebrews Return to Canaan	United Monarchy	Division of Kingdom and Wars with Neighboring Empires	Babylonian Captivity	Postexilic Period, Reestablishment of Jewish State	Maccabean Kingdom	Roman Rule in Judea	

Moses

Assyrians destroy Israel 722 B.C

Babylonians conquer Judah

Alexander the Great conquers Judah 332 B.C.

Pompey conquers Judah

Romans destroy Jerusalem

agreement, with Abraham to protect his family and bring prosperity to his offspring if they agreed to obey his divine commands. The outward sign of this contract was the circumcision of all male children. Although he was associated with nature and conceived of as the source of all natural goods, the Hebrew deity differed from other Mesopotamian deities in his commitment to justice and righteousness. He was an ethical god and sought to impose ethical principles on humans.

Egypt, Exodus, and Moses   The Hebrews enjoyed many prosperous decades in Canaan, but then something disrupted their life—perhaps a drought, a changed economy, or the attraction of a better life elsewhere. Whatever the reasons, in about 1500 B.C. a group of Hebrews migrated south into Egypt, which had recently been overrun by the Hyksos, a Semitic people with whom the Hebrews shared language and cultural traits. Over the next few centuries the Hebrews thrived and came to exercise some degree of political power in Egypt until the Egyptians reconquered their land and enslaved both the Hyksos and the Hebrews. In about 1250 B.C. the extraordinary leader Moses arose among the Hebrews and tried to negotiate their release from the Pharaoh. Thwarted in his efforts, Moses rallied the Hebrews in defiance of the Pharaoh and led them on the exodus from Egypt— one of the most significant events in Jewish history. Hebrew scriptures describe Moses as a savior sent by God.

For many years the Hebrews wandered in the desert on the Sinai peninsula between Egypt and Canaan. During this time Moses molded his followers into a unified people under a set of ethical and societal laws. Like other ancient peoples, the Hebrews believed that the laws Moses received were given to them by God. What made the laws of Moses unique was their grounding in the covenant between the Hebrews and God. Also unique was the fact that no distinction was made between religious and secular offenses. All crimes were seen as sins and all sins as crimes. Those who committed crimes could not simply make reparations to their victims; they also had to seek forgiveness from God. There were some crimes, such as murder, that were so offensive to God that they could not be forgiven by human beings alone. Furthermore, human life was seen as sacred, because it was given by God, who created and owned all things, and individual humans were precious because they were made in God's image.

The core of Mosaic law was the Ten Commandments, which set forth in summary form the proper behavior of human beings toward God and other human beings (Table 6.1). The commandments became the basis of a renewed covenant, which was now extended beyond Abraham and his descendants to include the entire people. The Hebrew God was a jealous god who tolerated no rivals; he was seen as the sole, omnipotent creator and ruler of the universe. If individuals followed his laws and worshiped him alone, they would be rewarded, and if they strayed, they would be punished. Likewise, if the tribe followed the divine commands, they would prosper, and if they disobeyed, they would meet adversity. As the mediator of the covenant between God and the Hebrew people, Moses played a crucial role in shaping Judaism into a comprehensive system of ethical monotheism.

While they were in the Sinai desert, the deity revealed a new name for himself—YHWH, a name so sacred that pious Jews never speak or write it. In the late Middle Ages, European scholars rendered YHWH as Jehovah, but today this term is generally considered a false reading of the sacred letters. In modern English, YHWH is usually rendered as Yahweh. In biblical times, Jewish priests called the deity Adonai, the Semitic term for Lord.

MAP 6.1
Ancient Israel

TABLE 6.1 THE TEN COMMANDMENTS

1. You shall have no other gods before me.

2. You shall not make for yourself a graven image, or any likeness of any thing that is in heaven above, or that is on the earth beneath, or that is in the water under the earth. . . .

3. You shall not take the name of the Lord your God in vain. . . .

4. Observe the sabbath day, to keep it holy, as the Lord your God commanded you. . . .

5. Honor your father and your mother. . . .

6. You shall not kill.

7. Neither shall you commit adultery.

8. Neither shall you steal.

9. Neither shall you bear false witness against your neighbor.

10. Neither shall you covet your neighbor's wife . . . or anything that is your neighbor's.

Source: The Bible, Revised Standard Version, Deuteronomy 5:6–21.

The Hebrews carried with them the stone tablets on which the Ten Commandments were carved as they wandered in the desert. The tablets were kept in a sacred decorated box called the Ark of the Covenant. Details of how to craft the Ark and all the other sacred objects used in worship were dictated to Moses by Yahweh (Figure 6.1). Yahweh also revealed hundreds of precepts, statutes, and laws to Moses during this time, covering every aspect of Hebrew life from the appointment of judges and the proper conduct toward slaves to diet, hygiene, and sexual relations.

After forty years of wandering, followed by Moses' death, the Hebrews finally found their way back to Canaan, the Promised Land pledged by Yahweh to their forefathers. Over the next two centuries, the Hebrews won Canaan, sometimes in war but primarily by infiltration and peaceful occupation. As they extended their control over the entire Promised Land, they came to be known as Israelites, a term derived from an early patriarch, Jacob, who had taken on the name Israel.

FIGURE 6.1 Stone Menorah. Second Century A.D. Height, 46 cm. Israel Museum, Jerusalem. *Although this particular menorah dates from the second century A.D., the seven-branched candelabrum had been in use as a religious symbol for centuries. According to Jewish beliefs, God gave Moses explicit instructions on how to craft the menorah, which was made for the tabernacle, or house of prayer. Later the menorah came to symbolize knowledge and understanding as well as the light of God protecting the Jews.*

The Kingdom of Israel   In about 1000 B.C. the Israelites established a monarchy, and from the late eleventh century to the end of the tenth century B.C. the nation flourished under a series of kings—Saul, David, and Solomon. The popular king David rallied the scattered Israelite tribes and centralized the government. During his reign the economy shifted toward commerce, trade, and farming and away from herding.

Solomon, David's son, brought the Israelite kingdom to its pinnacle of power and prestige. He signed treaties with other states, expanded Israel's trade across the Middle East, and raised the standard of living for many of his subjects. He completed the building of Jerusalem begun by David which, with its magnificent public structures, rivaled the glory of other Middle Eastern cities. Solomon's ambitious building program included a large and sumptuous palace, numerous government offices, and a splendid temple. The Temple of Solomon housed Israel's holy relics, including the Ark of the Covenant, and became the focal point of the nation's religion.

King Solomon considered himself a learned man and a patron of literature and the arts, and under his rule Hebrew culture branched out in several directions, notably in law, writing, music, and dance. As the Hebrews became conscious of their increased status in the eyes of the world, they turned their attention to their past. Their oral traditions gave way to written records, and Hebrew authors now wrote down their laws and their earliest histories, which are preserved in the first books of the Bible (Figure 6.2). These Hebrew works predate by five centuries the writings of the great Greek historians, Herodotus and Thucydides. But unlike the Greek writers, the Hebrew historians made God the central force in human history and thus transformed the unfolding of earthly events into a moral drama with cosmic significance.

Solomon's political success, economic gains, and cultural achievement came at a heavy price, for they undermined his people's religious foundations, intensified class divisions, and tended to divide the northern and southern tribes. When Solomon died in 926 B.C., the tensions between the regions intensified and the United Monarchy split into two separate states: Israel in the north, with its capital at Samaria, and Judah in the south, with its capital at Jerusalem.

During the period of the two Hebrew kingdoms, a new type of religious leader, known as a prophet, appeared. When the prophets saw the Hebrew people in both nations forsaking Yahweh and turning to other deities, they warned of the fatal conse-

FIGURE 6.2 Ancient Scroll of the Pentateuch. *The ancient Hebrews recorded their scriptures on parchment scrolls. Today, a copy of the Pentateuch, or Torah, is preserved on scrolls in every synagogue.*

quences of breaking his commandments. As successive prophets castigated the erring, these religious spokesmen also added an international dimension to Yahweh. In predicting the downfall of surrounding non-Hebrew states, the prophets asserted that God was now using peoples other than the Hebrews to fulfill his divine plan in history.

The prophets also demanded social justice for the helpless and the downtrodden. In the face of a widening gulf between the rich and the poor, the prophets called on the powerful and wealthy to aid the less fortunate. They predicted that if the well-off did not change their habits, Yahweh would bring down the evil rulers and, sometime in the future, punish the selfish and reward the sufferers. But the words of the prophets, such as Hosea and Amos in Israel and Isaiah and Jeremiah in Judah, seemed to go unheeded.

Defeat and Exile: The Babylonian Captivity Although Israel enjoyed its moments of prosperity and power, it could not compete with its neighbors or remain isolated from the larger empires, especially Egypt and Assyria, that wanted to control the military and trade routes crossing this part of the Fertile Crescent. In 722 B.C. the tiny nation of Israel was destroyed by the Assyrians. Judah, the southern half of the old United Monarchy, endured for two hundred years after the fall of Israel. Like Israel, Judah had some successful years, but the small state could not withstand external threats forever. In 586 B.C. the Babylonians conquered Judah, destroyed Solomon's Temple in Jerusalem, and deported most of the Hebrews to Babylonia. The approximately forty years of exile, known as the Babylonian Captivity, became one of the major turning points in Jewish history.

The Postexilic Period At the end of the sixth century, the Jews (as the Hebrews were called after the Babylonian Captivity) were freed by the triumphant Persians, who were sweeping across the ancient world under Cyrus (see Chapter 2). Returning to Judah, the Jews rebuilt their temple and restored their towns. Believing that God had rescued them, they established a theocratic state—a government ruled by those who are recognized as having special divine guidance and approval. They then dedicated themselves to the correct formulation and observation of their religious beliefs and rituals. The Jews welcomed back many exiles returning to their homeland from around the Mediterranean, reestablished their commercial ties, and revived their handicraft industries. But many exiles, uprooted by the successive destructions of Israel and Judah, remained outside their homeland and became known as Jews of the *Diaspora*, or the Dispersion.

After their return from Babylon, in the postexilic period, the Jews expanded their views of Yahweh. Probably under the indirect impact of the increasingly popular Persian religion, Zoroastrianism, the Jews began to envision a cosmic dualism in their beliefs. The Zoroastrian description of the twin forces of good and evil or Light and Dark thus crept into some aspects of the Jewish faith. The Hebrews' earlier perception of themselves as a chosen people under a universal deity was reinforced as they concluded that Yahweh had used the Persians to free them. Furthermore, the Jews started to interject two new features into their religion: *eschatology,* or the concern with the end of the world, and an interest in *apocalypse,* prophecies about the coming of God and a day of judgment. This future world would be led by a *Messiah,* or Anointed One, who would bring peace and justice to all.

The Hellenistic and Roman Periods As theological debates heated up in the reconstituted state of Judah, a new foreign menace appeared on the horizon. Alexander the Great conquered the region in 332 B.C., and after his death the area became part of the Seleucid kingdom, the successor state centered in Syria. Hellenistic culture and ideas gained ground in Judah and deeply affected Jewish life. Growing tensions between the Jews and the Hellenistic leaders erupted into a serious crisis in 168 B.C. when the Seleucid king Antiochus IV tried to impose the worship of Greek gods on the Jews. He placed a statue of Zeus in the Second Temple in Jerusalem, converting the holiest site in Judaism into a pagan shrine. Antiochus's violation of the sacred place enraged the Maccabean clan, whose inspired leadership and bravery led to a successful revolt and the recapture of the temple.

After the defeat of Antiochus, the Maccabean family ruled Judah as an independent commonwealth for approximately one hundred years, thus ensuring internal Jewish cultural and political freedom. Then in 63 B.C. the Roman general Pompey conquered most of the Middle East, including Judah, or what was now called Palestine. In Palestine, the Romans experimented with several forms of government, which only intensified the political turmoil and religious tensions among the various Jewish groups. Under Augustus, Rome incorporated Judah into its empire as Judea and placed the Jewish lands under client kings.

Appointed to these kingships were members of the Herod dynasty, a family of Jews who had gained favor with the Romans. Herod the Great, who ruled from 37 to 4 B.C., rebuilt Jerusalem, including the Temple, and promoted Hellenistic culture among the Jews (Figure 6.3). But conditions under the

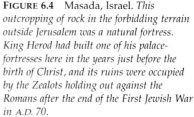

FIGURE 6.3 Model of the Third Temple (Herod's Temple) in Jerusalem. *This model of the Third Temple shows the strong influence of Hellenistic-style architecture, particularly in the colonnaded arcades, the decorative frieze, and the tall, slender Corinthian columns flanking the main entryway. The Third Temple was destroyed by Roman legions in A.D. 70, but one wall was left standing. The first two temples had also been destroyed by armies attacking Jerusalem.*

FIGURE 6.4 Masada, Israel. *This outcropping of rock in the forbidding terrain outside Jerusalem was a natural fortress. King Herod had built one of his palace-fortresses here in the years just before the birth of Christ, and its ruins were occupied by the Zealots holding out against the Romans after the end of the First Jewish War in A.D. 70.*

Romans became unbearable to the Jews, and in A.D. 66 a rebellion broke out. After four years of turmoil and bitter fighting, called the First Jewish War, the Romans captured Jerusalem and destroyed the Third Temple (A.D. 70). A revolutionary group known as Zealots held out until 73 at Masada, a sheer-sided mesa on the shores of the Dead Sea (Figure 6.4). When their cause became hopeless, they committed suicide rather than surrender to the Romans.

One wall of the Third Temple in Jerusalem remained standing, the famous Wailing Wall, which came to symbolize the plight of the Jewish people. As described in Chapter 5, Titus, the victorious Roman general and later emperor, returned to Rome with the holy Jewish relics (see Figure 5.26). To make sure that the Jews would no longer be a problem, the Roman government in the late first century A.D. ordered the dispersal of the Jews throughout the em-

pire. However, this second Diaspora did not end the Jews' cultural, intellectual, and religious existence. On the contrary, the Jewish way of life continued despite persecutions by the Romans.

The Bible

The Jews enshrined their cultural developments in the Bible, their collection of sacred writings, or **scriptures.** Known as the Old Testament to Christians, the Hebrew Bible (from the Greek word for book) contains history, law, poetry, songs, stories, prayers, and philosophical works. Evolving out of a rich and long oral tradition and compiled over several centuries by unknown writers, the Hebrew Bible was collected, edited, and authenticated by state officials and Jewish scholars.

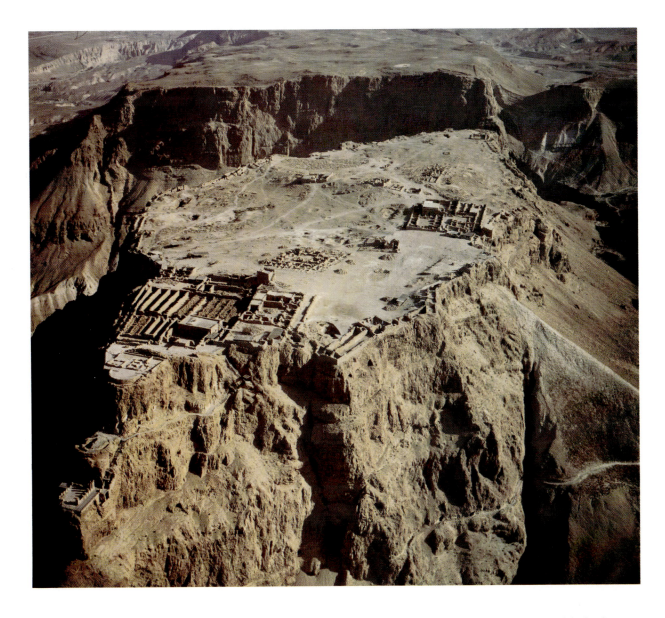

The Bible probably began to take its earliest written form during the United Monarchy in the tenth century B.C. By then the Hebrews had an alphabet that, like the Greek version, was probably derived from the Phoenicians. Having acquired a written language and a unified political state, the Hebrews shared a consciousness of their past and desired to preserve it. After the collapse of the United Monarchy, they assembled and wrote down various historical accounts, songs, and stories, plus the sayings of the prophets. Sometime in the fifth century B.C., after the Babylonian Captivity, Jewish scholars and religious leaders canonized (officially accepted) parts of these writings—the first five books, known as the Torah or the Pentateuch—as divinely inspired. Another portion of these scriptures was given canonical status by 100 B.C. The Hebrew Bible's ultimate form was reached in A.D. 90 when a council of Jewish scholars meeting in Jamnia in Judea added a last set of writings to the *canon.*

Another important development in the transmission of the Hebrew scriptures was their translation from Hebrew into other languages. A major step in this direction occurred in the third century B.C., after many Jews had fallen under the spell of Hellenistic culture: A group of scholars in Alexandria collected all of the authenticated Jewish writings and translated them into Greek. This Hebrew Greek Bible was called the Septuagint, from the Latin word for seventy, so named because of the legend that it was translated by seventy scholars.

The final version of the Hebrew Bible is divided into three parts: the Law, the Prophets, and the Writings (Table 6.2). (Christians arrange the books differently and divide the Old Testament into four parts.) The Law (also called the Torah or the

Pentateuch) consists of the first five books (Genesis, Exodus, Leviticus, Numbers, and Deuteronomy) and recounts the story of God's creation of the world and the early history of the Hebrews. More important, it details the establishment of the covenant and the foundation of the moral and ritualistic codes of personal and societal behavior that underlie Judaism.

The Torah was canonized in the fifth century B.C. at the time of the return from the Babylonian Captivity and the building of the Second Temple.

The Prophets, canonized in the first century B.C., provide records about Israel and Judah and expand the Hebrews' ideas about God's nature and their relationship to him. They recount the conquest of Ca-

TABLE 6.2   BOOKS OF THE HEBREW BIBLE AND THE CHRISTIAN BIBLE OLD TESTAMENT

HEBREW BIBLE		CHRISTIAN BIBLE OLD TESTAMENT	
The Law (Torah)		**The Pentateuch**	
Genesis	Numbers	Genesis	Numbers
Exodus	Deuteronomy	Exodus	Deuteronomy
Leviticus		Leviticus	
The Prophets		**The Historical Books**	
(Early Prophets)		Joshua	2 Chronicles
Joshua	Joel	Judges	Ezra
Judges	Amos	Ruth	Nehemiah
1 Samuel	Obadiah	1 Samuel	Tobit*
2 Samuel	Jonah	2 Samuel	Judith*
1 Kings	Micah	1 Kings	Esther
2 Kings	Nahum	2 Kings	1 Maccabees*
(Later Prophets)	Habakkuk	1 Chronicles	2 Maccabees*
Isaiah	Zephaniah		
Jeremiah	Haggai	**The Poetical or Wisdom Books**	
Ezekiel	Zechariah	Job	
Hosea	Malachi	Psalms	
		Proverbs	
The Writings		Ecclesiastes	
Psalms	Esther	Song of Solomon (Songs)	
Proverbs	Daniel	Wisdom*	
Job	Ezra	Sirach*	
Song of Songs	Nehemiah		
Ruth	1 Chronicles	**The Prophetical Books**	
Lamentations	2 Chronicles	Isaiah	Obadiah
Ecclesiastes		Jeremiah	Jonah
		Lamentations	Micah
		Baruch*	Nahum
		Ezekiel	Habakkuk
		Daniel	Zephaniah
		Hosea	Haggai
		Joel	Zechariah
		Amos	Malachi

*Roman Catholics include these books in the canon and refer to them as deuterocanonical ("second canon"); Protestants sometimes place them in an appendix with other Apocrypha.

naan, the events of the era of the Judges and the period of the United Monarchy, and the fate of Judah after the Babylonian Captivity up to about 400 B.C., when the theocratic state was founded. The Torah and the Prophets constitute the most essential sections of the Bible.

The Writings reflect diverse viewpoints and contain many types of literature, including poetry, wise sayings, stories, and apocalyptic visions of the end of time. Some of these books, such as Job, Ecclesiastes, and Proverbs, reflect the influence of other cultures on Jewish beliefs. The Writings were not deemed canonical until A.D. 90, with the exception of Psalms, a collection of poems, which was given sacred status by 100 B.C.

In addition to the Hebrew Bible, there is a body of Jewish literature outside the canon. The Apocrypha are books written between 200 B.C. and A.D. 100 that include wisdom literature, stories, and history, including the history of the Maccabees. Though not part of the Jewish canon, these books were included in the Septuagint, the Greek translation of the Hebrew Bible, and accepted by the Roman Catholic church as part of the Christian Old Testament. Another group of Jewish writings outside the canon, dating from between 200 B.C. and A.D. 200, is known collectively as the Pseudepigrapha and contains a variety of legends, interpretations, and apocalyptic literature.

Copies of many Jewish works, both canonical and noncanonical, were found in a cave near the Dead Sea in 1947. These documents, dating from about 200 B.C. to A.D. 100 and known as the Dead Sea Scrolls, were almost a thousand years older than any other existing manuscripts of the Bible and confirmed that the books had been transmitted faithfully for centuries (Figure 6.5). The scrolls also provided scholars with material about nonmainstream Jewish religious practices in the period before and during the earliest Christian period.

The Hebrew Bible provides Judaism with many of its beliefs and values and much of its world view. It contrasts a changing view of God with a rather consistently negative opinion of human nature. Examples abound of humans who, like Adam and Eve or David, fail on occasion to uphold their side of the covenant by disobeying Yahweh, worshiping other gods, exploiting the unfortunate, or breaking moral and social codes. Given the weakness of human nature and Yahweh's strict demands, it is unlikely that happiness can be attained by most mortals. Perhaps happiness would be reached when Yahweh's kingdom was established on earth, but no one knew when that would happen or in what form. The individual's life was made more perplexing because no mortal could comprehend the power of Yahweh. Human beings could only try to follow Yahweh's commandments—knowing that they would sin—and hope for happiness through his forgiving.

In biblical Judaism the hope for happiness depended on another aspect of the covenant: Jews believed that they would be forgiven for their sins. Redemption by God had occurred over and over in history, and the Bible sustained human hope while revealing Yahweh's love and mercy. Yet such qualities often seemed inconsistent with the Lord's vengeful manner. Consequently, the hearts of worshipers were torn between hope and fear. Their hope was strengthened through the covenant's promise that Yahweh would protect humanity as long as they lived just lives.

FIGURE 6.5 The Dead Sea Isaiah Scroll (detail). First Century B.C.–First Century A.D. *The Dead Sea Scrolls are believed to be the work of a Jewish sect known as the Essenes. Living in a monastic community called Qumran, this radical group rejected the leadership of the Jews in Jerusalem and practiced a militant, separatist form of Judaism. The scrolls represent their copies of the Hebrew Bible as well as previously unknown works. The Dead Sea Isaiah Scroll preserves all sixty-six chapters of the Bible's longest book.*

Early Jewish Art and Architecture

Jewish culture was profoundly shaped by the Second Commandment, which forbids the making of images or likenesses of God. In art, this meant that Yahweh could not, by definition, be depicted in any recognizable form. Furthermore, creation and creativity are considered the exclusive domain of God and reserved for him alone. Thus, there is no official Jewish sculpture or painting.

The scattered surviving artifacts of the Hebrews from the period before the United Monarchy can seldom be distinguished from the works of their neighbors. Because of the early Hebrews' nomadic existence, what sacred objects they had were transportable and kept in tents. These early works were not for public display because of the very holiness of Yahweh and the Hebrews' sense of their deity's power. Only a few persons were even permitted to see or be in the vicinity of these sacred objects. Once the tribes were united, however, Solomon enshrined the Ark of the Covenant and other ritualistic items in the splendid Temple he built in Jerusalem.

Solomon's Temple was completely destroyed by the Babylonians when they carried off the Jews in the early sixth century B.C. The description of the Temple in 1 Kings makes it sound similar to the "long-house" temples found in other civilizations of that time and probably indicated the influence of foreign neighbors. According to the Bible, Solomon's Temple was a rectangular building comprising three sections: a porch, a sanctuary, or main hall, and an inner sanctum that housed the Ark of the Covenant. Artists and craftspeople decorated the interior with carvings of floral designs and cherubs, highlighting these with gold. The building was made of ashlars and two large free-standing columns were placed at the entranceway. The Temple may have been raised on a platform. A court surrounded the Temple, and a large altar stood inside the court. Solomon meant the Temple to be the central national shrine of the Hebrews and a symbol of his dynasty for his subjects and other nations to admire.

When the Jews were released from the Babylonian Captivity by the Persians, they returned to their homeland and reconstructed the capital city of Jerusalem and its temple. The Second Temple, completed in the late sixth century B.C., exhibited a simpler design and decoration scheme than that of Solomon's Temple. Meanwhile, the Jews of the Diaspora gathered in Hellenistic cities to read the Torah and to pray in buildings that became synagogues, or houses of worship. No record survives of how these synagogues looked or how they might have been decorated until the third century A.D.

Greek influences became apparent in Jewish architecture during Hellenistic times. One Maccabean ruler, John Hyrcanus [hear-KAY-nuhs] (135–106 B.C.), constructed a fortress-palace at present-day Araq el Emir in Jordan that shows this influence clearly. The facade of the palace blended Greek columns and oriental carvings, typical of the Alexandrian architectural and decorative style (Figure 6.6). The edifice and its carvings were probably similar to the Second Temple in Jerusalem. One of the few decorations remaining from this palace is a lion fountain (Figure 6.7). Carved in high relief, the lion is well proportioned and conveys a sense of power, with its raised front paw and open mouth.

FIGURE 6.7   Lion at the Palace of John Hyrcanus. Second Century B.C. Araq el Emir, Jordan. *This lion, Greco-Oriental in style, was carved deeply into the stone's surface to create a high-relief work. The lion's tail, wrapped around his right rear leg, is balanced by the raised left front leg, creating a feeling of strength and agility.*

FIGURE 6.8   Tomb of Bene Hezir. Early First Century B.C. Kidron Valley, Israel. *The Tomb of Bene Hezir (on the left) shows the influence of Greek architecture in its post-and-lintel construction and its Doric columns. Even though the area was subject to Roman impact at this time, Roman influence is not apparent in the architecture. The members of the priestly Hezir family, as recorded in the First Book of Chronicles, chapter 24, were buried in what has been determined to be the oldest tomb in Israel's Kidron Valley. Scholars disagree over whether the structure in the center with the pyramidal roof belonged to the Bene Hezir tomb.*

The lingering influence of late Greek architecture on Jewish structures can also be seen in a set of tombs dug out of the soft limestone rocks east of Jerusalem in the Kidron Valley. According to the inscription, these tombs contained the remains of priests from the Hezir family (Figure 6.8). The tomb on the left displays Doric columns, and the one in the center fuses Greek Ionic columns and an Egyptian pyramidal roof. Several other tombs in the vicinity reveal a similar melding of styles.

During the reign of King Herod the Great (37–4 B.C.), architecture in Judea exhibited a further mix of Greek styles with Jewish motifs. King Herod's magnificent fortress-palace at Masada may have been a conscious blending of both cultures in an effort to bridge the gap between the Roman and Jewish worlds. It was the ruins of this fortress that the Zealots occupied during the war with the Romans. The various buildings in Herod's complex contained many representative Greco-Roman features, including fluted Corinthian columns and marble facings (Figure 6.9). In Herod's palace, Classical patterned mosiacs were combined with traditional Jewish decorations of flowers, fruits, and intertwined vines and branches (Figure 6.10).

Herod also built palaces at Jericho and in Jerusalem, but they were destroyed, and their remains have not been uncovered. The king also supervised

◀ **FIGURE 6.9** Hall of Herod's North Palace. Late First Century B.C. Masada, Israel. *These Corinthian columns were originally plastered over and painted. Carved directly out of the hill's rock, they formed a natural corridor around the banqueting hall. Herod built this and other splendid palaces to impress the Jews and win their political sympathy, but he failed to do either.*

the construction of the Third Temple in Jerusalem, whose large dimensions and impressive features were recorded in the writings of the Jewish historian Josephus in his works *The Jewish War* and *Jewish Antiquities* (see Figure 6.3). Like the previous temples, this one contained many rooms, including the Holy of Holies with the menorah and the table where the priests placed the consecrated, unleavened bread eaten during Passover, the festival that commemorates the exodus from Egypt. Whatever may have been Herod's motives in constructing this new temple, the results were short-lived. When the Romans finally crushed the Jewish revolt in A.D. 70, the Third Temple was almost totally destroyed and its sacred objects transported to Rome.

CHRISTIANITY

Like Judaism, Christianity rose from obscurity and gained much of its power from the tremendous moral force of its central beliefs and values. But Christianity went on to become the dominant religion of Western culture. From its origins in isolated Judea, Christianity slowly spread until by the end of the fourth century A.D., it had become the official faith of Rome. When Rome lost control of the western provinces at the end of the fifth century A.D., Christianity's ideas and institutions survived as rays of hope in the surrounding darkness. In the following century, Christians gradually gained the upper hand. Their triumph was powerfully symbolized in the Early Middle Ages when church authorities revised the old Roman calendar to make the birth of Christ the pivotal event in history. Thus, the period before Jesus' birth is known as B.C., or before Christ; and the era after his birth is termed A.D., or *Anno Domini*, Latin words meaning "in the year of the Lord," the title of respect given to Jesus by Christians. Although Christianity and the church have de-

◀ **FIGURE 6.10** Mosaic from Herod's Palace. Late First Century B.C. Masada, Israel. *The Greek practice of mosaic making was adopted by both the Romans and the Jews. The patterned designs around the borders of this mosaic from Herod's Palace are typically Greek, and the more organic image in the center is typically Jewish.*

clined from their zenith in the Middle Ages, the Christian calendar remains in effect throughout the West as well as in many other parts of the world—a symbol of the continuing power of this creed.

The Life of Jesus Christ and the New Testament

The only surviving near-contemporary sources for the origin of the Christian religion are writings in Greek by early believers who were openly partisan in their accounts. According to them, Christianity began within the Jewish faith among the followers of Jesus, a deeply pious and charismatic Jew who failed in his efforts to purify his own faith but succeeded in founding a new and dynamic religion.

Jesus was born to Mary and Joseph in Judea in about 4 B.C.—a date fixed by modern scholars that reflects changes in the Christian calendar made since its inauguration. After narrating the events surrounding his birth, the accounts of Jesus' life are almost silent until he reaches full maturity, when, at the age of about thirty, he commenced a teaching mission that placed him squarely in conflict with prevailing Jewish beliefs and authorities. The poor and outcast in Jewish society heard Jesus' message, and he soon had a small group of followers who came to believe that he was the Messiah, the Anointed One who would deliver the Jews, promised by God to the prophets. He was also termed the Christ, a term used interchangeably with Messiah, taken from the Greek for "the anointed one." Performing miracles and healing the sick, he preached that the apocalypse, or the end of the world, was near. In anticipation of what he called the coming of the kingdom of God, he urged his followers to practice a demanding and loving ethic.

Growing discord between the Jewish establishment and this messianic band caused Roman leaders to take notice of Jesus, whom they classified as a political rebel. In about A.D. 30, Jesus, denounced by his Jewish enemies and betrayed by his own disciple Judas, was crucified by the Romans—an ignoble form of death usually reserved for common criminals (Time Line 6.2). Three days later, some of his followers reported that Jesus had risen from the dead and reappeared among them. His resurrection became the ultimate miracle associated with his teachings, the sign that immortal life awaited those who believed in him as the son of God and as the Messiah. After a few days on earth, during which time Jesus appeared to some of his supporters, he ascended into heaven, though not before pledging to return when the world ended.

TIME LINE 6.2   CHRISTIANITY TO A.D. 284

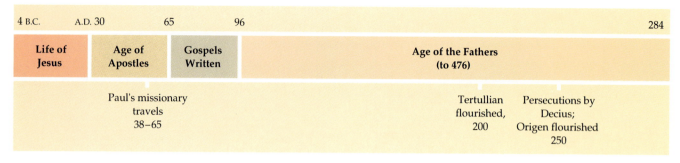

This outline of Jesus' life is set forth, with some slight variations among the different accounts, in the first three books, called *Gospels*, of the Christian scriptures. The early Christian community believed that these writers, known as Matthew, Mark, and Luke, were witnesses to Jesus' message, and hence they were called *evangelists* after the Greek word *evangelion*—for those who preached the gospel, or the good news. The Gospels, although providing evidence for the historical Jesus, were not intended as histories in the Greco-Roman sense because they were addressed to Christian converts. Mark's Gospel was the earliest, dating from around 70, Matthew's account was written between 80 and 90, and an early version of Luke's narrative probably appeared about the same time. The works of Matthew, Mark, and Luke are known as the synoptic Gospels (from the Greek *syn* for "together" and *opsis* for "view") because they correspond so closely, taking essentially the same point of view toward their subject.

Between 90 and 100 a fourth Gospel appeared— that of John—which paints a somewhat different picture of Jesus. In contrast to the synoptic Gospels, which describe Jesus as preaching the end of the world, John's account treats him as a wisdom teacher, a revealer of cosmic truths. The author of the Fourth Gospel has Jesus teach the possibility of being born again to eternal life.

The synoptic Gospels reflect a schism, or split, in the early Christian church. Peter, one of Jesus' original disciples, headed a Judaising group who stressed the necessity of first becoming a Jew before becoming a Christian, and Paul, a Jew who converted to Christianity after the death of Jesus, led a group who welcomed gentile, or non-Jewish, members. Mark's Gospel was written in part to support Paul's gentile faction against the Judaising group and therefore takes a negative tone toward Jews. Matthew was written (again, in part) as a corrective to Mark and made Peter the "rock" on which the church was founded—the biblical source for the belief that Peter was in effect the first pope. Luke's Gos-

pel was an effort by the early Roman church to deny, after the fact, that a schism had ever existed.

The author of Luke also wrote the Acts of the Apostles, the earliest account of the fledgling Christian community. This work records the activities of Jesus' followers immediately after his resurrection and defines some of the church's first rituals and beliefs. Of all of the matters touched on by the writer of Acts, however, the most important was the opening of Christianity to Gentiles, or non-Jews. Led by Peter's vision and abetted by Paul's example, the apostles were portrayed in Acts as rejecting the Jewish dietary laws and the practice of circumcision. Nevertheless, Christianity's open-membership policy was more important for the faith in the long term than in the short term because Paul and other missionaries preached mainly in the Jewish communities that were scattered across the Roman Empire. There they worked through synagogues among Greek-speaking Jews and Jewish converts.

The meaning of Jesus' life and teachings was further clarified for the early church by Paul, who had persecuted the Christians of Judea before joining the new faith. Between the years 50 and 62, Paul set forth his ideas in epistles, or letters, the earliest writings among the Christian scriptures although only seven of the fourteen so-called Pauline epistles are generally recognized by modern scholars as being by him. These epistles also constitute Christianity's first *theology*, or the study of the nature of religious truth. Paul directed his letters to churches he either founded or visited across the Roman Empire: Ephesus, Galatia, and Colossae (Asia Minor), Philippi and Thessalonica (Macedonia), Corinth (Greece), and Rome (Map 6.2). In these letters Paul addressed both local issues and broader theological concerns.

Paul's interpretation of the life of Jesus was based on the "Suffering Servant" section of the book of Isaiah in the Old Testament. The Suffering Servant was described as noble and guiltless but misunderstood and suffering on behalf of others. Paul's favorite term for Jesus, the Christ, reflected his identification of Jesus with Isaiah's image. Paul set forth the doctrine of the Atonement, whereby a blameless Christ suffered on the cross to pay for the sins of humankind. Christ's life and death initiated a new moral order by holding out hope of salvation to depraved human beings who otherwise were doomed to eternal death and punishment by Adam's first sin. But, according to Paul, human redemption was not automatically given, for a sinner must have faith in Jesus Christ and his sacrifice.

A second major aspect of Paul's teachings was his belief that the resurrection was the heart of Christian beliefs, an argument that echoed the synoptic Gospels. For him, Christ's resurrection guaranteed everlasting life for others. Pauline Christianity made a radical break with Judaism by nullifying the old law's authority. Paul claimed that the true heirs of Abraham were not the Jews but the followers of Christ. Paul also affirmed that obedience to Christ led to righteousness. Such righteousness demanded ascetic living, with particular stress on sexual chastity. Marriage was a second best condition, since it was better to marry than to burn with lust. From Paul's writings came the Roman church's teaching that sexuality, except for reproductive purposes, was inherently sinful.

The final section of the Christian scriptures was the Book of Revelation, dating from about 95. Written in the tradition of Jewish apocalyptic literature, this scripture projected the end of the world and the institution of a new moral order on the occasion of Jesus' return and final judgment. Revelation's picture of Rome as a corrupt Babylon destined for destruction expressed and fueled the early church's hatred of the existing political and social order. But the book, filled with enigmatic sayings and symbols, proved controversial from its origin, and not all ancient church communities accepted its authority.

Map 6.2
The Early Christian World

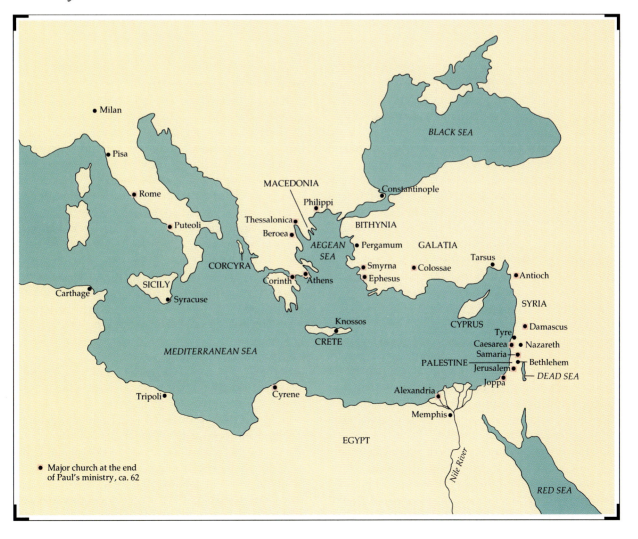

TABLE 6.3   BOOKS OF THE NEW TESTAMENT

GOSPELS	ACTS OF THE APOSTLES	EPISTLES	CHRISTIAN APOCALYPSE
Matthew	Acts	Romans	Revelation
Mark		1 Corinthians	
Luke		2 Corinthians	
John		Galatians	
		Ephesians	
		Philippians	
		Colossians	
		1 Thessalonians	
		2 Thessalonians	
		1 Timothy	
		2 Timothy	
		Titus	
		Philemon	
		Hebrews	
		James	
		1 Peter	
		2 Peter	
		1 John	
		2 John	
		3 John	
		Jude	

By the mid–second century the four Gospels, the Acts of the Apostles, the fourteen Pauline epistles, the seven non-Pauline epistles, and Revelation were accepted as the canon of Christian scriptures, or New Testament (Table 6.3). Believing themselves to be the new Israel, the early Christians also retained the Hebrew scriptures, which they called the Old Testament. Although the spoken language of the Jews in Palestine was Aramaic, a Semitic tongue, the Christian canon was composed in Greek, like the Hebrew Septuagint. The use of Greek reflected the triumph of Paul and the gentile party as the church turned away from Jerusalem and toward the Greco-Roman world.

Christians and Jews

Despite the distinctive features of early Christianity, many Jewish ideas, thought patterns, and rituals contributed to the new religion. The manner in which Christians envisioned Yahweh was rooted in Judaism: a single, creating, universal God who spoke through sacred texts (the canon) and who demanded moral behavior from all humans. Both Jewish and Christian ethical standards required social justice for individuals and for the community. Likewise, the Christian image of Jesus as Messiah was framed within the context of Jewish prophetic literature. Christian apocalyptic writing, such as Revelation,

also shared a common literary form with Jewish models like the book of Daniel.

Even when Christians rejected specific Jewish ideas as, for example, the sanctity of the Mosaic law, the early church continued discussions on human righteousness and sin in terms familiar to Jews. The Christians probably adapted their rite of baptism from a similar ceremony that the Jews of the Dispersion practiced. Christians also kept the idea of the Sabbath but changed it from Saturday to Sunday; they transformed the festival of Passover (a celebration of the Hebrews' escape from Egypt) to Easter (a festival celebrating Jesus' resurrection); and they made Shavuot (a harvest festival and a celebration of the giving of the Mosaic law) into Pentecost, a celebration of the coming of the Holy Spirit. The church sanctuary as a focal point for prayer and learning evolved out of the Jewish synagogue, as did Christian priests from the Jewish elders. And the Christian *liturgy*, or the service of public worship, borrowed heavily from the Jewish service with its hymns, prayers, and Bible reading.

Judaism also influenced Christian thought by transmitting certain ideas from Zoroastrianism acquired during Persia's rule of Palestine. From Zoroastrian dualism came such concepts as Satan as the personification of evil, demons both good and bad who enter human bodies, heaven and hell as the twin destinies of humankind, and a divine savior who would appear at the end of time. Jesus and the dominant Jewish sect, the Pharisees, though enemies, both partook of these Persian ideas and integrated them into their religious outlooks.

Despite their common heritage, however, relations between Christians and Jews were stormy at best. After the Council at Jamnia in Judea in 90, when the Jews established the final version of their sacred canon, there was no place in Judaism for the Christian message. As revealed in Paul's letters, the Jews viewed the followers of Jesus Christ as apostates, people who had abandoned or renounced their true religion. Accordingly, the Jews tried to deny the Christians the protection that Jewish leaders had negotiated with Roman authorities regarding emperor worship and their own unique beliefs and rituals. In some cases Jews resorted to reporting individual Christians to the Roman authorities, which at times resulted in persecutions and death. Until the end of the second century, Jews and Christians occasionally engaged in violent clashes. Possibly the strong anti-Jewish bias found in a few of the Christian books like the Gospel of Mark reflected the tensions and violence of these years.

Christianity and Greco-Roman Religions and Philosophies

Besides Jewish and Zoroastrian influences, Christianity benefited from its contacts with Greco-Roman mystery cults and philosophies. Whether or not the rituals of the cults of Cybele, Isis, or Mithra directly influenced Christianity, they all shared religious ideas that were common to this age—for example, salvation through the sacrifice of a savior, sacred meals, and hymns. Christianity, as a monotheistic religion, paralleled movements within the cults of the second and third centuries that were blending all deities into the worship of a single divinity. Among the Greco-Roman philosophies, Stoicism and Neo-Platonism both influenced Christianity as the church moved away from its Jewish roots and became hellenized. For example, the Stoics taught the kinship of humanity, and the Neo-Platonists praised the spiritual realm at the expense of the physical world.

Christians in the Roman Empire

Whatever may have been the connections between early Christianity and Greco-Roman civilization, and notwithstanding the complexities of Judaic-Christian relationships, the Romans eventually came to view

and to treat Jews and Christians separately and differently. Initially, the Romans regarded the Christians as a Jewish sect, but during the First Jewish War, which resulted in the destruction of Herod's Temple in 70, the Christians evidently held aloof from the struggle. The Christian attitude seemed to be that the Jews had brought calamity upon themselves through their rejection of Christ. Similarly, Christians remained untouched during later persecutions of Jews by Romans in 115–117 and in 132–135.

Christians began to experience troubles from the Romans as their faith expanded and separated itself from Judaism. During the first century, individual Christians suffered at the hands of the Romans, though no state policy of searching out Christians and forcing them to meet a test was introduced. However, if suspected Christians came to the notice of secular officials, they were punished if they did not renounce their beliefs. The same pattern of localized, random persecution continued until the mid–third century, reminding the Christians of their vulnerability to attack. The church, having increased dramatically in membership and accumulated property in buildings and cemeteries, profited from the indifference of imperial and local authorities. As long as economic prosperity and political stability lasted, the Christians seemed safe. Rumors even claimed that the emperor Alexander Severus [suh-VIER-uhs] (228–235) kept in his palace an image of Jesus along with statues of Apollo and other gods.

However, as the chaos of the Barrack Emperors descended on Rome, the Christians were blamed for all the empire's troubles. The fury of the Roman state was unleashed against the Christians by Decius [DEE-she-uhs] (249–251) when he mounted a wide-ranging political test that required all citizens (men, women, and children) to make a token sacrifice to the emperor. When the Christians refused to honor the emperors in this manner, hundreds of them died, including several of their local leaders or bishops. Decius's sudden death ended this assault, but in 257 Valerian (253–260) renewed the struggle, which resulted in the martyrdom of the bishop of Rome and the age's leading intellectual, Cyprian. Christians were beheaded, buried alive, or burned alive during this persecution. The killings eventually ceased, but for the rest of the century the Christian church survived under strenuous circumstances and faced an uncertain future in which its acceptance depended on a muted existence.

Despite persecutions from the authorities, the Christian church drew much sustenance from Roman culture. The language of the church in the western provinces became Latin, and in the eastern provinces the religious leaders adopted Greek. The canon law that governed the internal workings of the church was based on the Roman civil law. Most importantly, the church modeled itself on the Roman state: The bishops had jurisdiction over territories called dioceses just as the secular governors controlled administrative dioceses.

In addition, the church was moving toward a monarchical form of government. At first, the bishop of Jerusalem played a decisive role in church discipline until the fall of the city in 70. Thereafter, because the authority of the officeholders was believed to descend from Jesus' faithful supporters, those bishoprics established by apostles—such as the one in Rome that tradition claimed was founded by both Peter and Paul—emerged as the most powerful.

From an insignificant number of followers at the end of the first century, the church attained a membership of perhaps five million, or about a tenth of the population of the empire, by the end of the third century. The smallest communities were scattered along the frontiers, and the largest congregations were in Rome and the older eastern cities. Social composition of the church evolved from primarily lower-class foreign women and slaves, particularly those recruited from among the Jewish communities of the Diaspora, to progressively higher classes. By the late second century the middle classes, especially merchants and traders, were joining the church. Aristocratic women sought membership, but men of the highest classes tended to remain unconverted, although a few aristocratic converts prepared the way for future adherents.

Early Christian Literature

By the end of the second century the status of the church had risen sufficiently in popular esteem to attract the attention, if not always the approval, of leading Roman intellectuals, such as the philosopher Celsus and the physician Galen. Celsus (second century) ridiculed the Christian notion of the resurrection of the body and the new religion's appeal to women and slaves. On the other hand, Galen (about 130–about 201) found merit in Christianity because of its philosophical approach to life and its emphasis on strict self-discipline.

Christian literature, from its birth in Paul's letters until 284, remained closed off from the secular world. Because of their beliefs and values, Christian writers were excluded from public discourse, but their work, which addressed the evolving needs of this underground religion, began to circulate among the faithful. Of the many Christian writers active during this time, Tertullian [tehr-TULL-yuhn]

(about 160–about 230) and Origen [AHR-uh-juhn] (about 185–about 254) had the most enduring effect because their writings helped to define Christianity's relation to humanistic learning.

Tertullian's life and writings showed the uncompromising nature of Christianity. Trained in Stoic philosophy in Roman Carthage, he later converted to the new faith after he witnessed the serenity of Christians dying for their religion. The strength of his beliefs made him a spokesperson for North Africa, where a cult of martyrs made the area the "Bible belt" of the Roman world. Writing in Latin, he helped to shape the Western church's voice in that language. His diatribes against the pleasures of the theaters and arenas and his intense denunciation of women as sexual temptresses became legendary. In the severest terms he rejected the Greco-Roman humanistic heritage, preferring the culture of Christianity. Such fundamentalist thinking eventually drove this restless intellect into heretical, or false, beliefs. His vehement detestation of the secular world and the institutional church proved to be a thorny legacy for Christianity.

Origen of Alexandria shared Tertullian's puritanical zeal and his defiance of spiritual authority but, unlike Tertullian, he did not repudiate humanistic learning. In his mature writings, composed in Greek, Origen brought Christian thought into harmony with Platonism and Stoicism. Origen's Jesus was not the redeemer of the Gospels but the *logos* of Stoicism (see Chapter 4). The *logos*, or reason, liberated the human soul so that it might move through different levels of reality in order to reach God. Plotinus, Origen's contemporary, argued similarly in his Neo-Platonic philosophy (see Chapter 5). Origen's Platonism led him to reject the notion of the resurrection of the body as described in the Gospels and Paul's letters and to assert instead that the soul is eternal. Not surprisingly, Origen's ideas were condemned as heretical by later popes. Nevertheless, his philosophic writings, which continued to be read in secret, helped free Christianity from its Jewish framework and appealed to intellectuals.

Early Christian Art

Had Christians obeyed the Second Commandment, no figurative art would have been produced for this religion. Indeed, the earliest Christian writers, including Tertullian and Origen, condemned the depiction of religious subjects as blasphemous. Notwithstanding these objections, pious Christians, attracted by the pull of humanism, commissioned frescoes for underground burial chambers and sculp-

FIGURE 6.11 *The Good Shepherd.* Mid–Third Century A.D. Fresco. Crypts of Lucina, Catacomb of Callixtus, Rome. *This third-century fresco shows one of the popular religious symbols used by early Christians to disguise evidence of their faith from prying and perhaps hostile eyes. The "Good Shepherd" as an image of Jesus persisted in Christian art until the end of the fifth century.*

tures for their *sarcophagi*, or marble tombs. Starting from modest beginnings, Christian painters and sculptors slowly fused their religious vision with the Greco-Roman tradition, a style that would dominate the art of the late empire. After the fall of Rome, religious values remained paramount in Western art for almost a thousand years, until the Italian Renaissance.

In imperial Rome, Christians, Jews, and followers of other beliefs had the legal right to bury their dead in underground rooms beside the Appian Way, the city's chief thoroughfare. No evidence of Christian burials has been found earlier than the late second century. By that date, some of the tombs displayed Christian symbols and subjects, suggesting the increased confidence of the new religion in an otherwise hostile Roman environment. In the so-called Catacomb of Callixtus, a third-century fresco depicts a shepherd as a symbol of Jesus (Figure 6.11). This depiction, which is the most popular surviving image in the Christian art of this period, is based on the idea of Jesus as the kindly shepherd of his flock of followers, an image derived from many biblical sources, including the Twenty-third Psalm: "The Lord is my shepherd." Holding a sheep across his shoulders with his left hand, the shepherd carries in his right hand a pot of milk—the "milk" of instruction to the Christian initiate.

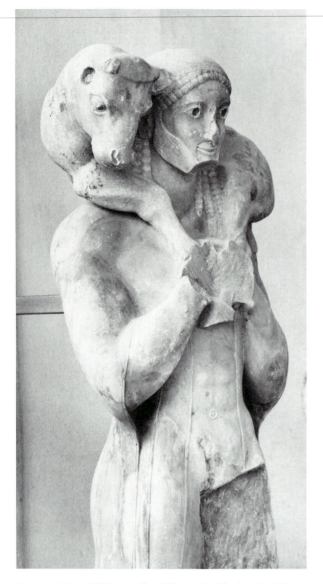

FIGURE 6.12 *Calf Bearer.* Ca. 570 B.C. Marble, height, 65".
Acropolis Museum, Athens. *This sixth-century B.C. Greek
statue shows a young man carrying a calf probably intended for a
ritual sacrifice. The statue is executed in the kouros style, popular
in the Archaic Age, as indicated by the frontality, stiffness, and
stylized beard. The shepherd image became associated with Jesus
in the early Christian period.*

FIGURE 6.13 *Christian Good Shepherd.* Second Century.
Marble. Vatican Museum. *This graceful statue blends Greek
influences with a Christian subject. The casual pose of the
shepherd with his easy contrapposto and dreamy gaze shows that
the influence of Praxiteles, the fourth-century B.C. Greek sculptor,
was still active after more than five centuries. The short cloak
worn by the figure was a typical costume of shepherds in the art of
the times.*

FIGURE 6.14   Panel from Sarcophagus of Baebia Hertofila. Late Third Century A.D. Museo delle Terme, Rome. *Other panels on this sarcophagus, including images of the Good Shepherd and Jonah, helped to establish the subject of this relief: the communion meal. The diners seem inappropriately boisterous, and in fact a passage in one of Paul's letters (I Corinthians 11:20–22) chastised those who behaved this way during the sacrament. This relief shows that attitudes more appropriate to Greek or Roman revels persisted among early Christian converts.*

Even though the shepherd and sheep convey a Christian message, the image adapts a familiar Greco-Roman theme—known in both art and literature—that identified such diverse figures as the philosopher Pythagoras and the Orphic cult leader Orpheus with shepherds. The pose of the youth carrying an animal on his shoulders appeared in Archaic Greek sculpture as early as the sixth century B.C. (Figure 6.12). The painter of the good shepherd fresco portrays the shepherd as a beardless youth without distinctive, godlike traits. A statue of a shepherd from the second century attests to the widespread use of this image (Figure 6.13). By such representations as these, the artists in effect declared the limits of their art in penetrating behind the mystery of Jesus as both God and man.

A relief panel sculpted on the marble sarcophagus of Baebia Hertofila, dating from the third century, also expresses a disguised Christian message (Figure 6.14). The panel portrays a communion meal, symbolized by the round loaves of bread below the table and in the basket. The seven figures are partaking of a Christian meal instead of a Roman funeral feast, although the rowdiness of the scene does not suggest a Christian rite. The figures' crude features, especially the open-mouthed man on the right, demonstrate the sculptor's feeble technique. Yet the emotional impact of this simplified cartoon is quite effective.

The Legacy of Biblical Judaism and Early Christianity

The entire Jewish tradition has evolved from the early history of the Hebrews—their wandering without a homeland, their role as outsiders in other cultures, their brief period in control of the promised land of Canaan, and, above all, their deep and abiding sense of being the chosen people of the almighty God, Yahweh. Under the Romans, the Jews were punished for their religious views, a portent of the anti-Semitism and violent attacks that have dogged their existence down through the twentieth century. Despite adversity, the Jews have survived and today have the longest continuous history of any group of people in Western civilization.

Unlike the Greco-Roman deities, who were seen as encouraging and supporting human achievement and excellence in many areas of life, the God of the Hebrews was primarily concerned with the ethical conduct of human beings and their obedience to his laws. Yahweh's jealousy extended to all forms of human expression insofar as they detracted from his worship. As a consequence, the arts and humanities, when allowed in Judaism, tended to be subordinated to religious concerns. Ultimately, Jewish culture found its voice in the ideals of the Bible, among the highest moral standards of any ancient people. The Jewish ethical vision, which still drives Western reformers and revolutionaries today, demanded social justice for every person, no matter how poor or powerless, within the human community.

Inheriting this conception of God and culture, the Christians reinterpreted it and gave it their distinctive stamp. After the fall of Rome, when Christianity emerged as the religion of the West, the Judeo-Christian tradition merged with the Greco-Roman heritage to form the basis of Western civilization. Following the teaching of Jesus, the early Christians perpetuated the Jewish emphasis on God's unity and omnipotence as well as the demands for stringently ethical behavior. Accordingly, Jesus' golden rule—to treat others as one would like to be treated—became the goal of devout Christians. The first Christians also laid great emphasis on taking care of the sick, the impoverished, and the homeless—a tradition that has given rise in Western civilization to a wide variety of private and public social relief programs.

The early Christians, rejecting the relatively closed nature of Judaism, turned their religion into a missionary faith; in the first generation of missionaries, Paul and other church leaders took Jesus' message to all people, addressing them as individuals regardless of their racial and ethnic backgrounds. Today, after two thousand years, nearly one-third of the world's population subscribes—at least nominally—to Christian beliefs.

Under the early Roman Empire, Christian thought also became a transnational, or international, belief system that expressed uncompromising hostility to Greco-Roman culture and to the Roman state. Those Christian writers who, like the author of the Book of Revelation, described Rome as "the great whore" and forecast that city's destruction simply expressed the collective yearnings of the faithful in the early church. Under the onslaught of the Roman persecutions, the Christians anticipated a new order ruled by God's values. Thus, early Christians adopted Greco-Roman ideas not for their own sake but only for their usefulness to the Christian religion.

The hostility of the early church to humanism and secular thought was but the opening assault in a running battle between two ways of looking at the world. For the moment, in imperial Rome humanism was triumphant among the people who counted—the aristocrats, the intellectuals, and the ruling class. But by the end of the fourth century the balance had swung over in favor of Christianity, and the non-Christian intellectuals were rapidly disappearing. This state of affairs prevailed until the Italian Renaissance; then, artists, writers, and intellectuals challenged the reigning Christian world view by reviving humanistic learning and the Greco-Roman past. As the modern world has taken shape, Christianity has found itself assaulted from many sides and has never regained the preeminence that it held from the time of the fall of Rome to the coming of the Renaissance.

KEY CULTURAL TERMS

covenant	*canon*
Diaspora	*Gospels*
eschatology	*evangelists*
apocalypse	*theology*
Messiah	*liturgy*
scripture	*sarcophagus*

SUGGESTIONS FOR FURTHER READING

PRIMARY SOURCES

EUSEBIUS. *The History of the Church from Christ to Constantine.* Translated by G. A. Williamson. New York: Penguin, 1965. Though a partisan account written by a credulous observer, this work is the major source of early Christian history.

JOSEPHUS. *The Jewish War.* Translated by G. A. Williamson. New York: Penguin, 1974. Josephus, a Jew who served Rome, wrote one of the few surviving accounts of this period.

Holy Bible, New Testament, Old Testament. There are many translations of these sacred books, ranging from the King James version of the early seventeenth century to various twentieth-century translations based on recent scholarship. The Douay edition is the official Bible of the Roman Catholic church.

7

LATE ROMAN
CIVILIZATION

What were the forces that brought the Roman Empire to an end? This chapter focuses on Rome's final era, from 284 to 476, when political, social, and economic crises seemed increasingly beyond human control and spiritual and cultural changes indicated growing disillusionment with the old Roman ways. The chapter suggests some causes for Rome's fall after more than twelve hundred years, during the last seven hundred of which it dominated the Mediterranean basin. Since the fate of Rome was inextricably tied up with the development of Christianity, the chapter also traces the growth of the church and offers reasons for its triumph (Figure 7.1). From the interweaving of Christianity and Classical humanism—the legacy of Greece and Rome—a new Western cultural ideal emerged.

THE LAST DAYS OF
THE ROMAN EMPIRE

When the Roman general Diocletian [die-uh-KLEE-shun] seized power as emperor in 284, the empire appeared to be ungovernable. Twenty-seven rulers had preceded Diocletian in the previous fifty years, and most of them were killed by the army, either at the hands of rival factions or by their own troops. The office of emperor now depended on the army's approval, for the autocratic imperial regime had successfully stifled all other forms of political life.

Although Diocletian faced other dangers as great as having to pacify a fickle army, Rome's military problems seemed to touch on and to intensify most of the problems that were threatening to bring down the state. Throughout the third century, more and more soldiers were required to police the frontiers to turn back the Germanic invaders in the north and the Persians in the east. Military pay for these larger armies drained the imperial treasury, which was caught between increasing inflation and a declining economy. Unpaid and ill-equipped troops forced civilians to supply them with food and goods that the state could no longer provide. Population in the urban areas fell as thousands fled into the countryside to avoid military duty and burdensome taxes. Of those who remained in the towns and cities, most still clamored for the amenities of Roman life, including bread and circuses. They seemed oblivious that their demands, when they were able to be met, were a drain on precious state resources.

That segment of the populace finding hope and consolation in the Christian religion presented yet another problem to Rome: Christian converts often refused to enroll in the military on the grounds that killing someone in battle was murder, an act forbidden by the Fifth Commandment. With the pool of young men available for the army reduced, the government recruited soldiers from among barbarians who had been allowed to remain inside Roman territory—a course of action that further weakened the loyalty of the military.

◀ Church of Sta. Costanza. Fourth Century. Rome.

FIGURE 7.1 *Young Christ. Third Century. Museo delle Terme, Rome. Early Christian art focused on biblical scenes and especially images of Jesus Christ. Lacking a clearcut tradition for portraying Jesus, church leaders simply borrowed from Classical art, making its tradition their own, as in this portrait of a young Christ. Like the gods on the Parthenon's frieze (see Figure 3.24), Christ is portrayed as a beardless youth, dressed in a Greek garment and seated in repose, his left foot resting against a chair leg. The image of Christ as a beardless youth persisted in the church until the fall of Rome, when it was supplanted by the image of an older, bearded man.*

Faced with this situation, Diocletian began a series of reforms that virtually refounded the Roman state and gave the empire a new lease on life. The almost two-hundred–year period of late Roman civilization may be divided into two phases: (1) Diocletian's reforms and the triumph of Christianity, lasting from 284 until 395 and (2) Christian Rome and the end of the empire in the West, extending from 395 until 476 (Time Line 7.1). In these years, basic social and cultural changes were set in motion that became integral to European civilization for centuries to come.

Diocletian's Reforms and the Triumph of Christianity, 284–395

Diocletian (284–305) stands as the creator of late Rome just as Augustus does of the early empire. Unlike Augustus, however, Diocletian insisted on divine status, building on the sun god cult that dated from the Severan dynasty (193–235). Isolating himself behind walls of curtains when with his subjects and bestowing grand titles on his representatives, he inflated the image of emperor to enhance the political power of the office.

Diocletian ruled as a god, but when he turned to the problems facing Rome, he showed that he had the soul of a bureaucrat. Possessed of an iron will, he inaugurated reforms that reined in the rebellious army, contained barbarian incursions, restored calm to Rome, restructured the empire, and returned modest prosperity to the economy for most of the fourth century. His efforts to restructure the governing apparatus met with mixed success. His greatest triumph was in dividing the empire into two separate areas. In the West, Rome still served as the cer-

TIME LINE 7.1   LATE ROME, 284–476

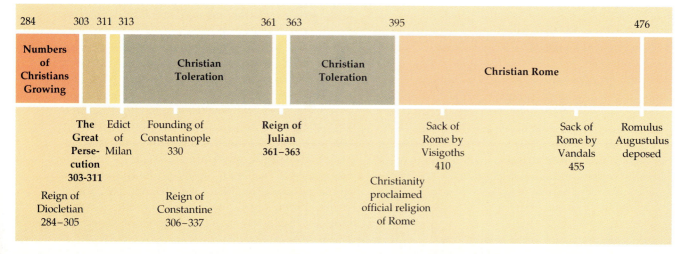

284	303	311	313		361	363		395		476
Numbers of Christians Growing			**Christian Toleration**		**Christian Toleration**			**Christian Rome**		
	The Great Persecution 303-311	**Edict of Milan**	Founding of Constantinople 330		**Reign of Julian 361–363**			Sack of Rome by Visigoths 410	Sack of Rome by Vandals 455	Romulus Augustulus deposed
							Christianity proclaimed official religion of Rome			
Reign of Diocletian 284–305			Reign of Constantine 306–337							

MAP 7.1

The Roman Empire in the Fourth Century

Prefecture of Gaul

Prefecture of Italy

Prefecture of Illyricum

Prefecture of the East

Line of division between East and West

emonial capital, though the actual capital depended on the emperor's movements. For example, Ravenna, on the Italian Adriatic coast, became the imperial residence for several decades. The Eastern Empire was centered first in Nicomedia in Asia Minor, but the capital was later shifted to Byzantium (now Istanbul, Turkey) and renamed Constantinople by Diocletian's successor, Constantine (Map 7.1).

Diocletian's plan for administering the vast empire under a tetrarchy, or a rule by four, proved unworkable, however. His reform called for each half of the empire to be governed by two tetrarchs, an Augustus supported by a Caesar, but the civil war that often broke out among rival tetrarchs only made an already confused situation worse (Figure 7.2).

FIGURE 7.2 *Diocletian's Tetrarchy. Ca. 300. Height, ca. 51".* St. Mark's Cathedral, Venice. *In this group portrait of the tetrarchs, the four rulers—two Augusti, or leaders, joined by their two Caesars, or successors—stand clasping shoulders to signify their unity and loyalty. By this time, the political leaders were no longer wearing imperial togas, as can be seen in the figures' cloaks, tunics, and hats, but the eagle-headed swords and decorated scabbards show that fine workmanship in armor was still practiced in late Rome. Despite the solidarity suggested by the sculpture, the tetrarchy was not a successful reform of the imperial administration.*

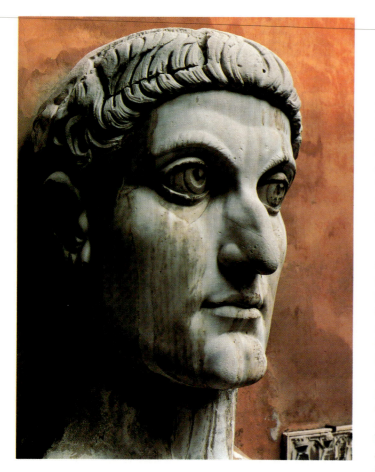

FIGURE 7.3 Colossal Statue of Constantine. Ca. 313. Marble, height, 8'. Palazzo dei Conservatori, Rome. *Like Diocletian, Constantine consciously nurtured the image of the emperor as a larger-than-life figure. To enhance this image, he commissioned a huge statue of himself, perhaps ten times life size, to stand in the gigantic basilica (which he had also built) in the Roman forum. All that remains of the statue today are the head, which measures over 8 feet tall, a hand, and some pieces of the limbs. The monument signaled the climax of the emperor cult and the beginning of its decline. With the spread of Christianity, rulers were no longer viewed as gods.*

A third reform of Diocletian's—grouping the provinces into dioceses—achieved his goal of making the state more centralized and hierarchical. But a side effect of this step was reduced efficiency since the empire became more bureaucratized as officials multiplied at all levels.

In addition, Diocletian could never hold in check the catastrophic inflation. He tried to freeze wages and prices, a policy that failed from the start. Moreover, the old tax system simply could not pay the costs of supporting the enlarged army and an expanded state bureaucracy. His plan for filling the empty treasury was to chain citizens to their private occupations and public offices, forcing social immobility on sons who inherited their fathers' tax burdens as well as their careers. This new tax code sped the process by which rural laborers attached themselves to landed estates and caused the final disappearance of the small independent farmer—the class that had made republican Rome great. Diocletian also recognized that money had virtually passed out of circulation, and his tax reforms moved the economy along toward barter, or exchange of goods. Thus, citizens now paid taxes in meat, leather, or wool; in bricks or building stone; in labor; or in army recruits.

The Great Persecution and Christian Toleration   One area of Roman life remained untouched by Diocletian for most of his reign: the problem posed to a polytheistic state by the growing number of monotheistic Christian citizens. But in 303, for reasons that are not quite clear, he began what the Christians called the Great Persecution. For eight years—though Diocletian himself retired in 305—the imperial policy was to stamp out Christianity. In a series of six edicts the emperors forbade Christians to worship and ordered their churches and books destroyed and their bishops arrested. Christian leaders and suspected church members were forced to sacrifice to the ruler under penalty of death. Roman cities were ordered to rebuild pagan temples and to impose a religious test on all citizens. Then in 311 the assault was called off as suddenly as it had begun. How many Christians perished in the Great Persecution cannot be reliably determined, and certain areas, such as Britain and Gaul, were untouched. Whatever the number, the government's policy failed in its purpose, for the killings strengthened rather than weakened the church, and the courage of Christian martyrs won many new converts.

The Great Persecution had barely ceased when the Christians gained a stunning victory. In 313 toleration was restored to Christians by the Edict of Milan, also known as the Peace of the Church, at the order of the emperor Constantine (Figure 7.3). His reason for this action has been a source of wide speculation—was he a genuinely devout convert to Christianity, as has been claimed, or a politically acute opportunist who foresaw how powerful Christians would become, or perhaps a mixture of both? Regardless of his motives, the Christian community welcomed this opportunity to advance their interests in the state. Priests joined soldiers in army units, and bishops attended the imperial court. Constantine undertook a campaign throughout the empire to expand the restored faith, returning confiscated property to the church, building new churches, and giving tax exemptions to bishops.

The greatest indication of Christianity's new power was that Constantine, who after 324 ruled in both the East and the West, built his eastern capital, Constantinople, as a fully Christian city. Dedicated in 330 on the site of ancient Byzantium, Constantinople was endowed with churches and other religious monuments along with a Senate house and mansions for its senators. These magnificent buildings were surrounded on three sides—the fourth side overlooked the water—by thick walls that turned the city into an almost impregnable fortress. But Constantine's new capital was more than a Christian city; the choice of its site showed Constantine's recognition of the superior vitality and wealth of the East when compared with the Western empire.

The successors to Constantine, all of them Christians except Julian, supported the spread of the church. By 395 most of the population was nominally Christian, including senators and other aristocrats. Christianity adapted to Rome's values, promising victory to Roman armies and a bountiful life to believers. But more importantly, the Christian religion attracted followers who responded to its ideal of charity and its belief in the spiritual worth of the poor.

Early Christian Controversies   As Christians became a majority within the empire, their success generated problems stemming from the deep divisions within the faith. Unlike other cults, Christianity developed a creed, or set of authorized doctrines, which church leaders imposed on believers. Those who differed from the creed were excommunicated as heretics. Moreover, since the emperors were now Christians, the state became entangled in the new religion's problems. Distressed by church squabbles, Constantine tried to end a major controversy over the relationship of Jesus to God. The followers of the priest Arius [uh-RYE-uhs] (about 250–about 336) maintained that Jesus' nature was similar to the divine, a belief that came to be known as Arianism. Those who supported deacon, later bishop, Athanasius [ath-uh-NAY-zhus] (about 296–373) believed that the natures of Jesus and God were identical. Although non-Christians found the quarrel over "similar" and "identical" natures ridiculous, fundamental issues were at stake, such as whether Jesus was eternal and whether God had made the ultimate sacrifice for humanity. To bring about harmony among the competing factions, Constantine, in 325, called a church council at Nicaea in Asia Minor. Under his guidance, the council issued the Nicene Creed, which proclaimed in favor of Athanasius.

Arianism, though condemned, divided the church for decades and remained strong in the church's ruling hierarchy. Arianism also triggered a crisis among new believers because most of the Germanic tribes who were moving into the empire became Christians through the efforts of Ulfilas [UHL-fuh-las], a fellow barbarian and an Arian bishop. Ulfilas's converts were treated as enemies of the true faith, for orthodox Christians, ever intolerant, recognized no difference between pagans and Christian heretics.

Despite these difficulties, Christianity continued to gain converts and grow in prestige. At the same time, an ascetic Christian movement was sweeping across the empire. Inspired by the sterner ideas of Jesus and Paul, this asceticism had two forms, both of which first arose in Roman Egypt during the early fourth century. Both groups of ascetics believed that the world was evil and must be shunned, but they differed over the best way to achieve salvation. Pachomius [puh-KOH-me-uhs] founded an isolated community in which a band of followers pursued perfection through a life of self-denial and moral rigor. His contemporary Antony chose the life of a hermit, seeking union with God through his individual efforts. The harsh messages of both Pachomius and Antony aroused favorable responses among the Romans, but ultimately the community style rather than the solitary style became the dominant form of Christian asceticism, evolving into monasticism in succeeding decades.

The end of paganism came with the reign of the emperor Theodosius I [the-uh-DOH-she-uhs], called the Great (379–395). The emperor and the law courts now ignored the rights of non-Christians and enforced Christian conformity. After Theodosius, little remained to complete the Christian triumph. In 407 the destruction of non-Christian images and temples was ordered, thus placing paganism outside the law and making Christianity the state religion. Although paganism was eradicated in the urban areas, it survived in the countryside, kept alive by oral traditions, protected by an engrained conservatism, and hidden behind a Christian veneer.

Christian Rome and the End of the Western Empire, 395–476

Despite the success of Diocletian's reforms, Rome faced basic problems that ultimately proved insoluble: the progressive barbarization of the army, the growing bureaucratization of the state, and a constantly shrinking tax base. When fresh waves of Germans began to sweep through the Western Empire in the fifth century, the Roman rulers were without plans for assimilating the intruders. The Visigoths menaced Rome in 410, demanding tribute. When the Senate refused, Rome was sacked for the first time since 390 B.C., and a chagrined Senate paid a hefty ransom to the barbarians. This Germanic tribe moved on to France and eventually settled in Spain to found a kingdom.

While Visigoths attacked Rome, Saxons, Angles, and Jutes invaded Britain and ended that island's ties to the empire. Vandals raged through France and Spain, finally creating a North African kingdom in 442. From there they managed to launch an attack on Rome and sacked the city in 455. Burgundians settled in France in the middle Rhone Valley after 430. Elsewhere, minor tribes exploited Roman weakness.

Western society radically changed. Town life had all but disappeared earlier, leaving only noisy metropolises and the silent countryside. After the barbarians seized so much land and further disrupted the economy and tax structure, city life, even with its public dole and entertainments, became as untenable as life in the towns. Powerful landowners assumed many of the functions of local government officials, while their isolated and relatively secure estates attracted desperate city people fleeing to these rural refuges. The beginning of the economic and social institutions of the Middle Ages may be seen in these developments.

The Roman Senate and the church responded to the disintegrating conditions in quite different ways. The Senate had long ago ceased to be a factor in imperial affairs, and, when, in the fourth century, Ravenna became the working capital of the Western Empire and the home of the official bureaucracy, it was reduced to the status of a ceremonial body. Yet the senators could still collect rents on their estates, doubling the fees where possible. The church's response was more praiseworthy than the Senate's. Some church leaders used the crisis to stamp out troublesome heresies, but, more positively, others offered shelter for the homeless, food for the hungry, and comfort to the grieving.

The end of the empire in the West came swiftly when Odoacer [oh-doh-AH-suhr], the leader of a troop of Germans, defeated a Roman army in 476 and sent the young ruler, Romulus Augustulus, into exile. Instead of taking the imperial title, as was usual in such an event, Odoacer dispatched the symbols of office to the Eastern emperor in Constantinople, thereby signaling that centralized rule had ended in the West. Like other Germanic leaders in the western states, Odoacer prepared to rule not as a Roman emperor but as a barbarian king in northern Italy. The empire in the West was in ruins, leaving barbarian kingdoms in its place.

THE TRANSITION FROM CLASSICAL HUMANISM TO CHRISTIAN CIVILIZATION

Between 284 and 476 Roman civilization moved through two stages, both of which bristled with bitter pagan and Christian tensions. The first phase, which coincided with Diocletian's reforms, was paganism's last flowering, and the second phase, which began when the empire started to break apart after Constantine's reign, was a dynamic Christian age.

Literature, Theology, and History

During Rome's last two centuries, secular writers and Christian writers competed for the hearts and minds of educated Romans through poems, treatises, letters, and essays. The secular authors, who felt threatened by Christian activity and thought, preserved Classical forms and values in their writings. They turned to the humanistic tradition for inspiration and guidance because they believed that their morals and culture were undergirded by Rome's old religion and the farmer-soldier values. Nonetheless, these writers' views of the past were distorted by their romantic imaginations into nostalgia for a Rome that either was no more or had never been (Figure 7.4).

Secular literature in the late empire paled in comparison to that of earlier periods. Secular writers never experimented with new styles or attempted to modify established forms. No one wrote plays, novels, or epics. As a group the secular Roman authors reflected a growing sense of a lost age, convinced as they were that a civilized life was possible by studying and venerating the past. With the exception of a few poets, they never seemed able to define or to analyze the profound changes occurring in their own lifetime.

The other group of writers, the Christians, looked to the future and a new world to come. They were convinced that Rome was not only dying but was not worth saving. After Constantine decreed toleration for Christians in 313, these authors moved into the mainstream and slowly began to overshadow their pagan rivals. The bitter differences of opinion between them and the pagans, which characterized the late fourth century, faded away in the early fifth century. By then Christian literature had triumphed, though it remained deeply indebted to Greco-Roman thought and letters.

FIGURE 7.4   The House of Amor and Psyche (Replacement Copy of Statuary). Fourth Century. Ostia, Italy. *The non-Christian elite of late Rome still revered their Classical past, as shown by this sculpture of Amor and Psyche, the famed lovers from Greek legend, found in the private residence of a wealthy Roman. The erotic pair stood in one of four elegantly decorated, intimate bedrooms, which were dimly lit by small windows and lined in white marble. The tale still caught the fancy of sophisticated Romans living in isolated splendor, perhaps reminding them of the glories of a former age.*

The Fathers of the Church   By about 300 Christian writers began to find a large, well-bred audience as their religion continued to win converts among the educated. Although they extolled the virtues and benefits of the new faith, they did not necessarily abandon Classical philosophy and literature; they believed that some of these writings conveyed God's veiled truth prior to the coming of Christ, and thus they combined Classical with biblical learning. No longer persecuted, these Christian writers lived either as interpreters of God's word or as bishops. Revered by later ages as the Fathers of the church, they set examples in their personal lives and public deeds. The three most famous church Fathers were Ambrose, Jerome, and Augustine. Due to their superior talents, resolute convictions, and commanding personalities, the Fathers were not only powerful figures within the church but often intervened in secular matters, instructing the local authorities and even the emperors. Moreover, their writings laid the foundation of medieval Christian doctrine and philosophy.

The first of these men, Ambrose (about 340–397), devoted his life to affairs of the church (Figure 7.5). Born into a well-established Christian family (his sister was a nun), he was trained in the Greco-Roman classics, from which he drew material for sermons, tracts, and letters. Ambrose vigorously opposed the Arian heresy, and as Bishop of Milan he aided the urban poor and the victims of barbarian assaults. In scholarly sermons, he took the emperors to task, condemning them for the social injustices of their reigns. His letters shed light on problems of church government, and his treatises analyzed controversies dividing the church. Ambrose's hymns, perhaps his most memorable contribution, introduced to the Western church another way for Christians to praise their God and enrich their ceremonies.

FIGURE 7.5 *Ambrose. Ca. 470. Church of Sant'Ambrogio, Chapel of San Vittore in Ciel d'Oro, Milan. This portrait of Ambrose conveys some of the spiritual intensity of the powerful fourth-century Bishop of Milan. The work is one of few mosaics that survived the destruction brought by the barbarian assaults in northern Italy. Although the artist shows some feeling for the shape and movement of the body, the mosaic strongly reflects the artistic ideals developing in the eastern provinces: frontality, flatness, enlarged eyes, and stylized pose.*

The second major church Father, Jerome (about 340–420), wrote extensively on religious issues, but his most enduring work was his translation of the Bible into Latin from Greek and Hebrew sources. The Vulgate (from *vulgus*, common people), as his version is called, was composed in the common speech of his day; the mark of his Bible's success is that, with some revisions, it remains the standard of the Roman Catholic church today. Like Ambrose, Jerome received a Classical education. Later, after settling in Bethlehem, he founded a monastery, where he devoted most of his days to his translations of the scriptures. His reclusive habits and his harshly critical opinions of Roman society made him an unattractive figure to his enemies. Yet, like the other Fathers, Jerome's ascetic life inspired both his own generation and later Christians to emulate his strict denial of personal pleasure.

Of all the Fathers, Augustine (354–430) exercised the greatest influence on Christianity. In his youth in North Africa he studied Classical literature and thought, including Neo-Platonism (see Chapters 5 and 6). Augustine then journeyed, via Rome, to Milan, where he met Ambrose, whose persuasive sermons assisted in his conversion. Augustine, convinced of Christianity's intellectual integrity and spiritual vitality, retired to North Africa and dedicated himself to the spread of his new faith. However, his winning personality and administrative skills soon propelled him into church politics.

Augustine's confrontational nature led him to join in the debates raging in the church. During his lifetime his writing came to represent the voice of orthodox beliefs. He opposed the Donatists, who claimed that a priest's sin would make the sacraments useless. Augustine's position—that each sacrament worked in and of itself—became the church's official stand. But his greatest fury was against Pelagianism, which asserted that good works could earn salvation for a sinner. Augustine's argument—that salvation can be achieved only by God's grace—rested on his rejection of free will and his insistence on original sin. Once again, he spoke for orthodoxy.

During a long, active life, Augustine wrote many different kinds of religious works, but looming over them all are his two major achievements: his *Confessions* and *The City of God*. The *Confessions*, written at the end of the fourth century, trace his search for intellectual and spiritual solace and detail his dramatic conversion. In this spiritual autobiography he castigates himself for living a sinful, sensual life. Although he was remorseful and laden with guilt for not having found God sooner, he came to believe that his efforts to understand the world by studying Greco-Roman philosophy, literature, and religion affirmed his desire to search for life's ultimate truths.

His conversion occurred in a garden in Milan, where he heard a child's voice command him to read the scripture. Opening the Bible at random, he read from Paul, who directed him to arm himself with Jesus Christ as a way of combating the sins of the flesh. Upon reading this passage Augustine wrote: ''. . . the light of confidence flooded into my heart and all the darkness of doubt was dispelled.'' Now certain of his faith, he dedicated himself to his new mission, adopted an ascetic style of life, and, ultimately, accepted church leadership as the Bishop of Hippo, in North Africa. Augustine's convictions, so forcefully expressed, helped to raise the standards of Christian literature in the dying years of the Roman empire.

In contrast to the autobiographical *Confessions*, *The City of God* offered a theological interpretation of history. In this work Augustine addresses the central question confronting the Romans of that generation: Why was their empire subjected to so many catastrophes? He wrote the book soon after the Visigoths sacked Rome in 410, a calamity that dramatized the decline of the empire. To those who blamed the Christians, he replied that the decline of Rome was part of God's plan to prepare the world for the coming of a divine kingdom on earth. If the city fell, it was best for the human race. Augustine expounded and reinforced this argument in the first ten books of *The City of God* as he attacked Greco-Roman philosophies and religions.

In the concluding twelve books of the work he elaborated his view of world history, which relied on the Hebrew experience and Christian sources. At the heart of his argument lay what he called the two cities in history, the City of God and the City of Man. The inhabitants of the City of God were predestined to be saved, but the citizens of the City of Man were condemned to hell. Augustine predicted that the future would eventually expose the nature of the two cities: The City of Man would be destroyed, but the City of God—composed of Christians on their way to heaven—would last forever. In the City of God, the saved would enjoy an eternal happiness that paganism had promised but could not deliver.

Augustine completed *The City of God* shortly before his death and as the barbarians were approaching his own city of Hippo. When Augustine's view of history seemed to be validated by the fall of Rome, his fame began to mount. For many centuries he was venerated by Christians as the supreme authority on nearly every major theological issue.

Church History   In addition to theology, early Christian writing included a new literary genre—church history. Eusebius [you-SEE-be-uhs] (about 260–about 340), Bishop of Caesarea in Palestine from 314 until his death, made no claims to impartiality in his *History of the Christian Church*. This history of the church from the earliest times until 324 makes the bishops the heroes, for Eusebius believed that they ensured the truth of Christianity. He also charted the church's spiritual, intellectual, and institutional life in its martyrs, thinkers, and leaders. While he is generally reliable in his discussions, modern scholars fault him for siding with the faction that was working to make the Bishop of Rome the head of the church in the West.

Written in Greek, Eusebius's history was inspired by the secular Greco-Roman historians, and he followed them in quoting from written sources. He consulted both the Old and New Testaments, Christian scholars, and the Greek classics, including Homer and Plato. Eusebius's historical account of the early church gained authority from his background. Having been jailed twice and having survived the Great Persecution, his life appeared to prove God's power in the world. He also baptized Constantine and delivered the opening oration at the Council of Nicaea.

The Visual Arts

In late Rome secular and Christian art underwent major transformations. In terms of patronage, tastes shifted as the emperors' dictates were first challenged by the early Christian communities and then forced to bow to the triumphant church. In aesthetic terms, Classical forms and values yielded to a *symbolic realism* in imperial secular art and, later, to abstract spiritual values in Christian works. In geographic terms, church art and architecture in the Eastern Empire moved further away from Greco-Roman ideals, even though the artists and builders continued to modify Classical forms and subjects to fit their faith's themes and needs (Figure 7.6). A striking example of this trend is the art and architecture of Ravenna, the working capital of the Western Empire. Ravenna naturally had strong political ties with the East, and Ravenna's artistic monuments borrowed heavily from Eastern styles and schools.

FIGURE 7.6 *Christian Orpheus with Animals.* Fifth Century. Archaeological Museum, Istanbul. *This mosaic appears to have a secular theme: the mythological Greek figure Orpheus bringing harmony to the animal kingdom with the music he plays on his lyre. But Christians used Orpheus as a symbol of Christ, the Messiah, who brings universal peace and harmony. Because this mosaic was found in a small chapel in Jerusalem, it is identified as a work of Christian art.*

Architecture In the late third century, Diocletian revitalized architecture, following an unproductive period during the previous fifty years of political turmoil. As a part of his efforts to restore centralized rule, Diocletian used art, specifically architecture, as a sign of his new power. Constantine followed Diocletian's lead until the Edict of Milan in 313, after which he promoted Christian architecture and art. He then launched a building campaign of churches and shrines across the empire. Except for the brief reign of Julian (360–363), who renounced Christianity and tried to restore paganism, the later emperors patronized Christian forms and styles, and pagan tastes and schools faded away.

During the fifth century, the bishops began to vie with the emperors in erecting Christian centers of worship. The invisible forms of the underground church—rooms in private homes, isolated buildings, and converted pagan temples—were abandoned in favor of new standardized structures such as baptisteries and basilicas. Architects, craftspeople, and artists traveled throughout the empire, directing their energies into glorifying the new official religion.

As part of his imperial reforms, Diocletian built a palace on the Dalmatian coast (Croatia) where he spent the last twelve years of his life. Strategically located halfway between the Western and Eastern centers of power, his residence resembled a Roman camp in its orderly, mathematical layout (Figure 7.7). The palace serves as a fitting monument for this soldier who restored law and order to a world racked by civil war and weakened by incompetent rulers.

Visitors entered the palace by the main gate on the north side and walked along a path lined with columns across the central intersection and into the *peristyle*, or colonnaded courtyard (Figure 7.8). Those who traveled this far would be reminded of the emperor's presence by such architectural features as the long entranceway, the domed vestibule, and the grandiose courtyard. Beyond the vestibule, on the south side bordering the sea, were the imperial apartments, the guards' barracks, rooms for private audiences, and banquet halls. This residence incorporated nearly all of the major designs and techniques, including the arch and mortar mixtures, known to Roman builders. More important, its impressive splendor symbolized divine authority combined with secular political power.

Just as Diocletian's palace was one of the last pagan edifices, the Arch of Constantine was literally the last pagan triumphant arch (Figure 7.9). The arch was erected to celebrate the emperor's victory in 312 which led to the issuing of the Edict of Milan. This well-proportioned monument with its triple arches evolved from the Arch of Titus with its single open-

FIGURE 7.7 Floor Plan of Diocletian's Palace. Ca. 300. *The almost square enclosure of the palace, surrounded by four high walls and anchored by tall towers at each corner and at each side of the entrance gates, contained the living quarters of the emperor, his tomb, and a temple to Jupiter that is probably the last surviving pagan shrine. A thoroughfare running from the east to the west gate and intersecting the main north-south road in the center of the complex divided the fortress-palace into four sections.*

ing (see Figure 5.17). The circular *medallions* set between the detached columns on the side arches helped to balance the smaller left and right arches with the central arch. The decorated *attic*, or crown of the arch, with its statues of barbarians, blended in well with the lower sections. The Senate and the Roman people, according to the inscription, gratefully dedicated this arch to Constantine for his deeds as their liberator from civil war and as their new emperor.

Much of the decoration was borrowed from other monuments; for example, some of the reliefs and carvings came from works honoring the victories of Trajan, Hadrian, and Marcus Aurelius, and where a likeness of the emperor is intended, the original has been remodeled to resemble Constantine. In spite of Constantine's celebrated conversion to Christianity, however, the arch clearly reflected a strong pagan influence. The symbols and figures stress human action, and only one small frieze hints at divine intervention.

The shift from pagan to Christian architecture began after 313 under Constantine's inspiration and patronage. He ordered the building of churches as places of worship for congregations and as memorials

FIGURE 7.8 Diocletian's Palace. Ca. 300. Split, Croatia. *The peristyle, or colonnaded courtyard, screened off the buildings on the left and right, enhanced the enclosed atmosphere, and focused attention on the vestibule. Behind the peristyle, on the left, stood Diocletian's tomb (now a church) and, on the right, the Temple to Jupiter (now the Baptistery of St. John).*

N

Aisle

Aisle

Atrium

Nave

Aisle

Aisle

Transept

Apse

FIGURE 7.10 Floor Plan of Old St. Peter's Basilica. Ca. 330. Rome. *Old St. Peter's Basilica was the most important structure in Christian Europe until it was demolished in the early sixteenth century to make way for the present St. Peter's. Constantine dedicated Old St. Peter's on the spot believed to be the burial site of Peter, whom the church considered the successor to Jesus. Of the original basilica nothing remains, but sixteenth-century drawings show that it was cruciform in shape, had a wide central nave with two aisles on either side, and was fronted by an atrium where worshipers washed their hands and faces before entering the sanctuary.*

at holy spots in Rome, Palestine, and other parts of the empire. Financed and supported by the state, this ambitious enterprise resulted not only in the spread of Christianity but also in the founding of new artistic values and architectural forms. The basic design of the churches that Constantine had constructed was derived from the *basilica*, a large enclosed rectangular structure that dated back to the second century B.C. and by the early empire was often built to house marketplaces or public assembly halls.

Although basilicas varied in detail, the basic form used for churches was simple: an oblong hall with an *apse*, or curved wall, at the eastern end. Two rows of parallel columns usually divided the hall into a central area, or *nave*, and two side *aisles*. The roof was taller over the nave section, and *clerestory windows* were set high in the outside nave walls to let in light. The apse, where ceremonies were performed or where the holy relics were placed, was often screened off from the worshipers, who stood in the nave. In some structures there was an *atrium*, or open courtyard, in front of the main hall.

No fourth-century Roman basilica churches remain, but drawings, such as that of the floor plan of the basilica of Old St. Peter's, suggest their appearance (Figure 7.10). St. Peter's Basilica, built as a memorial to mark the grave of the apostle who, by tradition, founded the church in Rome, included a *transept*, or crossing section, that intersected the nave at the apse end of the building, making it *cruciform* (cross-shaped). This first St. Peter's Basilica served as a shrine for thousands of pilgrims and, in its early years, as a burial ground for Christians.

Constantine ordered the construction of many similar buildings around the empire. In the provincial outpost of Trier, an important administrative and commercial center on the Moselle River (in modern Germany), Constantine erected a complex of government buildings, including an imperial residence and a large basilica that was used as an assembly hall (Figure 7.11). Originally an atrium fronted the basilica, and the hall connected to other buildings. Its heavily emphasized vertical supports, two tiers of rounded windows, and large apse established certain basic features that were incorporated

◀ **FIGURE 7.9** Arch of Constantine. 312–315. Rome. *The frieze that winds around the monument narrates the emperor's preparations for war, his victory, and his triumphant entry into Rome. The scenes depicted on the Arch of Constantine, like those on Trajan's Column, memorialized the Roman ruler's presence at every stage of a military campaign.*

172

FIGURE 7.11 Constantine's Basilica in Trier. 310. Trier, Germany. *This basilica served first as an audience hall for Roman officials, then as a medieval castle, and today it is a Lutheran church. Although it is an impressive 220 feet long, 91 feet wide, and 100 feet high, its plan is simple: a narrow hall without aisles and an apse at the eastern end. Around the exterior of the apse, two stories of round arched windows give a graceful appearance by creating the impression of an arcade. That such a monumental basilica was erected so far from the Roman capital showed the impact of imperial art in the distant provinces.*

FIGURE 7.12 Sta. Maria Maggiore. 432–440. Rome. *This early church shows the way that builders adapted Greco-Roman forms. The Ionic columns and mosaics are Greek in origin, and the basilica is a Roman structure. In this way Christians not only satisfied their own religious needs but kept alive the Greco-Roman architectural tradition.*

FIGURE 7.13 Church of Sta. Costanza. Fourth Century. Rome. *The twelve pairs of columns were carved specifically for the rotunda, the circular area beneath the dome, rather than taken from other buildings, as was often the case in late Rome. The columns support the arches, above which are windows placed in the drum. The niches, or recessed openings, in the walls and the ceiling above the columns are decorated with mosaics with religious themes.*

into later churches, such as Sta. Maria Maggiore in Rome, built by a fifth-century pope (Figure 7.12). By this date not only had Christians taken over Classical learning as a tool for studying God's word, but they had also Christianized the pagan basilica.

A second important design in Christian architecture was the round or polygonal structure topped by a dome. One of the earliest circular buildings (according to tradition, erected by Constantine as a tomb for his daughter) still stands in Rome. Now known as the Church of Sta. Costanza, the round edifice is a drum with a covering dome (Figure 7.13). As these structures evolved, they came to serve primarily as *baptisteries*, that is, a place set aside for baptism. The baptistery was usually separated from the basilica because Christians believed that the unbaptized were unworthy to enter the sanctuary and mingle with the members. This design, whose origins go back to the domed rooms of public baths and to funerary architecture and whose most impressive realization was the Pantheon (see Figure 5.13), became standardized as an octagon with a domed roof (Figure 7.14).

Sculpture   During Diocletian's reign and before Christianity's conquest of the Roman arts, the late empire produced some unique and monumental works, such as the group portrait of Diocletian's tetrarchy, carved in red porphyry (see Figure 7.2) and the colossal statue of Constantine, a composite of marble and metal (see Figure 7.3). The generalized features of these figures show the trend to symbolic representation characteristic of the art of the late empire and the movement away from the idealized or realistic faces of Classical

FIGURE 7.14 Baptistery at Frèjus. Fifth Century. Frèjus, France. *The Baptistery at Frèjus is one of the earliest surviving examples of the octagonal building. The eight-sided structure has a central dome resting on a solidly constructed drum pierced with windows. At one time it was believed that this style was imported from the east, but now evidence indicates it originated in the west, probably in France.*

FIGURE 7.15 *The Last Pagan.* Ca. 380–400. Museo Ostiense, Ostia, Italy. *Evidently this Roman, clad in the toga of an earlier era, has academic interests since a set of bound books rests beside his right foot. The drapery is cut at severe angles, which increases the overall effect of this care-laden man. The statue is of Greek marble and stands just over 6 feet tall.*

sculpture. These public works are clearly forms of propaganda art. But Roman artists also continued to sculpt statues for private citizens, whose changing tastes were typified in a statue of a bedraggled scholar (Figure 7.15). Here the artist has fashioned a realistic work that delves into the psychology of his subject. The man's lined features, worried look, and weary slouch convey resignation and defeat. Symmachus, one of the last learned non-Christians, often visited Ostia, where this statue was found, and the sculptor may have been depicting this Roman intellectual.

In addition to free-standing sculptures, relief sculptures continued to be popular in late Roman art. In the Western Empire the best of these surviving reliefs are the original carvings on the Arch of Constantine. The carvings, coarse and yet stylized, reflect the impact of provincial art on Rome and signify a marked change in the long tradition of secular sculpture in the West. In one of the reliefs, Constantine and those around him are portrayed as distributing the fruits of the empire—a typical theme in Roman art (Figure 7.16). But the figures are depicted more as stereotypes than as real individuals.

Christian sculpture was undergoing aesthetic changes similar to those taking place in secular art. By the end of the third century, Christian art was symbolic in content and *impressionistic* in style (see Chapter 6). Simple representations of Jesus and the apostles had become common in the underground church. In 313, when the Peace of the Church brought Christian art literally above ground, artists began to receive the support of the Roman state.

Christian Rome's reshaping of the humanistic tradition can be seen in the carvings on sarcophagi. The Roman anxiety about life after death and the pursuit of intellectual matters easily evolved into Christian images and themes. The growing acceptance of inhumation, or burial, rather than cremation and the resultant increased demand for sarcophagi afforded many artists new opportunities to express themselves. After about the second century, rich Roman families commissioned artists to decorate the sides of these marble boxes with images of Classical heroes and heroines, gods and goddesses, military and political leaders, and scenes of famous events and battles. The Christians borrowed many of these subjects and transformed them into religious symbols pertaining to salvation and life after death. Thus, although the content of sarcophagus art became Christian after the Peace of the Church, the style remained Classical for some time.

Roman sarcophagi also depicted abstract concepts. For example, a carving of a seated philosopher, surrounded by attentive men and women, represents the life of the mind, its attention directed toward more important matters than earthly delights (Figure 7.17). The carvings, finely executed and well-balanced, capture this philosophical idea through superbly realized human characters. Meanwhile, biblical scenes, in particular those detailing the life and miracles of Jesus, began to appear on sarcophagi throughout the empire, illustrating the complex themes and messages of the new faith. One relief, probably from a Roman sarcophagus, weaves together events from the Old and New Testaments (Figure 7.18). On the left, Adam and Eve are expelled from the Garden of Eden; on the right Peter baptizes

FIGURE 7.16 *The Imperial Bounty*, from the Arch of Constantine. 312–315. Rome. *The style for this relief derived from Trier in Gaul. Unlike Classicism, this provincial style conveyed its message with cartoon-like directness. Constantine, enthroned in the center, divides the panel in two, as officials above dispense coins to the citizens below. Some of the crowd show their eagerness through their upturned heads and reaching hands.*

FIGURE 7.17 The Plotinus Sarcophagus. Late Third Century. Lateran Museum, Rome. *This relief may depict Plotinus, a founder of Neo-Platonism, and his admirers. If so, then the scene is ironic, for Neo-Platonist philosophy rejected realistic art, claiming that art should be viewed with the inner eye. This Neo-Platonist belief influenced Christian mysticism, which, in turn, helped to create the symbolic art of the Middle Ages, an art that used traditional images to express religious faith.*

FIGURE 7.18 Relief from Christ–Peter Sarcophagus. 320–330. Lateran Museum, Rome. *This panel, crowded with biblical scenes and figures, reflects the primacy of religious values in Christian art. Nonetheless, the anonymous artisan knew Roman sarcophagus art, as shown by the depiction of Jesus as Apollo (center) and the deep, stylized folds of the draped clothing.*

FIGURE 7.19 Illumination from Vergil's *Aeneid*. Fifth Century. Vatican Library, the Vatican. *This page from an illustrated manuscript of Vergil's* Aeneid *shows Dido, the Queen of Carthage (center), flanked by Aeneas (left), and a guest. The scene depicts the banquet, described at the end of Book I, that Dido gave in honor of the newly arrived Trojans. After the meal Aeneas recounted his escape from Troy and seven subsequent years of wandering. Faithful to the* Aeneid's *description, the painting represents Aeneas speaking to Dido while she appears to be calling for the attendant, in the lower right corner, to wash the hands of the diners. That such works were being commissioned in fifth-century Christian Rome showed that not everyone was partaking of the new religion and its symbols. After the fall of Rome, however, decorated manuscripts became a favorite form of art for Christians.*

two soldiers. A beardless Christ—the typical image of Jesus in ancient art—stands in the center. In this relief the emphasis on Christ and Peter conveys the theme of Christ's message and deeds being spread by his most trusted disciple. Although there is a striking resemblance between this relief and the relief from the Arch of Constantine (see Figure 7.16), the similarity is only in style and composition; the purpose and content of the two sculptures are quite different.

Painting and Mosaics Unlike architecture and sculpture, painting exhibited no changes directly caused by the Peace of the Church. In the fourth century, Christian frescoes flourished in the Roman catacombs and continued the symbolic, impressionist style of the previous era (see Chapter 6). Non-Christian paintings are extremely scarce from the fifth century, except for a few works such as a collection of illustrations for Vergil's *Aeneid*, probably painted for a wealthy patron. This extensive picture cycle (Figure 7.19), numbering over 225 scenes, recalls the style of earlier paintings, but it is also an early example of a new medium, the illustrated book. Books were now written on vellum, a parchment made from animal skins, and bound in pages rather than written on scrolls. In the Middle Ages, this type of decorated, or illuminated, book became a major art form. In the late empire, however, the form was in its infancy.

A more vital art form was the mosaic, which, as in other art forms, Christians ultimately turned to their own ends. Pagans continued to place mosaics on both floors and walls, but Christians more often put them on the walls. Christian artists also replaced the stone chips with bits of glass that reflected light, thus adding a glittering, ethereal quality to the basilicas and other buildings.

FIGURE 7.20 *Female Athletes.* Detail from Mosaic. 350–400. Villa at Piazza Armerina, Sicily. *This scene may show a female version of games that continued to be conducted in the Christian empire. The mosaic conveys a grace and lightheartedness somewhat at odds with this troubled age and with the changing artistic ideals of Christian art.*

In the late Roman mosaics, pagan and Christian subjects stand in sharp contrast. Among the many pagan mosaics that survive, one depicting young female athletes from a country villa in Sicily indicates the continued interest of the Romans in the body as the temple of the mind and as an object of admiration (Figure 7.20). The artist has captured the energy and playfulness of these (probably professional) performers in a variety of feats: dancing, running, and exercising. Their movements are realistic, graceful, and strikingly modern. In contrast to these worldly women, the mosaic of the church father Ambrose emphasizes his spiritual, other-worldly qualities (see Figure 7.5). Where their movements are fluid, his pose is static, and where their bodies are celebrated, the shape of his body is completely concealed under his clothing, in accordance with the church teaching that the body is sinful and should be hidden from view.

Mosaics became one of the dominant art forms in the Eastern Empire and those areas influenced by the Eastern rulers beginning late in the fifth century. In Ravenna, the small cruciform tomb of Galla Placidia [GALL-uh pluh-SID-e-uh], daughter of Theodosius the Great, contained some splendid mosaics that prefigured the Byzantine style of the next century. In succeeding centuries the Byzantine style dominated Christian art in the Eastern Empire. In the mosaics in the tomb of Galla Placidia, scrolls of vines and leaves wind around the ceiling, large flowers, or rosettes, decorate other sections, and animals and saints adorn parts of the curved walls. Over the entranceway stands the youthful shepherd watching over his flock (Figure 7.21). By the fifth century the rich and the powerful, such as the relatives of Galla Placidia, now honored the Good Shepherd in their

sanctuaries as the giver of eternal life. The mosaics in the tomb of Galla Placidia clearly show the adaptation of Classical models to Christian purposes.

Music

The music of late Rome was in decline, but Christian music was just beginning to take shape. The Christians took the principles of Greco-Roman music and united them with the Jewish tradition of singing the psalms and the liturgy to make music an integral and dynamic part of their church rituals. In later times this Christian practice gave birth to a rich body of sacred music which included both singers and instrumentalists.

In late Rome, however, sacred music was limited to chanting and unaccompanied singing. The Antioch church, inspired by the singing in Jewish synagogues, developed a new musical genre, the hymn, a song of praise to God. From Antioch the practice of hymn singing spread to Constantinople and Milan and eventually was integrated into the Christian liturgy everywhere. A few hymns survive from the period before Constantine, but only a fragment of musical notation has come to light. As with other ancient music, how it actually sounded can only be a matter of speculation.

Ambrose, bishop of Milan, stands out among the earliest hymn writers as one of the founders of the Western sacred song. His hymns, which were written in Latin, coincided with a new era in the church; up until the fourth century the liturgy of the early church was in Greek. Ambrose's Latin hymns were probably meant to be sung antiphonally, that is, with lines sung alternately between a leader and chorus.

FIGURE 7.21 *The Good Shepherd.* Ca. 450. Mausoleum of Galla Placidia, Ravenna, Italy. *The young, beardless Christ, which was still the accepted image of the Christian savior in the fifth century, supports himself with the cross and feeds the sheep, the symbol of the church, with his right hand. Foliage and plants in the background tie in with similar decorations on the mausoleum's ceilings and walls. Upon entering the small tomb, worshipers would immediately be confronted with this large figure of Christ.*

WHY DID ROME FALL?

When the Western Empire collapsed in 476, many forces had been at work in undermining Rome since the end of the second century. During these three centuries the mounting pressures from the barbarians, the incompetence of the bureaucracy, the politically inert masses, the rampant inflation, the crushing and inequitable tax system, and, above all, the problems associated with a heterogeneous and uncontrollable army had together brought havoc on the state and society. Taking all of these difficulties into consideration, the wonder is that the empire was able to be propped up by Diocletian after 284 and to last as long as it did.

Nevertheless, all of the above forces, while playing an important role, were not as paramount a cause of Rome's decline and fall as was the change in the Roman constitution from a republic to an empire. This theory—which was first advanced by the French philosopher and historian Montesquieu in the eighteenth century—blamed Rome's fall on the moral consequences of the constitutional shift. According to Montesquieu, under the healthy republic, with its separation of political powers, the citizens actively decided their own future. But pressed down by a diseased empire, with power centered in one man in one city, the citizens became pawns of the ruling autocrat. Consequently, toward the end of the empire corruption engulfed all elements of society, from megalomaniacal emperors, to aristocrats wallowing in luxury, to the masses clamoring for handouts, to the aliens selling their votes for favors.

What effect did the triumph of Christianity have on the fall of Rome? This issue was first raised in the eighteenth century by English historian Edward Gibbon in his *Decline and Fall of the Roman Empire.* Gibbon's thesis was that the coming of Christianity was a major contributing factor in Rome's fall. Gibbon blamed the Christians for focusing on life in heaven rather than on earth and for sapping the military will of the Roman people. A careful review of Rome's last years reveals that Gibbon oversimplified events. Some Christians did avoid military service because of their pacifist ideas, and few Christians felt loyalty to the forms of pagan life. But by the time Christianity was firmly fixed as the official religion, in 395, the empire was already tottering on the brink of annihilation. Thus, there was very little that the Christians, or for that matter any other group, could do to prevent the fall of Rome.

The Legacy of Late Roman Civilization

Late Roman civilization, as we have described it, constituted the legacy of the ancient world to the next era, the Middle Ages. That legacy was neither the unadulterated humanism of Greece nor the Idea of Rome as formulated in the pre-Christian centuries. Rather, late Roman culture reflected a synthesis of Christian and Greco-Roman values achieved in a changing world. The intellectual voices of Christianity saw the wisdom of Greco-Roman thought as important for the support it lent to the spiritual values that were now considered primary. Late Roman art and architecture also reflected this synthesis of traditions.

Besides the amalgam of Christianity and humanism, the late Roman period also contributed much of the structure of everyday life to the medieval world. From late Rome came the sharp division of society into aristocratic landowners and dependent agricultural laborers, the emergence of the church in society as a state within the state, the rise of a barter economy, and the development of the military power of large-scale landed proprietors. In effect, the late Classical world was the womb from which would emerge the next incarnation of Western institutions as well as the Western humanities.

KEY CULTURAL TERMS

symbolic realism
peristyle
medallion
attic
basilica
apse
nave

aisles
clerestory windows
atrium
transept
cruciform
baptistery
impressionistic

SUGGESTIONS FOR FURTHER READING

PRIMARY SOURCES

ST. AUGUSTINE. *Confessions*. Translated by R. S. Pine-Coffin. New York: Penguin, 1966. One of the enduring books of Western literature; reveals the anguish and achievements of this influential thinker.

———. *The City of God*. Edited by D. Knowles. New York: Penguin, 1972. A monumental work that illustrates Augustine's blending of Classical and Christian thought.

STANIFORTH, M., Trans. *Early Christian Writings: The Apostolic Fathers*. New York: Penguin, 1968. Useful introduction to the issues and personalities of the early Christian church.

8

THE SUCCESSORS OF ROME

Byzantium, Islam, and the Early Medieval West

When Rome fell in 476, a power vacuum developed in the western Roman lands. Gradually, three new civilizations—Byzantium, Islam, and the Early Medieval West—emerged to compete for control of the Mediterranean basin. Although none succeeded in reviving Roman grandeur or uniting the Mediterranean world, these three contrasting civilizations developed religious and cultural values that today dominate half the globe.

Of the three, the Byzantine Empire (the former Eastern Roman Empire) seemed in 476 to have the greatest prospects for dominance and longevity, with its autocratic government, stable farm economy, Greek intellectual heritage, and what came to be called Orthodox Christianity. (The Eastern Empire is called "Byzantine" because Constantinople was founded on the site of the ancient Greek city of Byzantium.) In contrast, Islam did not appear until the seventh century, when it began a meteoric rise and quickly spread across the Mediterranean world. Building on Arabic roots and the new faith propounded by Muhammad, Islamic civilization borrowed freely from the Greco-Roman and Persian heritages to attain a brilliant culture superior in many respects to those of Byzantium and Western Europe.

At the same time, civilization in the West was all but eclipsed, its political and economic systems in disarray and its people huddled in wooden huts beside armed fortresses. In the midst of this chaos,

however, a new world was being born, built on Classical ruins, spurred by Germanic energies, and animated by the new Christian ethos. This chapter traces the development of these three varied civilizations (Map 8.1).

THE EASTERN ROMAN EMPIRE AND BYZANTINE CIVILIZATION, 476–1453

The end of centralized rule in Rome's western lands in 476 had little effect on the Eastern Roman Empire. Diocletian's division of the empire into two administrative halves in the third century had already set the eastern region on a different path. During its one-thousand–year existence, the empire took its Roman heritage and became an autocratic, static entity in a world of great upheaval and movement of populations. The changing boundaries of the Byzantine world tell the story of an empire under continual siege. Byzantium's borders reached their farthest western limits in the sixth century and then contracted more or less steadily for the next eight hundred years. The empire lost territory to the Arabs in the east and to the Bulgars and other groups in the west. Finally, no longer able to defend even the city of Constantinople itself, the empire fell to the Ottoman Turks in 1453.

Although Byzantium was buffeted by rapid and sometimes catastrophic upheavals, great wealth and economic resources gave the state the means to

◄ Scene from the *Khamsah* (Five Poems) of Amir-I Khusrau. 1485. Chester Beatty Library, Dublin.

MAP 8.1

The Byzantine, Carolingian, and Islamic Empires, ca. 814

survive. The rulers, like those of the late Western Empire, kept a tight rein on their subjects' economic affairs, a policy that ensured that state interests were placed above individual gains. A rich and varied urban life developed, centered especially in Constantinople, the empire's capital and preeminent city, made virtually impregnable by its fortresslike site (Figure 8.1).

Beyond Constantinople the countryside was dotted with walled towns and vast farming estates owned by aristocrats and tilled by *coloni*, or serfs. Agriculture remained Byzantium's basic source of wealth, with grains, fruits, livestock, and timber the chief crops. Wine made from fermented grapes in Cappadocia in Asia Minor was prized across the empire.

Even though the frontiers of the empire expanded and contracted over the centuries, its heartland in Greece and Asia Minor remained basically stable. Here, a relatively uniform culture evolved that differed markedly from late Rome and from the West. The Byzantine world gave up its pagan and Latin roots to become a Christian, Greek civilization. The Orthodox church, led by the patriarch of Constanti-

nople, emerged as a powerful force in society, but without the independence from secular rulers enjoyed by the Western church and the pope. Greek became the language of church, state, and scholarship in Byzantium, just as Latin served these functions in the West. But, like late Rome and unlike the West, Byzantium remained a state characterized by ethnic and racial diversity for most of its history; new peoples, such as the Serbs and the Bulgarians, helped to ensure this diversity as they were slowly assimilated into the Byzantine way of life.

History of the Byzantine Empire

The history of Byzantium reflects the fluctuating fortunes of the empire in relation to its hostile neighbors. In the first major period of Byzantine history, 476 to 641, the emperors, motivated by dreams of the Roman past and inspired by a sense of Christian mission (Time Line 8.1), made a valiant but ultimately futile effort to recover the lost western provinces.

The most memorable early emperor was Justinian (527–565), who conquered several of the Germanic

FIGURE 8.1 ISIDORE OF MILETUS AND ANTHEMIUS OF TRALLES. Hagia Sophia, Exterior. 532–537. Istanbul. *The Byzantine emperors transformed their capital into a glittering metropolis that easily outshone ravaged Rome. The most magnificent building in the city was Hagia Sophia ("Holy Wisdom"), originally built by Justinian as a church. The building's 101-foot-diameter makes it the largest domical structure in the world. Two half-domes at either end double the interior length to more than 200 feet. The beauty of Hagia Sophia made the domed church the ideal of Byzantine architecture.*

kingdoms that had sprung up in the former Western empire (Figure 8.2). He extended the borders of the empire to encompass Italy, southern Spain, and North Africa. Justinian's wars stretched the empire to its limit and exhausted the state treasury, leaving his successors unable to maintain the empire they inherited.

Between 641 and 867, the second period of Byzantine history, the empire was ill served by a series of weak rulers who lost all of the western lands that Justinian had recovered. The emperors were also

TIME LINE 8.1   **THE BYZANTINE EMPIRE**

476	641	867	1081	1261	1453
	Revival of Empire	Withdrawal and Renewal	The Golden Age	The Challenge from the West	The Paleologian Emperors	
The fall of Rome					The fall of Constantinople

FIGURE 8.2 *Justinian and His Courtiers. Sixth Century. Ravenna, Italy. This mosaic represents a contemporary portrait of Justinian with his courtiers, including the Patriarch of Constantinople, who is holding the bejeweled cross. The luxurious trappings of office—purple robes, jeweled crown, and golden scepter—were calculated to enhance the emperor's earthly dignity. The Byzantine Empire's union of church and state is symbolized by the juxtaposition of the soldiers on the emperor's right with the ecclesiastical officials on his left.*

forced to yield much of Asia Minor to their Arab foes, and in 687 a Bulgarian kingdom was carved out of Byzantine territory in the Balkans.

Byzantium now became more militarized as a way of fending off enemy assaults. In the provinces, generals were given vast military and civil powers, and they began to replace the aristocrats as landowners. In time a style of feudalism—vast estates protected by private armies—arose, similar to the feudal developments in the West. Despite the changes in the social fabric, however, important cultural developments occurred, including a major revision of the law code and the establishment of a second university in Constantinople.

With the reign of Basil I (867–886), a new dynasty of capable rulers—called Macedonian because of their geographic origins—led Byzantium into its golden age (867–1081), the third major period in Byzantine history. Once again expanding the borders of the empire, these rulers restored the state to economic health as taxes from newly conquered, prosperous subjects filled the treasuries. The Bulgarian state, whose populace had earlier been converted to Orthodox Christianity, became a part of the empire. Orthodox missionaries, working among other Slavic tribes like the Serbs, eventually tied the peo-

ples of eastern Europe to the religion and civilization of Byzantium, and in the late tenth century Byzantine missionaries introduced Christianity to Russia. As a result, medieval Russia became a spiritual and cultural client of Byzantium; after the fall of Constantinople, the Russian state claimed to be the principal heir to Byzantine civilization.

In 1081 an extraordinarily able feudal general, Alexios Comnenus [kahm-NEE-nuhs] (1081–1118), seized the throne and launched a new phase in Byzantine history, a period characterized by increasing pressure from the West (1081–1261). Despite the energy of the new dynasty, the empire was living on borrowed time, and Comnenus and his successors were unable to solve the social problems that now plagued the state. Under this dynasty, Byzantium became fully militarized and feudalized. The free peasantry disappeared, having been transformed into a vast population of serfs forced to labor on the landlords' estates.

The Comneni rulers, surrounded by enemies—Normans, Seljuk Turks, Hungarians, Serbs, Bulgars, and, after 1095, the European Crusaders who made Constantinople their first destination on their way to the Holy Land—tried to win allies, but in vain. In 1204 the soldiers of the Fourth Crusade conquered

Constantinople and parceled out the remaining lands among themselves. The empire appeared to be finished except for scattered holdings in Asia Minor. But, in 1261, Michael Paleologus [pay-lee-AHL-uh-guhs] (1261–1282), the ruler of one of these states, regained Constantinople and breathed some new life into the feeble empire. His dynasty ruled over the Byzantine world during the fifth and last phase of its history (1261–1453).

Michael Paleologus extended his power into the Greek peninsula and stabilized relations with the Bulgars and Serbs in the Balkans. Although Michael's successors continued to search for ways to strengthen the empire, they were forced to recognize that the empire was little but a diminished and ramshackle Greek state. From 1302 onward the Ottoman Turks—named for their leader Osman—built an empire on the ruins of the Byzantine empire. By 1330 this new state had absorbed Asia Minor, and by 1390 Serbia and Bulgaria were Turkish provinces. In 1453, when the Turks finally took Constantinople, they ravaged the city for three days, searching for booty and destroying priceless art treasures. Thus ended the last living vestige of ancient Rome. From the ashes of Byzantium rose the Ottoman Empire, which anchored the southeastern corner of Europe for nearly five hundred years until 1912, when revolutions and wars destroyed it.

Byzantine Culture: Christianity and Classicism

Byzantium inherited from Rome a legacy of unresolved conflict between Christian and Classical ideals that, in the wider Byzantine culture, revealed itself in the division between secular and religious forms of expression. The secular forms sometimes showed a playful or humorous side of Byzantine life,

whereas the religious forms were always deeply serious. However, Byzantine culture, whether secular or religious, tended to follow Classical values by stressing serenity, dignity, and restraint. This timeless and even majestic quality was cultivated, perhaps, in compensation for the beleaguered nature of the Byzantine state.

The Orthodox Religion   At the same time that the bishop of Rome was becoming the head of the Christian church in the West, the bishop of Constantinople was rising to power over the Eastern (Orthodox) church in Byzantium. As patriarch (the title taken by eastern bishops) he functioned as the Orthodox faith's spiritual and doctrinal head. Many differences existed between the two Christian churches. Besides disagreeing over whether the pope or a patriarch should lead the church, they differed in language (Latin in the West, Greek in the East), religious practices (Roman priests were celibate, Orthodox priests could marry), and fine points of religious doctrine. In 1054 the patriarch of Constantinople refused to yield to the Roman church's demand for submission, and a final, permanent schism, or split, ended all ties between the two faiths (Time Line 8.2).

The patriarch of Constantinople had to deal with challenges from the pope, from rival patriarchs in other eastern cities, such as Antioch and Alexandria, and from the Byzantine emperors themselves, who viewed the church as an arm of the government. Although they made great claims for themselves and for the Orthodox church, the patriarchs never had the kind of power enjoyed by the popes. The Eastern church was also plagued by internal dissension and a variety of heresies that even persecution by the emperors, who desired a unified state with a common creed, did not always eliminate.

The most serious issue to confront the Orthodox church was the Iconoclastic Controversy (726–843),

TIME LINE 8.2   RELIGIOUS DEVELOPMENTS IN THE ORTHODOX CHURCH

FIGURE 8.3   An Iconoclast Whitewashing an Image. Miniature from the Chludov Psalter. Ninth Century. Public Library, Moscow. *This miniature painting from the period of the Iconoclastic Controversy is historically inaccurate. It portrays an iconoclast attired as a monk, wearing a flowing robe and sporting a beard. In reality, however, the monks favored icons and protested their destruction. That the artist has depicted a monk desecrating a religious picture may indicate that the manuscript it appeared in was commissioned by a patron from the imperial circle, where images were despised.*

FIGURE 8.4   Mount Athos, Greece. *Since the tenth century, Mount Athos, located on a forty-mile-long peninsula in northern Greece, has been the site of a thriving monastic community. During that interval, the monks have enforced a strict code that excludes females, whether human or animal. Within the Mt. Athos complex each monastery was a self-governing unit that maintained order over its inmates, houses, and lands.*

which erupted when the emperor Leo III commanded the removal and destruction of all religious images (Figure 8.3). The iconoclasts, or image-breakers, believed that the devotion paid to sacred pictures was blasphemous and idolatrous. This belief may have been inspired by contacts in the Middle East with Judaism or Islam, for both religions strongly condemned the use of religious images. Siding with the iconoclastic emperors were the bishops, the army, and the civil service; opposed were the monks. Many monks lost their lives in the civil unrest that seized the empire. In the West the papacy refused to join the iconoclastic frenzy and broke relations with Byzantium during most of this period. The controversy lasted for over a hundred years, and, by the time the Byzantine rulers restored the veneration of icons, nearly all religious pictures had been destroyed by zealous reformers.

Monasticism, which furnished the chief foes of the iconoclastic emperors, was a basic expression of Orthodox piety. Monastic practices began in late Roman Egypt and quickly spread across the Roman world, adapting to local conditions (see Chapter 7). Like western ascetic practices, Byzantine monasticism took two forms, hermitic (or isolated) and communal. Communal monasticism in Byzantium was similar to monastic life in the West. The monastic communities were basically places where people retreated from the world to lead strictly disciplined lives. For centuries the monasteries received immense gifts of land and wealth from rulers, merchants, and peasants alike, and eventually they achieved a powerful economic position in Byzantine society.

The most important monastic complex in Byzantium was the one at Mount Athos, founded in 963 (Figure 8.4). Early in its history this mountain retreat in northern Greece, which during its heyday in the thirteenth century included over one hundred houses and about eight thousand monks, achieved relative independence from the secular authorities, which may explain how it survived into the twentieth century. The style of Mount Athos—self-governing, self-contained, and committed to study and prayer—influenced monastic development in the Orthodox world.

Law and History   From the viewpoint of Western culture, Byzantium's greatest accomplishment was the codification of the Roman law made under the emperor Justinian in the sixth century. The Justinian Code, which summarized a thousand years of Roman legal developments, not only laid the foundation of Byzantine law but also furnished the starting point for the revival of Roman law in the West in the eleventh century. This law code preserved such legal principles as requiring court proceedings to settle disputes, protecting the individual against unreasonable demands of society, and setting limits to the legitimate power of the sovereign. Through the Justinian Code, these ideals permeated Byzantine society and served as a restraint on the autocratic emperors. When the West revived the study of the Roman law in the Middle Ages, these principles were adopted by the infant European states. Today, in virtually all of the Western states, these principles continue to be honored.

From the viewpoint of world culture, Byzantium was noteworthy for contributing one of the first known works of history by a woman: the *Alexiad* by Anna Comnena [kawm-NEE-nuh] (1083–about 1153), daughter of Emperor Alexius I Comnenus. Joining Christian and Classical knowledge and following the rigorous method pioneered by the Greek historian Thucydides (see Chapter 3), the *Alexiad* is a scholarly study of the reign of Anna's father, Alexius. Flawed by such shortcomings as the author's obvious bias toward her father and confused chronology, the work is nevertheless the best source for this period in Byzantine history. Especially valuable for Western readers is its portrait of the soldiers, saints, and hangers-on of the First Crusade (1096) passing through Constantinople on the way to Jerusalem. To Anna Comnena's non-Western eyes, the European Crusaders were a crude violent bunch, more greedy for loot than concerned about salvation.

Architecture and Mosaics Besides law and history, the other great achievement of the Byzantine world was in architecture. Byzantine architecture was committed to glorifying the state and the emperors along with spreading the Christian message. Most of the secular Byzantine structures, whether palaces or state buildings, were either destroyed in the fifteenth century or have since fallen into ruins, but many Byzantine churches still survive and attest to the lost grandeur of this civilization.

By the seventh century the **Byzantine style** had been born, a style that drew from Greek, Roman, and Oriental sources. From the Greco-Roman tradition came the basic elements of Byzantine architecture: columns, arches, vaults, and domes. Oriental taste contributed a love of rich ornamentation and riotous color. Christianity fused these ingredients, provided wealthy patrons, and suggested subjects for the interior decorations. The **Greek cross**, which has arms of equal length, came to be the preferred floor plan for most later Byzantine churches.

Despite their borrowings, the Byzantines made one significant innovation that became fundamental in their architecture: They invented **pendentives**—supports in the shape of inverted concave triangles—that allowed a dome to be suspended over a square base (see Figure 8.5). As a result of this invention, the domed building soon became synonymous with the Byzantine style, notably in churches.

The Byzantine obsession with the dome probably stemmed from its central role in the magnificent church Hagia Sophia, or Holy Wisdom, in Constantinople (Figure 8.5). The dome had been employed in early Christian architecture (see Figure 7.14), and Romans had used the dome in important temples like the Pantheon (see Figure 5.13). Erected by Justinian, Hagia Sophia was intended to awe the worshiper with the twin majesties of God and the emperor. The central dome measures more than 101 feet in diameter and rests on four pendentives that channel the weight to four huge pillars. Half-domes cover the east and west ends of the aisles.

In the vast interior, the architects showed that they were divided about the Classical legacy. On the one hand, they used such Classical features as vaulted aisles, well-proportioned columns, and rounded arches. But they ignored the basic rules of Classical symmetry; for example, they failed to harmonize the floor columns with the columns in the second story gallery. Their goal was not to produce a unified effect but rather to create an illusion of celestial light. Glittering walls covered with polychrome marbles and brilliant mosaics, which have since disappeared or been covered with whitewash, suggested shimmering cloth to early viewers and contributed to the breathtaking effect of this magnificent church.

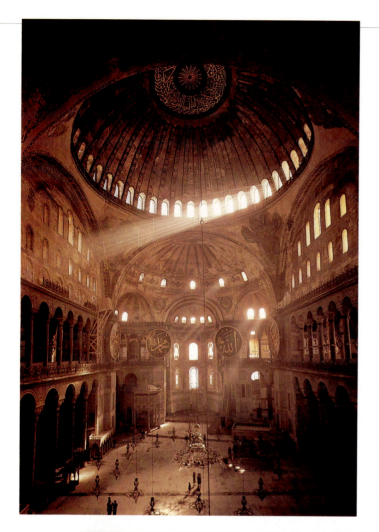

FIGURE 8.5 ISIDORE OF MILETUS AND ANTHEMIUS OF TRALLES. Hagia Sophia, Interior. 532–537. Istanbul. *Hagia Sophia was the mother church of the Orthodox faith. After the Ottoman conquest, the church became an Islamic mosque, and some of the trappings, such as the calligraphic writings, still survive from this stage of the building's life. Today, Hagia Sophia is a museum, and its striking mixture of Byzantine and Islamic elements makes it a vivid symbol of the meeting of West and East.*

Although many later Byzantine architects adopted Hagia Sophia as their model—a floor plan that unites the early Christian longitudinal basilica with a central square surmounted by a dome or domes set upon drums—they also built churches that did not make use of the dome, particularly in Ravenna in Italy. Ravenna, a seaport on the northeast Adriatic coast, enjoyed the best of both Roman worlds. The Western emperors began to rule from there in 404 and to turn their new capital into an artistic jewel. In the late fifth century Ravenna fell into the hands of Germanic invaders, who continued to add to the city's splendor.

When the city became a Byzantine outpost under Justinian, two new churches were built there, San

FIGURE 8.6 San Vitale, Exterior. 526–547. Ravenna, Italy. *Ravenna's church of San Vitale, with its octagonal plan and domed central core, is the prototype of the domed church that became standard in Byzantine civilization. From the outside, San Vitale's dome is not visible because it is covered by a timber and tile roof. This church inspired Charlemagne's Royal Chapel in Aachen (see Figure 8.21).*

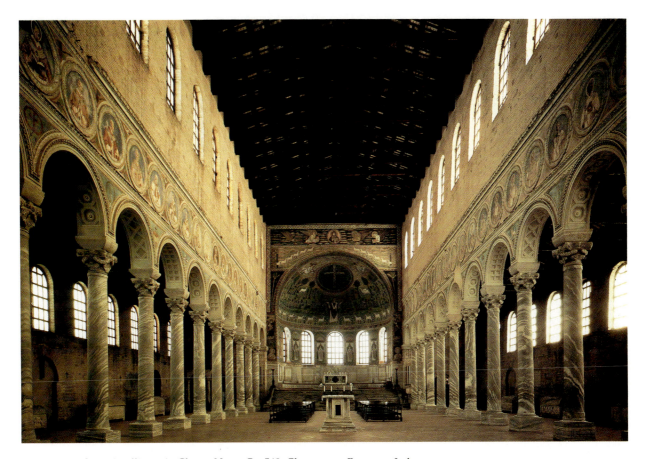

FIGURE 8.7 Sant' Apollinare in Classe, Nave. Ca. 549. Classe, near Ravenna, Italy.
Dedicated in 549 by the Bishop of Ravenna, the church of Apollinare was built about three
miles outside the walled city of Ravenna at the local port of Classe. Today, the harbor has
long since silted up and the church presides like a sentinel over the surrounding
farmlands. Sant' Apollinare's glittering interior mosaics and splendid marble columns
remind the visitor that this country church was once at the center of the Byzantine world.

Vitale and Sant' Apollinare in Classe (Ravenna's port). San Vitale was domed (Figure 8.6), but Sant' Apollinare in Classe imitated late Roman styles with its basilica shape and its symbolic mosaics (Figure 8.7). The Western Classical ideal was visible in the harmonious nave of this church, where twenty-four perfectly proportioned columns were echoed above by precious marbles, which no longer exist. But the architect turned to Oriental sources for his imaginative treatment of the columnar capitals in the nave. Instead of using stylized Corinthian capitals, he twisted and curled the acanthus leaves into fanciful shapes, as if blown by a stiff wind. The overall result was an artful blending of the Western and Eastern traditions.

Mosaic making had experienced a lively flowering in late Rome, and in Byzantium it became a major form of artistic expression. Unlike the Roman mosaics, which were of stone and laid in the floor, the Byzantine mosaics were usually of glass and set into the walls. Of the Byzantine mosaics, the most beautiful and the most perfectly preserved are those in the churches of Ravenna.

The church of San Vitale is home to a pair of impressive mosaics, one depicting Justinian and his courtiers (see Figure 8.2), the other depicting Justinian's empress, Theodora, and her retinue (Figure 8.8). In both these mosaics, debts to late Roman art may be seen in the full frontal presentation of each figure, their large and staring eyes, and their long gowns. But the two-dimensional rendering of the figures reveals the new Byzantine aesthetic; the rulers and their companions seem to float in space, their feet pointing downward and not touching any surface. In various ways, the mosaics make a comparison between Justinian and Theodora and Christ and the Virgin Mary. For example, Justinian is surrounded by twelve companions, and the lower portion of Theodora's robe shows the three Wise Men bearing gifts to the Christ Child.

FIGURE 8.8 *Theodora and Her Attendants.* Ca. 547. San Vitale, Ravenna. *This mosaic depicting the Empress Theodora and her attendants from the church of San Vitale faces the panel of her husband, Justinian, with his courtiers (see Figure 8.2). Together these mosaics communicate the pageantry and the luxury of this age. The man on Theodora's right draws back a curtain, inviting the imperial party into some unseen interior. His gesture may mean that this scene was part of a religious procession.*

During the Iconoclastic Controversy, the emperors destroyed virtually all figurative religious art that was under their control. After the conclusion of the controversy, a formalized repertory of church decoration evolved that characterized Byzantine art for the rest of its history. The aim of this religious art was strictly theological. For instance, Christ Pantocrator (Ruler of All) dominated each church's dome (Figure 8.9). In these portraits Christ was presented as the emperor of the universe and the judge of the world. Accordingly, he came to be pictured with a stern and forceful countenance, in contrast to Western portrayals, which increasingly focused on his suffering.

FIGURE 8.9 *Christ Pantocrator.* Central Dome, Church of Dafni. 1100. Dafni, near Athens. *In early Christian art Christ had been portrayed as a beardless youth, often in the guise of the Good Shepherd or Orpheus. In Byzantine art, starting in the seventh century, Christ began to be depicted as a mature man with a full beard, as in this mosaic. Part of the change was a result of a fashion for full beards at this time, but, more important, the bearded figure reflected Orthodox theology's focus on Christ as the stern judge of the world.*

THE ISLAMIC WORLD, 600–1517

Islamic civilization, another successor to the territories once controlled by Rome, was born at approximately the same time as Byzantine culture and in the same part of the world, the eastern Mediterranean. In Arabic, the word "islam" means submission (to God); a "muslim" is one who has submitted. Arabic religion and culture are known collectively as Islam, and those who practice the faith are known as Muslims. At its height, Islamic civilization extended over an enormous area that included southern Spain, Sicily, North Africa, Syria, Palestine, Mesopotamia, Persia, and the Arabian peninsula. The peoples living in these areas retained many elements of their native traditions but adopted the Islamic religion in a complex, two-way process of cultural assimilation. All of these territories have remained Islamic up to the present day, with the exceptions of southern Italy and Sicily, which fell to the Normans in the eleventh century; Spain, which the Christians won in the fifteenth century; and Palestine, which became the Jewish state of Israel after World War II.

The pre-Islamic Arabs inhabited the Arabian peninsula, a harsh land of treeless steppes and waterless deserts wedged between the Red Sea and the Persian Gulf. Their tradition traces their ancestry to Abraham and the Hebrew patriarchs, and their Semitic tongue, Arabic, is related to Hebrew as well as to Syriac and Coptic, the chief languages of Syria and Egypt, respectively, at this time.

Geography accounted for the differences between the two major groups of pre-Islamic Arabs on the Arabian peninsula. In the north, nomadic Bedouins lived in the desert, herding sheep and goats. Tribal membership provided identity and social cohesion. In contrast, the southern Arabs lived in cities and made their living through trade with their neighbors. Age-old caravan routes crossed Arabia, connecting India and the Roman world; local Arab merchants made the most of the opportunities created by the passing traffic, sometimes accumulating great fortunes.

Jews and Christians settled in southern Arabia as farmers and artisans and served as major sources for cultural interchange. From them the Arabs acquired knowledge of weaponry, textiles, food and wine, and writing. The Arabs also learned that their polytheism conflicted with Jewish and Christian monotheism. A meeting place for all these peoples was Mecca, the leading commercial city of southern Arabia. Because of its central location on the rich overland route between the Indian Ocean and the Mediterranean, Mecca flourished as the chief marketplace for the exchange of goods between travelers and the local populace.

History of Islam

At the beginning of the seventh century, political and social life in Mecca was dominated by a wealthy merchant aristocracy of the Quraish tribe (Time Line 8.3). Into this society in about 570 was born Muhammad, the founder of Islam and one of the most commanding figures in all of history. Descended from an obscure, albeit respectable, branch of the Quraish, he became a wealthy merchant. At the age of 40 he had a vision in which he felt himself called by God to be a prophet to the Arab people, just as Moses and Jesus had been prophets before him. Declaring that there was but one God (Allah), Muhammad attacked the polytheistic beliefs of his fellow Arabs and condemned the Kaaba, a local pagan shrine that housed a sacred black stone, perhaps a meteorite.

Since the Kaaba was a source of revenue from the business generated by the thousands of pilgrims who visited it every year, the Quraish leaders reacted to Muhammad's message with mounting suspicion and alarm. When he began converting others

TIME LINE 8.3   THE WORLD OF ISLAM, 600–1517

500	600	632	800	1000	1258	1517
Pre-Islamic Culture		Islamic Empire			Decline and Disintegration	
	Age of Muhammad 600-632					Triumph of the Ottoman Turks

to his views, notably the poorer Arabs, Quraish hostility was translated into persecution. Under these threats Muhammad and his followers accepted an invitation to travel to Yathrib, a neighboring city in southwestern Arabia. This flight, or Hegira, transformed Muhammad's message of reform into a call for a new religion. This historic event in 622 marks the beginning of the Arab calendar, just as the birth of Christ marks the beginning of the Christian era in the West. Yathrib was later renamed Medina, "the city of the Prophet."

In Yathrib, Muhammad's followers began to record the religious messages he received from Allah, and these writings became the Koran, the sacred book of Islam. Prominent among the divine words given to Muhammad was the *jihad,* the command to "holy war." Armed with this sacred order, Muhammad launched a religious and military movement that quickly conquered Arabia as both urban Arabs and desert Bedouins submitted to his authority. In 630 his forces defeated the Quraish, and a triumphant Muhammad reentered Mecca, making it his capital. The Kaaba shrine, now purified of pagan and other religious images, kept its sacred rock and thus remained an object of veneration for Muslims; this action ensured the willing cooperation of the newly converted business community who had at first bitterly opposed him. When Muhammad died in 632, he left an Arab state united around his prophecies.

In the century or so after the death of Muhammad, from 632 to 750, the energies awakened by his mission were unleashed in a series of military campaigns. Motivated by the lure of plundered wealth, the pressures of overpopulation, and the command to make holy war, the Arabs built a world state whose extent rivaled that of the Roman Empire. By 650 the Arabs ruled Syria, Mesopotamia, Egypt, and Persia, and by 740 North Africa had been added along with most of Spain. Only the militant kingdom of the Franks in the west and impregnable Constantinople in the east were able to withstand this Arab fury. At its height, the Arab empire stretched from the Indus River and the borders of China in the east to the Atlantic in the west and from the Taurus Mountains in the north to the Sahara in the south (see Map 8.1).

During the Abbasid dynasty (754–1258) Islamic civilization attained its golden age. A fusion gradually occurred between conquerors and conquered as the Arabs adapted other cultures to their own needs, and Arabic became the common cultural language throughout the empire. Millions converted to Islam, although Jews and Christians were allowed to retain their beliefs because they, like Muslims, were "people of the book." Trade with Europe, China, Russia, and Scandinavia generated great wealth for merchants and aristocrats, though the mainstay of the economy was agriculture, which, as always, depended on the backbreaking labor of an army of peasants working on small farms. This vast Islamic empire was a theocracy, autocratically ruled by a Caliph, or deputy, of the prophet Muhammad.

After the Abbasid era the Islamic world declined economically and politically as feudal agriculture replaced the commercial economy. In place of a unified caliphate, mutually hostile Islamic states confronted one another, and after 1453 the eastern Mediterranean area was clearly ruled by the Ottoman Turks from Constantinople. Eventually, in 1517, the Turks added Egypt and Syria to their holdings.

Islamic Religious and Cultural Developments

The Islamic civilization that flowered from the ninth to the twelfth century was more brilliant than that of either the West or Byzantium. Original learning flourished in science, mathematics, and law. Arab medicine was recognized in the West and in Byzantium as superior, and Islamic scholars made their civilization a successor to the Hellenic tradition by translating Greek philosophy, mathematics, and science into Arabic.

Nevertheless, religion, then as now, dominated Islamic life. Not only did the Koran serve as a guide for public and private morality, but the interpretation of koranic scriptures influenced the creation of such major cultural forms as jurisprudence and history. To the fundamentalist Muslim, religion, science, history, law, and theology were all different aspects of the same thing: God's divine word (Figure 8.10).

Islamic Religion   The two central beliefs of Islam are that there is but one God and that Muhammad is his prophet. Muslims worship the same God as Jews and Christians, but the Muslims alone recognize Muhammad as the *final* prophet of a tradition that goes back to Abraham and Moses in Judaism and also includes Jesus Christ as the giver of the Christian message. For the devout Muslim, Muhammad's voice is the culminating revelation from God that continues and perfects his earlier messages to Jews and Christians.

Muhammad's prophecies were recorded in the Koran during the generation after his death. Following no chronological pattern, this sacred book divides his revelations into chapters and verses beginning with the longest chapters and ending with the shortest. Muhammad's utterances reveal the prophet as a master of literary expression and of rhetorical skills. Within a century of Muhammad's death, a collection of his sayings and practices appeared that

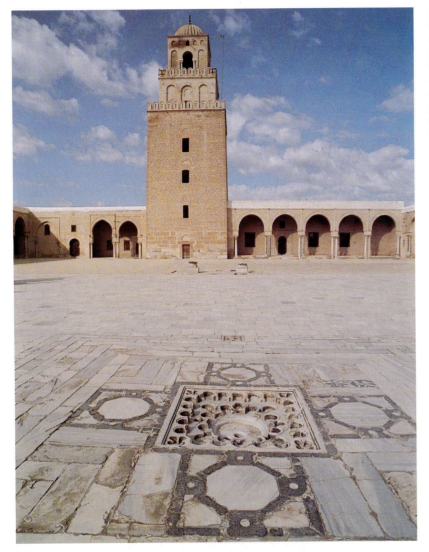

FIGURE 8.10 The Great Mosque of Kairouan, Tunisia. Ninth Century. *As in the other civilizations of this period, the dominant building type in Islam was the house of worship. The Great Mosque of Kairouan in Tunisia, with its plain walls and square tower for calling the faithful to prayer, reflects the puritanical style of early Islam. Inside the walls a large unadorned courtyard serves as a praying area.*

had been preserved by the faithful and that came to be known as the Hadith, or the Tradition. Together, the Tradition and the Koran became the infallible guide to God's will on earth for Muslims.

The core of Muslim religious life rests on the five Pillars of the Faith, which include one basic statement and four required devotional practices. The affirmation of faith states: "There is but one God, Allah, and Muhammad is his Prophet." The four acts of devotion are to pray five times a day facing Mecca, to fast during the lunar month of Ramadan, to give alms to the poor, and to make the pilgrimage to Mecca. Islam, like Christianity, promises salvation in heaven for the good and damnation in hell for the wicked. Besides the five Pillars of the Faith, the Muslim who desires God's favor has to meet many other religious, ethical, legal, and social obligations which form the basis of the *Shari'a,* or holy law, which is rooted in the Koran and the Tradition.

History   Because of Muhammad's supreme significance to Islam, lives of the Prophet and histories of his era appeared soon after his death. In time the Islamic world developed a great demand for historical writings, and diverse historical genres appeared, including accounts of territorial conquest, family genealogies, and town histories. Of the Islamic historians the greatest was Ibn Khaldun [ib-uhn kal-DOON] (1332–1406). His fame rests on the three-volume *Muqaddima,* or Prolegomena, which sets forth his scientific theory of history. In this work he reasoned that the best history should downplay the role of divine forces and instead focus on the role of human activity. He believed that historians who probed beneath the surface explanations would discover that human beings are motivated not by religious or idealistic impulses but by status concerns and desires to identify with certain groups. One of the founders of modern scientific history, Ibn Khaldun deserves wider recognition.

Science Muslim scientists form a link in the cultural chain that connects the ancient Greek thinkers to modern science. The linkage runs from Hellenic Greece to the Hellenistic world to ancient Rome to the Arabs and back to the West during the High Middle Ages. Not only did Muslim intellectuals translate the Greek texts into Arabic and thus preserve them, they also used the Greek heritage to lay the foundation for Muslim mathematics, astronomy, physics, geography, chemistry, and medicine. Medieval Christian Europe obtained most of its knowledge of Greek thought and science from Arabic sources. During Islam's golden age her scholars made more scientific advances than had been made since the Hellenistic period.

The outstanding areas of Muslim science were medicine and mathematics. Many works of Islamic scholars were translated into Latin by Western writers, an indication of the deep respect Christians accorded these Muslim specialists. Muslim doctors obtained their medical knowledge from the ancient Greek texts and from their training in the hospitals that dotted the Islamic world. Islamic medicine's commitment to observation and experimentation extended the frontiers of medical science. For example, Muslim doctors added many new drugs to the pharmacopeia, stressed the role of diet in the treatment of various illnesses, and were the first to make the clinical distinction between measles and smallpox.

In mathematics, however, the Muslims did their most original work. The great figure in this science was Al-Khwarizmi [al-KWAHR-iz-me] (780–850), who made several important contributions. Al-Khwarizmi (from whose name the word "algorithm" is derived) founded the algebraic system by adopting and expanding the hints thrown out by a Hellenistic Greek thinker. Al-Khwarizmi's study of quadratic equations introduced algebra to the West, and in translation this work became a standard textbook used in Western universities from the twelfth to the eighteenth centuries. He made celestial observations that were used for centuries, and he measured the length of a terrestrial degree. Finally, Al-Khwarizmi took from Hindu mathematics the idea of zero and the numeration system that became more widely known as Arabic numerals.

Art and Architecture Islamic art and architecture borrowed freely from other cultures, but the borrowings were always adapted to Arabic tastes in complex and exotic ways. From Greco-Roman architecture came the column and the *arcade*. From Byzantine architecture came the pendentive, which allowed the dome to become a prominent feature of the Islamic style. And from Persian art and architecture came the miniature painting, the vaulted hall, the pointed arch, and floral and geometric ornament.

The course of Islamic art was dramatically affected by the Koran's prohibition against the representation of living creatures. Large-scale paintings and sculptures were not produced, and lifelike figures, whether of humans or animals, largely disappeared from art. In compensation, perhaps, artists were abundantly inventive in the use of nonrepresentational forms. The *arabesque*—a complex figure made of intertwined floral, foliate, or geometrical forms—became a highly visible sign of Islamic culture (Figure 8.11). Geometric shapes, floral forms, and *calligraphy*, or writing, decorated walls, books, and mosaics (Figure 8.12).

In architecture, the dominant structure was the *mosque*. Plain in exterior decoration and rectangular in shape, mosques were distinguished from secular buildings by their interior features and spaces—basins and fountains for ritual hand washing, porticoes for instruction, and an open area for the group prayers. Sometimes the mosque was crowned with a dome, as in the Byzantine churches, but the Islamic

FIGURE 8.11 Arabesque Detail. Great Mosque of Cordoba. 785–987. Cordoba, Spain. *This arabesque is used as a decorative feature above the portal of the Great Mosque of Cordoba. The arabesque had its origins in the Arabic world's love of designs. These elaborate and elegant decorations were constructed either from geometrical features or from floral motifs. The geometric features, as seen here, were rarely based on nature but were meant to make viewers think of values other than those of their surrounding world.*

FIGURE 8.12 Arabic Calligraphy. Page from Koran of Sultan Uljaytu, in Gold Jalil Script, Northern Iraq. 1310. British Library, London. *Because Islam forbade the representation of figures in art, artists and artisans focused on decoration, design, and other nonrepresentational forms of expression. Besides the popular arabesques, Arabic calligraphy was the other major form available to Muslim artists. This handwritten page from a fourteenth-century Koran shows the exquisite beauty that this painstaking art could achieve.*

dome's high melon shape distinguished it from the more spherical Byzantine form (Figure 8.13). The mosque was also identified by a thin pointed tower, or **minaret**, from whose top a Muslim official called the faithful to prayer five times a day. Inside the mosque, from the earliest times, rich decorations assaulted the eyes of the worshipers, reminding them of the beauty of paradise. Brilliant mosaics and Oriental carpets emblazoned the floors, facings and calligraphic friezes beautified the walls, and overhead metal lamps cast a twilight glow onto the faithful at night.

In early Islam, the congregational mosque developed in response to the devotional practices and ritualistic needs. It housed the Friday worshipers in a central courtyard with a domed fountain for ablutions. The ninth-century Ibn Tulun Mosque at Cairo is an imposing example of this type (Figure 8.14). Four rows of arcades stand between the faithful and the east wall (the direction of Mecca), and portals of pointed arches open into the arcaded area (Figure 8.15). A minaret with a winding stair rises just beyond the mosque, which is built of brick faced with stucco. In later Islamic mosques the pointed arches and decorated stucco work became basic features of this style. Later, during the Christian Middle Ages, Western architects adapted the pointed arch to their own needs, using it to perfect the Gothic style of architecture.

FIGURE 8.13 The Tomb of Timur Lenk (Tamerlane). Ca. 1403. Samarkand, Uzbekistan. *Islamic architects imposed domes not only over prayer halls in mosques but also over the tombs of rulers and holy men. The dome of Timur Lenk's tomb has the characteristic high melon shape of Islamic architecture; in addition, the dome is decorated with ribs that break up the play of light on its surface. Below the dome on the cylindrical drum are letters in Kufic (Timur Lenk's language) that say, "Allah [alone] is permanent."*

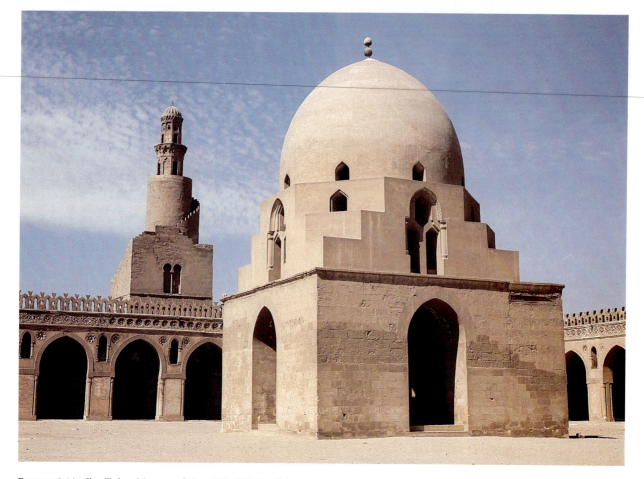

FIGURE 8.14 Ibn Tulun Mosque, Cairo. 876–879. *Ibn Tulun, a governor who founded a short-lived Egyptian dynasty independent of the caliphate in Baghdad, built this mosque in the congregational style created by Muhammad. The view is from inside the courtyard, with a domed fountain, used for ritual washing, standing in the foreground. Outside the walls rises the spire of the minaret with its encircling staircase. The finest surviving example of this style, the Ibn Tulun Mosque was imitated throughout the Muslim world.*

In the eleventh century the mosque evolved from a place for group prayer to a place for teaching, but the basic rectangular shape remained the same. In the teaching mosque, four large enclosed teaching halls with vaulted ceilings replaced the covered arcades on the perimeter of the courtyard, each opening into the central space.

Islamic artisans also excelled in palace architecture, and no more beautiful example exists than the Alhambra in Granada, the residence of the last Muslim rulers of Spain. Its exterior of plain red brick contrasted dramatically with its interior of restless splendor. The palace's asymmetrical plan included ornately decorated rooms, splendid courts, and formal gardens. The decoration of the Alhambra—variegated marbles, lustrous tiles, and painted stucco—

FIGURE 8.15 Floor Plan of Ibn Tulun Mosque. *This diagram shows the main features of the Ibn Tulun Mosque, a prototype of the congregational mosque that flourished in Islamic civilization in its early history. Constructed basically as an open rectangular area, the mosque has passageways (1) on three sides that lead through an arcaded area (5) into a central courtyard dominated by a domed fountain (2). In the middle of the eastern wall is the mihrab (3), a decorated niche indicating the direction of Mecca. Opposite the mihrab, on the western side, stands a minaret (4), a tower used by an official for calling the faithful to prayer.*

created a fantastic illusion of airiness. The Court of the Lions illustrates vividly the meaning of the term *arabesque*, with its calligraphic carvings, slender columns, geometric and floral shapes, and lacey decoration (Figure 8.16). The fountain surrounded by stone lions is a rare example of Islamic representational sculpture.

Notwithstanding the koranic prohibition, one branch of Islamic art, Persian *miniatures*, usually depicted realistic scenes. After the thirteenth century, illustrated manuscripts were produced in Persia under the patronage of the Mongol sultans, who had replaced the caliphs as rulers. Although the Mongols brought Chinese influences to the Persian miniatures, the Muslim artists rejected the openness of Chinese space and created their own ordered reality, as shown in a superb example from the fifteenth century (Figure 8.17). The painter records each object with painstaking naturalistic detail. The painting's high horizon and its rectangular format placed the two figures into a precise setting. Like all Persian miniatures, this exquisite work is characterized by fine detail, naturalistic figures and landscape, and subtle colors.

FIGURE 8.17 Scene from the *Khamsah* (Five Poems) of Amir-I Khusrau. 1485. Chester Beatty Library, Dublin. *During the fifteenth century, the age of the Mongol rulers in Persia, the art of Persian miniatures achieved its classic expression in paintings such as this. These small works are immediately recognizable by their rectangular designs, their representation of the human figure as being about one-fifth the height of the painting, and their use of extremely refined detail.*

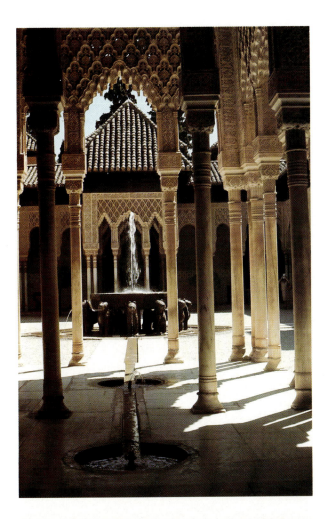

FIGURE 8.16 Court of the Lions. The Alhambra. Thirteenth and Fourteenth Centuries. Granada, Spain. *The Alhambra is the only Muslim palace surviving from the medieval period. Because of its location in the West, this fairy-tale palace has made Granada a popular destination for tourists. As a result, the ornate Alhambra has played a pivotal role in developing a taste for the arabesque among many Westerners.*

THE EARLY MEDIEVAL WEST

Since the Italian Renaissance, it has been customary to describe the fall of Rome as marking the end of the ancient world and inaugurating the thousand-year era known as the medieval period, or the Middle Ages. Although Renaissance intellectuals used the word *medieval* as a negative term, today's scholars believe the civilization of the Middle Ages to be as worthy of study as the ancient and modern worlds. The rest of this chapter is devoted to the first phase of this era, the Early Medieval period, dating from about 500 to about 1000.

The Early Middle Ages: A Romano-Germanic Christianized World

In the first years after the fall of Rome, life in the West was precarious for most people. There was a return to an essentially agrarian form of existence, accompanied by a decline in trade and commerce and a lowering of the standard of living. Villages operated at the simplest economic level, and barter became the primary medium of exchange. What little security there was in this world was provided by the Christian church, with its bishops and priests, its increasingly powerful pope in Rome, and its spreading network of monasteries and convents.

By about 500 Western life stabilized to some slight degree. Three Germanic tribes occupied and ruled vast parts of the old Western Roman Empire: the Visigoths in Spain, the Ostrogoths in Italy and southern Germany, and the Franks in France and western Germany. Meanwhile, the Angles and Saxons made themselves dominant in England, the Vandals in North Africa, and the Burgundians in southern France; other Germanic tribes claimed land in central Europe, the Scandinavian peninsula, and along the Baltic Sea. In what is present-day France, especially, life was being redefined in ways that would have a profound impact on the course of Western civilization.

At the same time that a Germanic tribe known as the Lombards was gaining control of the Italian peninsula, another Germanic tribe, the Franks, was achieving a semblance of centralized rule in Roman Gaul (modern-day France) under Clovis, the first important ruler of the Merovingian dynasty. An early convert to Latin Christianity, Clovis supported missionaries in newly conquered territories and thus strengthened political ties between Gaul and the pope (Time Line 8.4).

During these years of political expansion in the Frankish kingdom, some sense of security and order gradually developed, especially in and around the rulers' fortress-palaces. As the barbarian invasions subsided in the late sixth century, manorialism developed as a new economic system. Most of the Germanic invaders settled down as farmers on the manors, or landed estates, of the Frankish warrior class. There they became serfs, indentured servants who were bound to the land. Their value as workers earned them the protection of the lord of the manor in time of war.

The Frankish political and economic systems reflected a society composed of three well-defined ranks: those who fought, those who prayed, and those who worked. Each social rank was divided into a rigidly defined hierarchy of subgroups. The warrior class, headed by the king, consisted of the lords of the great manors and their families and, under them, their courtiers and bureaucrats, the less wealthy knights, and the lords of small manors. The upper clergy, who shared the high social status of the warriors, consisted of the archbishops, bishops, and abbots; the lower clergy comprised priests, monks, and

TIME LINE 8.4   THE KINGDOM OF THE FRANKS

476	481		680		700			800	843
End of Western Roman Empire	Frankish Self-Rule	Merovingian Line		Carolingian Line					

| End of Western Roman Empire | Clovis 481–511 | | | | Pepin II 680–714 | Charles Martel 714–741 | Pepin the Short 741–768 | Charlemagne 768–814 | Division of Charlemagne's Empire |

nuns and the clerical scribes and secretaries. Socially lower than either the warriors or the clergy were the workers, consisting of free farmers, artisans, and a few merchants, and the vast population of peasants, serfs, and a few slaves at the bottom.

In Frankish society the status of women declined sharply from what it had been in the Roman world. On the manors, noblewomen enjoyed few personal or property rights since, under Frankish law, land was passed through the male line. The noblewoman's primary function became the bearing of sons, and the peasant woman was simply another laborer. The only outlet for women who wanted a leadership role in this society was in the nunneries, for women traditionally ruled themselves in these religious institutions.

After 700 the Merovingians gradually lost control of the Frankish kingdom to the Carolingians, a family of ambitious landowners who served as court advisors to the Merovingians. Under Charles Martel ("Charles the Hammer"), Carolingian troops halted the advance of the Muslims at the Battle of Tours in southern France in 732, thereby ensuring the future of Europe as a Christian land.

The Carolingian dynasty triumphed over all its rivals in the reign of Pepin the Short (741–768), the son of Charles Martel. In 751, Pepin, with the approval of the pope and with the votes of the Frankish nobles, was declared King of the Franks. Three years later a new pope traveled to St. Denis, near Paris, crowned Pepin, and anointed him as defender of the church. This ceremony, cementing an alliance between the popes and the Franks, set the course for church-state relationships in the West.

In exchange for papal recognition of his royal title, Pepin crushed the Lombards who ruled most of Italy and gave the newly conquered lands in central Italy to the pope. These territories, which later became known as the Papal States, were conveyed in one of the most famous documents of the Early Middle Ages, the Donation of Pepin. The alliance symbolized by the Donation of Pepin benefited both parties: The pope's authority was enhanced, and the church was given a stronger economic foundation; the Frankish kings gained legitimacy and a claim to be the hereditary protectors of Rome. Of more lasting effect, this union redirected the church's interests away from the Eastern Empire and linked Rome's destiny with western Europe.

Besides the Donation of Pepin, another famous papal document dates from this period, the Donation of Constantine. Unlike the Donation of Pepin, which was genuine, the Donation of Constantine was a forgery, probably devised at the papal court. It claimed that Constantine, the fourth-century Ro-

man emperor, had granted the church extensive territories in Italy. During the early Renaissance, this document was proven fraudulent (see Chapter 11).

Charlemagne ("Charles the Great") (768–814), the son of Pepin the Short, established the first real empire in medieval Europe and challenged the Byzantine rulers' claims to the western Roman lands. A man of imposing stature and personality, Charlemagne was, without question, the most powerful ruler in the Early Middle Ages. Historians have named a dynasty and an age for him—Carolingian, from *Carolus,* Latin for Charles. Charlemagne conquered vast expanses of land, fighting the Lombards in Italy, the Saxons in Germany, and the Muslims in Spain. He followed up his victories by colonizing most of these areas, converting the populace to Christianity, and installing his own representatives as a link with the local authorities.

As a reward for his military and religious activities, Pope Leo III (795–816) crowned Charlemagne as "Charles Augustus, Emperor of the Romans" on Christmas Day, 800. With this act, Leo may have hoped to assert the authority of the church over the state, but Charlemagne continued to believe in the supremacy of the state. The coronation widened the rift between Byzantium and the West while reinforcing Charlemagne's reputation as a "new Constantine" who would set Western civilization on a new path.

Charlemagne created the most efficient and centralized state the West had seen since the Roman Empire. He built up a capable bureaucracy, instituted a fair judicial system, and brought learned people to his court as part of a revival of the arts and humanities. He granted large tracts of land to local warriors and then held them responsible for maintaining law and order in their domains. This administrative system represented a fusion of the Roman approach to governing an empire with the Germanic warrior tradition, and it worked as long as Charlemagne lived.

The end of the Carolingian era began in 843 when Charlemagne's grandsons divided the empire into three parts, a move that also hastened the splintering of western Europe into smaller kingdoms. In the ninth and tenth centuries, the divided Frankish kingdoms could not hold back the rampaging Vikings from Scandinavia and the Magyars from the Hungarian plains, the final wave of barbarian invasions into western Europe. By the end of the tenth century, however, two new kingdoms—the germs of modern France and Germany—were emerging out of the political chaos.

The first of these kingdoms was France, which developed from the ambitions of Hugh Capet (987–996),

FIGURE 8.18 Church of St. Pantaleon. 966–980, Restored 1890–1892. Cologne, Germany. *Otto the Great founded this church for a Benedictine monastery in Cologne where his brother was Archbishop. As a builder of churches, Otto was following in Charlemagne's footsteps, identifying himself as God's chosen instrument intent on expanding both the Christian faith and his own empire. Of the original fortresslike church, only the westworks with three towers survive. Like so many other churches of the tenth century, St. Pantaleon was flanked by two tall towers and an enclosed entrance. The rest of the church was restored at the end of the nineteenth century.*

a noble landowner who was crowned king of the western Franks with the approval of the local bishops and counts. From their power base in Paris, the Capetian kings slowly spread their authority and enlarged their domains by consolidating their grip over the other feudal lords.

The second emerging state in western Europe was that of Otto the Great (936–973), who was elected king of the Germans and Saxons. A superb military leader and dedicated church reformer, Otto halted the Magyar advance in the east and extended his kingdom into Italy in the south. There he released

the papacy from the control of corrupt Roman families and forced the pope, in return, to recognize him as emperor. In founding his empire and seeking papal sanctions, Otto was clearly following the dream of Charlemagne—to restore the lost Roman world (Figure 8.18).

Religion and Culture in the Early Middle Ages

During the Early Middle Ages literature, art, and architecture degenerated from the already low standards of late Rome. There was a brief, bright moment in the early ninth century under Charlemagne when literature, learning, and the arts flourished, but by the mid–ninth century this renaissance faded in the wake of political disintegration and foreign invasions. Later, Otto the Great encouraged the cultivation of letters within his empire. Notwithstanding their sporadic nature, these intellectual and artistic developments helped to blend the Germanic and Greco-Roman worlds into an emerging Christian Europe.

Christianity: Leadership and Organization Regardless of internal dissension and external foes in the period between 500 and 1000, Christianity strengthened itself and its hold on society. The early popes faced heresy, disorganization, and a vast world of unbaptized men and women. The energetic and dedicated Pope Gregory the Great (590–604) was the most successful of the early medieval pontiffs. He reformed the clergy, whose poor training and lax habits, in particular their sexual behavior, worked against the church's efforts to set high moral standards. Tradition claims he standardized the use of music in the service of worship, so that the Gregorian chants became synonymous with the medieval church. He encouraged the founding of new monasteries among the Germanic peoples. Abroad, he sent missionaries to England, thus ensuring the triumph of Christianity among the Anglo-Saxons. Despite the successes and reforms of Gregory and the later popes, however, they could not break the grip of secular power over church affairs, a thorny problem that awaited solution in the High Middle Ages.

The church found a new source of strength in monasticism. Western monks followed the guidelines that were laid down by St. Benedict (480–543) and observed in the Benedictine order's first monastery at Monte Cassino, south of Rome. The Benedictines, after a period of rigorous intellectual training and self-denial, vowed to lead lives of chastity, obedience, and poverty. They divided their days into alternating periods of work, prayer, and study. The

FIGURE 8.19 Plan of St. Gall Monastery. Ca. 820. *One of the most prominent monasteries of the ninth century was the Benedictine House at St. Gall in Switzerland. Although the monastery no longer exists, its original plan, perhaps by Linhard, has been preserved. The plan reveals the self-sufficient system of the monastery, with its school, hospital, dormitories, poor house, and various buildings and plots of land.*

monks were known as the regular clergy, because they followed a *regula*, or rule.

The monasteries that spread across Europe served many purposes. They were havens for the populace during times of invasion. They were centers for copying ancient literary and philosophical texts, which were then studied in their libraries. The monks often established schools for the local young men. Finally, the self-sufficient monasteries were often models of agricultural productivity and economic resourcefulness (Figure 8.19).

Literature, History, and Learning Writers during this period were more interested in conserving the past than in composing original works. Consequently, literature—all of it written in Latin—was eclectic, blending Christian ideas with Classical thought and often mixing genres, such as history, biography, science, philosophy, and theology.

The most highly educated scholar of the Early Middle Ages was Boethius [bo-E-the-uhs] (about 480–524), a Roman aristocrat and a courtier of Theodoric, the Ostrogoth king in Italy. A rarity in this age, an intellectual who knew Greek, Boethius translated much of Aristotle's vast writings into Latin. In the later Middle Ages, from the sixth through the eleventh centuries, all that Latin scholars knew of Aristotle was through Boethius's translations.

Boethius rose to prominence in Theodoric's court but then fell from favor and was eventually executed. While in prison he wrote the *Consolation of Philosophy,* a work widely read throughout the Middle Ages and beyond. In it he described his mental struggle with despair at life's cruel turn of events. He personified Philosophy as a learned woman with whom he argued many issues in search of the meaning of happiness. In the face of imminent death, Boethius finally concluded that true contentment was reserved for those who combined intellectual inquiry with Christian beliefs.

Although several scholars wrote historical chronicles, only Gregory of Tours and Bede can be classified as historians. Both consulted written documents and other sources and in general strove for (but did not always achieve) objectivity and historical accuracy. Gregory of Tours (about 538–593) left the single surviving record of the sixth-century Merovingian kingdom in his *History of the Franks.* Gregory's account lacks historical cohesion and shows stylistic confusion, but he manages to capture the flavor of his times in his lively and humane character sketches of the Frankish rulers. In Anglo-Saxon England, Bede [BEED] (673–735), an English monk and scholar, composed the *Ecclesiastical History of the English People,* which described the missionary activities that led to the founding of the English church. Written in a pure Latin style, his *History* is a major source for the chronology of this troubled age.

When Charlemagne came to power, cultural life revived and enjoyed its greatest flowering in the Early Middle Ages. The Carolingian Renaissance, which represented Europe's first genuine rebirth of Classical studies within the context of Christian beliefs, had its roots in educational reform. Recognizing that ignorance posed a threat to his regime, Charlemagne founded a palace school at his residence at Aachen, in present-day western Germany. To this school he invited the most learned men of the day to train his own staff and to teach the sons of the nobility. Leading scholars from England, Ireland, and Italy answered this call, settling down in Aachen, where they pursued their scholarship. Foremost among them was Alcuin [AL-kwin] of York (735–804), who led the palace school, giving instruction in Latin, composing his own textbooks, and overseeing the copying of manuscripts.

Another important scholar at Aachen was Einhard [INE-hart] (about 770–840), who came from Gaul and served Charlemagne in many ways. His lasting contribution was his brief and simple biography of the famed ruler, the *Vita Caroli* (the *Life of Charles*). Modeled on the lives of the Caesars by the Roman historian Suetonius, this work is a major literary achievement of the Early Middle Ages and still gives today's readers a vivid portrait of Charlemagne and his times.

One of the important achievements of the palace school was a significant innovation in handwriting. Trained scribes developed a flowing style consisting primarily of rounded lowercase letters that became the standard form for all later handwriting styles in the West. With the development of this legible and uniform Latin script, known as Carolingian minuscule, educated men and women gained access to written material, and monks, in transcribing books, were liable to fewer errors (Figure 8.20).

As Charlemagne's reign passed into golden memory during the turbulent ninth and tenth centuries, the light of civilization seemed to glow dimmer, ex-

FIGURE 8.20 Carolingian Minuscule. Ninth Century. Bibliothèque Nationale, Paris. *Because Christianity relied heavily on written works, legible texts were important, but the prevailing style of writing, which used separately formed lowercase letters, was almost impossible to read. To overcome this difficulty, scribes during Charlemagne's reign perfected a new style of writing—the Carolingian minuscule—which was characterized by clearly formed letters linked into words, spaces between words, and capital letters at the beginning of sentences, as shown in this manuscript. All subsequent Western handwriting styles follow from this tradition.*

cept in monasteries in Ireland and Germany where many monks and nuns kept the humanities alive. Especially noteworthy among the monastic scholars who balanced Christian faith with the Classics was Hrotswitha [rawts-VEE-tar] (about 935–about 975), a canoness (a nunlike vocation that did not require vows for life) at Gandersheim convent in Saxony. The first German playwright, Hrotswitha wrote six plays, in Latin, modeled on those of Terence, the Roman dramatist (see Chapter 5), but infused with erudite religious ideas. Rejecting the themes of Roman comedy as spiritually unhealthy, these Christian dramas focused on fall and conversion themes, as in *Abraham*, which tells of a prostitute rescued by a saintly monk. Literary exercises, these plays were probably never performed, except perhaps as recitations with mimed action. Hrotswitha's writings, forgotten until the Renaissance, were rediscovered in about 1500 by German humanists who recognized them as major monuments of medieval drama.

Music   Music became an integral part of the church liturgy during the Early Middle Ages and kept alive the Greek heritage of music as an art form. From this religious nursery ultimately arose all of the sacred and secular music of the modern West. The name of Pope Gregory the Great is preserved in the most famous early medieval musical form, the **Gregorian chant**, which became the official liturgical music of the early church—that is, used in the Mass (the celebration of the eucharist) and other services of the yearly cycle of public worship. The chants consisted of a single melodic line sung in unison, without instrumental accompaniment, by male voices. They had an impersonal, nonemotional quality and served religious rather than aesthetic or emotional purposes. Notwithstanding this aim, the chants cast a spell over their listeners, evoking in them feelings of otherworldliness, peace, and purity.

In the ninth century, one of the most important advancements in music history occurred, the rise of polyphony—two lines of melody which are sounded at the same time. Polyphony, unlike the monophonic Gregorian chants, gave music a vertical as well as a horizontal quality. But further musical developments would have to await more settled social and political conditions.

Architecture   The overall decline of living conditions in western Europe took its toll in architecture and art as patronage evaporated, skills fell into disuse, and artistic talents were necessarily directed to more pragmatic ends. The few artisans and builders who were still in business traveled across western Europe constructing churches and chapels in protected places.

FIGURE 8.21   Charlemagne's Palace Chapel. Ca. 792–805. Aachen, Germany. *Odo of Metz designed the Royal Chapel for Charlemagne, and Pope Leo III probably dedicated it in 805. Although the chapel is inspired by Byzantine architecture, the decorative scheme and the roof design make it a Roman rather than a Byzantine building. From the tenth to the sixteenth centuries the Germans crowned their kings in this chapel.*

Charlemagne gave full support to the construction of impressive churches and palaces, especially his own royal residence. Today, most of the original apartments and offices of his palace are restored rather than original, but the Palace Chapel remains largely as it was first built (Figure 8.21). Inspired by the design of San Vitale in Ravenna, this magnificent room reflects the architect's reinterpretation of the graceful Byzantine style to incorporate the massive solidity of Roman monuments and the vigor of Germanic taste. Octagonal in shape, the chapel stands two stories tall. Heavy square pillars support the second level, where galleries are framed by graceful

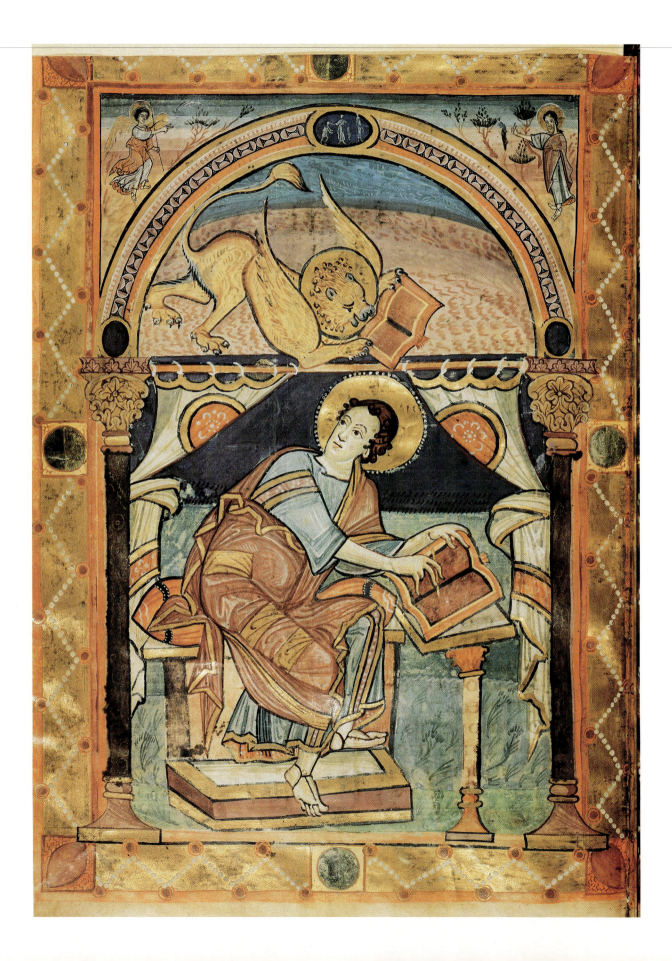

◀ **FIGURE 8.22** *St. Mark,* from the Gospel Book of St. Medard of Soissons. Early Ninth Century. Bibliothèque Nationale, Paris. *The so-called Italo-Alpine style of painting is evident in this portrait of St. Mark because it includes Roman decorations, in particular the columns derived from the Corinthian order. Although this gospel book was made for Charlemagne, it ended up in the abbey of St. Medard by 827 as a gift to the monks from Louis the Pious, Charlemagne's heir. Painted on vellum, it measures 14 by 10 inches.*

arches and columns brought from Italy. The bronze gratings and mosaic floor were also brought to Aachen from Italy. An ***ambulatory***, or passageway for walking, extends around the circumference of the central space behind the pillars. Spiral steps lead up to the upper floor, where the tribune, or emperor's throne, was located. From here, Charlemagne observed and participated in the services and ceremonies of the church and was in turn observed by his subjects, enthroned as Christ's representative on earth.

Painting: Illuminated Manuscripts   Although nearly all of the murals, frescoes, and mosaics from this period have vanished, the surviving ***illuminated manuscripts*** offer an excellent view of the early medieval painting ideal. The art of manuscript illumination was influenced by the barbarian practice of decorating small objects and the Classical tradition of fine metal work that had been maintained in Italy. During the Early Middle Ages, gifted artists and dedicated monks joined these disparate artistic elements to produce richly illustrated books and bejeweled book covers. Most of these decorated books were used in the liturgy of the Mass, such as the psalters, the collections of the psalms, and the gospel books, which were the texts of the first four books of the New Testament. For three centuries, in monasteries and abbeys from Ireland to Germany, scribes copied the Bible and their fellow artists adorned the pages with geometric and foliage designs, mythical animals, Christian symbols, and portraits of biblical characters and saints.

Manuscript illumination became both more symbolic and more realistic in the Carolingian Renaissance, partly because Italian artists were now influencing Frankish tastes. For example, the gospel of St. Medard of Soissons follows Italian practice in being filled with Christian symbols and religious icons as well as making visual references to Classical architecture. In a portrait of St. Mark, the painter decorates the page with the lion, St. Mark's symbol, and frames the saint with a rounded arch, Corinthian columns, and folded curtains (Figure 8.22). In this small

FIGURE 8.23   *St. Luke,* from the Gospel Book of Otto III. Ca. 1000. Bayerische Staatsbibliothek, Munich. *In this illumination from a gospel book, the biblical symbols and images above St. Luke dominate the earthly and human forms. The unnatural colors and placement of the figures suggest a mystical meaning. This portrait of St. Luke measures about 8 inches by 10 inches.*

work the figure of St. Mark exhibits a dynamic sense of life in his energetic body and tilted head.

At the end of the Early Middle Ages, the style of manuscript illumination became even more elaborate and richer in tone, as in the Gospel Book of Otto III, a product of the German Reichnau school. The miniaturist who painted this manuscript represents the figure of St. Luke in a state of religious ecstacy. Enthroned, St. Luke supports a host of Jewish prophets and heavenly messengers; books from the Old Testament are stacked in his lap. Hovering above the saint's head is his symbol, the ox (Figure 8.23).

The Legacy of Byzantium, Islam, and the Early Medieval West

When Constantinople fell, Byzantine civilization left a profound legacy to the West, some of which is still alive today. In Eastern Europe, the Orthodox church continues to influence the Slavic population. Western law owes a great debt to the Code of Justinian, which became the standard legal text studied in medieval universities. Elements of Byzantine art appeared in Renaissance art in Italy, and the Italian cities of Venice, Genoa, and Pisa became major cultural centers in the fifteenth century because of the wealth they had accumulated from Byzantine trade.

Byzantium also served conserving functions for the West. The Byzantine state acted as a buffer against the militant Arabs in the seventh century and against the Seljuk Turks in the twelfth century. Byzantine scholars preserved the ancient Greek texts, many of which were carried to Italy, England, and elsewhere in the mid–fifteenth century. When these works were reintroduced into the West, they intensified the cultural revival already underway.

Islamic civilization's impact on Western culture has been significant, though not as direct as that of Byzantium. Of all of the benefits passed on from Islam, the transmission of the basic philosophical and scientific texts from the ancient world is probably the most important. Original Muslim contributions in algebra and other mathematical concepts have also been central to the rise of the modern scientific tradition in the West.

The civilization of the Early Medieval West, of course, has been most decisive for the direction of Western culture. Most of the heritage from this first medieval period was simply a transmission of what had been formed earlier in the ancient world: the Christian church, the papacy, the Latin language, the educational ideal embodied in the arts and the sciences, building and artistic techniques, Greek thought, and Greco-Roman literary and artistic forms. Most of these ancient legacies were reshaped in some way, as for example in the reform of monasticism along Benedictine lines.

What was added to the Western legacy in the Early Middle Ages was basically the uniting of Classical, Germanic, and Christian elements into a new civilization, a civilization that was centered in Europe rather than in the Mediterranean basin. This new version of Western culture was born in the reign of Charlemagne, and its memory lingered on in the monasteries and other isolated quarters. When the barbarian invasions were over, a more enduring Western culture was born.

KEY CULTURAL TERMS

Byzantine style	*mosque*
Greek cross	*minaret*
pendentive	*miniature*
arcade	*Gregorian chant*
arabesque	*ambulatory*
calligraphy	*illuminated manuscript*

SUGGESTIONS FOR FURTHER READING

PRIMARY SOURCES

BEDE. *A History of the English Church and People.* Translated by L. Sherley-Price. New York: Penguin, 1955. Written in A.D. 731, this account of the church in Saxon England is an important source for understanding early Christian society and attitudes in England.

BOETHIUS. *The Consolation of Philosophy.* Translated by V. E. Watts. New York: Penguin, 1969. An account, combining verse and prose and written in the early sixth century, that shows how Christian faith and pagan philosophy enabled the author to accept both his fall from power and death.

COMNENA. *The Alexiad of Anna Comnena.* Translated and with a brief introduction by E. R. A. Sewter. New York: Penguin, 1979. A fresh, modern translation of this Byzantine classic work of history, with notes, a map, appendices, and genealogical tables; some of the author's digressions are consigned to footnotes.

EINHARD AND NOTKER THE STAMMERER. *Two Lives of Charlemagne.* Translated by L. Thorpe. New York: Penguin, 1969. A useful introduction and many footnotes enlighten the student about these two brief but important contemporary biographies by, respectively, the head of Charlemagne's palace school and a monk.

GREGORY, BISHOP OF TOURS. *History of the Franks.* Translated by L. Thorpe. New York: Penguin, 1974. An engrossing account of this chaotic time by an eyewitness.

HROTSWITHA. *The Plays of Hrotsvit [Hrotswitha] of Gandersheim.* Translated and with an introduction by K. Wilson. New York: Garland, 1989. A lively and authoritative translation of these early medieval plays, with scholarly notes.

9

THE HIGH MIDDLE AGES
The Christian Centuries

Although the ambitious hopes of Charlemagne for Europe were blasted by the barbarian invasions of the ninth and tenth centuries, society had grown more settled by the early eleventh century, and a brighter era began to unfold in the West. Between 1000 and 1300—the period called the High Middle Ages—a new foundation was laid that would support the future development of Western civilized life.

During this time the Christian church grew in influence to become the dominant institution of the medieval world. At the same time, feudalism was established as the principal military, economic, and political system, and feudal monarchies in France, England, and central Europe began to form the germs of future European states. Despite the prevalence of the feudal system, town life revived to an extent unseen in the West since the declining years of the Roman Empire, and a new urban class was born. Midway between the feudal aristocrats and the peasants, this middle class included merchants, moneylenders, and skilled artisans, among others—virtually any free persons associated with town life.

These momentous changes in the political, social, and economic realms were reflected in the cultural interests of the time. Theologians, writers, and architects worked to harmonize the opposing trends of the time, the secular and the spiritual. Their achievement was a stunning but short-lived synthesis that seemed to resolve many contradictions. Moving from rugged warrior values, supreme between 1000

and 1150, Western culture became more refined, learned, and increasingly secular between 1150 and 1300. The earlier 150-year-period is associated with monastic and feudal themes in literature and the Romanesque style in architecture. The later period saw a growing trend toward urban and courtly themes in literature and the rise of the Gothic style in architecture, the most spectacular realization of which was the Gothic cathedral.

FEUDALISM

Out of feudalism—a military and political system based on personal loyalty and kinship—arose a new social order, a code of conduct, and an artistic and literary tradition. In the beginning, feudalism restored law and order to western Europe, even though local lords often exploited those under them. But the nature of feudalism changed during the High Middle Ages; the feudal nobility slowly lost power to the feudal kings, who laid the foundations of the early modern national monarchies. As a result, by the early 1300s feudalism no longer served its original function and was being superseded in many areas by different political, social, and economic forms.

The Feudal System and Feudal Society

With origins in both Roman and German practices, feudalism evolved in the Early Middle Ages under the Franks and expanded under Charlemagne. As a

◀ Nave. Amiens Cathedral. View from the West. Amiens, France. Ca. 1220–1236.

military system it offered some protection from barbarian invaders but at the cost of fragmenting society into rival states. As the feudal chiefs began to pass their lands on to their eldest sons, Europe became dominated by a military aristocracy (see Chapter 8).

Feudal wealth was reckoned in terms of land—the feudal estate included lands, manor houses, and the serfs who worked the land. The feudal lords attracted warriors, called vassals, to their private armies by offering them landed estates, and thus feudalism depended on the manorial economy. The feudal estate, called a fief, enabled the warrior to outfit himself with the proper military equipment, including horses and attendants, and to live in a style worthy of an aristocrat.

Mature feudalism was a complex web of agreements, obligations, and rituals. A written agreement spelled out the mutual duties and obligations of the lord and the vassal. Typically, the lord gave military protection to his vassal and settled quarrels among his supporters through his court. The vassal in turn offered his lord "aid and counsel" by furnishing military or financial aid and sitting as counsel in the lord's court. Despite guarantees and safeguards, conflicts often arose between a lord and his vassal. Sometimes differences were settled by peers before the lord in his court; more often they resulted in civil wars that inflicted loss of life and goods on innocent parties as well as on the belligerents.

Throughout Europe the vassal-lord relationship was the heart of feudalism, but the specific form of the institution varied geographically. Feudalism's prototype was that of northern France, around Paris; from there it spread westward into Normandy and eastward into Champagne. From France feudalism radiated out across Europe, from Normandy over the English Channel to the British Isles, southward into Sicily, eastward into central Germany and Poland, and across the Alps into northern Italy. Each area modified the French form to suit its local needs. Those who profited from feudalism held on to the institution as long as possible, so that well into the twentieth century its vestiges were evident in central Europe and Russia and were eliminated only by revolution.

The hierarchical social order spawned by feudalism was defined and elaborated in the unwritten rules of conduct known as the *chivalric code*. In the early eleventh century, chivalry (from the French word *cheval*, meaning "horse") was largely a warrior code, although one rooted in Christian values. More an ideal than a reality, it nevertheless inspired the vassal to honor his lord and to respect his peers. He was also expected to protect the weak from danger and to practice his ideals—bravery, strength, and honesty—with all members of society.

In the early eleventh century, under the growing power of the church, chivalry evolved into a more refined code. The French clergy initiated the Peace of God, a call for an end to fighting at certain specified times, and other clerics were encouraging the knights to show more humane treatment to certain people, especially women, clergy, and peasants. By the twelfth century both the Peace of God and the notion of protected classes—notably women—were incorporated into the warrior code. Especially influential in altering the status of women was the rise of

FIGURE 9.1   *Count Eckhart and Uta.* Naumburg Cathedral. Ca. 1245. Naumburg, Germany. *In this representation of a feudal lord and lady, the most striking features are the woman's chaste beauty, reflecting her role as the queen of chivalry and linking her to the Virgin Mary, and the man's great heraldic shield and sword, symbolizing his position as an aristocratic warrior and defender of honor. These two figures are among several that stand in Naumburg Cathedral, representing noble men and women associated with the founding of the cathedral. The Naumburg statues are considered among the most beautiful sculptures from this period.*

FIGURE 9.2 *Labors of the Months. Amiens Cathedral. Ca. 1220–1230. Amiens, France. These carefully observed depictions of peasant life from the western portals of Amiens Cathedral show peasants engaged in their daily rounds. These three quatrefoils— four-leafed shapes—represent the summer months and the tasks of harvesting, threshing, and pruning.*

courtly love, a movement at first centered in the aristocratic courts of southern France and later spreading to courts across Europe. Perhaps the greatest contribution of medieval civilization, courtly love encouraged the intermingling of the sexes in social settings where dancing, music, and conversation were enjoyed in accordance with the rules of courtesy. Thus, after 1200 the protection of women was enshrined at the heart of a more courtly version of the chivalric code. Much of the secular literature, art, and music of the High Middle Ages was inspired by these values. Because they were identified with the Virgin Mary, women were idealized and venerated with an almost holy respect (Figure 9.1). A contradictory and equally unrealistic trend was the association of women with evil because of their descent from Eve, who tempted Adam to eat the forbidden fruit and brought the burden of original sin to humanity.

Whatever the image of woman in medieval society, however, on a practical level her position was determined by the social status of her husband or father. A few women—such as Eleanor of Aquitaine, wife of King Henry II of England in the twelfth century—sometimes influenced a spouse's decisions or wielded power on behalf of a son. But their rarity as rulers in their own right testifies to how little power women really had in the Middle Ages, despite their glorified image.

Peasant Life

Feudalism and chivalry were designed to serve the best interests of the relatively few members of the noble classes. Life was very different in the timeless world of the peasants, who made up the vast majority of the population. Some of them were free, but many were bound in service. The two most common

forms of servitude, slavery and serfdom, were legacies from Rome. Slavery was a dying institution because the church's teachings had convinced the feudal lords of its inhumanity. But serfdom, which bound peasants to their lord's service by inheritance, was firmly entrenched by the twelfth century and restricted the movements of those caught up in it. Law and tradition allowed each lord to control completely the world of the peasants on his manor.

The routine of the serfs and the free peasants was laid down by custom and regulated by daily and seasonal events (Figure 9.2). Living in wooden huts, they eked out a bare subsistence from their tiny plots of land, raised their children, and found relief in the frequent Holy Days and feast days set by the church calendar. In time, as farming innovations were introduced (such as three-field crop rotation, which allowed the land to replenish itself), the plight of the serfs improved. Increasing the productivity of the soil brought economic benefits to the lord of the manor, and he in turn could undertake such measures as paying the peasants in coin and selling them tracts of land.

As serfs gained a few legal rights, they could become economically independent and win their freedom from the manorial system. These trends, however, were confined to western Europe, notably England and France. In central and eastern Europe, serfs continued to be exploited, in some areas for centuries to come.

The Rise of Towns

Despite the dominance of the feudal system, a new trend was beginning that ran counter to all the principles of feudalism: the rise of urban areas where free individuals pursued their own economic goals. Although the rural manors provided work and

FIGURE 9.3 *Street Scene in a Medieval Town.* Bibliothèque Nationale, Paris. *Four businesses are crowded together into this narrow street. In the background, three furriers await customers. Other merchants have hung out signs to advertise their trades, such as the barber who displays four "barber bowls"—a device placed over the head during a haircut. In the left foreground, tailors stitch clothing, and, on the right, a storekeeper arranges goods in front of his shop. Most tradesmen lived above their stores, which meant that the town was filled with people both day and night.*

security for approximately 90 percent of the population, town life was beginning to flourish. Triggered in part by changes in agriculture, the population of Europe nearly doubled between 1000 and 1300, from thirty-five million to almost seventy million, and many people sought economic opportunities in the new and revitalized urban areas. These centers sprang up in various locations: at the sites of old Roman towns, near the castles of local feudal lords, around regional markets or the seats of bishops, or simply along rivers or roads where trade routes crossed (Figure 9.3). From this point on, the future of the West lay with the town dwellers, who expanded in steadily increasing numbers regardless of the uncertainties of the economy and the turmoil of urban living.

As town populations increased and urban life became more competitive, the residents formed associations, called guilds, to protect their special interests. The artisan and craft guilds, for example,

regulated working conditions, created apprenticeship programs, and set wages, and the merchant and banking guilds approved new businesses and supervised trade contracts. The artisan and the merchant guilds often quarreled over issues inside the town walls, but they joined hands against the intrusions of the church and the local nobility.

Because this kind of economic life was so at odds with the feudal system, urban dwellers, led by the guilds, founded self-governing towns, called communes, often with written documents (charters) that specified their political and economic rights in relation to the feudal lords. A serf, for example, could become a freeman if he lived in a chartered town for a year and a day. By about 1200, many towns in northern and western Europe had charters, and their political independence spurred economic growth. Moreover, these charters symbolized the fact that town life was protected and to some degree independent of the feudal world.

Artisans who crafted goods and merchants who sold them needed buyers, secure trade routes, and markets for their products if they were to prosper. The earliest trade routes were the rivers and old Roman roads. As demand increased in the West for luxury items from the Orient, new trade routes opened between Europe and the East. Italian cities—Venice, Pisa, and Genoa—took the lead in this international commerce, trading the luxurious woolen cloth of Flanders for the silks of China and the spices of the Middle East (Map 9.1). Along the overland leg of this route in Europe, local lords promised to give traders safe passage through their territory for a fee. Some nobles as well as a few strategically located towns in central France sponsored fairs as a lure for this rich international trade.

The role of women in this urban world was still subordinate to that of men, as it was on the feudal manor. Indeed, in this hierarchical society sex roles became hardened through custom and legislation.

As a consequence, females could neither hold governmental office nor have any public voice in politics. The few women with economic power—such as those directly involved in manufacturing and trade or the occasional rich widow who kept her husband's business afloat—were exceptions to this general exclusionary rule.

The Feudal Monarchy

Politically, feudalism was leading to a new form of rule. By about 1100 some powerful feudal lords began to expand their holdings into larger and larger kingdoms. As these ambitious rulers subdued weaker lords, they often sealed their victories through marriages with the conquered families. Over the ensuing generations, the heirs extended and consolidated their lands, always trying to win the loyalty of their new subjects.

MAP 9.1

Principal Trading Routes and Towns of Europe, 1300

TIME LINE 9.1   THE FRENCH FEUDAL MONARCHY IN THE HIGH MIDDLE AGES

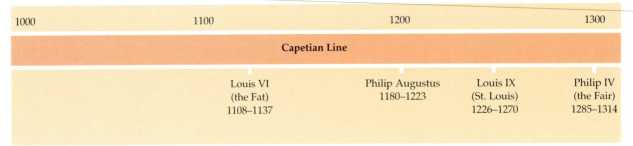

1000	1100	1200	1300
		Capetian Line	
	Louis VI (the Fat) 1108–1137	Philip Augustus 1180–1223	Louis IX (St. Louis) 1226–1270 · Philip IV (the Fair) 1285–1314

Unlike modern states, these feudal monarchies were simply clusters of feudal lands that the monarchs were constantly trying to control. The major domestic problem faced by a feudal monarch was building a centralized rule while keeping his (or in some instances, her) kingdom from disintegrating into a set of separate, warring states. During the High Middle Ages, four feudal monarchies dominated the West: the French monarchy, the English monarchy, the Holy Roman Empire, and the papal monarchy, which in its political aspect closely resembled the three secular monarchies.

The French Monarchy   The origins of modern France stem from the late tenth-century reign of Hugh Capet,

FIGURE 9.4   *Harold's Oath of Allegiance.* Panel from the Bayeux Tapestry. Third Quarter of the Eleventh Century. Wool embroidery on linen, height 20". Bayeux, France. *Probably stitched by English women and today housed in the Cathedral of Bayeux, this famous embroidery provides an important historic record of the events leading up to the Battle of Hastings. In its emphasis on the disastrous consequences of betrayed loyalties, it clearly reflects the feudal world view. Harold is cast as a villain who breaks his oath of allegiance to William and loses the English crown as a result of this treachery. In the panel, a seated William points to Harold, who is taking an oath while touching two shrines holding relics. The tapestry thus presents a justification for the Norman conquest of England.*

who exercised power over a part of the old Frankish kingdom (see Chapter 8). From him arose the Capetian dynasty, a line of resolute successors each of whom stubbornly continued to call himself King of the Franks. By the early eleventh century, the Capetians, having fought off their rivals, had founded a feudal monarchy in central France, with Paris as its center.

During the twelfth and thirteenth centuries, a series of able monarchs managed to consolidate and expand the Capetian power base and control the great vassals by forming alliances, at different times and in different ways, with the lesser nobles, the middle class, the clergy, and the papacy. The establishment of central authority in France was a slow and difficult process, but by the time of the reign of Philip IV (called "the Fair") in 1285, France was the most powerful feudal kingdom in Europe and the French tradition of royal absolutism was well established (Time Line 9.1).

The English Monarchy   Like the French kings, the English monarchs methodically amassed power at the expense of the feudal landowners, but otherwise the two kingdoms evolved quite differently. The English rulers never controlled their kingdom in the same manner or to the same degree as did their counterparts in Paris. Moreover, because some of the English kings made grievous mistakes, England's feudal barons won pivotal battles against the crown. In addition, judicial reforms and the growth of advisory councils tended to limit, not to expand, the English kings' power.

Three major events determined the course of English history during this period. The first was the French invasion of England. For five centuries England had been ruled by an Anglo-Saxon monarchy. When Edward the Confessor died in 1066 without a clear successor, Duke William, the ruler of the duchy of Normandy in northern France, invaded England to claim the throne. At the battle of Hastings in 1066, William conquered the Anglo-Saxon contender, Harold, and became king of England (Figure 9.4). For the rest of the High Middle Ages England was ruled by Norman kings and their French successors.

TIME LINE 9.2   THE ENGLISH FEUDAL MONARCHY IN THE HIGH MIDDLE AGES

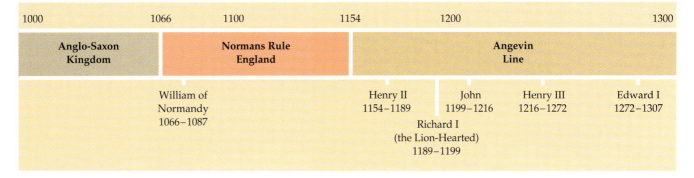

1000	1066	1100	1154	1200	1300
Anglo-Saxon Kingdom	**Normans Rule England**		**Angevin Line**		

William of Normandy 1066–1087

Henry II 1154–1189

Richard I (the Lion-Hearted) 1189–1199

John 1199–1216

Henry III 1216–1272

Edward I 1272–1307

During this time the conquerors and the conquered were blended into one nation and one culture (Time Line 9.2).

The second event occurred in 1215 when the English feudal barons forced King John (1199–1216) to sign the Magna Carta ("great charter"), a document that limited royal authority by guaranteeing that the king would not do certain things and that the barons had certain financial and governmental control over the crown. The signing of the Magna Carta was primarily a victory for the barons, but in the long run all freemen gained, for the document promised them certain judicial rights, such as trial by jury.

The third event occurred during the reign of John's son, Henry III (1216–1272), when Parliament, today Great Britain's national legislative body, made its first appearance. Faced by renewed hostility from his English barons, Henry agreed to convene the Great Council, an ancient but little-used body. Two representatives from each county and two from each town were summoned together to talk, and thus Parliament (from the French word *parler*, "to talk") began to advise the king. At first, Parliament was part of the royal government, but, in time, it came to speak for the people against the crown, and England moved further along the road to a limited feudal monarchy.

The Holy Roman Empire   While France and England grew into unified feudal monarchies, the Holy Roman Empire struggled and failed to achieve a centralized state. The Holy Roman Empire began as the Ottonian empire in the late tenth century. From the early eleventh to the early twelfth centuries, the empire prospered and trade expanded. During these same years, however, a conflict with the papacy arose that would undermine the empire. The conflict concerned the European-wide practice of lay investiture—the appointment of priests, bishops, and archbishops by local lords and nobles, not infrequently for money. By mak-

ing such appointments, the secular rulers were able to some extent to control the wealth and influence of the church within their own territories. The conflict was prolonged and complicated, but the central issue was this: Are the bishops and archbishops the servants of the pope or of the secular ruler?

The specific issue of lay investiture was settled by the Concordat of Worms in 1122, which allowed the pope to confer spiritual authority on the clergy and the emperor to invest them with land and secular authority. But the rivalry between the Holy Roman rulers and the papacy would not die. Under the empire's next dynasty, the Hohenstaufens, a new issue emerged. Were the popes or the emperors to control central Europe? The Hohenstaufens produced two able rulers, Frederick Barbarossa and Frederick II, but neither was able to achieve the German dream of an empire reaching from the Baltic Ocean in the north to Sicily in the south. Under their incompetent successors, the papacy resumed its sway over Italian politics, and the Holy Roman Emperors ceased to play a major role in European affairs for many years (Time Line 9.3).

The Papal Monarchy   The papacy during the High Middle Ages closely resembled the feudal monarchies in Europe, with the exception that it was guided by the ideal of Christendom—a universal state ruled by the popes under God's law. The church's most powerful claim to authority was that only through the clergy—those trained and ordained to administer the sacraments—could a Christian hope to reach everlasting life. The church defined and upheld society's moral standards by both teaching and example at the same time that it participated in the politics of the period.

The key to the church's power during the High Middle Ages was a reform movement that had originated in the monastery at Cluny, France, and swept through Europe in the 900s. Prior to this movement the church had been riddled with scandal and

TIME LINE 9.3   THE HOLY ROMAN EMPIRE IN THE HIGH MIDDLE AGES

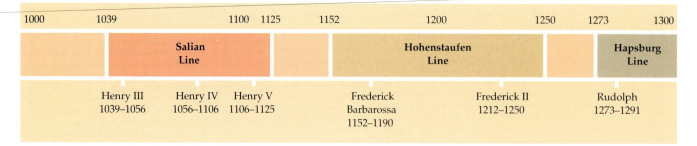

| 1000 | 1039 | | 1100 | 1125 | 1152 | | 1200 | | 1250 | 1273 | 1300 |

	Salian Line			Hohenstaufen Line			Hapsburg Line

Henry III 1039–1056   Henry IV 1056–1106   Henry V 1106–1125   Frederick Barbarossa 1152–1190   Frederick II 1212–1250   Rudolph 1273–1291

corruption. Many clergy were poorly trained—some barely literate—and lived less than exemplary lives. Bishops often acted as if they were the vassals of local feudal lords rather than agents of the church, a reflection of the entrenched nature of lay investiture. The buying and selling of church offices, a practice known as simony, meant that positions often went to the highest bidder. Worst of all, many clergymen expressed blatant disregard for the sacraments.

The monastery at Cluny was founded in 910 by the Benedictine order of monks. Free of feudal obligations and loyal only to the pope, the monastery inaugurated reforms that raised the moral level of the clergy and rid the church of scandal. Little by little, these Cluniacs impressed Europe with their superior spirituality. Encouraged by their success, the Cluny monks quickly established new monasteries and reformed others.

As the Cluniac reforms spread, the church began to be revivified. Campaigns were undertaken within the church to eliminate corrupt practices and to reimpose celibacy on the clergy. A landmark occurred in 1059 when the College of Cardinals was founded with sole responsibility for electing the popes, thus freeing the papacy from German and Italian politics. By late in the eleventh century the reformed popes had arrived at a point where their political power rivaled that of the feudal monarchs.

Of the great medieval popes, the two most powerful were Gregory VII and Innocent III (Time Line 9.4). Gregory VII (1073–1085) was brought to St. Peter's chair by the Cluniac revival. Once enthroned, he purified the wayward clergy, demanding full obedience to canon law. Although he was less effective in freeing the church from feudalism, he was able to liberate many church offices from local lay influence.

Innocent III (1198–1216), the second of these medieval popes, was probably the most powerful pontiff in the history of the church. He excommunicated kings, intervened at will in the secular affairs of England, France, and the Holy Roman Empire, and preached crusades against the Muslims abroad and heretics at home (Figure 9.5). Motivated by the ideal of Christendom, his aim was to unite Europe under the papal banner.

Pope Boniface VIII (1294–1303) unwittingly undid the three centuries' work of his predecessors. By his extravagant papal claims, he made a mockery of his office. In 1302, he issued the papal bull (from the Latin for *bolla*, or seal) known as *Unam sanctam*, a proclamation of papal superiority over all secular rulers. The French crown's answer to this papal challenge was swift: Philip IV (the Fair) sent an army to arrest the pope. In the melée that followed, an unnerved Boniface VIII had to flee for his life and died soon thereafter. This episode revealed that the popes

TIME LINE 9.4   THE PAPAL MONARCHY IN THE HIGH MIDDLE AGES

| 1000 | | 1100 | | 1200 | | 1300 |

Gregory VII 1073–1085   Innocent III 1198–1216   Boniface VIII 1294–1303

FIGURE 9.5 *Pope Innocent III.* Thirteenth Century. *This handsome mosaic portrays Innocent III in his crown and vestments—the rich trappings of papal monarchical power. The artist, influenced by the Byzantine style, has depicted him with large staring eyes—a sign of piety. In actuality, however, Innocent III was a realistic and somewhat ruthless ruler when it came to dealing with his adversaries.*

were no match for the feudal kings. Boniface VIII's humiliation precipitated a decline in papal prestige from which the papacy did not fully recover until the sixteenth century.

MEDIEVAL CHRISTIANITY AND THE CHURCH

In addition to its political significance, the institution of the church had incalculable influence in the High Middle Ages, bringing Christian values to bear on virtually every facet of medieval life. The church owed its influence not only to the maneuverings of the popes but to the tireless work of the clergy and the powerful effect of the Christian belief system.

By this time in its history the church had evolved an elaborate organization to carry out its work. The pope, as the spiritual leader of Christianity, stood at the head of a strict hierarchy. Supporting him was the papal curia—a staff of administrators, financial experts, secretaries, clerics, and legal advisors. A system of ecclesiastical courts handled the church's judicial functions and interpreted canon law, the church's law code based on the Bible. These courts were technically restricted to cases involving clerical personnel, but in actuality their jurisdiction was broader because of the huge number of people enmeshed in the workings of the church. The church's judicial branch rivaled the feudal courts in jurisdiction, and canon law sometimes challenged the authority of feudal law.

Tithes, taxes, and special collections provided the funds needed by the church to carry on its daily operations as well as to meet its charitable obligations. Given the absence of modern financial methods, the system was relatively efficient, and as long as the church spent the funds wisely, the populace kept up its generous contributions.

Christian Beliefs and Practices

A great part of the immense authority of the church sprang from the belief shared by the overwhelming majority of the medieval population that the church held the keys to the kingdom of heaven and provided the only way to salvation. By attempting to adhere to the Christian moral code and by participating in the rituals and ceremonies prescribed by the church, Christians hoped for redemption and eternal life after death.

These rituals and ceremonies were basically inseparable from the doctrines of the religion. They had been derived from the teachings of Jesus and Paul, clarified by the church fathers, particularly Augustine, and further defined by medieval theologians. Finally, the Fourth Lateran Council of 1215 under Pope Innocent III had officially proclaimed the sacraments as the outward signs of God's grace and the only way to heaven.

As established by the council, the sacraments numbered seven: baptism, confirmation, the Eucharist (Holy Communion), penance, marriage, last rites, and ordination for the priesthood. Baptism, the Eucharist, and penance were deemed of primary importance. In baptism the parents were assured that the infant had been rescued from original sin. In the Eucharist, the central part of the Mass, the church taught that a miracle occurred whereby the priest turned the bread and wine into the body and blood of Jesus. Known as the doctrine of transubstantiation, this miracle gave the priest additional prestige. That the outer appearance of the bread and wine remained the same while their inner nature changed was explained by medieval philosophers. For the uneducated congregation, however, the Mass and the miracle were simply another sign of the church's spiritual power.

The third of these primary sacraments, penance, evolved into a rather complicated practice. First, sinners confessed their sins individually to a priest; the priest conveyed God's forgiveness for the mortal penalties of sin, so that hell could be avoided; the priest then directed that an earthly punishment—the penance—be carried out in an effort to erase the effects of the sin. Depending on the severity of the sin, penance could range from saying a few prayers to going on a pilgrimage or a crusade. This sacrament was made even more complex by its association with purgatory.

With the groundwork laid by Augustine in the fifth century and Pope Gregory the Great in the sixth century, the doctrine of purgatory was given more explicit form by the papacy and scholastic thinkers of the High Middle Ages. Neither hell nor heaven, purgatory was a third place reserved for those souls whose sins were such that they could avoid damnation but whose good deeds were insufficient to merit immediate salvation. All souls in purgatory were ultimately destined for heaven; penance was a means of reducing time in purgatory. Thus the living could do penance on earth in hope of spending less time in purgatory.

Confession and penance became widespread practices of the eleventh-century church. By 1300 both were integral parts of Christian rituals and beliefs. In political terms, penance, along with the Mass, became effective means for controlling the moral behavior of church members.

Religious Orders and Lay Piety

Crucial to the workings of the church were the clergy, who were the most visible signs of the church's presence in everyday life. The "secular" clergy (from *saeculum*, Latin for "world") moved freely in society, and the "regular" clergy lived apart from the world in monasteries under a special rule (*regula* in Latin). The monasteries served as refuges from the world, as schools, and as places of study where manuscripts could be copied and traditional learning maintained. They also gave rise to the reform movements that periodically cleansed the church of corruption.

FIGURE 9.6 *St. Francis of Assisi.* Ca. 1274. Attributed to School of Berlinghieri. Tempera on panel, 81 × 51 cm. Accademia, Florence. *Many miraculous events were reported to have occurred in the life of Francis, the founder of the Franciscan order. In this painting, completed some fifty years after the saint's death, he is portrayed as receiving the stigmata, or the wounds of Christ—a sign to Christians that Francis was a man marked in a special way by God.*

As noted earlier, the Benedictines at Cluny originated the reform movement that helped to establish the moral and political authority of the medieval church. After Cluny other waves of reform followed, the most important of which was represented by the founding of the Cistercian order in the twelfth century. Bernard of Clairvaux [KLER-VOE] (1090–1153), a saint, a mystic, and one of the most forceful personalities of the period, personally founded over 160 Cistercian abbeys. Unlike the moderate Benedictines, the Cistercians observed a severe rule, living usually in isolated monasteries where the brothers worked with the local peasants. The Cistercians also simplified their worship services, stripping them of elaborate ceremonies.

For women, the religious impulse found an outlet in convents and nunneries. Here, women could devote themselves to Christ and follow ascetic lives filled with prayer, contemplation, and service. Convents had existed since the time of Charlemagne, although seldom with the large endowments monasteries enjoyed or with as much influence in local affairs.

Another type of religious order appeared in the thirteenth century with the rise of two major mendicant, or begging, orders, the Franciscans and the Dominicans. These new churchmen, called *friars*, were originally dedicated to working among the urban poor, but their mission changed, and by 1250 they were dominating higher education. For example, Thomas Aquinas, the age's leading scholar, was a Dominican friar. In the fourteenth century the two orders became notorious for their association with the Inquisition, the church court charged with stamping out heresy.

While both orders of friars made important contributions, the Franciscans had a greater impact on medieval society, largely because of the gentle nature of the order's sainted founder, Francis (1182–1226). Many people still find Francis's piety, selflessness, and legendary humility the personification of a sublime Christian (Figure 9.6).

As monastic reform slowed in the late twelfth century, a wave of lay piety swelled up from the lower social ranks. These unorthodox movements, usually rooted in social and economic causes, quickly ran into trouble with the church. At first, the clergy tried to direct this new populist energy along established lines, but church officials condemned the new groups as heretics when they appeared to be growing uncontrollable.

The most powerful of these heretical sects was the Albigensian, which was centered at Albi in southern France. The Albigensians were also known as the Cathari, from the Greek word for "pure." Their unorthodox beliefs were derived partly from Zoroastrianism, the source of their concept of a universal struggle between a good God and an evil deity, and partly from Manicheism, the source of their notion that the flesh is evil. The Albigensians stressed that Jesus was divine and not human, that the wealth of the church was a sign of its depravity, and that the goal of Christian living was to achieve the status of Cathari, or perfection.

These unorthodox beliefs spread rapidly across much of southern France, permeating the church and the secular society at all levels. In 1214 Pope Innocent III called for the destruction of the hated beliefs. His message found eager hearers among the feudal nobles who were greedy for the heretics' lands. The repression of the Albigensians was carried out with incredible ferocity and cruelty. Many Cathari were slaughtered and their property confiscated, while others were tried by the Inquisition and burned at the stake. Actions like these reflected the less benign face of the medieval church and gave one more measure of its immense power.

THE AGE OF SYNTHESIS: EQUILIBRIUM BETWEEN THE SPIRITUAL AND THE SECULAR

Between 1000 and 1300 Christian values permeated all aspects of European cultural life. The Christian faith was a unifying agent that brought together and reconciled the opposing realms of the spiritual and the secular, the immaterial and the material—as symbolized in many cities and towns by the soaring spires of the *cathedral* (Figure 9.7). Medieval culture drew from the arts and humanities of the Classical world, the heritage of the various European peoples, and, to a lesser extent, the traditions of Byzantium and Islam. Because of these diverse influences, the culture of the High Middle Ages was by no means uniform. What many writers, thinkers, and artists shared was a set of common concerns and interests, most notably the quest for forms that could transcend and bring together the contradictions of the age.

A historical watershed occurred in the mid–twelfth century that was reflected in architecture, sculpture, music, learning, and literature. Before 1150, Western culture tended to express the rugged virtues of the feudal castle and the cloistered monastery; the militant warrior and the ascetic monk were the social ideals; and women were treated as chattel, or property. After 1150, the urban values of the new towns became paramount along with a more courtly attitude toward women. The church indirectly encouraged this trend with the rise of the cult of the Virgin Mary; Mary's status became so great that she was revered almost as much as Christ.

Learning and Theology

From about 1000 onward, scholars revived the school system that had flourished briefly under Charlemagne in the Early Middle Ages. These few monastic schools—along with many new cathedral schools—appealed to an age that was hungry for learning and set Europe's intellectual tone until about 1200. During these two centuries, the only serious rival to the schools were the handful of

FIGURE 9.7 Chartres Cathedral. Aerial View. Ca. 1220–1225. Chartres, France. *Looming over the town and dominating the countryside for miles around, the Gothic cathedral symbolized the preeminent role of the Christian Church in medieval life. No other building could soar past its spires, either literally or figuratively. People worshiped inside it, built their houses right up to its walls, and conducted their business affairs within the shadows of its towers. Thus, the cathedral also symbolized the integration of the secular and the sacred in medieval life.*

independent scholars who drew crowds of students to their lectures in Paris and elsewhere. By 1200, new educational institutions arose—the universities—that soon surpassed the monastic and cathedral schools and forced the independent masters out of business. Since then, the universities have dominated intellectual life in the West.

Cathedral Schools and the Development of Scholasticism During the twelfth century the new cathedral schools reached the height of their power, with Chartres and Paris leading the way. Schooling, with rare exceptions, was the exclusive province of men who were preparing for careers in either the church or the dynastic states. For the next three hundred years the curriculum stayed the same as that codified by Boethius in the sixth century: the trivium (grammar, logic, and rhetoric) and the quadrivium (arithmetic, astronomy, geometry, and music)—the seven liberal arts—which, in turn, were based on the works of the Classical authors and those of the early church fathers. Teachers and pupils communicated in Latin, and students read the Christian works in the original Latin. In contrast, Classical writings were known only from misleading Latin summaries until they were replaced in the twelfth century with more accurate Latin versions made from Arabic translations.

The introduction of the new versions of the Classical texts, notably those of Aristotle, caused a revolution in education and elevated the Greek thinker to the status of an authority whose word could not be questioned. By 1300 Aristotle's writings virtually monopolized the curriculum at every educational level. The revival of Aristotle contributed to the development of a body of thought known as ***scholasticism***. In general, the aim of a scholastic thinker was to bring Aristotle's thought into harmony with the Christian faith. Scholasticism was also a system of reasoning that had been perfected in oral debates in the schools. In the scholastic method, a scholar divided each problem into three parts. First, a question was set forth for intellectual analysis; next, a discussion thoroughly summarized the arguments for and against the question, usually citing the Bible, the church fathers, Aristotle, and other ancient authors; finally, a solution was offered, reinforced with support from religious and secular sources.

The scholastic method was not meant to discover new knowledge; rather, it used deductive logic to clarify existing issues and to explore the intellectual ramifications of a topic. This aspect of scholasticism, which tended to uphold rather than to question religious beliefs, was discarded in favor of an inductive, mathematically based style of reasoning in the seventeenth century.

Peter Abelard The primacy of the cathedral schools of Chartres and Paris in the twelfth century was challenged by a few independent masters who pitted their own intellects against the authority of the faculty of these institutions. Of this daring breed of scholars, Peter Abelard (in French, Pierre Abélard) [AB-uh-lard] (1079–1142) was the most brilliant and controversial. More important, he was one of the first medieval thinkers to proclaim a clear distinction between reason and faith. Intellectually curious and reveling in provocative disputes, Abelard attended the lectures of William of Champeaux [SHAHM-POE] (about 1070–1121), the most revered teacher in the cathedral school of Paris. Dissatisfied with what he was hearing, Abelard began his own lecture series before William's course was completed. Overnight, Abelard became the sensation of Paris and his words found eager listeners. A master logician, Abelard demolished William's arguments and drove his rival into a monastery.

What divided Abelard and William of Champeaux was the problem of universals, the supreme intellectual issue between 1050 and 1150. This controversy revolved around the question of whether or not universal terms, or generalities, like "human being" and "church" truly existed. At stake in this dispute between the two schools of thought, known as *Realism* and *Nominalism*, were basic Christian ideas, such as whether Jesus' sacrifice had removed the stain of original sin from each individual. The Realists, following Plato, reasoned that universal terms did exist and were more "real" than separate entities. Hence, "humanity," for example, was constantly present in each and every individual. In opposition, the Nominalists denied the existence of universals and claimed that only separate things and individual persons were actual. Hence, "church" and "human being" existed only in particular instances.

In these debates, Abelard showed that William's extreme Realism denied human individuality and was thus inconsistent with church teachings. For his part, Abelard taught a moderate Realism that held that the universals existed, but only as mental words, and hence could be used as an intellectual convenience. Later in the century, when new translations of Aristotle became available, thinkers discovered that Abelard and the Greek genius agreed on universals, a discovery that further enhanced Abelard's fame. In the next century, Abelard's moderate Realism was adopted by Thomas Aquinas, the greatest mind of the High Middle Ages.

The Rise of the Universities   After 1100 a period of cultural ferment erupted that a modern historian has called the twelfth-century renaissance. Even though this term is exaggerated, the century spawned some of the finest achievements of medieval times, including the founding of the universities. By 1200, conditions were ripe for the rise of universities at Bologna, at Paris, and at Oxford, the first Western schools of higher education since the sixth century. Unlike the ancient universities in Athens and Alexandria, these medieval institutions were organized into self-governing corporations with charters. A century later, similar centers of learning were springing up elsewhere in Italy, France, and England, as well as in Spain, Portugal, and Germany. The University of Paris was the most celebrated institution of advanced learning during the High Middle Ages. Divided into faculties by specialization, it awarded degrees in both civil law and canon law, medicine, theology, and the liberal arts. The liberal arts degree was basically devoted to mastering the new translations of Aristotle. Other universities taught a similar curriculum, but their faculties lacked the international renown of the Parisian professors.

Intellectual Controversy and Thomas Aquinas   More and more of Aristotle's works became available in the late twelfth and early thirteenth centuries. Between 1150 and 1200 a few hardy Christian scholars traveled to centers of learning off the main track, such as Muslim Sicily and Toledo, Spain—freed from Muslim control only in 1085—to meet Islamic and Jewish scholars and study Aristotle's writings. There they learned Arabic and translated the Greek and Arabic philosophical and scientific works into Latin, the form in which they entered the mainstream of European medieval thought.

At the University of Paris, the introduction of these improved and more complete versions split the intellectual community into two camps. On one side was the theological faculty, who welcomed the Arabic writings but wanted to reconcile them to Christian thinking. Arrayed against them were the members of the arts faculty, who advocated that reason be fully divorced from faith, or, in other words, that philosophy be separated from theology. The leaders of the arts faculty were called Latin Averroists because they claimed inspiration from the Arabic philosopher Ibn Rushd [ib-uhn-RUSHT], known in the West as Averroes [uh-VER-uh-weez].

Faced with the skeptical Latin Averroists, the Parisian theologians devised two ways to relate the new learning to orthodox beliefs. The more traditional view was set forth by Bonaventure [bahn-uh-VEN-chur] (1221–1274), who was later made a saint. Denying that knowledge was possible apart from God's grace, Bonaventure, following Augustine's mode of reasoning, argued that truth had to begin in the supernatural world and thus could not arise in the senses, as Aristotle had argued. A new and brilliant theological view, and the one that carried the day, was set forth by Thomas Aquinas [uh-KWI-nus] (1226–1274), a Dominican friar who taught at Paris from 1252 to 1259 and again from 1269 to 1272. Within a generation of his death, he was made a saint, and six hundred years later, in 1874, the papacy declared his thought the official basis of Roman Catholic beliefs. Avoiding the pure rationalism of the Latin Averroists and the timidity of Bonaventure, Thomas Aquinas steered a middle path, or **via media**, that gave Aristotle a central role in his theology while honoring traditional Christian beliefs. Known as Thomism, this theological system in its complex design and sheer elegance remains one of the outstanding achievements of the High Middle Ages.

Of Thomas Aquinas's two monumental *summas*—comprehensive summaries of Christian thought—the *Summa Theologica* is his masterpiece. In this work he showed that God had given human beings two divine paths to truth: reason and faith. Following Aristotle, he made the senses the only source for human knowledge—a bold step that sharpened the difference between reason and faith. As a long-range result, Thomism outdistanced Bonaventure and the Augustinians, who muddled the distinction between the worlds of revelation and reason. At the same time, Thomism escaped the rationalism of the Latin Averroists by denying that philosophy, or reason, could answer all theological questions. Aquinas claimed that reason based on sensory knowledge could prove certain truths, such as the notion that God exists and that the soul exists, but that reason had limits and that faith was necessary for those truths that were beyond sensory proof, such as the belief in the soul's immortality.

Thomas Aquinas's contributions to medieval thought extended far beyond theology into political and economic matters. He saw the secular state as a natural and necessary support to human life. He believed that the natural law—which derived from a divine rational order—offered a correct guide to individuals and to society, even if sin prevented people from achieving the good life in the here and now. Rejecting Augustine's notion of the state as a sign of God's punishment for Adam and Eve's sin, he followed Aristotle in claiming that a settled society with justice for all is the highest human goal on earth. For Aquinas, politics had an ethical root, and this thought allowed him to write in his *Summas* about everyday life. For example, he reasoned that church law should be used to regulate economic behavior, putting controls on usury (the practice of charging exorbitant interest) and setting a just price for consumer goods.

Aquinas and the other theologians of the High Middle Ages held differing views on a number of subjects, but all of them shared a confidence in human reason and its ability to comprehend the world. Even though the role of reason was carefully circumscribed and often had to give way to revelation, there was still a genuine rationalist tradition during this period—one that originated in ancient Greece, was transmitted into Renaissance thought, and finally helped to bring about the Scientific Revolution that inaugurated modern times.

Literature

Beyond the rarefied atmosphere of scholastic thought, writing was finding its own way. The literature of the High Middle Ages falls naturally into two chronological parts, with the dividing line at about 1150. The first half, which coincides with Romanesque art, perpetuates the feudal and monastic values of the Early Middle Ages. The second half, which parallels the Gothic style, introduces urban and courtly themes while moving away from the world of the monasteries.

Monastic and Feudal Writing   Between 1000 and 1150 most authors were monks, writing in Latin and imitating late Roman literary models such as hymns, sermons, lives of the saints, and historical chronicles. Perhaps most distinctive was the Latin lyric poetry composed during this time, which has been called the best literary work of the Latin-speaking Middle Ages. These poems were rich in metric subtleties, extremely learned in content, and filled with Classical and Christian allusions. Some of the poets have been identified as *goliards*, or roaming scholars, but most were probably clerics. Addressing an audience of church intellectuals, these poets often wrote on religious and moral topics. They also wrote lighthearted love poems, however, which appeared to have had a wider audience and whose themes certainly appealed to more secular interests. Even though the love poems sang of carnal pleasure, these verses were not personal, nor were the poets' erotic yearnings directed to real women.

While the monks sang of love in Latin, lay poets at the feudal courts of northern France were developing a new literary genre, the **chanson de geste**, or song of brave deeds. Written in the *vernacular*, or popular, spoken language, the *chansons de geste* chiefly honored the heroic adventures of warriors who lived in France under Charlemagne and his heirs. These medieval epics often memorialized a minor battle or, more rarely, even a defeat. They took Christian values for granted, but supernatural and magical elements were commonly a part of their plots. Of the many *chansons de geste*, the masterpiece is the *Song of Roland*, which became the standard for the genre (Figure 9.8).

Much of the *Song of Roland* was passed down orally for three hundred years, and it did not reach

FIGURE 9.8 *Charlemagne Panels.* Stained Glass Window, Chartres Cathedral. Chartres, France. Ca. 1220–1225. *The Song of Roland was so well known and well loved that scenes from the poem were depicted in the stained glass windows of Chartres Cathedral, constructed in the thirteenth century. The Charlemagne panels are among the most famous windows in the cathedral. Even though they were inspired by a secular poem, they were situated in the ambulatory behind the main altar, one of the cathedral's most sacred areas. In one scene, Charlemagne is shown arriving too late to save Roland's life. Other panels depict him donating a church and traveling to Constantinople.*

its final written form until around 1100. The narrative claims to be based on a historical event, telling first of the destruction of a troop of Frankish warriors led by Count Roland, one of Charlemagne's vassals, and second of Charlemagne's revenge for this massacre. Superimposed on this supposedly Carolingian tale are the later values of the High Middle Ages, such as chivalry, militant Christianity, and primitive nationalism. For example, Roland and his men obey the chivalric code, showing devotion to their ruler, to God, and to their personal honor—an ideal unknown in Charlemagne's day. Likewise, the religious zeal of Charlemagne's army against their enemies, the Spanish Muslims, probably derived from the First Crusade in 1095; indeed, modern scholars have shown that Charlemagne's actual enemies in Spain were Christians. Finally, this poem portrayed the Franks as ready to die for "sweet France," a sentiment that would have been incomprehensible to Charlemagne but that was encouraged by the twelfth-century French kings who used the popular *Song of Roland* to further their political ambitions.

Vernacular and Courtly Writing   Between 1150 and 1300 Latin continued to hold pride of place in the universities, but elsewhere lay writers, composing in the vernacular, were beginning to win new audiences and to develop new genres.

For example, inspired by Latin lyric verse, vernacular lyric poetry began to appear in the eleventh century in the Provençal tongue of southern France.

This vernacular poetry reached its zenith in the next two centuries. Its supreme expression was the **canzone**, or love poem, the ancestor of all later Western love poetry. At the educated feudal courts of southern France, professional *minstrels*, or entertainers, sang the songs before the assembled court; the poems' composers—called *troubadors*—were often local nobles. Addressed to court ladies whose identities were thinly disguised in the poem, these troubador songs made devotion to a highborn woman the passionate ideal of the chivalrous knight. In the mature Provençal lyrics, adulterous passion was the central theme, and women were idolized and made the masters over men. Where previously adoration had been reserved for God, the troubadour lyrics now celebrated the worship of women.

As the influence of Provençal poetry spread, the status of women in Western literature was revolutionized, a development paralleled in the church, where the cult of the Virgin Mary was beginning to flourish. For the moment, most real-life medieval women were unaffected by these literary and religious changes; their happiness depended on submitting to the limited roles that the masculine society allowed them to fill. After 1400, though, these cultural changes encouraged upper-class women to play a more prominent role in society, as hostesses and as arbiters of social decorum.

After 1150 courtly *romances* quickly replaced the feudal *chansons de geste* in popularity. The romances were long narratives of the chivalric and sentimental adventures of knights and ladies. The name *romance* arose from the mistaken belief that the medieval authors were imitating a Roman literary form. Their subjects derived from stories of ancient Troy and Celtic legends from the British Isles, the most enduring of which proved to be the Celtic stories of King Arthur and his knights of the Round Table.

The first poet to make Arthur and his court his subject was Chrétien de Troyes [KRAY-tyan du-TRWAH], whose versions set the standard for later romances. Chrétien (about 1148–about 1190) wrote his romances for the feudal courts of northern France. His treatment of the adulterous love of the knight Lancelot and Arthur's queen, Guinevere, is characteristic of the way romances combined aristocratic, courtly, and religious themes. In this version, Lancelot rescues Queen Guinevere after experiencing many adventures and personal humiliations for her sake; this humbling of Lancelot is necessary to teach him to love Guinevere with unquestioning obedience.

A curiosity for modern readers is that Chrétien identifies Lancelot with Christ, so that many episodes echo scenes of Jesus' suffering and death. While the work avoids sacrilege, the net effect is unsettling in its mixing of the sacred with the profane. Chrétien describes Lancelot and Guinevere's passion without judging their behavior. Such moral neutrality was unacceptable to other Christian writers, who believed adultery to be a deadly sin. In an English prose version of this tale—Thomas Malory's *Le Morte d'Arthur*, published in 1485—the lovers were blamed for the collapse of Arthur's court. Perhaps because today's world tends to agree with Malory's more judgmental view, his story of Lancelot is the one better known by modern readers.

Another literary genre that flourished simultaneously with the romance was the *lay* (French, *lai*), a short lyric or narrative poem meant to be sung to the accompaniment of an instrument such as a harp. The oldest lays are the twelve surviving by Marie de France (flourished about 1170), a poet from Brittany who lived most of her life in England. Based on Celtic legends, including those of Arthur, Marie de France's lays were stories of courtly love, often adulterous (for instance, a young wife kept under close watch by a jealous old husband), usually faced with conflict, always with a moral lesson. Writing in Old French, Marie addressed the French-speaking nobility of post–Norman Conquest England, an audience that may have included King Henry II and Queen Eleanor of Aquitaine. Marie's lays, along with her fables and other works, were part of the outpouring of writing in the twelfth century that made Old French the most influential literature in Europe until the rise of Italian literature in the age of Dante.

Dante Vernacular writing appeared late in Italy; not until the thirteenth century did Italian poetry begin to emerge. But, despite its later start, Italy brought forth by 1300 the greatest literary figure of the High Middle Ages, Dante Alighieri [DAHN-tay ahl-eeg-YEH-ree] (1265–1321). A native of Florence in the province of Tuscany, Dante was the first of a proud tradition that soon made the Tuscan dialect the standard literary speech of Italy.

Born into a minor aristocratic family, Dante was given an excellent education with a thorough grounding in both Greco-Roman and Christian classics. Attracted to the values of ancient Rome, he combined a career in public office with the life of an intellectual—a tradition of civic duty inherited from the ancient Roman republic. When Dante's political allies fell from office in 1301, he was exiled from Florence for the rest of his life. During these years, when he suffered from poverty and wandered about Italy, he composed the *Commedia*, or *Comedy*, which stands as the culmination of the literature of the Middle Ages. The *Comedy*'s sublime qualities were immediately recognized, and soon its admirers attached the epithet "divine" to Dante's masterpiece.

Divided into three book-length parts, the *Divine Comedy* narrates Dante's fictional travels through three realms of the Christian afterlife. Led first by the ghost of Vergil, the ancient Roman poet, Dante descends into hell, where he hears from the damned the nature of their various crimes against God and the moral law. Vergil next leads Dante into purgatory, where the lesser sinners expiate their guilt while awaiting the joys of heaven. At a fixed spot in purgatory, Vergil is forced to relinquish his role to Beatrice, a young Florentine woman and Dante's symbol of the eternal female. With Beatrice's guidance, Dante enters paradise and even has a vision of the almighty God.

The majestic complexity of Dante's monumental poem, however, can scarcely be conveyed by this simple synopsis. Written as an allegory, the *Divine Comedy* was meant to be understood on several levels at the same time. Read literally, the poem bears witness to the author's personal fears as a moral sinner yet affirms his hope for eternal salvation. Read allegorically, the poem represents a comprehensive synthesis of the opposing tendencies that characterized medieval culture, such as balancing the Classical with the Christian, Aristotle with Aquinas, the ancient with the new, the proud with the humble, and the secular with the spiritual.

Of the great cultural symbols that abound in the *Divine Comedy*, the richest in meaning are the central figures of Vergil and Beatrice, who represent human reason and divine revelation, respectively. In the poem Vergil is made inferior to Beatrice, thus revealing Dante's acceptance of a basic idea of Thomas Aquinas—reason can lead only to awareness of sin; revelation is necessary to reach God's ultimate truth. Besides this fundamental Christian belief, the two figures convey other meanings. Vergil stands for Classical civilization and the secular literary life; Beatrice (Italian for "blessing") symbolizes spiritualized love and Christianized culture. By turning Beatrice into an image of God's grace, Dante revealed that the High Middle Ages were open to new symbols of Christian truth. (By the time of the Catholic Counter-Reformation in the sixteenth century, however, Dante's image was considered blasphemous and was censured by religious critics.)

Dante's spiritual odyssey is set during the season of Easter. The poet's journey through hell coincided with Jesus' descent into hell on Good Friday, and Dante's ascent up the Mount of Purgatory happens at Easter dawn—the time of Jesus' resurrection. Thus Dante's allegory has the religious aim of forcing his readers to meditate on the fate of their own immortal souls.

Dante's vision of the afterlife underscored his belief that humans have free will. Predestination had no place in his system, as his picture of hell shows. With one exception, all of the damned earned their fate by their deeds on earth. Excepted were the people consigned to Limbo—the pious pagans—who lived prior to Jesus and thus were denied his message of hope. Moreover, those in Limbo, such as Aristotle and Plato, were not subjected to any punishment other than being removed from God's presence.

The intricate structure of Dante's massive poem owes much to numerology, a pseudoscience of numbers that absorbed the medieval mind. The numbers three and nine, for example, occur prominently in the *Divine Comedy*. Three is a common symbol of the Christian Trinity (the union of the Father, the Son, and the Holy Ghost in one God), and the poem is written in a three-line verse form called **terza rima** (an interlocking rhyme scheme in three-line stanzas, as *aba, bcb, cdc, ded*, and so on, ending in a rhyming couplet), which was Dante's invention. The other number, nine, symbolizes the Trinity squared. More important, Dante identified the number nine with the dead Beatrice, whose soul lived on in the ninth heaven, the one nearest to God. He also divides hell, purgatory, and paradise into nine sections each.

Despite its allegorical and theological features, the *Divine Comedy* is a deeply personal poem. Dante rewards and punishes his Florentine friends and foes by the location that he assigns each in the afterlife. He also reveals his private feelings as he enters into discussions with various saints and sinners along the way. Beyond his desire for salvation, his most cherished idea is to bring about a harmony between the church and the secular state on earth.

Architecture and Art

Just as scholars and writers devoted their efforts to exploring and elaborating on religious concerns and Christian values, artists, artisans, and architects channeled their talents into glorifying the Christian house of worship. Because the dominating physical presence of the church made it a ubiquitous symbol in both the countryside and the towns, architecture ranked higher than the other arts in medieval life. Indeed, the arts lacked an independent status, for they were regarded as mere auxiliary sources of church decoration—statues, stained glass windows, and wall paintings, most of which portrayed saints and biblical heroes. In this respect, these art forms conformed to the church's teachings that the purpose of art was to represent Christian truth.

Even though the church dominated art and architecture, it did not prevent architects and artists from experimenting. In about 1000 an international style emerged called the **Romanesque** that was the first in

FIGURE 9.9 Floor Plan of a Typical Romanesque Church. *This floor plan identifies the characteristic features of a Romanesque church with its cruciform floor plan: (1) narthex, (2) towers, (3) nave, (4) side aisles, (5) transept, and (6) apse.*

FIGURE 9.10 Church of Sainte-Marie-Madeleine, Vézelay, France. View from the West. Ca. 1089–1206. *This church conveys the fortress-like quality that was typical of Romanesque architecture and reflects the harsh style of life of twelfth-century Europe. The church's facade is massive, pierced only by doorways at ground level and arched openings above. Highlighting its impressively stark exterior is a simple plan of decoration consisting largely of sculptures over the central portal and on pillars and in niches in the central upper section.*

a succession of uniform styles to sweep over Europe. The Romanesque, carried along by the monastic revival, was favored until about 1200. But by 1150, the *Gothic* style was already being born in Paris; it was to become the reigning style of the towns for the remainder of the Middle Ages, succumbing finally to Renaissance fashion in about 1500.

Romanesque Churches and Related Arts The Romanesque style earned its name from the ancient Roman building features that had characterized the churches of the Early Middle Ages. These Roman features, along with Christian influences, had flourished briefly in some churches built during the Carolingian era (see Figure 8.21). The Romanesque church architects revived such basic Roman elements as the basilica plan and employed rounded arches, vaulted ceilings, and columns for both support and decoration (see Figure

7.10). They also perpetuated early Christian ideas by pointing each basilica toward Jerusalem in the east and curving the building's eastern end into an apse to house the altar. A transept, or crossing arm, was added at the church's eastern end in order to convert the floor plan into a cruciform shape to symbolize the cross (Figure 9.9). Other Christian beliefs dictated such practices as having three doorways in the western facade, which symbolized the Trinity, and building the baptistery apart from the church to keep the unbaptized out of sacred space.

In its origins, the Romanesque is associated with the Cluniac monastic order because the headquarters church at Cluny in eastern France was built in

FIGURE 9.11 View of Nave, Looking East. Church of Sainte-Marie-Madeleine, Vézelay, France. Ca. 1089–1206. *Vézelay's nave was made unusually long so that religious pilgrims might make solemn processions along its length. A reliquary, or an area for displaying holy relics, was later set aside in the choir. Within the choir, the design of the ambulatory provided ample space for masses of pilgrims to view all the relics at one time.*

this style. The extravagant success of the Cluniac movement in the eleventh century led to the spread of the Romanesque style over the map of Europe. In appearance, the Romanesque style reflected both the needs of the monastic communities and the physical demands created by the unsettled conditions of the day. These churches were sturdy and earth hugging, with massive walls and very few windows. They looked like the spiritual fortresses that they indeed were (Figure 9.10).

Many Romanesque churches were pilgrimage churches—destinations for pilgrims traveling vast distances to see and venerate holy relics, very often the supposed bones of saints. The foremost pilgrimage churches had to be built to accommodate the hordes of religious tourists, and this was usually done by building ambulatories, semicircular or polygonal aisles behind the apse.

A celebrated pilgrimage church in the Romanesque style is Sainte-Marie-Madeleine in Vézelay, France. Attached to a Cluniac convent, this church attracted penitents eager to view the bones of Mary

Magdalene. Vézelay's builders followed a basilica design with a cruciform floor plan. Inside, the most striking feature is the nearly 200-foot-long nave, which could hold a large number of pilgrims as well as allow religious processions (Figure 9.11). Typical of the Romanesque style, the nave is divided into sections called **bays**. Each bay is framed by a pair of rounded arches constructed from blocks of local pink and grey stones. These colors alternate in the overhead arches and create a dazzling effect for which this church is famous. The ceiling of each bay is a groin vault—a Roman building technique. The support system for the tall nave walls was also taken from Roman architecture—a series of arches resting on clusters of columns.

Vézelay's Romanesque builders used sculpture to provide "sermons in stone" for illiterate visitors. Symbolic rather than idealistic or realistic, the Romanesque figures were designed to convey religious meanings. For example, instead of copying the ancient Greco-Roman columns, the artisans created their own style of decorated column. The capitals, or

FIGURE 9.12 *Angel Subduing Demon.* Decorated Column Capital. Church of Sainte-Marie-Madeleine, Vézelay, France. Ca. 1089–1206. *The Vézelay capitals survive in near-immaculate condition. Late medieval moralists considered their vivacity and gaiety inappropriate in God's house, and the offending sculptures were plastered over. When they were uncovered during a nineteenth-century restoration of the church's interior, the capitals were revealed in their charming originality.*

FIGURE 9.13 *The Ascension and the Mission to the Apostles.* Tympanum over Central Portal. Church of Sainte-Marie-Madeleine, Vézelay, France. 1125–1135. *The subject of this tympanum, Jesus' missionary charge to his disciples, was especially appropriate for Sainte-Marie-Madeleine. Two crusades against the Muslims who occupied the holy places in the Middle East were preached and begun from this church.*

tops, of the interior columns are sculpted with religious scenes and motifs, such as one that shows an angel subduing a demon (Figure 9.12). Both figures have wings, suggesting that the demon is a fallen angel. Because people in the High Middle Ages feared devils of all kinds, the art often depicted such triumphs of divine, or even magical, power over evil.

Other carvings in this church, however, show a more mature art. The stone *tympanum* over the central doorway in the *narthex* depicts Jesus' ascension into heaven and a symbolic rendering of his mission to the Apostles (Figure 9.13). Jesus' lively draperies and pose reflected the dynamism and stress on mystical truth that were typical of Romanesque art. Each Apostle, feet pointing downward, holds a gospel, showing that he accepts his missionary role. On the lintel below are depicted various real and legendary peoples, the recipients of the Christian message. Above the semicircular panel in framed units are portrayed biblical events, zodiac signs, and peasant scenes—a visual symbol of the integration of sacred and profane learning.

Besides church building and church decoration, the Romanesque style was also used in manuscript illumination. Originated in late Rome and developed in the Early Middle Ages, this art remained a cloistered activity in this age of monasticism (see Chapter 8). Perhaps only cloistered painters had the leisure to pursue this painstaking skill. During the High Middle Ages, new local styles arose, inspired by regional tastes and by a knowledge of Byzantine painting brought from the East by Crusaders. The English monks probably developed the finest of these local styles.

The Bury Bible, painted at Bury St. Edmunds monastery, reflects an English taste that is calmer and less exuberant than continental styles. Two panels from the Bury manuscript, set off by a border of highly colored foliage, show an episode in Moses' life (Figure 9.14). Borrowings from Byzantine art may be detected in the elongated figures, the large eyes, the flowing hair, and the hanging draperies. The naturalness of these scenes presented a vivid contrast with the spirited agitation of French Romanesque art.

Gothic Churches and Related Arts   The word *Gothic* was invented by Renaissance scholars who preferred

Greco-Roman styles. They despised medieval architecture, labeling it *Goth-ic*—meaning a barbaric creation of the Goths, or the Germanic peoples. Modern research, however, has shown that this Renaissance view is false. In fact, the Gothic grew out of the Romanesque and was not a German art. Nevertheless, the term *Gothic* is still used today, although its negative connotation has long since been discarded.

Gothic architecture sprang from the religious revival of the twelfth century, when the clergy wanted to bring God's presence more tangibly to their urban congregations. As a result, clerics began to demand taller churches with more windows than were

Figure 9.14 *Moses Expounding the Law of the Unclean Beasts.* The Bury Bible. 1130–1140. Bury St. Edmunds, England. Master and Fellows of Corpus Christi College, Cambridge. *These panels depict Moses delivering the dietary laws to the ancient Hebrews. The responses of his audience reveal the sure hand of the artist, known only as Master Hugo. For example, in the upper panel one figure pulls at his nose, while a nearby companion looks skeptical. Moses' head is depicted with horns, which reflected a biblical mistranslation of the term for the radiance that surrounded him after receiving God's law.*

FIGURE 9.15 Principal Features of a Typical Gothic Church. *In this schematic drawing, the features are numbered from the nave outward: (1) nave arcade, (2) pointed arch, (3) vault, (4) clerestory, (5) flying buttress, (6) buttress, and (7) gargoyle.*

available in the relatively dark Romanesque churches. To the medieval mind, height and light were symbols of the divine. Another impetus behind the Gothic was the rise of the middle class, who wanted churches that reflected their growing economic power. Thus spiritual and economic forces were united in pushing architects to seek a new kind of architecture.

Two problems with the Romanesque stood in the way: The groin vaults were so heavy that the nearly windowless walls had to be extremely thick in order to support their great weight, and the rounded arches limited the building's height to less than 100 feet. During the early twelfth century, builders constantly sought solutions to these problems.

Eventually, between 1137 and 1144, the Gothic style was created by Suger [SUE-ZHAY] (about 1081–1151), the Abbot of the royal Abbey Church of St. Denis, near Paris, and an advisor to the French kings. Suger's approach to architecture grew out of his religious faith, as in his words, "Through the beauty of material things we come to understand God." The brilliant innovation employed by Suger and the architects and artisans he hired was to change the vaulting problem from one of weight to one of stress. First, they replaced the groin vault with a *ribbed vault*; this step allowed lighter materials to be placed between the stone ribs, thus reducing the weight. Next, they abandoned the rounded arch in favor of the Muslim pointed arch. The combination of pointed arch and ribbed vault permitted an increase in the building's height as well as a rechanneling of the ceiling's stresses downward and outward to huge *piers* internally and, in later buildings, to *flying buttresses* externally that formed a bridge between the upper nave walls and the nearby tall pillars (Figure 9.15). With the support skeleton transferred to the building's exterior, the builders could easily insert stained glass windows into the non-weight-bearing walls.

The glory of the Gothic church—the *choir*—was all that remained to be built. The plan and inspiration for the choir (the part of the church where the service was sung) were the pilgrimage churches, like Vézelay, that had enlarged their apses to accommodate religious tourists. In Suger's skillful hands, the east end of St. Denis was now elaborated into an oval-shaped area—the choir—ringed with several small chapels (Figure 9.16). At the heart of the choir was the apse, now arcaded; a spacious ambulatory area divided the apse from the chapels (Figure 9.17).

St. Denis gave only a foretaste of the triumphant art that was called the Gothic. Between 1145 and 1500 the Gothic style presented an overwhelming image of God's majesty and the power of the church. A Gothic exterior carried the eye heavenward by impressive vertical spires. A Gothic interior surrounded the daytime worshiper with colored, celestial light; the soaring nave ceiling, sometimes rising to more than 150 feet, was calculated to stir the soul. In its total physicality the Gothic church stood as a towering symbol of the medieval obsession with the divine.

During the High Middle Ages, the Gothic style went through two stages, the Early and the High. The Early Gothic style lasted until 1194 and was best represented by Notre Dame cathedral in Paris. The High Gothic style flourished until 1300 and reached perfection in the cathedral at Amiens, France.

EARLY GOTHIC STYLE, 1145–1194   The cathedral of Notre Dame ("Our Lady," the Virgin Mary) in Paris made

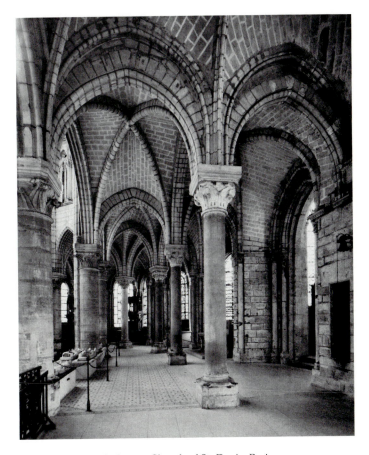

FIGURE 9.16   Ambulatory. Church of St. Denis, Paris. Ca. 1145. *This interior view of the choir of St. Denis shows a portion of the ambulatory, the passageway that allowed pilgrims to walk around and view the chapels in the apse. The evenly spaced support columns and the pointed arches enabled the builders to construct this flowing, curved space. The ribbed arches in the ceiling are also central to the Gothic skeletal construction.*

FIGURE 9.17   Floor Plan, Ambulatory. Church of St. Denis, Paris. Ca. 1145. *This floor plan, based on a similar design used in the pilgrimage churches, became the basis for the reordering of interior space in the Gothic choirs. The features include (1) choir, (2) apse, (3) ambulatory, (4) transept, and (5) chapel.*

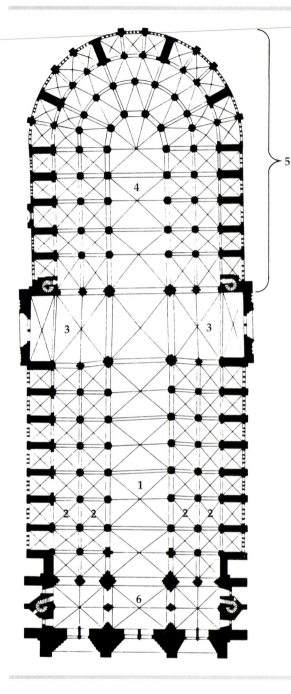

FIGURE 9.18   Floor Plan of Notre Dame, Paris. 1163–ca. 1250. *This drawing shows the principal features of Notre Dame Cathedral: (1) nave, (2) aisle, (3) transept, (4) apse, (5) choir, and (6) narthex.*

FIGURE 9.19   Western Facade. Notre Dame, Paris. 1220– 1250. *In the gallery above the western portals are twenty-eight images of the kings of Judah, including David and Solomon. These sculptures, which are typical of Gothic churches, are more than decorations: They are reminders that Mary and Jesus were descended from royalty. In the medieval mind, this religious idea was meant to buttress the monarchical style of government.*

popular the Early Gothic style, making it a fashion for other cities and towns. Begun in 1163, the cathedral was the most monumental work erected in the West to this time. Its floor plan was cruciform, but the length of the transept barely exceeded the width of the aisle walls (Figure 9.18).

Part of Notre Dame's beauty stems from the rational principles applied by the builders, notably the ideal of harmony, best expressed in the integration of sculpture and decorative details with building units. For instance, the west facade is divided into three equal horizontal bands: the three doorways, the *rose window* and *blind arcades*, and the two towers (Figure 9.19). Within each subdivision of this facade, figurative sculpture or architectural details play a harmonizing role, from the rows of saints flanking each of the portals to the *gargoyles*, or grotesque demons, peering down from the towers.

Inside Notre Dame, the spectacular nave reveals the awe-inspiring effects of Early Gothic art at its best (Figure 9.20). The strong vertical lines and the airy atmosphere represent the essence of this taste. With its ribbed vaults and pointed arches, the nave rises to a height of 110 feet from the pavement to the ceiling. Like the harmonious west facade, the nave is divided into three equal tiers: the nave and double

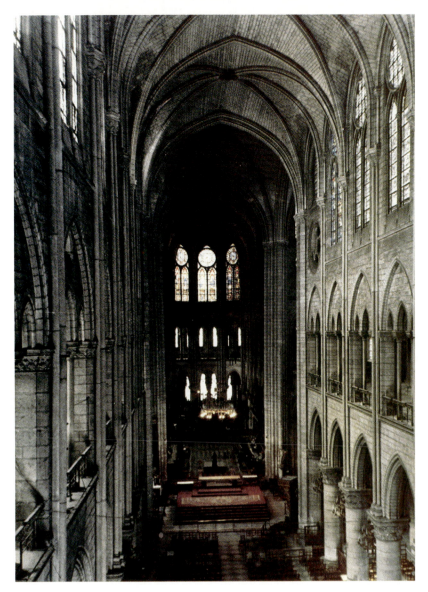

FIGURE 9.20 Nave. Notre Dame, Paris. View from the Height of the Western Rose Window. 1180–1250. *The nave is clearly not aligned properly. The choir bends perceptibly to the north, which probably reflected the different building times for various parts of the cathedral. The transept and the choir were finished first, after which the nave and the double aisles were added. The western facade was completed last.*

FIGURE 9.21 Choir. Notre Dame, Paris. View from the East. 1163–1182. *Notre Dame's choir was originally built without chapels and flying buttresses—a sign of its Early Gothic origins. Paris's greatest church caught up with the High Gothic style in the fourteenth century, when these architectural features were added.*

aisles, the open spectator *gallery* above the aisles, and, at the top, the clerestory, as the window area is called.

Notre Dame reveals that the choir was coming to dominate the entire Early Gothic church. Notre Dame's choir is almost as long as the nave, so that the transept virtually divides the church into two halves. At first, the choir's walls had no special external supports, but as cracks began to appear in the choir's walls during the thirteenth century, flying buttresses were added to ensure greater stability—a feature that would later characterize High Gothic churches (Figure 9.21).

The down-to-earth Gothic sculptures that decorate Notre Dame differ from the exuberant Romanesque style. The Romanesque's animated images of Jesus have given way to the Gothic's more sober figures. In addition, the Gothic figures are modeled in three dimensions, and their draperies fall in natural folds. At the same time, the rise of the cult of the

FIGURE 9.22   *The Last Judgment.* Central Portal, West
Facade. Notre Dame, Paris. Ca. 1210. *This tympanum
represents Jesus enthroned and presiding over the Last Judgment.
Surrounding him are the Apostles, the prophets, the church
fathers, and the saints—arranged in descending order of their
importance in relation to Jesus himself. Like all of the sculptures
of Notre Dame's first story, the entire scene was gilded with gold
paint until the mid–fifteenth century.*

FIGURE 9.23 North Rose Window. Notre Dame, Paris. Ca. 1255. *This masterwork by Jehan de Chelles is the only original of Notre Dame's three rose windows. The nineteenth-century restoration genius Viollet-le-Duc recreated the other two. Measuring 43 feet in diameter, the window was installed after workers first removed sections of the existing wall. The bits of predominantly blue glass, encased in iron settings, were then placed inside the stone frame.*

Virgin meant an increased number of images of Mary as well as of female saints (Figure 9.22). The name "Notre Dame" itself testifies to the appeal of the Virgin cult. Despite these visual differences, however, the Gothic remained true to the symbolic purposes of Romanesque art.

Before Notre Dame was finished, its architects began to move in new directions, refining the traditional features into a new style, called **Rayonnant**, or Radiant. In the *Rayonnant* style, the solid walls gave way to sheets of stained glass framed by elegant **traceries**, or rich ornamentation, of stone. This radiant effect was especially evident in the north transept facade, which was rebuilt in this new style. With the addition of this transept's imposing rose window, organized so as to suggest the rays of the sun, the cathedral's interior was bathed in constantly shifting colors, giving it a mystical atmosphere (Figure 9.23).

236

FIGURE 9.24 Amiens Cathedral. Aerial View. Amiens, France. Ca. 1220–1270. *This aerial photograph shows the brilliantly articulated exterior skeleton of Amiens Cathedral. The Gothic churches openly displayed the exterior support system that made their interior beauty possible. In the Renaissance, this aspect of Gothicism was decried for its clumsiness. Renaissance architects preferred Classical structures that hid their stresses and strains.*

FIGURE 9.25 Nave. Amiens Cathedral. View from the West. Amiens, France. Ca. 1220–1236. *Gothic architecture was built to appeal to the emotions. The overwhelming height and the celestial light were intended to create a spiritual environment. Even in a photograph of the nave of Amiens Cathedral this spiritual feeling may be sensed. The dramatic contrast between the human elements—the chairs—and the voluminous space is a reminder of the frailty of mortals.*

HIGH GOTHIC STYLE, 1194–1300   The High Gothic style is a tribute to the growing confidence of the builders of the thirteenth century. These builders took the Gothic ingredients and refined them, creating grander churches than had been erected earlier. In comparison with Early Gothic architecture, High Gothic churches were taller and had greater volumes; artistic values now stressed wholeness rather than the division of space into harmonious units. Rejecting the restrained decorative ideal used in the Early Gothic style, the High Gothic architects covered the entire surface of their churches' western facades with sculptural and architectural designs.

The cathedral in Amiens is a perfect embodiment of the High Gothic style. Amiens was planned so that flying buttresses would surround its choir and march along its nave walls (Figure 9.24). Instead of trying to disguise these supports, the architect made the exterior skeleton central to his overall plan. As a result, more spacious window openings could be made in the nave and the choir walls than had been the case in Notre Dame. Furthermore, the design of Amiens' nave was also changed so that the entire space was perceived as a homogeneous volume. The division of the nave walls into three equal horizontal bands was eliminated, and the system of arches and bays overhead became less emphatic (Figure 9.25). Amiens' overall floor plan was conservative, however, for it resembled that of Notre Dame; for example, its transept bisected a choir and nave of equal length (Figure 9.26).

The western facade of Amiens shows how decoration changed in the High Gothic style (Figure 9.27). Amiens' western wall and towers are pierced with rich and intricate openings. The elegant tracery has the effect of dissolving the wall's apparent solidity. What surface remains intact is covered with an elaborate tapestry of architectural devices and sculptural figures (Figure 9.28).

The finest stained glass from the High Gothic era is from the cathedral in Chartres, a bishopric in Hugh Capet's old lands. Indeed, Chartres' windows are often recognized as the most exquisite of all Gothic stained glass. Chartres has 176 windows, and most are the thirteenth-century originals. Outstanding examples of this art are the Charlemagne panels depicting scenes from the *Song of Roland*, illustrated earlier in this chapter (see Figure 9.8). Each figure is precisely rendered, though many are cropped off at the edge of the pictorial space. The glass itself is brilliant, notably in the dominant blue tones.

High Gothic painting survives best in the manuscript illuminations of the late thirteenth century. By this time, these small paintings were being influenced by developments elsewhere in Gothic art. Under this influence, the Gothic illuminators abandoned the

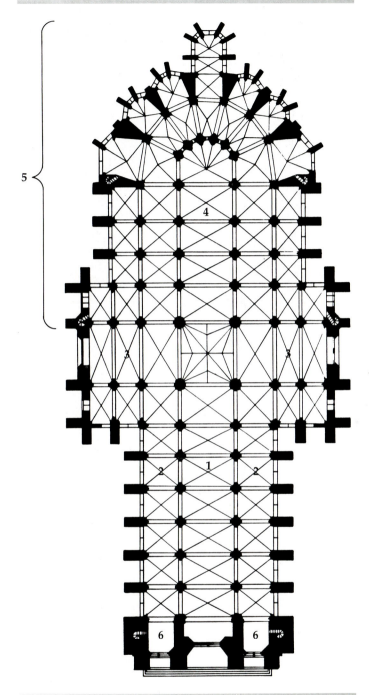

FIGURE 9.26   Floor Plan of Amiens Cathedral. Amiens, France. Ca. 1220–1236. *This drawing shows the principal features of Amiens Cathedral: (1) nave, (2) aisle, (3) transept, (4) apse, (5) choir, and (6) narthex.*

lively draperies of the Romanesque and instead showed gowns hanging in a natural manner. More important, they sometimes allowed the architectural frame to dominate the painting, as in the Psalter of St. Louis IX of France. Commissioned by the sainted French king, this volume contains seventy-eight

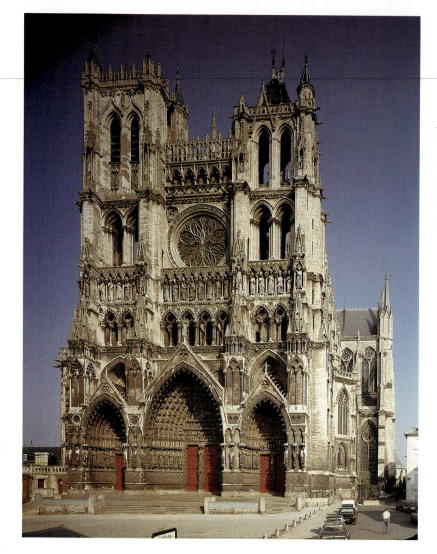

FIGURE 9.27 Western Facade. Amiens Cathedral. Amiens, France. Ca. 1220–1236. *Comparison of Amiens' facade with that of Notre Dame in Paris shows how the High Gothic differs from the Early Gothic. The basic form remains the same, but Amiens' surface is richer in detail and more splendid overall. The pointed features, as in the arches over the portals and in the peaked openings in the towers, are the most characteristic visual element in the High Gothic style.*

full-page paintings of scenes from the Old Testament. Of these paintings, "Balaam and his Ass" is a typical representation of the anonymous painter's style (Figure 9.29). The scene unfolds before a High Gothic church; two gables with rose windows are symmetrically balanced on the page. Although this painting owes much to changes in Gothic sculpture, the animated figures of the men, the angel, and the ass are reminiscent of the exuberant Romanesque style.

Music

As with the other arts, the purpose of music during the High Middle Ages was understood to be the glo-

FIGURE 9.28 *Golden Virgin.* Amiens Cathedral. Amiens, France. Ca. 1260. *The* Golden Virgin *of Amiens, so-called because it was originally covered with a thin layer of gold, is one of the most admired works of Gothic art. The artist has depicted Mary as a loving earthly mother with fine features, a high forehead, and a shy smile. This sculpture shows the new tenderness that was creeping into art during the High Middle Ages as part of the rise of the cult of the Virgin.*

rification of God. At the beginning of this period the monophonic (single-line) Gregorian chants were still the main form of musical expression, but two innovations—the introduction of tropes and the development of polyphony—pointed the way to a different sound in the future.

The *tropes*, or turns, were new texts and melodies that were inserted into the existing Gregorian chants. Added for both poetic and doctrinal reasons, these musical embellishments slowly changed the plain chants into more elaborate songs. Culminating in about 1150, this musical development coincided with the appearance of the richly articulated Gothic style churches.

The tropes also gave a powerful impetus to Western drama. From the practice of troping grew a new musical genre, the *liturgical drama*, which at first was sung and performed in the church but gradually moved outdoors. From the twelfth century onward these works were staged in the area in front of the church as sacred dramas or mystery plays ("mystery" is derived from the Latin for "action"). As their popularity increased, they began to be sung in the vernacular instead of Latin. Ultimately, the liturgical drama supplied one of the threads that led to the revival of the secular theater.

Gregorian chants were also being modified by the development of *polyphony*, in which two or more lines of melody are sung or played at the same time. In the early eleventh century polyphony was extremely simple and was known as *organum*. It consisted of a main melody, called the *cantus firmus*, accompanied by an identical melody sung four or five tones higher or lower. By about 1150, the second line began to have its own independent melody rather than duplicating the first. During the thirteenth century, two-voiced organum gave way to multivoiced songs called *motets*, which employed more complex melodies. In the motets, the main singer used the liturgy as a text while up to five other voices sang either commentaries or vernacular translations of the text. The result was a complex web of separate voices woven into a harmonious tapestry. By about 1250 the motet composers had laid the foundations of modern musical composition.

Notwithstanding these developments in sacred music, the church could not stop the rise of secular music any more than it could prevent the spread of courtly love. Indeed, the first secular music was associated with the same feudal courts where the *chansons de geste* and the troubador songs flourished in the twelfth century. At first, France was the center of this musical movement, but in the early thirteenth century, German poets took the lead. At the same time, music began to be practiced not just by aristocratic poets but by middle-class minstrels, and

FIGURE 9.29 *Balaam and His Ass.* Psalter of St. Louis IX. 1252–1270. Bibliothèque Nationale, Paris. *The architectural details in this miniature painting show a correspondence with the Rayonnant architectural style: the two gabled roofs, the two rose windows with exterior traceries, the pointed arches, and the pinnacles. Just as Gothic style architects emphasized the decorative aspects of their buildings, so did this anonymous miniature painter. The story of Balaam and his ass (from Numbers 22: 22–35 in the Old Testament) was a beast fable—a popular literary genre in the Middle Ages. In the biblical story, the ass could speak and see things of which his master, Balaam, was ignorant. In the painting, the ass turns his head and opens his mouth as if to speak.*

new musical instruments—some, such as the *lute* (a multistringed instrument with neck and soundbox) and the bagpipe, banned by the church—started to find their way into secular music (Figure 9.30).

The High Middle Ages also gave rise to some innovations which made modern music possible. The great reformer in this area was Guido of Arezzo [GWEE-doe/uh-RET-so] (about 995–about 1050), an Italian monk, who modernized musical notation by his invention of the music staff, the set of five horizontal lines and four intermediate spaces on which notes may be drawn. Guido also began the practice of naming the musical tones by the syllables *ut* (or *do*), *re, mi, fa, sol*, and *la*, a step which greatly simplified the teaching of music. The music composed according to Guido's system can be reproduced by today's music historians; thus, Western music may be said to descend in an unbroken line from the music of this period.

FIGURE 9.30 Embellished Letter ''B.'' Psalter from Würzburg-Ebrach. Early Thirteenth Century. Universitäts Bibliothek, Munich. *In illuminated manuscripts the initial letter of a sentence was often embellished with intricate details, drawn from the artist's imagination and experience. In this particular example from a thirteenth-century German psalter, the letter ''B'' is interwoven with a band of musicians playing instruments typical of the era: organ (with bellows), bells, ivory horn, flute, stringed instruments, and an instrument for bows. The artist who painted this miniature scene has captured the liveliness of a musical performance, depicting several players in the act of singing.*

The Legacy of the Christian Centuries

The grandeur of this age of synthesis declined after 1300, when the secular and the spiritual began to go their separate ways. But the legacy of the Christian centuries survives, particularly in the writings of Dante, the theology of Thomas Aquinas, and the Gothic cathedrals. Of Dante's works, the *Divine Comedy* is his most enduring gift to world literature; his poetic style and literary forms influenced Italian writers for centuries. Furthermore, Dante's love for Beatrice has deeply influenced Western literature by encouraging poets to seek inspiration from a living woman.

The Roman Catholic world is the most significant beneficiary of the philosophy of Thomas Aquinas. Since the late nineteenth century Thomism has been regarded as the basis of orthodox beliefs. As for the Gothic style, it ceased to be practiced after about 1500, although it was revived in the nineteenth century as part of the Romantic movement, and even today universities often adopt Gothic elements in their official architecture.

Besides these great gifts, the Christian centuries have left the modern world other significant cultural legacies. First and foremost was the birth of the courtly love movement that glorified individual romantic affection—the idea that *this* man loves *this* woman. Vernacular literature finally found its voice during this time in the first European poetry. Of special note, the vernacular writers created one of the richest literary traditions in the West through the stories of King Arthur and the knights of the Round Table. The basic theoretical system for composing music was developed during this period under the auspices of the church. Outside the church, the ancestor of all Western love songs was invented by the Provençal poets. In Gothic sculpture, artists began to move away from symbolic representation to a more realistic art.

Notwithstanding these innovations, the Christian centuries transmitted many of the legacies that had been received from ancient and other sources. The liberal arts, the Christian religion, the rationalist tradition, Muslim science, and the entire Greco-Roman heritage are only the major ingredients of this invaluable legacy to later ages.

KEY CULTURAL TERMS

chivalric code
friars
cathedral
scholasticism
Realism
Nominalism
via media
goliard
chanson de geste
vernacular language
canzone
minstrel
troubador
romance
lay
terza rima
Romanesque style
Gothic style
bay

tympanum
narthex
ribbed vault
pier
flying buttress
choir
rose window
blind arcade
gargoyle
gallery
Rayonnant
tracery
trope
liturgical drama
polyphony
organum
motet
lute

SUGGESTIONS FOR FURTHER READING

PRIMARY SOURCES

CHRÉTIEN DE TROYES. *Arthurian Romances.* Translated by W. W. Comfort. New York: Everyman's Library Edition, 1955. A good prose version of Chrétien's romances, including *Lancelot.*

DANTE. *The Divine Comedy. The Inferno. The Purgatorio. The Paradiso.* Translated by John Ciardi. New York: New American Library, 1982. The best contemporary English translation; lively and with good footnotes.

The Lais of Marie de France. Translated and with an introduction by R. Hanning and J. Ferrante. Durham: The Labyrinth Press, 1982. A modern, free-verse translation of these Old French poems; with notes and an extremely useful introductory essay.

ST. THOMAS AQUINAS. *Summa Theologica.* 3 vols. Translated by Fathers of the English Dominican Province. New York: Benziger, 1947. A good English version of St. Thomas's monumental work, which underlies Roman Catholic theology today.

The Song of Roland. Translated by P. Terry. Indianapolis, Ind.: Bobbs-Merrill, 1965. A recent translation that is readable and modern but still captures some of the language and drama of the original.

TIERNEY, B. *The Crisis of Church and State, 1050–1300.* Englewood Cliffs, N.J.: Prentice-Hall, 1964. Primary documents linked together by sound interpretations and explanations.

10

THE LATE MIDDLE AGES
1300—1500

People living during what a modern historian has termed the "calamitous" fourteenth century were thrown into confusion and despair. Many believed that the biblical apocalypse had arrived, attended by plague, famine, and war, for these were among the calamities that rained down on them. Amid the turbulence of this century, the unique culture of the High Middle Ages, which had blended the spiritual with the secular, began to come undone. In the Late Middle Ages, significant changes were affecting the achievements of the previous era. The church had to give up its dream of Christendom—a united Christian commonwealth—when faced with the reality of rival European states at war with each other. New military tactics and weapons rendered chivalry obsolete, and the chivalric code began to take on the colors of romantic fiction. In the universities, new intellectual currents drove a wedge between philosophy and theology, which had been so carefully integrated by Thomas Aquinas. And the balanced High Gothic style in art and architecture gave way to the florid Late Gothic style.

This chapter examines the third and final phase of medieval civilization during the period between 1300 and 1500. It also explores the explosion of secular interests that was occurring in this contradictory age and the technological and artistic innovations that were beginning to point the Western world

in a new direction. Chapter 11 returns to the fifteenth century to focus on the specific developments that ushered in the Renaissance and the modern era.

HARD TIMES COME TO EUROPE

Shortly after the opening of the fourteenth century, Europe entered a disastrous period of economic depression, accompanied by soaring prices and widespread famine. Against the backdrop of the Hundred Years' War, social unrest increased, with urban riots and peasant revolts, and renegade feudal armies ravaged much of western Europe for decades. The church, in disgrace and disarray for much of this period, was unable to provide moral or political leadership. As old certainties evaporated, the optimistic mood of the High Middle Ages gave way to a sense of impending doom.

Ordeal by Plague, Famine, and War

Of all the calamities that now befell Europe, the worst was the plague, which first appeared in northern Italy in 1347. Imported from the East along newly opened trade routes, the plague bacillus was carried over sea and land by fleas, which in turn were transported by rats (Map 10.1). From Italy, the

◄ HUBERT AND JAN VAN EYCK. *Adoration of the Lamb.* Detail of the *Ghent Altarpiece.* Ca. 1432. St. Bavo Cathedral, Ghent, Belgium.

MAP 10.1

Progress of the Black Death across Europe in the Fourteenth Century

FIGURE 10.1 *Burial of Plague Victims. Mid–Fourteenth Century. The devastating plague of the mid–fourteenth century caused an air of melancholy to hover over the waning years of the Late Middle Ages. This small painting shows the gruesome burial rites, including interment in mass graves, that were a familiar sight in the regions hardest hit by the disease.*

disease spread rapidly over most of Europe, halted only by the frost line in the north. Amazingly, a few cities and areas—like Milan and central Germany—were free of plague. But in other places the plague raged from 1348 until 1351, and further onslaughts occurred at random throughout the century and into the next. So deadly was the disease that more than a third of Europe's 70 million people died in the first epidemic alone (Figure 10.1). The later outbreaks were less severe, but the West did not regain a population of 70 million until 1470.

The mechanism of disease transmission was not fully understood, and the medieval plague created panic and hysteria. Using medieval accounts of the disease, modern researchers have detected three different forms of plague: bubonic (infected lymph nodes), pneumonic (infected lungs), and septicemic (blood poisoning). The diseases were all extremely painful, and death could come within a matter of hours or a few days. People in the Late Middle Ages referred to these disease types collectively as "the plague"; in the sixteenth century historians began to label this medieval epidemic the "Black Death," which has become the generally accepted term.

The Black Death cast a long shadow over the Late Middle Ages. Many writers and artists reflected the melancholy times, occasionally brightening their dark works with an end-of-the-world gaiety. The age's leading image became the Dance of Death. In literature and in art, death was portrayed as a skeleton, democratically joining hands with kings, queens, popes, merchants, peasants, and prostitutes as they danced their way to destruction. In the direct manner of medieval thinking, this symbol forcefully showed the folly of human ambition and the transitoriness of life (Figure 10.2).

The crisis atmosphere surrounding the plague was compounded by growing famine conditions across the European continent. Starting in 1315, agricultural harvests failed with some regularity for more than a century. Besides raising the death rate, these famines weakened the populace and made them more susceptible to diseases.

Climatic changes or cyclic shifts in ocean currents may have occasioned the bad harvests, but the food shortages were probably triggered by the economic adjustments that had to be made because of the previous era's overproduction and too-rapid expansion. The new farmlands that had been opened after 1250 were now abandoned. Increased demand for meat caused farmers to turn to raising cattle rather than growing cereal and grain crops. Besides, cheap imported cereals from Italy and Germany severely depressed grain prices in other areas. Lower prices led

FIGURE 10.2 *The Dance of Death.* Fifteenth Century. *In the wake of the Black Plague, art and literature became filled with themes affirming the biblical message that life is short and death certain. One of the most vivid images of this theme was the* Danse Macabre, *or Dance of Death, which took many artistic and literary forms. In this example, a miniature painting taken from a Spanish manuscript of the fifteenth century, the corpses are shown nude, stripped of their human dignity, and dancing with wild abandon.*

farmers to specialize—in wines, fruit, or flax—rather than to invest in multiple crops. The Italian hinterland and the German lands along the Baltic became Europe's breadbasket, and when plague disturbed these areas, famine spread across the continent.

In addition to plague and famine, war also disrupted the pattern of social and economic life. By 1450 the kings of Aragon in eastern Spain had defeated and replaced the French rulers of Naples, Sicily, and Sardinia. The increasingly powerful northern Italian cities waged war among themselves for commercial and political advantage. Farther east, from 1347 on, the Ottoman Turks were on the move, occupying Greece and the Balkan peninsula and finally conquering Constantinople in 1453. As the century ended, the Turks were marching westward, menacing Bohemia and Hungary. In the west, England and France fought the seemingly endless Hundred Years' War intermittently from 1337 to 1453. The Dukes of Burgundy were frequently parties to this struggle, as they attempted, but failed, to carve out a "middle kingdom" between France and the German empire.

One of the side effects of this almost constant warfare was a growing number of soldiers loose in the land from renegade mercenary armies. The countryside was filled with bands of roving knights—nobles, younger sons or bastards of aristocratic families, and outlaws—who blackmailed landowners and peasants alike in Aragon, France, and Italy. All over Europe these dangerous circumstances in the countryside compelled town dwellers to retreat behind their city walls.

Depopulation, Rebellion, and Industrialization

The major consequence of the plagues, famines, and wars was depopulation, which caused the commercial map of Europe to be redrawn. In general, the regions hardest hit economically were those that had benefited most in the earlier boom, particularly France. New centers now rose to economic importance, including Bohemia, Poland, Hungary, Scandinavia, and Portugal. The northern Italian cities, the largest cities in Europe—Florence, Genoa, and Venice—rallied from the plague's devastating losses in the fifteenth century to make a remarkable economic recovery.

Population decline also caused dramatic social dislocations. Plague-free regions lost settlers as healthy people flocked to plague-stricken areas, where laborers were in great demand. Europe experienced a sharp decrease in the density of the rural population. Thousands of villages simply disappeared as peasants abandoned their farms and settled in the towns, causing a rise in the number of urban dwellers. A short-term effect of depopulation and the shifts in population was to widen the gap between rich and poor and to foster deep class hatred. As class cohesion declined, the established social order broke down, and society now experienced warfare between peasants and landowners, guildsmen and merchants, and town laborers and middle-class elites. These social uprisings often had an anticlerical element, with the rebels attacking church property and denouncing the collection of tithes.

Starting in Flanders in 1296, social unrest mounted across Europe. In 1358 conditions in France reached a critical juncture when the *Jacquerie,* or rural renegades, made common cause with Parisian malcontents and killed many nobles. Across the English Channel in 1381, during the brief Peasants' Revolt, insurgents seized and occupied London. Among their demands was that the English king abolish the nobility. In the end, these uprisings failed to make any lasting impact on the social order. Fighting on foot and using farm tools as weapons, the poorly organized and ill-equipped rebels were no match for troops of armored knights on horseback.

While the immediate consequence of the demographic crisis was to intensify social unrest, the long-term effect was to produce a higher standard of living for the survivors. Peasants in western Europe found their labor more in demand and their bargaining positions with the landowners improved. Many were able to break out of servitude and become rent-paying farmers. Others, less fortunate, moved from the status of serf to sharecropper. As a result, by 1500 manorialism was dying out in western Europe except for minor obligations. But in central and eastern Europe—Poland, Bohemia, and Hungary, where the plague was less devastating and the landlords could hold firm—the peasants were not so lucky. On the contrary, estate owners there, and in Germany and Russia, bound the serfs ever more tightly to their farm labors.

As farming changed, so did Europe's fledgling industrial life. Textile manufacture, performed on hand looms, remained the leading industry, but its production and distribution centers shifted. Cut off by war from their former wool supplies and their retail markets, the Flemish and French weavers were challenged by woolen manufacturers from northern Italy, the Rhineland, and Poland. The greatest change in textile manufacturing, however, was ultimately precipitated by England's shift from the export of raw wool to the export of finished cloth, a change that disrupted the traditional rural way of life. Entrepreneurs wishing to escape the confining regulations of the town guilds devised the "putting out system," whereby raw wool was consigned to peasant families who wove it into cloth within their own cottages. As the new system prospered, the demand increased for raw wool, and many landowners turned English farmland into pasture for sheep in order to accommodate this need.

New industries also grew up around the production of rag paper, a Chinese invention perfected by the Arabs and manufactured widely in Spain after 1300; of salt, distributed by Venice and Lisbon and used in tanning leather and preserving food; and of iron, in demand for weapons, armor, and horseshoes. The development of movable type in the mid–fifteenth century was the most significant of these technological innovations; it gave rise to the printing and publishing industries and had enormous repercussions for education and literature. Additional breakthroughs occurred elsewhere. The suction pump helped increase productivity in the mines, the spinning wheel radically improved the turning of wool into thread, and new casting methods led to a superior bronze for cannons. Older inventions, such as eyeglasses, clocks, and gunpowder, were now perfected in this age of rapid change.

The Secular Monarchies

France and England maintained their positions as the leading states of Europe, but they exhausted their economies with wasteful wars. The Hundred Years' War, as the group of conflicts between the mid–fourteenth and the mid–fifteenth century is called, arose over feudal entanglements, dynastic rivalries, and military alliances dating from the High

TIME LINE 10.1   ROYAL DYNASTIES IN LATE MEDIEVAL FRANCE

Middle Ages. The war was fought entirely on French soil. The French crown under the Valois dynasty had to contend not only with England, but with the Dukes of Burgundy, who threatened to break away from their French ties and set up an independent kingdom. The Burgundian Dukes aimed for a royal crown, either that of France or one authorized by the Holy Roman Emperor. Whatever may have been its final political goal, the Duchy of Burgundy by the 1400s encompassed vast territories on the northeast border of France. Like the French kings, these dukes adopted a centralized state structure that included a treasury, a judiciary, and a standing army. The Burgundian court at Dijon was the most brilliant in northern Europe, attracting the leading artists and humanists of the age.

Despite the ravages of the Hundred Years' War, the Valois kings emerged from the conflict with more territory than when the hostilities began. Except for the port of Calais, England was forced to cede her overseas lands to the French crown. Burgundy remained a threat somewhat longer, until King Louis XI (1461–1483) brought the dukes under his control. The last major territory that had escaped the French crown was gained by Charles VIII (1483–1498) when he married the heiress to the County of Brittany. With the acquisition of Brittany, the contour of modern France was now complete (Time Line 10.1).

While the Hundred Years' War raged on the continent, life in England was disrupted by feudal rebellion, peasant unrest, and urban strife. Like France, England was also emerging from the feudal system but moving in a different direction from her rival across the channel. The English Parliament gained power at the expense of the king, meeting frequently when summoned and representing the interests of the nobles, the towns, and the rural counties. Parliament also expressed popular feelings when laws curbing papal power in England were passed.

When Henry VII (1485–1509) became king, it soon was apparent that part of the reason for the dominance of Parliament during this period was the weakness of the kings. This founder of England's brilliant Tudor dynasty abandoned foreign wars, lived off his own estates, and relied on his own advisers—all issues that had led to violent quarrels between his predecessors and Parliament. Henry VII's policies deflated parliamentary power, keeping the representative body subservient to the crown and making Henry as potent as his contemporaries in France (Time Line 10.2).

The success of the French and English kings in centralizing their states attracted many imitators. Their ruling style—with royal secretaries, efficient treasuries, national judiciaries, and representative assemblies—was adopted in part by other states. Spain was the most successful in achieving unity. Dynastic politics and civil war kept the states of central Europe and Scandinavia from becoming strong and centralized. The Holy Roman Empire was the least successful of these political entities, and Germany remained divided into combative states with weak centralized rule.

The Papal Monarchy

From its pinnacle of power and prestige in 1200 under Pope Innocent III, the church entered a period of decline in about 1300. In 1303, Pope Boniface VIII's

TIME LINE 10.2   ROYAL DYNASTIES IN LATE MEDIEVAL ENGLAND

reign ended in abject failure (see Chapter 9). For most of the next century or more, the church was beset with dislocation, schism, and heresy.

Papal dislocation occurred in 1309 when Pope Clement V abandoned Rome. For almost seventy years the seat of the papacy was in Avignon, a papal fief on the Rhone River. This step, unique in the almost two-thousand-year history of the church, was taken because the papacy sought relief from Rome's factional politics. The Avignon popes found the Rhone valley a safer, more hospitable place from which to rule the church than the banks of the Tiber. The relocation provoked voices, which soon became legion, speaking against these popes for being in the pocket of the French crown.

The chief success of the Avignonese popes was to centralize the papacy, an accomplishment comparable to what was happening in the secular kingdoms. These popes reorganized the church's financial system and changed payments from kind to money. At the same time, unfortunately, they rarely made moral reforms. Their reigns lapsed into worldliness and greed, which made the papacy more vulnerable to criticism.

The Avignonese papacy had barely ended in 1378 when a new calamity, the Great Schism, threw the church into even more confusion. Under Pope Gregory XI, the papacy had returned to Rome in 1377, and the cardinals had elected an Italian pope when Gregory died. The French cardinals did not approve of this pope, and they withdrew and elected another pontiff to rule from Avignon. This scandalous situation divided western Christendom into two obediences with two popes, two Colleges of Cardinals, two curias, and two church tax systems. The rising power of the secular states became evident as rulers cast their support along political lines. France, Sicily, Scotland, Castile, Aragon, and Portugal rallied behind the Avignon pope; England, Flanders, Poland, Hungary, Germany, and the rest of Italy stayed loyal to the Roman pope. During these political shenanigans, the papal office was the real loser; the pope's authority diminished as pious Christians became bewildered and disgusted.

The worst was yet to come. In 1409 both sets of cardinals summoned a church council in Pisa to heal the fissure. The Pisan Council elected a new pope and called on the other two to resign. When they both refused, the church was faced with *three* rulers claiming papal authority. The Great Schism was finally resolved at the Council of Constance (1414–1418), convened by the Holy Roman Emperor. This council deposed the Avignon ruler, accepted the resignation of the Roman claimant, ignored the earlier conciliar choice, and elected a new pope, Martin V.

With the success of the Council of Constance, the supporters of conciliar rule (that is, rule by councils) as a way of curbing the power of the popes seemed to be gaining ground in the church. But Martin V (1417–1431) quickly rejected this idea as soon as he was elected to the papal throne. Nevertheless, the conciliar movement remained alive until the mid–fifteenth century, when strong popes once again reasserted the monarchical power of their office.

Having surmounted their earlier crises by the restoration of the papal monarchy, the popes in the mid–fifteenth century turned their interest to the arts and humanities rather than to pressing moral and spiritual issues. Moreover, they were vitally concerned with the trappings of political power. They plunged into Italian politics more deeply than ever, ruling as secular princes in their papal lands. Their worldly interests and blatant political maneuvers only intensified the mounting disapproval of the papacy and provided the church's critics with more examples of the institution's corruption and decline.

THE CULTURAL FLOWERING OF THE LATE MIDDLE AGES

The calamitous political, social, and economic events of the Late Middle Ages were echoed in the cultural sphere by the breakdown of the medieval synthesis in religion, in theology, in literature, and in art. New secular voices began to be heard, challenging traditional views, and the interests of the bourgeoisie started to have an impact on art and architecture. Although the church remained the major financial supporter of the arts, rich town dwellers, notably bankers and merchants, were emerging as the new patrons of art (Figure 10.3). Their conspicuous art patronage was a way of establishing their cultural credentials in society.

Religion

Monastic reform had been a major force within the church in the High Middle Ages, but such collective acts of devotion were largely unknown in the Late Middle Ages. Dedicated and virtuous monks and nuns were increasingly rare, and their influence was waning. Innovative forms of religious expression did not come from members of religious orders but from lay people, inspired perhaps to protest and react against what they perceived as the increasing

FIGURE 10.3 Jacques Coeur's House. 1443–1451. Bourges, France. *Coeur was an immensely successful entrepreneur who at one point was bankrolling the French kings. His magnificent mansion at Bourges spawned many imitations among wealthy businessmen across Europe. The building's high, spiky turrets, fanciful balconies, and highly decorated windows are all secular adaptations of the Late Gothic style more commonly seen in church architecture. Coeur conducted his continent-wide financial and commercial dealings from this house, sending messages by carrier pigeons released through the holes on the roof.*

By 1400 other groups, such as the Brethren and Sisters of the Common Life and the Friends of God, were rising in the Rhineland, the Low Countries, and Flanders. This lay movement constituted the **devotio moderna**, or the "new devotion," with its ideal of a pious lay society. Disappointed with traditionally trained priests, members of these groups often rejected higher education and practiced the strict discipline of the earlier monastic orders, but without withdrawing into a monastery. Among the most important expressions of this new devotion was *The Imitation of Christ* by Thomas à Kempis (1380–1471). His manual, with its stern asceticism, reflected the harsh ideals of the Brethren of the Common life, the group of which Kempis was a member.

Within the pietistic movement, extreme ascetic practices that verged on heresy mounted in these turbulent years. The bizarre behavior of the flagellants, for example, was triggered by the plague. They regarded this disease as God's judgment on an evil society, and they engaged in ritual whippings in an attempt to divert divine wrath away from others (Figure 10.4).

The flagellants managed to escape official censure, but those more openly critical of the church did not. The leaders who attempted to reform the church in England and Bohemia met stout resistance from the popes. The English reform movement sprang from the teachings of John Wycliffe (about 1320–1384), an Oxford teacher whose message attracted the nobility as well as the common folk. Wishing to purify the church of worldliness, Wycliffe urged the abolition of

FIGURE 10.4 *Flagellation Scene. Annales of Gilles Le Muisit.* Bibliothèque Royale Albert Ier, Brussels. *This miniature painting represents a scene that became a familiar sight across Europe during the plague years. The penitents, depicted with bare backs and feet, marched through the towns scourging themselves with whips. By this self-punishment, they hoped to atone for their own and society's sins and thus bring the plague to an end.*

worldliness of the church and the declining commitment of many clergy.

Lay piety was thus one of the most significant developments in the religious landscape. The beguine movement, which encouraged lives devoted to helping the needy, had begun in the thirteenth century among lay women in northern France. Now, the beguines, along with male lay brethren called beghards, spread to Germany and the Netherlands, usually in proximity to Dominican monasteries. Medieval Germany's finest devotional writer, Meister Eckhart (about 1260–1328), composed tracts and sermons to guide these lay people's religious impulses into orthodox ways. A subtle thinker, Meister Eckhart's prose works reveal him to be one of the great mystics of the Christian tradition.

ecclesiastical property, the subservience of the church to the state, and the denial of papal authority. The most lasting achievement of Wycliffe's movement was the introduction of the first complete English-language Bible, produced by scholars inspired by his teaching. After his followers (known as Lollards) were condemned as heretical, the secular officials launched savage persecutions that resulted in the murder of those supporters who did not recant.

The Bohemian reformers in the Holy Roman Empire were indebted to Wycliffe, whom some had met at Oxford, but, more importantly, their strength was rooted in the popular piety and evangelical preachers of mid-fourteenth-century Prague. The heresy became identified with Jan Hus (about 1369–1415), a Czech theologian who accepted Wycliffe's political views but rejected some of his religious teachings. Hus was invited to the Council of Constance in 1415, where his ideas were condemned, and he was burned at the stake by state authorities. His death outraged his fellow Czechs, many of whom, including the powerful and wealthy, now adopted his views. Hussite beliefs became a vehicle for Czech nationalism, as his ethnic comrades fought against German overlords and attacked church property. Because of the backing of powerful lay leaders, the Hussites survived into the next century. They gained more followers during the Protestant Reformation and exist today as the Moravian Brethren.

Although the secular authorities, instigated by the church, could usually be counted on to put down the heresies, the church had a more powerful internal weapon at its disposal: the Inquisition (from the Latin *inquisitio*, meaning "inquiry"). Born in the aftermath of the Albigensian heresy in the twelfth century (see Chapter 9), the Inquisition was a religious court for identifying and condemning heretics. The Inquisition reached its cruel height during the Late Middle Ages, particularly in Italy and Spain.

Because of its procedures, the Inquisition became the most notorious instrument ever created by the Christian church. Ignoring the basic ideals of Roman law, this church court allowed suspects to be condemned without ever facing their accusers. Confessions made under torture were also allowed to serve as evidence against other persons. Forbidden by the Bible to shed blood, the leaders of the Inquisition turned convicted heretics over to the state authorities, who then executed them by burning. By modern estimates, thousands of men and women perished in this way.

The Inquisition was also used to rid society of women—and to a lesser extent of men—who were suspected of being in league with the devil. The belief in witchcraft, an occult legacy of the ancient world, was next to universal during the Middle Ages. Many educated people sincerely believed that certain women were witches and that magical devices could protect the faithful from their spells. Consequently, hundreds of suspected individuals were killed by the Inquisition or by unruly mobs. Fear of witchcraft persisted as a dangerous part of popular lore into the eighteenth century.

Theology, Philosophy, and Science

Although the popes betrayed their spiritual mission in these years, the church was not without dedicated followers who cared deeply about theological issues. Many of these clerical thinkers were affiliated with the universities, principally in Paris and at Oxford. Their major disputes were over Thomism, the theological system of Thomas Aquinas, which in the Late Middle Ages was losing supporters and coming increasingly under attack. At the same time, the ongoing philosophical struggle between Realism and Nominalism finally ended with a Nominalist victory. In the long run, those who questioned Thomism and those who accepted Nominalism set philosophy and theology on separate paths and thus paved the way to the Renaissance and the Scientific Revolution.

The Via Antiqua *versus the* Via Moderna   The opening round in the theological war against Thomism began soon after the death of Thomas Aquinas in 1274 and before the High Middle Ages was over. In 1277, church officials in Paris condemned the Latin Averroists at the local university for their rationalist ideas. As part of their attack on extreme rationalism, the church authorities rejected some of Aquinas's arguments. The censure of Thomism led to a heated controversy that raged for much of the Late Middle Ages among university scholars. In particular, Thomas's fellow Dominican friars waged an acrimonious battle with the Franciscan masters, their great rivals in theological studies.

During these theological debates, new labels were invented and assumed by the opposing sides. Aquinas's *via media* came to be termed by his opponents the **via antiqua**, or the old-fashioned way. Broadly speaking, the *via antiqua* followed Thomism in urging that faith and reason be combined as the correct approach to divine truth. In contrast, the **via moderna**, or the modern way, made a complete separation of biblical beliefs and rationalism. In time the *via moderna* prevailed, driving the *via antiqua* underground until it was rescued from oblivion in the modern period.

Duns Scotus and William of Ockham   The conflict between the *via antiqua* and the *via moderna* was best exemplified in the writings of John Duns Scotus and William of Ockham, respectively. The first of these commentators was sympathetic to the theology of Thomas Aquinas, but the second scholar was unmistakably hostile and tried to discredit Thomism.

Duns Scotus [duhnz SKOAT-us] (about 1265–1308), the most persuasive voice of the *via antiqua*, was a Scottish thinker who was trained as a Franciscan and lectured at the universities in Oxford, Paris, and Cologne. Even though he was a supporter of Thomism, Duns Scotus unwittingly undermined Aquinas's synthesis by stressing that faith was superior to reason, a shift in focus that arose from his belief in God's absolute and limitless power. Pointing out that God's existence could not be proven either through the senses or by reason, he asserted that faith was the only way to explain the divine mystery. Furthermore, Duns Scotus concluded that because the theologian and the philosopher have different intellectual tasks, theology and science (that is, the study of nature) should be independent fields of inquiry.

What Duns Scotus unintentionally began, William of Ockham (about 1300–about 1349) purposely completed. Under the assaults of Ockham's keen intellect, the Thomist theological edifice collapsed. An Oxford-trained theologian, he recognized the importance of both reason and faith, but, like Scotus, he did not see how reason could prove God's existence. Both thinkers believed that only personal feelings and mystical experiences could reveal God and the divine moral order. Yet Ockham went further than Scotus by asserting that reason, the senses, and empirical evidence could enable human beings to discover and hence understand the natural world. To Ockham, faith and reason were both valid approaches to truth, but they should be kept apart so that each could achieve its respective end.

In the seemingly endless medieval debate between the Realists and the Nominalists, Ockham's reasoning swept Nominalism to its final victory. Like the Nominalists of the twelfth century, Ockham denied the existence of universals and claimed that only individual objects existed. He concluded that human beings can have clear and distinct knowledge only of specific things in the physical world; no useful knowledge can be gained through reason or the senses about the spiritual realm. Ockham's conclusion did not mean that human beings were cast adrift without access to the world of God. A corollary of his approach was that understanding of the spiritual realm rested solely on the truths of faith and theology.

In his reasoning, William of Ockham asserted a principle of economy that stripped away all that was irrelevant: Arguments should be drawn from a minimum of data and founded on closely constructed logic. "It is vain to do with more what can be done with fewer," he says in one of his works. Ockham's "razor" of logic eliminated superfluous information that could not be verified, thus enabling a student to cut to the core of a philosophical problem. The Ockhamites, following their mentor's logic and empiricism, challenged the Realists and dominated the intellectual life of the universities for the next two hundred years.

Developments in Science   Ockham's ideas broadened the path to modern science that had been opened by two thirteenth-century thinkers. In that earlier time, Robert Grosseteste [GRO-stest] (about 1175–1253), a Franciscan at Oxford University, had devised a scientific method for investigating natural phenomena; using step-by-step procedures, he employed mathematics and tested hypotheses until he reached satisfactory conclusions. Roger Bacon (about 1220–1292), another Franciscan and a follower of Grosseteste, advocated the use of the experimental method, which he demonstrated in his studies of optics, solar eclipses, and rainbows and in his treatises on mathematics, physics, and philosophy. From the modern standpoint, Bacon was perhaps the most original mind of this otherwise barren period in the history of science.

In the fourteenth century, other thinkers, with Grosseteste and Bacon as guides and Ockham's logic as a weapon, made further contributions to the advance of science. Outstanding among these men was one bold Parisian scholar who took advantage of the growing interest in the experimental method, Nicholas Oresme [O-REM] (about 1330–1382). Oresme answered all of Aristotle's objections to the idea that the earth moved. Using pure reason and applying theoretical arguments, he concluded that it was as plausible that the earth moved around the sun as that it was fixed. Having used reason to show that the earth may move, however, Oresme then chose to accept church doctrine, denying what he had demonstrated. Nevertheless, Oresme's arguments, along with Ockham's separation of natural philosophy from theology and Bacon's formulation of the experimental method, foreshadowed the end of the medieval concept of the physical and celestial worlds.

Literature

The powerful forces that were reshaping the wider culture—the rising new monarchies, the growing national consciousness among diverse peoples, the emerging secularism, and the developing urban environment—were also transforming literature in the Late Middle Ages. The rise of literacy produced a growing educated class who learned to read and

FIGURE 10.5 FRANCESCO TRAINI. *Triumph of Death.* Detail. Ca. 1350. Pisa, Italy.
Like the storytellers in The Decameron, *these well-dressed travelers have left their
plague-stricken city, perhaps in search of safety or hoping for a day's pleasant diversion in
the countryside. Instead, they come on three corpses rotting in coffins—even the dogs are
afraid—and a hermit who points out the lesson: Death triumphs over all. This detail is
from a huge fresco painted on the wall of the cemetery next to the Pisa Cathedral.*

write the local languages rather than Latin, and a
shift to vernacular literature began to occur. Two
new groups—the monarchs and their courts and the
urban middle class—started to supplant the nobility
and the church as patrons and audiences. And, ultimately most important of all, in the mid–fifteenth
century Johann Gutenberg developed a practicable
method of using movable type to print books. This
invention helped to seal the doom of medieval civilization and signaled the commencement of the
modern world.

Northern Italian Literature: Petrarch and Boccaccio
New literary forms emerged in the areas where the
chivalric and feudal modes were weakest—northern
Italy and England. Petrarch and Boccaccio, both Florentines, like Dante, grew up in a Christian world that
was rapidly being secularized. These two writers captured the mood of this transition era as Florence and
the other Italian city-states shed their medieval outlook. Both authors looked back to the Classical world
for inspiration, and yet both found in the bustling
world of the nearby towns the materials and characters
for their stories. Of the two, Petrarch was the more
dedicated Classicist and often used ancient themes in
his writings.

Francesco Petrarch [PEE-trark] ("Petrarca" in
Italian) (1304–1374), though Florentine by birth and
in spirit, flourished in Avignon amid the splendor

and learning of the papal court. As a diplomat for
popes and Italian princes, he won fame and wealth,
but his reputation arose from his career as a professional man of letters. Rejecting the age's trend toward the vernacular, he dedicated his life to Latin
writing and to the recovery of ancient manuscripts,
although the work for which he is most famous today, a collection of love lyrics and sonnets called
Canzoniere, or *Songbook,* is written in Italian. His devotion struck a responsive chord among his fellow
Italians, who in 1341 proclaimed him poet laureate
for his lyrics, sonnets, treatises, and epics. In many
ways, Petrarch, despite preparing for a clerical career though never becoming a priest, shows the typical secular interests of his times. A conventional
Christian, he only occasionally addressed religious
issues in his works.

A religious theme is touched on in *Secretum,* or
My Secret, in which Petrarch deals with the state of
his soul. In this dialogue, "Augustinus," or St. Augustine, hounds "Franciscus," or Petrarch, about his
innermost thoughts and desires, charging him with
all the deadly sins. Freely admitting his moral lapses,
Franciscus pleads that he is the same as any other
man—driven by a love of learning, a weakness for
fleshly attractions, and an appetite for personal comforts. Despite this confession, the dialogue shows
that Petrarch could not liberate himself fully from
medieval values.

Even more than his lifelong friend Petrarch, Giovanni Boccaccio [bo-KACH-e-o] (1313–1375) was a man of the world. The son of a banker, Boccaccio began his literary career by penning prose romances along with poetic pastorals and sonnets, many of which were dedicated to Fiammetta, a young woman who was both his consuming passion and his literary muse. His early efforts, however, were overshadowed by his Italian prose masterpiece, *The Decameron.* Written in about 1351, this work reflects the grim conditions of the Black Death, which had just swept through Florence (Figure 10.5). In *The Decameron* (from the Greek for "ten days"), Boccaccio describes how ten young men and women, in their efforts to escape the plague, flee the city to a country villa, where they pass the time, each telling a story a day for ten days. Most of their one hundred tales were based on folk stories and popular legends. While some tales deal lightly with social mores and a few contain moral messages, the majority simply entertain the listener. Boccaccio, speaking though a cross section of urban voices and relying on well-known stories, helped develop a form of literature that eventually led to the modern short story.

English Literature: Geoffrey Chaucer   Like its Italian counterpart, English literature rapidly matured into its own forms during the Late Middle Ages. The development of an English literary style was aided immensely by the evolution of a common language. Until this time most educated English people read and spoke French, but a rising sense of national consciousness, triggered by the Hundred Years' War and by an emerging educated urban class, hastened the spread of a native tongue. England's kings came to see themselves as different from their French ancestors and purposely began to speak English instead of French; they also made English the official language of government.

By 1300 important works in English were beginning to appear, such as *The Vision of Piers Plowman,* a moral allegory probably written by William Langland (about 1332–1400) that graphically exposes the plight of the poor and calls for a return to Christian virtues. This work provides insight into England's social and economic system and, through the author's anguish, reveals the social tension around the time of the Peasants' Revolt in 1381.

English literature was still establishing its own identity and a common language was slowly emerging when Geoffrey Chaucer (about 1340–1400) appeared on the scene. He wrote in an East Midland dialect of English that became the standard form for his generation as well as the foundation of modern English. The son of a wealthy London merchant, Chaucer spent his professional life as a courtier, a diplomat, and a public servant for the English

crown. The profession of "writer" or "poet" was unknown in Chaucer's day. But his poetry brought him renown, and when he died he was the first commoner to be buried in Westminster Abbey, a favored burial spot for English royalty.

Chaucer began composing his most famous work, *The Canterbury Tales,* in 1385. He set the tales in the context of a pilgrimage to the tomb of Thomas à Becket, the twelfth-century martyr. Even though the journey has a religious purpose, Chaucer makes it plain that the travelers intend to have a good time along the way. To make the journey from London to Canterbury more interesting, the thirty-one pilgrims (including Chaucer himself) agree to tell tales—two each going and returning—and to award a prize for the best story told.

Chaucer completed only twenty-three tales and the general Prologue, in which he introduces the pilgrims. Each person on the pilgrimage not only represents an English social type but is also a unique and believable human being. In this poetic narrative about a group of ordinary people, the spiritual is mixed with the temporal and the serious with the comic.

Chaucer drew his pilgrims from nearly all walks of medieval society. The Knight, in this late stage of feudalism, personified much that was noble and honorable in the chivalric code; his bravery could not be questioned, but he was also a mercenary and cruel to his enemies. Certain representatives of the church are also somewhat skeptically treated. The Prioress, the head of a convent and from the upper class, is more concerned about her refined manners and polished language than the state of her soul. Similarly, the Monk lives a life of the flesh and enjoys good food, fine wines, and expensive clothing. The Friar seems the very opposite of his sworn ideals; he is eager to hear a confession for a fee, and he never goes among the poor or aids the sick. Yet, in the country Parson Chaucer portrays a true servant of God who preaches to his parish, looks after the infirm and dying, and never takes more than his share from his religious flock.

Among the secular travelers the most famous is the Wife of Bath. A widow five times over, this jolly woman is full of life and loves to talk. She has been on many pilgrimages and not only knows about foreign places but has a keen insight into people (Figure 10.6).

As for the tales they tell, the pilgrims' choices often reflect their own moral values. The worthy Knight tells a chivalric love story, but the Miller, a coarse, rough man well versed in lying and cheating, relates how a young wife took on a lover and deceived her husband—an example of the popular medieval tale known as a *fabliau.* Thus the pilgrims'

FIGURE 10.6 *The Wife of Bath.* Ellesmere Manuscript. Early Fifteenth Century. Bancroft Library, University of California at Berkeley. *In the Ellesmere Manuscript, an early edition of* The Canterbury Tales *issued soon after Chaucer's death, each story was accompanied by a sketch of the pilgrim who was narrating it. This portrait of the Wife of Bath shows her riding an ambler, a horse that walks with an easy gait, and wearing a wimple, the typical headdress of nuns as well as lay women of the period.*

stories, based on folk and fairy tales, romances, classical stories, and beast fables, reveal as much about the narrators as they do about late medieval culture.

French Literature: Christine de Pizan   France was also touched by the winds of change blowing through Europe during the Late Middle Ages. Christine de Pizan, the leading French writer of the day, began to explore in her works the status and role of women, giving birth in the process to one of the major issues that helps define the Post-Modern world (see Chapter 21). She also contributed to the triumph of vernacular over Latin language by writing in a graceful French with the learnedness of Latin.

Christine de Pizan (sometimes written as "de Pisan" or "of Pisa") (1364–about 1430) was by birth an Italian whose literary gifts blossomed under the patronage of the French kings and dukes of Burgundy. With close ties to the French court, she began a life of study and learning only after the death of

her husband, a royal official, in 1389, leaving her with a family to support. The first known Western woman to earn a living through her writings, Christine is a pioneer who blazed the trail for today's female authors.

Christine wrote on diverse topics, ranging over the well-established literary genres of her day, including love poems, lays, biography, letters, political tracts, and moral proverbs. Two themes dominate her writing: calls for peace and appeals for the recognition of women's contributions to culture and social life. Both themes reflect the era in which she lived—an age beset by civil strife and a time in which women were scarcely allowed to express an opinion in public.

The work of Christine's that has excited the most interest among modern readers is *The Book of the City of Ladies* (1405), a book that forcefully tries to raise the status of women and to give them dignity. Offering one of the first histories of women and arguing that women have the right to be educated, this book seems almost feminist in a modern sense. However, a close reading of the work shows that Christine is not a modern feminist but is writing within a medieval framework. Nowhere in this book nor in any other writings does she advocate that women abandon their traditional roles and strike out on a new path. It is proper nevertheless to claim that Christine de Pizan is the first Western writer to raise "the woman question," the modern term for the issue of women's rights in society and culture.

FIGURE 10.7   The Church of St. Maclou. 1435–ca. 1514. Rouen, France. *St. Maclou's exterior illustrates the ornate Late Gothic style. Its west facade, unlike a square High Gothic front, fans out to form a semicircular entrance. There are five portals (rather than the usual three), two of which are blind, and set above them are steeply pitched stone arches of intricate design.*

Art and Architecture

The Gothic style continued to dominate architecture throughout this period (see Chapter 9), but the balanced and unified High Gothic of the thirteenth century was now replaced with the ornate effects of the *Late Gothic style*. Virtuosity became the chief aesthetic goal, as the architects took basic forms and pushed them to the stylistic limits. The spires of churches soared ever higher, and building facades dissolved into fantastic surfaces of delicate, lacy details.

Late Gothic sculpture and painting also became more virtuosic. Statues and sculpted figures were given willowy, swaying bodies, rendered in exquisite details, and illuminated manuscripts and painted wooden panels became ever more refined. At the same time, Giotto, an early fourteenth-century Florentine painter, was revolutionizing art with a new approach to painting. The trend toward naturalism embodied in his works was the most significant new artistic development of this period and was destined to be the wave of the future.

Late Gothic Architecture   France—the home of the Gothic style—remained a potent source of architectural innovation. French architects now abandoned the balanced ideal of the High Gothic and made extravagance their guiding principle, creating a Late Gothic style typified by ever-greater heights and elaborate decoration. This tendency culminated in fifteenth-century France in the *Flamboyant style,* so named for its flamelike effects. French churches built in this style had sky-piercing spires, and their facades were embroidered with lacy or wavy decorations that obscured the buildings' structural components (Figure 10.7).

During the fourteenth century the Late Gothic spread from France to other areas and became an international style. All across Europe the focus shifted to fanciful designs: The churches were smaller, the roofs and towers taller, the naves wider, and the decorations more luxuriant. Regional tastes, however, made for local variations in the general style.

In England the Late Gothic was called *Perpendicular* because of its dramatic emphasis on verticality. This Perpendicular style was characterized by an increased use of paneled decorations on the walls and overhead vaults, resulting in a variation of rib vaulting called *fan vaulting,* in which stone ribs arch out from a single point in the ceiling to form a delicate pattern. This style also increased the number of window openings, which necessitated additional flying buttresses. The best example of the English Perpendicular is the cathedral in Gloucester.

In the choir the vertical lines, extending from the floor to the ceiling, where the tracery is interwoven,

FIGURE 10.8   Choir of Gloucester Cathedral. Ca. 1330–1357. Gloucester, England. *The choir and apse of Gloucester Cathedral were rebuilt in the Perpendicular Gothic style in about 1330, when King Edward III chose the church as the burial shrine for his murdered father, Edward II. The architects made the earlier Norman apse into a square and filled the east end with glass panels. Inside, the builders redesigned the support system, using thin vertical piers; these piers were attached to the walls and laced together on the ceiling, creating elaborate patterns that complemented the glass decorations.*

unite the building's interior into an upward-moving volume (Figure 10.8). Just as impressive and overpowering as the interior is the nearby cloister with its fan tracery vaulting that weaves a pattern overhead while tying the walls and ceiling into a complex unit (Figure 10.9).

In Italy the Gothic had put down only shallow roots because the Italians felt that the French builders had little to teach them about architecture. Italian Gothic has strong affinities with the Romanesque Style—the large hall with its basilica floor plan and massive walls. In addition, most of the key Gothic features are missing from the Italian Gothic, such as the flying buttresses, the twin towers, and the vast numbers of stained glass windows.

One of the best of the few examples of the Late Italian Gothic is the cathedral in Siena. Filled with civic pride, Siena's citizens urged their leaders to build a cathedral more splendid than those of their neighbors. Begun in the mid–thirteenth century, the cathedral was constructed over the next hundred

FIGURE 10.9 South Cloister of Gloucester Cathedral. Ca. 1370. Gloucester, England. *Fan vaulting, an intricate pattern in which ribs arch out from a single point in the ceiling, first appeared at Gloucester Cathedral and inspired many imitations. Although the ribs may appear to be structurally necessary, they are really a richly decorative device carved from stone. In Gloucester's south cloister, the tracery fans out from the top of each column and then merges in the center of the ceiling, giving the impression of a delicate screen.*

FIGURE 10.10 Siena Cathedral. 1250–1400. Siena, Italy. *Extant records and floor plans show that the Sienese changed their minds several times before deciding on the cathedral's final shape. At one time, about 1322, a commission of architects advised that the existing cathedral be demolished because the foundations and walls were not strong enough to support new additions. Nonetheless, construction went forward, and the cathedral is still standing after more than six hundred years.*

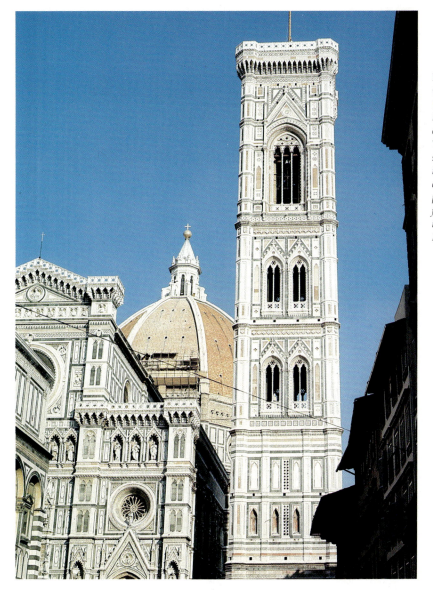

FIGURE 10.11 GIOTTO. Campanile of the Florentine Cathedral. Ca. 1334–1350. Florence, Italy. *Giotto's Tower, as this campanile is known in Florence, is one of the city's most cherished landmarks. Today, its bells still toll the time. The two sets of windows in the central section and the taller openings at the top give the campanile a strong sense of balanced proportion. Thus, despite being built in the fourteenth century, the tower anticipates the Classical ideal that was revived in the Renaissance.*

and fifty years, and, as a result, the building complex shows a mixture of styles: The *campanile*, or bell tower, is executed in the Italian Romanesque, but the overall cathedral complex is Italian Gothic (Figure 10.10). The facade, for the first time in Italy, incorporated nearly life-size figures into the total design, thus heightening its resemblance to the French Gothic. However, many features distinguish Siena from the French taste. For example, the decorative statues on Siena's facade were placed above the gables and not set in niches. Furthermore, the Sienese builders put mosaics into the spaces in the gables and above the central rose window.

Florence, Siena's greatest military and trade rival, refused to be outdone by its nearby competitor. The Florentine city fathers asked Giotto [JAWT-toe], the city's most renowned painter, to design a campanile for their own cathedral. Today, the first story of the bell tower—with its carvings, interlaced patterns of pink and white marble, and hexagonal inlays—still stands as conceived by Giotto (Figure 10.11). Giotto's

plan, as left in a drawing, called for an open tower with a spire on top, as in a French Gothic tower. But later architects constructed a rectangular top instead and decorated it with marble—making it distinctively Italian rather than reminiscent of the French.

Late Gothic Sculpture   During the Late Middle Ages, sculpture, like architecture, continued to undergo stylistic changes, among which two general trends may be identified. One trend centered in Italy, notably in Siena, where the Pisano family began to experiment with sculptural forms that foreshadowed Renaissance art, with its return to Classical themes and values (see Chapter 11). Outstanding among the members of the gifted Pisano family was Giovanni Pisano [pee-SAHN-o] (1245–1314), who designed the intricate Late Gothic facade of the Siena Cathedral (see Figure 10.10). Giovanni's great artistic reputation is largely based on the massive marble pulpit that he carved for the cathedral at Pisa. Using Classical themes derived from Roman art (as Renaissance artists were to do), he designed the

◀ **FIGURE 10.12** GIOVANNI PISANO. Pulpit in the Pisa Cathedral. Ca. 1302–1310. Pisa, Italy. *Pisano built and carved this massive (17-foot-high) pulpit late in his life but at the height of his reputation. A superb artist but a quarrelsome man, Pisano recorded his frustrations in the lengthy inscription around the pulpit's base. In this message to posterity, he claimed that he had achieved much, had been condemned by many, and took full responsibility for this work of art. Pisano's advance from the shadows of anonymity to a position of great artistic repute was typical of a new breed of artist appearing in Italy in the fourteenth century.*

pulpit to rest on acanthus leaves at the top of eight Corinthian columns (Figure 10.12). The lions that support two of the columns were modeled on those on an ancient Roman sarcophagus. Just as late Roman art blended Christian and Classical symbols, so Giovanni's treatment of the pulpit's base mixed images of the cardinal virtues, such as Justice and Temperance, with the figure of the Greek hero Herakles.

FIGURE 10.13 GIOVANNI PISANO. Nativity Scene. Pulpit in the Pisa Cathedral. Ca. 1302–1310. Pisa, Italy. *In this Late Gothic sculpture, Pisano cut deeply into the marble's surface to give a nearly three-dimensional effect. His many figures all seem involved in their own tasks but are nevertheless linked with one another around the Madonna and Child. For example, the two shepherds (the head of one has been lost) in the upper right-hand corner appear to be listening to the angels approaching from the left, while in the lower right-hand corner, sheep rest and graze. Such balanced placements are evidence of Pisano's classicizing tendencies. Despite such classicizing, Pisano's relief panel retains a prominent Gothic feature by presenting the Virgin and Child twice, once in the central scene and again in the lower left-hand corner, where a seated Mary, balancing the baby Jesus on her right leg, stretches her left hand to test the temperature of the water in an elaborate basin.*

◄ **FIGURE 10.14** CLAUS SLUTER. Moses, from *The Well of Moses*. Ca. 1395–1406. Chartreuse de Champmol, Dijon, France. *Sluter followed the allegorical tradition of medieval art in this portrait of the Hebrew prophet Moses. The book in Moses' right hand and the scroll over his left shoulder symbolize the Word of God. Sluter also depicted Moses with "horns" growing out of his forehead as was characteristic in medieval representations.*

Pisano's octagonal pulpit includes eight panels in high relief that depict scenes from the lives of either John the Baptist or Christ. Of these panels, the scene depicting the Nativity ranks as his finest work. In this scene, he portrays a natural vitality through the careful balance and orderly spacing of the animals and people (Figure 10.13). The placement and the calm actions of the surrounding figures frame the Virgin and Child so that the viewer's attention is focused on these two central figures. Giovanni's swaying figures with their smooth draperies were rooted in Late Gothic art, but their quiet serenity attested to his classicizing manner.

The other trend in sculpture during this time centered in Burgundy, where Philip the Bold (1364–1404) supported scholars and artists at his ducal court in Dijon. Preeminent among these was Claus Sluter [SLUE-tuhr] (about 1350–1406), a sculptor of Netherlandish origin who helped to define this last phase of Gothic art. Sluter's masterly sculptures are still housed in a monastery near Dijon, and his most famous work, *The Well of Moses*, was commissioned for the cloister of this monastic retreat.

The Well of Moses, which was designed as a decorative cover for an actual well in a courtyard, is surrounded at its base with Old Testament prophets symbolizing the sacraments of communion and baptism. The most beautifully rendered of the surviving life-size statues is Moses, encased in a flowing robe and standing erect with a finely chiseled head (Figure 10.14). Sluter's sense of the dramatic moment, of the prophet's personal emotions, and of the individual features make the statue nearly an individual portrait. Sluter rendered Moses' beard and the unfurled scroll in precise detail and carved the figure to twist and bend in the pronounced, swaying manner of the Late Gothic style.

Late Gothic Painting and the Rise of New Trends Of all the arts, painting underwent the most radical changes in the Late Middle Ages. Illuminated manuscripts maintained their popularity, but their themes became more secular under the patronage of titled aristocrats and wealthy merchants. At the same time, painters of frescoes and wooden panels introduced new techniques for applying paint and mixing colors.

Stylistically, painters preferred to work in the extravagant Late Gothic manner with its elegant refinement and its undulating figures. Nevertheless, as mentioned earlier, Giotto and other Italian painters discovered fresh ways of depicting human figures that started to revolutionize art.

ILLUMINATED MANUSCRIPTS The Burgundian court played a pivotal role in the production of one of the outstanding illuminated manuscripts of the medieval period, the *Très Riches Heures du Duc de Berry*. This famous collection of miniatures was painted by the three Limbourg brothers for the Duke of Berry, brother of Philip the Bold of Burgundy. These illustrations stand above the rest of their time for their exquisite detail, general liveliness, and well-managed crowd scenes—some of the marks of the Late Gothic style.

The *Très Riches Heures*, or the *Very Rich Hours*, represents a type of small prayer book that was a favorite of nobles and businessmen. These personal books of worship, with their litanies and prayers, were often handsomely hand-illustrated to enhance their value. The Duke of Berry's prayer book contained some 130 miniature paintings, including scenes from the life of Christ and the calendar cycle. In the calendar series each tiny painting, finely detailed and colored in jewel-like tones, notes a seasonal activity appropriate for each month. Some paintings represent the brilliant court life of the duke, and others depict the drudgery of peasant life, sharply differentiated from the court scenes by their action and color. The illustration for the month of January shows the Duke of Berry surrounded by his well-dressed courtiers enjoying a sumptuous feast (Figure 10.15).

NEW TRENDS IN ITALY: GIOTTO Regardless of the lasting appeal of the illuminated miniatures, this type of art was overshadowed by what was occurring in Italy. The paintings of Giotto (about 1276–1337) are generally recognized as having established a new direction in Western art, one that led into the Renaissance. In Giotto's own day, Dante praised him and the citizens of Florence honored him. Later, Vasari, the famous sixteenth-century painter and biographer, declared that Giotto had "rescued and restored" painting.

Giotto's revolution in painting was directed against the prevailing *Italo-Byzantine style*, which blended Late Gothic with Byzantine influences. He turned this painting style, with its two-dimensional, lifeless quality, into a three-dimensional art characterized by naturalism and the full expression of human emotions. Partly through the innovative use of light and shade, Giotto was able to create realistic-looking figures, rather than the flat, ornamental

◀ **FIGURE 10.15** LIMBOURG BROTHERS. Month of January, from the *Très Riches Heures du Duc de Berry*. 1413–1416. Ca. 8½ × 5½". Musée Condé, Chantilly, France. *This miniature painting provides insightful social history in its exquisite details. The duke, seated in the right center, is dressed in a blue patterned cloak and is greeting his guests for what was probably a New Year's celebration. Behind the duke stands a servant. Over the servant's head are written the words "aproche, aproche," a welcome that is the equivalent of "Come in, come in." Above this festive scene the zodiac signs of Capricorn and Aquarius identify the month as January.*

FIGURE 10.16 CIMABUE. *Madonna Enthroned*. Ca. 1280. Tempera on panel, 12'7½" × 7'4". Uffizi Gallery, Florence. *Although Cimabue was experiencing the same desire for freedom in art as the sculptor Giovanni Pisano, this painting of the Madonna shows that he still was strongly under the spell of the Italo-Byzantine tradition. Rather than showing the intense feeling of Giotto's portraits, Cimabue's Virgin and Child remain medieval and mystical.*

◄ **FIGURE 10.17** GIOTTO. *Madonna Enthroned*. Ca. 1310. Tempera on panel, 10′8″ × 6′8″. Uffizi Gallery, Florence. *Giotto's Madonna Enthroned, so revolutionary in its composition and spatial dimensions, has been called the most influential painting of the fourteenth century. Especially innovative in this altarpiece is the realistic treatment of the Virgin's eyes. They are shaped like ordinary eyes and peer out at the viewer rather than gazing into the distance, as in the Italo-Byzantine style.*

depictions found in most illuminated manuscripts or the Italian altar paintings.

A painting by one of Giotto's contemporaries, Cimabue [chee-muh-BU-a] (about 1240–1302), the *Madonna Enthroned*, reveals the state of Italian painting at this time (Figure 10.16). The angels on the side are rendered stiffly, aligned vertically without any sense of space between them, and placed flat on the wood panel without any precise relationship with the four prophets below them. Although Cimabue's angels were balanced in their placement and the depiction of the figures of the Madonna and Christ child offered some sense of rounded form, the overall effect of the work confirms its debt to the two-dimensional tradition of Italo-Byzantine art.

In contrast, Giotto's *Madonna Enthroned*, painted about twenty years after Cimabue's, shows how Giotto was transforming Florentine art (Figure 10.17). Giotto's Madonna seems to be actually sitting on her throne, and the angels around her chair are placed to give a sense of space and volume. The angels' gazes are highly expressive, suggesting feelings of wonder and respect. The Virgin resembles an individual woman and Christ a believable baby, not a shrunken adult. Although Giotto uses Gothic touches—the arch and the applied gold leaf—the natural rendering of the figures points toward the great changes coming in art.

Giotto was a prolific artist whose paintings adorned churches in Florence and cities all over Italy. At the Arena Chapel in Padua Giotto painted his masterpiece, two sets of frescoes, one of the life of the Virgin and the other of the life of Christ. These thirty-eight scenes show Giotto at the height of his powers, rendering space with a sense of depth and organizing figures so as to create dramatic tension. An outstanding scene from the Padua frescoes is the *Pietà*, or *Lamentation* (Figure 10.18). This scene, which portrays the grief for the dead Christ, expresses total despair through the mourners' faces and gestures, from Mary who cradles the body of Jesus, to John who stands with arms outstretched, to the hovering angels. In the fresco's stark and rugged landscape, even nature seems to mourn, notably in

the barren tree that symbolizes the wood of the cross on which Jesus was crucified. When Giotto died in 1337, no painter for the rest of the century was able to match his remarkable treatment of nature and human emotions.

FLEMISH PAINTING: JAN VAN EYCK AND HIERONYMUS BOSCH
When Philip the Good (1419–1467) became Duke of Burgundy, he expanded his territories to include the wealthy counties of Holland, Zeeland, and Luxembourg. Philip was the greatest secular patron of the arts of his day. Of the artists encouraged by his patronage, the brothers Jan and Hubert van Eyck are the most famous, and their religious works and portraits established the Flemish style of art. Little is known of Hubert, but Jan van Eyck [van-IKE] (about 1370–about 1440) is considered the founder of the Flemish school.

As a general principle, Flemish art sought reality through an accumulation of precise and often symbolic details, in contrast to Italian art which tended to be more concerned with psychological truth as in Giotto's frescoes in the Arena Chapel. This national style, primarily expressed through painting with oils on wood panels, turned each artwork into a brilliant and precise reproduction of the original scene. The finest detail in a patterned carpet, the reflected light on a copper vase, or the wrinkled features of an elderly patron were laboriously and meticulously recorded. The Flemish style, with its close attention to detail, was widely appreciated and quickly spread to Italy and England.

Jan van Eyck, probably with his brother's help, painted the *Altarpiece of the Lamb* for the cathedral at Ghent, Belgium. This large work—originally commissioned to beautify the high altar—still remains in its original place. The twenty panels are hinged together so that when opened twelve are visible. These twelve panels are divided into two levels—heavenly figures and symbols on the upper level and earthly figures on the lower level. On the ends of the upper level are nude portraits of Adam and Eve, next to angels singing and playing musical instruments. Mary on the left and John the Baptist on the right flank a portrayal of God the Father, resplendent in a jewel-encrusted robe and triple crown. Below, on the lower level, are human figures who are depicted as moving toward the center panel. Those on the left are knights and judges, riding on horseback, while, on the right, pilgrims and hermits approach on foot (Figure 10.19).

The focus of the *Ghent Altarpiece*, when opened, is the lower center panel, the *Adoration of the Lamb*. In this work, the sacrificial death of Jesus is symbolized by the cross, the baptismal font in the foreground, and the blood issuing from the lamb into the

FIGURE 10.19 HUBERT AND JAN VAN EYCK. *Ghent Altarpiece*. Ca. 1432. Oil on panel, 11′3″ × 14′5″. St. Bavo Cathedral, Ghent, Belgium. *This large altarpiece, measuring 15 by 11 feet, may seem to be a collection of separate paintings, but the work is united in themes and symbolism. What links the panels is their portrayal of Christ's redemption of humanity. From the sin of Adam and Eve to the mystic Adoration of the Lamb, all of the paintings touch in some manner on Christ's sacrifice.*

◄ **FIGURE 10.18** GIOTTO. *Lamentation*. Ca. 1305–1310. Arena Chapel, Padua, Italy. *Works like this won for Giotto his reputation as the modern reviver of realistic art—a tradition that had been lost with the fall of ancient Rome. In this fresco he created three-dimensional space in ways that even the Greeks and Romans had not used. Giotto's illusion of depth was conveyed by surrounding the dead Christ with numerous figures and, in particular, by placing two mourners in the foreground with their backs to the viewer. Although this was achieved without mathematical precision, Giotto's perspective was convincing to his generation.*

FIGURE 10.20   HUBERT AND JAN VAN EYCK. *Adoration of the Lamb,* Detail of the *Ghent Altarpiece.* Ca. 1432. St. Bavo Cathedral, Ghent, Belgium. *This lower center section of the opened altarpiece dramatically shows how the Flemish school could use religious symbolism to evoke a mystical effect. The exquisitely refined details, which derived from the tradition of manuscript painting, make this scene both credible and otherworldly at the same time.*

communion chalice. The surrounding worshipers include holy virgins, martyrs, and prophets, plus the four Evangelists and the twelve Apostles, who stand and kneel in groups amid unusual plants and trees (Figure 10.20).

In contrast to this mystical work, Jan van Eyck painted a decidedly secular but still symbolic work in his *Arnolfini Wedding Portrait* (Figure 10.21). In this painting, nearly every object—the lighted candle, the shoes, the fruit, the dog—refers to a wedding custom or belief. Yet, the details—for example, the mirror on the rear wall reflecting the couple's backs, the artist, and a fourth person—create a worldly setting. Van Eyck's painting is not an imaginary scene but a recording of an actual event, for Arnolfini was an Italian businessman who lived in Bruges. Thus, the commerce and wealth of Burgundy and the Italian cities are symbolically united by van Eyck in this wedding portrait.

A second outstanding Flemish artist in the Late Middle Ages was Hieronymus Bosch [BOSH] (about 1450–1516), whose personal life is a mystery and whose paintings still puzzle modern experts. Treat-

ing common religious subjects in bizarre and fantastic ways, he earned a reputation even among his contemporaries for being enigmatic.

Much of Bosch's distinctive art may be explained by the changes taking place during his day. His late fifteenth-century world was radically different from that of Jan van Eyck, who died in 1441. In 1477, the dream of the Dukes of Burgundy to convert their duchy into a kingdom came crashing down, with Burgundy's absorption into France—and aristocratic patronage began to decline. At the same time, a feeling of dread, born perhaps of the periodic ravages of the plague, stalked northern Europe, causing preachers, writers, and artists to take up the theme of the Dance of Death (see Figure 10.2). And across northern Europe, serious religious trouble was brewing that would end with the revolt of Martin Luther (see Chapter 13). Influenced by the foregoing forces and also perhaps subjected to his own private demons, Bosch created a body of art that defies strict classification in the stylistic sense.

FIGURE 10.21   JAN VAN EYCK. *Arnolfini Wedding Portrait.* 1434. Panel painting, 33 × 22½". National Gallery, London. *This work is a perfect expression of the symbolic realism that dominated northern European painting in the Late Middle Ages. The wedding is celebrated in a room filled with religious symbols of the marriage rite. For example, the bride and groom stand barefooted, indicating that they are in holy space, and above them is a chandelier with a single lighted candle, a sign of God's presence.*

FIGURE 10.22 HIERONYMUS BOSCH. *Garden of Earthly Delights.* Ca. 1510–1515. Prado, Madrid. *Careful study of the minute details of this triptych has uncovered the major sources of Bosch's artistic inspiration—namely, medieval folklore, common proverbs, exotic learning, and sacred beliefs. For example, folklore inspired the ravens and owl (left panel), traditional emblems of nonbelievers and witchcraft, respectively; the Flemish proverb "Good fortune, like glass, is easily broken" is illustrated by the lovemaking couple under the glass globe; allusions to exotic learning may be seen in the egg shapes (all three panels), symbolic of the world and sex in the pseudoscience of alchemy; and Christian belief is evident throughout the triptych, but especially in the right panel showing the punishment of sinners.*

In his paintings, Bosch seems torn between the declining Late Gothic style and the soon-to-be-born Mannerist (see Chapter 13). His addiction to precise detail and his frequent use of sweeping landscapes are clear signs of the debt he owed Flemish art and, in particular, the age's illuminated manuscripts; but his tendency to endow his works with ambiguous, or even cynical, moral messages points to the Mannerist works of later Dutch artists, such as Pieter Bruegel the Elder (see Chapter 13). Perhaps the best way to look at Bosch is as an artist whose originality was so pronounced that he stands outside of any historical period.

Of Bosch's thirty or more paintings, the most recognizable and controversial is *The Garden of Earthly Delights*, a work in oil on three wood panels, called a **triptych** (Figure 10.22). When open, the triptych displays three separate but interrelated scenes, organized around the theme of the creation, fall, and damnation of the human race. Most confusingly, the center and right-hand panels are crowded with

tiny figures—mostly human, though some are grotesquely monstrous—performing a variety of peculiar actions. Although no scholarly consensus exists as to the ultimate meaning of this work, certain features can be identified that may help the viewer understand it.

The left panel of *The Garden of Earthly Delights* shows the Garden of Eden, with Adam and Eve in the foreground and the first plants and animals (including "natural" animals but also weird monsters) scattered around. Contrary to the Bible, Jesus holds the newly created Eve's hand and introduces her to Adam. Many scholars interpret this panel as making Eve the source of original sin.

The center panel—the dramatic focus of the triptych—depicts the sins of the flesh in lurid and metaphorical detail. In the top horizontal band, the waters of the earth converge to make a fountain, an image that has been identified as a false symbol of human happiness; in the middle band, naked young women cavort in a pool while a parade of naked youths riding animals partly realistic, partly fantastic encircles them; and in the lower band, more naked men and women engage in various sex acts or are involved with huge birds, fruits, flowers, or fish. The diverse images in this central panel symbolize Bosch's vile perspective on the human condition: perpetual enslavement to the sexual appetite unleashed by Adam and Eve's first sin. Also worthy of note is that this crowded scene includes many black males and females, an early instance of nonwhites in Western art.

The triptych's right panel is a repulsive portrait of Hell and the pains human beings must suffer for their sins. A horrific scene of fiery ruins and grisly instruments of torture, this panel proclaims Bosch's hopeless vision of the futility of life on earth. For the artist, human beings cause their own destruction through wicked desires. At no point in the entire work is there a hint of salvation.

A few scholars reject this gloomy view of Bosch's message by trying to link the triptych to the beliefs of the underground, heretical sect of Adamites. If their interpretation is correct, then the central panel may be understood as the Adamites' unusual vision of Paradise. Most scholars reject this view, however, and hold instead that Bosch was a stern moralist, mocking the corrupt society of his day.

The Legacy of the Late Middle Ages

All historical eras are periods of transition, but the changes of the Late Middle Ages were especially momentous. The medieval world was dying, and the modern era was struggling to be born. Dating from this turbulent period were many of the cultural tensions that defined the history of Europe for the next four hundred years.

The most revolutionary happening in the Late Middle Ages was the release of a powerful secular spirit that began to make its presence felt everywhere. The upsurge of vernacular literature, the rise of literary themes questioning the low status of women, and the divergence of philosophy and theology are three examples of this new development. But the greatest impact of the rise of secularism on cultural life was that painting and sculpture began to be liberated from the service of architecture. The first stirrings of this change were expressed in the works of Giotto and other Italian and Flemish artists. By the next century, painting in Italy had freed itself from the tutelage of architecture and become the most important artistic genre in the West.

This period also saw the emergence of a new breed of secular ruler who was prepared to mount a sustained drive against the church's combined political and spiritual powers. The victories of the English and the French kings over the papacy—each ruler was able to secure control over his national church—were signs of the breakup of Christendom.

Another important legacy of these years is that the towns, led by their bourgeois citizens, began to exercise their influence over the countryside. From today's perspective, the growth of the middle class as a dominant force in society was perhaps the single most critical development of this age. Finally, this period witnessed the unusual spectacle of the common people revolting against the aristocratic control of the culture and society. Their sporadic efforts failed, but the seeds of future revolution were planted.

KEY CULTURAL TERMS

devotio moderna
via antiqua
via moderna
Late Gothic style
Flamboyant style

Perpendicular style
fan vault
campanile
Italo-Byzantine style
triptych

SUGGESTIONS FOR FURTHER READING

PRIMARY SOURCES

BOCCACCIO, G. *The Decameron.* Translated by M. Musa and P. E. Bondanella. New York: Norton, 1977. An updated translation of the hundred stories—some learned, some coarse, but all humorous—that make up this work; first published about 1351.

CHAUCER, G. *The Canterbury Tales.* Edited by N. Coghill. New York: Penguin, 1978. Of many versions of these bawdy and lighthearted tales, Coghill's is one of the most readable and enjoyable; the original work dates from 1385.

CHRISTINE DE PIZAN. *The Book of the City of Ladies.* Translated by E. J. Richards. New York: Persea Books, 1982. An accessible, modern translation of this late medieval work, which argues that the political and cultural dignity of women depends on their being educated properly, just as men are; first published in 1405.

LANGLAND, W. *The Vision of Piers Plowman.* Translated by H. W. Wells. New York: Sheed and Ward, 1959. A good modern version of Langland's work criticizing the religious establishment of his day and calling for a new order; written between 1362 and 1394.

11

THE EARLY RENAISSANCE: RETURN TO CLASSICAL ROOTS

1400—1494

Believing they were living in a period that had broken radically with the past, Italian artists and intellectuals in the fifteenth century began to speak of a rebirth of civilization. Since the nineteenth century, the term *Renaissance* (meaning "rebirth") has been used by historians and others to describe the cultural and artistic activities of the fourteenth and fifteenth centuries that began in Italy and eventually spread to other European countries.

The Renaissance profoundly altered the course of Western culture, and, since the mid–nineteenth century, scholars have made a specialty of the Renaissance, studying and analyzing its culture. They have not always agreed on their findings, however, and several schools of thought have arisen concerning the definition and significance of this first modern period.

THE RENAISSANCE: SCHOOLS OF INTERPRETATION

In the middle of the nineteenth century, Swiss historian Jacob Burckhardt laid the foundation for Renaissance studies. Agreeing with the fifteenth-century Italians, he asserted that an actual rebirth of ideas began in their time after centuries of cultural

stagnation. He maintained that a new way of understanding the world emerged during this period when the Italians began to look back to ancient Greece and Rome for inspiration and declared themselves part of a revitalized civilization that was distinctive and superior to the immediate past.

By the middle of the twentieth century, Burckhardt's view began to be reexamined. Pronouncing it too simplistic, some historians pointed out that the break with the past was not as dramatic as Burckhardt claimed; what changes did take place simply modified trends and attitudes that had been prevalent in Italian culture for centuries. These scholars claimed that the Italians, after the fall of Rome, never lost sight of their Classical roots and that the revival of learning in the fifteenth century was more a shift in educational and cultural emphasis than a rediscovery of antiquity. They also noted that the Renaissance passed through at least two phases, the Early and the High, and that each phase was distinct in its nature and contributions. Furthermore, these scholars insisted that the world of the Renaissance must be broadened geographically to include other states in Italy besides Florence, notably the Republic of Venice, and other regions outside of Italy, especially the Duchy of Burgundy.

Since 1960 a third school of interpretation has come to dominate Renaissance studies. This latest view contends that the word *Renaissance* should be used exclusively to describe what was happening in learning and the arts and should not be applied to politics and society. Moreover, this interpretation

◄ DONATELLO. DAVID. Ca. 1430–1432. Bronze, height 62¼". Bargello, Florence.

FIGURE 11.1 DOMENICO GHIRLANDAIO. *Old Man with a Child.* Ca. 1480. Panel, 24½ × 18". Louvre. *This double portrait by the Florentine artist Ghirlandaio summarizes many of the new secular values of the Early Renaissance, such as its human-centeredness and its preference for simple scenes. Further, the work's subject, possibly a man with his grandchild, indicates the important role that the family played in the life of the times. In addition, the age's commitment to direct observation of the physical world is evident in the treatment of the man's diseased nose and the landscape glimpsed through the open window. Finally, the painter has made the exterior scene realistic by using linear and atmospheric perspective—two new techniques invented during the period.*

holds that the label should be used with extreme caution, because only now are historians beginning to comprehend the events of this complex age.

We tend to agree with the third group of scholars who say that the fifteenth-century Italians were misguided in the belief that they had made a profound break with the Middle Ages. In terms of politics, economics, and society, Italy in the 1400s was roughly like Italy in the 1300s. In *cultural* terms, however, the Italians of the 1400s did start down a new path (Figure 11.1).

This chapter examines the first phase of this new cultural style, the Early Renaissance (1400–1494). Chapter 12 is devoted to the brief High Renaissance (1494–1520) and to Early Mannerism (1520–1564), an anti-Classical phase of the Renaissance. Finally, Chapter 13 considers a number of developments including the religious reformations of the early sixteenth century and Late Mannerism (1564–1603), when Renaissance style was slowly undermined by new trends (Time Line 11.1).

EARLY RENAISSANCE HISTORY AND INSTITUTIONS

For most of the fifteenth century, the Italian peninsula was freed from threats of foreign invasion and intrusion into its domestic affairs. The major central European powers were distracted by their own problems, and southeastern Europe became Muslim as the Ottoman Turks solidified their conquests with the capture of Constantinople in 1453. The Muslim presence was to have important long-range repercussions for eastern and southern Europe as well as for the Italian interests in the Mediterranean. But overall these events had little impact on Italian affairs until 1494, when a French army led by Charles VIII entered Italy in the hope of furthering French monarchic ambitions.

Italian City-States during the Early Renaissance

During the Early Renaissance five Italian states competed for political mastery: in the north, the Republic of Venice, the Duchy of Milan, and the Republic of Florence; in the center, the Papal States, led by a rejuvenated post-Schism papacy; and, in the south, the Kingdom of Naples, including the island of Sicily. Besides these five powers, some smaller states like Ferrara and Modena were important artistic and intellectual centers that played minor but crucial roles in Italian affairs (Map 11.1).

In the first half of the fifteenth century the Italian states waged incessant wars among themselves, shifting sides when it was to their advantage, and no single principality could rule over the rest. Eventually, the Peace of Lodi, signed in 1454, established a delicate balance of power among Milan, Florence, and Venice, drawn together by their common fear that Italy might be invaded by foreigners. The Peace of Lodi coincided with the end of the Hundred Years' War and the fall of Constantinople—three

TIME LINE 11.1   STAGES OF THE ITALIAN RENAISSANCE

1400		1494	1520	1600
	Early Renaissance	High Renaissance		Late Renaissance

pivotal events in European history. The decision of the Kingdom of Naples to join the northern Italians in this defensive pact ensured that Italy was tranquil for forty years, until the French invasion.

The impact of these deadly wars of the first half of the century, coupled with a changing economy, led to the emergence of autocratic rulers, or despots, across the map of Italy. The age of despots spelled the end of the great medieval legacy of republicanism in Venice, Milan, and Florence and the rise to power of either ruling families or elitist factions in these territories as well as in the Papal States and the Kingdom of Naples. What influence guilds, business leaders, and middle-class cliques had wielded in the fourteenth century now gave way to the despots,

also called *signori*. Taking advantage of economic and class tensions, these autocrats pledged to solve local problems and in so doing proceeded to accumulate power in their own hands.

Under the despots, military tactics were rapidly changing because technological developments in weaponry affected the ways that wars were waged, troops were recruited, and generals were chosen. Campaigns were now fought with mercenary troops led by soldiers of fortune, called *condottieri*, who sold their military expertise to the highest bidder. Since professional warriors were loyal only to themselves, they often changed sides in the heat of battle and thus affected the final military outcome. In addition, a state's victory was sometimes jeopardized by the

MAP 11.1

The States of Italy during the Renaissance, ca. 1494

rivalries between local factions and families—the curse of every Italian city-state.

The most significant change in Renaissance warfare was the emergence of diplomacy as a peaceful alternative to armed struggle. The Italian regimes began to send representatives abroad to serve state interests. As a result, it became customary for diplomats, during a pause in the fighting, to set about making a peace settlement, although these negotiated arrangements seldom lasted very long—with the notable exception of the Peace of Lodi. The Italian method of establishing diplomatic ties slowly spread over the continent and became the standard of the European states in the following century.

A major factor in Italy's politics in this period was the shifting fortunes of the once-thriving economy. Emerging from the High Middle Ages in 1300 as Europe's leading commercial center and top manufacturer of finished woolens (see Chapter 9), the northern Italian city-states lost the economic race to the north Europeans by 1500. During these two hundred years, however, Italy's economy did not move in a downward spiral. In fact, the worst years were in the 1300s, when the peninsula suffered terrible population losses and a sharp decline in productivity due to the Black Death and the birth of the English woolen industry.

After this low point, the Italians made a remarkable, though limited, recovery in the 1400s. Venice, the most powerful of these mercantile states, renewed control of Mediterranean trade, and Florence, after subduing Pisa in 1405, gained a seaport. Other states made a niche for themselves in the luxury market by producing such items as ceramics, glassware, and lace. But the flow of history was moving against the north Italian cities. The woolen trade was lost forever to England and Flanders; although Florence countered this loss with a highly successful local silk industry, it was forced to give up its leadership in textiles. Even the Italian domination of international banking was being challenged by German businessmen. What finally sealed the Italians' economic doom were three events over which they had no control: the fall of Constantinople, Portugal's opening of the trade routes around Africa to India, and the discovery of the New World.

As more powerful secular rulers emerged in Europe, some used their powers to advance their political and economic interests beyond the geographical limits of continental Europe. Portugal led the way in the late fifteenth century as its ships opened the sea route to India around Africa's Cape of Good Hope. Spain was not far behind as the crown supported the Genoese sailor Christopher Columbus in his voyage to the West Indies in 1492. These explorations

FIGURE 11.2   ROGIER VAN DER WEYDEN. *Portrait of Francesco d'Este.* Ca. 1455–1460. Tempera and oil on wood, 11¾ × 8". Metropolitan Museum of Art. Bequest of Michael Friedsam, 1931. The Friedsam Collection. *Ferrara, situated between Bologna and Venice, was home to the Este family, who dominated the city's political and cultural life. Through generous patronage, this family founded a public library and attracted leading Renaissance artists and scholars to their splendid court. This portrait was painted by the Flemish artist Rogier van der Weyden, who helped to introduce the Italians to the use of oil paints.*

launched a maritime revolution that resulted, in the sixteenth century, in the shifting of the focus of international trade from the Mediterranean to the Atlantic.

The long-range prospect for Italy's economy may have been bleak, but in the short run unprecedented levels of wealth were enjoyed by the upper-class families of the fifteenth century. Led by this elite, the city-states followed an urban way of life that had first appeared along with the revival of commerce as early as 1100. The culture of the Early Renaissance was substantially determined by the patronage of these families, who used their money to cultivate their tastes in literature and art (Figure 11.2). The courts of local rulers, or *grandi,* served as the centers of this way of life where educated men, and, on occasion, women, gathered to exchange ideas and to discuss philosophical issues.

Time Line 11.2   PHASES OF FLORENTINE POLITICS

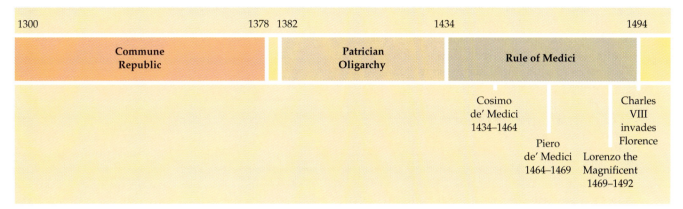

Another prominent characteristic of Italy's urban way of life was the reverence paid to the family by both the noble elite and the wealthy merchant class. On a practical level, middle-class parents had to make sure that sons were properly educated to carry on the family businesses and that daughters were prepared to be loyal wives. In the average family, the condition of women did not improve appreciably, but many more females were educated now than in earlier times. The marriages of both daughters and sons were arranged by the parents, and a costly dowry usually accompanied the prospective bride. Brides wed in their teens, but grooms waited until their mid-thirties. Because of this age discrepancy among the well-to-do, many women became rich and fairly young widows with substantial social power.

A few outstanding women at the ducal courts exhibited some degree of independence and exercised a certain amount of political influence. For example, Lucrezia Borgia [loo-KRET-syah BOR-juh] (1480–1519), who held court in Ferrara and was the illegitimate daughter of Pope Alexander VI, married three times, supported writers and artists, and in her late years devoted herself to charitable causes. But most women did not have the opportunity to be independent.

Florence, the Center of the Renaissance

Amid the artistic and intellectual activity occurring throughout the Italian peninsula, Florence, the capital of the Tuscan region, stands head and shoulders above the other city-states. Florence's political system evolved through several stages after 1300—from republic to oligarchy to family rule. Simultaneously with these turbulent political activities, Florentine artists and writers made their city-state the center of the Early Renaissance to 1450.

The first phase of Florence's political evolution was the republic, which was born in the fourteenth century. But no sooner was the republic set up with its hopes for political equality than it fell into the hands of a wealthy oligarchy. This oligarchy, composed of the rich bankers and merchants as well as the more successful guildsmen and craftsmen, ruled until the early fifteenth century, when the Medici family gained control of the state. The Medici dominated Florentine politics and cultural life from 1434 to 1494. The Medici period, which sometimes amounted to a mild despotism, constituted the third phase of Florentine political life during this time (Time Line 11.2).

The Medici arose from modest circumstances, lending money to poor Florentines and supplementing their income with profits from the woolen trade. Giovanni di Bicci de' Medici [jo-VAHN-nee dee-BET-chee day-MED-uh-chee] (1360–1429) amassed the family's first large fortune by setting up branch banks in major Italian cities and forming close financial ties with the papacy. His son Cosimo [KOH-zee-moh] (1389–1464) added to the Medici's wealth and outmaneuvered his political enemies, becoming the unacknowledged ruler of Florence. As a matter of policy, he persuaded others through appeals to their self-interest and spent his money on those things that pleased him—books, paintings, sculptures, and palaces. This astute Florentine, who always claimed to be the common man's friend, was eventually awarded the title *Pater patriae,* Father of his Country—an ancient Roman title revived during the exuberance of the Renaissance.

Piero, Cosimo's son, ruled for only a short time. He was succeeded by his son, Lorenzo (1449–1492), called the Magnificent because of his grand style of living. Lorenzo, well-educated, vigorous, and accomplished, lived a full life. He controlled Florence with his brother Giuliano until Giuliano was assassinated in 1478 by the Pazzi family, the long-standing rivals of the Medici. Lorenzo, barely escaping death, brutally executed the conspirators and then governed alone in an autocratic manner for the next fourteen years. In foreign affairs, he used diplomacy to inaugurate an era of peace but at a high cost, since taxes were raised, thereby draining the city's resources and piling up debts owed to rich families.

Within two years of Lorenzo's death, the great power and prestige that Florence had achieved began to weaken. Two events are symptomatic of this decline in Florentine authority. First, in 1494 a French army led by Charles VIII marched into Florence, thereby instigating a political and cultural decline that would eventually overtake Italy, whose small city-states simply could not withstand the incursions of the newly powerful European monarchies. The French army drove the Medici family out of Florence; they remained in exile until 1512.

The second was the iconoclastic crusade against the city's pleasure-loving tradition led by the Dominican monk Fra Savonarola [sav-uh-nuh-ROH-luh] (1452–1498). He was opposed to the Medici's de facto rule of the city and wanted to restore a republican form of government. In his fire-and-brimstone sermons he denounced Florence's leaders and the city's infatuation with the arts. He eventually ran afoul of the papacy and was excommunicated and publicly executed, but not before he had had an enormous effect on the citizens—including even the painter Botticelli, who is said to have burned some of his paintings while under the sway of Savonarola's reforming zeal.

The Resurgent Papacy, 1450–1500

The Great Schism was ended by the Council of Constance in 1418 and a tattered Christendom reunited under a Roman pope (see Chapter 10). The popes tried to suppress conciliar ideas and to reassert their full control over the church, and by 1447 they were back in command. Thereafter and well into the next century the papacy was in the hands of the so-called Renaissance popes (Table 11.1). Turning their attention to consolidating the Papal States, they became caught up in the pursuit of power. Like the secular despots whom they resembled, these pontiffs engaged in war and, when that failed, conducted diplomacy. They brought artistic riches to the church but, at the same time, lowered its moral tone. Masters of political deceit, they accepted bribes for church offices or filled them with kinsmen. But above everything else, these popes patronized Renaissance culture. Three of the most aggressive and successful of these church rulers were Nicholas V (1447–1455), Pius II (1458–1464), and Sixtus IV (1471–1484).

TABLE 11.1   POPES OF THE EARLY RENAISSANCE

Nicholas V	1447–1455
Pius II	1458–1464
Sixtus IV	1471–1484

Nicholas V founded the Vatican Library, an institution virtually unrivaled for its holdings of manuscripts and books. As the former librarian for Cosimo de' Medici, he was naturally attracted to scholarship, collecting manuscripts and bringing Classical scholars to Rome. He also continued the rebuilding of Rome begun by his predecessors.

Pius II, often considered the most representative of the Renaissance popes because of his interest in the Greek and Roman classics and his poetry, which had won him fame as a young man, rose rapidly through the ecclesiastical ranks to the papal throne. Understanding the dynamics of war and diplomacy, this clever politician practiced both with astounding success. As a student of the new learning and as a brilliant Latin writer, Pius II attracted intellectuals and artists to Rome. His personal recollections, or *Commentaries*, reveal much about himself and his turbulent times.

The third Renaissance pope, Sixtus IV, came from the powerful della Rovere family. Growing up in an atmosphere of intrigue, he learned to scheme to get rid of his enemies. He urged on the Pazzi family in Florence in its feud with the Medici and was implicated in the failed Pazzi conspiracy to kill Lorenzo. Furthermore, Sixtus IV increased his personal power through nepotism, the practice of giving offices to relatives, which he brought to a state of near perfection. Sixtus IV was also a great art connoisseur and continued the papal tradition of making Rome the most beautiful city in the world. His greatest achievement was the construction of the Sistine Chapel, whose walls and ceiling were later adorned with paintings by Botticelli and Michelangelo, making it the jewel of this extraordinary age (see Chapter 12).

THE SPIRIT AND STYLE OF THE EARLY RENAISSANCE

Drawing inspiration from ancient Greek and Roman models, the thinkers and artists of the Early Renaissance explored such perennial questions as, What is human nature? How are human beings related to God? and What is the best way to achieve human happiness? While they did not reject Christian explanations outright, they were intrigued by the secular and humanistic values of the Greco-Roman tradition and the ways in which they might be brought to bear on these questions. They also rightfully claimed kinship with certain fourteenth-century predecessors such as the writer Petrarch and the artist Giotto (see Chapter 10).

Those identified with the Early Renaissance and who embodied its spirit were linked, through shared tastes and patronage, with the entrepreneurial nobility, the progressive middle class, and the secular clergy. Until about 1450 most artistic works were commissioned by wealthy patrons for family chapels in churches and for public buildings; later, patrons commissioned works for private dwellings, where paintings and sculptures were made for the delight of the domestic household.

Even though artists, scholars, and writers stamped this age with their fresh perspectives, old cultural traits remained amid the developing new ones. Unsettling secular values emerged in the midst of long-accepted religious beliefs to create contradictions and tensions within the society. In other ways, however, the past held firm, and certain values seemed immune to change. For example, Early Renaissance thought made little headway in science, and church patronage still strongly affected the evolution of the arts and architecture, despite the growing impact of the urban class on artistic tastes.

Humanism, Scholarship, and Schooling

Toward the end of the 1300s, a positive mania developed in Italy's educated circles for ancient Roman civilization. Inspired by Petrarch's interest in Latin literature and language, scholars began to collect and translate Roman manuscripts uncovered in monastic libraries and other out-of-the-way depositories. There was a shift in emphasis from the church Latin of the Middle Ages to the pure Latin style of Cicero, the first-century B.C. Roman writer whose eloquent essays established a high moral and literary standard.

In the 1400s these scholars spoke of their literary interests and new learning as **studia humanitatis**. They defined this term, which may be translated as humanistic studies, as a set of intellectual pursuits that included moral philosophy, history, grammar, rhetoric, and poetry. At first, the men who studied these disciplines read the appropriate works in Latin, but after the Greek originals began to appear around 1400 and the study of ancient languages spread, they learned from the Greek texts as well.

In response to the demand for humanistic learning, new schools sprang up in most Italian city-states. In these schools was born the Renaissance

ideal of an education intended to free or to liberate the mind—a liberal education. To this end, study was based on the recently recovered Latin and Greek works rather than on the more narrowly defined curriculum of scholasticism and Aristotelianism that had been favored in the Middle Ages.

The first Renaissance scholars, who were primarily searching for original Latin manuscripts, were philologists, that is, experts in the study of languages and linguistics. In time, they came to call themselves humanists because of their training in the *studia humanitatis*. These early humanists created a branch of learning now called textual criticism that compares various versions of a text in order to determine which one is most correct or authentic. They recognized that knowledge of the evolution of language was necessary in order to make a critical judgment on the authenticity of a text. As a result of their studies, they revealed writing errors committed by medieval monks when they copied ancient manuscripts—revelations that, in the case of religious documents, raised grave problems for the church.

The most spectacular application of textual criticism was made by Lorenzo Valla (1406–1457), who exposed the Donation of Constantine as a forgery. Throughout the Middle Ages this famous document had been cited by the popes as proof of their political authority over Christendom. By the terms of the document, the Roman emperor Constantine gave the popes his western lands and recognized their power to rule in them. But by comparing the Latin of the fourth century, when Constantine reigned, with the Latin of the eighth century, when the document first came to light, Valla concluded that the Donation must have been produced in the later century and not when it was claimed.

Other humanists played an active role in the life of their states, modeling themselves on the heroes of the Roman Republic. Outstanding among them is Leonardo Bruni (1374–1444). In his professional career, Bruni typifies the practical, civic humanist. A one-time chancellor, or chief secretary, of Florence's governing body, or *signoria*, Bruni also worked for both the Medici and the papacy and wrote the *History of the Florentine People*. This work reflected his humanistic values, combining as it did his political experience with his knowledge of ancient history. To Bruni, the study of history illuminated contemporary events. Bruni and the other civic humanists, through their writings and their governmental service, set an example for later generations of Florentines and helped infuse them with love of their city. Moreover, by expanding the concept of humanistic studies, they contributed new insights into the ongoing debate about the role of the individual in history and in the social order.

An important consequence of humanistic studies was the rise of educational reforms. Of those humanists who experimented with the educational curriculum, Vittorino da Feltre [veet-toe-REE-no dah-FEL-tray] (1378–1446) made the most significant contributions. Vittorino favored a curriculum that exercised the body and the mind—the ideal of the ancient Greek schools. His educational theories were put into practice at the school he founded in Mantua at the ruler's request. At this Mantuan school, called the Happy House, Vittorino included humanistic studies along with the medieval curriculum. A major innovation of his was the stress on physical exercise, which arose from his emphasis on moral training. At first, only the sons and daughters of Mantuan nobility attended his school, but gradually the student body became more democratic as young persons from all classes were enrolled. Vittorino's reforms were slowly introduced into the new urban schools in northern Europe, and their model—the well-rounded student of sound body, solid learning, and high morals—helped to lay the foundation for future European schools and education.

Thought and Philosophy

The Italian humanists were not satisfied with the answers medieval thinkers had offered to the perennial inquiries of philosophy because those answers did not go beyond Aristotelian philosophy and Christian dogma. Casting their nets wider, the Renaissance thinkers concluded that the ancients had been concerned with many of the same issues as Christians and had given worthwhile responses that should not be dismissed simply because they were non-Christian.

Renaissance scholars came to advocate more tolerance toward unorthodox beliefs and began to focus on the important role played by the individual in society. Fulfillment of the individual became a leading Renaissance idea and remains a central notion in Western thought today. During the Renaissance, the growing emphasis on the individual resulted in a more optimistic assessment of human nature—a development that in time led to a rejection of Christianity's stress on original sin.

After the fall of Constantinople in 1453 and the flight of Byzantine scholars bearing precious manuscripts, the humanists began to focus increasingly on Greek literature, language, and, in particular, philosophy. The philosophy of Plato found a home in Italy in 1462 when Cosimo de' Medici established the Platonic Academy at one of his villas near Florence. Here, scholars gathered to examine and to discuss the writings of Plato as well as the Neo-Platonists

FIGURE 11.3 SANDRO BOTTICELLI. *The Birth of Venus.* 1480s. Tempera on canvas, 5'8" × 9'1". Uffizi Gallery, Florence. *With the paintings of Botticelli, the nude female form reappeared in Western art for the first time since the Greco-Roman period. Botticelli's* Venus *contains many Classical echoes, such as the goddess's lovely features and her modest pose. But the artist painted such pre-Christian images to convey a Christian message and to embody the principles of Ficino's Neo-Platonist philosophy.*

whose reinterpreted Platonism had influenced early Christian theology. The Academy was under the direction of the brilliant humanist Marsilio Ficino [mar-SILL-e-o fe-CHEE-no] (1433–1499), whom Cosimo commissioned to make Latin translations of Plato's works.

In two major treatises Ficino made himself the leading voice of Florentine *Neo-Platonism* by harmonizing Platonic ideas with Christian teachings. Believing that Platonism came from God, Ficino began with the principle that both thought systems rested on divine authority. Like Plato, Ficino believed that the soul was immortal and that complete enjoyment of God would be possible only in the afterlife, when the soul was in the divine realm. Ficino also revived the Platonic notion of free will. In Ficino's hands, free will became the source of human dignity because human beings were able to choose to love God.

However, Ficino had the most powerful impact on the Early Renaissance when he made Plato's teaching on love central to Neo-Platonism. Following Platonism, he taught that love was a divine gift that bound all human beings together. Love expressed itself in human experience by the desire for and the appreciation of beauty in its myriad forms. Platonic love, like erotic love, was aroused first by the physical appearance of the beloved. But Platonic love, dissatisfied by mere physical enjoyment, could not rest until it moved upward to the highest spiritual level, where it finally met its goal of union with the Divine. Under the promptings of Platonism, the human form became a metaphor of the soul's desire for God. Many Renaissance writers and artists came under the influence of Ficino's Neo-Platonism, embracing its principles and embodying them in their works. Sandro Botticelli, for example, created several allegorical paintings in which divine love and beauty were represented by an image from pre-Christian Rome—Venus, goddess of love (Figure 11.3).

Ficino's most prized student, Pico della Mirandola [PEE-koh DAYL-lah me-RAHN-do-lah] (1463–1494), surpassed his master's accomplishments by the breadth of his learning and the virtuosity of his mind. Pico—a wealthy and charming aristocrat—

impressed everyone with his command of languages, his range of knowledge, and his spirited arguments. He set as his goal the synthesis of Platonism and Aristotelianism within a Christian framework that also encompassed Hebraic, Arabic, and Persian ideas. Church authorities and traditional scholars attacked Pico's efforts once they grasped the implication of his ambitious project— that all knowledge shared basic common truths and that Christians could benefit from studying non-Western, non-Christian writings.

Pico's second important contribution—the concept of individual worth—had been foreshadowed by Ficino. Pico's *Oration on the Dignity of Man* gives the highest expression to this idea, which is inherent in the humanist tradition. According to Pico, human beings, endowed with reason and speech, are created as a microcosm of the universe. Set at the midpoint in the scale of God's creatures, they are blessed with free will, which enables them either to raise themselves to God or to sink lower than the beasts. "Constrained by no limits," individuals possess the power to make of themselves what they wish. This liberty to determine private fate makes human beings the masters of their individual destinies and, at the same time, focuses attention on each human being as the measure of all things—a Classical belief now reborn. What others had only hinted at, Pico boldly crystalized into a major motif that knit together many of the underlying themes of the humanistic movement.

Architecture, Sculpture, and Painting

It was in architecture, sculpture, and painting that the Renaissance made its most dramatic break with the medieval past. The *Early Renaissance style* was launched in Florence by artists who wanted to make a complete break with the Late Gothic style (Figure 11.4). Led by the architect Filippo Brunelleschi [bru-nayl-LAYS-kee] (1377–1446), this group studied the ruins of Classical buildings in Rome and other cities along with surviving ancient works of sculpture in order to unlock the secrets of their harmonious style. They believed that once the Classical ideals were rescued from obscurity, new works could be fashioned that captured the spirit of ancient art and architecture, without slavishly copying it.

Artistic Ideals and Innovations Guided by Brunelleschi's findings, architects, sculptors, and painters made the Classical principles of balance, simplicity, and restraint the central ideals of the Early Renaissance style. The heaviest debt to the past was owed by the architects, for they revived the Classical orders—the Doric, the Ionic, and the Corinthian. The new buildings, though constructed to accommodate modern needs, were symmetrical in plan and relied on simple decorative designs. The theoretician of Early Renaissance style and its other guiding light was Leone Battista Alberti [ahl-BAIR-tee] (1404–1472), who wrote at length on Brunelleschi's innovations and published a

FIGURE 11.4 LEONE BATTISTA ALBERTI. *Tempio Malatestiano (Malatesta Temple) (Church of San Francesco).* Ca. 1450. Rimini, Italy. *Although unfinished, this church strikingly demonstrates the revolution in architecture represented by Early Renaissance ideals. Nothing could be further from the spires of Late Gothic cathedrals than this simple, symmetrical structure with its plain facade, post-and-lintel entrance, rounded arches, and Classical columns. Designed by the leading theoretician of the new style, the Malatesta Temple served as a model for artists and architects of the later Renaissance.*

highly influential book on the new painting. Alberti believed that architecture should embody the humanistic qualities of dignity, balance, control, and harmony and that a building's ultimate beauty rested on the mathematical harmony of its separate parts.

Sculpture and painting, freed from their subordination to architecture, regained their ancient status as independent art forms and in time became the most cherished of the visual arts. Renaissance sculptors and painters aspired to greater realism than had been achieved in the Gothic style, and so both sought to depict human musculature and anatomy with a greater degree of credibility. Sculptors, led by this period's genius, Donatello [dah-nah-TEL-lo] (about 1386–1466), revived Classical practices that had not been seen in the West for more than a thousand years: the free-standing figure; the technique of contrapposto, or a figure balanced with most of the weight resting on one leg (see Figure 3.21); the life-size nude statue; and the equestrian statue representing both horse and rider.

While architecture and sculpture looked back to ancient Greek and Roman traditions, developments in painting grew from late medieval sources. In the

early fourteenth century, Giotto had founded a new realistic and expressive style (see Chapter 10) that Florentine painters at the opening of the fifteenth century began to build on. Much of Giotto's genius lay in his ability to show *perspective*, or the appearance of spatial depth, in his frescoes, an illusion he achieved largely through the placement of the figures (see Figure 10.18). Now, approximately one hundred years after Giotto, painters learned how to enhance the realism of their pictures by the use of linear perspective, the most significant artistic innovation of the age.

The invention of linear perspective was another of the accomplishments of Brunelleschi. Using principles of architecture and optics, he conducted experiments in 1425 that provided the mathematical basis for achieving the illusion of depth on a two-dimensional surface (and, coincidentally, contributed to the enhancement of the status of the arts by grounding them in scholarly learning). Brunelleschi's solution to the problem of linear perspective was to organize the picture space around the center point, or *vanishing point*. After determining the painting's vanishing point, he devised a structural grid for placing objects in precise relation to each other within the picture space. He also computed the ratios by which objects diminish in size as they recede from view, so that pictorial reality seems to correspond visually with physical accuracy. He then subjected the design to a mirror test—checking its truthfulness in its reflected image.

When the camera appeared in the nineteenth century, it was discovered that the photographic lens "saw" nature according to Brunelleschi's mathematical rules. After the 1420s, Brunelleschi's studies led to the concept of Renaissance space, the notion that a composition should be viewed from one single position. For four hundred years, or until first challenged by Manet in the nineteenth century, linear perspective and Renaissance space played a paramount role in Western painting.

A second type of perspective, atmospheric or aerial, was perfected by painters north of the Alps in the first half of the fifteenth century, although the Italian painter Masaccio was the first to revive atmospheric perspective in the 1420s, based on the Roman tradition. Through the use of colors, these artists created an illusion of depth by subtly diminishing the tones as the distance between the eye and the object increased; at the horizon line, the colors become grayish and the objects blurry in appearance. When atmospheric perspective was joined to linear perspective, as happened later in the century, a greater illusion of reality was achieved than was possible with either type used independently.

FIGURE 11.5 FILIPPO BRUNELLESCHI. Cathedral Dome, Florence. 1420–1436. *After the dome of the Florence Cathedral was erected according to Brunelleschi's plan, another architect was employed to add small galleries in the area above the circular windows. But the Florentine authorities halted his work before the galleries were fully installed, leaving the structure in its present state.*

Again commenting on the innovations of Brunelleschi was Alberti, who published a treatise in 1435 that elaborated on the mathematical aspects of painting and set forth brilliantly the humanistic and secular values of the Early Renaissance. Alberti was an aristocratic humanist with both a deep knowledge of Classicism and a commitment to its ideals. In his treatise he praised master painters in rousing terms, comparing their creativity to God's—a notion that would have been considered blasphemous by medieval thinkers. He asserted that paintings, in addition to pleasing the eye, should appeal to the mind with optical and mathematical accuracy. But paintings, he went on, should also present a noble subject, such as a Classical hero, and should be characterized by a small number of figures, by carefully observed and varied details, by graceful poses, by harmonious relationships among all elements, and by a judicious use of colors. These Classical ideals were quickly adopted by Florentine artists eager to establish a new aesthetic code.

Architecture In the High Middle Ages, most architects were stonemasons and were regarded as artisans, like shoemakers or potters. But by the fifteenth century the status of architects had changed. Because of the newly discovered scientific aspects of their craft, the leading architects were now grouped with those practicing the learned professions of medicine and law. By 1450 Italian architects had freed architecture from Late Gothicism, as well as from the other arts—and vice versa. Unlike Gothic cathedrals adorned with sculptures and paintings, these new buildings drew on the Classical tradition for whatever simple decorative details were needed. This transformation became the most visible symbol of Early Renaissance architecture.

Although Brunelleschi established the new standards in architecture, most of his buildings have either been destroyed or altered considerably by later hands. However, the earliest work to bring him fame still survives in Florence largely as he had planned it—the dome of the city's cathedral (Figure 11.5). Although the rest of the cathedral—nave, transept, and

FIGURE 11.6 FILIPPO BRUNELLESCHI. Design for Construction of Dome of Florence Cathedral. *Brunelleschi designed the dome of the Florence Cathedral with an inner and outer shell, both of which are attached to the eight ribs of the octagonal-shaped structure. Sixteen smaller ribs, invisible from the outside, were placed between the shells to give added support. What held these elements together and gave them stability was the lantern, based on his design, that was anchored to the dome's top sometime after 1446.*

FIGURE 11.7 FILIPPO BRUNELLESCHI AND OTHERS. Exterior, Pazzi Chapel, Santa Croce Church. 1433–1461. Florence. *The Pazzi Chapel's harmonious facade reflects the Classical principles of the Early Renaissance style, that is, symmetry and simplicity. By breaking the rhythm of the facade with the rounded arch, the architect emphasizes its surface symmetry so that the left half is a mirror image of the right side. Simplicity is achieved in the architectural decorations, which are either Greco-Roman devices or mathematically inspired divisions.*

choir—was finished prior to 1400, no one had been able to devise a method for erecting the projected dome until Brunelleschi received the commission in 1420. Using the learning he had gained from his researches in Rome as well as his knowledge of Gothic building styles, he developed an ingenious way for raising the dome, which was virtually completed in 1436.

Faced with a domical base of 140 feet, Brunelleschi realized that a hemispheric dome in the Roman manner, like the dome of the Pantheon, would not work (see Figure 5.13). Traditional building techniques could not span the Florentine cathedral's vast domical base nor could the cathedral's walls be buttressed to support a massive dome. So he turned to Gothic methods, using diagonal ribs based on the pointed arch. This innovative dome had a double shell of two relatively thin walls held together by twenty-four stone ribs, of which only eight are visi-

ble. His crowning touch was to add a lantern that sits atop the dome and locks the ribs into place (Figure 11.6). The dome's rounded windows echo the openings in the upper nave walls, thereby ensuring that his addition would harmonize with the existing elements. But the octagonal-shaped dome was Brunelleschi's own creation and expresses a logical, even inevitable, structure. Today the cathedral still dominates the skyline of Florence, a lasting symbol of Brunelleschi's creative genius.

Brunelleschi's most representative building is the Pazzi Chapel, as the chapter house, or meeting room, of the monks of Santa Croce is called. This small church embodies the harmonious proportions and Classical features that are the hallmark of the Early Renaissance style. In his architectural plan, Brunelleschi centered a dome over an oblong area whose width equals the dome's diameter and whose length is twice its width and then covered each of the chap-

FIGURE 11.8 FILIPPO BRUNELLESCHI. Interior, Pazzi Chapel, Santa Croce Church. Ca. 1433–1461. Florence. *Decorations on the white walls of the Pazzi Chapel's interior break up its plain surface and draw the viewer's eye to the architectural structure: pilasters, window and panel frames, medallions, capitals, and dome ribs. The only non-architecturally related decorations are the terra-cotta sculptures of the four evangelists and the Pazzi family coat of arms, mounted inside the medallions and modeled by Luca della Robbia, one of a famous Florentine family of sculptors.*

el's elongated ends with a barrel vault. Double doors opened into the center wall on one long side, and two rounded arch windows flanked this doorway. A loggia, or porch, which Brunelleschi may not have designed, preceded the entrance (Figure 11.7). Inside the chapel, following the Classical rules of measure and proportion, Brunelleschi employed medallions, rosettes, *pilasters* (or applied columns), and square panels. In addition to these Classical details, the rounded arches and the barrel vaults further exemplify the new Renaissance style (Figure 11.8). His Classical theories were shared by Florence's humanist elite, who found religious significance in mathematical harmony. Both they and Brunelleschi believed that a well-ordered building such as the Pazzi Chapel mirrored God's plan of the universe.

The other towering figure in Early Renaissance architecture was Alberti, although, as is the case with Brunelleschi's work, few of his buildings survive as originally planned. Despite the influence of his ideas, which dominated architecture until 1600, no completed building remains based on his design. A splendid unfinished effort is the Tempio Malatestiano in Rimini (see Figure 11.4), a structure that replaced the existing church of San Francesco. Rimini's despot, Sigismondo Malatesta, planned to have himself, his mistress, and his court buried in the refurbished structure, and he appointed Alberti to supervise the church's reconstruction.

Alberti's monument represents the first modern attempt to give a Classical exterior to a church. Abandoning the Gothic pointed arch, he designed this church's unfinished facade with its three rounded arches after a nearby triumphal arch. He framed the arches with Corinthian columns, one of his favorite decorative devices. Although the architect apparently planned to cover the church's interior with a dome comparable to Brunelleschi's on the Florentine cathedral, the fortunes of Malatesta failed, and the projected temple had to be abandoned. Nevertheless, Alberti's partly finished church was admired by later builders and helped to point the way to the new Renaissance architecture.

Sculpture Like architecture, sculpture blossomed in Florence in the early 1400s, and no major Italian rivals appeared for the rest of the century. Donatello (1386–1466), the leader of the sculptural revival, was imbued with Classical ideals but obsessed with realism. He used all sorts of techniques—expressive gestures, direct observation, and mathematical precision—to reproduce what his eyes saw. Donatello accompanied Brunelleschi in his forays to Rome to study ancient art, and he adapted linear perspective as early as 1425 into a small *relief* called *The Feast of Herod* (Figure 11.9).

The subject is the tragic end of John the Baptist, Florence's patron saint, as recounted in Mark 6:20–29. In this square bronze panel, Donatello carved the saint's severed head being displayed on a dish to King Herod at the left, while the scorned Salome stands near the right end of the table. A puzzled guest leans toward the ruler, Herod recoils with upraised arms, two children at the left back away from the bloody head, and a diner leans back from the center of the table—all depicted under the rounded arches of the new Brunelleschian architecture. The sculpture's rich details point up the horror of the scene and thus achieve the heightened realism that was among the artistic goals of this era. The use of linear perspective gives astonishing clarity to the story. The scene's vanishing point runs through the middle set of arches, so that the leaning motions of the two figures in the foreground not only express their inner turmoil but cause them to fall away from the viewer's line of sight.

FIGURE 11.9   DONATELLO. *The Feast of Herod.* Ca. 1425. Gilt bronze, 23½" square. Baptismal Font, San Giovanni, Siena. *The first low-relief sculpture executed in the Early Renaissance style,* The Feast of Herod *is a stunning example of the power of this new approach to art. Its theatrical force arises from the successful use of linear perspective and the orderly placement of the figures throughout the three rooms.*

Donatello also revived the free-standing male nude, one of the supreme expressions of ancient art. Donatello's bronze *David*, probably executed for Cosimo de' Medici, portrays David standing with his left foot on the severed head of the Philistine warrior Goliath—a pose based on the biblical story (Figure 11.10). The David and Goliath story was often allegorized into a prophecy of Christ's triumph over Satan. But Donatello's sculpture undermines such an interpretation, for his *David* is less a heroic figure than a provocative image of refined sensuality, as suggested by the undeveloped but elegant body, the dandified pose, and the incongruous boots and hat. His *David* is a splendid modern portrayal of youthful male power, self-aware and poised on the brink of manhood.

Like other Renaissance masters, Donatello owed debts to Classical artists, but he also challenged them by adapting their principles to his own times. For example, the Roman statue of Marcus Aurelius (see Figure 5.10) inspired Donatello's bronze called the *Gattamelata*, the first successful equestrian sculpture in over 1200 years (Figure 11.11). As Donatello's David portrays the subtleties of adolescent male beauty, his Gattamelata pays homage to mature masculine power. This work honored the memory of

Erasmo da Narni, a Venetian *condottieri* nicknamed Gattamelata, or "Honey Cat." The warrior's pose resembles the Roman imperial style, but, in almost every other way, the sculptor violates the harmonious ideals of ancient art.

Most significantly, the rider's face owes its sharp realism—firm jawline, bushy eyebrows, widely set eyes, and close-cropped hair—to fifteenth-century sources, especially to the cult of the ugly, an aesthetic attitude that claimed to find moral strength in coarse features outside of the Classical rules (Figure 11.12).

FIGURE 11.10   DONATELLO. *David.* Ca. 1430–1432. Bronze, height 62¼". Bargello, Florence. *This sculpture had a profound influence on later sculptors, who admired Donatello's creation but produced rival interpretations of David. Donatello and his successors used the image of David to pay homage to male power— a major preoccupation of Renaissance artists and intellectuals.*

FIGURE 11.11   DONATELLO. *Equestrian Monument of Erasmo da Narni, Called "Gattamelata."* 1447–1453. Bronze, ca. 11 × 13'. Piazza Del Santo, Padua. *This equestrian statue of the* condottieri *was funded by his family but authorized by a grateful Venetian senate in honor of his military exploits. Conceiving of the dead military leader as a "triumphant Caesar," Donatello dressed him in Classical costume and decorated his saddle and armor with many allusions to antique art, such as flying cupids and victory depicted as a goddess.*

FIGURE 11.12   DONATELLO. Detail of *"Gattamelata."* 1447–1453. Piazza Del Santo, Padua. *Donatello deliberately designed the monument's stern, deeply lined, and serious face to conform to the Renaissance ideal of a strong military commander.*

FIGURE 11.13 LORENZO GHIBERTI. *The Annunciation.* Panel from the North Doors of the Baptistery. 1403–1424. Gilt bronze. Florence. *Ghiberti's rendition of the Annunciation was typical of his panels on the north doors. The figures of Mary and the Angel were placed in the shallow foreground and were modeled almost completely in the round. The background details, including a sharply foreshortened representation of God on the left, were scarcely raised from the metal. The contrast between these two design elements greatly enhanced the illusion of depth.*

Consequently, since this work was commissioned after the hero's death and since Donatello had no way of knowing how the soldier looked, he sculpted the face to conform to his notion of a strong-minded general. The massive horse, with flaring nostrils, open mouth, and lifted foreleg, seemed to be an extension of the soldier's forceful personality.

The only serious rival to Donatello in the Early Renaissance was another Florentine, Lorenzo Ghiberti [gee-BAIR-tee] (about 1381–1455), who slowly adapted to the new style of art. In 1401 he defeated Brunelleschi in a competition to select a sculptor for the north doors of Florence's Baptistery. The north doors consist of twenty-eight panels, arranged in four columns of seven panels, each depicting a New Testament scene. These doors, completed between 1403 and 1424, show Ghiberti still under the influence of the International Gothic style that prevailed in about 1400. Illustrative of this tendency is the panel of *The Annunciation* (Luke 1:26–38) that depicts the moment when Mary learns from an angelic messenger that she will become the mother of Christ (Figure 11.13). The Gothic quatrefoil, or four-leafed figure, was standard for these panels, and many of Ghiberti's techniques are typical of the Gothic style—the recessed area, or niche, in which the Virgin stands, her swaying body, and the angel depicted in flight. Nevertheless, Ghiberti always exhibited a strong feeling for Classical forms and harmony, as in the angel's well-rounded body and Mary's serene face.

The artistic world of Florence was a rapidly changing one, however, and Ghiberti more and more adapted his art to conform to the emerging Early Renaissance style of his younger rival, Donatello. Between 1429 and 1437, Ghiberti brought his mature art to its fullest expression in the east doors, the last of the Baptistery's three sculpted portals. These panels, larger than those on the north doors, depict scenes from the Old Testament, such as the story of Jacob and Esau (Figure 11.14). Most of the Gothic touches are eliminated, including the framing quatrefoils,

FIGURE 11.14 LORENZO GHIBERTI. *The Story of Jacob and Esau.* Detail from the East Doors of the Baptistery (the "Gates of Paradise"). Ca. 1435. Gilt bronze, 31¼ × 31¼". Florence. *This exquisite panel from the Florence Baptistery's east doors is a testament to Ghiberti's absorption of Early Renaissance taste. He followed Brunelleschi's new rules for linear perspective by placing the vanishing point in the middle of the central set of arches, and he adhered to Alberti's principle of varied details by adding the hunting dogs, the fleeing snake, and the woman with the basket on her head.*

which are now replaced with rectangular panels. In many other ways the Jacob and Esau panel on the east doors shows Ghiberti's growing dedication to Classical ideals: the graceful contrapposto of the standing figures and the Brunelleschian architecture, for example. In a daring move, Ghiberti sculpted a figure on either side of the panel whose mass extends beyond the frame. This work translates Albertian aesthetics into bronze, observing proportional relationships and creating an illusion of depth. So sublime was Ghiberti's accomplishment that Michelangelo, in the next century, is said to have referred to these doors as "the Gates of Paradise."

Painting   The radical changes taking place in architecture and sculpture were minor compared to what was happening in painting. Inspired by Classicism though lacking significant examples from ancient times, painters were relatively free to experiment and to define their own path. As in the other arts of the 1400s, Florentine painters led the way and established the standards for the new style—realism, linear perspective, and psychological truth. This movement climaxed at the end of the century with the early work of Leonardo da Vinci. After 1450 Florence's dominance was challenged by Venetian painters who were forging their own artistic tradition. Venice, having only won her freedom from the Byzantine Empire in the High Middle Ages, was still in the thrall of Byzantine culture (see Chapter 8). As a result, Venetian painters and their patrons showed a pronounced taste for the stylized effects and sensual surfaces typical of Byzantine art.

North of the Alps, a third Early Renaissance development was taking place in Burgundy and the Low Countries. There, the painters pursued an art more religious than that of Italy and closer in spirit to the Late Gothic. The northern artists concentrated on minute details and landscapes rather than on the problems of depth and composition that concerned Italy's painters. This survey confines itself to the major figures in the two generations of painters in the Florentine school.

The guiding genius of the revolution in painting in the earlier Florentine school was the youthful Masaccio [mah-ZAHT-cho] (1401–1428), whose career was probably cut short by the plague. He adopted mathematical perspective in his works almost simultaneously with its invention by Brunelleschi. In the history of Western painting, Masaccio's *Holy Trinity* fresco, painted in 1425, is the first successful depiction in painting of the new concept of Renaissance space.

Masaccio's design for this fresco in the church of Santa Maria Novella, Florence, shows that he was well aware of the new currents flowing in the art of

FIGURE 11.15   MASACCIO. *The Holy Trinity.* 1427 or 1428. Fresco, 21'10½" × 10'5". Santa Maria Novella, Florence. *Masaccio achieved a remarkable illusion of depth in this fresco by using linear and atmospheric perspective. Below the simulated chapel he painted a skeleton in a wall sarcophagus (not visible in this photograph) with a melancholy inscription reading, "I was once that which you are, and what I am you also will be." This momento mori, or reminder of death, was probably ordered by the donor, a member of the Lenzi family. His tomb is built into the floor and lies directly in front of the fresco.*

his day. The painting offers an architectural setting in the style of Brunelleschi, and the solidity and vitality of the figures indicate that Masaccio had also absorbed the values of Donatello's new sculpture. Masaccio's fresco portrays the Holy Trinity—the three divine beings who make up the Christian idea of God—within a simulated chapel (Figure 11.15).

Jesus' crucified body appears to be held up by God the Father, who stands on a platform behind the cross; between the heads of God and Jesus is a dove, symbolizing the Holy Spirit and completing the Trinitarian image. Mary and Saint John, both clothed in contemporary dress, flank the holy trio. The only gesture in the painting is Mary's, as she points dramatically to the Savior. Just outside the chapel's frame, the donors kneel in prayer—the typical way of presenting patrons in Renaissance art.

In the Trinity fresco Masaccio uses a variety of innovations to create a startlingly original painting. He is the first painter to show light falling from a single source, in this instance, from the left, bathing the body of Christ and coinciding with the actual lighting in Santa Maria Novella. This realistic feature adds to the three-dimensional effect of the well-modeled figures. The use of linear perspective further heightens the scene's realism. Finally, the perspective, converging to the midpoint between the kneeling donors, reinforces the hierarchy of beings within the fresco: from God the Father at the top to the human figures at the sides. In effect, mathematical tidiness is used to reveal the divine order—an ideal congenial to Florence's intellectual elite.

A second fresco by Masaccio, *The Tribute Money,* painted in the Brancacci Chapel of the church of Santa Maria del Carmine, Florence, is recognized as Masaccio's masterpiece (Figure 11.16). This fresco illustrates the Gospel account (Matthew 17:24–27) in which Jesus advises Peter, his chief disciple, to pay the Roman taxes. A biblical subject virtually unrepresented in Christian art, this painting was probably commissioned by a donor to justify a new and heavy Florentine tax. Whether the fresco had any effect on tax collection is debatable, but other artists were captivated by Masaccio's stunning technical effects: the use of perspective and *chiaroscuro*, or the modeling with light and shade.

The Tribute Money fresco follows the continuous narrative form of medieval art. Three separate episodes are depicted at the same time—in the center, Jesus is confronted by the tax collector; on the left, Peter, as foretold by Jesus, finds a coin in the mouth of a fish; and, on the right, Peter pays the coin to the Roman official. Despite this Gothic effect, the fresco's central section is able to stand alone because of its spatial integrity and unified composition. Jesus is partially encircled by his apostles, and the tax gatherer, viewed from the back, stands to the right. In this central group, the heads are all at the same height, for Masaccio aligned them according to Brunelleschi's principles. Fully modeled in the round, each human form occupies a precise, mathematical space.

Painters like the Dominican friar Fra Angelico (about 1400–1455) extended Masaccio's innovations. Fra Angelico's later works, painted for the renovated monastery of San Marco in Florence and partially funded by Cosimo de' Medici, show his mature blending of biblical motifs in Renaissance space. *The Annunciation* portrays a reflective Virgin receiving the angel Gabriel (Figure 11.17). Mary and Gabriel are framed in niches in the Gothic manner, but the other elements—the mastery of depth, the simplicity of gestures, the purity of colors, and the integrated

◀ **FIGURE 11.16** MASACCIO. *The Tribute Money.* Ca. 1425. Fresco, 8'2⅜" × 19'8¼". Santa Maria del Carmine, Florence. *This fresco represents the highest expression of the art of Masaccio, particularly in his realistic portrayal of the tax collector. This official, who appears twice, first confronting Christ in the center and then receiving money from Peter on the right, is depicted with coarse features—a typical man of the Florentine streets. Even his posture, though rendered with Classical contrapposto, suggests a swagger—a man at home in his body and content with his difficult occupation.*

FIGURE 11.17 FRA ANGELICO. *Annunciation.* 1438–1445. Monastery of San Marco, Florence. *Fra Angelico's portrayal of the Virgin at the moment when she receives the news that she will bear the baby Jesus is a wonderful illustration of the painter's use of religious symbols. Mary's questioning expression and her arms crossed in a maternal gesture help to establish the painting's subject. Moreover, the physical setting of the scene, bare except for the rough bench on which she sits, suggests an ascetic existence—an appropriate detail for the painting's original setting, a monastery.*

scene—are rendered in the new, simple Renaissance style. The painting's vanishing point is placed to the right of center in the small barred window looking out from the Virgin's bedroom. The loggia, or open balcony, in which the scene takes place was based on a new architectural fashion popular among Florence's wealthy elite. Religious images abound in this painting; the enclosed garden symbolizes Mary's virginity, and the barred window attests to the purity of her life. Because of his gracious mastery of form and space, Fra Angelico's influence on later artists was pronounced.

One of those influenced by Fra Angelico was Piero della Francesca [PYER-o DAYL-lah frahn-CHAY-skah] (about 1420–1492), a great painter of the second Florentine generation, who grew up in a Tuscan country town near Florence. His panel painting, *The Flagellation,* shows the powerful though mysterious aesthetic effects of his controversial style (Figure 11.18). The sunlight flooding the scene unites the figures, but the composition places them in three distinct areas. At the extreme left sits Pilate, the judge, on a dais. The painting's subject—the scourging of Christ before his crucifixion—is placed to the left rear. Reinforcing this odd displacement are the figures on the right, who are apparently lost in their own conversation. Aesthetically this strange juxtaposition arises because Piero has placed the horizon line around the hips of the figures beating Christ, causing the three men on the right to loom in such high perspective. As a result, the men in the foreground appear to be indifferent to Christ and unaware of his importance. The effect is distinctly unsettling in a religious scene. The modern world, which loves conundrums, has developed a strong passion for the private vision of Piero della Francesca as represented in his art.

Sandro Botticelli [baht-tuh-CHEL-lee] (1445–1510) is the best representative of a lyrical aspect of this second generation and one of the most admired painters in the Western tradition. One of the first Florentine artists to master both linear and atmospheric perspective, he was less interested in the technical aspects of painting than he was in depicting languid beauty and poetical truth.

Until the 1480s Botticelli's art was shaped by the Neo-Platonism of the Florentine Academy, and thus he often allegorized pagan myths, giving them a Christian slant. Especially prominent in Neo-Platonic thought was the identification of Venus, the goddess of love, with the Christian belief that "God is love." Taking inspiration from this idea, Botticelli, with the support of his patrons, notably the Medici family, made the Roman goddess the subject of two splendid paintings, the *Primavera* and *The Birth of Venus*. In this way female nudes once again became a proper subject

◀ **FIGURE 11.18** PIERO DELLA FRANCESCA. *The Flagellation.* 1460s. Oil on panel, 23 × 32". Galleria Nazionale della Marche, Palazzo Ducale, Urbino. *A secondary religious message may be found in this work. In 1439 the Orthodox Church discussed union with Rome at the Council of Florence but later repudiated the merger when the Byzantine populace rioted in favor of Turkish rule. The hats on Pilate and the third man from the right are copies of Greek headdresses that were worn at the council. In effect, these figures suggest that the Greek church is a persecutor of true Christianity, for the papacy regarded the Greek Orthodox faith as schismatic.*

for art, though male nudes had appeared earlier in Donatello's generation (see Figure 11.10).

Botticelli's *Primavera,* or Allegory of Spring, presents Venus as a Christianized deity, dressed in a revealingly transparent gown (Figure 11.19). At first glance, the goddess, standing just slightly to the right of center, appears lost amid the general agitation, but on closer view she is seen to be presiding over the revels. Venus tilts her head coyly and holds up her right hand, establishing by these commanding gestures that this orange grove is her garden and

the other figures are her familiars, or associates, all of them symbolically linked with divine love.

Even though the *Primavera* is one of the most beloved works of Western art, in technical terms the painting shows that Botticelli was out of step with the Early Renaissance. He has placed the scene in the near foreground, stressing this area's extreme shallowness by the entangled backdrop of trees and shrubs. The figures are flattened, and the background appears more decorative than real.

An even more famous work by Botticelli, and one of the great landmarks of Western art, is *The Birth of Venus* (see Figure 11.3). Painted in an even more flattened style than the *Primavera,* this masterpiece was probably intended as a visual complement to it. In Neo-Platonic terms, Venus is an image of beauty and

FIGURE 11.19 SANDRO BOTTICELLI. *Primavera.* Ca. 1482. Tempera on panel, 6'8" × 10'4". Uffizi Gallery, Florence. *Botticelli's lyricism is evident in his refined images of human beauty. His figures' elegant features and gestures, such as the sloping shoulders and the tilted heads, were copied by later artists. The women's ropelike hair and transparent gowns are typical of Botticelli's style.*

◀ **FIGURE 11.20** LEONARDO DA VINCI. *The Virgin of the Rocks.* 1483. Oil on panel, ca. 6′3″ × 3′7″. Louvre. *Two slightly different versions of this work exist, an early one dating from 1483 and now hanging in the Louvre and a later one done in 1506 and on view in the National Gallery in London. The Louvre painting, with its carefully observed botanical specimens, is the culmination of the scientific side of the Early Renaissance. It also points to the future, the High Renaissance, with its arbitrary features—the grotto setting and the unusual perspective—which call attention to Leonardo's confident genius.*

love as it is born and grows in the human mind; the birth of Venus corresponds to the baptism of Jesus, because baptism is a symbol of rebirth.

In the 1480s Florentine art was moving toward its culmination in the early works of Leonardo da Vinci (1452–1519). Leonardo is the quintessential representative of a new breed of artist: the Renaissance Man who takes the universe of learning as his province. Not only did he defy the authority of the church by secretly studying human cadavers, but he also rejected the Classical values that had guided the first generation of the Early Renaissance. He relied solely on empirical truth and what the human eye could discover. His notebooks, encoded so as to be legible only when read in a mirror, recorded and detailed his lifelong curiosity about both the human and natural worlds. In his habits of mind, Leonardo joined intellectual curiosity with the skills of sculptor, architect, engineer, scientist, and painter.

Among his few surviving paintings from this period, the first version of *The Virgin of the Rocks* reveals both his scientific eye and his desire to create a haunting image uniquely his own (Figure 11.20). In this scene, set in a grotto or cave, Mary is portrayed with the infant Jesus, as a half-kneeling infant John the Baptist prays and an angel watches. The plants underfoot and the rocks in the background are a treasure of precise documentation. Nevertheless, the setting is Leonardo's own invention—without a scriptural or a traditional basis—and thus stands as a testimony to his creative genius.

Leonardo's plan of *The Virgin of the Rocks* shows the rich workings of his mind. Ignoring Brunelleschian perspective, he placed the figures according to ideas of his own. He also developed a pyramid design for arranging the figures in relation to one another; Mary's head forms the pyramid's apex while her seat and the other three figures anchor its corners. Within this pyramid he creates a dynamic tension by using gestures to suggest a circular motion: The angel points to John the Baptist who, in

turn, directs his praying hands toward Jesus. A second line of stress, this time vertical, is seen in the motioning hands of Mary, the angel, and Christ. Later artists so admired this painting that its pyramidal composition became the standard in the High Renaissance.

No prior artist had used chiaroscuro to such advantage as Leonardo does in this work, causing the figures to stand out miraculously from the surrounding gloom. And unlike earlier artists, he colors the atmosphere, softening the edges of surfaces with a fine haze called **sfumato.** As a result, the painting looks more like a vision than a realistic scene. Leonardo's later works are part of the High Renaissance (see Chapter 12), but his early works represent the fullest expression of the scientific spirit of the second generation of Early Renaissance painting.

Music

The changes affecting the cultural life of fifteenth-century Europe naturally also affected the music of the time. The impetus for a new musical direction, however, did not spring from Classical sources because ancient musical texts had virtually perished. Instead, the new music owed its existence to the meetings between English and continental composers at the church councils that were called to settle the Great Schism (see Chapter 10) and the continental composers' deep regard for the seductive sound of English music. The English composer John Dunstable [DUHN-stuh-bull] (about 1380–1453) was a central figure in the new musical era that began with the opening of the fifteenth century. Working in England and in France, he wrote mainly religious works—motets for multiple voices and settings for the Mass—that showed his increasingly harmonic approach to polyphony. The special quality of his music is its freedom from the use of mathematical proportion—the source of medieval music's dissonance.

Dunstable's music influenced composers in France, in Burgundy, and in Flanders, known collectively as the Franco-Netherlandish school. This school, which became the dominant force in fifteenth-century music, blended Dunstable's harmonics with north European and Italian traditions. The principal works of this group were Latin *Masses,* or musical settings of the most sacred Christian rite; motets, or multivoiced songs set to Latin texts; and secular **chansons,** or songs, with French texts, including such types as the French ballade and the Italian madrigal, poems set to music for two and six voices, respectively. Together, these polyphonic compositions established the musical ideal of the Early Renaissance: multiple voices of equal importance singing **a capella** (without instrumental accompaniment) and stressing the words so they could be understood by listeners.

Between 1430 and 1500, the continent's musical life was guided by composers from the Franco-Netherlandish school, the most important of whom was Josquin des Prez [zho-SKAN-day-PRAY] (about 1440–1521). A Burgundian, Josquin was influential in his day and is now recognized as one of the greatest composers of all time. He was the first important composer to use music expressively so that the sounds matched the words of the text, thereby moving away from the abstract church style of the Middle Ages. One of his motets was described at the time as evoking Christ's suffering in a manner superior to painting. Josquin also began to organize music in the modern way, using major and minor scales with their related harmonies. All in all, he is probably the first Western composer whose music on first hearing appeals to modern ears.

The Legacy of the Early Renaissance

Today, modern times are thought to begin with the Early Renaissance, but primarily in Italy and only in high culture, that is, with the study and practice of the arts and the humanities. Under humanism's powerful stimulus, the liberal arts were restored to their primacy over religion in the educational curriculum, a place they had not held for a thousand years, or since Christianity's triumph in the fourth century. With humanism also came a skeptical outlook that expressed itself in a new regard for the direct role of human causality in history and the rise of textual criticism.

The greatest cultural changes took place in the arts and in architecture, largely under the spell of humanistic learning. Now freed from subordination to architecture, sculpture and painting became independent art forms. Fifteenth-century architects, inspired by the Greco-Roman tradition, adapted Classical forms and ideals to their own needs. For the next four hundred years, until the Gothic revival in the nineteenth century, Classicism was a ruling force in a succession of architectural styles. Sculpture also used its Classical roots to redefine its direction, reviving ancient forms and the practice of depicting male and female nudes. Of all the visual arts, however, painting was least influenced by the Classical tradition, except for its ideals of simplicity and realism. Perhaps as a consequence of its artistic freedom, painting became the dominant art form of this era and continues to hold first rank today.

KEY CULTURAL TERMS

Renaissance
studia humanitatis
Neo-Platonism
Early Renaissance style
perspective
vanishing point
pilaster

relief
chiaroscuro
sfumato
Mass
chanson
a capella

SUGGESTIONS FOR FURTHER READING

PRIMARY SOURCES

CASSIRER, E., KRISTELLER, P. O., and RANDALL, J., eds. *The Renaissance Philosophy of Man*. Chicago: University of Chicago Press, 1948. Selections from Pico, Valla, and other Renaissance scholars accompanied by a useful text.

PICO DELLA MIRANDOLA. *On the Dignity of Man*. Indianapolis, Ind.: Bobbs-Merrill, 1956. A succinct statement on Renaissance thought by one of its leading scholars.

SUGGESTIONS FOR LISTENING

DUNSTABLE (or DUNSTAPLE), JOHN (about 1380–1453). Dunstable's sweet-sounding harmonies helped inaugurate Early Renaissance music. Predominantly a composer of sacred music, he is best represented by motets, including *Veni Sancte Spiritus—Veni Creator Spiritus* and *Sancta Maria, Non Est Similis*. He also wrote a few secular songs of which the two most familiar are *O Rosa Bella* and *Puisque M'Amour*.

JOSQUIN DES PREZ (1440–1521). Josquin's Masses, motets, and *chansons* all illustrate his skill at combining popular melodies with intricate counterpoint and his use of harmonies commonly heard today. The motet *Ave Maria*, the *chanson Faulte d'argent*, and the Mass *Malheur me bat* are good examples of his style.

12

THE HIGH RENAISSANCE AND EARLY MANNERISM

1494—1564

Between 1494 and 1564, one of the most brilliantly creative periods in Western history occurred in Italy. During this span of seventy years there flourished three artists—Leonardo da Vinci, Raphael, and Michelangelo—and a writer—Machiavelli—whose achievements became legendary in their own time and whose names today spark instant recognition among educated people everywhere. The works of these geniuses, along with the works of a small group of other talented but less well-known artists and intellectuals, affected the basic Western concept of art and fundamentally influenced the way we understand ourselves and the world.

The first phase of this seventy-year period is called the *High Renaissance*; lasting from 1494 to 1520, it represents the zenith of the cultural renewal known as the Renaissance. During the High Renaissance the Classical principles that had begun to be revived in Italy in the early fifteenth century—beauty, balance, order, serenity, harmony, rational design—reached a state of perfection. At the same time, the center of culture shifted from Florence, the heart of the Early Renaissance, to Rome, where the popes became the leading patrons of the new style. Florence had begun to decline in 1494, when the French invaded and took control of northern Italy. While Florence languished, a papal campaign to make Rome the world's most beautiful city gained

momentum, and the popes used their wealth and prestige to attract the age's most talented artists into their service. Florence even had to yield the services of Michelangelo, its favorite son, to the Roman pontiffs (Figure 12.1).

After 1520, however, the Renaissance veered away from the humanistic values of Classicism toward an antihumanistic vision of the world. This new phase is labeled *Mannerism* because of the self-conscious, or "mannered," style adopted by its artists and intellectuals. Mannerist art and culture endured from 1520 until the end of the century, although this chapter covers the story of this style only until the end of its first phase in 1564, with the death of Michelangelo. Chapter 13 traces the path of the Renaissance in northern Europe and also picks up the thread of later changes in Mannerism, particularly focusing on the impact of religious controversy on Mannerism until its demise at the end of the sixteenth century.

THE RISE OF THE MODERN SOVEREIGN STATE

The most important political development in the first half of the sixteenth century was the emergence of powerful sovereign states in the newly unified and stabilized kingdoms of France, England, and Spain. This process was already underway in the last part of the fifteenth century (see Chapter 10), but it now

◀ RAPHAEL. *Sistine Madonna.* 1513. Oil on canvas, 8'8½" × 6'5". Gemäldegalerie, Dresden.

FIGURE 12.1 MICHELANGELO. *"Dying Slave."* 1513–1516. Marble, ca. 7'5". Louvre. *Michelangelo's so-called Dying Slave embodies the conflicting artistic tendencies at work between 1494 and 1564. The statue's idealized traits—the perfectly proportioned figure, the restrained facial expression, and the body's gentle S-curve shape—are hallmarks of the High Renaissance style. But the figure's overall sleekness and exaggerated arm movements—probably based on one of the figures in the first-century A.D. Laocoön Group, which had only recently been rediscovered—were portents of Early Mannerism.*

TABLE 12.1 FRENCH AND SPANISH RULERS, 1494–1564

FRANCE	SPAIN
Charles VIII, 1483–1498	Ferdinand V, 1479–1516 and Isabella, 1474–1504
Louis XII, 1498–1515	
Francis I, 1515–1547	Charles I, 1516–1556 (also Holy Roman Emperor, 1519–1556)
Henry II, 1547–1559	
Francis II, 1559–1560	Philip II, 1556–1598
Charles IX, 1560–1574	

ests of Spain and the Holy Roman Empire until his abdication in 1556 (Table 12.1). England, the other emerging strong sovereign state, kept virtually aloof from continental affairs during this time.

After 1519 especially, the French and Spanish rulers dispatched their armies and allies into the weaker states, where they fought and claimed new lands as their own. As these sovereign monarchs gained power at home and abroad, the medieval dream of a united Christendom—pursued by Charlemagne, preached by the popes, and cherished by the Holy Roman Emperors—slowly faded away.

The source of the strength of these new states was that they were united around a ruler who exercised more and more central control. Within these new monarchies the kings devised varied techniques for increasing and centralizing their power. Although most claimed to rule by divine right, their practical policies were actually more important in increasing their power than any divine claims. They surrounded themselves with ministers and consultative councils, both of which depended on the crown. The royal ministers were often chosen from the bourgeois class, who were more trustworthy than the independent-minded feudal nobility. These ministers, many of whom grew rich and powerful, advised the rulers on such weighty matters as religion and war and ran the developing bureaucracies. The bureaucracies in turn strengthened centralized rule by extending the king's jurisdiction into areas formerly reserved to the feudal nobility, such as the justice system.

The crown further eroded the status of the feudal nobles by completing a process begun in the Late Middle Ages: The king's armies no longer relied on the warrior class but depended on standing mercenary armies. In order to pay the mercenary troops, the kings were forced to consult with representative bodies, such as Parliament in England, and to make them a part of their regular administration.

Rivalry between France and Spain—under Spanish and, later, Hapsburg rulers—plunged the Euro-

began to have a profound effect on the course of international affairs. The ongoing rivalries of these aggressive national powers brought into existence the concept of the balance of power—a principle that has dominated politics ever since.

During this seventy-year period Europe's international political life was controlled, either directly or indirectly, by France and Spain. France's central role was the result of the policies of a series of strong Valois kings, the dynasty that had governed France since the early fourteenth century. Spain's fortunes soared during this period, first under the joint rule of Ferdinand V and Isabella and then, after 1516, under Charles I. In 1519 Charles I was also elected Holy Roman Emperor as Charles V, thus joining the inter-

pean continent into wars for much of the sixteenth century. Between 1494 and 1529, Italy was a battleground where foreign armies acted out the dreams of ambitious rulers, ravaging the peninsula in the process. The conflict over Italy ended in 1529 with the triumph of the Holy Roman Emperor, Charles V, over the French king. But no sooner was Charles V victorious in Italy than he extended his war to Europe north of the Alps in the name of uniting Christendom. Between 1530 and 1559 central Europe was the stage for another series of exhausting dynastic wars. In the last forty years of the sixteenth century, from 1560 on, any hope for a united Europe was swept away by a rising tide of national consciousness, intensified dynastic rivalries, and bloody religious and civil wars (see Chapter 13).

The Struggle for Italy, 1494–1529

Italy's relative tranquility, established by the Peace of Lodi in 1454, was shattered by the French invasion in 1494. For the next thirty-five years, France, Spain, and the Holy Roman Empire fought among themselves, as well as with the papacy and most of the Italian states, for control of portions of this wealthy peninsula. The struggle began when a newly unified France, anxious to reassert a hereditary claim to Naples and southern Italy, gladly accepted Milan's call for aid in a controversy involving Naples, Florence, and the pope. The French king, Charles VIII (1483–1498), took Florence in 1494, then advanced to Rome and finally to Naples, wreaking havoc as he went.

But the Italians did not back down. Joined by Venice and the pope and supported by the Holy Roman Emperor and the Spanish monarch, they drove the French from Italian soil. The aid of these two foreign rulers was not simply altruistic, however; each had his own goals in Italy. The Spanish king wanted to keep his Sicilian lands intact, and the Holy Roman Emperor was determined to protect his long-standing political interests in Italy.

After the French ruler died, his successor, Louis XII (1498–1515), returned to Italy in 1499 to activate a hereditary claim to Milan. Once again the Spanish and the Germans joined with the Italians to drive the French from Italy. The inability of either side to resolve these conflicts with finality led to intermittent, but inconclusive, invasions of Italy over the next decades under both Louis XII and, after 1515, France's new king, Francis I (1515–1547). In the course of their campaigns, the French rulers, who were enamored of the Italian Renaissance, brought the new artistic and intellectual ideals to northern Europe (Figure 12.2).

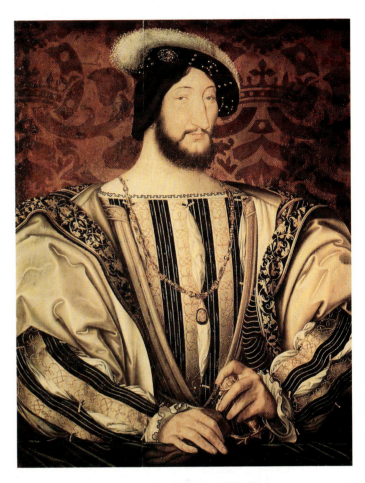

FIGURE 12.2   JEAN CLOUET. *Francis I.* Ca. 1525. Oil on panel, 37¾ × 29⅛". Louvre. *During his thirty-two-year-long reign, Francis I was a major force in sixteenth-century European affairs. He also embarked on a massive artistic program, inspired by the Italian Renaissance, to make his court the most splendid in Europe. Under his personal direction, Italian artworks and artists, including Leonardo da Vinci, were imported into France. Unfortunately, this rather stylized portrait by Jean Clouet, Francis's chief court artist, fails to do justice to this connoisseur of Italian culture. Indeed, the likeness owes more to the conventionalized portraits of the Gothic style than it does to the realistic works of the Italian Renaissance.*

In 1522 full-scale hostilities broke out between France and the Holy Roman Empire over Italy's future. This struggle, the first of several wars fought in different locations, pitted the old Europe against the new. The Holy Roman Empire, ruled by Charles V (1519–1556) of the royal house of Hapsburg, was a ramshackle, decentralized relic from the feudal age. France, under the leadership of the bold and intellectual Francis I of the royal house of Valois, was the epitome of the new sovereign state.

The first Hapsburg-Valois war was the only one to be fought in Italy. Its most notorious moment occurred in 1527 when the troops of Charles V ran riot in Rome, raping, looting, and killing. The sack of

Rome had two major consequences. First, it cast doubt on Rome's ability to control Italy—long a goal of the popes—for it showed that the secular rulers no longer respected the temporal power of the papacy. Second, it ended papal patronage of the arts for almost a decade and thus weakened Rome's role as a cultural leader. It also had a chilling effect on artistic ideals and contributed to the rise of Mannerism.

In 1529 the Treaty of Cambrai brought to a close this first phase of the Hapsburg-Valois rivalry. Twenty-five years of invasions and wars left most of Italy divided and exhausted. Some cities, like Florence and Rome, suffered nearly irreparable harm.

Florence, because it had so much to lose, fared the worst. The city never regained its former power and prestige after opening its gates to the French in 1494. By the 1530s the Medici rulers had resumed power as the Dukes of Florence, but in the power politics of the mid–sixteenth century, they were little more than puppets of the foreigners who controlled much of the peninsula.

In the aftermath of the Treaty of Cambrai, the only important Italian state to keep its political independence was Venice. Because it eluded the ravages of war and because of its stable government and extensive commercial activity in the Mediterranean, this

MAP 12.1

European Empire of Charles V

state became the last haven for artists and intellectuals in Italy for the rest of the sixteenth century.

Charles V and the Hapsburg Empire

By 1530 the struggle between the Valois and the Hapsburgs over the balance of power shifted to central Europe. The French felt themselves to be hemmed in by the Spanish in the south, the Germans to the east, and the Dutch to the north—peoples all ruled by the Hapsburg Emperor Charles V. In French eyes Charles had an insatiable appetite for power that expressed itself through his determination to surround France and to control the Continent through wars and alliances. In contrast, the Hapsburg ruler considered the French king a land-hungry upstart who stood in his way of a Europe united under a Christian prince—in other words, the dream of Christendom. These opposing perceptions prevailed until 1559 when, after a number of exhausting wars and a series of French military victories, the belligerents signed the Treaty of Cateau-Cambrésis. This treaty, recognizing that neither side could prevail, had the happy effect of ushering in a brief period of peace (Map 12.1).

The man who stood in the center of most of these events, Charles V, lived a life filled with paradoxes and ironies (Figure 12.3). Because of the size of his empire, he was in theory one of the most powerful rulers ever to live; but in actuality, again because of the vastness of his lands, he never quite succeeded in gaining complete control of his empire. In some ways, he was the last of medieval kings, for around him were gathered those who wanted a united Christian Europe; on the other hand, he foreshadowed a new age driven by sovereign kings, standing armies, diplomatic agreements, and strong religious differences.

Charles V's unique position at the center of Europe's political storm was the result of a series of timely deaths, propitious births, and politically astute arranged marriages. These circumstances, even before Charles came on the scene, had already permitted the Hapsburg line of rulers, which had existed since the thirteenth century, to accumulate more and more power, wealth, and land. Now, at the opening of the sixteenth century, Charles came into possession of an enormous empire. Born in 1500 to a German father and a Spanish mother, he was the grandson of both the Holy Roman Emperor Maximilian I and the Spanish King Ferdinand V. At the age of six he inherited Burgundy and the Low Countries from his father; at sixteen he received Spain and the Spanish Hapsburg territories in Italy, along with the unimaginable riches of the recently acquired

FIGURE 12.3   TITIAN. *Charles V with a Dog.* Ca. 1533. Oil on canvas, 6'3" × 3'8". Prado, Madrid. *Titian's full-length, standing portrait of Charles V was painted when the Hapsburg emperor was at the height of his power. By rendering the "ruler of the world" in* contrapposto, *his fingers casually holding the collar of his dog, Titian endows the emperor with a natural grace. The lighting that illuminates Charles from the dark background and the breathless hush that seems to envelope the man and dog are trademarks of Titian's style.*

lands in the New World, from his maternal grandfather; and at nineteen he acquired Germany and Austria from his paternal grandfather, which set the stage for his successful bid to become the Holy Roman Emperor. By 1519, Charles V—simultaneously Charles I of Spain—ruled the largest empire the world has ever known. He was referred to by many of his subjects as "ruler of the world."

For most of his life, Charles traveled from one of his possessions to another, fighting battles, arranging peace treaties, and attempting to unify his empire by personal control and compromise. He frequently found that his attention was divided, for he might have to confront the French to the west and at the same time counter a threat from the Ottoman Turks in the east. Thus Charles would find himself caught between two powerful foes who drained both his personal energies and his imperial resources.

Within the Holy Roman Empire, the princes of the German principalities often took advantage of his prolonged absences and his preoccupation with the French and the Turks. They were especially able to gain political power at the emperor's expense after Martin Luther's revolt and the beginning of the Protestant Reformation (see Chapter 13). Charles made matters even worse by his contradictory policies, which often depended on the military pressures he was experiencing: At times he angered the disaffected German princes by meddling in their affairs and condemning Lutheran doctrines, and at other times he angered the popes by making concessions to the Protestants.

Exhausted and disillusioned by his inability to prevail in Europe, Charles abdicated in 1556 and retired to a monastery, leaving his possessions to be divided between his heirs. His brother Ferdinand took control of the German-Austrian inheritance and was soon elected Holy Roman Emperor. His son Philip assumed control of the Spanish Hapsburg holdings, including Spain, the New World territories, and the Netherlands. He became Philip II of Spain. Thus ended Charles's vision of a united Europe and Christendom, which, because of forces beyond his control, had turned into a nightmare of endless meetings, gory battles, and false hopes of peace and unity.

ECONOMIC EXPANSION AND SOCIAL DEVELOPMENTS

By the late fifteenth century Europe was well on the way to full recovery from the impact of the plague (see Chapter 10). The sixteenth century continued to be a time of growing population and increasing prosperity. The center of commerce now shifted from the Mediterranean to the Atlantic coast, making cities like London and Antwerp financial and merchandising centers. Skilled craftspeople turned out quality products, and enterprising merchants distributed these finished goods in increasing quantities across much of western Europe north of the Alps. At the same time, the first steps toward a worldwide market were taken, following the daring sailing expeditions and discoveries of the late fifteenth and early sixteenth centuries. New raw materials from America and innovative ways of manufacturing spurred economic growth.

Although the data are scattered and often unreliable, enough evidence is available to show that the population of Europe increased from about 45 million in 1400 to 69 million in 1500 and to about 89 million by 1600. In a few regions, the population grew at an accelerated pace, as in the Holy Roman Empire, where it rose from about 12 to 20 million. There was also a major population shift from rural to urban areas. This shift was reflected in the rise in the number of cities with populations of over 100,000 from five to eight between 1500 and 1600. Rome, for example, grew from about 50,000 in 1526—the year before the sack—to 100,000 by the end of the century.

Prosperity brought a higher standard of living to most of the urban middle class, but the expanding economy also created some serious problems. The basic problem was that throughout much of the century prices rose faster than wages. Those who were not profiting from increased economic growth, such as poor peasants and impecunious nobles living on unproductive farms, individuals with fixed incomes, and persons in outmoded jobs, suffered the most. In those areas of Europe hardest hit by inflation or agricultural and commercial stagnation, economic crises often became intertwined with social and religious matters that intensified long-standing regional and local differences.

Yet the boom offered economic opportunities to many people. Merchants who were engaged in a variety of businesses and financial arrangements made fortunes for themselves and provided employment for others. These merchants and the bankers who offered loans were also accumulating capital, which they then invested in other types of commercial activity. The campaigns of Charles V were financed by wealthy bankers operating in a well-organized money market. The amassing of surplus capital and its reinvestment ushered in the opening phase of commercial capitalism that laid the foundation for Europe's future economic expansion.

During the first half of the sixteenth century the abundance of raw materials and the vast market potential of the New World had only just begun to affect Europe's economy. South American gold and silver played an important role in the upward price revolution—a development that would go on for decades. Only later, after 1650, would New World agricultural products, such as tobacco, cotton, and cocoa, lead to the production of new manufactured goods and profoundly alter consumer habits.

In one area, however, a major economic change now occurred. Some Europeans, taking advantage of the institution of slavery and the existing slave trade in western Africa, mercilessly exploited the local Africans by buying and shipping them to European colonies in the New World. The slaves were put to work in the gold and silver mines of Central and South America and on the cotton and sugar cane plantations in the West Indies, where they became a major factor in the production of these newly discovered forms of wealth.

FROM HIGH RENAISSANCE TO EARLY MANNERISM

The characteristics of High Renaissance style were largely derived from the visual arts. Led by painters, sculptors, and architects who worshiped ancient Classical ideals, notably those of late-fifth-century B.C. Greece, the High Renaissance was filled with images of repose, harmony, and heroism. Under the spell of Classicism and the values of simplicity and restraint, artists sought to conquer unruly physical reality by subjecting it to the principle of a seemingly effortless order.

Although the visual arts dominated the High Renaissance, literary figures also contributed to this era. From Classicism the High Renaissance authors appropriated two of their chief aesthetic aims, secularism and idealism. Like their ancient predecessors, historians showed that contemporary events arose from human causes rather than from divine action—unmistakable evidence of a mounting secular spirit. Actually, secularism more deeply affected the writing of history than the arts and architecture, where church patronage and religious subjects still held sway. A rising secular consciousness can also be seen in the popular manuals on manners that offered advice on how to become a perfect gentleman or lady. Although they have no coun-

TABLE 12.2   POPES OF THE HIGH RENAISSANCE

Alexander VI	1492–1503
Julius II	1503–1513
Leo X	1513–1521

terpart in ancient literature, these books nevertheless have the Classical quality of treating their subject in idealized terms.

What distinguished the High Renaissance preoccupation with the Classical past from the Early Renaissance's renewed interest in ancient matters was largely a shift in creative sensibility. The Early Renaissance artists, in the course of growing away from the Late Gothic style, had invented new ways of recapturing the harmonious spirit of ancient art and architecture. The geniuses of the next generation, benefiting from the experiments of the Early Renaissance, succeeded in creating masterpieces of disciplined form and idealized beauty. The High Renaissance masters' superb confidence allowed them to produce works that were in harmony with themselves and the physical world—a hallmark of Classical art.

Regardless of its brilliance, the High Renaissance existed for only a fleeting moment in the history of Western culture—from the French invasion of Italy in 1494 until the death of Raphael in 1520 (preceded by the death of Leonardo in 1519) (Time Line 12.1). In this era, the Renaissance popes spared no expense in their patronage of the arts and letters (Table 12.2). After the disasters of the fourteenth century, the papacy seemed to have restored the church to the vitality that it had enjoyed in the High Middle Ages. In reality, however, the popes of the early sixteenth century presided over a shaky ecclesiastical foundation. To the north, in Germany, a theological storm

TIME LINE 12.1   ITALIAN CULTURAL STYLES BETWEEN 1494 AND 1564

1494		1520			1564
	High Renaissance		Early Mannerism		
French Invasion of Northern Italy 1494	Sistine Chapel ceiling frescoes by Michelangelo 1508–1512	Death of Raphael 1520 / Death of Leonardo da Vinci 1519	Publication of Machiavelli's *Prince* 1532	*Last Judgment* fresco in Sistine Chapel by Michelangelo 1536–1541	Death of Michelangelo 1564

was brewing that would eventually split Christendom and destroy the papacy's claim to rule over the Christian world (see Chapter 13). This religious crisis, coupled with increasing tendencies to exaggeration in High Renaissance art and the sack of Rome in 1527, contributed to the development of Mannerism and its spread through Italy and later across western Europe.

Mannerist painters, sculptors, and architects moved away from two of the guiding principles of the High Renaissance: the imitation of nature and the devotion to Classical ideals. In contrast to the High Renaissance masters, Mannerist painters deliberately chose odd perspectives that called attention to the artists' technical effects and their private points of view. Mannerist sculptors, rejecting idealism, turned and twisted the human figure into unusual and bizarre poses to express their own notions of beauty. Likewise, Mannerist architects toyed with the emotions and expectations of their audience by designing buildings that were intended to surprise. Behind the Mannerist aesthetic lay a questioning or even a denial of the inherent worth of human beings and a negative image of human nature, along with a sense of the growing instability of the world.

Literature

The leading writers during the High Renaissance in Italy were all solidly grounded in the Greco-Roman classics, from which they drew their themes and values. Their artistic vision sprang from the Classical virtue of *humanitas*—a term coined by Cicero in antiquity (see Chapter 5) that can be translated as "humanity," meaning the wisdom, humor, tolerance, and passion of the person of good sense. With some reservations, they also believed in Classicism's basic tenet that human nature is inherently rational and good. But even as High Renaissance literature was enjoying its brief reign, the Mannerist works of the Florentine author Niccolò Machiavelli began to appear, at the heart of whose thought is an anti-Classical spirit. Despite his education in Classicism and his strict rationalism, Machiavelli concluded that the human race was irremediably flawed. The contrast between the idealizing spirit of the High Renaissance and the antitraditionalist views of Mannerism can be clearly seen by placing the work of the diplomat and courtier Baldassare Castiglione beside that of Machiavelli. Each wrote a book that can fairly be described as a manual of behavior—but there the resemblance ends.

Castiglione   The reputation of Castiglione [kahs-teel-YOH-nay] (1478–1529) rests on *The Courtier,* one of the most influential and famous books of the High Renaissance. Intended for Italian court society, *The Courtier* was published in 1528 and translated into most Western languages by the end of the century. It quickly became the bible of courteous behavior for Europe's upper classes and remained so over the next two hundred years. Even today, in the late twentieth century, Castiglione's rules for civilized behavior are still not completely outmoded.

A Mantuan by birth, Castiglione (Figure 12.4) based his manual of manners on life at the north Italian court of Urbino, where, between 1504 and 1517, he was the beneficiary of the patronage of its resident duke, Guidobaldo da Montefeltro. Impressed by the graceful conversations of his fellow courtiers and most especially taken with the charms of Urbino's duchess, Elisabetta, Castiglione was moved to memorialize his experiences in writing. *The Courtier* is composed as a dialogue, a literary form originated by Plato and favored by Cicero. Castiglione's dialogue is set in Urbino over a period of four evenings

FIGURE 12.4   RAPHAEL. *Baldassare Castiglione.* 1514. Oil on canvas, 32¼ × 26½". Louvre. *Castiglione was memorialized in this handsome portrait by Raphael, one of the great portrait painters of the High Renaissance. Raphael's debt to Leonardo's portrait style, especially as represented by the* Mona Lisa, *is evident in the half-length, seated pose and the direct gaze of the subject. Elegantly groomed and completely at ease, Castiglione appears here as the age's ideal courtier.*

and peopled with actual individuals for whom he invents urbane and witty conversations that suit their known characters. Despite this realistic touch, his book's overall tone is definitely idealistic and hence expressive of High Renaissance style.

Castiglione's idealism shines forth most clearly in the sections in which the invited company try to define the perfect courtier or gentleman. Under Duchess Elisabetta's eye, the guests cannot agree on which aspect of the ideal gentleman's training should take precedence: education in the arts and humanities or skill in horsemanship and swordplay. Some claim that a gentleman should be first a man of letters as well as proficient in music, drawing, and dance. In contrast, others believe that a courtier's profession was first to be ready for war, and hence athletics should play the central role. At any rate, both sides agreed that the ideal courtier should be proficient in each of these areas. A sign that the Renaissance had raised the status of painting and sculpture was the group's expectation that a gentleman should be knowledgeable about both of these art forms.

The Courtier also describes the perfect court lady. In the minds of the dialogue participants, the ideal lady was a civilizing influence on men, who would otherwise be crude. To this end, the perfect lady should be a consummate hostess, charming, witty, graceful, physically attractive, and utterly feminine. She ought to be well versed in the same areas as a man, except for athletics and the mastery of arms. With these social attributes, the cultivated lady could then bring out the best in a courtier. But she must not seem his inferior, for she contributed to society in her own way.

Castiglione's book turned away from medieval values and led his followers into the modern world. First, he argued that social relations between the sexes ought to be governed by Platonic love—a spiritual passion that surpassed physical conquest—and thus he rejected medieval courtly love and its adulterous focus. Second, he reasoned that women in society should be the educated equals of men, thereby sweeping away the barrier that had been erected when women were excluded from the medieval universities. In the short run, the impact of Castiglione's social rules was to keep women on a pedestal, as courtly love had done. But for the future, his advice allowed women to participate actively in every aspect of society and encouraged their education in much the same way as men's.

Machiavelli   In contrast to Castiglione's optimism, the Florentine Machiavelli [mak-ee-uh-VEL-ee] (1469–1527) had a negative view of human nature and made human weakness the central message of his writings. If *The Courtier* seems to be taking place in a highly re-

fined never-never land where decorum and gentility are the primary interests, Machiavelli returns the reader to the solid ground of political reality. His Mannerist cynicism about his fellow human beings sprang from a wounded idealism, for life had taught him that his early optimism was wrong. His varied works, by means of their frank assessments of the human condition, were meant to restore sanity to a world that he thought had gone mad.

Except for Martin Luther (see Chapter 13), Machiavelli left a stronger imprint on Western culture than any other figure who lived between 1494 and 1564. His most enduring contribution was *The Prince,* which inaugurated a revolution in political thought. Rejecting the medieval tradition of framing political discussions in Christian terms, Machiavelli treated the state as a human invention that ought not necessarily conform to religious or moral rules. He began the modern search for a science of politics that has absorbed political thinkers and policy makers ever since.

Machiavelli's career in sixteenth-century Italy, like that of many writers in antiquity, was split between a life of action and a life of the mind. Between 1498 and 1512 he served the newly reborn Florentine republic as a senior official and diplomat, learning statecraft firsthand. During these turbulent years he was particularly impressed by the daring and unscrupulous Cesare Borgia, Pope Alexander VI's son. In 1512, after the fall of the Florentine republic to the resurgent Medici party, Machiavelli was imprisoned, tortured, and finally exiled to his family estate outside the city. There, as he recounts in one of his famous letters, he divided his time between idle games with the local farmers at a nearby inn and nightly communion with the best minds of antiquity in his study. From this background issued in 1513 the small work known as *The Prince,* which circulated in manuscript until after his death. In 1532 it was finally published.

Machiavelli had several motives in writing this masterpiece. Despairing over Italy's dismemberment by the French and the Spanish kings, he hoped the book would inspire an indigenous leader to unify the peninsula and drive out the foreigners. Enlightened by his personal experience in Florence's affairs, he wanted to capture in writing the truth of the politics to which he had been a witness. And, of equal importance, by dedicating *The Prince* to the restored Medici ruler, he hoped to regain employment in the Florentine state. Like other writers in this age, Machiavelli could not live by his wits but had to rely on secular or religious patronage.

Machiavelli's work failed to gain its immediate objectives: The Medici despot brushed it aside, and Italy remained fragmented until 1870. But as a work that exposed the ruthlessness needed to succeed in practical politics, *The Prince* became an instant, though controversial, success. The book was denounced by religious leaders for its amoral treatment of political power and read secretly by secular rulers for its sage advice. In the prevailing climate of opinion in the sixteenth century, which was still under the sway of Christian ideals, the name "Machiavelli" became synonymous with dishonesty and treachery, and the word *machiavellianism* was coined to describe the amoral notion that "the end justifies any means."

From the modern perspective, this negative valuation of Machiavelli is both too simplistic and too harsh. Above all else he was a clear-eyed patriot who was anguished by the tragedy unfolding in Italy in his day. *The Prince* describes the power politics that the new sovereign states of France and Spain were pursuing in Italian affairs. Machiavelli realized that the only way to rid Italy of foreigners was to adopt the methods of its successful foes. Seeing his countrymen as cowardly and greedy, he had no illusions that a popular uprising would spring up and drive out Italy's oppressors. Only a strong-willed monarch, not bound by a finicky moral code, could bring Italy back from political chaos.

The controversial heart of Machiavelli's political treatise was the section that advised the ruler on the best way to govern. He counseled the prince to practice conscious duplicity, since that was the only way to maintain power and to ensure peace—the two basic goals of any state. By appearing virtuous and upright while at the same time acting as the situation demanded, the prince could achieve these fundamental ends. Machiavelli's startling advice reflected both his involvement in Italian affairs and his own view of human nature.

Painting

In the arts, the period between 1494 and 1564 was preeminently an age of painting, though several sculptors and architects created major works in their respective fields. The Classical values of idealism, balance, and restraint were translated by High Renaissance painters into harmonious colors, naturally posed figures with serene faces, realistic space and perspectives, and perfectly proportioned human bodies. After 1520, Mannerist tendencies became more and more evident, reflected in abnormal subjects, contorted figures with emotionally expressive faces, and garish colors.

Leonardo da Vinci The inauguration of the High Renaissance in painting is usually dated from Leonardo's

The Last Supper, which was completed between 1495 and 1498 (Figure 12.5). Painted for the Dominican friars of the church of Santa Maria delle Grazie in Milan, *The Last Supper* heralded the lucidity and harmony that were the essence of High Renaissance style. In executing the fresco, Leonardo unfortunately made use of a flawed technique, and the painting began to flake during his lifetime. Over the centuries the work has been touched up frequently and restored several times, most recently in the past decade. Nevertheless, enough of his noble intention is evident to ensure the reputation of *The Last Supper* as one of the best known and most beloved paintings of Western art.

Leonardo's design for *The Last Supper* is highly idealized—a guiding principle of the High Renaissance. The fresco depicts the moment when Jesus says that one of the twelve disciples at the table will betray him. Ignoring the tradition that integrated this symbolic meal into an actual refectory, Leonardo separated the scene from its surroundings so that the figures would seem to hover over the heads of the clergy as they ate in their dining room. Idealism is also evident in Leonardo's straightforward perspective. The artist makes Jesus the focal center by framing him in the middle window and locating the vanishing point behind his head. In addition, the arrangement of the banqueting party—Jesus is flanked by six followers on either side—gives the painting a balanced effect. This harmonious composition breaks with the medieval custom of putting the traitor Judas on the opposite side of the table from the others.

A final idealistic touch may be seen in the way that Leonardo hides the face of Judas, the third figure on Jesus' right, in shadow while illuminating the other figures in bright light. Judas, though no longer seated apart from the rest, can still be readily identified, sitting cloaked in shadows, reaching for the bread with his left hand and clutching a bag of silver—symbolic of his treason—in the other hand. For generations admirers have found Leonardo's fresco so natural and inevitable that it has become the standard version of this Christian subject.

Leonardo's setting and placement of the figures in *The Last Supper* are idealized, but his depiction of the individual figures is meant to convey the psychological truth about each of them. Jesus is portrayed with eyes cast down and arms outstretched in a gesture of resignation, while on either side a tumultuous scene erupts. As each disciple reacts to Jesus' charge of treason, Leonardo reveals the inner truth about each one through bodily gestures and facial expressions. Beneath the visual tumult, however, the artistic rules of the High Renaissance are firmly in place. Since neither biblical sources nor sacred tradition offered an ordering principle, Leo-

FIGURE 12.5 LEONARDO DA VINCI. *The Last Supper*. 1495–1498. Oil-tempera on wall, 13'10" × 29'7½". Refectory, Santa Maria delle Grazie, Milan. *Classical restraint is one of the defining characteristics of this High Renaissance masterpiece. Instead of overwhelming the viewer with distracting details, Leonardo reduces the objects to a minimum, from the austere room in which the meal is being celebrated to the simple articles on the dining table. The viewer's gaze is thereby held on the unfolding human drama rather than on secondary aspects of the scene.*

nardo used mathematics to guide his arrangement of the disciples. He divides them into four groups of three figures; each set, in turn, is composed of two older men and a younger one. In his conception not only does each figure respond individually, but each interacts with other group members.

Besides mastering a narrative subject like *The Last Supper*, Leonardo also created a new type of portrait when he painted a half-length view of the seated *Mona Lisa* (Figure 12.6). As the fame of this work spread, other painters (and later, photographers) adopted Leonardo's half-length model as a basic artistic format for portraits. This painting, perhaps the most famous portrait in Western art, was commissioned by a wealthy Florentine merchant. Avoiding the directness of *The Last Supper*, Leonardo hints at the sitter's demure nature through her shy smile and the charmingly awkward gesture of having the fingers of her right hand caress her left arm. In her face, celebrated in song and legend, he blends the likeness of a real person with an everlasting ideal to create a miraculous image. Further heightening the

FIGURE 12.6 LEONARDO DA VINCI. *Mona Lisa*. 1503. Oil on panel, 30¼ × 21". Louvre. *Leonardo's* Mona Lisa, *a likeness of the wife of the merchant Giocondo, illustrates the new status of Italy's urban middle class. This class was beginning to take its social cues from the fashionable world of the courts, the milieu described by Castiglione. Leonardo treats his middle-class subject as a model court lady, imbuing her presence with calm seriousness and quiet dignity.*

FIGURE 12.7   MICHELANGELO. Sistine Chapel Ceiling. (Restored.) 1508–1512. The Vatican. *Michelangelo's knowledge of architecture prompted him to paint illusionistic niches to hold the Hebrew prophets and the pagan sibyls on either side and low pedestals as seats for the nude youths that frame the nine central panels. Neo-Platonism inspired his use of triangles, circles, and squares, for these geometric shapes were believed to hold the key to the mystery of the universe. These various framing devices enabled him to give visual order to the more than three hundred figures in his monumental scheme.*

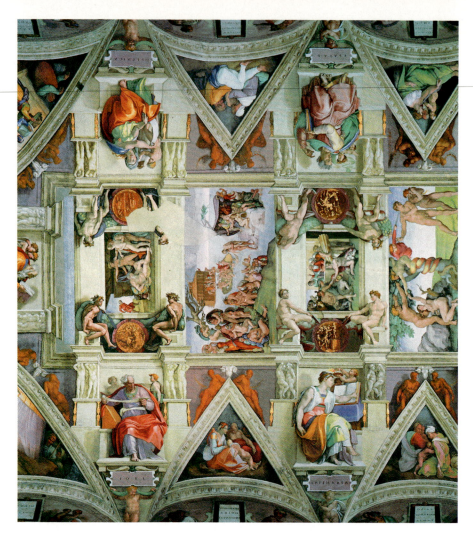

painting's eternal quality, the craggy background isolates the figure in space and time, in much the same way that the grotto functioned in Leonardo's *Virgin of the Rocks* (see Figure 11.20). Finally, he enhances the *Mona Lisa's* mystery by enveloping her in the smoky atmosphere called *sfumato*—made possible by the oil medium—that softens her delicate features and the landscape in the background.

During the High Renaissance, Leonardo's great works contributed to the cult of genius—the high regard, even reverence, that the age accorded to a few select artists, poets, and intellectuals. *The Last Supper* earned him great fame while he was alive. The history of the *Mona Lisa* was more complicated since it was unseen while he lived and found among his effects when he died in 1519. After his death, as the *Mona Lisa* became widely known, first as a possession of the King of France and later as a jewel in the Louvre collection, Leonardo was elevated to membership among the immortals of Western art.

Michelangelo   While Leonardo was working in Milan during most of the 1490s, Michelangelo Buonarroti [my-kuh-LAN-juh-lo bwo-nahr-ROH-tee] (1475–1564) was beginning a career that would propel him to the forefront of first the Florentine and later the Roman Renaissance as well as make him the most formidable

artist of the sixteenth century. Michelangelo's initial fame rested on his sculptural genius, which manifested itself at the age of thirteen when he was apprenticed to the Early Renaissance master Ghirlandaio and then, one year later, taken into the household of Lorenzo the Magnificent, the Medici ruler of Florence. In time Michelangelo achieved greatness in painting and architecture as well as in sculpture, but he always remained a sculptor at heart.

Michelangelo's artistic credo was formed early, and he remained faithful to it over his long life. Sculpture, he believed, was the art form whereby human figures were liberated from the lifeless prison of their surrounding material. In this sense, he compared the sculptor's creativity with the activity of God—a notion that would have been judged blasphemous in prior Christian ages. Michelangelo himself, unlike the skeptical Leonardo, was a deeply pious man given to bouts of spiritual anxiety. His art constituted a form of divine worship.

Central to Michelangelo's artistic vision was his most celebrated image, the heroic nude male. Like the ancient Greek and Roman sculptors whose works he studied and admired, Michelangelo viewed the nude male form as a symbol of human dignity. In the High Renaissance Michelangelo's nudes were based on Classical models, with robust bodies and

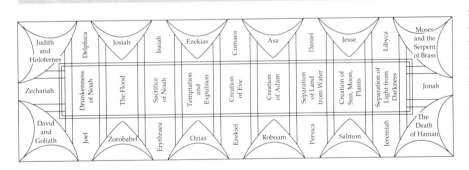

FIGURE 12.8 Plan of Ceiling Frescoes, Sistine Chapel. 1508–1512. *The paintings on the Sistine Chapel ceiling may be grouped as follows: (1) the central section, which presents the history of the world from the creation (called "The Separation of Light from the Darkness") through the "Drunkenness of Noah"; (2) the gallery of portraits on both sides and at either end, which depict biblical prophets and pagan oracles; and (3) the four corner panels depicting Jewish heroes and heroines who overcame difficulties to help their people survive.*

serene faces. But in the 1530s, with the onset of Mannerism, the growing spiritual crisis in the church, and his own failing health, Michelangelo's depiction of the human figure changed. His later nudes were distorted in their bodily proportions and had unusually expressive faces.

In 1508 Michelangelo was asked by Pope Julius II to decorate the Sistine Chapel ceiling. Michelangelo tried to avoid this commission, claiming that he was a sculptor and without expertise in frescoes, but the pope was unyielding in his insistence. The chapel had been built by Julius II's uncle, Pope Sixtus IV, in the late 1400s as a private chapel, and most of the walls had already been covered with frescoes. Mi-

chelangelo's frescoes were intended to bring the chapel's decorative plan closer to completion.

The task presented to Michelangelo by the Sistine Chapel ceiling was enormous, for it was almost 70 feet from the floor, its sides were curved downward, necessitating numerous perspective changes, and its area covered some 5,800 square feet. Michelangelo overcame all of these difficulties, teaching himself fresco technique and working for four years on scaffolding, to create one of the glories of the High Renaissance and unquestionably the greatest cycle of paintings in Western art (Figure 12.7).

Michelangelo, probably with the support of a papal advisor, designed a complex layout (Figure 12.8)

FIGURE 12.9 MICHELANGELO. *The Creation of Adam*, Detail (restored) of the Sistine Chapel Ceiling. 1511. The Vatican. *One of the most celebrated details of this fresco is the outstretched fingers of God and Adam that approach but do not touch. By means of this vivid symbol, Michelangelo suggests that a divine spark is about to pass from God into the body of Adam, electrifying it into the fullness of life. The image demonstrates the restraint characteristic of the High Renaissance style. The Vatican's ongoing restoration of the Sistine Chapel frescoes has revealed the brilliant colors of the original, apparent in this detail.*

for the ceiling frescoes that combined biblical narrative, theology, Neo-Platonist philosophy, and Classical allusions. In the ceiling's long center, running from the altar to the rear of the chapel, he painted nine panels that illustrate the early history of the world, encompassing the creation, fall, and salvation of the human race. Framing each of these biblical scenes were nude youths, whose presence shows Michelangelo's belief that the male form is an expression of divine power. The recent cleaning of the ceiling frescoes, although controversial, has brought out the original color harmonies that had faded over time.

On the long sides he depicted Hebrew prophets and pagan sibyls, or oracles—all foretelling the coming of Christ. The pagan sibyls represent the Neo-Platonist idea that God's word was revealed in the prophecies of pre-Christian seers. At either end of the ceiling he placed four Old Testament scenes of violence and death that had been allegorized as foreshadowing the coming of Christ. Michelangelo unified this complex of human and divine figures with an illusionistic architectural frame, and he painted a plain background to make the figures stand out simply and boldly to the viewer.

The most famous image from this vast work is a large panel from the central section, *The Creation of Adam* (Figure 12.9). In the treatment of this episode from the book of Genesis, Michelangelo reduces the scene to the fewest details, in accordance with the High Renaissance love of simplicity. Adam,

stretched out on a barely sketched bit of ground, seems to exist in some timeless space. Michelangelo depicts Adam as a pulsing, breathing human being. Such wondrous vitality in human flesh had not been seen in Western art since the vigorous nudes of ancient Greek art. In a bold move, Michelangelo ignored the Genesis story that told of God's molding Adam from dust. Instead, the artist paints Adam as half-awakened and reaching to God, who will implant a soul with his divine touch—an illustration of the Neo-Platonic idea of flesh yearning toward the spiritual.

By the 1530s Michelangelo's Mannerist style was in full bloom, triggered by his disappointment with Florence's loss of freedom and his own spiritual torment. In this new style he replaced his heroic vision with a fearful view of the world. A compelling example of this transformation is *The Last Judgment*, a fresco painted on the wall behind the Sistine Chapel's altar. *The Last Judgment* conveys both his own sense of sinfulness as well as humanity's future doom (Figure 12.10). Executed twenty-five years after the ceiling frescoes, *The Last Judgment*, with its images of justice and punishment, also reflects the crisis atmosphere of a Europe divided into militant Protestant and Catholic camps. Michelangelo depicts Jesus as the divine and final judge, standing with right arm raised in a commanding gesture. At the bottom of the fresco, the open graves yield up the dead, and the saved and the damned (on Jesus' right and left, respectively) rise to meet their fate.

FIGURE 12.10 MICHELANGELO. *The Last Judgment.* 1536–1541. 48 × 44'. Sistine Chapel, the Vatican. *This Last Judgment summarizes the anti-Classicism that was sweeping through the visual arts. Other painters studied this fresco for inspiration, borrowing its seemingly chaotic composition, its focus on large numbers of male nudes, and its use of bizarre perspective and odd postures as expressions of the Mannerist sensibility. This fresco was recently restored, its colors returned to the vivid primary colors of Michelangelo's original design and the draperies removed which had been added during the Catholic Reformation; however, problems with the commercial dealer who is negotiating the photography rights with the Vatican prevent the use of an image of the restored painting at this time.*

In this painting Michelangelo abandons the architectural framework that had given order to the earlier ceiling frescoes. Instead, the viewer of *The Last Judgment* is confronted with a chaotic surface on which a circle of bodies seems to swirl around the central image of Jesus. Michelangelo elongates the bodies and changes their proportions by reducing the size of the heads. There is no classical serenity here; each figure's countenance shows the anguish provoked by this dreaded moment. Faced with judgment, some gesture wildly while others look beseechingly to their savior. One of the damned, fearfully and bewilderedly gazing straight ahead, cowers with an upraised hand partly covering his face. In this Mannerist masterpiece, simplicity has been replaced by exuberant abundance and order has given way to rich diversity.

Raphael   The third member of the trio of great High Renaissance painters is Raphael [RAFF-ee-uhl] Santi (1483–1520). Lacking Leonardo's scientific spirit and Michelangelo's brooding genius, Raphael nevertheless had such artistry that his graceful works expressed the ideals of this style more than any other painter. Trained in Urbino, Raphael spent four years (from 1504 to 1508) in Florence, where he absorbed the local painting tradition, learning from the public works of both Leonardo and Michelangelo. Inspired by what he saw, Raphael developed his artistic ideal of well-ordered space in which human beauty and spatial harmony were given equal treatment.

Moving to Rome, Raphael was showered with artistic patronage, especially from the popes. At the heart of Raphael's success was his talent for blending the sacred and the secular, and in an age in which a pope led troops into battle or went on hunting parties, this gift was appreciated and rewarded. Perhaps Raphael's most outstanding work in Rome was the cycle of paintings for the *stanze,* or rooms, of the Vatican apartment—one of the finest patronage plums of the High Renaissance. Commissioned by Julius II, the *stanze* frescoes show the same harmonization of Christianity and Classicism that Michelangelo had brought to the Sistine Chapel ceiling.

Raphael's plan for the four walls of the Stanza della Segnatura in the papal chambers had as their subjects philosophy, poetry, theology, and law. Of these, the most famous is the fresco devoted to philosophy called *The School of Athens* (Figure 12.11). In this work, Raphael depicts a sober discussion among a group of ancient philosophers drawn from all periods. Following Leonardo's treatment of the disciples in *The Last Supper,* Raphael arranges the philosophers in groups, giving each scholar a characteristic gesture that reveals the essence of his thought. For example, Diogenes sprawls on the steps apart from the rest—a vivid symbol of the arch Cynic's contempt for his fellow man. On the right, Euclid, the author of a standard text on geometry, illustrates the proof of one of his theorems. In his careful arrangement of this crowd scene, Raphael demonstrates that he is a master of ordered space.

The School of Athens has a majestic aura because of Raphael's adherence to Classical forms and ideas. The architectural setting, with its round arches, medallions, and coffered ceilings, is inspired by Classical architectural ruins and also perhaps by contemporary structures, though Raphael's conception is not so exact as to be capable of being built. Perfectly balanced, the scene is focused on Plato and Aristotle, who stand under the series of arches at the painting's center. Raphael reinforces their central position by placing the vanishing point just above and between their heads. The two thinkers' contrasting gestures symbolize their philosophies: Plato, on the left, points his finger skyward, suggesting the world of the Forms, or abstract thought, and Aristotle, on the right, motions toward the earth, indicating his more practical and empirical method. Raphael then uses these two thinkers as part of his ordering scheme for dividing philosophy into the arts and sciences. On Plato's side are gathered the poetic thinkers under the statue of Apollo, the Greek god of music and lyric verse; Aristotle's half includes the scientists under the statue of Athena, the Greek goddess of wisdom.

Of even greater fame than Raphael's narrative paintings are his portraits of the Virgin Mary. Raphael's paintings of the Virgin set the standard for this form of portraiture with their exquisite sweetness and harmonious composition. The *Sistine Madonna* is probably the best known of this group (Figure 12.12). This painting shows Raphael at his best, borrowing

from several sources yet creating his own convincing style. It is composed in the pyramid shape first popularized by Leonardo da Vinci (see Figure 11.20). The Virgin's head forms the apex of the pyramid, Pope Julius II (whom the painting memorializes) stands bareheaded on her right, and St. Barbara on her left; the drape of the curtains underscores the pyramidal design. In this funeral scene, Barbara's presence is justified, for she is the patron saint of the arrival of death. Raphael relieves the scene's somber mood by painting below the hovering figures two mischievous

FIGURE 12.12 RAPHAEL. *Sistine Madonna.* 1513. Oil on canvas, 8'8½" × 6'5". Gemäldegalerie, Dresden. *Raphael's use of the rules of Classical art in the* Sistine Madonna *is nowhere more evident than in the painting's balanced composition. Bracketing the central image of the Virgin and Child are a variety of pairings: At the top, two curtains are drawn open; toward the middle, two human figures kneel in prayer; and the open space between the draperies above is echoed by the two angels below. These artful pairings not only give visual variety to the simple scene, but also outline and define the sacred space surrounding the Virgin and Child.*

◄ **FIGURE 12.11** RAPHAEL. *The School of Athens.* 1510–1511. Fresco, 18 × 26'. Stanza della Segnatura, the Vatican. *Much of Raphael's success stemmed from the ease with which he assimilated the prevailing ideas of his age. For instance, the posture of the statue of Apollo against the wall on the left is probably derived from Michelangelo's ''Dying Slave'' (see Figure 12.1), which he must have seen in early drawings. For all of his artistic borrowings, however, Raphael could be very generous, as indicated by the conspicuous way he highlights Michelangelo's presence in this fresco: The brooding genius sits alone in the foreground, lost in his own thoughts and oblivious to the hubbub swirling about him.*

putti, or angels, who look upward, unimpressed with the scene-stealing baby Jesus. Raphael's assured confidence in handling these complex effects makes the *Sistine Madonna* a glowing masterpiece of the High Renaissance.

The Venetian School: Titian   Venice maintained its autonomy during the High Renaissance both politi-

FIGURE 12.13   TITIAN. *Martyrdom of St. Lawrence.* 1550s. Oil on canvas, 16′5½″ × 9′2″. Chiesa dei Gesuiti, Venice. *Even though Titian worked within the High Renaissance style, he was dissatisfied with the symmetry advocated by Classical rules and chose to deviate from strict regularity in his works. In this painting, the temple's columns recede along a diagonal line, creating a sense of deep space in the foreground; within this space, elements are arranged in a triangular shape with the celestial light source at the apex. By using diagonal and triangular lines, as he often did in his religious works, Titian was able to achieve dramatic and emotional effects without sacrificing coherence or meaning.*

cally and culturally. Despite the artistic pull of the Roman and Florentine schools, the Venetian artists stayed true to their Byzantine-influenced tradition of sensual surfaces, rich colors, and theatrical lighting. The greatest of the Venetian painters was Titian [TISH-uhn] (about 1488–1576), who in his later years was revered as Europe's supreme painter. Titian's paintings were prized not only for their easy grace and natural lighting—characteristics of the Venetian High Renaissance—but for the masterful use of rich color to create dramatic effects (see Figure 12.3).

Titian's adherence to the principles of High Renaissance style is evident in such narrative paintings as his *Martyrdom of St. Lawrence* (Figure 12.13). Titian's careful arrangement of this complicated scene of torture and martyrdom reflect his commitment to the principle of simplicity. In the foreground, he depicted St. Lawrence being roasted on a grill; to the right, he painted a pagan temple, rendered in sharply receding perspective, thereby framing the early Christian saint's death scene. The juxtaposition of the dying saint and the Classical temple reminds the viewer that pagan culture had failed in its bid to stamp out Christians and their religion.

Titian's choice of subject in the martyrdom of St. Lawrence was probably inspired by the excesses of the religious wars then raging between Protestants and Catholics, but he resisted the temptation to treat the topic in an exaggerated Mannerist style. Here, as elsewhere in his paintings, Titian builds most of his dramatic effect through the use of rich color. Indeed, his great artistic discovery was that color could express various perceptions of light. In this painting, Titian illuminated the saint's body from scattered light sources—the glowing coals, the flickering torches, and the divine emanation from heaven—to achieve spectacular effects.

The School of Parma: Parmigianino   Parma in northern Italy was another center of High Renaissance art, but the city's best-known artist is Parmigianino [pahr-mee-jah-NEE-noh] (1503–1540), a founder of Mannerism. The *Madonna with the Long Neck* shows Parmigianino's delight in ambiguity, distortion, and dissonance and his love of eccentric composition (Figure 12.14). Mary is portrayed with sloping shoulders and long arms in the manner of Botticelli, and her sensuous figure is not quite hidden under diaphonous draperies—a disturbing mix of sacred and profane love. A similar confusion exists in the depiction of the infant Christ: The bald baby Jesus appears more dead than alive, so that the subject invokes the Pietà image of the dead Christ stretched on his mother's lap along with the image of the Virgin and Child. On the left, five partially dressed figures stare in various directions, apparently not in-

FIGURE 12.14   PARMIGIANINO. *Madonna with the Long Neck.* 1534–1540. Oil on panel, 7'1" × 4'4". Uffizi Gallery, Florence. *This Madonna by Parmigianino is one of the landmark works in the rise of the Mannerist style. Ignoring Classical ideals, Parmigianino exaggerates the Virgin's body proportions, especially the slender hands and long neck, and elongates the body of the sleeping Jesus. This anti-Classical portrait was greatly at odds with the prevailing High Renaissance image of the Madonna established by Raphael.*

teracting with Mary and Jesus. In the background, unfinished columns and an old man reading a scroll, perhaps an allusion to biblical prophecies of Jesus' birth, add to the feeling of multiple focuses and contradictory scales. Unlike the simple and balanced art of the High Renaissance, which offered readily understood subjects, this Mannerist painting, with its uneasy blend of religious piety and disguised sexuality, is exaggerated and enigmatic.

Sculpture

Michelangelo's art is as central to the High Renaissance style in sculpture as it is in painting. An early sculpture that helped to inaugurate this style was the *Pietà,* executed when he was twenty-one (Figure 12.15). The pathetic subject of the **Pietà**—Mary holding the body of the dead Christ—struck a responsive chord in Michelangelo, for he created several

◄ **FIGURE 12.15** MICHELANGELO. *Pietà*. 1498–1499. Marble, ht. 5'8½". St. Peter's, the Vatican. *This* Pietà *is the only one of Michelangelo's sculptures to be signed. Initially it was exhibited without a signature, but, according to a legend, when Michelangelo overheard spectators attributing the statue to a rival sculptor, he carved his signature into the marble strap that crosses and binds Mary's bosom.*

sculptural variations on the Pietà theme during his lifetime.

The first *Pietà*, executed in 1498–1499 at about the same time as Leonardo's *Last Supper*, shows Michelangelo at the height of his creative powers. He has captured completely a bewildering sense of loss in his quiet rendering of Mary's suffering. Everything about the sculpture reinforces the somber subject: the superb modeling of Jesus' dead body, with its heavy head and dangling legs; Mary's outstretched gown, which serves as a shroud; and Mary's body, burdened by the weight of her son. Like some ancient funeral monument, which the *Pietà* brings to mind, this sculpture of Mary and Jesus overwhelms the viewer with its sorrowful but serene mood.

In 1501, two years after finishing the *Pietà*, Michelangelo was given the commission by the city of Florence for the sculpture that is generally recognized as his supreme masterpiece, the *David* (Figure 12.16). Michelangelo was eager for this commission because it allowed him to test himself against other great sculptors who had tackled this subject, such as Donatello in the Early Renaissance (see Figure 11.10). Moreover, Michelangelo, a great Florentine patriot, identified David with the aggressive spirit of his native city. Michelangelo's *David* was instantly successful, and the republic of Florence adopted the statue as its civic symbol, placing the work in the open square before the Palazzo Vecchio, the town hall. Damage to the statue through weathering and local unrest caused the civic leaders eventually to house it indoors, where Michelangelo's most famous sculpture remains today.

Michelangelo's *David*, rather than imitating Donatello's partly clothed and somewhat effete version,

FIGURE 12.16 MICHELANGELO. *David*. 1501–1504. Marble, ht. 14'3". Accademia, Florence. *Michelangelo's colossal David—standing more than 14 feet tall—captures the balanced ideal of High Renaissance art. The "closed" right side with its tensed hanging arm echoes the right leg, which supports the figure's weight; in the same way, the "open" left side with its bent arm is the precise counterpart of the disengaged left leg. Further tension arises from the contrast between David's fixed stare and the grasping motion made by the right fist, which holds the stone. Through these means, Michelangelo reinforces the image of a young man wavering between thought and action.*

FIGURE 12.17 MICHELANGELO. *Pietà*. Before 1555. Marble, ht. 7'8". Santa Maria del Fiore, Florence. *The rage that seemed to cloud Michelangelo's Mannerist vision in* The Last Judgment *appears purged in this* Pietà—*the work he was finishing when he died at the age of eighty-eight. Mannerist distortions are still present, particularly in the twisted body of the dead Christ and the implied downward motion of the entire ensemble. But the gentle faces suggest that serenity has been restored to Michelangelo's art.*

portrays the young Jewish warrior as a completely nude, Classical hero. Taking a damaged and abandoned block of marble, Michelangelo carved the colossal *David* as a muscular adolescent with his weight gracefully balanced on the right leg in Classical contrapposto. The *David* perfectly represents Michelangelo's conception of sculpture; imagining a human figure imprisoned inside marble, he simply used his chisel to set it free.

Michelangelo also made minor deviations from Classical principles in his rendition of David in the name of higher ideals, just as ancient artists had done. David's large hands, for example, are outside Classical proportions and suggest a youth who has yet to grow to his potential. And his furrowed brow violates the Classical ideal of serene faces but reflects his intense concentration.

Michelangelo's later sculpture is Mannerist in style, as is the case with his later paintings. A second *Pietà* group—with Christ, Mary, Mary Magdalene, and Joseph of Arimathea—shows in dramatic fashion his altered notion of the human form (Figure 12.17). In this somber scene, Michelangelo's anti-Classical spirit is paramount. Jesus' body is severely elongated and twisted in death; the other figures, haltingly and with great difficulty, struggle to support his dead weight. But rather than detracting from the sculpture's impact, the awkward body adds to the scene's heavy emotional interest—an aim of Mannerist art, which did not trust the viewer to respond to more orderly images. Joseph, the rich man who, according to the Gospel, donated his own tomb to Jesus, has Michelangelo's face—a face that is more a death mask than a human countenance.

Architecture

The architectural heir to Alberti in the early sixteenth century was Donato Bramante [brah-MAHN-tay] (1444–1514), who became the moving force behind the High Renaissance in architecture. Trained as a painter, Bramante rejected the reigning building style, called **scenographic**, which saw buildings as composed of discrete, individual units. Instead, by concentrating on space and volume, Bramante created an architecture that was unified in all of its components. Furthermore, he wanted a strict Classicism that followed the rules of the Classical orders.

The clearest surviving expression of Bramante's architectural genius is the Tempietto, or little temple, in Rome (Figure 12.18). This small structure was designed both as a church, seating ten worshipers, and as a building marking the site of the martyrdom of St. Peter. Copied from the circular temples of ancient

Rome, this small domed building became the prototype of the central plan church popularized in the High Renaissance and later.

Bramante's design for the Tempietto sprang from ancient Classical principles. Foremost was his belief that architecture should appeal to human reason and that a building should present a severe appearance and not seek to please through specially planned effects. Further, he thought that a building should be unified like a piece of sculpture and that ornamentation should be restricted to a few architectural details.

In accordance with this artistic credo, the Tempietto functions like a work of sculpture; it is raised on a pedestal with steps leading up to its colonnaded porch. In the absence of sculptural decorations, the temple's exterior is accented with architectural details: the columns, the *balustrade*, or rail with supporting posts, and the dome with almost invisible ribs. The proportions of its various features, such as the ratio of column widths to column heights, were computed using ancient mathematical formulas. Unfortunately for Bramante's final conception, the plan to integrate the small temple into a circular courtyard of a nearby church was never completed. Despite the absence of this crowning touch, the Tempietto is one of the jewels of the High Renaissance. Bramante had been commissioned by Pope Julius II to rebuild St. Peter's basilica, the world's most famous church, but he died before his plans could be carried very far.

The supervision of the rebuilding of St. Peter's fell into other architects' hands, and eventually Michelangelo, at the age of seventy-one, was given this vital task. From 1546 until his death in 1564, Michelangelo, among his other artistic tasks, was occupied with St. Peter's, especially with the construction of the dome. Over the years other building projects had come his way, but nothing could compare with the significance of this one. Although the dome was completed after his death, and with some slight modifications, it remains Michelangelo's outstanding architectural monument and a splendid climax to his career.

Michelangelo's sculptural approach to architecture is similar to that of Bramante. In an attempt to integrate the dome of St. Peter's with the rest of the existing structure, Michelangelo uses double Corinthian columns as a unifying agent. Because the facade of St. Peter's was altered in the 1600s, the best location to observe Michelangelo's dome is from the southwest (Figure 12.19). Beginning at ground level,

FIGURE 12.18 BRAMANTE. Tempietto. After 1502. San Pietro in Montorio, Rome. *Bramante's Tempietto is the earliest surviving High Renaissance building and an exquisite example of this style. Fashioned from pure Classical forms, the building is almost devoid of decoration except for architectural features, and the separate parts—dome, cylindrical drum, and base— are brought into a harmonious whole. The only significant missing feature (since High Renaissance buildings were always planned in relation to their enveloping space) is the never-finished courtyard.*

FIGURE 12.20 PALLADIO. Villa Rotonda (Villa Capra). Begun 1550. (Completed by Vincenzo Scamozzi.) Vicenza. *Despite its harmonious proportions and Classical features, the Villa Rotonda belongs to the Mannerist style. Unlike High Renaissance buildings, which were designed to be an integral part of their setting, this boxlike country house stands in an antagonistic relationship to its surrounding garden space. Furthermore, the Mannerist principle of elongation is apparent in its four long stairways. But the Villa Rotonda's most striking Mannerist feature is the surprise inherent in a plan that includes four identical porches, each resembling a Roman temple facade.*

the Corinthian order provides the artistic cement that pulls the entire building together. Sometimes as columns, sometimes as pilasters, and sometimes as ribs, the double Corinthian units move up the walls, eventually up the dome's drum, and up the dome itself.

This plan for St. Peter's shows that Michelangelo the architect differed from Michelangelo the painter and sculptor. In painting and sculpture he had by the 1530s become a Mannerist in his love of exaggeration and expressive effects. But in architecture he stayed faithful to the High Renaissance and its ideal of harmonious design.

The preeminent architect of the Mannerist style was Andrea di Pietro (1508–1580), known as Palladio [pah-LAHD-yo], whose base of operations was Vicenza in northern Italy. The name Palladio derives from Pallas, a name for Athena, the goddess of wisdom. Palladio's artistic creed was rooted in Classicism, but his forte was the richly inventive way in which he could arrange the Classical elements of a

building to guarantee surprise. He played with the effects of light and shadow, adding feature on top of feature, to create buildings that possess infinite variety in the midst of a certain decorative solemnity.

Palladio's most influential domestic dwelling was the Villa Capra, more commonly called the Villa Rotonda because of its central circular area and covering dome (Figure 12.20). Inspired by ancient Roman farmhouses, the Villa Rotonda is a sixteenth-century country house built of brick and faced with stucco and located on a rise overlooking Vicenza. A dome provides a central axis from which four symmetrical wings radiate. Each of the four wings, in turn, opens to the outdoors through an Ionic-style porch raised on a pedestal. The porticoes, or covered porches supported by columns, then lead to the ground level through deeply recessed stairways. Statues stand on the corners and peak of each of the four pediments, while others flank the four stairways (Figure 12.20).

◀ **FIGURE 12.19** MICHELANGELO. Dome of St. Peter's. View from the Southwest. 1546–1564. (Completed by Giacomo della Porta, 1590.) Rome. *Its harmonious design and its reliance on Classical forms made Michelangelo's dome an object of universal admiration when it was completed in 1590, after his death. From then to the present day, other architects have used his dome as a model, hoping to reproduce its Classical spirit.*

Palladio's Mannerist spirit can be seen at work in the design of this building. Although the coldly formal porches are Classical in appearance, no Greek or Roman temple would have had four such identical porches, one on each side of the building (Figure 12.21). Palladio's design incorporates the unexpected and the contradictory within an apparently Classical structure.

Besides designing buildings, Palladio also wrote about architecture in his treatise *Quattro Libri dell'Architettura*, or *The Four Books of Architecture*. Through its English translation, this work gained wide currency and led to the vogue of Palladianism in the English-speaking world. English aristocrats in the eighteenth century commissioned country houses built on Palladian principles, as did plantation owners in America's ante-bellum South.

Music

No radical break separates the music of the High Renaissance from that of the Early Renaissance. Josquin des Prez, the leading composer of the dominant Franco-Netherlandish school, had brought to a climax the Early Renaissance style of music while he was employed in Italy by the popes and local aristocrats (see Chapter 11). Josquin's sixteenth-century pieces, which consist chiefly of religious Masses and motets along with secular *chansons*, or songs, simply heightened the ideal already present in his earlier works: a sweet sound produced by multiple voices, usually two to six, singing a capella and expressing the feelings described in the text. Despite his interest in music's emotional power, Josquin continued to subordinate the song to the words—thus reflecting the needs of the church, the foremost patron of the age. This balancing act between the music and the words, resulting in a clearly sung text, was also evidence of the Classical restraint of his High Renaissance style. A striking feature of this style was the rich multichoral effect produced when the singing group was subdivided into different combinations of voices.

Experimentation with choral effects was carried into the next generation by Adrian Willaert [VIL-art] (about 1490–1562), a member of the Netherlandish school and a disciple of Josquin's. After the death of

FIGURE 12.21 PALLADIO. Floor Plan of the Villa Rotonda. *Palladio designed the Villa Rotonda to further the social ambitions of its wealthy Venetian owner, so he made its most prominent interior feature a central circular area, or rotunda. Surmounted by a dome, this area was ideal for concerts, parties, and other entertainments. Palladio surrounded the rotunda with four identically shaped sets of rooms on two levels where the family lived and guests were housed. Passageways led to the four porches, where villa residents could obtain relief from the summer's heat and enjoy diverting views of the surrounding countryside.*

FIGURE 12.22 HANS BURGKMAIR. *Maximilian with His Musicians.* Illustration from *Der Weisskunig.* Sixteenth Century. Woodcut. Metropolitan Museum of Art, New York. Gift of William Loring Andrews, 1888. *This woodcut depicts the Holy Roman Emperor Maximilian surrounded by his court musicians. Among the instruments being played are an organ, a flute, a harp, and a harpsichord-type instrument. On the table top at the right are a viol, recorders, and a cromorne (a curved instrument with a double reed), and piled together in the right foreground are a lute, drums, a kettledrum, and an ancestor of the slide trombone. Rounding out this musical scene is the quartet of singers in the upper left.*

his mentor, Willaert was probably Europe's most influential composer. He made his mark on musical history from his post as chapel master of the cathedral of St. Mark's in Venice, and he is considered the founder of the Venetian school of music. Taking advantage of St. Mark's two organs and the Venetian practice of blending instruments with voices, he wrote music for two choirs as well. By a variety of musical mechanisms, such as alternating and combining voices, contrasting soft and loud, and arranging echo effects, Willaert created beautiful and expressive sounds that were the ancestor of the splendid church concertos of the Baroque era. A benefit of Willaert's innovations was that the organ was released from its sole dependence on vocal music.

Except for the stylistic perfection brought about by Josquin and Willaert, the musical scene during this period witnessed only minor changes from the

Early Renaissance. Instrumental music still played a secondary role to the human voice, though Josquin and Willaert composed a few pieces for specific instruments, transposing melodies that had been originally intended for singers.

The development that had the most promise for the future was the invention of families of instruments, ranging from the low bass to the high treble, which blended together to make a pleasant sound (Figure 12.22). In most cases, these families, called **consorts**, consisted either of recorders or viols. This step was important because the consorts represented the principle of the mixed instrumental ensemble, and from this beginning would emerge the orchestra. Recorders and viols could also be blended together to make an agreeable sound; when human voices were added to the mixture, the conditions were ripe for opera.

The Legacy of the High Renaissance and Early Mannerism

From a contemporary perspective, the seventy-year period during which the High Renaissance and Early Mannerism flourished is the golden age of the West in certain artistic and humanistic areas. In the visual arts—painting, sculpture, and architecture—standards were set and indelible images created that have not been surpassed. In political theory, this age produced the Mannerist thinker Machiavelli, who is the founder of modern political thought, just as Plato and Aristotle launched the ancient tradition of political speculation.

Beyond these achievements, two other important steps were being taken on the road to the modern world. On a political level, the beginnings of the modern secular state may be seen in the changes taking place in France, Spain, and England. What was innovative, even revolutionary, for these countries in the early sixteenth century has become second nature to the states of the twentieth century, both in the Western world and beyond. On a social level, a new code of behavior appeared in the Italian courts and was in time adopted throughout Europe. Not only did the rules of courtesy finally penetrate into the European aristocracy and alter their behavior, but they eventually trickled down to the middle classes. By our day, the behavior of Castiglione's courtier and lady, though in diluted form, has become the model for all Western people with any shred of social ambition.

Another new idea was beginning to develop now as well. The Classical and medieval worlds had praised what was corporate and public, in conformity with traditional, universal values. But in the 1500s a few artists and humanists, along with their patrons, began to revere what was individual and private. The supreme example of free expression and of the "cult of genius" in the High Renaissance was Leonardo da Vinci, whose encoded notebooks were meant for his personal use and not for general publication. Early Mannerism carried individual expression to extremes by finding merit in personal eccentricities and unrestrained behavior. That patrons supported the new works of these artists and humanists demonstrates the rise of the belief that free expression is both a social and a private good. The High Renaissance and Early Mannerism both encouraged the daring idea of individualism and thereby set in motion a trend that has been building in Western culture ever since.

KEY CULTURAL TERMS

High Renaissance
Mannerism
machiavellianism
putti

Pietà
scenographic
balustrade
consort

SUGGESTIONS FOR FURTHER READING

PRIMARY SOURCES

CASTIGLIONE, B. *The Book of the Courtier.* Translated by G. Bull. New York: Penguin, 1967. A flowing translation; includes a helpful introduction and descriptions of characters who participate in the conversations recorded by Castiglione; first published in 1528.

MACHIAVELLI, N. *The Prince.* Translated by G. Bull. New York: Penguin, 1971. The introduction covers Machiavelli's life and other writings to set the stage for this important political work; written in 1513.

SUGGESTIONS FOR LISTENING

WILLAERT, ADRIAN (about 1490–1562).
Willaert is particularly noted for his motets, such as *Sub tuum praesidium,* which reflect the Renaissance humanist ideal of setting the words precisely to the music. His *Musica nova,* published in 1559 and including motets, madrigals, and instrumental music, illustrates the complex polyphony and sensuous sounds that made him a widely imitated composer in the second half of the sixteenth century.

13

THE RELIGIOUS REFORMATIONS, NORTHERN HUMANISM, AND LATE MANNERISM

1500—1603

While Italy was experiencing the High Renaissance, Germany became the epicenter of the spiritual earthquake called the *Reformation*, a movement that forever shattered the religious unity of the West. Like the Renaissance, the Reformation looked to the past for inspiration and ideals. But unlike the artists and intellectuals of the Renaissance, who found models in the Classical world of Greece and Rome, the religious leaders of the Reformation looked to the early Christian church before it became hierarchical and bureaucratic to clarify their beliefs and to purify ecclesiastical practices. Almost immediately they met with unbending resistance from the contemporary church and its officials. From the ongoing confrontations between these hostile groups emerged the labels the two sides still wear today: the Protestants, who wanted a complete renovation of the church, and the Roman Catholics, who were largely satisfied with things as they were.

The Catholics did not oppose all change. In the second half of the sixteenth century they conducted their own reforms, known as the *Counter-Reformation*, purifying the church and setting it on the path that it followed until the 1960s. In contrast, the Protestants disagreed over basic Christian doctrines and soon split into rival sects that went their separate ways. This sectarian tendency has remained an element in Protestantism until the present day.

This chapter brings to conclusion the story of the Renaissance, which first began in Italy in about 1400. The Renaissance, now in its Mannerist phase, moved north and to Spain in the early sixteenth century. The early stages of the Northern Renaissance and the Protestant Reformation unfolded within the broader political context examined in the last chapter. As the reforming zeal spread from Germany to France, Switzerland, the Low Countries, Scandinavia, England, and Scotland, the movement became bound up with local and international politics. Soon both the Protestants and the Catholics were swept into the dynastic and religious wars that dominated foreign affairs during this period.

This chapter picks up the thread of these events with the beginning of the reign of Charles V's son, Philip II, in Spain in 1556. For the rest of the century Europe's quarreling royal houses were polarized into two religious camps, with both sides looking for help from their coreligionists. Generally, the Catholics were led by Philip II, while the Protestants rallied around German princes or the English monarch Elizabeth I. The forces supporting the popes and the church managed to stop the expansion of Protestantism and win back many adherents, though not without widespread religious wars. By 1603 the religious map of Europe had settled into the Protestant and Catholic pattern that still exists today.

◀ PIETER BRUEGEL THE ELDER. *Wedding Dance.* 1566. Oil on panel, 47 × 62". Detroit Institute of Arts.

TIME LINE 13.1   THE RELIGIOUS REFORMATIONS OF THE SIXTEENTH CENTURY

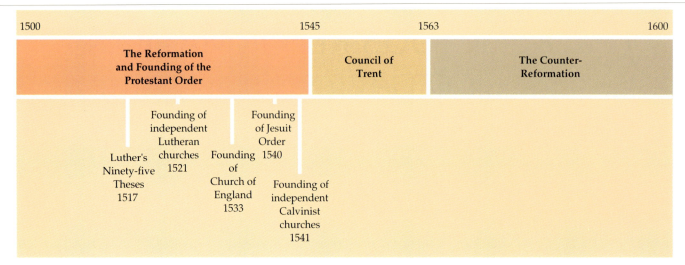

MAP 13.1

The Religious Situation in Europe in 1560

THE BREAKUP OF CHRISTENDOM: CAUSES OF THE RELIGIOUS REFORMATIONS

Although the reasons for the breakup of Europe's religious unity are complicated and the ensuing events of the sixteenth century often confusing, two basic causes for this change are nevertheless clear: the radical reshaping of Western society and culture that began in about 1350 and the timeless spiritual yearnings of human beings. After 1500 these two forces came together in Germany to make conditions ripe for a religious explosion.

What made some modification in religion seem unavoidable were the historical trends that had become entrenched features of Europe during the Late Middle Ages. Especially contributing to the growing need for change were the presence of unrelieved corruption and abuses inside the church, the rise of sovereign states, the decay of medieval thought, and the revival of humanism.

The church had been plagued with problems since the Avignon papacy and the Great Schism of the fourteenth century and the challenges to its time-honored practices posed by the growth of heretical groups like the Hussites (see Chapter 10). Without firm guidance from the popes, many clergy led less than exemplary lives, particularly those inside the monasteries. Lay writers, now unafraid of the church, delighted in describing clerical scandals, and the populace gossiped about their priests' latest sins. Everywhere anticlericalism seemed on the rise.

Perhaps the church could have reformed the clergy and stemmed the tide of anticlericalism if the papacy had been morally and politically strong, but such was not the case. By 1500 the popes were deeply distracted by Italian politics and fully committed to worldly interests. Another factor leading to the church's decline was its loss of power to secular rulers who were determined to bring all of their subjects under state control. By 1500 the English and French kings, to the envy of other rulers, had made their national churches free of papal control in major ways. In England the crown regulated clerical assignments and forbade judicial appeals to Rome. France was even more independent, for the kings gained control of priestly appointments, along with the ecclesiastical courts and taxes.

In Germany, however, where no unified nation-state developed, the local political leaders did not have the power to dictate terms to the church, a fact that only intensified anticlericalism and hatred of Rome. The German princes, perceiving the popes and their Italian representatives as power hungry and greedy for gain, made church reform a rallying cry. Rebuffed by ecclesiastical officials, these German rulers, who already were struggling to be free from the control of Holy Roman Emperor Charles V, now turned against Rome and made the first rupture with the church. As events unfolded, the popes proved incapable of preventing these princes from converting their lands into independent states outside of papal jurisdiction (Map 13.1).

The Protestant Order

Rooted in the problems confronting the church and spurred on by theological issues, Protestantism erupted in Germany, where Martin Luther led a first generation to found a new religious sect in the 1520s. In the 1530s a second generation acted on the opportunity created by Luther. John Calvin, a French scholar, formed an independent church in Geneva, Switzerland, and King Henry VIII removed the English church from Roman rule (Time Line 13.1).

Luther's Revolt One of the church's most glaring abuses, dating from the High Middles Ages, was the buying and selling of indulgences, which were pardons that reduced part or all of the time that Christians had to spend doing penance in atonement for their sins. The practice was based on the idea of a Treasury of Merit that held the inexhaustible surplus grace of Jesus and the saints. Through the sacraments of confession and penance, people could be forgiven for their sins during their lifetime, but after they died they still had to spend time in purgatory. To limit the time spent doing penance either on earth or in purgatory and thus speed up admission to heaven, the popes established indulgences, drawn on the Treasury of Merit. Indulgences were given to those who performed good deeds, such as going on crusades, and to those who gave money to the church.

THE NINETY-FIVE THESES In 1517 the Archbishop of Mainz offered indulgences for sale to raise money, and Martin Luther (1483–1546), a monk teaching at nearby Wittenberg University, responded by compiling his famous Ninety-five Theses (Figure 13.1). These were questions and arguments about the legitimacy of indulgences, and they implicitly challenged the sacraments of confession and penance and the authority of the pope. Luther had simply hoped to arouse a debate in the university, but instead he ignited a firestorm of criticism against the church and placed himself in the vanguard of a reform movement.

FIGURE 13.1   LUCAS CRANACH THE ELDER. *Martin Luther.* 1520. Copper engraving, 138 × 97 mm. The Metropolitan Museum of Art, New York. Gift of Felix Warburg, 1920. *This portrait of Martin Luther, with its vivid rendering of his steel jaw and piercing eyes, shows some of the qualities that made him such a force to be reckoned with during the Reformation. The admiring likeness was done by the German artist Lucas Cranach, a supporter of the new faith and a close friend of Luther's. At the time of this engraving, the Reformation was barely underway; the thirty-seven-year-old Luther was still in communion with the church in Rome and a member of a monastic order.*

The church's response to Luther was initially hesitant, but in 1520 Pope Leo X excommunicated him. When Luther burned the papal document of excommunication in public, the church branded him a heretic and an outlaw. During this trouble and later, Luther survived because he was under the protection of his patron, Elector Frederick the Wise of Saxony. Frederick's support was based on mixed motives, since he also led the German princes who opposed the Holy Roman Emperor (Figure 13.2).

Luther's attack on indulgences arose from a spiritual quest that he had begun many years earlier. Obsessed by his sins, Luther had become a monk but had failed to find peace of mind. Through study, however, he reached the understanding that salvation came not because of good works but from God's unmerited love, or grace, or, as Luther phrased it, "justification by faith alone." "The just shall live by faith" (Romans 1:17) were the words that finally calmed Luther's soul; salvation would be achieved only by faith in Jesus' sacrificial death. Luther's belief led him to conclude that buying indulgences was trying to buy salvation—a direct contradiction of the biblical truth he had experienced in his theological studies.

LUTHER'S BELIEFS   In his theology, which came to be known as *Lutheranism*, Luther tried to revive primitive Christianity—practices and beliefs based on biblical precedents and reminiscent of the early church. He believed that the sole source of religious authority was the Bible, not the pope or church councils. He also thought that people could lead simple lives of piety and repentance without the benefit of priests to mediate with God. Since he viewed good works as unnecessary for salvation, he rejected such age-old practices as viewing relics, fasting, making pilgrimages, and abstaining from meat on Fridays. Along with indulgences, he repudiated the mystical definition of the sacraments, the notion of purgatory, the adoration of the saints, and Masses for the dead. In his pared-down sacramental system he retained only baptism and the Lord's Supper, as he called the Eucharist. Preaching in German became the heart of the liturgy, replacing the Latin Mass in importance.

SOCIAL AND POLITICAL IMPLICATIONS OF LUTHER'S REVOLT The Ninety-five Theses circulated widely throughout Germany, and in 1521 Lutheran churches sprang up in Wittenberg and in most other German towns. Simultaneously, radical followers fomented new problems,

FIGURE 13.2   ALBRECHT DÜRER. *Elector Frederick the Wise.* 1524. Copper engraving. Print collection, Miriam and Ira D. Wallach Division of Art, Prints, and Photographs, The New York Public Library, Astor, Lenox, and Tilden Foundations. *Dürer's portrait captures the princely bearing of Frederick the Wise, the ruler of Electoral Saxony and Luther's great patron. Ironically, Frederick owned one of the largest collections of relics in Christendom. It has been estimated that the 17,443 artifacts in the Elector's collection in 1518 could reduce the time in purgatory by 127,799 years and 116 days.*

FIGURE 13.3 HANS BROSAMER. *Katherine von Bora.* Second Quarter of the Sixteenth Century. Woodcut, 37.1 × 28.9 cm. The British Museum, London. *Katherine von Bora was one of a dozen nuns liberated from a convent near Wittenberg in the heady days of 1523. She joined the mixed collection who lived with Luther in the Black Cloisters, his old monastery given him by Frederick the Wise. Despite Luther's protests, she determined to become his wife, and she did. He treated her with great deference, calling her "My lord Kate," though he poked fun at her supposed greed for property.*

powerful than their predecessors, since their powers were not limited by Rome.

LUTHER'S BIBLE   Luther's voluminous writings constitute the largest legacy of any German author. Luther's German Bible holds first place, in terms of its enduring influence, among his vast output of tracts, essays, and letters. Although nineteen German Bibles were in print by 1518, Luther's version quickly drove the others from the field and gradually left its stamp on the German language. The secret of Luther's approach was his pithy style, which engaged the reader's emotions with everyday images and idiomatic speech.

The Reforms of John Calvin   The first generation of Protestant reformers now gave way to a second generation, active in the 1530s. The most influential reformer among this second generation was John Calvin (1509–1564) (Figure 13.4). After earning a law degree in Paris, he experienced a religious conversion and cast his lot with the cause of the Reformation. Coming under the suspicion of the French authorities, he fled to

FIGURE 13.4   ANONYMOUS. *John Calvin.* 1550s. Bibliothèque Publique et Universitaire de Geneva. *This anonymous portrait of Calvin shows the way that he probably wanted to be viewed rather than a natural likeness. Still, the angular features, the intense gaze, and set mouth suggest that the reputation Calvin had for strict discipline was justified. The florid beard and fur collar, although typical of middle-class fashion of the era, create an ironic contradiction in this otherwise austere portrait.*

causing riots, driving priests from their homes, closing down monasteries, and destroying religious images. In his sermons Luther made it clear that he rejected this violence and advocated moderation. He did accept the abolition of monasticism, however, dropping the monk's habit in 1523 and two years later marrying Katherine von Bora, a former nun (Figure 13.3). When he and his wife had children, he created a familial tradition for Lutheran clergy.

Luther distanced himself not just from violence but from the political and social reforms espoused by some of his followers. In 1523 a brief Peasants' War erupted under the banner of Luther's faith, but Luther responded with a diatribe urging suppression of the workers by any means, thereby clearly showing his preference for the status quo. His reliance on Saxony's rulers for protection set the model for his religion; in the Lutheran faith, the church acted as an arm of the state, and the clergy's salaries were paid from public funds. Luther's revolt did not embrace individualism in the political or social arena; indeed, the Protestant princes were more

Basel, Switzerland, a Lutheran center, where he began to publish *The Institutes of the Christian Religion*. In its final form, this work became a theological document of immense importance.

CALVIN'S BELIEFS In his theology (*Calvinism*), Calvin, like Luther, advocated beliefs and practices having biblical roots. Calvin agreed with most of Luther's positions regarding the proper Christian faith, but because Calvin differed from Luther over the nature of God, church-state relations, and Christian morals, he blazed a new religious path. Calvin's religious thought rested on his concept of an awesome, even angry, God, which led him to make predestination (the belief that God predestines certain souls to salvation and others to damnation) a central tenet of his faith. Calvin also espoused a theocratic state in which the government was subordinate to the church. Within this state, he favored strict ethical demands that went beyond routine civic laws, regulating everything from laughter in church to public shows of affection between the sexes. Because of these and similar rules, which later became associated with the religious reform movement known as *Puritanism*, Calvinism acquired the reputation for being a joyless creed.

THE IMPACT OF CALVIN'S BELIEFS ON SOCIETY More important than the puritanical streak in Calvin's theology was the impact his thought had on political, social, and economic life in the sixteenth century and beyond. Calvin's ascetic rules for good Christian behavior encouraged the qualities of thrift, industry, sobriety, and discipline—precisely the same traits that made for business success. Calvin's teachings had the effect of spurring on the Christian capitalist in his accumulation of wealth, so that gradually there developed the idea that worldly success was tantamount to God's approval and poverty a sign of God's disfavor.

THE SUCCESS OF CALVINISM Of all the new sects, Calvinism was the most international, as reformed congregations spread across Europe, with Scotland and the Netherlands representing the greatest successes (see Map 13.1). The readiness of Calvin's followers to oppose tyranny with arms made them dangerous everywhere. In France, Calvinist nobles resisted the power of the French crown, and in England the Puritans questioned Queen Elizabeth's royal prerogative. Less disruptive and smaller minorities also emerged in Poland, Hungary, and Transylvania.

The Reform of the English Church A second major religious reformer in the 1530s was King Henry VIII (1509–1547), who founded the Church of England, or the Anglican church, as it is also known. As was the

case with the other Protestant sects, the formation of this church was bound up with politics. In 1529 Henry asked the pope to annul his marriage to Catherine of Aragon, who, though she had given him a daughter, had failed to produce a male heir. In Henry's eyes, Catherine's failure was a divine punishment for his sin of having married his dead brother's widow—an incestuous union in the eyes of the church. In favorable times, the pope might have given Henry a dispensation, but now his hands were tied. The troops of Holy Roman Emperor Charles V, Catherine's nephew, had just sacked Rome and virtually imprisoned the pontiff. And because Charles opposed any step that would nullify his aunt's marriage and make her daughter a bastard, Henry had to seek relief elsewhere. In 1533,

FIGURE 13.5 MARCUS GHEERAERTS THE YOUNGER. *Elizabeth I.* Late Sixteenth Century. Oil on panel, 7'11" × 5'. National Portrait Gallery, London. *The so-called Ditchley portrait presented Queen Elizabeth in all her Renaissance finery. Following the Spanish fashion, the queen wears a neck ruff and yards of pearls, and she carries a fan. Her impossibly thin waist underscores her well-known vanity. She stands atop a map of England, even as in life she ruled her troubled land with compassion and firmness.*

after four years of failed strategies, Henry pushed through Parliament the laws setting up the Church of England with himself as the head.

Although *Anglicanism* was founded by Henry VIII, the ground had been prepared locally by Christian humanists and English Lutherans. The work of both these groups led to the so-called Reformation Parliament (1529–1535), which had begun to reform the English church even before Henry made the decisive break with Rome.

After Henry's death, religious turmoil followed, and the fate of the English reformation stayed in doubt until his daughter Elizabeth (1558–1603) became queen (Figure 13.5). In 1559 Elizabeth resolved the religious crisis, with the aid of Parliament, by steering a middle course between Catholicism and Calvinism, which had gained many English converts. With Elizabeth as its head, the Anglican church honored only the sacraments of baptism and the Lord's Supper, allowed clerical marriage, and adopted English as the language of worship. Anglican beliefs were summarized in the Thirty-nine Articles, and people who wished to sit in Parliament, earn university degrees, or serve as military officers had to swear allegiance to them. Hence, Calvinists (who in England were known as nonconformists and dissenters) and Roman Catholics were legally excluded from English public life and remained so for almost 275 years. Elizabeth refrained from persecuting nonconformists, however, as long as they publicly observed certain rituals of the Church of England.

The Counter-Reformation

Before Martin Luther took his stand in Germany, a Roman Catholic reform movement had begun quietly in isolated parts of Europe. But with the surprising successes of the various Protestant groups, the centuries-old church was forced to fight for its very existence. Spurred on by the loss of virtually half its members to Protestantism, the Roman Catholic church, as it was now called, struck back with a Counter-Reformation. By 1600 this superbly organized campaign had slowed Protestantism and won back many adherents. The Catholics held on to southern Europe and most of central Europe, halting Protestantism's spread in Poland, France, and Switzerland and limiting the movement to the northern third of Europe plus Scotland and England.

The Counter-Reformation proceeded simultaneously on three fronts: a revitalized papacy, new monastic orders, and an effective reforming council. Together these forces confronted the Protestant threat

TABLE 13.1   THE COUNTER-REFORMATION POPES

Paul III	1534–1549
Julius III	1550–1555
Marcellus II	1555
Paul IV	1555–1559
Pius IV	1560–1565
Pius V	1566–1572
Gregory XIII	1572–1585
Sixtus V	1585–1590
Gregory XIV	1590–1591
Clement VIII	1592–1605

and purified the church of abuses and reorganized its structure.

The Reformed Papacy   With the reign of Pope Paul III (1534–1549), there appeared a series of reform-minded popes who reinvigorated the church (Table 13.1). To counter the inroads made by Protestantism, Paul enlisted the support of the full church by convening a council representative of Roman Catholic clergy from all over Europe and launched new monastic orders that tapped the springs of religious enthusiasm bubbling up among the faithful.

Paul's successors perpetuated his policies, supporting the work of the council and implementing its decrees. As a result, they reclaimed the moral leadership of the church and reorganized the internal workings of the papal bureaucracy so that discipline was now enforced throughout the ecclesiastical hierarchy. Sensing that Protestantism would not go away and recognizing the increasing availability of books and other written material now that the printing press had appeared, these popes tried to isolate the church from deviant ideas. A committee of churchmen was established for the purpose of drawing up a list of books that were forbidden to Roman Catholic readers because they were thought to be prejudicial to faith or morals. The first Index of Forbidden Books, as this list was called, included the works of Luther, Calvin, and other Protestants, along with writings that were condemned as obscene. In the long run this tactic failed to suppress hated ideas, but the Index continued to be brought up to date until the 1960s.

New Monastic Orders   The second major way in which the Counter-Reformation was effected was through the work of new religious orders. Since the High Middle Ages monastic reform had played only a small role in the life of the church. Indeed, the growth of Pietism in northern Europe during the Late Middle Ages could be, and was, read as a criticism of the existing monastic system. Suddenly in the sixteenth century it was as if a dam had burst, and new monastic groups arose to fill a variety of needs, such as preparing men and women to minister directly to the masses and reclaiming lapsed believers to the faith.

The most significant and influential new order was the Society of Jesus, commonly known as the *Jesuits*. Founded during the pontificate of Paul III, the Jesuits had emerged by 1600 as the church's major monastic order with special blessings from the popes. The dedicated members helped to curb Protestantism in Europe, and their missionary efforts

abroad represented the first steps in making Roman Catholicism a global faith. After a shaky beginning, their rise to power was quick, and their success depended very much on the order's founder, Ignatius Loyola.

The life of the Spaniard Ignatius Loyola (about 1493–1556) was imbued with more than a touch of medieval knight errantry (Figure 13.6). His first calling was as a professional warrior, defending his country from invaders. When in 1521 a battle wound left him crippled for life, he underwent a religious conversion that eventually led him to become a "soldier" in the army of Christ. Overpowered with a need to serve God but uncertain of the path to take, he cast about for a number of years until he settled on founding the Society of Jesus. This society resembled a military company more than a monastic order in its rigid hierarchy, close discipline, and absolute obedience to the founder. Pope Paul III gave the order his official recognition in 1540.

The Jesuits were initially concerned with working among the unchurched and the poor, focusing especially on teaching their children. But their mission changed somewhat in the 1540s when they began to take the Christian message to the lands just being reached by European explorers and adventurers. Guided by the Spaniard Francis Xavier [ZAY-vee-uhr] (1506–1552), they established outposts in the Far East and converted thousands to the Christian faith. Other Jesuits had similar success in missions to North and South America.

What especially set the Jesuits apart from other monastic orders was their special vow of loyalty to the pope, a relationship that in later years led them to be called "the shock troops of the papacy." Because of this special connection and their expertise in education, the Jesuits soon became the church's chief weapon against the Protestants. In their writings, the Jesuits answered the church's critics, setting forth their orthodox beliefs in a clear and straightforward manner.

FIGURE 13.6 ATTRIBUTED TO JUAN DE ROELAS. *St. Ignatius Loyola*. 1622. Oil on canvas, ca. 7'3" × 5'6". Museo Provincial de Bellas Artes, Seville, Spain. *This portrait, painted the year Loyola was canonized and nearly seventy-five years after his death, evokes the determination and strength of the founder of the Society of Jesus. In his right hand Ignatius holds the graphic symbol of Jesus' name, and under his left arm he carries a Bible. Posthumous portraits such as this one were not intended to be exact likenesses but were designed to confirm the high status of the distinguished subject.*

The Council of Trent The third force contributing to the Counter-Reformation was the reform established by the council conducted at Trent in northern Italy, meeting in three separate sessions between 1545 and 1563. Dominated by papal supporters, Italian delegates, and the Jesuits, the Council of Trent offered no sympathy to the Protestants and thus accepted the split in Christian Europe as an unfortunate fact of life. The council reaffirmed all of the practices comdemned by the Protestants, such as monasticism, indulgences, and relics, though mechanisms were set in motion for purifying them of abuses. Clerical reform, notably strengthening education, was another step taken at Trent.

The basis of the council's unyielding position in regard to the Protestants arose from the belief that the Bible and church tradition—not the Bible alone as advocated by the Protestants—were the bases of authority and the word of God. To the council, the Vulgate was the official and only Bible as interpreted by the church, and all other versions were rejected. The council agreed that salvation should be sought by faith *and* by good works—not by faith alone, as the Protestants claimed. The council also reaffirmed the seven sacraments. The power of the bishops was expanded at the diocesan level, but the bishops now came under additional papal influence as the pontiffs tightened their control. The moral, doctrinal, and disciplinary results of the Council of Trent laid the foundations for Roman Catholic policies and thought right up to the present.

Warfare as a Response to Religious Dissent, 1520–1603

As religious dissent spread, the secular rulers watched with mounting fears stemming from the obvious threats associated with heresy and from the unquestioned assumption that a single religion should exist within each community and buttress its institutions, especially the state. Until 1530 compromise between the Lutheran rebels and the dominant faith seemed possible, but with the constant growth of mutually hostile sects, warfare became the usual means for secular rulers to deal with the crisis.

In Chapter 12 the wars of Charles V were presented from the viewpoint of clashing dynastic houses—the Hapsburgs versus the Valois—but these struggles also had a religious aspect, especially within Charles's German lands. Charles played for time in dealing with the crisis caused by the growth of Protestantism, thus allowing the Protestant and Catholic princes and cities to form mutual defense leagues. War between Charles's armies and the Lutheran forces finally erupted in 1546 (the year Luther died) and lasted until 1555, when the Religious Peace of Augsburg brought it to an end. This armistice granted toleration to the Lutheran states, but on strict terms. The ruler's religion became the official faith of each territory; members of religious minorities, whether Roman Catholic or Lutheran, could migrate and join their coreligionists in nearby lands. But the rights of other minority sects were ignored, and hence the Peace of Augsburg contained the seeds of future wars.

In 1556, when Charles V abdicated, Philip II, who inherited the Spanish crown, became the head of the Roman Catholic cause. Besides Spain, Roman Catholic regimes now ruled Italy, Portugal, and Austria;

TABLE 13.2 THE RELIGIOUS WARS, 1559–1603

WAR	OUTCOME
The Spanish–Netherlands War, 1567–1609	The United Provinces become an independent Protestant state.
Civil War in France, 1562–1593	France remains Roman Catholic with a large Protestant minority.
Anglo–Spanish War, 1588	England turns back invasion of the Spanish Armada and remains a Protestant state.
Franco–Spanish War, 1589–1598	Spanish designs are frustrated by the conversion of French king to Roman Catholicism in 1593; France remains a Roman Catholic state.

Protestants reigned in Scandinavia. Elsewhere the religious rivals vied for supremacy. For the rest of the century, until 1603, Germany was at peace, but western Europe now suffered religious violence (Table 13.2).

Philip II (1556–1598), backed by the riches of Mexico and Peru, dominated European politics during his reign. His highly trained and well-equipped armies won victory after victory, enabling him to control much of Europe. At first, Philip II seemed unstoppable. He expelled suspected Muslims from Spain and defeated the Turks in the Mediterranean; he invaded Portugal and joined that country to Spain. But his fortunes began to decline when he launched a bloody campaign against the seven religiously disaffected provinces of the northern Netherlands. Eventually, in 1609, the United Provinces, as this new state was called, won freedom from Spain and kept its Calvinist faith. Even as the Dutch war was winding down, Philip had turned his gaze on Protestant England, a supporter of the Dutch revolt.

In Philip's eyes, only England stood between him and a reunited Christendom. Already, Spain and England were engaged in a scramble for the precious metals of the New World. This rivalry now escalated, bringing Philip to plan an English invasion. In 1588 his scheme ended in disaster as the Spanish Armada was defeated by a lethal combination of English sea power and a violent storm.

Philip II's goal of a reunited Christendom had been an impossible dream from the beginning. The Protestant world was too determined, the growth of national consciousness too powerful, and the rise of a sovereign state system too far advanced for any one monarch to succeed in unifying Europe under a single banner or cause. When Philip died in 1598, Spain was already declining, and Europe was divided into independent states and several religions.

NORTHERN HUMANISM

Northern Europe and Spain moved almost directly from the Late Gothic style into the Mannerist phase of the Renaissance. A major exception to the age's all-encompassing Mannerism was the literary movement known as *Christian humanism*, which shared some of the aesthetic values of the High Renaissance such as idealism, rationalism, and a deep love for Classical literature. Unlike the humanist movement in Italy, the northern humanists were preoccupied with the condition of the church and the wider Christian world. For these northern thinkers, the study of Christian writings went hand in hand with research on the Greco-Roman classics, and their scholarship was simply meant to further the cause of ecclesiastical reform (Time Line 13.2).

Like the Pietists, from whom they drew inspiration, the northern humanists approached their faith in simple terms. They taught that any Christian who had a pure and humble heart could pray directly to God. These scholars further strengthened the appeal of this simple creed by claiming that it was identical with Christ's scriptural message, which they were discovering in their vernacular translations of the New Testament.

The thinking of the Christian humanists, notably in Germany, was tinged with national feeling and hostility toward Italian interference in their local religious affairs. Their Christian humanism with its simple faith led them to believe that by imitating the early church—freed of corrupt Italian leaders—they could revitalize Christianity and restore it to its original purpose.

A notable French humanist was François Rabelais [RAB-uh-lay] (about 1494–1553), who wrote two sa-

tirical adventure stories, *Pantagruel* and *Gargantua*. In these works Rabelais vigorously attacked the church's abuses and ridiculed the clergy and theologians. Beneath the satire he affirmed the goodness of human nature and the ability of men and women to lead useful lives based on reason and common sense. However, his skepticism and secularism, as well as the ribald humor, obscene references, and grotesque escapades of his gigantic heroes, put Rabelais in a unique category, well outside the mainstream of northern humanism.

The outstanding figure among the northern humanists—and possibly the outstanding figure among *all* humanists—is the Dutch scholar Desiderius Erasmus. Called the prince of humanists in his day, Erasmus, because of his coolness under pressure, remains one of the most attractive personalities of this unfortunate century (Figure 13.7).

Erasmus (about 1466–1536) was fully prepared for the great role that he played in the Christian humanist movement. He studied in the pietistic atmosphere surrounding a school run by the Brethren of the Common Life, where he was introduced to the Greek and Roman classics. He later completed his education at the University of Paris. This training was supposed to lead to a church career, but although he was ordained, he never wore clerical garb or lived as a priest. On the contrary, with the aid of patrons he patiently pursued a writing career, enjoying the comforts of a scholarly life. He also traveled widely throughout western Europe, eventually finding a second home in England among the intellectual circle gathered around Thomas More, England's Lord Chancellor and another well-known humanist.

As a humanist, Erasmus believed in education in the *humanitas* sense advocated by Cicero, emphasizing study of the Classics and honoring the dignity of the individual. As a Christian, he promoted the "philosophy of Christ" as expressed in the Sermon on the Mount and in Jesus' example of a humble and virtuous life. Erasmus earnestly felt that the church could reform itself and avoid division by adopting the moderate approach that he advanced.

TIME LINE 13.2   NORTHERN HUMANISM IN THE SIXTEENTH CENTURY

1500		1552
Christian Humanist Literature		
Publication of *The Praise of Folly* by Erasmus 1516	Publication of *Gargantua* and *Pantagruel* by Rabelais 1532–1552	

FIGURE 13.7   HANS HOLBEIN THE YOUNGER. *Erasmus of Rotterdam*. Ca. 1523–1524. Oil on panel, 16½ × 12½". Louvre. *This sensitive likeness of the great humanist was painted by one of the most successful northern European portraitists of the sixteenth century, Hans Holbein. The artist has conveyed the humanity and intellectual authority of his subject by depicting him engaged in writing one of his many treatises. At the same time, Holbein reveals his Mannerist tendencies by placing Erasmus in a shallow space, by creating a stark contrast between the light hands, face, and paper and the darker, patterned background, and by presenting him in profile, forever cut off from the viewer.*

Despite a prodigious output of books that include treatises, commentaries, collections of proverbs, a manual for rulers, and a definitive edition of the Greek New Testament, Erasmus's fame rests on his most popular work, *The Praise of Folly*, written in 1516. This lively book, filled with learned humor, captures the gentle grace and good sense of the Christian humanists. Even this work's Latin title, *Encomium Moriae*, reflects a lighthearted spirit, for it is a punning reference to the name of More—the English friend to whom the book is dedicated.

In this work Erasmus pokes fun at the human race by making his mouthpiece the goddess Folly—an imaginary creation who symbolizes human foolishness. In a series of sermons, Folly ridicules every social group, from scholars and lawyers to priests and cardinals. Erasmus's jolly satire, especially in its exposure of clerical hypocrisy, struck a responsive

chord among educated people. But with the outbreak of Protestantism such cultivated criticism only got Erasmus in trouble. Roman Catholics felt betrayed by his mild barbs, and Protestants accused him of not going far enough. In the end, this mild reformer and gentle scholar sadly witnessed the breakup of his beloved church while being denounced by both sides.

For a time, Luther had hoped for the support of Erasmus in his reforming crusade. But that changed in 1524 when Erasmus asserted, contrary to Luther, that the human will was free; otherwise, according to Erasmus, the Bible would not have urged sinners to repent. Erasmus's argument so enraged Luther that he countered with a tract in which he declared that the human will was irrevocably flawed; in Luther's view, only God's free grace could save any man or woman from the fires of hell. So intemperate was Luther's reply that the two scholars never communicated again. Erasmus's calming voice went unheeded amid the wild rhetoric and religious mayhem that characterized this age.

LATE MANNERISM

Despite the influence of Christian humanism and the persistence of High Renaissance ideals in some areas of expression, Mannerism was the prevailing artistic style in Europe in the second half of the sixteenth century. The most significant expressions of Mannerism appeared in literature and painting. The Mannerist style originated in the north in about 1520, the same time that it emerged in Italy, although there was at first no direct link between the two developments (Time Line 13.3).

Northern Mannerism was affected not only by the religious revolution but also by the survival of late medieval trends, such as Gothic forms and mysticism. Together, these forces helped to create a self-conscious vision that opposed the natural and harmonious outlook of the High Renaissance.

Mannerist Literature in Northern Europe

The sixteenth century was truly an amazing period in literature, for the vernacular tongues now definitively showed that they were the equal of Latin as a vehicle for literary expression. In the High Middle Ages, the Italian Dante led the way with his *Divine Comedy*; now, other authors writing in the vernacular found their voices. Montaigne, writing in French,

TIME LINE 13.3 EARLY AND LATE MANNERISM IN NORTHERN EUROPE AND SPAIN, AND LATE MANNERISM IN ITALY

1500		1564		1600
	Early Mannerism		Late Mannerism	

Last of Dürer's
self-portraits
1500

Death of
Michelangelo
1564

Montaigne's
Essays
1590–1593

Brueghel's
*Peasant
Wedding
Dance*
1566

El Greco's
*The Burial
of
Count Orgaz*
1586

Shakespeare's
plays
performed
in London
1590–1610

Tintoretto's
*The Last
Supper*
1592–1594

and Shakespeare, writing in English, left such a rich legacy that, by common consent, each is revered as the outstanding writer of his respective tradition.

Michel de Montaigne Like an ancient Roman senator, Michel Eyquem de Montaigne [mee-SHEL ek-em-duh mahn-TAYN] (1533–1592) balanced a public career with a life devoted to letters. While he served as a judge and a mayor, he wrote constantly on his lifelong project, which he called *Essays*. This collection of discursive meditations is essentially the autobiography of his mind and is thus representative of the individualistic spirit of the Renaissance. What emerges is a self-portrait of a man who is both intellectually curious and fascinated by his own mental processes and personality. He describes his contradictions, accidental as well as deliberate, though he writes that his loyalty is always to truth. What keeps the *Essays* from falling into sterile self-absorption is Montaigne's firm sense that in revealing himself he is speaking for others.

But the *Essays* are more than an early example of modern confessional literature. They also constitute, in the French tradition, the earliest work of *moralisme*, or moralism, and the beginning of modern skepticism. In terms of morality, Montaigne attached little importance to Christian ethics, since cruelty and barbarism in the name of religion were justified equally by Protestant and Catholic. His musings reflected France's chaotic condition during the religious wars, causing him to question the Renaissance's natural optimism. Montaigne searched for, without ever discovering, a moral code that was centered on a human world and that no one could deny.

In his skeptical outlook Montaigne rejected the Renaissance view of humanity as a microcosm of the universe. Indeed, he claimed that he saw nothing except vanity and insignificance in human beings and their reasoning—a distinctly Mannerist conclusion. Montaigne, however, avoided total skepticism, for although he denied to humans perfect knowledge, he held that practical understanding was possible.

William Shakespeare Montaigne wrote during a period when religious wars were brutalizing France, but England at the same time was enjoying a relatively calm period of cultural exuberance, the Age of Elizabeth. Under Queen Elizabeth I, who reigned from 1558 to 1603, London rose to an eminence that rivaled that of Florence of the Early Renaissance. English playwrights rescued tragedy and comedy from the oblivion that had befallen them with the collapse of Rome. As in ancient Greece, tragedy and comedy again became part of popular culture. A purely secular and commercial theater now emerged, with professional playwrights and actors, playhouses, and a ticket-buying public (Figure 13.8).

The revived popularity of the theater represented a dramatic reversal of a cultural outlook that had prevailed in the West since the time of Augustine in the fifth century (see Chapter 7). Christian scholars had condemned the stage for its wicked displays and seductive delights. On occasion, medieval culture had spawned morality plays and dramas with biblical themes, but these edifying works remained primitive in form with little care given to language, character, or plot. A play like the fifteenth-century

The Globe Playhouse 1599–1613

A Conjectural Reconstruction
by C. Walter Hodges

KEY

AA Main entrance
B   The Yard, where the 'groundlings' stood (for one penny admission)
CC Entrances to lowest gallery (on payment of another penny)
D   Entrances to staircase and upper galleries
E   Corridor serving the different sections of the middle gallery
F   Middle gallery (The 'Twopenny Rooms')
G   'Gentlemen's Rooms' or 'Lords' Rooms'
H   The stage
J   The hanging being put up round the stage (N.B. In some theatres this was boarded in)
K   The 'Hell' under the stage
L   The stage trap, leading down to the Hell
MM Stage doors, leading into the tiring-house
N   Curtained 'place behind the stage', sometimes opened for special scenes
O   Gallery above the stage, used as required sometimes by musicians, sometimes by spectators, and often as part of the play (e.g. *Romeo and Juliet*)
P   Back-stage area (the tiring-house)
Q   Tiring-house door
R   Dressing rooms
S   Wardrobe and storage
T   The hut housing the machine for lowering enthroned gods, etc., to the stage
U   The 'Heavens'
W   Hoisting the playhouse flag

G (Position of)
G (Position of)

Position of Staircase

C. Walter Hodges
1965

FIGURE 13.8 Reconstruction of the Globe Playhouse, 1599–1613. *When the Globe Playhouse of London was razed in 1644 to make way for new buildings, one of the most significant monuments of Renaissance England disappeared: the theater where most of Shakespeare's plays were first performed. This cutaway drawing, made by C. W. Hodges, a leading expert on the theaters of the period, attempts to depict the Globe Playhouse as it appeared in Shakespeare's day. As shown in the drawing, the Globe was a sixteen-sided structure with the stage erected in an open courtyard surrounded on three sides by three tiers of seats.*

Everyman, for example, was intended mainly to reinforce Christian values and only incidentally to entertain or to provoke thought. Under Elizabeth, many able dramatists began to appear, such as Thomas Kyd (about 1557–1595) and Christopher Marlowe (1564–1593). These Elizabethan playwrights revolutionized drama in a single generation. However, first honors must be given to William Shakespeare, the greatest dramatist in the English language and one of the literary immortals.

Shakespeare (1564–1616) was born in Stratford-upon-Avon, a market-town, and educated in its grammar school. By 1590 his plays were being performed on the London stage, and his active public career continued until 1610, when he returned home to Stratford to enjoy a life of leisure in the country. His early retirement reflected the success that he had achieved as an actor, a theater owner, and a playwright. But it was as the age's leading dramatist that he earned undying fame, mastering the three different genres of history plays, comedies, and tragedies. These thirty-seven dramas constitute his legacy to the world. Just as tragedies ranked higher than comedies in ancient Greece, so have Shakespeare's tragedies enjoyed a reputation superior to his other writings. Of the eleven tragedies, many are regarded as masterpieces; *King Lear, Othello, Julius Caesar, Macbeth,* and *Romeo and Juliet* are constantly performed on the stage and often presented in films, in English as well as other languages. Perhaps the Shakespearean tragedy that stands above the rest, however, and is reckoned by many as his supreme achievement is *Hamlet.*

Shakespeare's *Hamlet* is a **revenge tragedy,** among the most popular dramatic forms in the Elizabethan theater. The revenge play had its own special rules, consisting chiefly of a murder that requires a relative of the victim, usually with the prompting of a ghost, to avenge the crime by the drama's end. The origin of this type of play, with its characteristic violence and suspense, has been obscured by time, although Seneca's Roman tragedies, which were known and studied in England, are almost certainly a source.

The basic plot, characters, and setting of *Hamlet* are drawn from a medieval chronicle of evil doings at the Danish court. Elizabethan theatergoers had seen an earlier dramatized version (now lost) before Shakespeare's play was performed in 1600–1601. Shakespeare thus took a well-known story but stamped it with his own genius and feeling for character. In its basic conception, *Hamlet* is a consummate expression of the Mannerist style. Shakespeare presents Hamlet from shifting perspectives in the Mannerist way, preferring ambiguity, rather than portraying him from a single vantage point in accordance with the Classical ideal. By turns, Hamlet veers from madman to scholar to prince to swordsman, so that a unified, coherent personality is never exposed to the audience. Because of Hamlet's elusive character, it is no wonder that he has become the most frequently analyzed and performed of all Shakespeare's heroes.

Another Mannerist aspect of this play is the self-disgust that seems to rule Hamlet's character when he is alone with his thoughts. While the High Renaissance reserved its finest praise for the basic dignity of the human being, Hamlet finds little to value in himself, in others, or in life. Instead, he offers a typically Mannerist, contradictory vision:

> It goes so heavily with my disposition that this goodly frame, the earth, seems to me a sterile promontory; this most excellent canopy, the air . . . this majestical roof fretted with golden fire, why, it appears no other thing to me but a foul and pestilent congregation of vapours. What a piece of work is a man, how noble in reason, how infinite in faculty; in form and moving how express and admirable, in action how like an angel, in apprehension how like a god! the beauty of the world, the paragon of animals!

> And yet to me what is this quintessence of dust? Man delights not me. . . .

> (Act 2, Scene 2)

In its construction, the tragedy of *Hamlet* is typical of Shakespeare's plays. All of his dramas were written for commercial theater troupes and were not intended especially for a reading public. Only after Shakespeare's death were his plays published and circulated to a general audience and thus regarded as "literature."

Mannerist Painting in Northern Europe

The influence of the Protestant Reformation on the arts began in the 1520s and reached its zenith in the middle of the century. Part of this impact was negative: Some Protestants looked on the enjoyment of the visual arts as a form of idol worship and began to destroy statues, paintings, and stained glass that portrayed biblical figures and saints. Luther rejected such iconoclasm, but the purifying zeal spread among the new sects.

Mannerist painting had begun to appear in northern Europe as a result of the partial loosening of ties to the Flemish school and a growing awareness of the new Italian painting. Moreover, the general air of cultural crisis felt by the Italian artists was shared by their northern colleagues. The combined influences of Mannerism and Protestantism produced three artists of unique stature who reflected the turbulent world of post-Lutheran Europe in quite different ways: Dürer, Grünewald, and Bruegel.

Albrecht Dürer   Albrecht Dürer [AHL-brekt DYOU-ruhr] (1471–1528), the son of a goldsmith, pursued a career as an engraver and painter. After studying in Germany, he traveled widely in Italy, where he absorbed the lessons of Renaissance art. Between 1510 and 1519 he earned great fame for the works that he executed for the Holy Roman Emperor, but he also discovered that his true artistic bent was for engraving, either on wood or metal. His engravings, which were issued in multiple editions, enhanced his reputation, and as a result he received many commissions throughout Germany and the Netherlands. Near the end of his life Dürer became a Lutheran, and some of his last paintings indicate his new faith.

Fully aware of himself and his place in the world, Dürer showed a Mannerist sensibility in his ambiguous self-portraits, especially in the famous work in which he depicts himself as a Christ figure (Figure 13.9). In this stunning image—the intense stare suggests that it was painted while the artist was looking

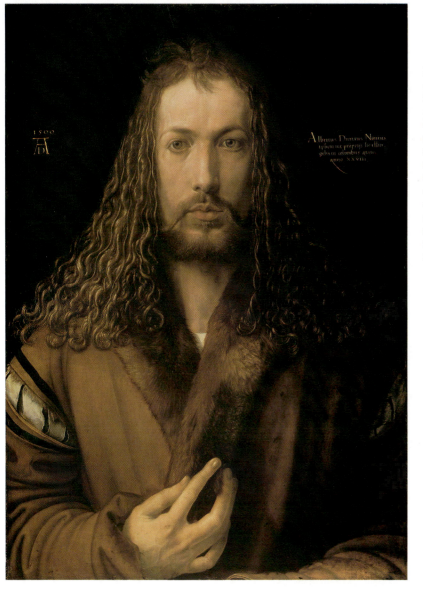

FIGURE 13.9 ALBRECHT DÜRER. *Self-Portrait.* 1500. Oil on panel. 26¼ × 19¼″. Alte Pinakothek, Munich. *Dürer's preoccupation with his own likeness showed that he had absorbed the questing spirit of the Renaissance. In a series of self-portraits, starting at the age of thirteen, he examined his face and upper torso and rendered them with astonishing details reflective of his passing age and moods. This self-portrait is the last of the series and suggests that he has taken the role of artist upon himself in much the manner that Jesus had taken the role of Savior.*

in the mirror—Dürer blends a dandified likeness of himself with a standard Flemish representation of Christ. Such an identification of his artistic self with Jesus' divine power would have been unthinkable before the Renaissance. Nevertheless, Dürer remained true to the spirit of the Middle Ages, for he was also following the tradition of mysticism in which he saw himself as striving to imitate the example of Christ.

While Dürer's paintings brought him recognition and wealth in his day, his engravings constitute his greatest artistic legacy. At the time of Luther's revolt, Dürer engraved the scene called *Knight, Death, and the Devil* (Figure 13.10). This magnificent engraving shows a knight riding through a forest, ignoring both the taunts of Death, who holds up an hourglass to remind him of his mortality, and the fiendish Devil who watches nearby. The knight is probably meant as a symbol of the Christian who has to live in the practical world.

Dürer's *Knight, Death, and the Devil* combines Late Gothic and Renaissance elements to make a disquieting Mannerist scene. From the northern tradition are derived the exquisite details, the grotesque demon, and the varied landscape in the background. From Renaissance sources comes the horse, which Dürer copied from models seen during his Italian tour.

Matthias Grünewald   A second major German artist in this period is Matthias Grünewald [muh-THI-uhs GREW-nuh-vahlt] (about 1460–1528), who was less influenced by Italian art and more northern in his techniques than Dürer. His paintings represent a continuation of the Late Gothic style rather than a northern development of Mannerist tendencies.

Grünewald's supreme achievement is the altarpiece painted for the church of St. Anthony in Isenheim, Germany. The *Isenheim Altarpiece*, as this work is known, includes nine painted panels that can be

FIGURE 13.10 ALBRECHT DÜRER. *Knight, Death, and the Devil.* 1513. Engraving, 250 × 192 mm. The Fogg Art Museum, Harvard University. Gift of William Gray from the Collection of Francis Calley Gray. *Dürer's plan for this work probably derived from a manual by Erasmus that advised a Christian prince on the best way to rule. In his version, Dürer portrays the Christian layman who has put on the armor of faith and rides steadfastly, oblivious to the various pitfalls that lie in his path. The knight is sometimes identified with Erasmus, whom Dürer venerated.*

displayed in three different positions, depending on the church calendar.

When the *Isenheim Altarpiece* is closed, the large central panel depicts the Crucifixion (Figure 13.11). By crowding the five figures and the symbolic lamb into the foreground and making Christ's body larger than the rest, Grünewald followed the Late Gothic style. This style is similarly apparent in every detail of Christ's tortured, twisted body: the gaping mouth, the exposed teeth, the slumped head, and the torso raked by thorns. And Grünewald's Late Gothic emotionalism is evident in his treatment of the secondary

FIGURE 13.11 MATTHIAS GRÜNEWALD. *The Crucifixion,* from the *Isenheim Altarpiece.* 1515. 9'9½" × 10'9". Musée d'Unterlinden, Colmar, France. *Jesus' suffering and death were a central theme in North European piety, particularly after the plague of the fourteenth century. Northern artists typically rendered Christ's death in vivid and gory detail. Grünewald's* Crucifixion *comes out of this tradition; Christ's broken body symbolizes both his sacrificial death and the mortality of all human beings.*

FIGURE 13.12 PIETER BRUEGEL THE ELDER. *Peasant Wedding Feast.* Ca. 1567–1568. Oil on panel, 44⅞ × 64″. Kunsthistorisches Museum, Vienna. *Bruegel had personally witnessed the details of peasant life that he painted. A member of the upper middle class, Bruegel enjoyed making outings into the countryside in disguise and participating in local celebrations and drinking parties. The attentiveness with which he records the behavior of the peasants reduces the otherwise somewhat negative tone of his scenes.*

figures in this crucifixion panel. On the right, John the Baptist points toward Jesus, stressing the meaning of his sacrificial death. John the Baptist's calmness stands in stark contrast to the grieving tableau on the left, including Mary Magdalene, who kneels at Jesus' feet, and the Apostle John, who supports a swooning Mary. The swaying bodies of these three figures reinforce their anguished faces.

Pieter Bruegel the Elder The life and work of Pieter Bruegel [BREW-gul or BROY-gul] the Elder (about 1525–1569) indicate that new winds were blowing through northern European art in the mid–sixteenth century. The great German artists Dürer and Grünewald were now dead, and German art, which dominated northern Europe in the early sixteenth century, had gone into decline. Protestant iconoclasm had taken its toll, and the demand for religious art had markedly diminished. Within this milieu, Bruegel chose a novel set of artistic subjects—landscapes, country life scenes, and folk narratives—and in the process became the first truly modern painter in northern Europe. Bruegel's subjects, rooted in the Flemish tradition, were often devoid of overt religious content and presented

simply as secular art, although he also painted a number of pictures on standard religious themes such as the adoration of the Magi.

Bruegel's most memorable paintings are his scenes of peasant life. The peasants are always depicted in natural settings, neither romanticized nor patronized. Rather, Bruegel represents the common folk as types, never as individuals, and often as expressions of the blind forces of nature. For some viewers, these scenes also convey a pessimism tinged with grudging admiration about human nature as reflected in the peasants' simple, lusty behavior—an ambiguous perspective typical of the Mannerist style.

A painting that illustrates Bruegel's attitude toward country folk is his *Peasant Wedding Feast* (Figure 13.12). This banquet scene is set in a barn converted to a dining hall for the occasion. Bruegel's Mannerist values lead him to take the focus off the bride and groom and make the gathering itself the subject of the painting. He accomplishes this by placing the banqueting table along a diagonal, thrusting several figures into the foreground: the server pouring beer into jugs, the rustics carrying new dishes on

FIGURE 13.13 PIETER BRUEGEL THE ELDER. *Wedding Dance.* 1566. Oil on panel, 47 × 62". Detroit Institute of Arts. *Bruegel has made a sensuous arrangement out of the dancers and bystanders at this country wedding. The line of dancers winds from the foreground back through the trees, where it reverses itself and returns to its original starting point. The sense of lively movement is reinforced by the vivid red colors in the hats and vests and by the stomping feet and flailing arms.*

a barn door, the child licking the plate clean with his fingers, and beyond them, the bagpipers standing beside the diners. Against the side wall under a makeshift banner, the quietly smiling bride sits with eyes half-closed and hands clasped before her.

Another of Bruegel's scenes of peasant life is his lively *Wedding Dance* (Figure 13.13). The painting records the exuberant revels of the lusty men and the kerchief-wearing women. The bride and groom cannot be distinguished from the other dancers. In a typical touch, Bruegel uses a high horizon and a high point of view, so that we look at the scene from above. This effect, along with the crude faces of the peasants, serves to underscore the impression that these are types and not individuals. The painting's composition reinforces the sense of peasant types in the way that the swirling figures in the foreground are repeated in the background in ever-diminishing size.

Mannerist Painting in Spain

The strongest impact of the Counter-Reformation on the arts did not begin until after the close of the Council of Trent in 1563. Nowhere was Trent's influence greater than in Spain, and no Catholic artist expressed the spirit of Trent more than El Greco (1541–1614) in his Spanish paintings after 1576. These works, with their visionary style, also symbolize the spirit of Late Mannerism. El Greco's real name was Domenikos Theotokopoulos. A native of Crete, he had lived in Venice, where he had absorbed the colorful styles of the painters of the Venetian school. Unsuccessful as a painter in Venice, he also failed to find rich patrons in Rome, though he learned from the works of Michelangelo and the Mannerists. He arrived in Toledo, Spain, in about 1576, and there he

found an appreciative public among the wealthy nobility, but much to El Greco's despair, he never became a favorite of the Spanish ruler, Philip II, who found the Greek painter's works too bizarre.

For his select audience of aristocrats and Roman Catholic clergy, however, El Greco could do no wrong. They believed that his paintings of saints, martyrs, and other religious figures caught the essence of Spanish emotionalism and religious zeal—the same qualities that had led Loyola to found the Jesuits. In effect, El Greco's extravagant images gave visible form to his patrons' spiritual yearnings. In his paintings, he rejected a naturalistic world with conventional perspective, especially when a divine dimension was present or implied; his spiritualized vision came to be distinguished by elongated bodies, sharp lines in the folds of cloth, and luminous colors.

El Greco's masterpiece is *The Burial of Count Orgaz,* which was painted to honor the founder of the church of Santo Tomé in Toledo (Figure 13.14). This painting was designed to fit into a special place beside the church's high altar. Its subject is the miraculous scene that, according to legend, occurred during the count's burial when two saints, Augustine and Stephen, appeared and assisted with the last rites.

From this legend, El Greco has fashioned an arresting painting. The large canvas is divided into two halves, with the lower section devoted to the count's actual burial and the upper section focused on the reception of his soul in heaven. Except for two men who tilt their faces upward, the town dignitaries seem unaware of what is happening just above their heads. El Greco has devised two distinct styles to deal with these different planes of reality. The dignitaries below are rendered in realistic terms, down to the precise fashions of El Greco's era, such as the neck ruffs, mustaches, and goatees. The heavenly

FIGURE 13.14 EL GRECO. *The Burial of Count Orgaz.* 1586. Oil on canvas, 16′ × 11′10″.
Church of Santo Tomé, Toledo, Spain. *A Manneristic invention in* The Burial of Count
Orgaz *was the rich treatment of the robe of St. Stephen, the first Christian martyr and, in this
painting, the beardless figure supporting the body of the dead count. Embroidered onto
Stephen's garment is a picture of the stoning of St. Stephen, an episode narrated in the New
Testament. By depicting one event inside another, El Greco created an illusionistic device—
a typical notion of Mannerist painters, who were skeptical about conventional reality.*

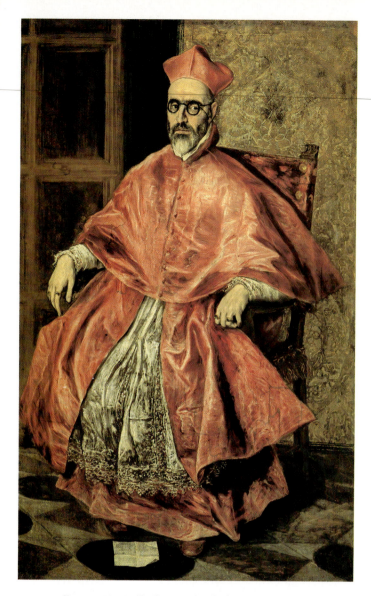

FIGURE 13.15 EL GRECO. *Cardinal Guevara.* 1596–1600. Oil on canvas, 67¼ × 42½". The Metropolitan Museum of Art, New York. Bequest of Mrs. H. O. Havemeyer, 1929. The H. O. Havemeyer Collection. *El Greco's painting of Cardinal Guevara illustrates his mastery of Mannerist portraiture. Disturbing details are visible everywhere. Guevara's head is almost too small for his large body, made even grander by the red cardinal's robe, and the divided background—half wooden panel, half rich tapestry—sets up a dissonant effect. Even the chair the cardinal sits in contributes to the air of disjointedness, for its one visible leg seems barely to touch the floor.*

►

FIGURE 13.16 SOFONISBA ANGUISSOLA. [Formerly ~~attributed to Alonzo Sánchez Coello.~~] *Portrait of Don Carlos.* Ca. 1560. Oil on canvas, 42¹⁵⁄₁₆ × 34³⁄₁₆". Prado, Madrid. *This painting of Prince Don Carlos shows typical features of the artist's personal style. Like most women of the period, Anguissola was skilled in the needle arts, and she reveals this knowledge in the painstaking detail she has lavished on the prince's court costume—her trademark, according to one scholar. She also had a signature way of rendering hands—in a "square-U" pattern, so that the index and little fingers are parallel and act as the raised portions of a "U" connected by an imaginary line—which may be seen in both of Don Carlos's hands.*

seems to have an uneasy conscience, as betrayed by the shifty expression of the eyes, the left hand clutching the chair arm, and the general sense that the subject is restraining himself. Through these means El Greco created another model for Mannerist portraiture.

Another Mannerist artist-in-exile working in Spain in the late sixteenth century was Sofonisba Anguissola [an-gwee-SOL-uh] (about 1532–1625), a northern Italian from Cremona who, along with El Greco, is credited with helping to introduce the Italian school of painting into Spanish culture. Praised and encouraged by the aging Michelangelo, Anguissola began her rise to international fame when King Philip II of Spain chose her to be his court painter, in 1559. Court painter for twenty years, she painted mainly portraits, as, for example, the *Portrait of Don Carlos* (Figure 13.16). In this three-quarter-length likeness of Spain's crown prince, Anguissola shows her mastery of the Mannerist style, including the challenging gaze of the young subject and the painting's highly polished surface and dark olive background. Another Mannerist feature of this work is the nonrealistic scene, visible through the open window: an eagle flying and holding a column—a Hapsburg emblem—in its talons. The column functions as an allegory, referring to Don Carlos' position as heir to the Spanish throne and to the very real power of the Hapsburg family. Such enigmatic puzzles as this scene were beloved by the spirit of Mannerism.

Anguissola's international acclaim was due, in part, to her aristocratic breeding and—rare for women of the times—education in Renaissance learning. This background, coupled with rich artistic gifts, enabled her to overcome the prejudices and guild restrictions that had previously kept women from pursuing careers in the arts. Anguissola is the ablest of the women artists who now begin to emerge in sixteenth-century Europe.

Italian Culture, 1564–1603

The Council of Trent had more impact on the arts, architecture, and music in Italy than in any other

spectacle is depicted in the spiritualized manner that he increasingly used in his later works.

El Greco also painted several portraits of church officials, of which the best known is that of *Cardinal Guevara* (Figure 13.15). This painting portrays the Chief Inquisitor, dressed in his splendid red robes. El Greco has captured the personality of this austere and iron-willed churchman who vigorously pursued heretics and sentenced them to die in an *auto-da-fé*, Portuguese for "act of faith"—that is, a public ceremony in which heretics were executed, usually by being burned at the stake. El Greco's likeness suggests much about the inner man: Cardinal Guevara artistic policy tended to clash with Mannerism, which was elitist and deliberately complex. Only with the rise of the Baroque after 1600 was there a style that could conform to the church's need for art with a mass appeal. In the meantime, the general influence of Trent on the last stage of Mannerism was to intensify its spiritual values.

Late Mannerist Painting in Italy: Tintoretto   With the death of Michelangelo in 1564, Venice displaced Rome as the dominant artistic center in Italy. From then until the end of the century, Venetian painters carried the banner of the Italian Renaissance, bringing Mannerism to a brilliant sunset. The leading exponent of **Late Mannerism** in Italy is Tintoretto [tin-tuh-RAY-toe] (1518–1594). This Venetian artist created a feverish, emotional style that reflected impetuosity in its execution. With his haste, Tintoretto was reacting against his famous Venetian predecessor Titian, who had been noted for extraordinary discipline in the way he painted. But in other respects, he learned from Titian, adopting his love of color and his use of theatrical lighting. The special quality of Tintoretto's art, which he reached in his earliest paintings, was to place his human figures into arrangements that suggest a sculptural frieze.

Tintoretto's rendition of the familiar biblical account of *The Last Supper* shows his feverish style (Figure 13.17). Unlike the serene, classically balanced scene that Leonardo had painted (see Figure 12.5), Tintoretto portrays an ethereal gathering, illuminated by eery light and filled with swooping angels. The diagonal table divides the pictorial space into two halves; on the left is the spiritual world of Jesus and his disciples, and on the right is the earthly realm of the servants. Tintoretto's depiction of these different levels of reality is reminiscent of a similar

Roman Catholic area because of the historic tradition of papal intrusion into Italian affairs. The council decreed that the arts and music should be easily accessible to the uneducated. In sacred music, for example, the intelligibility of the words should take precedence over the melody, and in architecture the building should create a worshipful environment. The church council envisioned paintings and sculptures that were simple and direct as well as unobjectionable and decent in appearance. Guided by this principle, the Counter-Reformation popes declared that some of the male nudes in Michelangelo's *Last Judgment* were obscene and ordered loincloths to be painted over them. General church policy now returned to the medieval ideal of an art and music whose sole aim was to serve and clarify the Christian faith.

Since the Roman Catholic Church after Trent wanted a simplified art that spoke to the masses, its

FIGURE 13.17   TINTORETTO. *The Last Supper.* 1592–1594. Oil on canvas, 12′ × 18′8″. San Giorgio Maggiore, Venice. *Nothing better illustrates the distance between the High Renaissance and Mannerism than a comparison of Leonardo's* Last Supper *(Figure 12.5) with that of Tintoretto. Everything about Tintoretto's spiritualized scene contradicts the quiet Classicism of Leonardo's work. Leonardo's painting is meant to appeal to the viewer's reason; Tintoretto's shadowy scene is calculated to stir the feelings.*

division in El Greco's *The Burial of Count Orgaz* (see Figure 13.14). Especially notable is Jesus' body, including the feet, which positively glows. *The Last Supper*, finished in Tintoretto's final year, is a fitting climax to Mannerist painting.

Music in Late Sixteenth-Century Italy and England

Unlike painting, Italian music remained under the sway of High Renaissance ideals, keeping to the path pioneered by Josquin des Prez (see Chapter 12). Nevertheless, the Council of Trent, along with other forces, led to the breakup of the High Renaissance style and created the conditions for the rise of the Baroque. For one thing, the council ruled that the Gregorian chant was preferable to polyphony for church liturgy and that the traditional chants should be simplified to ensure that the words could be easily understood. Most composers, considering the chants to be barbarous, continued to use polyphony but pruned its extravagant effects. The best of these composers and the chief representative of Counter-Reformation music was Giovanni Pierluigi da Palestrina [pal-uh-STREE-nuh] (about 1525–1594). His controlled style established the Roman Catholic ideal for the next few centuries—polyphonic masses sung by choirs and with clearly enunciated and enormously expressive texts.

Nevertheless, the future of Italian music lay outside the church. Ironically, secular vocal music was also moving toward an ideal in which the words took precedence over the sound, but secular composers, unlike those in the church, rejected polyphony because it did not allow the text to be fully understood. The move to make the words primary in secular music was triggered by Renaissance humanists who were convinced that ancient music's power stemmed from the expressive way that the setting suited the clearly articulated words of the text. The most evident signs of this humanistic belief were in the works of the Florentine *Camerata*, a group of musical amateurs. Rejecting polyphony, the Florentine musicians composed pieces for a text with a single line of melody accompanied by simple chords and sung in a declamatory style.

The trend to expressive secular music in Italy was reflected most completely in the *madrigal*, a song for four or five voices composed with great care for the words of the poetic text. The novelty of this vocal music was that it vividly illustrated the meanings and emotions in the words, rather than the structure of the music. Madrigals began to be written in the 1520s, but their heyday was the second half of the

sixteenth century. Late in the century they were imported to England and quickly became the height of fashion there. The success of madrigals in England had to do with the country's vogue for Italianate things, as is evident from the settings and sources of Shakespeare's plays and the translation into English of Castiglione's *Book of the Courtier* during this period.

England's leading madrigal composer was Thomas Weelkes [WILKS] (about 1575–1623), whose works often made use of the technique called ***word paintings***, or word illustrations, a musical illustration of the written text. For example, in the madrigal "As Vesta was from Latmos hill descending," Weelkes uses a descending scale for the word *descending*, an ascending scale for the words *a maiden queen ascending*, and a hill-shaped melodic phrase for the words *Latmos hill descending*. Such clever fusing of music and lyrics appealed to listeners, many of whom, in the spirit of the Renaissance, were amateur musicians themselves.

Madrigals eventually achieved a European-wide popularity, but this fashion ended with the Renaissance. Nevertheless, the musical technique of word painting continued to be a favorite of composers, down through Bach and Handel in the Age of the Baroque (see Chapter 14).

KEY CULTURAL TERMS

Reformation	*Jesuits*
Counter-Reformation	*Christian humanism*
Lutheranism	*revenge tragedy*
Calvinism	*Late Mannerism*
Puritanism	*madrigal*
Anglicanism	*word painting*

SUGGESTIONS FOR FURTHER READING

PRIMARY SOURCES

CALVIN, J. *Institutes of the Christian Religion.* Translated by F. L. Battles. Philadelphia: Westminster Press, 1960. A recent translation of Calvin's theological masterpiece.

ERASMUS, D. *Praise of Folly.* Translated by B. Radice. New York: Penguin, 1971. A lively translation of Erasmus's satire that ridiculed the hypocrisy of the age, especially in the church; originally published in 1516.

LUTHER, M. *Three Treatises.* Translations by various authors. Philadelphia: Fortress Press, 1960. Good versions of the short works that helped to make Luther an outstanding and controversial public figure in his day.

The Legacy of the Religious Reformations, Northern Humanism, and Late Mannerism

The period from 1520 until 1603 brings to a close the third and final phase of the Renaissance. This eighty-three-year–period, framed by the deaths of Raphael and Queen Elizabeth I, saw the foundations of early modern Europe move firmly into place. A world culture and economy, in embryo, begins during this period. This momentous development was foreshadowed in the shift of Europe's commercial axis from the Mediterranean to the Atlantic, as well as in the start of Europe's exportation of peoples, technology, religions, and ideas to colonies in Asia, Africa, and the Americas.

Probably the most important material change during this era was the rise of a system of sovereign and mutually hostile states. No single state was able to assert its authority over the others; the pattern set by their struggles would govern Western affairs until the emergence of global politics in the twentieth century. The European state system also spelled the doom of a united Christendom.

The reformations further split Christian Europe, dividing it into Protestant and Catholic armed camps. As a result, religious wars afflicted this century and the next, only fading away by about 1700. On a local level, religious differences led to intolerance and persecution. Although Europe's religious boundaries today remain roughly the same as they were in 1600, it took over three hundred years for Protestants and Catholics to accept that they could live together in harmony.

The reformations also left different cultural legacies to their respective Christian denominations. From Protestantism came a glorification of the work ethic, Puritanism, and a justification for capitalism. At the heart of the Protestant revolution, despite its insistence on the doctrine of original sin, was the notion that human beings can commune directly with God without church mediation. While Protestantism tended to view human beings as adrift in the universe, the Catholic church tried to control the spiritual and moral lives of its members and to insulate them from the surrounding world. This policy eventually placed the church on a collision course with the forces of modernity, but it nevertheless was followed by most of the popes until after World War II.

In the upheavals spawned by the religious crisis, the legacy of Northern humanism—rational morals allied to a simple faith—went unheeded by Protestants and Catholics alike. Not until the eighteenth century and the rationalist program of the Enlightenment did Christian humanist ideas find a willing audience.

In the arts and humanities, however, the legacy was clear: The Mannerist period left a rich and varied inheritance, including the work of Shakespeare, the most gifted and influential individual writer in the history of Western civilization.

MONTAIGNE, M. *Essays and Selected Writings*. Translated and edited by D. Frame. New York: St. Martin's Press, 1963. The *Essays* reveal Montaigne as one of the founders of French skepticism.

RABELAIS, F. *The Histories of Gargantua* and *Pantagruel*. Translated by J. M. Cohen. Franklin Center, Pa.: Franklin Library, 1982. An excellent modern version of this lusty masterpiece.

SHAKESPEARE. *Hamlet. Othello. King Lear. Romeo and Juliet. Antony and Cleopatra. Macbeth.* One of the best editions available of Shakespeare's tragedies is published by Washington Square Press. This series is inexpensive and profusely illustrated, and it offers the text with a facing page of editorial notes.

SUGGESTIONS FOR LISTENING

PALESTRINA, GIOVANNI PIERLUIGI DA (about 1525–1594).
A prolific composer of Masses, Palestrina is the major musical figure of the Counter-Reformation. Unlike the highly emotional style of Josquin, Palestrina's music is noted for its tightly controlled quality and its perfection of detail, as illustrated in such Masses as *Hodie Christus Natus Est, Assumpta Est Maria*, and *Ave Maria*.

WEELKES, THOMAS (about 1575–1623).
An English composer and organist, Weelkes is an important figure in Late Renaissance music. A composer of sacred vocal music and instrumental works for viols and harpsichord, he is best known for introducing the Italian madrigal to England and adapting it to the tastes of his compatriots. His madrigals were characterized by clever word paintings, as in *O, care, thou wilt despatch me* and *The Andalusian merchant* (both 1600).

14

THE BAROQUE AGE
Glamour and Grandiosity
1600—1715

As the Roman Catholic church feverishly pursued its goal of turning back Protestantism, and as the political system of powerful sovereign secular states took hold in Europe, a new age dawned in the early seventeenth century. Known as the *Baroque*, it was a period characterized by a love of grandeur, opulence, and vast, expanding horizons. For the church, Baroque art and architecture provided spectacular and compelling images with which to reassert its presence in the world and to dazzle and indoctrinate the faithful. For the secular rulers, the Baroque offered a magnificence that enhanced their political power and control. Art during the Baroque period became a propagandistic tool in a way that the Mannerist art of the previous period—with its focus on the personal, the distorted, and the eccentric—could never be.

The term "baroque" was coined in the eighteenth century by artists and scholars whose taste was attuned to the Classical ideals of the Renaissance. To them, much culture of the seventeenth century was imperfect, or "baroque," a term probably derived from the Portuguese word "barroco," meaning an irregular pearl. Not until the mid–nineteenth century did the word acquire a positive value. Since then, "Baroque" has gained currency as a label for the seventeenth century and its prevailing cultural style.

The Baroque period was an era of constant turmoil and momentous change. Hardly a year passed free from warfare. Until the middle of the century,

Europe was plagued by religious warfare, a legacy of the Reformation. In the second half of the century, the struggles had secular causes, notably territorial expansion and the extension of national boundaries. Further upheavals were caused by the continuing movement of peoples to the New World and by a growing race among the most powerful European states for overseas empires.

The seventeenth century was also a period of great scientific discoveries and intellectual change. Breakthroughs occurred that overturned age-old beliefs, and Western thought was freed from the errors of Greek science that had prevailed for more than two thousand years. Scholars revised their basic understanding of how the body functioned and how the universe was arranged. Because the Scientific Revolution, as this intellectual movement is called, had such an important influence on the making of the modern world, it is covered separately in Chapter 15, along with related philosophical ideas. This chapter focuses on the art, literature, and music of the Baroque age and their historical, political, and social context.

ABSOLUTISM, MONARCHY, AND THE BALANCE OF POWER

Although the Baroque style in art originated in Rome and from there spread across the continent, neither the Italian city-states nor the popes were any longer at the center of European political life. By the time

◀ ARTEMISIA GENTILESCHI. *Judith and her Maidservant.* Ca. 1613–1614. Pitti Palace, Florence.

MAP 14.1

Europe in 1714

House of Bourbon
House of Hapsburg
Boundary of the Holy Roman Empire

Europe had recovered from the first wave of religious wars in 1600, a new system of sovereign states had replaced the old dream of a united Christendom. Over the course of the Baroque age this system matured, and by 1715 there was a balance of power in Europe among five great military states—England, France, Austria, Prussia, and Russia (Map 14.1). The rise of the great military states in the 1600s was brought about by a new breed of ruler who was fas-

cinated with both the display and the exercise of power. Known as absolutists, these rulers wanted complete control over state affairs. In this respect they were unlike medieval monarchs, who had to share authority with the church and the feudal nobles. Steeped in the works of Machiavelli, the new monarchs buttressed their claims to power with theories of divine right and natural law. France's greatest monarch, Louis XIV, was the most spectacular in his claims, launching a propaganda campaign that glorified him as the Sun King—a title derived from the late Roman emperors (Figure 14.1).

In their bid for absolute power these monarchs founded new institutions and reformed old ones. For example, bureaucracies had existed since the High Middle Ages, when they were set up to deal with the kings' administrative and legal duties, and they had always attracted a few well-educated men of humble origin. Under the absolute monarchs, however, the bureaucracies were reformed to become the exclusive domain of university-trained career officials drawn from the middle classes. Moreover, these career bureaucrats began to displace the great lords who had dominated the kings' advisory councils up to this time. The alliance between these officials and the crown also served to weaken the fading authority of the feudal nobility.

A new institution founded by the absolute monarchs was a permanent diplomatic corps to assist in the conduct of foreign policy. Venice had first taken this step in the fifteenth century, and now the great states of Europe followed, establishing diplomatic missions in the major capitals. These diplomatic posts were staffed with trusted officials who served as their rulers' eyes and ears in foreign cities.

Another institution created by these kings was the standing army funded from state revenues. Led by noble officers and manned by lower-class soldiers, the new armies outperformed all armed forces since the time of the Roman legions. New weapons—the flintlock rifle and the bayonet—and an improved breed of horse made these armies even more efficient.

France: The Supreme Example of Absolutism

At the opening of the seventeenth century, France was ruled by Henry IV, the first of the Bourbon dynasty, who had converted from Calvinism to Catholicism in order to restore peace to his largely Roman Catholic state. Ruling like a medieval king, Henry shared authority with the feudal nobles, though he began to reward middle-class supporters with high office. A sign of his pragmatic spirit was that he felt no need to force his adopted faith on the Huguenots, as the French Calvinists were called. He allowed them limited freedom of worship, greater than that enjoyed by any other religious minority of the day. All of this changed when Henry was assassinated in 1610. Between then and 1715 France became the model absolutist state (Time Line 14.1).

Henry IV was succeeded by Louis XIII, but real authority passed to Cardinal Richelieu, who was the

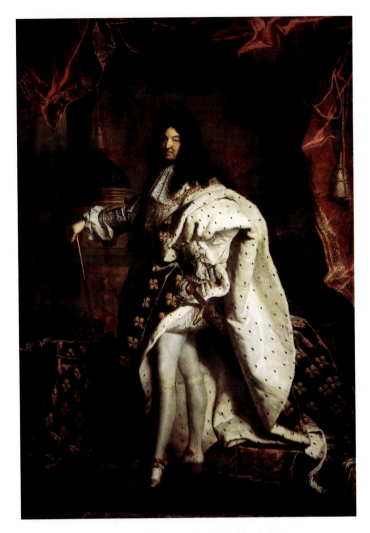

FIGURE 14.1 HYACINTHE RIGAUD. *Portrait of Louis XIV*. 1701. Oil on canvas, 9'2" × 7'10¾". Louvre. *Louis XIV had the longest reign of any European monarch, and the spirit of much of the seventeenth century was set by his concept of government. In this portrait by Louis's court artist, the love of grandeur and exaggeration characteristic of the Baroque age is apparent. The French monarch was barely 5 feet tall, but here he seems every inch the king, preening in his coronation robes. The Baroque love of theatricality is also evident in the placement of the king's feet— a pose inspired by the ballets and court dances in which he sometimes performed.*

virtual ruler of France from 1624 until his death in 1642. Gifted with political acumen, Richelieu was an outstanding statesman. As Louis's chief minister, he worked tirelessly to wrest power from the nobles. His pragmatic politics were exemplified by the different ways he treated Protestants at home and abroad. At home, in the name of centralized power, he reduced the freedom of the Huguenots; abroad, in order to curb Hapsburg influence, he fought on the side of the Protestant Swedes in the Thirty Years'

TIME LINE 14.1   KINGS OF FRANCE DURING THE BAROQUE PERIOD

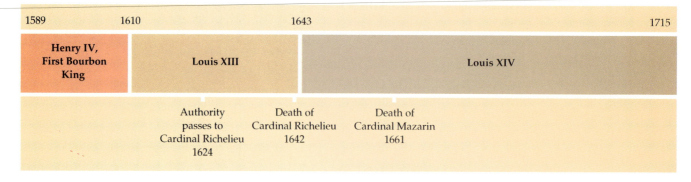

1589	1610	1643	1715
Henry IV, First Bourbon King	Louis XIII	Louis XIV	

Authority passes to Cardinal Richelieu 1624

Death of Cardinal Richelieu 1642

Death of Cardinal Mazarin 1661

War. Richelieu's pragmatic policies were continued by his protegé and successor, Cardinal Mazarin.

Mazarin's iron-fisted style moved France further in the direction of absolutism but also produced an aristocratic backlash known as the Fronde (1649–1653). This rebellion of nobles temporarily drove Mazarin from power and almost caused the death of the young Louis XIV, Louis XIII's son and heir. The Fronde eventually subsided, but it left a painful memory for Louis XIV, who never forgot this ill treatment by his nobles. Mazarin returned to favor and ruled France until his death in 1661. Mazarin's time in office coincided with the beginning of a golden age in France; for more than a century French politics and culture dominated Europe.

When Mazarin died, Louis XIV, aged twenty-three, decided to rule France in his own right, and he proved to be a tireless leader. Throughout his fifty-four-year personal reign, he made his private and public life the embodiment of the French state. "L'état c'est moi"—"I am the state"—is the remark he is said to have made about his concept of government. His public style—indeed, his every move—was calculated to impress both his subjects and his foreign visitors (see Figure 14.1).

Determined that nothing should escape his grasp, Louis XIV canceled what freedom remained to the Huguenots, persecuting them until they converted to Roman Catholicism, fled into exile, or were killed. As king, he perfected the policies of his Bourbon predecessors, becoming the chief of a bureaucratic machine that regulated every phase of French life from economics to culture. His economic policy was called mercantilism, a system that rested on state

TIME LINE 14.2   KINGS AND QUEENS OF ENGLAND DURING THE BAROQUE PERIOD

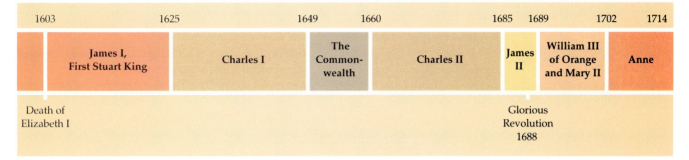

1603	1625	1649	1660	1685	1689	1702	1714
James I, First Stuart King	Charles I	The Common-wealth	Charles II	James II	William III of Orange and Mary II	Anne	

Death of
Elizabeth I

Glorious
Revolution
1688

control. Through his ministers, Louis regulated exports and imports, subsidized local industries, and set tariffs, custom duties, and quotas.

Louis waged a spectacular campaign of self-glorification and at the same time made France the center of European arts and letters. His palace at Versailles became the symbol of his regal style, one that no other noble in Europe could begin to emulate (Figure 14.2). He also encouraged the work of the academies that were emerging in this century, particularly the French Academy, founded in 1635 by Cardinal Richelieu to purify the French language and honor the state's most distinguished living authors, and the Royal Academy of Painting and Sculpture, founded by Cardinal Mazarin in 1648 to recognize the country's best artists. The latter academy was reconstituted in 1795 as the Academy of Beaux-Arts. Academies had first appeared in Italy in the sixteenth century, but it was the academies of seventeenth-century France that became the models for similar institutions in most Western states.

England: From Monarchy to Republic to Limited Monarchy

Like France, England seemed poised on the brink of absolutism at the beginning of the seventeenth century (Time Line 14.2). Following the death of Elizabeth I, a new dynasty, the Stuart, assumed the throne. King James I thought of himself as ruler by

◀ FIGURE 14.2   LOUIS LE VAU AND JULES HARDOUIN-MANSART. Palace of Versailles. 1661–1688. Versailles, France. *Versailles Palace, the seat of government and the center of fashionable society, is the greatest symbol of this age of kings. Nobles competed for Louis XIV's favors and a post at his royal court. He shrewdly rewarded them with menial positions and lofty titles and thus undermined their political influence. At the height of Louis's power, this complex of buildings could house 10,000 people—members of the royal court, hangers-on, and servants.*

divine right and even wrote a book on this subject. But certain aspects of English life served to hold royal power in check. Specifically, the English nobles were not isolated from the rest of society but made common cause with the middle-class members of Parliament; England's Parliament met regularly and considered itself the king's partner rather than his enemy; and England's Calvinist minority, called Puritans, were not despised by the Anglican majority, many of whom shared their purifying zeal. When England became embroiled in a constitutional crisis between Parliament and the headstrong Charles I, James I's successor, Puritans and Anglicans joined forces in a civil war, toppling the monarchy and setting up a republic, called the Commonwealth, in 1649. But the Commonwealth soon lost its allure when its leader, the Puritan Oliver Cromwell, turned it into a military dictatorship.

Having been disappointed by the republic, the English restored monarchy in 1660, recalling Charles I's son from exile in France to become Charles II, an event known as the Restoration. But they hedged the ruler's powers about with vague restrictions, such as the need for the king to consult Parliament regularly. Lack of clarity about the terms of the arrangement soon led to renewed conflicts between the crown and Parliament. In 1688 King James II, brother of Charles II, was expelled in a bloodless coup known as the Glorious Revolution, and his daughter and son-in-law, Mary II and William III of the Netherlands, became England's joint sovereigns. With the reign of William and Mary, England's constitutional crisis was finally resolved, for they understood that they could only rule if they recognized citizens' rights and Parliament's power over most financial matters. By 1715 England had become the classic example of limited monarchy under written laws. In the ensuing years, England's experience was to appeal to political philosophers who cited it as a successful example of the principle that government should rest on the consent of the people.

Warfare in the Baroque Period: Maintaining the Balance of Power

Warfare played an important role in establishing the configuration of the great powers because the most successful states were those in which the king could marshal his country's resources behind his military goals. But when one state began to stand out from the rest, the other states pursued policies designed to hold it in check, that is, to keep a balance of power. This system had a number of consequences. For one, it prevented any single state from gaining hegemony, or control, over the rest. Second, it was a practical way for discouraging the ambition of empires like that of the Ottoman Turks, because even though the great powers quarreled among themselves, they were willing to unite to stop Turkish expansion. Finally, this system relegated many countries to secondary power status, such as Spain and Poland, and at the same time it spelled the end of a significant international role for city-states like Florence and Venice.

The Thirty Years' War, 1618–1648   Most of the first half of the seventeenth century was consumed in the fighting of the destructive Thirty Years' War. This conflict, which was actually a series of four wars, was the last great European-wide struggle between the Protestants and the Roman Catholics (Table 14.1). Besides the great powers of Austria, France, and Brandenburg (soon to become Prussia), other states that were engaged in this war at one time or another included Denmark, Sweden, Spain, Venice, the United Provinces of the Netherlands, and Poland. But the German states, cities, and principalities, numbering about 360 and populated by both Catholics and Protestants, suffered the most, because the war was fought largely on German soil. The war wiped out a generation of Germans, inaugurating a century or more of cultural decline in Germany.

The Treaty of Westphalia, which ended the Thirty Years' War in 1648, nullified the religious objectives that had caused the war and also created the conditions for the rise of Brandenburg-Prussia to great power status. Germany itself remained divided, neither wholly Protestant nor wholly Catholic. Calvinism was now tolerated, but true religious freedom did not appear, for the principle established at Augsburg in 1555 was retained: The religion of each state was to be dictated by its ruler (see Chapter 13). A divided Germany served the interests of Brandenburg-Prussia and its rulers. Commencing with the Treaty of Westphalia, these Calvinist leaders began to amass additional territories, becoming kings of Prussia in 1701 and finally emperors of a united Germany in 1871.

The Thirty Years' War also had powerful consequences for the emerging system of great powers. The peace conference was the first in which decisions were arranged through congresses of ambassadors. The peace conference and the war itself revealed Spain's impotence, showing that it had fallen from its peak in the 1500s. In contrast, Sweden and the Netherlands gained advantages that made them major powers for the rest of the century. The Hapsburg rulers were forced to accept the fact that Protestantism could not be turned back in their German lands; henceforth they concentrated their attention on their Austrian holdings, ignoring the Holy Roman Empire, which now seemed a relic of the feudal age.

The country that profited the most from the Thirty Years' War was France, which was catapulted to the forefront of the great powers. By shifting sides to support first Roman Catholics and then Protestants, the French rulers demonstrated a shrewd understanding of power politics. Even after the religious wars were over, France continued to struggle against Roman Catholic Spain, concluding peace only in 1659. Two years later Louis XIV took control of the reins of power in France and launched a series of aggressive wars that lasted until his death in 1715.

The Wars of Louis XIV, 1665–1713   Under Louis XIV France reached the pinnacle of power in Europe's affairs. The king used various means, including marriage and diplomacy, to assert French might on the continent, but it was chiefly through warfare that he left his enduring mark. In his own mind, he fought for *la gloire* ("glory"), an elusive term that reflected his image as the Sun King and which in practice meant the expansion of France to imperial status.

Louis XIV fought the states of Europe in four separate wars and was finally brought down by a coalition that included virtually all of Europe's major and minor powers (Table 14.2). Because of its wide-ranging nature, Louis's last struggle, the War of the Spanish Succession, is generally regarded as the first of a type that later came to be called world wars. The

TABLE 14.1   THE THIRTY YEARS' WAR

PHASE	WAR	DATES
Phase One	The Bohemian War	1618–1623
Phase Two	The Danish War	1624–1629
Phase Three	The Swedish War	1630–1635
Phase Four	The French War	1635–1648

Treaty of Utrecht, signed in 1713, not only settled this last war but showed that the great power system was working.

The peace constructed at Utrecht was a reaffirmation of the balance of power principle. The victors set aside Louis's most extravagant acquisitions of land, but they allowed those additions to stand that still serve as France's borders today. A major concession to France's state interests was the installation of a Bourbon prince on the Spanish throne, but with the proviso that France and Spain remain independent of each other. Fear of Hapsburg power had been a major preoccupation of French rulers for almost two hundred years, and this arrangement was designed to lay those fears to rest. A major winner at Utrecht was Brandenburg-Prussia; its status as a great power was confirmed by new additions of territory. However, England emerged with the lion's share of the spoils, acquiring Gibraltar and the island of Minorca from Spain and important areas of Canada from France. From this augmented base, rich with commercial potential, England became the leader of world trade in the 1700s.

THE BAROQUE: VARIATIONS ON AN INTERNATIONAL STYLE

The Baroque mentality originated in a search for stability and order in a restless age. The previous century had seen a crisis in faith, a questioning of long-held beliefs, and the division of Christendom into Protestant and Catholic strongholds, accompanied by destructive wars. Mannerism had been in part a response to the disorder of the period.

Now, encouraged by the Catholic church, artists and writers sought to reveal the order they believed lay beneath the seeming chaos and instability of life. In this, they shared certain aims with the artists of the High Renaissance. But although both styles were devoted to order, they differed in their concept of how harmony was best achieved. The artists of the High Renaissance valued repose, a single, static perspective, and designs that were complete in themselves. Baroque artists, on the other hand, created dynamic, open-ended works that threaten to explode beyond their formal boundaries. These exuberant works are characterized by grand, sweeping gestures, flowing, expansive movement, and a love of curving lines and oval and elliptical shapes. Reflecting the excitement of overseas explorations and of the new discoveries in astronomy, Baroque art is fascinated with the concept of infinite space.

TABLE 14.2 THE WARS OF LOUIS XIV

WAR	FOUGHT AGAINST	DATES
The War of Devolution	England, Sweden, and the United Provinces of the Netherlands	1667–1668
The Dutch War	The United Provinces of the Netherlands, the Holy Roman Emperor, Spain, Lorraine, and Brandenburg-Prussia	1672–1679
The War Against the League of Augsburg	The league included the Holy Roman Emperor, Spain, Sweden, the United Provinces of the Netherlands, England, and various German principalities	1689–1697
The War of the Spanish Succession	England, the Holy Roman Emperor, the United Provinces of the Netherlands, and Brandenburg-Prussia	1702–1713

Despite religious differences among various regions of Europe, the Baroque style spread readily from its origin in Rome to the entire continent and to England. Lines of communication—through trade, diplomacy, and marriage—facilitated its spread, as did the persistence of Latin in scholarly works and diplomatic exchanges. Travel was also a factor in the export of Baroque ideals to the rest of Europe. Many Protestant families in northern and western Europe sent their sons, and sometimes their daughters, on grand tours to "complete their education." English travelers to Rome and other Catholic bastions included such faithful Protestants as poet John Milton and architect Christopher Wren.

Even though the Baroque was an international style, however, it was reinterpreted and adapted in different regions, so that three separate and distinct manifestations of the style emerged. The Florid Baroque, dominated by Roman Catholic religious ideals and motivations, was a product of the Counter-Reformation. This style developed in Italy and flourished there and in Spain and central Europe. The French Baroque, aristocratic and courtly, was a more restrained interpretation of Baroque ideals. French taste had been guided by the values of simplicity and harmony since the early 1500s, when Renaissance culture was first introduced into France. The preference for the Classical in the French Baroque (sometimes called "Classical-Baroque") fit well with the absolutist policies of Louis XIV, who promoted the adoption of strict rules in all aspects of cultural life as a way to reinforce his own obsession with order and control.

The third manifestation of this style was the Protestant Baroque, which arose in the middle-class United Provinces of the Netherlands and aristocratic England. Repelled equally by Catholicism and absolutism, the artists and writers of the Protestant Baroque cultivated a style in keeping with their own religious values, a style simpler and less ornate than either the Florid or the French Baroque.

The Florid Baroque

The most important formative influence on the evolution of the Baroque style in the arts and architecture was the Council of Trent (see Chapter 13). In this series of sessions held between 1545 and 1563, church leaders had reaffirmed all the values and doctrines rejected by the Protestants and called for a new art that would support their mission. They wanted an art geared to the teaching needs of the church and that set forth correct theological ideas easily understood by the masses. To achieve this goal, the popes of the late sixteenth century began to hold a tighter rein on artists and architects and to discourage the individualistic tendencies of the Mannerist style.

The seventeenth-century popes used their patronage powers to bring to life the *Florid Baroque*, a style that mirrored the church's new resolve. Once again, as in the Middle Ages, aesthetic values were subordinated to spiritual purposes. The popes enlisted architects, painters, and sculptors to glorify the Catholic message. Architects responded with grand building plans and elaborate decorative schemes that symbolized the power and richness of the church. Painters and sculptors represented dramatic incidents and emotion-charged moments, particularly favoring the ecstatic visions of the saints and the suffering and death of Jesus. They portrayed these subjects with a powerful realism intended to convey the physical presence and immediacy of the church's holiest figures. In everything, vitality and theatrical effects were prized over such Classical elements as restraint and repose.

Architecture The church of St. Peter's in Rome became the age's preeminent expression of the Florid Baroque building style. First conceived in the early 1500s by Bramante as a High Renaissance temple in the shape of a Greek cross, St. Peter's was now redesigned to conform to the ideals of the Council of Trent. Rejecting the Greek cross as a pagan symbol, Pope Paul V commissioned Carlo Maderno [mah-DAIR-noh] (1556–1629) to add a massive nave, thereby giving the floor plan a Latin cross shape (Figure 14.3). The

FIGURE 14.3 CARLO MADERNO AND GIANLORENZO BERNINI. Plan of St. Peter's Basilica with Adjoining Piazza. 1607–1615 and 1665–1667. *This plan of St. Peter's Basilica shows the design of Maderno for the church (left), dating from 1607–1615, and the adjoining piazza and colonnade (right) by Bernini, dating from 1665–1667.*

elongated nave not only satisfied the need to house the large crowds drawn to the mother church of Roman Catholicism, but the enormous size of the building signified the church's power.

St. Peter's exterior was basically finished after Maderno designed and built the building's facade, but the popes wanted to integrate this huge church into its urban setting—a Classical ideal that was now adapted to Baroque taste. For this task, Pope Alexander VII commissioned Gianlorenzo Bernini [bayr-NEE-nee] (1598–1680). Bernini's solution was a masterstroke of Florid Baroque design in which he followed the principle of abolishing all straight lines. He tore down the buildings that crowded up close to St. Peter's and replaced them with a huge public square where the faithful could gather to see and hear the pope. Bernini then outlined this keyhole-shaped space with a sweeping colonnade topped with a row of statues of saints (Figure 14.4). For those assembled in the square, the curved double colonnade stood as a symbol of the church's welcoming arms.

From its origin in Rome, the Florid Baroque style in architecture spread to Spain, Austria, and southern Germany. By 1650 this lush style had appeared

FIGURE 14.4 GIANLORENZO BERNINI. Piazza of St. Peter's. 1665–1667. The Vatican. *Bernini's plan for the piazza leading up to St. Peter's was instrumental in making exterior space a major concern of Baroque architects. The ancient Romans had integrated buildings into their urban settings, as had High Renaissance planners, but no architect had ever achieved such a natural blending of a monumental structure with its airy surroundings as Bernini did in this design.*

in Spanish and Portuguese colonies in the Americas, and there it flourished until well into the nineteenth century.

Sculpture   During the Baroque period, sculpture once again became a necessary complement to architecture, as it had been in medieval times. This change was hastened by the Council of Trent's advocacy of religious images to communicate the faith as well as the need to decorate the niches, recessed bays, and pedestals that were part of building facades in Florid Baroque architecture. The demand for sculpture called forth an army of talented artists, of whom the most outstanding was Bernini, the architect of St. Peter's.

Bernini brought the Florid Baroque to a dazzling climax in his sculptural works. His pieces, executed for such diverse projects as churches, fountains, and piazzas, or squares, often combined architecture with sculpture. His sculptural ideal was a dynamic

composition that used undulating forms to delight the eye. His sensuous sculptures with their implicit movement were the perfect accompaniments to Florid Baroque structures with their highly decorated walls.

The most famous sculptures by Bernini are the decorations that he made for the interior of St. Peter's, including altars, tombs, reliefs, statues, and liturgical furniture. For fifty years, commencing in 1629, the popes kept him employed on St. Peter's, executing sumptuous interior decorations. His masterpiece among these ornate works is the **baldacchino**, the canopy, mainly bronze and partly gilt, that covers the spot where the bones of St. Peter are believed to lie—directly under Michelangelo's dome. Combining architectural and sculptural features, the baldacchino is supported by four 14-foot-high columns whose convoluted surfaces are covered with climbing vines (Figure 14.5). Bernini crowned this

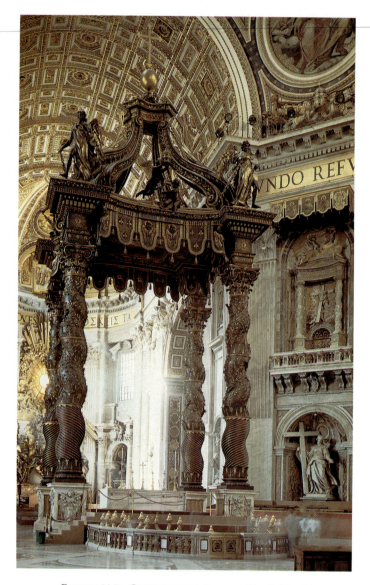

FIGURE 14.5 GIANLORENZO BERNINI. The Baldacchino. 1624–1633. Ht., ca. 100'. St. Peter's, Rome. *This magnificent canopy, a masterpiece of the Florid Baroque, reflects the grandiose ambitions of its patron, Pope Urban VIII, a member of the Barberini family. The Barberini crest was the source for the huge stylized bees displayed on the flaps of the bronze canopy. In his desire for worldly immortality, this pope shared a common outlook with the secular rulers of the Baroque age.*

colossal work with a magnificent display of four large angels at the corners, four groups of cherubs with linked arms in the centers of the sides, and between these figures four scrolls that rise to support a ball and cross at the top.

The baldacchino's corkscrew-like columns were modeled on the type that by tradition supported Solomon's temple in Jerusalem and had been used in the old St. Peter's basilica. Thus these columns symbolized the church's claim to be the true successor to the Jewish faith. So popular was Bernini's

Solomonic canopy that in southern Germany it inspired many imitators and became the standard covering for altars for the next two centuries.

The sculpture that marks the highest expression of Bernini's art is *The Ecstasy of St. Teresa* (Figure 14.6). Using stone, metal, and glass, he portrays the divine moment when the saint receives the vision of the Holy Spirit—symbolized here by the arrow with which the angel pierces her heart. In his conception, Bernini imagines the pair floating on a cloud and bathed by light from a hidden source; the light rays seem to turn into golden rods that cascade onto the angel and the saint. The intensity of the saint's expression, the agitation of the draperies, and the billowing clouds all work to create the illusion that the pair are sensuously real. By depicting St. Teresa's supernatural experience in physical terms, Bernini intended to force the viewer to suspend belief and accept the religious truth of the scene.

Painting   In the Baroque period painting once again became an integral part of church decoration. In pursuit of church ideals, the painters of this tradition tended to use rich color and unusual lighting effects to depict spectacular or dramatic moments. They represented nature and the human form realistically in order to make art intelligible and meaningful to the ordinary viewer.

The earliest great Florid Baroque painter was Michelangelo Merisi (1573–1610), better known as Caravaggio [kahr-ah-VAHD-jo]. Caravaggio rejected the antinaturalism of Mannerism in favor of a dramatic realism. His concern with realism led him to pick his models directly from the streets, and he refused to idealize his subjects. To make his works more dramatic and emotionally stirring, he experimented with light and the placement of figures. His paintings offer startling contrasts of light and dark—the technique known as chiaroscuro—and he banished landscape from his canvases, often focusing on human figures grouped tightly in the foreground.

A superb example of Caravaggio's work is *The Martyrdom of St. Matthew*, one of a series of works he painted on the life of this early Christian saint (Figure 14.7). His revolutionary use of chiaroscuro, whereby the light drenches the foreground figures and the darkness renders the background indistinct, makes the agony of the saint more dramatically vivid. The tension in the scene is intensified by the thrusting limbs of the various figures. Caravaggio had an enormous influence on other painters both in Italy and elsewhere, notably France, Spain, and the Netherlands.

Perhaps the most original of Caravaggio's Italian disciples—known as Caravaggisti—was Artemisia

FIGURE 14.6 GIANLORENZO BERNINI. *The Ecstasy of St. Teresa.* 1645–1652. Marble, Lifesize. Cornaro Chapel, Santa Maria della Vittoria, Rome. *Even though the subject of this sculpture is an ecstatic vision, its portrayal reflects the naturalism that was central to the Baroque style. Bernini based this work on the saint's personal account in which she described how an angel pierced her heart with a golden spear—a mystical moment the tableau faithfully reproduces.*

FIGURE 14.7 CARAVAGGIO. *The Martyrdom of St. Matthew.* 1602. Oil on canvas, 323 × 343 cm. Contarelli Chapel, San Luigi dei Francesi, Rome. *Caravaggio's paintings made monumentality an important feature of the Florid Baroque style. By presenting the human figures in close-up and giving full weight to their bodies, as in this painting, the artist made their presence an inescapable fact to the viewer. This approach gave his paintings a dramatic immediacy.*

Gentileschi [ahrt-uh-MEEZ-e-uh jain-teel-ESS-key] (1593–1653), his only female follower. Unlike most women artists of the early modern period who limited their art to portraits, such as the late sixteenth-century painter Sofonisba Anguissola (see Chapter 13), Artemisia made career choices similar to male artists of the times in that she concentrated on biblical and mythical subjects. Trained by her painter-father Orazio, himself a disciple of Caravaggio, Artemisia adapted the flamboyant and dramatic style of Caravaggesque realism and made it her own. In almost 30 surviving paintings, she followed this style's preference for "night pictures," dark scenes whose blackness is illuminated by a single internal light source.

What distinguishes Artemisia Gentileschi's art from that of the rest of the Caravaggisti is its female assertiveness, a highly unusual quality in the Baroque period, when women artists were still making their way without guild support or access to nude modeling. Female assertiveness is expressed throughout her works in an androgynous (having female and male characteristics) ideal, as may be seen in *Judith and her Maidservant* (Figure 14.8), a depiction of a scene from an apocryphal book of the Old Testament, the Book of Judith. The painting's central figure—Judith—is decidedly female (the vulnerable throat and curvaceous breasts) and yet exhibits masculine strength (the swaggering gesture accentuated by the lightly grasped sword). Judith, often treated in Italian painting and sculpture in the Renaissance and Baroque eras, is a perfect subject for Artemisia, since the biblical story describes a woman of destiny. In the story, Judith saves the Jewish people by beheading their enemy Holofernes, having first seduced him. In the painting, Holofernes's bloody head, visible in the basket, starkly dramatizes the point that Judith is a forthright woman who plans and acts, just as men do. Artemisia's Judith typifies an heroic female ideal who is endowed with the traits of that fuller humanity that by tradition had been allowed only to male figures. Through such dramatic works as this, Artemisia helped to spread the Caravaggesque style in Italy.

At about the same time that Caravaggio was creating his dramatic works, a new form caught the imagination of painters in the Florid Baroque tradition—the illusionistic ceiling fresco. In these paintings, artists constructed imaginary continuations of the architectural features already present in the room, expanding up through layers of carefully foreshortened, sculpted figures and culminating in patches of sky. Looking up as if at the heavens above, the viewer is overawed by the superhuman spectacle that seems to begin just overhead.

The superb example of this *illusionism* is the nave ceiling of the church of Sant' Ignazio (St. Ignatius) in Rome, painted by Andrea Pozzo [POE-tzo] (1642–1709). In this fresco, entitled *Allegory of the Missionary Work of the Jesuits*, Pozzo reveals a firm mastery of the technique of architectural perspective (Figure 14.9). The great nave ceiling is painted to appear as if the viewer were looking up through an immense open colonnade. Figures stand and cling to the encircling architectural supports and, in the center, an

expansive vista opens to reveal Ignatius, the founder of the Jesuit order, being received by an open-armed Christ. The clusters of columns on either side are labeled for the four continents—Europe, Asia, America, and Africa—symbolizing the missionary zeal of the Jesuits around the globe. Illusionism, infinite space, and spectacular effects make this a masterpiece of the Florid Baroque.

Outside Italy, the principal centers of Florid Baroque painting were the studio of Velázquez in Spain and the workshop of Rubens in Flanders (present-day Belgium). While Velázquez softened the Florid Baroque to his country's taste, Rubens fully embraced this sensual style to become its most representative painter.

The work of Diego Velázquez [vuh-LAS-kus] (1599–1660) owes much to the tradition of Caravaggio, but without the intense drama of the Italian's painting. Velázquez also used chiaroscuro, but he avoided the extreme contrasts that made Caravaggio's paintings controversial. Velázquez's works have a somber quietude that sometimes suggests that the subjects have been interrupted in what they are doing.

Velázquez's greatest work is *Las Meninas*, or *The Maids of Honor* (Figure 14.10). In his role as official artist to the Spanish court, Velázquez painted this group portrait of the Infanta, or princess, surrounded by her maids of honor (one of whom is a

FIGURE 14.8 ARTEMISIA GENTILESCHI. *Judith and her Maidservant.* Ca. 1613–1614. Oil on canvas, 46 × 36½". Pitti Palace, Florence. *Artemisia Gentileschi's style in this painting is strongly indebted to the cinematic manner of Caravaggio: The natural background is virtually eliminated and painted black, the central figures are shown in tight close-up, and the action is frozen like a single frame in a film sequence. The aesthetic impact of this cinematic method is to draw viewers into the scene and make the figures seem as real as life and with individual personalities. The artist's interest in the personal psychology of her characters is part of the general trend toward naturalism—''a coming down to earth,'' in the words of one scholar—that characterized Baroque culture in general.*

dwarf). What makes this painting so haunting is the artful play of soft light over the various figures. In the background, a man is illuminated by the light streaming through the open door, and even more abundant sunshine falls on the princess from the window on the right.

Velázquez also plays with space and illusion in this painting. On the left side he depicts himself, standing before a huge canvas with brush and palette in hand. The artist gazes directly at the viewer— or is he greeting the king and queen, who have just entered the room and are reflected in the mirror on the rear wall? The princess and two of her maids also look attentively out of the picture, but whether at the artist painting their portrait, at the royal couple, or at the viewer is left unclear. This fascination with illusion and with the effects of light and shade reveals Velázquez's links with Caravaggio and the art of the Florid Baroque.

In contrast to Velázquez's devotion to the ideal of grave beauty, the work of Peter Paul Rubens (1577– 1640) is known for its ripe sensuality and for his portrayal of voluptuous female nudes. Rubens had already forged a sensuous style before he visited Italy, but his encounters with Caravaggio's tradition impressed him deeply, causing him to intensify his use of explosive forms and chiaroscuro. From the Venetian painters, especially Titian, he derived his love and mastery of gorgeous color. In his mature works, he placed human figures in a shallow foreground, bathed them in golden light with dark contours, and painted their clothes and flesh in sensuous tones.

As the most sought-after artist of his day, Rubens was often given commissions by the kings of the great states, and he produced works for royalty, for the church, and for wealthy private patrons. As official painter to the French court, he was commissioned to paint a cycle of works glamorizing the life of Queen Marie de' Medici, widow of Henry IV and powerful regent for her son, Louis XIII. One of the typical works from this series was *The Landing of Marie de' Medici at Marseilles* (Figure 14.11). In this huge

FIGURE 14.9 ANDREA POZZO. *Allegory of the Missionary Work of the Jesuits.* Ca. 1621–1625. Ceiling fresco. Sant' Ignazio, Rome. *Pozzo was motivated by spiritual concerns when he painted this supernatural vision. He believed that the illusion of infinite space could evoke feelings of spiritual exaltation in the viewer. The observer, overwhelmed by the sight of St. Ignatius Loyola's ascent into heaven, could thus be transported into a religious rapture.*

FIGURE 14.10 VELÁZQUEZ. *Las Meninas (The Maids of Honor).* 1656. Oil on canvas, 10′5″ × 9′. Prado, Madrid. *Velázquez uses the mirror on the back wall, reflecting the Spanish king and queen, to enhance the dynamic feeling of the scene. This illusionistic device explodes the pictorial space by calling up presences within and outside the painting.*

canvas, Rubens transforms a relatively insignificant event in the life of a queen into a splendid pageant of the French monarchy. The scene depicts the moment at which the young Medici heiress first sets foot on French soil on her way to meet her bridegroom. Rubens flatters his subject by showing her accompanied by the ancient god Neptune with his retinue

while Fame soars above her head. All action in the painting is centered around the regal presence of the queen, as flags and clouds billow overhead and fleshy sea nymphs rise from the waters below. Rubens's mastery of both spiritual and secular subjects and the turbulent drama of his works made him the finest artist of the Florid Baroque.

FIGURE 14.11 PETER PAUL RUBENS. *The Landing of Marie de' Medici at Marseilles.* Ca. 1625. Oil on canvas, 12'11" × 9'8¼". Louvre. *The Medici cycle, of which this work is a superb example, not only established Rubens's European-wide reputation but defined historical narrative—the combining of a historical event with mythological motifs—as one of the great themes of Baroque art. By 1715 the French Academy had created a ranked set of painting subjects, of which historical narrative occupied the highest level.*

The French Baroque

Although the Baroque originated in Rome, the pronouncements of the church had little effect on the art and architecture of France. Here, the royal court was the guiding force in the artistic life of the nation. The rulers and the royal ministers provided rich commissions that helped to shape the *French Baroque*, giving this style a secular focus and identifying it with absolutism. A second powerful influence on the French Baroque was the pervasiveness in French culture of the Classical values of simplicity and grave dignity. Accordingly, French artists and architects found the Florid Baroque alien and even offensive; their adaptation of this style was more impersonal, controlled, and restrained.

Architecture   The palace of Versailles was the consummate architectural expression of the French Baroque. A hunting lodge under Louis XIII, Versailles was transformed by Louis XIV into a magnificent royal residence that became the prototype of princely courts in the West. At Versailles, where all power was concentrated in the royal court, were collected the best architects, sculptors, painters, and landscape architects as well as the finest writers, composers, and musicians that France could produce. The duty of this talented assemblage was to use their gifts to surround Louis XIV with the splendor appropriate to the Sun King.

The redesign of Versailles gave Louis XIV the most splendid palace that has ever been seen in Europe. The chief architects of this revamped palace were Louis Le Vau [LUH-VO] (1612–1670) and Jules Hardouin-Mansart [air-dwan MAN-sahrt] (1646–1708), but the guiding spirit was the Sun King himself. When finished, the palace consisted of a huge central structure with two immense wings (see Figure 14.2). The architecture is basically in the style of the Renaissance, with rounded arches, Classical columns, and porticoes inspired by Roman temples, but the overall effect is of restrained Baroque.

The most striking aspect of Versailles is its monumentality: The palace is only the most imposing building of an elaborate complex that includes a royal chapel and various support structures, all of which are set in an elaborate park over two miles long. Versailles' park, designed by André Le Nôtre [luh-NOH-truh] (1613–1700), is studded with a rich display of fountains, reflecting pools, geometric flower beds, manicured woods, exotic trees, statues, urns, and graveled walks—a gorgeous outdoor setting for royal receptions and entertainments (Figure 14.12).

The most famous room in Versailles Palace is the Hall of Mirrors, a central chamber with a tunnel-vaulted ceiling (Figure 14.13). The grandiose design of this hallway reflects its original function as the throne room of Louis XIV. Named for its most prominent feature, this long hall is decorated with Baroque profusion, including, in addition to the mirrors, wood parquetry floors of intricate design, multi-colored marbles, ceiling paintings depicting military victories and other deeds of Louis XIV, and gilded statues at the base of the paintings. In modern

FIGURE 14.13 CHARLES LEBRUN AND JULES HARDOUIN-MANSART. Hall of Mirrors, Versailles Palace. 1678–1684. Versailles, France. *Lebrun and Mansart designed this enormous hall to overlook the vast park at Versailles. Viewed through the floor-to-ceiling windows, which are placed along the width of the room, the majestic park becomes an extension of the interior space. The inside space, in turn, is enlarged by the tall mirrors that match the windows, echoing the outside view.* ▶

FIGURE 14.12 ANDRÉ LE NÔTRE, LANDSCAPE ARCHITECT, AND VARIOUS SCULPTORS. Versailles Gardens. The Pool of Latona with Adjacent Parterres. 1660s. Versailles, France. *This fountain, composed of four concentric marble basins, is named for its crowning statue of Latona, the mother of the sun god Apollo, who was the inspiration for Louis XIV's reign. On either side of the fountain may be glimpsed parterres, or flower gardens with beds and paths arranged into patterns. Beyond the fountain stretches an avenue flanked by wooded areas that culminates in the grand canal, which extends the view into infinity. The rich profusion of this scene is a hallmark of Baroque design.*

FIGURE 14.14 NICOLAS POUSSIN. *Et in Arcadia Ego.* Ca. 1640. Oil on canvas, 34 × 48". Louvre. *In sacred art, painters expressed the theme of the inevitability of death in portraits of the sufferings of Jesus and the saints, and in secular art, in depictions of skeletons and death's heads, or images of human skulls. But Poussin, whose art was fired by Classical ideals and who was thus more reflective than others of his age, treated death in a much more detached way, as in this painting. Poussin's puzzled shepherds are a gentle reminder that the reality of death always comes as a surprise in the midst of everyday existence.*

times, major political events have taken place in the Hall of Mirrors: The Germans proclaimed their empire from here in 1871 after having vanquished the French, and the peace treaty that ended World War I was signed here in 1919.

Painting   Classical values dominated Baroque painting in France even more completely than architecture. In pursuit of ancient Roman ideals (for Greek values were virtually unknown), French Baroque artists painted mythological subjects, stressed idealized human bodies, and cultivated a restrained style. The outstanding French Baroque artist was Nicolas Poussin [POO-SAN] (1594–1665), the finest Classical painter of the seventeenth century. Ironically, except for two disappointing years in Paris, Poussin spent his professional life in Rome, the home of the Florid Baroque. Although he was inspired by Caravaggio's use of light and dark, the style that Poussin forged was uniquely his own, a detached, almost cold approach to his subject matter and a feeling for the unity of human beings with nature.

A beautiful example of Poussin's detached style is *Et in Arcadia Ego,* a painting in which the human figures are integrated into a quiet landscape (Figure 14.14). In ancient mythology, Arcadia was a land of pastures and flocks. In Poussin's painting, four shepherds, modeled on ancient statuary and dressed to suggest Roman times, are portrayed standing around a tomb, evidently absorbed in a discussion provoked by the Latin words carved into the tomb: *Et in Arcadia Ego,* that is, "I too once dwelled in Arcadia." One shepherd traces the letters with his finger, spelling out the words. The magnificent stillness, the mythological subject, and the gentle melancholy evoked by this reminder of death were

central to Poussin's art and evidence of his Classical spirit. Typically Baroque are the use of chiaroscuro, which makes the exposed limbs and the faces of the shepherds stand out vividly from the shadowy middle ground, and the sensual tones and rich colors.

The Protestant Baroque

The Protestant culture of northern and western Europe created simpler works that humanized Baroque exuberance, appealed to democratic sentiments, and reflected common human experience. This style of art is called the **Protestant Baroque**, and it was founded by the painters and architects of the Netherlands and England.

Painting   The Calvinist Netherlands pointed the way in the arts in Protestant Europe until 1675. The Dutch Republic was ruled by a well-to-do middle class whose wealth was based largely on their dominant role in international shipping. Led by these sober-minded burghers, as the townspeople were called, the Netherlands was briefly one of Europe's great powers. During the middle of the century the Dutch virtually controlled northern Europe, using their military and naval might to fight England, check French ascendancy, and destroy Spanish sea power. Amsterdam became one of Europe's largest cities, and an important school of painting flourished there. In about 1675, a series of military disasters ended the Netherlands' economic expansion, and the state's fortunes declined sharply. By this time the great days of Dutch art were over.

During the heyday of the Dutch Republic a school of painters arose whose works defined the Protestant Baroque. Attuned to the sober values of their religion and sympathetic to the civic ideals of the republic, these artists created a secular style that mirrored the pious outlook of the ruling middle class. An important development that helped to shape the course of Dutch painting was the rise of an art market. Venice had shown some tendencies in this direction in the 1500s, but in the Netherlands in the 1600s the first full-fledged art market made its debut. The impact of this market on the Dutch school was instantaneous and dramatic. Driven by a demand for home decoration, especially small works to hang on the wall, the market responded with specific subjects—still lifes, landscapes, portraits, and genre, or "slice-of-life," scenes. Paintings were sold by dealers as wares, and buyers speculated in art objects. The market dictated success or failure; some painters pursued other careers as a hedge against financial ruin.

The greatest artist of the Dutch school and probably one of the two or three greatest painters of Western art was Rembrandt van Rijn (1606–1669). His early genius lay in his subtle and dramatic use of lighting and his forceful expressiveness—both qualities that reflected the distant influence of Caravaggio. He also was supremely gifted in his ability to portray the range of moods and emotions he found in humanity, as expressed through the ordinary people he used as models.

A splendid illustration of Rembrandt's early style is *The Blinding of Samson,* a work inspired by the biblical story of seduction and betrayal (Figure 14.15). In the biblical account, Samson was a powerful warrior whose hair—the source of his strength—was cut off by the beautiful Delilah; she then betrayed him to his enemies who were able to capture and blind him. This painting, with its lush colors and dramatic detail, reflects the Baroque vogue for sensuality and violent episode. Much of the scene is rendered in near darkness, but Rembrandt uses subtle lighting to focus attention on the central action and to stir the viewer's emotions. Light falls through the tent opening revealing soldiers wrestling with Samson, the Jewish hero. One figure bends over the struggling Samson putting out his eye while the figure with the pike stands guard. Behind the soldiers can be seen the figure of Delilah, brandishing Samson's shorn locks as she hastily exits from the tent. Through works such as this Rembrandt became one of the most successful painters working in Amsterdam.

The culmination of Rembrandt's early style is a painting entitled *The Militia Company of Captain Frans Banning Cocq* but commonly known as *The Night Watch* (Figure 14.16). The painting was commissioned by one of Amsterdam's municipal guard troops in a typical display of Dutch civic pride. Instead of painting a conventional group portrait, however, Rembrandt created a theatrical work filled with exuberant and dramatic gestures and highly charged chiaroscuro effects. He gave the composition added energy by depicting the guardsmen marching toward the viewer. The militia is led by Captain Cocq, the black-suited figure with the red sash and white ruff who marches with arm outstretched in the center foreground. On his left marches his attentive lieutenant, dressed in yellow, with his halberd in his hand. Behind them the members of the surging crowd, engaged in various soldierly activities and looking in different directions with expressive faces, seem ready to burst forth from

FIGURE 14.15 REMBRANDT VAN RIJN. *The Blinding of Samson.* 1636. Oil on canvas, 7'9" × 9'11". Staedelsches Kunstinstitut, Frankfurt. *The influence of Caravaggio on Rembrandt, particularly in his early works, can be seen in this painting. It is evident in the passionate energy, the handling of contrasts of light and shade, and the modeling of the bodies and faces of ordinary people. Later in his life, Rembrandt's style became less dynamic and sensual.*

FIGURE 14.16 REMBRANDT VAN RIJN. *The Night Watch (The Militia Company of Captain Frans Banning Cocq)*. 1642. Oil on canvas, 12′2″ × 14′7″. Rijksmuseum, Amsterdam. *Because of its murky appearance, this painting acquired its nickname,* The Night Watch, *in the nineteenth century. But a cleaning of the painting's deteriorated surface showed that it was actually set in daylight. Restored to its original conception, this work now reveals Rembrandt's spectacular use of light and dark.*

FIGURE 14.17 REMBRANDT VAN RIJN. *Self-Portrait*. 1669. Oil on canvas, 23¼ × 20″. Mauritshuis, The Hague. *In this last self-portrait, Rembrandt's eyes reveal the personal anguish of a man who has outlived wife, beloved mistress, and children. By this means, Rembrandt expresses one of the most popular themes of Baroque art, that of pathos—the quality that arouses feelings of pity and sorrow.*

FIGURE 14.18 JAN VERMEER. *The Lacemaker*. Ca. 1664. Oil on canvas, 9⅝ × 8¼". Louvre. *Unlike Rembrandt, Vermeer was not concerned with human personality as such. Rather, his aim was to create scenes that registered his deep pleasure in bourgeois order and comfort. In* The Lacemaker *he gives his female subject generalized features, turning her into a social type, but renders her sewing in exquisite detail, giving it a monumental presence. The painting thus becomes a visual metaphor of a virtuous household.*

the space in which they are enclosed. Of Rembrandt's vast repertory, this painting is one of his most representative.

In the later work painted in the mid–1640s, Rembrandt's style became more personal and simpler. His paintings now expressed a stronger naturalism and an inner calm, a change that paralleled the rise of the quieter French Baroque. This final stage of his art is most beautifully and movingly rendered in his last self-portrait (Figure 14.17). During his career he had often painted his own likeness, coolly revealing the effects of the aging process on his face. The last self-portrait is most remarkable for the expressive eyes, which, though anguished, seem resigned to whatever happens next. Rembrandt's pursuit of truth—inspired by his own meditations—is revealed here with clarity and acceptance. Looking into this time-ravaged face, the viewer recognizes the universality of growing old and the inevitability of death.

Another great Dutch artist was Jan Vermeer (1632–1675), who specialized in domestic genre scenes. His works reveal a calm world where ordinary objects possess a timeless gravity. Color was important for establishing the domesticity and peacefulness of this closed-off world; Vermeer's favorites were yellow and blue. These serene works evoked the fabled cleanliness of Delft, the city where he lived and worked.

One of the most beautiful of his domestic scenes is *The Lacemaker* (Figure 14.18). Like most of his thirty-five extant paintings, *The Lacemaker* depicts an interior room where a single figure is encircled by everyday things. She is lit by a clear light falling on her from the side, another characteristic of Vermeer's paintings. The composition (the woman at the table and the rear wall parallel to the picture frame), the basic colors (yellow and blue), and the subject's absorption in her task typified Vermeer's works. *The Lacemaker* also has a moral message, for a woman engaged in household tasks symbolized the virtue of domesticity for Vermeer.

England also contributed to the creation of the Protestant Baroque, but conditions there led to a style markedly different from that of the Dutch school. Unlike the Netherlands, England had no art market, was dominated by an aristocracy, and, most importantly, had as yet no native-born painters of note. Painting in England was controlled by aristocratic patrons who preferred portraits to all other subjects and whose taste was courtly but restrained. The painter whose style suited these aristocratic demands was a Flemish artist, Anthony van Dyck [vahn-DIKE] (1599–1641). A pupil of Rubens, van Dyck eventually settled in England and became court painter to Charles I.

Van Dyck's elegant style captured the courtly qualities prized by his noble patrons. He depicted

FIGURE 14.19 ANTHONY VAN DYCK. *James Stuart, Duke of Richmond and Lennox.* Ca. 1630. Oil on canvas, 7′1″ × 4′2¼″. Metropolitan Museum of Art, New York. Gift of Henry G. Marquand, 1889. *This pose, an aristocrat with his dog, had been established in the High Renaissance. Van Dyck transforms the arrangement into a Baroque work of art, making the figure of the animal as interesting in its own way as the handsome duke. The sinuous lines of the dog's body and his beseeching expression are perfect complements to his aloof and insipid master.*

his subjects' splendid costumes in all their radiant glory, using vibrant colors to reproduce their textures. He invented a repertory of poses for individual and group portraits that showed his subjects to their greatest advantage. Within a generation, his designs had become the standard for English portraiture. But van Dyck did more than cater to the vanity of his titled patrons. With superb sensitivity, he portrayed their characters in their faces, showing such qualities as intelligence, self-doubt, and obstinacy. His psychological insights make his courtly portraits into genuine works of art.

Van Dyck's fluent style is wonderfully shown in his portrait of *James Stuart, Duke of Richmond and Lennox,* one of the dandies at the court of Charles I (Figure 14.19). This likeness indicates the artist's sly

insight. The fashionable dress and the haughty expression establish the high social status of the Duke. But the vacant look in the eyes and the weak, untested face tell another story, namely, that the subject is a vapid young man. No painter in either the Florid Baroque or the French Baroque was capable of such measured insight.

Architecture   The architecture of the Protestant Baroque drew strongly on the Classical tradition. One of the most influential English architects of this period was Sir Christopher Wren (1632–1723), whose Baroque style had two sources. From the French Baroque of Versailles came his love of rich ornamentation, and from Bramante's High Renaissance style came his devotion to pure Classical forms, such as the dome and the Classical orders. Following these traditions, Wren created his own unique style, with spacious interiors and elaborately decorated facades.

Although Wren created many brilliant secular works, he is best known for his churches. His masterpiece is St. Paul's Cathedral in London (Figure 14.20). Intended as a Protestant rival to St. Peter's in Rome, St. Paul's has a longitudinal floor plan similar to St. Peter's and a dome reminiscent of Bramante's Tempietto (see Figure 12.18). The church has many Classical elements, such as the pairs of columns on two levels, the symmetrical towers and decorations, and the elaborate pediment. At the same time, its Baroque nature is revealed in the ornate facade punctuated by niches, the robust twin steeples with their shadowy recesses and staggered columns, and the dramatic play of light across the face of the building. The most outstanding feature of St. Paul's is the magnificent dome, inspired by the one designed by Michelangelo for St. Peter's (see Figure 12.19), with its encircling colonnade. This elegant dome still dominates the London skyline, a splendid reminder of Baroque glory.

Literature

The Council of Trent's decrees, which had such a powerful impact on artists and architects, were hardly felt by seventeenth-century writers. Nevertheless, a style of literary expression arose that is called Baroque and that became international in scope. The most enduring literary legacy of this period is drama. Baroque audiences delighted in works that blended different forms, and drama mixed literature, costume design, set painting, and theatrical spectacle. Tragedy, based on Roman models, was the supreme achievement of the Baroque stage, but comedies of all types, including satires, farces, and sexual comedies, were also important. After centu-

Figure 14.20 Christopher Wren. St. Paul's Cathedral. 1675–1710. London. *Christopher Wren was a true child of the Baroque age. An astronomy professor at Oxford University, he made discoveries that brought him to the attention of the age's greatest scientist, Isaac Newton. When opportunity called and Wren was given the royal commission to rebuild the churches of London, he approached this task with the same passionate love of geometry that had motivated his scientific researches. Wren's design for St. Paul's united his sense of beauty with his mathematical bent.*

ries of neglect, tragedy and comedy had been brilliantly revived in Elizabethan England, and their appearance in France was evidence of the continuing growth of secular consciousness. Another ancient literary genre that gained wide favor was the epic, a reflection of the love of power typical of the age. Finally, Baroque literature began to take notice of the world outside Europe, as may be seen in the rise of writings with a non-Western dimension. These non-Western aspects included settings (for example, Mexico in the poetry of the Mexican nun Sor Juana Inés de la Cruz (1648–1695]), characters (for example, the Aztec ruler Montezuma, the hero of the play *The Indian Emperor* [1665] by John Dryden [1631–1700]), and themes (especially the comparison of Western and non-Western customs in travel literature, as in *A New Voyage Round the World* [1697] by William Dampier [1652–1715] and *Travels in Persia* [1686] by Jean Chardin [1643–1713]).

Despite the variety of their works, the Baroque writers had common characteristics, including a love of ornate language and a fascination with characterization, either of individuals or of types. Baroque authors often dealt with emotional extremes, such as gross sensuality versus pangs of conscience. With such emotionally charged themes, Baroque writers could and did employ dynamic rhetoric, slipping occasionally into empty bombast.

The French Baroque Drama was France's greatest literary contribution to the literature of the Baroque period. Secular drama revived under the patronage of Louis XIII in the 1630s and reached a climax during Louis XIV's reign. Strict control was exercised over the

plays staged at the royal court, although comic playwrights were given more freedom, so long as they did not offend common decency or good taste.

The tragic playwrights were expected to obey the rules of literary composition laid down by the French Academy and based on the theories of Aristotle (see Chapter 3). The ideal play must observe the unities of time, place, and action—that is, it must take place during a twenty-four-hour time span, have no scene changes, and have a single uncomplicated plot. Furthermore, the plays were supposed to use elevated language and to focus on universal problems as reflected in dilemmas experienced by highborn men and women. Because of the playwrights' strict adherence to these rules, it is sometimes claimed that the dramas of this period are expressive of a Classical style. But the compulsive stress laid by the French on order, gravity, and severity was evidence of a Baroque sensibility—just as was the case in French Baroque painting and architecture.

The two great French tragedians of the Baroque period are Pierre Corneille [kor-NAY] (1606–1684) and Jean Racine [ra-SEEN] (1639–1699). Corneille wrote tragedies in verse based on Spanish legends and Roman themes. Drawing on the Hellenistic philosophy of Stoicism, his dramas stressed the importance of duty, honor, patriotism, and loyalty—ideals that appealed to his courtly audience. His finest work is *Le Cid*, based on a Spanish legend and concerned with the hero's choice between personal feelings and honor.

In Racine drama found a voice whose refined language and penetrating psychological insight have never been equaled in the French theater. Preoccupied with the moral struggle between the will and the emotions, Racine created intensely human characters in classically constructed plays. A subject that intrigued Racine was the doomed woman who was swept to her destruction by obsessive sexual passion. This Baroque theme was most perfectly expressed in his masterpiece, *Phèdre,* his version of the Greek tale of incestuous love first dramatized by Euripides in the fifth century B.C. Where Euripides makes fate a central reason for the heroine Phèdre's downfall, Racine portrays the unfortunate woman as a victim of her own passion for her stepson. Even though he explored other types of love in his plays, such as mother love and even political passion, it was in his study of sex as a powerful motive for action that Racine was most original.

The Baroque period in French drama also produced one of the comic geniuses of the Western theatre, Jean Baptiste Poquelin, better known as Molière [MOLE-YAIR] (1622–1673). Molière analyzed the foibles of French life in twelve penetrating satirical comedies that had the lasting impact of tragedy. He peopled his plays with social types—the idler, the miser, the pedant, the seducer, the hypochondriac, the medical quack, the would-be gentleman, the pretentiously cultured lady—exposing the follies of the entire society. To create his comedic effects, Molière used not only topical humor and social satire but all the trappings of farce, including pratfalls, mistaken identities, sight gags, puns, and slapstick.

Molière was appointed official entertainer to Louis XIV in 1658; even so, he made many enemies among those who felt they were the butt of his jokes. When he died, for example, the French clergy refused to give him an official burial because they believed some of his plays to be attacks on the church. The testament to Molière's enduring brilliance is that many of his comedies are still performed today, including *Tartuffe, The Miser, The Bourgeois Gentleman,* and *The Misanthrope,* and that when they are, they are still enormously entertaining.

The English Baroque   The outstanding contribution in English to the literature of the Baroque period was provided by John Milton (1608–1674), a stern Puritan who held high office in Cromwell's Commonwealth. The deeply learned Milton had a grand moral vision that led him to see the universe as locked in a struggle between the forces of darkness and the forces of light. Only an epic was capable of expressing such a monumental conception.

His supreme literary accomplishment was to Christianize the epic in his long poem *Paradise Lost.* Inspired by Homer's and Vergil's ancient works, but also intended as a Protestant response to Dante's *Comedy,* Milton's poem became an immediate classic. His grandiose themes in *Paradise Lost* were the rebellion of the angels led by Lucifer, the fall of Adam and Eve in the Garden of Eden, and Christ's redemption of humanity.

An astonishing aspect of *Paradise Lost* is Milton's portrait of Lucifer, which some readers have seen as a Baroque glamorization of evil. Lucifer is characterized as a creature of titanic ambition and deceitful charm. Despite his powerful presence, however, this epic story has moral balance. At the end, Adam, the author of original sin, is saved instead of being condemned to Hell. Adam's redemption occurs when he accepts Jesus as Lord. Adam's choice reflected Milton's belief in free will and the necessity of taking responsibility for one's actions.

In addition to its grand theme, *Paradise Lost* is Baroque in other ways. The mixing of Christian legend and ancient epic, for example, is typical of Baroque taste. Milton's convoluted style is Baroque with its occasionally odd word order, Latinisms, and complex metaphors. Most of all, Milton's epic is Baroque in its lofty tone and exaggerated rhetoric—literary equivalents, perhaps, of Rubens or Rembrandt.

A secondary achievement of the literary Baroque in England was that literature began to reflect the West's overseas expansion, as in the publishing of travel books, memoirs, and letters describing real and fictional contacts with peoples and lands around the globe. Part of a European-wide trend, the growth of English literature with a non-European dimension expressed the Baroque theme of pushing against the boundaries of life and art. A pioneering work on this Baroque theme was the short prose work *Oroonoko* (1688) by Aphra Behn (1640–1689), an English writer who exploited her firsthand experiences as a resident of Surinam (modern Suriname), to provide a vivid, exotic setting. Situated in South America and told with a blend of realism and romance, *Oroonoko* condemns the culture of slavery through the story of the doomed love affair between a black slave-prince and a slave woman. The author portrays the black hero as untutored in Western ways yet polished and educated on his own terms, and, above all, superior to the natural depravity of the European characters. This is an early version of the myth of the noble savage, the cultural archetype that reached its climax in the Romantic era (see Chapter 16). England's first professional woman writer, Behn also wrote about 20 comedies for the stage and a poem collection, but *Oroonoko* is her chief claim to renown.

Music

Unlike the Renaissance, when a single musical sound prevailed (see Chapter 12), the Baroque had no single musical ideal. Nonetheless, four trends during the Baroque period give its music distinctive qualities. First, the development of major and minor tonality, which had been prefigured in Josquin des Prez's music in the early 1500s, was a central feature of the works of this time, making it the first stage in the rise of modern music. Second, the mixing of genres, which has been noted in literature and the

FIGURE 14.21 JAN BRUEGEL. *Hearing.* Ca. 1620. Oil on canvas, ca. 2'3" × 3'6". Prado, Madrid. *One of a series of allegorical paintings representing the five senses, this work by Jan Bruegel depicts the sense of hearing. Set in a Renaissance interior framed by three rounded arches, it shows a variety of sources that make sounds pleasing to the human ear. Most prominent are the musical instruments, which collectively constitute an anthology of the instruments used in Baroque music.*

arts, also occurred in Baroque music. Third, the expressiveness that had entered music in the late 1500s now became even more exaggerated, being used to stress meanings and emotions in the musical texts that otherwise might not have been heard. And last, this was an age of *virtuosos*, master musicians, especially singers, who performed with great technical skill and vivid personal style, and of a growing variety of musical instruments (Figure 14.21). The musical form that drew these trends together was *opera*, making it the quintessential symbol of the age.

Opera originated in Italy in the late sixteenth century among a group of Florentine musicians and poets with aristocratic ties. The first great composer of opera was Claudio Monteverdi [mon-tay-VAIR-dee] (1567–1643), whose earliest opera, *Orfeo* (1607), was based on the legend of the ancient Greek poet-musician Orpheus. *Orfeo* united drama, dance, elaborate stage mechanisms, and painted scenery with music. Monteverdi wrote melodic arias, or songs, for the individual singers, and he increased the opera's dramatic appeal by concluding each of its five acts with a powerful chorus. His setting truly mirrored the text, using musical phrases to serve as aural symbols and thus to enhance the unfolding of events.

By the 1630s opera began to shed its aristocratic origins and become a popular entertainment. This change did not affect opera's focus on ancient myths and histories about noble men and women, nor did it halt the trend to brilliant singing called **bel canto**, literally "beautiful song." However, in order to appeal to a wider audience, operatic composers added elements from Italy's popular comic theater, such as farcical scenes and stock characters, notably humorous servants. By the end of this age, the operatic form was stylized into a recipe, including improbable plots, inadequate motivations for the characters, and magical transformations—signs of its Baroque nature.

Opera became immensely popular in Europe, especially in Italy, where it remains so today. By 1750 opera houses had been built in many major cities, with Venice leading the way with more than a dozen separate establishments. The rise of opera in Italy during the 1600s, like the founding of a commercial theater in London in the 1500s, presaged the downfall of the aristocratic patronage system and the emergence of entertainments with mass appeal.

The winding down of the Thirty Years' War allowed Italian opera to be exported to the rest of Europe. Only in France were composers able to defy the overpowering Italian influence and create an independent type of opera. This development was made possible by the grandeur of Louis XIV's court and French taste, which was more restrained than the opulent Italian. Nevertheless, French opera was founded by an Italian, Jean-Baptiste Lully [loo-LEE] (1632–1687), who later became a French citizen and Louis's court composer. Under Lully's direction, French opera developed its identifying features: dignified music, the full use of choruses, the inclusion of a ballet, and, most importantly, a French text. Lully's patron, the Sun King, sometimes performed in the opera's ballet sequences himself, dancing side by side with the composer. Lully's works, which dominated French music until 1750, ensured a powerful role for French music in the Western tradition.

Baroque music reached its climax after 1715 in Protestant northern Europe. Two German composers were responsible for this development—Bach in his homeland and Handel in England.

The greater of these late Baroque masters was Johann Sebastian Bach (1685–1750). A devout Lutheran who worked for German courts and municipalities far from the major cities, Bach created a body of sacred music that transcends all religious creeds and nationalities. Employing all of the Baroque musical genres, his works are distinguished by their inventiveness and complete mastery of major and minor tonality. His most memorable achievements are the Passions, the musical settings of the liturgy to be performed on Good Friday—the most tragic day in the Christian calendar. Composed around 1727, the

St. Matthew Passion expresses the collective grief of the Christian community for the death of Jesus. Bach used a German text with arias and choruses, making the music bring out all of the emotional implications of the words. Thus the *St. Matthew Passion* is more dramatic than most operas and a sublime religious experience in itself.

The other great late Baroque master was George Frederic Handel (1685–1759) who was renowned for his Italian-style operas. More cosmopolitan than Bach, Handel eventually settled in London, where he composed thirty-six operatic works. His operas succeeded in their day because of the brilliant way in which the music allows the singers to show their virtuosity, but they are generally not to the taste of modern audiences and have not found a place in the standard operatic repertory. In contrast, his mastery of sacred music, particularly the *oratorio*— an opera-like form but without any stage action— which he perfected, has made his name immortal. Of the oratorios, the *Messiah,* based on biblical texts and sung in English, holds first place. Its popularity stems from its Baroque qualities: the emotionally stirring choruses and the delightful embellishments the soloists are permitted in their arias. As a result, the *Messiah* is probably the best known work of sacred music in the English-speaking world.

The Legacy of the Baroque Age

The Baroque period left a potent legacy to the modern world in politics, economics, and religion. The system of great states governed by a balance of power dominated European affairs until 1945. From the Baroque period date the roles of France and England as Europe's trendsetters, both politically and culturally. The concept and practice of "world war" also dates from this period. The economic system known as mercantilism originated during the Baroque period and prevailed in Europe into the nineteenth century. The religious orientation of the European states became well established in the seventeenth century, along with the division of the vast majority of Westerners into Protestant and Catholic camps. The Baroque idea of spectacle is a thread that runs thoughout the culture of this period and helps to explain not only the propagandistic aspects of politics and religion but also the theatrical elements in the arts and entertainment.

Culturally, the Baroque is still with us, despite the fact that much about this style seems excessive to modern taste. Although Baroque operas are not often performed, the idea of opera originated in this age of spectacle. Other Baroque musical works, notably the majestic oratorios of Handel and the powerful compositions of Bach for church and court, are part of the regular concert repertoire in the West today. Some of the most admired and enduring artworks in Western history were created during this time, including Bernini's *Ecstasy of St. Teresa* and the paintings of Rembrandt. Many cities of Europe are still showcases of Baroque splendor. The church of St. Peter's in Rome, St. Paul's Cathedral in London, and the palace and gardens at Versailles are but three of the living monuments of this period, reminding us of the grand religious and political ideals of a very different age.

KEY CULTURAL TERMS

Baroque
Florid Baroque style
baldacchino
illusionism
French Baroque style

Protestant Baroque style
virtuoso
opera
bel canto
oratorio

SUGGESTIONS FOR FURTHER READING

PRIMARY SOURCES

BEHN, A. *Oroonoko and Other Stories*. Edited and introduced by M. Duffy. London: Methuen, 1985. A recent edition of Behn's stories, with a useful introduction; these short works prepared the way for the novel genre, born after 1700. *Oroonoko* was first published in 1678.

CORNEILLE, P. *The Cid*. Translated by V. J. Cheng. Newark: University of Delaware Press, 1987. An up-to-date version of Corneille's drama, recounting the story of a hero torn between honor and love; imitates the poetic form of the original, first staged in 1636.

MILTON, J. *Paradise Lost*. New York: Norton, 1975. Milton's Baroque epic about rebellion—Lucifer's revolt in heaven and Adam and Eve's defiance on earth; Scott Elledge provides a useful introduction and notes to the text, which was first published in 1667.

MOLIÈRE (POQUELIN, J. B.). *The Misanthrope*. Translated by R. Wilbur. London: Methuen, 1967. A good version by a leading American poet. Useful English versions by various translators of Molière's other frequently performed comedies are also available, including *The Miser* (New York: Applause Theatre Book Publishers, 1987), *Tartuffe* (London: Faber and Faber, 1984), and *The Bourgeois Gentleman* (New York: Applause Theatre Book Publishers, 1987).

RACINE, J. B. *Phaedra*. Translated by R. Wilbur. New York: Harcourt Brace Jovanovich, 1986. A solid translation of this French tragic drama.

SUGGESTIONS FOR LISTENING

BACH, JOHANN SEBASTIAN (1685–1750).
The greatest composer of the Baroque era, Bach is best known for his sacred music, which has tremendous emotional power. His church music for voices includes more than two hundred cantatas, or musical settings of biblical and chorale texts, such as *Jesu der du meine Seele (Jesus, Thou Hast My Soul)*, *Wachet Auf (Wake Up)*, and *O Haupt voll Blut und Wunden (O Sacred Head Now Wounded)*; six motets, such as *Jesu meine Freude (Jesus, My Joy)*; two passions, or musical settings of biblical passages and commentaries on the Easter season, such as the *St. Matthew Passion*; and a Mass, the *Mass in B Minor*. He also composed instrumental church music, notably about 170 organ chorales required by the liturgy for the church year. Besides sacred music Bach wrote secular music, including the "Little" *Fugue in G minor*, the *Brandenburg Concertos*, and *The Well-Tempered Clavier* (1722; 1740), a collection of works for clavier, or keyboard, that consisted of one prelude and fugue for each of the twelve major and minor keys.

HANDEL, GEORGE FREDERIC (1685–1759).
The German-born Handel, who lived and worked mainly in England, made eighteenth-century England a center of Baroque music. Of the thirty-six Italian-style operas that he composed and produced in London, three of the best known are *Rinaldo* (1711), *Giulio Cesare* (1724), and *Serse* (1738). His oratorios—including the *Messiah*—were performed in public theaters rather than churches and especially appealed to the rising middle classes. Handel also produced a body of instrumental music of which the most significant are the two suites known as the *Fireworks Music* (1749) and the *Water Music* (about 1717) and six concertos for woodwinds and strings.

LULLY, JEAN-BAPTISTE (1632–1687).
Lully's eleven operas helped to define the operatic genre in France, giving it an opening overture and a ballet movement. Of his operas, the best known are probably *Theseus* (1675) and *Amadis* (1684). Especially appealing to modern ears are the massed choruses and rhythmic dances of his operas.

MONTEVERDI, CLAUDIO (1567–1643).
A prodigious composer of madrigals and sacred music, Monteverdi is best remembered as one of the pioneers of opera. He composed his operas in a highly expressive style that matched the spirit of music to the meaning of words in the text, as in *Orfeo* (1607) and *The Coronation of Poppea* (1642).

THE BAROQUE AGE II

*Revolutions in Scientific
and Political Thought, 1600—1715*

The Baroque age was more than a time of political upheaval and artistic spectacle. It was also the period when the event known as the Scientific Revolution took place. As centuries-old beliefs were challenged by discoveries in astronomy and physics, a whole new way of viewing the universe—and the position of humanity in it—emerged. At the same time, in England, a revolution in political philosophy was going on, leading to the notion that states ought to be governed by the people rather than by paternalistic rulers. These momentous changes in the way people thought added to the pervasive restlessness of the times.

The climax of this revolutionary age occurred between 1685 and 1715, a period that witnessed what one twentieth-century historian has called "the crisis of the European conscience." For a handful of scholars, the balance swung away from traditional ideas to modern views. These early modern scientists and philosophers opposed faith with reason, dogma with skepticism, and divine intervention with natural law. They made mathematics their guiding star in the search for truth, accepting as true those things that could be proven mathematically and rejecting as untrue those that could not. Their new philosophy eventually concluded that the universe was like a great clock that operated according to universal laws. Although we today tend to discount this clock-

work image, we still owe a debt to these thinkers, who set Western culture on its present course and brought modernity into being.

THE BACKGROUND
OF THE SCIENTIFIC
REVOLUTION

The Scientific Revolution was both an outgrowth and a rejection of the Aristotelian cosmology that had held Western thinkers in thrall for two thousand years. The Aristotelian system, named for the fourth-century B.C. philosopher, was developed by the ancient Greeks and transmitted to the West through Roman and Islamic culture and the medieval scholastic tradition. The fundamental principle of this cosmology is *geocentrism*, the notion that the universe is earth-centered. Around the earth, according to the theory, revolved the five known planets (Mercury, Venus, Mars, Jupiter, and Saturn) and the sun and moon, each held aloft by a crystalline sphere. The earth, which did not move, was not considered a planet. Nearest the earth was the moon, and there was a complete division between the supralunar world, the region beyond the moon, and the sublunar world, the region beneath the moon (Figure 15.1). In the supralunar world, the planets moved in circular orbits and were made of an incorruptible element, aether; in the sublunar world, change was constant, motion was rectilinear, and matter was

◀ GODFREY KNELLER. *Sir Isaac Newton.* 1702. Oil on canvas, 29¾ × 24½". National Portrait Gallery, London.

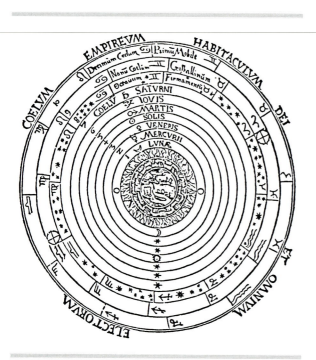

FIGURE 15.1 PETER APIAN. Geocentric Diagram of the Universe, from the *Cosmographia.* 1539. *The Bancroft Library, University of California, Berkeley. This schematic diagram illustrates the geocentric universe in the pre-Copernican era. The unmoving earth is placed at the center and is surrounded by nine moving spheres, containing, in sequential order, the moon, Mercury, Venus, the sun, Mars, Jupiter, Saturn, the fixed stars, and the empty sphere called the* primum mobile. *The ninth sphere, the primum mobile, was logically necessary in Aristotle's theory because it moved first and brought the other eight into motion. Beyond the ninth circle was the Empyrean, home of the Unmoved Mover in philosophy or of God in theology.*

composed of the four elements, earth, air, fire, and water. This system had an absolute up and down: Up referred to the area beyond the spheres inhabited by the Unmoved Mover—Aristotle's name for the source of all celestial motion—and down referred to the center of the earth.

In the second century A.D., the Egyptian scholar Ptolemy brought Aristotle's geocentric theory up to date with new astronomical data and improved mathematical calculations, and the system is now called the Ptolemaic system. During the golden age of Muslim culture (800–1000 A.D.), Arab intellectuals preserved this legacy, improving and refining it to reflect new planetary sightings. In the High Middle Ages (1000–1300), Western scholars recovered the Ptolemaic heritage—with its Muslim additions— and gave it a Christian interpretation: Medieval Christian scientists began to identify the Unmoved Mover as God and the space beyond the spheres as heaven. More importantly, the church became attached to the geocentric theory because the doctrine

of original sin seemed validated by it. In other words, the corrupt earth inhabited by fallen mortals corresponded to the sublunar world of decay and constant change.

Up to this point in the transmission of ancient knowledge, scientists simply made minor adjustments to Aristotle's original picture. But at the University of Paris in the 1300s a more self-assured and skeptical outlook arose among a few thinkers. Unconvinced by Aristotle's solution to the problem of motion (which was to attribute the forward motion of a projectile to air movement), the Parisian scholars offered an alternative explanation. They asserted that a projectile acquired "impetus," a propulsive quality that gradually diminished as the projectile moved through space. The theory of "impetus" commanded scholars' attention for centuries, leading them to consider a new range of scientific problems.

From the modern perspective, it matters little that the theory of "impetus" was untrue. As a first step away from the Aristotelian tradition, it made Western scientists aware that the great Greek thinker was not always right. And scholars at Paris and other universities began to advocate the application of mathematics to practical problems as well as the direct observation of nature, that is, collecting data (*empiricism*) and framing hypotheses from observable facts (*inductive reasoning*).

Aristotle had also used empirical data and inductive logic, but his writings had become so authoritative that for generations scholars did not examine his methodology and were afraid to tamper with his conclusions. Indeed, his followers relied on *deductive reasoning*; in other words, they only explored the ramifications of accepted truths. But with the new critical spirit that appeared in the Late Middle Ages, scholars looked at the world with new eyes. In time, this spirit led to the greatest achievement of Baroque science, the Scientific Revolution that overturned the Ptolemaic system and enthroned *heliocentrism*, the notion that the universe is centered around the sun.

THE SCIENTIFIC REVOLUTION: DISCOVERIES AND THEORIES

The term *Scientific Revolution* applies chiefly to astronomy and physics, the fields of study in which dramatic breakthroughs occurred in the Baroque age, although major advances were also made in medical science and lesser though still important gains occurred in chemistry, biology, and embryology. In addition, the Scientific Revolution gave rise to a type of

Time Line 15.1   REVOLUTIONS IN SCIENTIFIC AND POLITICAL THOUGHT

1543	1600	1700	1715

The Scientific Revolution and Early Modern Political Philosophy

Contributions of Copernicus and Tycho Brahe

Jamestown founded 1607

Galileo sights four moons of Jupiter 1610

Plymouth Colony 1620

Grotius's *The Law of War and Peace* 1625

Descartes's *Discourse on Method* 1637

Hobbes's *Leviathan* 1651

Bahamas Colony 1648

Pennsyl-vania Charter 1681

Newton's *Mathematical Principles* 1687

Locke's *Second Treatise* and *Essay Concerning Human Understanding* 1690

literature that treated the impact of the new science on secular and religious thought. Armed with the new learning and impelled by a need to make a clean break with the past, a few scholars and publicists composed literary works that redefined the place of human beings in the cosmos and the purpose of human life. The chief result was to bring to a climax the separation of philosophy from theology, a gap that had been widening since the 1300s (see Chapter 10). From this point, philosophy begins to address secular concerns, and theology is relegated to a minor cultural role (Time Line 15.1).

THE MAGICAL AND THE PRACTICAL IN THE SCIENTIFIC REVOLUTION

The Scientific Revolution is notable for the paradoxes and ironies that the movement gave rise to, some of which will be discussed in a later section of this chapter. A paradox that should be noted at the outset, however, is that this revolution in human thought, which ushered in modern science, was rooted in both magical beliefs and practical technological achievements. With one or two exceptions, the makers of the Scientific Revolution were motivated by two divergent and rather contradictory sets of beliefs. On the one hand, they followed the lead of late medieval science by collecting empirical data, reasoning inductively, and using mathematics to verify results. Significantly, the most startling changes evolved in those areas where mathematics was applied to long-existing intellectual problems, namely in astronomy, physics, and biology.

On the other hand, these thinkers were entranced by Neo-Platonism, the ancient Greek philosophy that was revived in the Early Renaissance (see Chapter 11). Like late medieval science, Neo-Platonism stressed the role of mathematics in problem solving, but Neo-Platonism also had a mystical streak—a legacy from Pythagoras—that led its devotees to seek harmony through numbers (see Chapter 2). Thinkers who followed Neo-Platonism believed that simplicity was superior to complexity in mathematical figuring because simplicity was the supreme sign that a solution was correct. This belief has become a guiding ideal of modern science, although other aspects of Neo-Platonism would be rejected today, such as the attribution of mysterious powers to the sun. One effect of Neo-Platonism's occult side was to tighten the link between astronomy and astrology, a connection as old as Greek science. Most of those who made the revolution in science supported this linkage, and a few even cast horoscopes for wealthy clients.

As for the role of technology in the Scientific Revolution, many of its achievements would have been impossible without the telescope and the microscope, both of which were invented in about 1600 in the Netherlands. These enabling devices were decisive for the success of the Scientific Revolution because without them scholars would have simply remained "thinkers," as they had been since the time of the ancient Greeks. But with the telescope and the microscope they could penetrate deep into hitherto inaccessible areas—outer space and the inner workings of the human body. Henceforward, scholars with a scientific bent allied themselves with the crafts tradition, becoming in the process experimenters and empiricists.

Astronomy and Physics: From Copernicus to Newton

The intellectual shift from the earth-centered to the sun-centered universe was almost 150 years in the making and involved an international community of scholars. Heliocentrism, the new model of the world, was first broached in modern times by the Polish thinker Copernicus in 1543, and incontrovertible mathematical calculations to prove this view were published by the English scholar Newton in 1687. Between these dates, major steps in the revolution in science were taken by Brahe of Denmark, Kepler of Germany, and Galileo of Italy. Newton spoke the truth when he claimed that he "stood on the shoulders of giants" (Table 15.1).

Nicolas Copernicus   When Nicolas Copernicus (1473–1543) published *Revolutions of the Heavenly Bodies* in 1543, he was reviving the discarded heliocentric theory of the third-century B.C. Greek thinker Aristarchus. In this highly technical work, Copernicus launched a head-on assault against Ptolemaic geocentrism. The main issue between Copernican astronomy and the older world view was not one of mathematical precision, for both were mathematically solid and thus equally able to predict planetary positions and solar and lunar eclipses. Rather, the basic question between the two systems was which one was simpler. Copernicus reasoned that a more convincing picture of the

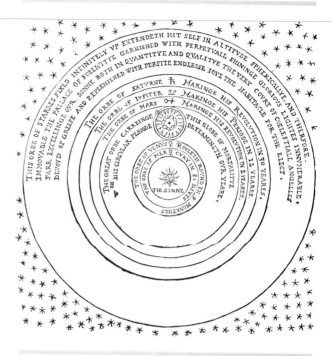

FIGURE 15.2   THOMAS DIGGES. The Sun-Centered Universe of Copernicus, from *A Perfit Description of the Celestiall Orbes.* 1576. The Huntington Library, San Marino, California. *This diagram drawn by the Englishman Thomas Digges agrees with the Copernican system except in one major way. Copernicus believed the universe was a finite, closed system, but Digges represents it as infinite. The infinitude is expressed in the stars scattered outside the orbit of fixed stars in the illustration.*

universe could be achieved by transposing the positions of the sun and the earth. Instead of the Ptolemaic notion of a finite world centered around a fixed earth, Copernicus envisioned a vastly expanded, but not infinite, universe with the planets orbiting the sun (Figure 15.2).

Recognizing the revolutionary nature of his hypothesis, Copernicus delayed printing his ideas until he was dying. In an attempt to mollify clerical critics, he dedicated his book to the pope, Paul III. At first, the pope and other religious leaders saw his views as ingenious speculation with no useful purpose, but later the religious establishment concluded that heliocentrism was dangerous and contrary to scripture; they therefore condemned it as a false system. What disturbed them was that when the earth was removed from the center of the universe, the place of human beings in the divine order was also reduced. In effect, human beings were no longer the leading actors in a cosmic drama, staged for them alone.

Catholics and Protestants alike denounced the ideas of Copernicus. Lutheran and Calvinist authorities condemned his views as unbiblical, and in 1610 the pope placed *Revolutions of the Heavenly Bodies* on

TABLE 15.1   EVOLUTION OF HELIOCENTRISM

DATE	EVENT
1543	Copernicus publishes *Revolutions of the Heavenly Bodies*
1571–1601	Tycho Brahe makes his observations
Ca. 1600	Dutch lens grinders develop the telescope
1609	Kepler publishes his first and second planetary laws in *On the Motion of Mars*
1609	Galileo perfects his own telescope
1610	Galileo sights the four moons of Jupiter
1619	Kepler publishes his third planetary law in *The Harmonies of the World*
1620	Bacon publishes *New Organon*
1632	Galileo publishes *Dialogues on the Two Chief Systems of the World*
1633	Galileo humiliated by the Inquisition
1637	Descartes publishes *Discourse on Method*
1687	Newton publishes *Mathematical Principles of Natural Philosophy*

the Index, the list of forbidden books created during the Counter-Reformation. Eventually the two religious groups came to a parting of the ways over this issue. For more than two hundred years, until 1822, the Roman Catholic church, with all of its considerable power and influence, opposed the sun-centered theory. In this policy the church reversed a centuries-old tradition of being open to innovative scientific thought. However, in Protestantism—where there was no focus of authority as there was in Roman Catholicism—some sects slowly accepted and adapted their beliefs to the new astronomy.

Johannes Kepler   The reception of Copernican astronomy by the scientific community was neither immediate nor enthusiastic. For example, the great Danish astronomer Tycho Brahe [TEE-ko BRAH-hee] (1546–1601) adopted a modified Copernicanism, believing that the other planets moved around the sun but that the earth did not. Brahe nevertheless made a major contribution to the ultimate triumph of heliocentrism because of his copious observations of planetary movement. So accurate were his sightings that they set a new standard for astronomical data.

Among Brahe's assistants was Johannes Kepler (1571–1630), a brilliant mathematician who dedicated his life to clarifying the theory of heliocentrism. When the Danish astronomer died, Kepler inherited his astronomical data. Inspired by Neo-Platonism to make sense of the regular and continuous sightings of Brahe, Kepler in 1609 published *On the Motion of Mars,* setting forth his solution to the problem of what kept the planets in their orbits. His findings were expressed in two scientific laws that were elegant in their simplicity. In the first planetary law, Kepler substituted the ellipse for the circle as the descriptive shape of planetary orbits. And his second planetary law, which was set forth in a precise mathematical formula, accounted for each planet's variable speed within its respective orbit by showing that nearness to the sun affected its behavior—the closer to the sun, the faster the speed, and the farther from the sun, the slower the speed. Together, these laws validated sun-centered astronomy, enabling Kepler to abolish the orbital deviations and the tangled calculations that had cluttered the Copernican system.

Kepler continued to manipulate Brahe's undigested data, convinced that other mathematical laws could be derived from observations of the heavens. In 1619, he arrived at a third planetary law, which, unlike his other two, had no equivalent in earlier astronomy. In the third law, he showed that the squares of the length of time for each planet's orbit are in the same ratios as the cubes of their respective mean distances from the sun. Through this formula, he affirmed that the solar system itself was regular and organized by mathematically determined relationships. This was the first expression of the notion that the universe operates with clocklike regularity, an idea that became an article of faith by the end of the Baroque age. Kepler took great pride in this discovery, because it confirmed his Neo-Platonist belief that there is a hidden mathematical harmony in the universe.

Galileo Galilei   While Kepler moved in the rarefied realm of theoretical, even mystical, science, one of his contemporaries was making major breakthroughs with experiments that relied on precise mathematics and careful logic. This patient experimenter was Galileo Galilei (1564–1642), whose most valuable contributions were his accurate celestial observations and his work in terrestial mechanics, the study of the action of forces on matter. Inspired by news that Dutch lens grinders had made a device for viewing distant objects, in 1609 Galileo made his own telescope, which enabled him to see stars invisible to the naked eye.

With these sightings Galileo demonstrated that the size of the universe was exponentially greater than that computed on Ptolemaic principles. Further, his observations of the moon's rough surface and the sun's shifting dark spots provided additional proofs against the ancient arguments that the heavenly bodies were perfectly formed and never changed. But his most telling discovery was that the planet Jupiter has moons, a fact that contradicted the Ptolemaic belief that all celestial bodies must move about a common center. Galileo's research affirmed that Jupiter's four satellites rotated around it in much the same way as the six planets orbited the sun. These telescopic sightings hastened the demise of the idea that the earth was the center of the universe.

Similarly, Galileo's research in terrestrial mechanics proved conclusively that both Aristotle and his fourteenth-century critics in Paris were wrong about one of the central questions of earthly motion, that is, the behavior of projectiles. Aristotle had claimed that projectiles stayed in flight because of the pushing motion of the air, and the Parisian scholars had countered with the theory of "impetus." Through experimentation, Galileo showed that a mass that is moving will go on moving until some force acts to stop it—the earliest expression of the modern law of inertia.

Galileo was probably the first scientist to make a clock a basic means for measuring time in his experiments. Like his contemporary Kepler, he reported his findings in the form of simple mathematical laws.

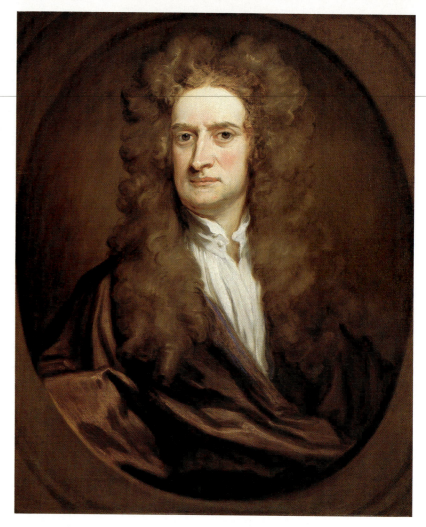

Galileo's work was later validated by the conclusions of Newton, who proved that the laws of mechanics on earth were the same as the laws of mechanics in the sky.

At the same time that Galileo was conducting the experiments that would make him a hero of modern science, he ran afoul of the religious authorities, who brought his career to a humiliating end. The church, as noted above, had by now abandoned its relative openness to ideas and was moving to stifle dissent. In 1633 Galileo was arrested by the Inquisition, the church court created in the thirteenth century to find and punish heretics. The great astronomer was charged with false teachings for his published support of the idea that the earth moves, a notion central to Copernicanism but untrue according to Aristotle and the church. Threatened with torture, Galileo recanted his views and was released. Despite living on for several years, he died a broken man. This episode abruptly ended Italy's role in the burgeoning revolution in science.

Isaac Newton Building on the research of the heirs to Copernicus, including Kepler's laws of planetary motion and Galileo's law of inertia, the English mathematician Isaac Newton (1642–1727) conceived a model of the universe that decisively overturned the Ptolemaic scheme and finished the revolution in astronomy begun by Copernicus (Figure 15.3). In Newton's world picture, there is uniform motion on earth and in the heavens. More significantly, Newton presented a satisfactory explanation for what held the planets in their orbits. Newton's solution was the force of gravity, and this topic formed the heart of his theory of the universe.

In a precise mathematical formula, Newton computed the law of universal gravitation, the formula whereby every object in the world exerts an attraction to a greater or a lesser degree on all other objects. By this law, the sun held in its grip each of the six planets, and each, in turn, lightly influenced the sun and the other planets. The earth and its single moon as well as Jupiter and its four satellites similarly interacted. In effect, because of gravity, the heavenly bodies formed a harmonious system in which each attracted the others.

Having described gravity and asserted its universal nature, Newton declined to speculate about what caused it to operate. For him, the universe behaved precisely as a machine, and his law was nothing but a description of its operation. Because Newton refused to speculate beyond what mathematics could prove, he has been called a "mind without metaphysics." Modern scientists have followed Newton's lead, preferring to ignore the *why* of things and to concentrate on the *how* and *what*.

Newton's views were set forth in his authoritative work, *Mathematical Principles of Natural Philosophy.* Known more familiarly as the *Principia* (the first word of its Latin title), this book quickly gained an authority that made Newton the modern world's equivalent of Aristotle. By the eighteenth century the English poet Alexander Pope could justifiably write:

> Nature and Nature's Laws lay hid in Night;
> God said, *Let Newton be!* and All was *Light.*

Even though Newton's work was the culmination of the revolution that brought modern science into being, he was not fully free of older attitudes. True, he believed that scientific truth was simply a matter of using methodical principles. He made mathematics his guiding ideal and used patient and careful observation. But Newton cared little for his own scientific achievement, believing that his lasting monument was his religious writings. A pious Christian, he devoted his last years to demonstrating that the prophecies in the Bible were coming true.

Newton also invented a form of calculus, a mathematical method of analysis that uses a symbolic notation. This breakthrough had huge potential for solving problems in physics and mechanics by providing a tool for computing quantities that had nonlinear variations. Newton's development of calculus, in contrast to his work in gravitation, was not a solo effort. He had to share this triumph with Gottfried Wilhelm von Leibniz [LIBE-nits] (1646–1716), a German thinker who, simultaneously and independently of Newton, invented another version of calculus. Indeed, Leibniz's notation proved more useful than Newton's cumbersome technique, so that by 1800 Leibniz's symbols had become the universally accepted language of calculus.

Medicine and Chemistry

At the same time that Western understanding of the universe at its outer limits was being radically altered, another revolution was taking place in knowledge of the workings of the human body. This revolution in anatomical knowledge involved the discovery of the true circulation of the human blood. Unlike developments in astronomy, this breakthrough in medical science happened largely without the aid of technology. Only during the last step in the solving of the mystery of the blood's circulation did early modern scientists use the newly invented microscope.

In 1600 knowledge of the workings of the human body was cloaked in darkness. There were many reasons for this, but the most powerful was that the church forbade the violation of corpses because of the teaching that the body would be resurrected. Biological research had been based on the dissection of animals with generalizations then applied, whether justified or not, to the human body. This practice had led to a great deal of misinformation and many half-truths.

Besides, in biology as in astronomy and physics, the authority of ancient Greek thinkers reigned supreme—Aristotle since the fourth century B.C. and Galen since the second century A.D. Galen's vast researches, collected in about 500 books and covering nearly all aspects of ancient medicine, were lost in the chaos of the fall of Rome, but some works were preserved by Arab scholars and were translated from Arabic into Latin by Western scholars from the eleventh century onward; filled with information unknown to European doctors, Galen's works became an uncritical authority in medieval medicine. Though offering rival theories, Aristotle and Galen shared many false ideas, namely the notions that air ran directly from the lungs into the heart, that blood flowed from the veins to the outer part of the body, and that different types of blood coursed in the arteries and veins. The birth of modern medical science had to await the dispelling of these myths.

The problem of the circulation of the blood was eventually resolved by scientists at the University of Padua in Italy, the most prominent of whom was Andreas Vesalius [vuh-SAY-lee-us] (1514–1564). His painstaking observations led him to deny Galen's theory that blood passed from one side of the heart to the other through the septum, an impermeable membrane. At the same time his work proved the need for further careful study of human anatomy (Figure 15.4).

The research of Vesalius and his successors set the stage for William Harvey (1578–1657), an English scientist who studied and taught at the University of Padua. In 1628 Harvey published his ground-breaking work, based on years of careful research, which overthrew the ancient theories and produced the correct view of circulation, including the role of the heart, the lungs, the arteries, and the veins. Mathematical calculation played a decisive role in this scientific triumph, just as it had in Newton's gravitation theory. Using arithmetic, Harvey proved that a stable quantity of blood constantly circulated throughout the body, thereby destroying Galen's

FIGURE 15.4 REMBRANDT VAN RIJN. *The Anatomy Lesson of Dr. Tulp.* 1632. Oil on canvas, 66¾ × 85¼". Mauritshuis, The Hague. *The pioneering work of Vesalius made the study of anatomy a central concern of medical science in the seventeenth century. In this painting, Rembrandt depicts Dr. Nicolas Tulp of Amsterdam as he demonstrates the dissection of the left arm. Rembrandt's use of Baroque effects, such as the dramatic light on the corpse, the contrast between Dr. Tulp's calm demeanor and the inquisitive faces of his pupils, and the flayed arm of the corpse, make this an arresting image.*

ebb-and-flow theory. Harvey lacked knowledge of the capillaries, the connectors between the arteries and the veins, but in 1661 the Italian scientist Marcello Malpighi [mahl-PEE-gee] (1628–1694) identified these tiny vessels with the aid of the microscope, and with this critical piece of information an essentially correct, modern description of the blood's circulation was complete.

Chemistry did not become a separate discipline in the Baroque age, but it was during this time that the English physicist Robert Boyle (1627–1691) laid the groundwork for modern chemistry. A major aspect of Boyle's thought linked him to Newton, for both believed that the universe is a machine. Boyle believed that the workings of nature could be revealed only through experimental study—the inductive method. Boyle's zeal for experimentation led him to study the behavior of gases and to formulate the famous law that bears his name. Boyle's law, which is still used in modern chemistry, is a method for computing the weight of compressed air in a tube.

Boyle was also one of the first to distinguish chemistry from alchemy, a set of magical practices that had been allied with chemistry since the time of the ancient Greeks. In medieval Europe, alchemy had led scholars to search vainly for the "philosopher's stone" that would miraculously turn a base metal like lead into gold. Rejecting alchemy's assumptions and methodology, Boyle sought to understand only those chemical reactions that happened naturally and could be analyzed in mathematical terms.

The Impact of Science on Philosophy

The Scientific Revolution had a profound influence on Western thought and also gave rise to a type of literature that reflected the impact of science on the wider culture. Three prominent contributors to this literature were the English jurist and statesman Francis Bacon and two brilliant French mathematicians,

René Descartes and Blaise Pascal, whose speculative writings continued the French rationalist tradition begun by Montaigne in the 1500s (see Chapter 13).

Francis Bacon   Francis Bacon (1561–1626) owes his fame to his ability to write lucid prose about science and its methodology. In a field that was dominated by scholars whose writings were accessible only to those learned in mathematics, Bacon's clear and eminently quotable prose opened the door to a curious and educated public. In the process of clarifying the techniques and the aims of the new science, he became the spokesman for the "experimenters," those who believed that the future of science lay in discarding Aristotle and seeing the world with fresh eyes. Condemning Aristotle for relying on deductive reason and unproven axioms, Bacon advocated the inductive method, the procedure that embraced the conducting of experiments, the drawing of conclusions, and the testing of results in other experiments. His claims were not new, but they were forcibly and memorably expressed; few scholars exhibited Bacon's optimism about the usefulness of science. He sincerely believed that the march of science inevitably led to mastery over the natural world, a view summarized in the famous phrase attributed to him, "knowledge is power." Bacon's slogan became the watchword of the forces of progress in the next century and remains so until the present day.

René Descartes   An outstanding critic of the belief that the experimental method was the correct path to knowledge was René Descartes [day-KAHRT] (1596–1650), a philosopher who urged a purely mathematical approach in science (Figure 15.5). Descartes's love of numbers came from a mystic side of his personality, as illustrated by his confession that a dream had inspired his belief that mathematics holds the key to nature. Descartes was the founder of analytic geometry, that branch of mathematics that describes geometrical figures by the formulas of algebra, and the author of a widely influential philosophical treatise, *Discourse on Method*, published in 1637.

In the *Discourse*, Descartes outlined four steps in his approach to knowledge: to accept nothing as true unless it is self-evident; to split problems into manageable parts; to solve problems starting with the simplest and moving to the most complex; and to review and reexamine the solutions. He used deductive logic in his method, only making inferences from general statements. But more important than his stress on deductive reasoning was his insistence on mathematical clarity. He refused to accept anything as true unless it had the persuasiveness of a proof in geometry.

FIGURE 15.5   FRANS HALS. *René Descartes.* After 1649. Oil on canvas, 30¾ × 26¾". Louvre. *Descartes had the good fortune to be memorialized in paint by a great Dutch portrait artist and contemporary of Rembrandt, Frans Hals. In this likeness, Hals has captured the complex personality of the great French philosopher and mathematician. Descartes's piercing gaze shows his skeptical spirit, and his disdainful presence and rough features reveal his early background as a soldier. Hals apparently felt no need to flatter his sitter in this compelling portrait.*

Descartes's most influential gifts to Western philosophy were skepticism and a dualistic theory of knowledge. He rejected the authoritarian method of medieval scholasticism and began with universal doubt in order to determine what was absolutely certain in the universe. Step by step, he questioned the existence of God, of the world, and of his own body. But he soon established that he could not doubt the existence of his own doubting self. He reached this absolute conclusion in the famous phrase "*Cogito ergo sum*"—I think, therefore I am. This datum became both Descartes's conclusion to his doubting and the starting point from which he erected his view of the world. Having first destroyed the age-old certainties, he then, through deduction, reestablished the existence of his own body, the world, and finally, God.

Descartes's speculations were aimed at identifying clear and distinct ideas that were certain for everyone, but his efforts had a deeply ironic result. In the long run his thought fostered the growing awareness among the educated elite that absolute truth was not possible. Many who read his *Discourse* were unimpressed by his rational arguments, but they nevertheless accepted his radical doubt, and some even became atheists. That his work contributed to the rise of atheism would have horrified Descartes, since, to his own way of thinking, he had proven the existence of God. He had used skepticism merely as a means of achieving certainty.

Descartes's other great legacy, dualism, made a division between the material world and the human soul or mind. According to him, mathematics permitted natural truths to be revealed to the human understanding. He thought, however, that the mind itself was beyond mathematical knowing and hence was not a fit subject for study. From this dichotomy arise two contrasting traditions, the scientists who reduce the natural world to order through mathematics and the thinkers who focus on human psychology. The second group—the psychologists—represent another ironic legacy, for through the study of such topics as depth psychology and alienation they want to prove that Descartes was wrong and that the human self is knowable in all of its irrationality.

Even though Descartes's speculations were aimed at achieving certainty, his focus on deductive logic has not withstood the test of time. This is because modern scientists think that inductive reasoning—building a model of truth on the facts—is more valid. But he was proven correct in assigning to mathematics its paramount role in establishing precision and certainty in science. Today, those sciences that have the greatest degree of mathematical rigor have higher reputations for accuracy and believability than those sciences whose formulations cannot be achieved mathematically.

This French intellectual also had a marked impact on the Scientific Revolution when he applied his method to terrestrial mechanics. It was he, rather than Galileo, who gave final expression to the law of inertia in all of its clarity. Descartes was able to reach this conclusion because he conceived of problems in geometrical terms, that is, as occurring in empty, directionless space. With this frame of reference, he concluded that a projectile would continue to move in a straight line until it was interrupted by some force. With this language Descartes finally got rid of the myth of circular motion. His definition of the law of inertia gained many supporters and became part of the scientific synthesis of Newton.

Blaise Pascal   Descartes's work was barely published before it elicited a strong reaction from Blaise Pascal [BLEHZ pas-KAHL] (1623–1662), an anguished thinker who made radical doubt the cornerstone of his beliefs. Like Descartes, Pascal left his mark in mathematics, notably in geometry and in the study of probability. Pascal was a Jansenist, a member of a Catholic sect that to some observers was Calvinistic because it stressed original sin and denied free will. This attachment set him on a different path from Descartes, one which in Pascal's case led to extreme skepticism. Pascal's Jansenism permeates his masterpiece, the *Pensées*, or *Thoughts*, a meditative work of intense feeling published in 1670, eight years after his death.

In the *Pensées* Pascal went beyond Descartes's skepticism, concluding that human beings can know neither the natural world nor themselves. Despite this seemingly universal doubt, Pascal still reasoned that there were different levels of truth. Regarding science, he thought that what he called the geometric spirit—that is, mathematics—could lead scholars to a limited knowledge of nature. Pascal's most controversial opinions, however, concerned human psychology. He felt that the passions enabled human beings to comprehend the truths about God and religion directly. He summed up this idea in his often quoted words, "The heart has reasons that reason does not know." In another passage he justified his continued belief in God, not by intellectual proofs in the manner of Descartes, but by a wager—a notion he derived from his probability studies. Pascal claimed his faith in God rested on a bet: If God exists, then the bettor wins everything, but if God does not exist, then nothing is lost. Pascal's fervent belief in God in the face of debilitating doubt makes him a forerunner of modern Christian existentialism.

Ironic Aspects of the Scientific Revolution

Ironies abound in the seventeenth century's most characteristic development, the Scientific Revolution. To begin with, it must be remembered that only a handful of thinkers contributed to the scientific changes, that the vast majority of the populace remained unaware of their findings, and that they could not have understood them even if they had been informed of them. Furthermore, those who made the scientific discoveries were primarily engaged in solving practical problems rather than in trying to build a new model of the universe. They also believed that what they were doing was entirely within an orthodox Christian framework (although some were aware that religious leaders might think otherwise), and few realized that their efforts would eventually lead to a conflict between religion and science.

Another irony was that the scientific advancements were not always completely original creations but were rooted in late medieval rationalism and the Renaissance revival of Classical learning. Indeed, the new thinkers were often more concerned with working out minor inconsistencies in the calculations of medieval scholars than in overturning the accepted picture of the universe.

Not only did Baroque science have roots stretching back to medieval science, but it also felt a continuing influence from superstitions and mystical beliefs. These intellectual relics from a bygone day may be conveniently summarized as medieval values, because it was during the medieval time that nonrational and arcane beliefs so mesmerized both the educated and the popular mind. During the Scientific Revolution even the greatest intellectuals still held firmly to superstitious medieval views. Brahe and Kepler, for example, supported their research by pursuing careers as court astrologers. Harvey imagined that the heart restored a "spiritous" quality to the blood during circulation. Newton and Boyle were both involved in secret experiments with alchemy, and Boyle wrote that metals and minerals "grew" in the earth. A mystical experience lay behind Descartes's mathematical zeal, while Neo-Platonism motivated the thought of Copernicus, Kepler, and Galileo. Many scholars were conventionally devout in their religious convictions. Copernicus was a canon at the cathedral in Frauenburg, and Newton tried to correlate biblical prophecy with history. Despite their medieval roots, these scholars nevertheless did point European thought in a new direction. In the next century, a new generation of intellectuals constructed a set of beliefs based on the achievements of the Scientific Revolution and their implications for the improvement of humanity.

THE REVOLUTION IN POLITICAL THOUGHT

Political philosophy reflected the nature of the shifting political, economic, social, and religious institutions of the seventeenth century. The Thirty Years' War, the Wars of Louis XIV, and the English Civil War (see Chapter 14) forced political theorists to reconsider such basic themes as the nature of government, the relations between rulers and subjects, the rivalries among sovereign states, and the consequences of war on society and the individual. Many of these thinkers were influenced directly by the breakthroughs in astronomy and mechanics; others were affected only indirectly.

Political writers, stimulated by the rise of the nation-state in the 1500s, addressed themselves in the 1600s to the fundamental questions of who holds the final sovereignty in a state and how power should be exercised. Realizing that new states were rapidly extinguishing the last vestiges of rights held by the feudal estates—those class divisions that became most prominent in the Middle Ages—these theorists tried to define the best form of government. They all supported their arguments with the same sources—the Bible, the concept of natural law, scientific discoveries, and their own views of human nature—but they came to widely differing conclusions.

Natural Law and Divine Right: Grotius and Bossuet

Hugo Grotius [GRO-she-us] (1583–1645) thought that natural law should govern the relations between states. He arrived at this belief chiefly because of his personal sufferings during the Thirty Years' War and the intolerance that he observed in religious disputes. A Dutch citizen but also an ambassador for Sweden, he saw at first hand the ambiguity of diplomatic relations between the great powers.

Drawing on the idea of natural law as set forth by the ancient Stoic thinkers, Grotius urged that the states should follow a law that applied to all nations, was eternal and unchanging, and could be understood by human reason. By this means he separated the basic concept of natural law from the Christian add-ons that had crept in during the Middle Ages and restored it to its ancient status.

Like the Stoics, Grotius was convinced that the natural law was founded on human reason and was not the gift of a loving God. He rejected original sin, believing instead that human beings were not motivated merely by selfish drives. He thought that because all mortals were rational, they wanted to improve themselves and to create a just and fair society. In his treatise, *The Law of War and Peace,* he applied this rational view of human nature to his description of sovereign states. He concluded that nations, like individuals, should treat each other as they would expect to be treated. Today, the writings of Grotius are recognized as the starting point of international law.

Taking a contrary point of view to Grotius was Bishop Bossuet [bo-SWAY] (1627–1704), who defended the theory that kings rule by divine right. This French church leader echoed the opinions of James I of England, who maintained that God bestowed power on certain national monarchs. The French bishop avowed that absolutism, as ordained by God in past societies, was now manifested in the rule of Louis XIV, king of France. Louis, as God's chosen vessel on earth, had the power to intervene in the lives of his subjects, not because of natural law but by divine right. According to this theory, for corrupt and sinful humans to rebel against the king was to go against God's plan. The bishop believed that the age's conflicts made autocratic rule a political necessity. Bossuet's belief in autocracy was also shared by the Englishman Thomas Hobbes who, however, explained absolute rule in different terms.

Absolutism and Liberalism: Hobbes and Locke   Thomas Hobbes (1588–1679) grew up in an England increasingly torn by religious, social, and political discord. A trained Classicist, Hobbes translated into English the work of the Greek historian Thucydides, whose reservations about Athenian democracy deeply impressed him (see Chapter 3). His study of the Greek geometer Euclid convinced Hobbes that certainty could be achieved only through geometrical reasoning, which in turn could be applied to topics such as human behavior and politics. The final stage of his intellectual initiation fell into place when he visited Galileo in Italy. Hobbes came away from this meeting certain that everything, including human beings and their social acts, could be explained by using mechanistic, natural laws to describe various states of motion or movement.

Hobbes's efforts to synthesize a universal philosophy founded on a geometric design and activated by some form of energy culminated in his best-known work, *The Leviathan*, published in 1651 (Figure 15.6). *The Leviathan* sets forth a theory of government based on the pessimistic view that individuals are driven by two basic forces, the fear of death and the quest for power. Hobbes imagined what life would be like if these two natural inclinations were allowed free rein and there were no supreme power to control them. Hobbes described human life under these circumstances as "solitary, poor, nasty, brutish, and short."

Hobbes thought that human beings, recognizing the awfulness of their situation, would decide to give up such an existence and form a civil society under the rule of one man. This first step in the evolution of government was achieved by means of a *social contract* drawn up between the ruler and his subjects. By the terms of this covenant the subjects surrendered all their claims to sovereignty and bestowed absolute power on the ruler. The sovereign's commands were then to be carried out by all under him, including the religious and civic leaders. Armed with the sword, the sovereign would keep peace at home and protect the land from its enemies abroad.

FIGURE 15.6   Frontispiece of *The Leviathan*. 1651. The Bancroft Library, University of California, Berkeley. *The original illustration for Hobbes's* Leviathan *conveys the political message of this controversial work in symbolic terms. Towering over the landscape is the mythical ruler, whose body is a composite of all of his subjects and in whose hands are the sword and scepter, symbols of his absolute power. Below this awesome figure is a well-ordered and peaceful village and countryside—Hobbes's political dream come true.*

Hobbes made no distinction between the ruler of a monarchy and the head of a commonwealth, for he was less concerned with the form of government than with the need to hold in check destructive human impulses. In the next generation, Hobbes's pessimistic philosophy provoked a reaction from John Locke, who repudiated absolutism and advocated a theory of government by the people.

Despite their contradictory messages, Hobbes and John Locke (1632–1704) had been subjected to similar influences. Both adapted ideas from the new science, witnessed the English Civil War, and sought safety on the Continent because of their political views. But Locke rejected Hobbes's gloomy view of humanity and his theory of absolutism; he taught instead that human nature was potentially good and that human beings were capable of governing themselves. The two thinkers originated opposing schools of modern political thought: From Hobbes stems the absolutist, authoritarian tradition, and from Locke descends the school of liberalism. Their works represent two of the most significant legacies of the Baroque age to the modern world.

Locke set forth his political theories in his *Two Treatises of Government,* which he published anonymously in 1690. In the *First Treatise* he refuted the divine right of kings, and in the *Second Treatise* he laid out the model for rule by the people. The latter work has become the classic expression of early *liberalism.* In it Locke described the origins, characteristics, and purpose of the ideal political system—a government limited by laws, subject to the will of its citizens, and existing to protect life and property.

Locke's treatise shared some of Hobbes's ideas, such as the view that human life is violent and disorderly in the state of nature, that human beings must form civil governments to protect themselves, and that a social contract is the necessary basis of civil society. But Locke believed that basic rights, including life and property, exist in the state of nature. He also believed that human beings possess reason, are fundamentally decent and law abiding, and are slow to want change. From these principles he concluded that human beings would contract together to create a limited government that had no other purpose than the protection of the basic natural rights of life and property.

Locke rejected the idea that by making a social contract citizens surrender their sovereignty to a ruler. He argued instead that the people choose rulers who protect their rights in a fiduciary trust; that is, they expect their rulers to obey the social contract and govern equitably. If the rulers break the agreement, then the people have the right to revolt, overthrow the government, and reclaim their natural rights. Unlike Hobbes, Locke asserted that rulers possess only limited authority and that their control must be held in check by a balanced governmental system and a separation of powers. In later years, Locke's tract greatly influenced political thinkers and patriots who used its ideas to support both the American and the French revolutions.

Locke was not only a political theorist but the preeminent English philosopher of his day. He grappled with many of the same problems as Descartes, although his conclusions were radically different from the French thinker's. In his important philosophical work *An Essay Concerning Human Understanding,* published in 1690 (the same year he published *Two Treatises of Government*), Locke addressed the question, How is knowledge acquired? Descartes had proposed that the germs of ideas were inborn and that people were born knowing certain truths; education required nothing more than the strenuous use of the intellect without concern for new information from the senses.

Locke repudiated these views and described the mind at birth as a **tabula rasa** (erased tablet) on which all human experiences were recorded. Locke maintained that all that human beings can know must first be received through their senses (a basically Aristotelian viewpoint) and then registered on their minds. The raw sensory data are manipulated by the mental faculties, such as comparing, contrasting, and so on, so that abstract concepts and generalizations are formed in the mind. According to Locke, individuals come to understand the world and to have ideas through a series of mental steps. As a result, reason and experience are united in human thought and together determine what is real for each person. Locke's explanation of the origin of ideas is the basis of modern empiricism—the theory that all knowledge is derived from or originates in human experience. His influence has been so great that many of his ideas seem to the modern reader to be just "common sense."

EUROPEAN EXPLORATION AND EXPANSION

The exploration begun in the late fifteenth century had led to a series of encounters with new peoples that slowly eroded the isolation and self-absorption of Europe. In the sixteenth century the pace of exploration quickened, and the globe was circumnavigated—events that intensified rivalries among the European states, increased the Continent's economic power, and diffused European culture and customs around the world.

The greatest success of European expansion was achieved through a series of permanent settlements in North and South America and by the opening of new trade routes to the Far East (Map 15.1). Expansion and colonization affected Europe in numerous ways: the introduction of new foodstuffs and other products, the establishment of innovative business methods, the disruption of old economic and social patterns, the introduction of novel ways of looking at the world, and the adoption of new symbols and themes in the arts. Whatever may have been the beneficial or harmful effects of these changes on European life, the negative impact on non-Europeans tended to outweigh the good that came with the introduction of Western culture. In Africa, the Europeans expanded the slave trade; in North, Central,

MAP 15.1

Expansion of Europe, 1715

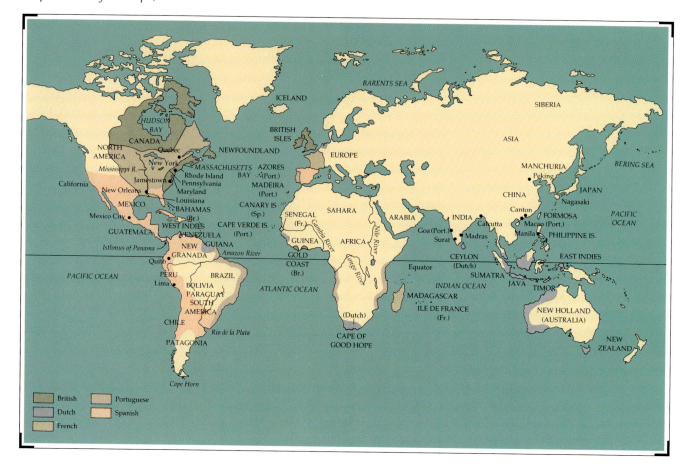

TABLE 15.2   **SETTLEMENTS IN THE NEW WORLD DURING THE BAROQUE AGE**

LOCATION	DATE OF FOUNDING	SETTLERS
Jamestown (Virginia)	1607	English
Quebec (Canada)	1608	French
Plymouth (Massachusetts)	1620	English
St. Kitts (West Indies)	1623	English
New Amsterdam (New York)	1624	Dutch
Barbados	1627	English
Brazil	1632–1654	Dutch
Curaçao (West Indies)	1634	Dutch
Honduras (Belize)	1638	English
Bahamas (West Indies)	1648	English
Jamaica (West Indies) (Captured from Spain)	1655	English

and South America and the Caribbean, they annihilated many native tribes; and everywhere they forced trade agreements favorable to themselves on the local people.

The earliest leaders in the European penetration of the Western Hemisphere were Spain and Portugal. Since the 1500s these two states had claimed South and Central America and the southern reaches of North America. Where possible, they mined the rich gold and silver veins, flooding Europe with the new wealth and gaining power and influence for themselves. But during the seventeenth century the mines were nearing exhaustion, and the glory days were a thing of the past.

While Spain's and Portugal's ties with the New World languished during the Baroque age, England, France, and the Netherlands were accelerating theirs, especially with North America. In 1607 English farmers settled along the Atlantic seaboard in Virginia, ready to exploit the land, and in 1620 English Puritans emigrated to New England in search of religious freedom. To the north, French explorers, missionaries, and fur traders founded Quebec in 1608 and then spread along the St. Lawrence river valley and southward into the Great Lakes region. At the same time, the French moved into the Caribbean basin, occupying many islands in the West Indies. After 1655 the English worked their way into the southern part of the Atlantic coast and the West Indies. These newly arrived colonists eventually either drove out the Spaniards or drastically reduced their influence. Meanwhile, the Dutch set up their own colonies in North America on the banks of the Hudson River and in scattered areas of the mid-Atlantic region (Table 15.2).

The English, French, and Dutch recognized the economic advantages of sending more explorers and families abroad and encouraged the founding of colonies. Relying chiefly on state or royal charters, they created large overseas settlements that soon led to a brisk trade in which raw products from the New World were exchanged for finished goods from the Old World. A typical example of the use of charters to encourage overseas growth was the governmental charter granted by England to William Penn (1644–1718) for the founding of Pennsylvania in 1681.

In the Far East, colonial developments relied less on charters than on joint stock companies, a private enterprise technique exploited by both England and the Netherlands. The English East India Company and the Dutch East India Company were the means whereby England and the Netherlands, respectively, opened trade routes and secured markets in the Far East. The two companies made lucrative contracts with Indian princes and Japanese and Chinese state officials.

RESPONSES TO THE REVOLUTIONS IN THOUGHT

The scientific discoveries, the growth of skepticism, the new political theories, and the overseas explorations provoked a variety of responses among the artists, intellectuals, and educated public of the 1600s. In the aristocracy, for example, a new social type appeared—the *virtuoso*, a person who dabbled in the latest science and gave it respectability. A new type of literature also appeared, in which scientific concepts and discoveries were popularized for the consumption of an educated elite. Overall, the innovations and changes of the seventeenth century found ample creative expression in the attitudes and images of the period.

The Spread of Ideas

In the exciting dawn of the Scientific Revolution, some scientists and intellectuals realized that new scientific findings needed to be given the widest dissemination possible, since the information would be of inestimable value to others who were engaged in their own research. Their enthusiasm for this task led them to share ideas in a variety of ways. At first, they exchanged information informally through personal contacts or by chance encounters in the universities. But by midcentury, the scientific society became the usual method for communicating new knowledge. The first one was in England, where King Charles II gave a charter to the Royal Society in 1662. Only a few years later, in 1666, Louis XIV supported the creation of the French *Académie des Sciences,* and in 1700 German scientists instituted the Berlin Academy of Science (Figure 15.7).

At the same time, many intellectually curious men and women, who wanted to learn more about the changes taking place in science and mathematics but who lacked specialized training, turned to writers who could demystify the new discoveries and explain them in popular language. One who responded to this interest was the French thinker Fontenelle [FOHNT-NEL] (1657–1757), the long-lived secretary of the *Académie des Sciences.* His *Conversations on the Plurality of Worlds* set the early standard for this type of popular literature (Figure 15.8). With learning and wit, Fontenelle created a dialogue between himself and an inquiring countess in which Newtonian physics and the new astronomy were explained in an informative and entertaining way. Through publicists like Fontenelle the new theories and ideas became available to a general public and entered the broader culture.

Another French publicist, Pierre Bayle [BELL] (1647–1706), created a famous work that launched the intellectual fashion for arranging ideas in systematic form, as in dictionaries and encyclopedias. Bayle's great popularizing work was called the *Historical and Critical Dictionary,* and it was probably the most controversial book of the Baroque age. For this encyclopedic work, Bayle wrote articles on biblical heroes, Classical and medieval thinkers, and contemporary scholars, many of which touched on and challenged Christian beliefs. Each article was a little essay with a text and lengthy footnotes. He approached the work with the aim of setting forth rival and contradictory opinions on each topic; if the result proved to be offensive to the pious, he pointed out that he himself was only following the Bible and the teachings of the Christian faith. Many readers responded to the essays by becoming skeptical about

FIGURE 15.7   J. GOYTON after a painting by S. Leclerc. *Louis XIV at the Académie des Sciences.* 1671. Engraving. Bibliothèque Nationale, Paris. *Science became fashionable during the Baroque age, and rulers provided funds to advance the new discoveries. Louis XIV, king of France, is shown here visiting the French Royal Academy of Science, the premier organization of scientists in France. From this period dates the close alliance between science and government, a linkage based on mutual self-interest and a prominent feature of modern Western life.*

the subjects, as Bayle clearly was. Others questioned Bayle's motives and accused him of atheism. The controversy over his works did not cease with his death. By 1750 his *Dictionary* had been reprinted many times and had spawned many imitations.

Bayle's *Dictionary* marked a new stage in the history of literature for two reasons. First, the work was sold to an audience of subscribers, for almost the first time anywhere. This step meant a turning away from the usual publishing method, which had prevailed since the dawn of printing, of issuing books under royal, aristocratic, or ecclesiastical patronage. Second, the extravagant success of his venture showed that a literate public now existed that would buy books if they appealed to its interests. Both of these facts were understood very well by authors in the next generation, who freed writing from the patron-

age system and inaugurated the world of modern literature with its specialized audiences.

Impact on the Arts

The innovations in science and philosophy coincided with and fostered a changed consciousness not only in the educated public but in artists and writers as well. New attitudes, values, and tastes reflecting these ideas are evident in the creative works of the Baroque period, many of which are discussed and illustrated in Chapter 14. First and foremost among the new ideas is the belief that there is a hidden harmony in nature that may be expressed in mathematical laws. This belief led to the guiding principle of order and wholeness beneath wild profusion, such as the geometric order that controls the gardens and grounds of Versailles or the theme of redemption that unifies Milton's sprawling epic, *Paradise Lost.*

A second reflection of the Scientific Revolution, and particularly of the discoveries in astronomy, is the feeling of infinite space, of limitless boundaries, that pervades Baroque art. The love of curving lines, elliptical shapes, and flowing contours may be related to the new, expansive views of the planets and the universe. The ultimate expression of these interests and feelings, of course, is the illusionistic ceiling painting.

A final effect of the Scientific Revolution was the elevation of analytic reasoning skills to a position of high esteem in the arts. Just as Newton's genius led him to grasp concepts and laws that had eluded others down through the ages, so artists and humanists were inspired to use their powers of analysis to look below the surface of human life and search out its hidden truth. Racine's plays, for example, reveal acute insight into human psychology, and Rembrandt's cycle of self-portraits shows his ability and his desire to reveal his innermost feelings. Baroque art and literature demonstrate that although the Scientific Revolution may have displaced men and women from the center of the universe, an optimistic and even glorious view of the human predicament was still possible.

FIGURE 15.8 Frontispiece of *Conversations on the Plurality of Worlds.* 1686. *In this original frontispiece of Fontenelle's classic work, the narrator and his young pupil sit in a formal Baroque garden. He points to the sky, where the new Copernican model of the universe can be seen. Wealth, leisure, and the new scientific knowledge are brought together in this idyllic setting, indicating how the Scientific Revolution was beginning to affect upper-class life.*

The Legacy of the Revolutions in Scientific and Political Thought

One historian of science claims that the Scientific Revolution "outshines everything since the rise of Christianity and reduces the Renaissance and Reformation to the rank of mere episodes . . . within the system of medieval Christendom." Although others hesitate to go that far in praise of this singular event, enough evidence exists to show that the revolution in science speeded up the onset of modern times and caused a dramatic shift in the way human beings viewed themselves and their world. The Newtonian system became the accepted view of the universe until the twentieth century. Likewise, the new methodology—collecting raw data, reasoning inductively to hypotheses, and verifying results with mathematics—remains the standard in modern science. Out of the gradual spread of this method of reasoning to other areas of thought have emerged the modern social sciences. Even certain disciplines in the humanities—such as linguistics, the study of language—have adopted scientific methods to the extent that is possible.

At the same time that science held out the promise that its methods could unlock the secrets of nature, it was also leading to a dramatic upsurge in skepticism. Since the end of the Baroque age virtually everything in Western culture has been subjected to systematic doubt, including religious beliefs, artistic theories, and social mores. Although many causes besides science lie behind this trend to question all existing standards, the Scientific Revolution created a highly visible model and ready tools for universal doubt. In effect, because Aristotle's and other ancient thinkers' ideas were proven false, modern scholars were inclined to question all other beliefs received from the past. This trend has encouraged the intellectual restlessness that is perhaps the most prominent feature of modern life.

The legacies left by the innovations in Baroque political thought and the expansion of European culture cannot compare with the effects of the rise of modern science. Nevertheless, the changes in political theory and in the relations of Europe with the rest of the world did have strong consequences for modern life. In general, the new political theories gave rise to two rival heritages, the authoritarian tradition, which claims that a strong centralized government is the best way to ensure justice for all citizens, and the liberal tradition, which holds that the citizens are capable of ruling themselves. From this time forward, politics in the West has been organized around the conflicting claims of these two points of view. In the twentieth century, until relatively recently, the symbol of this development was the division of the world between the supporters of the authoritarian Soviet Union and the supporters of the libertarian United States.

As for the colonizing efforts in the New World during the 1600s, this early step meant that these regions would later be dominated by Western peoples and values and thus served to extend the geographic limits of the West. As a result, Western ideas and technology may be found today even in the most far-flung reaches of the globe. A negative consequence of the opening of the New World was that slavery, an institution that had virtually died in Europe in the early Middle Ages, was reintroduced with all its destructive consequences for the non-Western people who became enslaved. We in the modern age are reaping the bitter harvest of this development.

KEY CULTURAL TERMS

geocentrism   Scientific Revolution
empiricism   social contract
inductive reasoning   liberalism
deductive reasoning   tabula rasa
heliocentrism   virtuoso

SUGGESTIONS FOR FURTHER READING

PRIMARY SOURCES

BACON, F. *The Essays.* New York: Penguin, 1985. Judicious editing of Bacon's highly readable text, dating from 1625, which contributed significantly to the rise of modern scientific thinking.

BAYLE, P. *Historical and Critical Dictionary: Selections.* Translated by R. H. Popkin and C. Brush. Indianapolis, Ind.: Bobbs-Merrill, 1965. Typical and controversial excerpts from one of the first modern dictionaries; a work originally published in 1697.

DESCARTES, R. *Discourse on Method.* Edited and translated by E. Anscombe and P. T. Geach. Indianapolis, Ind.: Bobbs-Merrill, 1971. A lucid translation of one of the key tracts of modern philosophy; Descartes's arguments and evidence are relatively easy to understand. First published in 1637.

LOCKE, J. *An Essay Concerning Human Understanding.* New York: Collier Books, 1965. A good edition, introduced by M. Cranston, of Locke's essay arguing that the mind is shaped by the environment, an assertion that made the progressive theories of the modern world possible; first published in 1690.

———. *Two Treatises of Government.* Cambridge: Cambridge University Press, 1967. An excellent edition with introduction and notes by the distinguished scholar P. Laslett; Locke's *Second Treatise,* making the case for the doctrine of government by consent of the governed, has become the bible of modern liberalism.

HOBBES, T. *The Leviathan.* Buffalo, N.Y.: Prometheus Books, 1988. A recent edition of Hobbes's most important work—first issued in 1651—advocating absolutist government without any restraint by the people; this work has inspired many modern forms of authoritarian rule.

16

THE AGE OF REASON

1700—1789

The scientific discoveries and philosophic ideas that made the seventeenth century such an intellectually exciting time bore fruit in the eighteenth century, a period often referred to as the Age of Reason. The work of the giants of the 1600s—Isaac Newton, Francis Bacon, René Descartes, and John Locke—led thinkers in the 1700s to believe they were living in a time of illumination and enlightenment. Committed to scientific methodology, mathematical reasoning, and a healthy skepticism toward traditional habits of thought, they fervently believed their ideas and proposals could lead to the improvement of both the individual and society.

The Age of Reason was marked by four different trends. The first was the growing concentration of political power in the great states, each of which was controlled by a ruling dynasty—a development that had begun during the Baroque era. France was the most powerful of these states, followed by Great Britain (the new name of a unified England and Scotland), Prussia, Austria, Russia, and the Netherlands (Map 16.1). The second was the return of the aristocracy to prominence after a century or more of decline. The ostentatious culture spawned by the resurgent aristocrats proved to be their swan song.

The third trend was the achievement of political and cultural eminence by the middle class after a centuries-long rise from their origins in medieval times (Figure 16.1). The middle class supported those progressive thinkers who advocated social

◄ ROBERT ADAM. Library, Kenwood House. Begun in 1767. London.

equality, social justice, and a thorough revamping of society. The intellectual and cultural movement spawned by these thinkers is called the *Enlightenment*, and it constitutes the fourth and most important trend that helped to reshape Western life in the 1700s.

At the same time that these trends were occurring, a reaction was setting in against the excesses of the Baroque style in art, architecture, and music. In the early years of the eighteenth century a new style was emerging in France that was lighter, more informal and graceful, less ponderous and oppressive than the Baroque. Known as Rococo, it suited the light-hearted pursuits of the reinvigorated French aristocracy. After about 1750, in reaction to both the Rococo and the Baroque, a very different style developed, known as Neoclassical. Unlike the Rococo, the Neoclassical style in art and architecture spread widely throughout Europe and to the United States. In music, the second half of the eighteenth century saw the development of a refined and elegant new style known as Classical; the period was graced by the incomparable presence of Mozart, arguably the greatest musical genius who ever lived.

THE ENLIGHTENMENT

Eighteenth-century thinkers derived their ideals and goals from a variety of sources. Following the example of ancient Greece and Rome, they rejected superstition, sought truth through the use of reason, and

MAP 16.1

Europe 1763–1789

viewed the world from a secular, human-centered perspective. Drawing on the Renaissance, they embraced humanism—the belief that a human being becomes a better person through the study and practice of literature, philosophy, music, and the arts. And from the seventeenth-century revolutions in science and philosophy, particularly the works of Newton, Bacon, Descartes, and Locke, they derived a reverence for rationalism, empiricism, skepticism, and the experimental method, along with a belief in the perfectibility of the individual through education and unlimited progress for humanity and society.

Despite the power of these ideas, the impact of the Enlightenment was limited to a relatively small percentage of Europe's population. It had its greatest effect in the major cultural capitals of France and Great Britain—Paris, London, and Edinburgh. Many aristocrats read the works of Enlightenment writers, as

did many members of the middle class, particularly educators, lawyers, journalists, and clergymen. Ultimately, enough literate and influential people were converted to the goals of the Enlightenment to have an effect on the revolutionary events that occurred later in the eighteenth century (Time Line 16.1).

The *Philosophes* and Their Program

The central figures of the Enlightenment were a small band of writers known as **philosophes**, the French word for philosophers. Not philosophers in a formal sense, the *philosophes* were more likely to be popularizers who wanted to transform the prevailing climate of opinion to make it accord with their point of view. They avoided the methods of

FIGURE 16.1 JEAN-BAPTISTE-SIMÉON CHARDIN. *Little Girl Playing Shuttlecock.* 1737. Oil on canvas, 31⅞ × 25⅝″. Uffizi Gallery, Florence. *This painting by Chardin serves as a symbol of the middle class, whose rise to cultural prominence in the Age of Reason was a foretaste of their political power in the nineteenth century. The young subject is dressed as a small adult, the typical way that children were treated at every social level in this century. On the other hand, Chardin's portrayal of the young girl as quietly absorbed in her thoughts, oblivious of everything else, reflects the home-loving values of the middle class.*

TIME LINE 16.1   THE AGE OF REASON

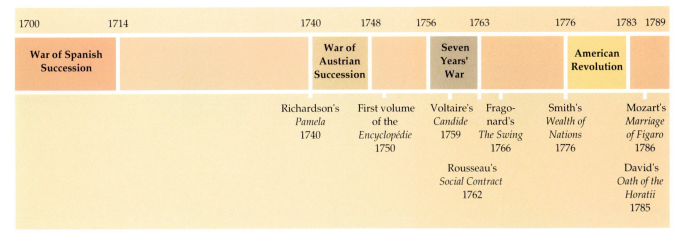

1700	1714		1740	1748	1756	1763		1776		1783	1789

War of Spanish Succession			War of Austrian Succession		Seven Years' War			American Revolution		

| | | Richardson's *Pamela* 1740 | First volume of the *Encyclopédie* 1750 | Voltaire's *Candide* 1759 | Frago-nard's *The Swing* 1766 | Smith's *Wealth of Nations* 1776 | Mozart's *Marriage of Figaro* 1786 |

Rousseau's *Social Contract* 1762

David's *Oath of the Horatii* 1785

academic scholars, such as engaging in philosophical debates or writing only for colleagues, and tried to reach large audiences through popular means such as novels, essays, pamphlets, plays, poems, and histories. In this they were following the lead of Fontenelle, who popularized the new astronomy in his *Conversations on the Plurality of the Worlds* (see Chapter 15). When possible, they openly attacked what they deemed to be the evils of society and supported those rulers who favored change, the so-called enlightened despots. When the censors threatened, however, they disguised their radical messages or else published their criticisms in the Netherlands—the most liberal state in Europe at the time.

The Enlightenment was essentially a product of French cultural life, and Paris was its capital. The principal *philosophes* were Voltaire, Diderot, Montesquieu—all French—and by adoption the French-speaking Swiss writer Rousseau. But the Enlightenment was much more than a French phenomenon. Major *philosophes* appeared all over Europe, in Great Britain, and in Britain's North American colonies. The most influential of these voices were the English historian Edward Gibbon, the American writer Benjamin Franklin, and two Scottish thinkers, the economist Adam Smith and the philosopher David Hume.

The *philosophes*, though never in complete agreement and often at great odds, shared certain assumptions. They had full confidence in reason; they were convinced that nature was orderly, fundamentally good, and could be understood through the empirical method; they believed that change and progress would improve society since human beings were open to perfectibility. Faith in reason led them to reject religious doctrine, in particular Roman Catholic dogma, to denounce bigotry and intolerance, and to advocate freedom of religious choice. Maintaining that education liberated humanity from ignorance and superstition, the *philosophes* called for an expanded educational system independent of ecclesiastical control.

The *philosophes* thought that the political, economic, and religious institutions should be reformed to bring "the greatest happiness for the greatest numbers"—a phrase that expresses a key Enlightenment ideal and that, in the nineteenth century, became the battle cry of the English thinker and reformer Jeremy Bentham (see Chapter 18). These theorists anticipated a general overhaul of society, leading to universal peace and a golden age for humanity. Few *philosophes* thought that they would witness these radical changes, but all passionately believed that the future would bring unlimited improvements in the human race. In effect, these eighteenth-century thinkers preached a secular gospel that happiness need not be delayed until after death but could be enjoyed here on earth.

Envisioning a rejuvenated society that guaranteed natural rights to its citizens, the *philosophes* were almost unanimous in thinking exclusively in terms of men and not of women. They still considered women their intellectual and physical inferiors and thus in need of male protection or guidance. Not until the next period were voices raised in the name of women's rights and only then under the inspiration of the French Revolution.

One of those moved by the revolutionary winds blowing from France was the English writer Mary Wollstonecraft (1759–1797) who, in *A Vindication of the Rights of Woman* (1792), used Enlightenment ideals to urge the liberation of her own sex. Like Rousseau, Wollstonecraft was a democrat and opposed to hierarchy in all forms: in the aristocracy, the military, and the clergy to the extent that promotion was based on obsequiousness. Unlike Rousseau, she was dedicated to the rights of women, whom she repeatedly called "one-half of the human race." Rejecting the "Adam's rib" explanation of woman's inferiority as being simply a male fabrication, she claimed that women were as rational as men and thus should be treated the same. The heart of this latter-day *philosophe's* argument was that women should abandon feminine artifice and cunning, especially the all-consuming need to be socially pleasing, and, through education, become equal partners with educated men. Starting in the nineteenth century, reformers gradually began to take up Wollstonecraft's challenge, particularly her call for female education and women's suffrage.

Deism

Newtonian science implied that God had set the universe in motion and then left it to run by its own natural laws. The *philosophes* accepted this metaphor of God as a clockmaker, and in place of traditional Christianity some thinkers now offered a version of Christianity called *Deism*. Deists focused on the worship of a Supreme Being, a God who created the universe and set the laws of nature in motion but who never again interfered in natural or human matters. Believing in this idea of a clockmaker God, the Deists rejected the efficacy of prayer and reduced the role of Jesus from that of savior to that of a good moral example.

Deism was espoused by only a relatively small percentage of Westerners, however, such as Benja-

FIGURE 16.2 Illustration from the *Encyclopédie*: Hand Manufacture of a Coach. 1751–1765. *As principal editor of the* Encyclopédie, *Diderot adopted Francis Bacon's notion that all knowledge is useful. Thus, the articles and the illustrations for this reference work focused on practical data such as soapmaking, human anatomy, and military drill. In this drawing, for example, the readers could peruse the interior of a shop in which horse-drawn coaches were made by hand.*

min Franklin in the British colony of Pennsylvania. Religions that ran counter to the Enlightenment's ideas—including the new sect of Methodists founded by John Wesley (1703–1791) in England—continued to attract most of the populace. Although it did not find wide acceptance, Deism's appeal marked another shift in religious attitudes and was added evidence of the growing secularization of European consciousness in the 1700s.

The *Encyclopédie*

The message of the *philosophes* was communicated by a variety of written and oral means, through pamphlets, essays, and books, through private and public discussions and debates, through the new journalistic press, and, especially in France, through the salon—the half-social, half-serious gatherings where the fashionable elite met to discuss ideas. But the outstanding voice of the *philosophes* was the *Encyclopédie*—the monumental project that remains the summation of the Enlightenment. Two earlier works, Chambers's *Cyclopedia* in England (1728) and Bayle's *Dictionary* in France (1697) (see Chapter 15) paved the way for the *Encyclopédie*, which surpassed its predecessors in size and impact. Begun in 1750 and completed in 1772, the original work comprised seventeen text volumes and eleven books of plates and illustrations (Figure 16.2). More than 161 writers wrote articles for this educational venture, which

was intended as a summary of existing knowledge in the arts, crafts, and sciences.

The editorship of the *Encyclopédie* was in the capable hands of Denis Diderot [DEED-uh-roh] (1713–1784), one of the giants of the Enlightenment. Diderot was constantly in trouble with the authorities because of the work's controversial essays, which he asserted were meant "to change the general way of thinking." Publication was halted in 1759 by the state censor but resumed secretly with the collusion of other government officials. Unlike many previous publications, the project was funded by its readers, not by the crown or the church. Even though there were only four thousand subscribers, the actual reading audience far exceeded that figure, for each paying household constituted many potential readers, and private circulating libraries rented the volumes to untold numbers of customers.

The Physiocrats

Under the broad umbrella of Enlightenment ideas, the *philosophes* were joined by a group of French writers who were concerned with economic matters—the *Physiocrats*, as they called themselves. (The term is a coined word, from Greek, meaning "rule of (or from) the earth.") The Physiocrats examined the general nature of the economy and, in particular, the strengths and weaknesses of mercantilism, the eighteenth century's prevailing economic system by which trade and production were regulated by the state for its own benefit. In the eyes of the Physiocrats, this state-run system had hindered, not helped, the growth of the economies of the various European countries. Contrary to its goals, mercantilism had lowered the productivity of workers, especially farmers, and had led to labor unrest and riots.

Guided by Enlightenment doctrine regarding the "natural laws" of society, the Physiocrats assumed that similar "laws" also applied to both economic growth and decline. After a thorough analysis of the French economy, they concluded that some fundamental principles did exist, such as the law of supply and demand, and that these laws operated best when free from governmental interference. Accordingly, they recommended the dismantling of mercantilism and the adoption of *laissez faire*, French for "to let alone"—in other words, an economy where the self-regulating laws of free trade were in effect. In addition, they argued that unrestricted enjoyment of private property was necessary for individual freedom. These French thinkers concluded that both the individual and the entire society automatically benefited from allowing all people to serve their own self-interests instead of working for the good of the state.

At about the same time, the Scottish economist Adam Smith (1723–1790) was developing ideas similar to those of the Physiocrats. He reported his conclusions in *An Inquiry into the Nature and Causes of the Wealth of Nations* (1776), a book that became the bible of industrial capitalism for the next two centuries. In this work, Smith blamed mercantilism for the economic woes of his time, identified the central role played by labor in manufacturing, and called for open and competitive trade so that the "invisible hand" of a free-market economy could operate. Smith's ideas were quickly absorbed by budding entrepreneurs and had an immediate impact on the changes being generated by the Industrial Revolution (see Chapter 17).

THE GREAT POWERS DURING THE AGE OF REASON

In comparison to the seventeenth century, the period between 1715 and 1789 was less turbulent. What wars occurred were usually fought for practical motives such as territorial gain rather than for ideological or religious reasons. National rivalries did trigger a few major conflicts on the Continent and in the overseas colonies, but they were usually brief due to

changes in military strategies, tactics, and organization; they were also less destructive to civilian populations, particularly in Europe. In addition, Europe experienced a slow but sound and steady economic expansion that was supported by a continuing increase in population. The prosperity fueled the rise of the middle classes, who now surged ahead, especially in Great Britain and Holland. In France, however, they made only modest gains, while in central and eastern Europe they constituted just a small fraction of the population.

Society: Continuity and Change

A major consequence of the century's modest economic growth was the growing urbanization of society. Although most Europeans still followed traditional lives on farms and in villages, cities and towns offered increasing opportunities for ambitious rural folk. The rural-to-urban shift originated in England, the home of the Industrial Revolution, and to a lesser extent in France. Only in the next century did it spread, and then slowly, to a few areas in central Europe and finally to the eastern European countries.

The traditional hierarchical social structure that had originated in medieval times continued to keep each class in its place. The aristocracy constituted only about 3 percent of the total population, but they possessed tremendous political, economic, and social power (Figure 16.3). Below them, the upper middle class—made up of rich merchants, bankers, and professionals—normally resided in the rapidly expanding cities and towns and exercised their influence in business and governmental affairs. In the broad middle class were the smaller merchants, shopkeepers, skilled artisans, and bureaucrats. Beneath the middle ranks came the lesser artisans and craftspeople, and below them, the metropolitan poor, who did the menial labor and were often unemployed.

In the countryside, the nobility and the more prosperous farmers owned large sections of the land and controlled the rural populace. The small cultivators, tenant farmers, landless workers, and indentured contract laborers made up a complex group whose legal, social, and personal rights varied widely across Europe. Next were the peasants, whose status ranged from freedom in western Europe to serfdom in Russia. (Serfs were bound to the land they worked, but they had customary rights, and strictly speaking they were not slaves.) These impoverished people often bore the brunt of the taxes and the contempt of the other classes.

FIGURE 16.3 François de Cuvilliés. Hall of Mirrors, Amalienburg. 1734–1739. Munich. *Despite the growing size and power of the middle class in the 1700s, the aristocracy still set the tone of life and dictated styles in the arts. In their royal courts, their town houses, and their country estates, they reigned supreme, surrounding themselves with luxury. This grandiloquent room is in the Amalienburg, a hunting lodge built for the Elector of Bavaria. Inspired by its namesake, the Hall of Mirrors at Versailles, the room reflects the delicate Rococo sensibility that dominated aristocratic European taste in the first half of the eighteenth century.*

With few exceptions, such as the upper-middle-class women who played influential roles in the salons, women remained subordinate to men. As mentioned earlier, the *philosophes*, who made such a thorough critique of society, failed to recognize women's contributions or champion their rights. Even Rousseau, who was often at odds with his fellow writers, agreed with the *philosophes* that women were inferior to men and should be submissive to them.

Another group who gained little from the Enlightenment were the black slaves in Europe's overseas colonies. During the eighteenth century, ships from England, France, and Holland carried about six million Africans to the New World and enslavement. Efforts to improve their conditions or abolish the slave trade proved futile despite the moral disapproval of the *philosophes* and the pleas of English Christians for the abolition of slavery.

Absolutism, Limited Monarchy, and Enlightened Despotism

The eighteenth century was the last great age of kings in the West. With a few exceptions, monarchs were everywhere the focus of the political system. In most countries the royal rulers followed proven policies even in the face of criticism or occasional opposition. Supported by inefficient bureaucracies and costly standing armies, they controlled the masses through heavy taxes and threats of brutality, while at the same time holding in check the aristocrats and other privileged groups that survived from the Middle Ages. Although a few monarchs attempted reforms in order to solve domestic problems, regardless of their strategies nothing finally seemed to work for these rulers. By the end of this period, most of the monarchies were showing signs of stress, as democratic sentiments continued to rise.

TABLE 16.1   WARS OF THE EIGHTEENTH CENTURY

War of the Austrian Succession	1740–1748
Seven Years' War (Known in North America as the French and Indian War)	1756–1763
American Revolution	1775–1783

In France, the kings struggled to uphold the power and prestige they inherited from Louis XIV. In Great Britain, the kings fought a losing battle against Parliament and the restrictions of constitutional monarchy. In Prussia and Austria, so-called enlightened despots experimented with reforms to strengthen their states, while in Russia the czars found new ways to expand absolutism.

By mid-century the dynastic ambitions and rival territorial claims of these monarchs plunged the continent into a series of brief wars that ended the several relatively peaceful decades Europe had enjoyed (Table 16.1). These continental conflicts soon escalated into commercial and colonial rivalries on a world scale that ended only with the termination of the American Revolutionary War (1775–1783).

France: The Successors to the Sun King   No French ruler was ever able to recapture the splendor that France had enjoyed under Louis XIV (Table 16.2). Louis XV (1715–1774), who succeeded to full political control at the age of thirteen, only compounded the problems of the French state. A charming man, Louis XV lacked a strong will to rule. He did not always pick talented, loyal subordinates, and he permitted his mistresses, who were not trained in government, to interfere in official matters. Even the king and his court seemed to sense that things were out of control. It is reported that when Louis XV, despairing over a military defeat, expressed his misgivings about the future of France to his royal favorite, Madame de Pompadour, she replied with the prophetic words, "Après-nous le déluge" ("After us, the flood").

TABLE 16.2   FRENCH KINGS DURING THE AGE OF REASON

Louis XV (Regency under Duke of Orleans 1715–1723)	1715–1774
Louis XVI	1774–1792

Life at Louis XV's court could not be sustained in the grand manner of the late Sun King. The nobles began to leave Versailles for Paris, where they exchanged their cramped quarters at the royal court for spacious town houses, called *hôtels*, in the capital. Whether at Versailles or elsewhere, educated aristocrats became fascinated by Enlightenment ideas. A large segment of top-ranked officials and their wives read the *Encyclopédie* and studied the writings of the *philosophes*. Upper-class women played influential roles in presiding over salons, where the enlightened thinkers and their admirers gathered to dine, gossip, and discuss the newest ideas, the latest literary works, and the current scandals. Even though the French elite debated the merits of reform and the more controversial topics raised by the *philosophes*, Louis XV clearly did not accept the movement's call for change. It is ironic that the country where the Enlightenment began failed to undertake any of its progressive reform. Indeed, when changes were introduced under Louis XVI (1774–1792), they were too little and too late.

Handicapped with a weak monarch, France found its preeminent position in foreign affairs threatened by challenges from Great Britain on the high seas and from Austria and Prussia on the Continent. Until 1756 France was at peace most of the time and the economy grew, but in that year the Seven Years' War began in which France suffered defeats in Europe and lost its holdings in both North America and India. During the American Revolution France sided with the colonists against Great Britain, her foe at home and overseas. France's aid to the American rebels further drained the diminishing financial resources and forced the nation deeper into debt.

While France's power declined abroad, at home the kings seemed unable to solve their domestic problems. This failure was the consequence of poor leadership, both at the top and among the royal officials, called *intendants*, who had the duty of coordinating the loose federation of provinces into a functioning French state. Similarly, the tax farmers (men empowered by the government to collect taxes, on which they made a profit) failed to provide adequate revenues for the state because of the corrupt tax system. And, most important of all, the crown was faced with a resurgent aristocracy determined to recover the feudal privileges taken from them by Louis XIV. Rather than joining in the reform efforts of the king, the nobility blocked the crown at every step. It was at this juncture that the middle class, who also wanted political power, joined forces with some sympathetic aristocrats and transformed what had been a feudal issue into a struggle for freedom in the name of the people. In 1789, during the reign of Louis XVI, the grandson of Louis XV, France started on a revolutionary course that united the nobility, the middle classes, and most of French society against the crown.

Great Britain and the Hanoverian Kings Great Britain under the Hanoverian kings was the nation that the French *philosophes* praised as the ideal model. To them, Britain seemed more stable and prosperous than the states on the continent, a success they attributed to the limited powers of the English monarchy imposed by Parliament during the Glorious Revolution of 1688. Furthermore, Britain's laws guaranteed to every Englishman certain political and civil rights, such as free speech and fair and speedy trials. Under the unwritten British constitution, new and often unpopular ideas could be openly debated and printed without fear of government censorship or church condemnation. Britain's economy, spurred on by enterprising merchants and progressive landowners, took the lead in an expanding global market and raised the standard of living for its steadily growing population.

After the death of Queen Anne in 1714, George, the Protestant ruler of the German principality of Hanover and a great-grandson of James I, succeeded to the English throne as George I. The Hanoverians inherited an English crown with certain rights and privileges, but they eventually lost most of them. This decline in royal powers happened because the first two of these kings seemed more interested in events in Hanover than in England (Table 16.3). The power vacuum left by the kings was quickly filled by factions who further eroded the crown's influence. In the end, the kings reigned in splendid isolation at the royal court, but the real power was in the hands of a coalition of London society and country landowners.

The first of the Hanoverian kings, George I (1714–1727), allowed Parliament to run the country. Under George II (1727–1760), Britain was drawn into the Seven Years' War but emerged victorious, the dominant presence in world trade. From this pinnacle of international power, Great Britain occupied center stage until the outbreak of World War I in 1914.

Nevertheless, Great Britain faced serious domestic problems once George III (1760–1820) was crowned because he set out to restore to the throne the powers lost to Parliament by his predecessors. This internal struggle affected foreign policy when the king and Parliament offered differing proposals to control the American colonies' economic development through export and import quotas, duties, and taxes. The differences between George III's and Parliament's plans hastened the onset of the American Revolution and probably contributed to Britain's eventual defeat. After the American struggle was settled in 1783, Great Britain had to face its most serious foreign crisis since the Hundred Years' War of the Late Middle Ages—the French Revolution.

Enlightened Despotism in Central and Eastern Europe The system of European states underwent some modifications during the Age of Reason. Great Britain and France now dominated western Europe because of their size, economic power, and military strength, and the less populous countries of Holland and Sweden declined from the powerful roles that they had played in the seventeenth century. Spain, whose glory years had been in the 1500s, turned more and more inward and all but disappeared from continental affairs. "Italy" was hardly more than a geographical expression, as it lay under Austrian and papal control and remained an economic backwater. Meanwhile, three states—Prussia, Austria, and Russia—jockeyed for control of central and eastern Europe. Under their absolutist rulers, these states pursued aggressive policies, seizing territories from one another and their weaker neighbors whenever they could. Although these rulers played at being enlightened despots, their planned reforms bore little fruit; their regimes remained committed to oppressive and authoritarian policies.

The kingdom of Prussia by 1740 had a solid economic base, a hardworking bureaucracy, and an efficient army—the necessary ingredients for a nation-state to succeed in the eighteenth century. Capitalizing on these advantages, Frederick II, known as Frederick the Great (1740–1786), turned Prussia into a leading European power. His pragmatic diplomacy, his brilliant military tactics, and above all his successful efforts to expand his territories added to his state's increasing authority and prestige. An admirer of French culture and a student of the Enlightenment, Frederick was an enlightened despot of the type so beloved by the *philosophes*. He even made an attempt (though it failed) to reform his state's agrarian economy and social system in accordance with the rational principle that all individuals have the natural right to choose personally the best way to live.

Prussia's chief rival in central Europe was Austria. In an age of states with relatively homogeneous ethnic populations, Austria was a relic from another

TABLE 16.3   **HANOVERIAN KINGS IN GREAT BRITAIN DURING THE AGE OF REASON**

George I	1714–1727
George II	1727–1760
George III	1760–1820

time. Throughout the 1700s Austria's struggled to govern a population that included large numbers of Germans, Hungarians, Czechs, and Slovaks along with generous sprinklings of Poles, Italians, and various Slavic minorities. At the same time, the emperors tried, with mixed success, to assert Austria's role as a great power. Two rulers stand out from the rest, shoring up the faltering Austrian presence in central Europe and thus serving to entrench their dynasty—the Hapsburg—over their multiethnic peoples. These Hapsburg emperors were Maria Theresa and Joseph, her son, who reigned between 1740 and 1790.

Unlike Frederick II of Prussia, Maria Theresa (1740–1780) was not attracted to the ideas of the *philosophes*. More important in her psychological outlook was her simple Roman Catholic faith, which led her to portray herself to her subjects as their universal mother. She was perhaps the most beloved monarch in this age of kings. Maria Theresa's reforming zeal sprang not from philosophic principle but from a reaction against Austria's territorial losses during military defeats. She used all of her royal prerogatives to overhaul the political and military machinery of the state. Along with universal military conscription, increased revenues, and more equitable distribution of taxes, she wanted a general reorganization of society that gave more uniform treatment to all citizens. Her efforts were not wasted, for her son Joseph II took up her uncompleted task and became the ultimate personification of enlightened despotism.

During a brief reign Joseph II (1780–1790) attempted the most complete reform program of any of the age's monarchs. Convinced that his country's economic and social institutions had to be fully modernized if Austria were to survive, he launched far-reaching changes to raise farm production and to provide more economic opportunities for the peasants. He abolished serfdom and passed decrees guaranteeing religious toleration and free speech. Although these reforms brought about some striking improvements, he alienated many nobles and religious leaders. In the 1790s much of what he had accomplished was undone by his successors who, fearing the excesses of the French Revolution, acted to restore aristocratic and ecclesiastic control and privileges.

Russia was the newest member of the family of great powers, having achieved this stature during the reign of Peter the Great (1682–1725). Abroad, Peter had made Russia's presence known, and at home he had begun to reform political, economic, and social institutions along Western lines. For the most part his eighteenth-century successors were in-

effective, if not incompetent, until Catherine the Great (1762–1796) became empress. She pursued the unifying policies of Peter, but unlike him she was able to win the powerful support of the large landowners. A patron of the Enlightenment, Catherine sought the advice of a few *philosophes*, including Diderot. She also made some efforts to improve the low farm productivity and the nearly enslaved condition of the peasants, but the vastness of Russia's problems and the reactionary autocratic government defeated any genuine reforms.

CULTURAL TRENDS IN THE EIGHTEENTH CENTURY: FROM ROCOCO TO NEOCLASSICAL

Even though the eighteenth century was dominated by the Enlightenment, other cultural trends also held sway. The Rococo style in the arts mirrored the taste of the French nobility; the succeeding Neoclassical style was adopted and supported by the progressive writers, artists, intellectuals, and ambitious members of the middle class. Meanwhile, innovations in literature were pointing the way toward the modern world.

The Rococo Style in the Arts

Conceived on a more intimate scale than the Baroque and committed to frivolous subjects and themes, *Rococo* taste arose in France in the waning years of the Sun King's reign. With his death in 1715 and the succession of his five-year-old heir, Louis XV, the nobility were released both from Versailles and from the ponderous Baroque style. Their exodus from Versailles made Paris once again the capital of art, ideas, and fashion in the Western world. There, the Rococo style was created for the French elite almost single-handedly by the Flemish painter and decorator Jean-Antoine Watteau.

The Rococo gradually spread to most of Europe, but its acceptance was tied to religion and class. It was embraced by the aristocracy in Germany, Italy, and Austria; Roman Catholic nobles in Austria developed a version of Rococo that was second in importance only to that of France. The English, on the other hand, rejected the Rococo, possibly because its erotic undercurrent and sexual themes offended the Protestant middle-class sensibility. Consequently, Rococo style is a purely continental phenomenon; there is no English Rococo.

FIGURE 16.4 JEAN-ANTOINE WATTEAU. *Departure from Cythera.* 1717. Oil on canvas, 4′3″ × 6′4½″. Louvre. *Watteau's aristocratic lovers, mesmerized by a brief moment of pleasure, represent the idealized image that the eighteenth-century elite wanted to present to the world. No hint of the age's problems is allowed to disturb this idyllic scene. From the court costumes to the hovering cupids, this painting transforms reality into a stage set—the ideal of Rococo art.*

Rococo Painting Jean-Antoine Watteau [wah-TOE] (1684–1721) specialized in paintings that depict **fêtes galantes,** or aristocratic entertainments. In these works Watteau portrays the intimate world of the aristocracy, dressed in sumptuous clothing and grouped in parks and gardens often accompanied by costumed actors, another of Watteau's favorite subjects. He filled these bucolic settings with air and lightness and grace—all of which were a contrast to the occasionally heavy-handed Baroque. Mythological allusions kept Watteau's works from being mistaken for scenes of ordinary life.

In 1717 Watteau became the first Rococo painter to be elected to membership in the Royal Academy of Painting and Sculpture in Paris. As required by the terms of election, he submitted as his diploma piece *Departure from Cythera* (Figure 16.4). The setting is Cythera, the legendary island of Venus, whose bust on the right is garlanded with her devotees' roses. Forming a wavering line, the lovers express hesitation as they make their farewells: The

couple under the statue are lost in reverie as a clothed cupid tugs at the woman's skirt; beside this group a suitor assists his lady to her feet; and next to them a gentleman accompanies his companion to the waiting boat as she longingly gazes backward. This melancholy scene, signified by the setting sun and the departing lovers, represents Watteau's homage to the brevity of human passion.

In *Departure from Cythera*, many of the new values of the Rococo style can be seen. Where the Baroque loved tumultuous scenes depicting the passions and ecstasies of the saints, the Rococo focused on smaller, gentler moments, usually involving love of one variety or another, whether erotic, romantic, or sentimental. Where the Baroque used intense colors to convey feelings of power and grandeur, the Rococo used soft pastels to evoke nostalgia and melancholy. The monumentality and sweeping movement of Baroque art were brought down to a human scale in the Rococo, making it more suited to interiors, furniture, and architectural details than to architecture

FIGURE 16.5 JEAN-ANTOINE WATTEAU. *The Sign for Gersaint's Shop.* Ca. 1720. Oil on canvas, 5'11⅝" × 10'1⅛". Schloss Charlottenburg, Berlin. *This painting of a shop interior illustrates the social dynamics of the emerging art market in the eighteenth century. The aristocratic customers act as if they own the place, turning it into a genteel lounge. The shop employees, on the other hand, have clearly inferior social roles; one brings forward a heavy painting for inspection, another holds a miniature work up to view, and a third stands downcast at the left. By using such clinical details, Watteau reveals the social gulf between classes that was implicit in the Rococo style.*

itself. *Departure from Cythera* shows the Rococo to be a refined, sensual style, perfect for providing a charming backdrop to the private social life of the eighteenth-century aristocracy.

In one of his last works, *The Sign for Gersaint's Shop,* Watteau removed all mythological and idyllic references (Figure 16.5). His subject, a shop where paintings are sold (François-Edmé Gersaint [1696–1750] was one of the outstanding art tradesmen of the eighteenth century), indicates the importance of the new commercial art market that was soon to replace the aristocratic patronage system. Within the store's interior, elegantly dressed customers browse, flirt, and study the shopkeeper's wares. The sexual motifs in the pictures on the walls and in the oval canvas on the right reinforce the sensuous atmosphere of this painting. But Watteau made this Parisian scene quite dignified by giving equal focus to the human figures and the role each plays in the overall composition. More than a shop sign, Watteau's painting is a telling metaphor of the end of an age and the beginning of another. This meaning can

be interpreted in the crating of the portrait of Louis XIV (on the left), a punning metaphor for the demise of the old political order and the style of Louis XIV. Art collecting in the age of Louis XIV had been restricted largely to kings, princes, and nobles, but, in the Rococo period, many new collectors came from the world of the upper bourgeoisie and shopped in commercial galleries like Gersaint's shop.

Watteau's paintings convey a dreamy eroticism, but those of François Boucher [boo-SHAY] (1703–1770) are characterized by outspoken sexuality. Boucher was the supreme exponent of the graceful Louis XV style, becoming official painter to the French crown in 1765. His voluptuous nudes, which were made more titillating by their realistic portrayal without Classical trappings, appealed to the king and to the decadent court nobility. Boucher's *Nude on a Sofa* is probably a study of one of Louis XV's mistresses (Figure 16.6). The casually suggestive pose, the rumpled bedclothes, and the delicate pastel shades are all designed to charm and to seduce. Boucher's art, though masterful, epitomizes the lax morals of French noble life that were becoming increasingly offensive even to other Rococo artists.

A different focus is evident in the Rococo portraits of Elisabeth-Louise Vigée-Lebrun [vee-ZHAY-luh-BROHN] (1755–1842), who became the leading society painter of the later eighteenth century and one of the relatively few women to gain independent fame as an artist. In 1783 she painted a famous portrait of Louis XVI's queen, Marie Antoinette, whom she served as court painter (Figure 16.7). Elements of the Rococo style can be seen in this elegant portrait in the soft colors, the graceful gestures, and the feeling of intimacy and informality. Many members of the court found it too informal, however, and demanded that it be withdrawn from public view. The queen had a well-known fondness for simplicity, and Vigée-Lebrun's depiction of her in a white muslin dress suggested that the queen was really just an ordinary woman—a notion that shocked and outraged the aristocrats. Despite the scandal it created at the time, the painting today is regarded as a masterpiece of Rococo portraiture.

The last great French Rococo painter, Jean-Honoré Fragonard [frag-uh-NAHR] (1732–1806), continued the style into the nineteenth century. Fragonard revived Watteau's graceful, debonair themes, as in *The Swing* (Figure 16.8). A lounging suitor motions to a young woman as a servant pulls her in a swing. The lady coyly kicks her dainty slipper toward the young man, who is strategically positioned to study her legs and underclothing. What is fresh in Fragonard's art and prefigures Romanticism is his treatment of the natural setting, which, although resembling the idealized, parklike backgrounds of Watteau, has a vivid, luxuriant life of its own. In Fragonard's painting, nature seems almost

◄ **FIGURE 16.8** JEAN-HONORÉ FRAGONARD. *The Swing*. 1766. Oil on canvas, 32 × 35". Wallace Collection, London. *This painting shows why Fragonard is regarded as the supreme interpreter of the Rococo subject of a young girl who is ardently pursued by an admirer. In Fragonard's art, nothing is ever coarse or brutal; everything is reduced to subtlety. Seduction is suggested and discrete gestures tell the story, as in the playful kick of the girl's leg and the answering salute of her suitor.*

ready to overwhelm the couple. Despite his interest in landscape, however, Fragonard remained faithful to the Rococo style even after it fell out of fashion. His paintings continued to focus on the playful themes of flirtation and pursuit in a frivolous, timeless world.

Rococo Interiors The decorative refinement and graceful detail of the Rococo style made it well suited to interior design. A major Rococo design element was **rocaille:** fanciful stucco ornaments in the shape of ribbons, leaves, stems, flowers, interlaces, arabesques, and elongated, curving lines applied to walls and ceilings. The effect of *rocaille* was to make solid surfaces look more like fleeting illusions. Mirrors further deceived the senses, and chandeliers provided jewel-like

lighting; all elements worked together to create a glittering, luxurious setting for an ultrarefined society.

Germain Boffrand [bo-FRAHN] (1667–1754), France's royal architect, helped to establish Rococo's popularity with his "Salon de la Princesse" in the Hôtel de Soubise in Paris (Figure 16.9). Exploiting the room's oval shape, Boffrand eliminated the shadows and omitted Classical details such as pilasters and columns, which had been part of decoration since the Renaissance. The floor-to-ceiling windows admitted light freely, and the strategically placed mirrors reinforced the airy feeling. Instead of a large overhead fresco, Boffrand divided the ceiling into many panel pictures. The characteristically nervous Rococo line—seen in the intricate designs of the gold edging—integrated the interior into a harmonious whole. The overall effect of airiness, radiance, and grace was worthy of a Watteau setting of aristocratic revelry.

FIGURE 16.9 GERMAIN BOFFRAND. "Salon de la Princesse," Hôtel de Soubise. Ca. 1735–1740. Paris. *The "Salon de la Princesse" was a reception room designed for the apartment of the Princess de Soubise. The graceful undulations of Boffrand's design represent the exquisite style of the Louis XV era. A typical Rococo design element is the blurring of the line between the walls and the ceiling.*

FIGURE 16.10 BALTHASAR NEUMANN AND OTHERS. Kaisersaal, the Residenz. View toward the South Wall. 1719–1744. Würzburg, Germany. *In this magnificent room, the ceiling fresco by Tiepolo is gorgeously framed with multicolored marble curtains pulled back by stucco angels. Other sumptuous details include ornate framed paintings, cartouches, and mirrors; gilded Corinthian capitals and arabesques; and crystal chandeliers suspended low over a polychrome marble floor.*

German decoration followed the French lead. The Residenz, a palace commissioned by the prince-bishop of the German city of Würzburg, is an example of Baroque architecture with Rococo interiors. Designed chiefly by Balthasar Neumann [NOI-mahn] (1687–1753), the building's glory is the main reception room called the Kaisersaal, or Emperor's Room (Figure 16.10). The ceiling frescoes are by Giovanni Battista Tiepolo [tee-AY-puh-loh] (1696–1770), an Italian-born Rococo master. His paintings combine the theatricality of the Italian Florid Baroque and the love of light and color characteristic of Rubens and the Flemish school. But Tiepolo's frescoes are only one facet of the riotous splendor of this room, which abounds in crystal chandeliers, gilt ornamentation, marble statues, gold-edged mirrors, and cartouches, or scroll-like frames. In rooms such as this, the age's painters and decorators catered to their patrons' wildest dreams of grandeur.

The English Response   In Great Britain, where the Rococo was condemned as tasteless and corrupt, the painter William Hogarth (1697–1764) won fame as a social satirist, working in a style quite different from that of his French contemporaries. Even though the appeal of his mocking works was to all social groups, the Protestant middle classes most enthusiastically welcomed his biting satires. In the paintings, which sometimes ridiculed idle aristocrats and always took a moralistic view of life, his bourgeois admirers discovered the same values that caused them to embrace the English novel. Taking advantage of his popularity, Hogarth made engravings of his paintings, running off multiple copies available for as many customers as wanted them—the first major artist to take this step in order to reach a new clientele.

Among the most popular of Hogarth's moral works was the series of paintings that depict the course of a loveless marriage between a profligate nobleman and the daughter of a wealthy middle-class businessman. Entitled *Marriage à la Mode*, this series comprises six scenes that show in exquisite detail the bitter consequences of an arranged marriage by following the husband and the wife to their untimely deaths. In the series, the married couple are no sooner yoked together than they begin their descent into degradation. By the fourth episode, called *The Countess' Levée*, or *Morning Party*, Hogarth portrays the wife plotting a rendezvous with a potential lover (Figure 16.11). In this scene, which was typical of the age's aristocratic entertainments, the hostess is having her hair curled while the would-be suitor lounges on a sofa, charming her with conversation. Nearby, guests, servants, and musicians play their supporting roles in this sad tale. Hogarth, never willing to let the viewers draw their own conclusions, provides the moral lesson. In the right foreground, a black child-servant points to a small horned creature—a symbol of the cuckold, or the deceived husband—thus alluding to the wife's planned infidelity. Even the paintings on the walls echo Hogarth's theme of sexual abandon.

The Challenge of Neoclassicism

Soon after the middle of the eighteenth century the Rococo began to be supplanted by a new style, known as *Neoclassical*. With its backward glance to the restrained style of antiquity, the Neoclassical had its origins both in a rejection of the Rococo and in a

FIGURE 16.11 WILLIAM HOGARTH. *The Countess' Levée*, or *Morning Party*, from *Marriage à la Mode*. 1743–1745. Oil on canvas, 27 × 35". The National Gallery, London. *Hogarth's painterly techniques—learned in France—have transformed a potentially banal topic into a glittering social satire. On the left, a pig-snouted musician is used to ridicule the popular* castrati—*men who were emasculated as youths in order to preserve their boyish tenor voices. Hovering over the* castrato *is a flutist—his coarse features demonstrating the artist's loathing for this social type. Other rich details, such as the tea-sipping dandy in hair curlers and the female guest who is gesticulating wildly, confirm Hogarth's contempt for the entire gathering.*

fascination with the new archeological discoveries made at mid-century. Excavations of Pompeii and Herculaneum—Roman cities buried by Mt. Vesuvius in A.D. 79 and only recently rediscovered—had greatly heightened the curiosity of educated Europeans about the ancient world. At the same time, scholars began to publish books that showed Greek art to be the original source of ancient Classicism. The English authorities James Stuart and Nicholas Revett pointed out the differences between Greek and Roman art in *The Antiquities of Athens*, published in 1762. In 1764 the German Johann Joachim Winckelmann (1717–1768) distinguished Greek sculpture from the Roman in his *History of Art*—a study that led to the founding of the academic discipline of art history. The importance of Neoclassicism is indicated by the decision made in 1775 by the Paris Salon—the biennial exhibition that introduced the lat-

est paintings to the public—to rebuff works with Rococo subjects and to encourage those with Classical themes.

Neoclassical Painting In 1775, the first year of Louis XVI's reign and the same year the Salon began to promote Neoclassicism, the king appointed Joseph-Marie Vien to head the *Académie de France* in Rome, a leading art school. A strict disciplinarian, Vien returned the study of art to the basics by instructing his students to focus on perspective, anatomy, and life drawing, efforts that resulted in the purified style of Jacques-Louis David [dah-VEED] (1748–1825), the principal exponent of the Neoclassical style.

David's response to a commission from Louis XVI for a historical painting was the *Oath of the Horatii*, a work that electrified the Salon of 1785 (Figure 16.12). Taking a page from the history of the early Roman

Republic, this painting depicts the Horatii brothers vowing to protect the state, even though their stand means killing a sister who loves one of Rome's enemies. The patriotic subject with its tension between civic duty and family loyalty appealed to the *philosophes*, who thereafter preferred Neoclassicism with its implicitly revolutionary morality to the Rococo with its frivolous themes.

David's *Oath of the Horatii* established the techniques and ideals that soon became typical of Neoclassical painting. His inspirational model was the seventeenth-century French artist Poussin, with his Classical themes and assured mastery of linear perspective. Rejecting the weightless, floating images of Rococo painting, David portrayed his figures as frozen sculptures, painted in bold primary colors. The Classical ideals of balance, simplicity, and restraint

served as a basis for many of David's artistic choices.

David showed his mastery of these techniques and ideals in *The Death of Socrates*, which was exhibited in the Salon of 1787 (Figure 16.13). Like Jesus in scenes of the Last Supper, Socrates is portrayed shortly before his death, encircled by those men who will later spread his message. Just as in the *Oath of the Horatii*, David's arrangement of the figures reflected the Classical ideal of balance. Surrounded by grieving followers, the white-haired Socrates reaches for the cup of poison and gestures toward his heavenly goal—serene in his willingness to die for intellectual freedom.

Neoclassical Architecture   No other painter could compare with David, but the Scotsman Robert Adam (1728–1792) developed a Neoclassical style in interior

◄ **FIGURE 16.12**   JACQUES-LOUIS DAVID. *The Oath of the Horatii.* 1784. Oil on canvas, 10'10" × 14'. Louvre. *David achieved a Classical effect in his works by arranging the figures so they could be read from left to right as in a sculptural frieze and by giving them the idealized bodies of Classical art. By omitting distracting details from the corners of his paintings, he further enhanced the sense that his central figures had been sculpted instead of painted.*

FIGURE 16.13   JACQUES-LOUIS DAVID. *The Death of Socrates.* 1787. Oil on canvas, 4'11" × 6'6". Metropolitan Museum of Art, New York. Wolf Fund, 1931. *Neoclassicism usually relied on ancient literature and traditions for inspiration, as in this painting by David. The general setting rests on Plato's dialogue* Phaedo, *though David has chosen to depict Plato present (at the foot of the bed), contrary to the literary account. Many of the domestic details are based on artifacts uncovered at Pompeii, such as the shoes, the lamp, and the bed.*

420

FIGURE 16.14 ROBERT ADAM. Kenwood House, Exterior, the North Front. 1764. London. *English architecture had been tinged with Classicism since the seventeenth century. Even St. Paul's Cathedral, the grandest Baroque English structure of the period, was deeply imbued with a Classical spirit. Adam's restrained style in the late eighteenth century represented a strong reinfusion of Classical principles into the English tradition. His style, with its reliance on the Classical orders and the Classical principles of balance and proportion, appealed to all classes but especially to the sober-minded middle class.*

decor that was the reigning favorite from 1760 until 1800. Classicism had dominated British architecture since the 1600s, and Adam reinvigorated this tradition with forms and motifs gathered during his archeological investigations. Kenwood House in London shows his application of Roman design to the exterior of a domestic dwelling, combining Ionic columns, a running frieze, and a triangular pediment to form a graceful portico, or porch, in the manner of a Roman temple (Figure 16.14). In the library Adam mixed Classical elements with the pastel colors of the Rococo to produce an eclectic harmony (Figure 16.15). To continue this

FIGURE 16.15 ROBERT ADAM. Library, Kenwood House. Begun in 1767. London. *Adam designed the library of Kenwood House with several basic elements of Classical architecture: columns, pilasters, and apses. By and large, he followed the Renaissance dictum of letting the architectural elements determine the chamber's decorative details. Nonetheless, he achieved a dazzling effect by his daring addition of mirrors and color.*

theme, he borrowed from Roman buildings with his barrel-vaulted ceiling and adjoining apse.

French architects too began to embrace the Neoclassical style in the late 1700s. The leader of this movement was Jacques Germain Soufflot [soo-FLOH] (1713–1780), who designed buildings based on Roman temples. Soufflot's severe Neoclassicism is characterized by its reliance on architectural detail rather than on sculptural decoration. Avoiding Adam's occasional intermingling of Rococo and Classical effects, Soufflot preferred pure Roman forms. The most perfect expression of Soufflot's style is the Pantheon in Paris. Soufflot's Classical ideal is mirrored in the Pantheon's basic plan, with its enormous portico supported by huge Corinthian columns (Figure 16.16). Except for the statues in the pediment, the building's surface is almost devoid of sculptural detail. The only other decoration on the stark exterior is a frieze of stone garlands around the upper walls. For the dome, Soufflot turned away from Roman models and found his inspiration in London—a sign that English architecture had come of age: The Pantheon's spectacular dome, with its surrounding Corinthian colonnade, was based on the dome of St. Paul's Cathedral in London (see Figure 14.20).

FIGURE 16.16 JACQUES GERMAIN SOUFFLOT. *The Pantheon.* 1755–1792. Paris. *By 1789 advanced thinkers in France had begun to appropriate Classical images for their movement, with David's Neoclassical paintings leading the way. When the revolution began, its leaders determined to build a suitable monument to house the remains of those philosophes whose works had furthered the cause of reform. Hence, it was natural that the revolutionary government turn Soufflot's Classical church—with its portico modeled from Roman styles—into a patriotic shrine.*

Political Philosophy

Modern political theory continued to evolve after its founding in the seventeenth century. Absolutism, the reigning form of government in the eighteenth century, still had many staunch defenders. Voltaire, convinced that the people lacked political wisdom, advocated enlightened despotism. But with this outstanding exception, the other leading *philosophes* of the Age of Reason rejected absolutism and supported alternative forms of government.

The Enlightenment's chief political theorists were Baron de Montesquieu and Jean-Jacques Rousseau, whose contrasting social origins probably to some extent account for their radically different definitions of the ideal state. Montesquieu, a titled Frenchman and a provincial judge, believed that rule by an enlightened aristocracy would ensure justice and tranquility. Rousseau, an impoverished citizen of the Swiss city-state of Geneva, advocated a kind of pure democracy. Of the two, Rousseau's ideas about who should control the state were more far-reaching and revolutionary.

Montesquieu [mahnt-us-KYOO] (1689–1755) most persuasively expressed his political ideas in *The Spirit of the Laws* (1748), a work that compares systems of government in an effort to establish underlying principles. He concludes that climate, geography, religion, and education, among other causes, account for the world's different types of laws as well as governmental systems. Despite his misunderstanding of the roles of climate and geography, Montesquieu's analytical approach identified influences on governments that had not been considered before his time. One enduring idea in *The Spirit of the Laws* is that a separation of governmental powers provides an effective defense against despotic rule. Montesquieu was an admirer of England's parliamentary democracy and of the work of the English political philosopher John Locke, whose influence is evident here. American patriots adopted this principle of the separation of powers in the 1780s when they framed the Constitution, dividing the federal government's power into executive, legislative, and judicial branches.

In contrast to Montesquieu's conservative views, Jean-Jacques Rousseau [roo-SOH] (1712–1778) framed his political theories within a more libertarian tradition. Rousseau set forth his model of the ideal state in *The Social Contract*, published in 1762. He agreed with John Locke that human beings were free and equal in nature, but he defined the "state of nature" as a paradoxical condition in which individuals could follow any whim and hence possessed no moral freedom. On the other hand, the state, which was founded on a social contract (an agreement among people), gave its citizens basic civil rights (freedom, equality, and property) and a moral purpose—precisely the things that they lacked in nature. That morality arose within the civil state was a function of the "General Will," his term for what was best for the entire community. If each citizen were to be granted the right to vote, and if each citizen voted on the laws in accord with the General Will, then the laws would embody what was best for the whole society. Thus, in Rousseau's thinking, the citizens who obeyed the laws became moral beings. (It should be noted that the questions and problems of who defines and implements the General Will and its relationship to individual freedom remain ambiguous in *The Social Contract*.)

In contrast to Locke's form of democracy, where a representative group like a legislature acted in the name of the people, Rousseau asserted that the people themselves collectively personified the state through the General Will. Rousseau's ideal state, therefore, had to be relatively small, so that all citizens could know and recognize one another. His ideal state was based on his experience as a citizen of the tiny Genevan republic. Nevertheless, Rousseau has had an incalculable influence on thinkers and politicians who had larger states in mind than his small model. Indeed, his impact in the nineteenth century extended far beyond democratic circles. Conservative philosophers like Hegel borrowed Rousseau's theory of the all-encompassing state, and radical theorists like Marx adopted his doctrine of the General Will (see Chapters 17 and 18).

Literature

Western literature in the Age of Reason was chiefly under the sway of French authors and the French language, which now replaced Latin as the international language of scholarship, diplomacy, and commerce. French writers made common cause with the progressive *philosophes,* sharing their faith in a glorious future. They wrote for the growing middle-class audience that was replacing the aristocratic patrons. Since these authors were under the constant threat of state censorship, they were often forced to disguise their more barbed social criticisms or to sugarcoat their beliefs. These restrictions did not, however, deter them from their mission to liberate the consciousness of their readers and usher in an enlightened society.

French Writers: The Development of New Forms   The two political philosophers whose works were discussed earlier—Montesquieu and Rousseau—were also prominent figures in French literature. Early in his career Montesquieu had written *Persian Letters,* a cleverly devised, wide-ranging critique of French institutions and customs in the guise of letters purporting to be written by and to Persian travelers during a trip to Paris. Through the eyes of the ''Persians,'' Montesquieu ridiculed the despotism of the French crown, the idle aristocracy, and the intolerance of the Roman Catholic church. His device of the detached observers of Western life was a safeguard against censorship, as was the decision to print the *Persian Letters* in the Netherlands. Montesquieu's publication inspired a new type of literature, a genre in which a ''foreign'' traveler voices the author's social criticisms.

Rousseau foreshadowed the Romantic sensibility of the next century with his intensely personal autobiography, *The Confessions.* Published after his death, this work was the frankest self-revelation that had yet been seen in print. It narrated Rousseau's lifelong follies and difficulties, including sexual problems, religious vacillation, a grotesque marriage, and his decision to place his five offspring in an orphanage as soon as each was born. Not only did he reveal his personal secrets, but he also tried to justify them, pleading with his audience that he not be judged too harshly. The revelations shocked many readers, but others praised him for his emotional truthfulness and were willing to overlook his rather high-handed treatment of a number of the actual facts of his own life. After Rousseau's candid admissions the genre of autobiography was never the same again.

The third great French writer of the eighteenth century was François-Marie Arouet, better known by his pen name, Voltaire (1694–1778)—the outspoken leader of the Age of Reason and the *philosophe* who best personifies the Enlightenment (Figure 16.17). A restless genius, Voltaire earned success in many forms, including dramas, essays, poems, histories, treatises, novels, a philosophical dictionary, letters, and the first work of history—the *Essay on Customs*—that surveyed civilization from a world perspective.

Of Voltaire's voluminous writings, only one work is still widely read today: the novel *Candide,*

FIGURE 16.17 JEAN-ANTOINE HOUDON. *Voltaire.* 1780. Bibliothèque Nationale, Paris. *Houdon's Neoclassical portrait in plaster of Voltaire shows the sculptor's determination to portray his subject as an ancient Roman. Houdon seated Voltaire in an armchair copied from ancient models and draped him in an ample robe that suggested Roman dress (but was actually based on the robe worn by the great* philosophe *to keep out the cold). He then endowed his aging subject with a vivid sense of life, as may be seen in the fine details and the expressive face.*

published in 1759. The most popular novel of the Age of Reason, *Candide* exhibits Voltaire's urbane style, his shrewd mixture of philosophy and wit, and his ability to jolt the reader with an unexpected word or detail. Beneath its frivolous surface, this work has the serious purpose of ridiculing the fashionable optimism of some eighteenth-century thinkers who, Voltaire believed, denied the existence of evil and insisted that the world was essentially good.

At one time an optimist himself, Voltaire altered his beliefs about evil after the 1755 Lisbon earthquake, a calamity that figures prominently in *Candide*. This comic adventure tale recounts the coming of age of the aptly named Candide, who is introduced to optimism by Dr. Pangloss, a caricature of a German professor. The naive hero suffers many misfortunes—war, poverty, religious bigotry, trial by the Inquisition, shipwreck—and through them all holds fast to Pangloss's teaching that "this is the best of all possible worlds." But finally, faced with mounting incidents of pain and injustice, Candide renounces optimism. The story ends with the hero's newly acquired wisdom for combating the evils of boredom, vice, and want: "We must cultivate our gardens."

Neoclassicism in English Literature In England, the presence of a Protestant middle class, which was growing larger and increasingly literate, created a demand for a literature that was decorous, conservative, and basically moralistic and religious in tone, even if that religion were little more than deference to nature and nature's God. The poetry of Alexander Pope and the monumental historical work of Edward Gibbon are typical of this style of literature, which is referred to as Neoclassical.

Alexander Pope (1688–1744) is the most representative voice of the English Neoclassical style. His poems celebrate the order and decorum that were prized by the middle classes—the social group from which he sprang. He became his age's leading spokesman for humane values such as reason, Classical learning, good sense and good taste, and hatred of hypocrisy and ostentation. His verses, marked by their satirical tone and sophisticated wit, made Pope the supreme inspiration of the Age of Reason until the Romantics, led by William Wordsworth in the 1790s, turned away from the Neoclassical ideal.

Pope wrote many kinds of poetry—pastorals, elegies, satires, among others—but the work closest to the spirit of the Age of Reason is his *Essay on Man*, a didactic work combining philosophy and verse, published in 1733–1734. Issued in four sections and composed in rhymed couplets, this poem brings together one of the age's central ideas, optimism, with some notions inherited from antiquity. In the first section of this poem Pope argues that God in his infinite power has created the best possible world—not a perfect universe—and that God's design rests on the concept of the great chain of being: Reaching from God to microscopic creatures, this chain links all living things together. Human beings occupy the chain's midpoint, where the human and animal species meet. Because of this position, two different natures fight in the human breast: "Created half to rise, and half to fall; / Great lord of all things, yet a prey to all; . . ."

Since humanity's place is unchanging, human reason is limited, and God does not make mistakes, humans therefore should not question the divine plan. Pope concludes that "Whatever is, is right." From this fatalistic principle it follows that what humans perceive as evil is simply misunderstood good. This unabashed optimism was satirized by Voltaire in *Candide* through the character of Dr. Pangloss.

Having established a fatalistic outlook in the first section of *Essay on Man*, Pope became more optimistic in the remaining sections. Although God's ways may be unknowable, he reasoned that some truths may still be learned by human beings: "The proper study of mankind is man." From this belief he concluded that a paradise could be created on Earth if human beings would think and act rationally—an attitude dear to the hearts of the *philosophes*.

Edward Gibbon's (1737–1794) *History of the Decline and Fall of the Roman Empire* appeared in six volumes between 1776 and 1788. Gibbon's recognition was instant and universal; he was hailed across Europe both for the breadth of his historical knowledge and the brilliance of his style. His subject, the history of Rome, appealed to the age's Classical interests, and his skepticism, notably regarding the Christian faith, echoed the sentiments of the *philosophes*. Although Gibbon's authority as a scholar was eclipsed in the next century because of the progress of historical science, his work remains one of the Enlightenment's genuine literary masterpieces.

Gibbon's massive work reflects both the ancient historical tradition as well as the ideals of the Enlightenment. Following the ancient historians, he wrote with secular detachment and offered reasons for historical change based on human motives and natural causes. From the Enlightenment, he determined that history should be philosophy teaching through example. These influences come together in his history when he attributes Rome's decay to an unpatriotic and subversive Christian faith along with the barbarian invasions. In effect, Gibbon's history praises secular civilization and covertly warns against the perils of religious enthusiasm.

The Rise of the Novel Despite the contributions of Pope and Gibbon to Western letters, the most important literary development in England during the Age of Reason was the rise of the modern novel. The hallmark of the early English novel was its realism. In the spirit of the Scientific Revolution, the new authors broke with the past and began to study the world with fresh eyes. Previous writers had based their plots on historical events or fables, but now individual experience became the keystone of the writer's art, and authors turned away from traditional plots in favor of an accurate representation of real-life events.

The English novel was realistic in several ways. It focused on individual persons rather than universal types and on particular circumstances rather than settings determined by literary custom. Furthermore, its plots followed the development of characters over the course of minutely observed time. The sense of realism was complete when the author adopted a narrative voice that contributed to the air of authenticity.

The novel captured the wholehearted attention of the reading public, many of them women. The works of Samuel Richardson and Henry Fielding especially appealed to these new readers. The writings of these two Englishmen helped to define the modern novel and at the same time set the standards for later fiction. For centuries, tragedy, with its plots about aristocratic heroes and heroines, had been regarded as the highest literary form. But since the age of Richardson and Fielding the novel, with its focus on ordinary men and women, has been and remains the dominant literary genre.

The novels of Samuel Richardson (1689–1761) focus on love between the sexes. For more than a thousand pages in *Pamela, or Virtue Rewarded* (1740) and almost two thousand pages in *Clarissa Harlowe* (1747–1748), he tells the contrasting stories of two young women whose virtue is sorely tested by repeated seduction attempts. Pamela, a resourceful and somewhat calculating maidservant, eventually finds happiness in marriage to her prosperous would-be seducer. Clarissa, from a higher social class but of weaker mettle, runs off with her seducer and dies of shame.

In contrast to Richardson's sentimental domestic dramas, the novels of Henry Fielding (1707–1754) depict a robust world of comedy and adventure. His best work is *The History of Tom Jones, a Foundling* (1749), a comic masterpiece that has been called the finest English novel. Tom, the hero, is a high-spirited young man who makes little effort to resist the temptations that come his way. His wealthy guardian rejects him for his immoral behavior, but Tom is shown to be good-hearted and honest and thus worthy of the good fortune that befalls him at the novel's end when he has learned the virtues of moderation. The novel contains a great deal of amusing satire, aimed particularly at the upper classes.

Music

The standard in music in the early part of the eighteenth century was set by the French, as it was in art and decoration. Rococo music, like Rococo art, represented a reaction against the Baroque. Instead of the complex, formal structure of Baroque music, eighteenth-century French composers strove for a light and charming sound with graceful melodies over simple harmonies. Known as the **style galant** (gallant style), this music was particularly fashionable during the reign of Louis XV.

The perfect instrument for Rococo music was the harpsichord, a keyboard instrument whose strings are plucked, giving it a delicate, refined sound. At the same time, improved instruments, such as brasses and woodwinds, were joining the musical family (Figure 16.18), and the violin was perfected by Antonio Stradivari. The earliest piano was invented in the first decade of the eighteenth century by Bartolommeo Cristofori, who installed a mechanism in a harpsichord that would strike the strings with hammers rather than pluck them. With this new instrument, a player could vary the loudness of the sound depending on the force exerted on the keys, something impossible to do on the harpsichord— thus the name *pianoforte*, from the Italian for "soft" and "loud."

The two outstanding composers of Rococo music were the Frenchmen François Couperin and Jean-Philippe Rameau. Couperin [koop-uh-RAN] (1668–1733) set the tone in court society for the early part of the eighteenth century. His finest works were written for the harpsichord; many contain dance pieces and are noted for their rhythmic virtuosity. His highly ornamented compositions are the perfect musical counterpart to Watteau's painting.

Rameau [rah-MOH] (1683–1764) shared Couperin's fascination with the harpsichord and small-scale works, but his major achievement was as a composer of dramatic operas. Following in the footsteps of the French-Italian operatic composer Jean-Baptiste Lully, he made a ballet sequence with a large corps of dancers a central feature of his operatic works. The best of his operas was *Hippolyte and Aricie* (1733), based on the French playwright Racine's tragedy *Phèdre*. Rameau heightened the tension of the gripping plot through his expressive music, underscoring the sexual tension between the doomed heroine and her stepson.

FIGURE 16.18 Illustration from the *Encyclopédie*: A Brazier's Workshop. 1751–
1765. *This engraving shows the interior of a workshop where braziers (metalsmiths) are
making copper musical instruments. Depicted in the figure are the various steps in the
manufacture of a hunting horn. A workman first hammers a piece of copper around a form
attached to the wall, turning the copper into a tube (fig. 1); a flared mouth is then soldered
onto the tube at a forge (fig. 2); next, the tube is filled with molten lead to make it more
malleable (fig. 3); and finally, the tube is curved upon itself like a snail (fig. 4). Two
finished hunting horns can be seen on the wall. Such illustrations served to demystify the
crafts by making practical knowledge readily accessible to educated readers.*

Like Rococo art, Rococo music was supplanted in
the second half of the eighteenth century by the new
Classical style, in which more serious expression
seemed possible. An important characteristic of
Classical music was its emphasis on form and structure. The most versatile and widely used form to
emerge was the **sonata form**, in which a musical
piece is written in three main sections, known as the
exposition, the development, and the recapitulation.
In the first, melodies and themes are stated; in the
second, the same material is expanded and changed
in various ways; and in the third, the themes are
stated again but with richer harmonies and more
complex associations for the listener.

The sonata form was also used as the basis for
whole compositions, including the **symphony** (a
composition for orchestra), the **concerto** (a piece for
a solo instrument and orchestra), and the **sonata** (a
work for a small group of instruments). Such pieces
often had three movements varying in **key, tempo,**

and **mood**. The first was usually the longest and had
a quick tempo. The second was slow and reflective,
and the third was as quick as the first if not quicker.
If there were four movements, the third was either a
minuet, based on a French dance, or a **scherzo**, a
lively Italian form. The sonata form provided general principles of composition that governed each
movement and yet allowed composers to express
their own ideas. Classical music retained the Rococo
love of elegant melodic lines and clear, simple harmonies, but by using the sonata form, composers
were able to add length and depth to their works.

Franz Joseph Haydn [HIDE-'n] (1732–1809) is the
first master of the Classical style. Haydn spent almost thirty years as music director at the palace of a
Hungarian noble family, where his status was that
of a skilled servant to the reigning prince. At his
death, however, he was both comfortably off and famous throughout Europe. He is largely responsible
for the development of the sonata form, and his 104

symphonies helped to define the standard, four-movement symphony. Despite their formal regularity, the symphonies show Haydn's inventiveness and sense of freedom as he experiments with a large and imaginative variety of moods and structures.

Similarly, Haydn's more than seventy string quartets, each composed for first and second violins, viola, and cello, became the accepted norm for this type of chamber music. His supreme innovation was to allow each instrument to show its independence from the rest. Although the first violin had the most prominent role, the musical effect of a Haydn quartet is of four persons conversing.

However prodigious Haydn's efforts, they are overshadowed by the greatest exponent of the Classical style, Wolfgang Amadeus Mozart (1756–1791). From the age of six he wrote music, alternating composing with performing. His travels around Europe as a child prodigy exposed him to the musical currents of his day, which he eagerly adapted into his own works. For nine years of his adult life he was a court musician in the service of the archbishop of Salzburg, a post that caused him great anguish because of its low social position. Unlike Haydn, he would not accept the conventional position of musicians as liveried (uniformed) servants of wealthy patrons. The last decade of his life was spent as a freelance musician in Vienna, where he died in extreme poverty. Despite his brief and tragic life, Mozart left a huge body of music that later generations have pronounced sublime.

Mozart's gift was not for creating new musical forms; Mozart already had at hand the sonata, the opera, the symphony, and the quartet. Rather, his inimitable talent was for composing music with a seemingly effortless line of melody, growing naturally from the opening bars until the finale. His disciplined and harmonious works embody the spirit of the Enlightenment.

The transparency of Mozart's composing technique allowed him to give a unique stamp to every type of music that he touched, and he composed in every genre available to him, including concertos, symphonies, trios, string quartets and quintets, serenades, divertimentos, and an unfinished requiem Mass, or service for the dead.

The fullest expression of Mozart's genius was reached in his operas, especially his comic operas, where he gave free rein to the playful side of his temperament, blending broad humor with dramatic characterization. His masterpiece in this genre is probably *The Marriage of Figaro*, based on a play by the French *philosophe* Pierre Beaumarchais [boh-mahr-SHAY] (1732–1799). Since its first performance in 1786, *Figaro*'s knockabout humor and rich musical texture have made it one of the most popular works in the entire operatic repertory. Beneath the farcical scenes and the enchanting melodies, however, lies a serious theme: By allowing the servant, Figaro, to outwit his arrogant master, Mozart joined the growing ranks of those who criticized the privileged classes and attacked the injustices of their times. In Mozart's other music, his personal presence was always obscured. But in *Figaro* the disgruntled servant-musician who chafes at his hard lot speaks with Mozart's authentic voice.

The Legacy of the Age of Reason

After the Enlightenment, Western civilization was never the same. By the end of the period, the prevailing form of government—absolutism—was on the defensive, facing condemnation from all sides. Supporters of absolutism argued for enlightened despotism, aristocratic critics advocated a division of centralized rule into rival branches, and democrats wanted to abolish monarchy and give the power to the people. Under these assaults, absolutist governments began to crumble.

Another development in the eighteenth century with long-term consequences was the emergence of the middle classes as a potent force for change. By and large, the Enlightenment reflected their political, social, and economic agenda, though their advocates claimed to speak for all people regardless of background. The rise of the middle classes also opened the door to popular forms of culture, such as the novel. Today this democratizing tendency continues and is one of the hallmarks of modern civilization.

Many of the ideas and principles of the Enlightenment are now articles of faith in the Western heritage. From it come the beliefs that governments should rest on the consent of the people, that the least amount of state interference in the lives of citizens is best, and that all people are created equal. More fundamentally, from the Enlightenment come the views that human nature is good and that happiness is the proper goal of human life.

Although the Enlightenment pointed the way to the future, we must not be misled by the modern-sounding language of the times. The *philosophes* wrote endlessly in support of free speech and religious toleration, and yet censorship and bigotry remained the normal condition of existence for most Europeans. Despite their brave words, most of these enlightened thinkers did not move from ideas to action, believing that ideas would triumph because of their inner logic and inherent justice. Moreover, they thought that the ruling classes would surrender their privileges once reason had shown them the error of their ways. The Enlightenment was the last era in which such simplistic beliefs held sway. The world in 1789 stood poised on the brink of an era in which ideas became politicized through action, war, and social agitation. In the postrevolutionary world, the radical power of ideas would be understood by all.

KEY CULTURAL TERMS

Enlightenment
philosophes
Deism
Physiocrats
Rococo style
fête galante
rocaille
Neoclassical style
style galant
pianoforte

Classical style (in music)
sonata form
symphony
concerto
sonata
key
tempo
mood
scherzo

SUGGESTIONS FOR FURTHER READING

PRIMARY SOURCES

DIDEROT, D. *The Encyclopedia: Selections.* Edited and translated by S. J. Gendzier. New York: Harper & Row, 1967. Well-chosen selections from the most influential work of the Enlightenment; originally published between 1750 and 1772.

FIELDING, H. *The History of Tom Jones, A Foundling.* Middleton, Conn.: Wesleyan University Press, 1975. A recent edition of this rollicking novel about an orphan who through personal charm, good looks, and honesty survives misadventures and is finally restored to his rightful inheritance; first issued in 1749.

GIBBON, E. *The History of the Decline and Fall of the Roman Empire.* Abridged by M. Hadas. New York: Putnam, 1962. One of the landmarks of the Enlightenment, Gibbon's history attributes the fall of Rome to the rise of Christianity; published between 1776 and 1788.

HARDT, U. H. *A Critical Edition of Mary Wollstonecraft's* A Vindication of the Rights of Woman, with Strictures on Political and Moral Subjects. Troy, N.Y.: Whitston, 1982. An authoritative text of one of the books that helped launch the modern feminist movement.

MONTESQUIEU, BARON DE. *The Persian Letters.* Translated by G. R. Healy. Indianapolis: Bobbs-Merrill, 1964. An excellent recent English version of this novel that satirizes European customs through the eyes of imaginary Persian travelers; the original dates from 1721.

————. *The Spirit of the Laws.* Translated and edited by A. M. Cohler, B. C. Miller, and H. S. Stone. New York: Cambridge University Press, 1989. A good recent English version of this groundbreaking work that claims people's choices are influenced by such matters as climate, geography, and religion.

POPE, A. *An Essay on Man.* Edited by M. Mack. London: Methuen, 1964. A poetic statement of the ideals of the Enlightenment by the leading English poet of the age.

RICHARDSON, S. *Pamela.* London: Dent, 1962. A recent edition of one of the earliest novels in the English language, recounting the tale of a servant girl whose fine moral sense enables her to prevail over adversity and rise to the top of aristocratic society.

ROUSSEAU, J.-J. *Basic Political Writings.* Translated and edited by D. A. Cress. Indianapolis: Hackett, 1987. Includes selections from *First Discourse* (1750), *The Social Contract* (1762), *Emile* (1762), and other writings.

————. *Confessions.* Translated by J. M. Cohen. New York: Penguin, 1954. One of the most original books ever written; bridges the Enlightenment and the Romantic period.

SMITH, A. *The Wealth of Nations: Representative Selections.* Indianapolis: Bobbs-Merrill, 1961. The basic writings that set forth the theory of free market economics; first published in 1776.

VOLTAIRE. *Candide.* Translated and edited by P. Gay. New York: St. Martin's Press, 1963. The most popular novel of the eighteenth century; contains the original French as well as an English text; first published in 1759.

SUGGESTIONS FOR LISTENING

COUPERIN, FRANÇOIS (1668–1733).
The harpsichord, with its delicate and lively sounds, was the symbol of Rococo music; Couperin's more than two hundred harpsichord works, composed usually in highly stylized and stately dance rhythms, helped to define the Rococo musical style. Typical works are *La Visionaire (The Dreamer)* and *La Misterieuse (The Mysterious One)*, both from 1730.

RAMEAU, JEAN-PHILIPPE (1683–1764).
Rameau's musical fame rests largely on his operas, which combine late Baroque forms with Rococo elegance and grace. His best known operas include *Hippolyte et Aricie* (1733), *Les Indes galantes (The Gallant Indies)* (1735), and *Castor et Pollux* (1737).

HAYDN, FRANZ JOSEPH (1732–1809).
Over a long and laborious career, Haydn honed his approach to music, moving from late Baroque forms until he established the sonata form of composition as the basic ingredient of the Classical musical style. Of the string quartets, those in Opus 17 and 20, composed respectively in 1771 and 1772, show his pure Classical style; the quartets he wrote in the 1790s (Opus 76 and 77) illustrate his later style, bursting with rhythmic vitality and harmonic innovation. Good examples of his more than one hundred symphonies are Symphony No. 45 *(Farewell)* (1772), Symphony No. 85 *(La Reine) (The Queen)* (1785), Symphony No. 94 in G major *(Surprise)*, and Symphony No. 103 *(Drum Roll)* (1795). Besides instrumental music, Haydn composed religious works, notably the oratorios for orchestra and massed chorus, *The Creation* (1798) and *The Seasons* (1801)—inspired by Handel's *Messiah.*

MOZART, WOLFGANG AMADEUS (1756–1791).
The most gifted composer of the period, Mozart helped to define the Classical style in virtually all forms of musical expression, including the symphony, the piano sonata, the concerto for piano and orchestra, the string quartet, and the comic opera. Mozart's religious music includes Masses, motets, and settings of sacred songs, such as *Solemn Vespers of the Confessor* (1780), with its serene "Laudate Dominum" section, as well as the *Epistle Sonatas* for organ and orchestra, composed between 1767 and 1780 as part of the Mass. Among his best-loved compositions are his last two symphonies, Nos. 40 and 41, composed in 1788; the six concertos for piano and orchestra written in 1784; the six string quartets in Opus 10 (1785), dedicated to Haydn; the opera *Don Giovanni* (1787) in Italian, combining comic and dramatic elements; and the comic operas *The Marriage of Figaro* (1786) and *Cosi Fan Tutti (They All Do It This Way)* (1790) in Italian and *The Magic Flute* (1791) in German.

17

REVOLUTION, REACTION, AND CULTURAL RESPONSE

1760—1830

The Age of Reason was a time of radical talk and little action, but before the eighteenth century was over, three revolutions had changed the face of the Western world forever. So turbulent was the period between 1760 and 1830 that today it is considered a historical watershed. The Industrial Revolution created new ways of producing wealth; with this event, industrialism replaced agriculture as the soundest basis for the economic well-being of a state. The American Revolution demonstrated that government for and by the people was a viable alternative to monarchy. And the French Revolution showed that the time was ripe for sweeping changes in the distribution of political power in Europe.

These changes were not welcomed by all. Many groups attempted to hold on to old ways and tried in particular to prevent the spread of revolutionary political ideas. The middle class, known as the bourgeoisie, benefited the most from these revolutions, in some cases challenging aristocrats in wealth and power. Emboldened by their newly acquired status, the middle classes asserted themselves as the new standard bearers of culture, embracing Neoclassicism at first and then shifting their allegiance to the powerful new spirit and style of the age—Romanticism.

◄ CASPAR DAVID FRIEDRICH. *The Chalk Cliffs of Rugen.* 1818. Oil on canvas, 90 × 70 cm. Museum Stiftung Oskar Reinhart, Winterthur, Switzerland.

THE INDUSTRIAL REVOLUTION

Even before the birth of the Industrial Revolution, changes in agriculture had occurred in England that made industrialization possible. One of these was the change in land use called enclosure, whereby common lands were fenced off by their wealthy owner and consolidated into one large estate. This practice brought hardship to smaller farmers but ultimately resulted in increased farm productivity. There were also improvements in farming techniques that increased crop yields and farm income, such as growing cash crops that replenished the soil instead of letting fields lie fallow to replenish themselves. Finally, better technology was leading to improved tools and farm implements, such as the iron plow and the reaper.

Industrialization in England

By the middle of the eighteenth century, changes both at home and abroad had created conditions that made England ripe for industrialization. An increase in population provided both a labor force and a market of consumers. Money to invest was available because of surplus capital generated by sound private and public fiscal practices. Several decades of peace had created an atmosphere conducive to economic growth, and the government's policies promoted

FIGURE 17.1 MICHAEL ANGELO ROOKER. *The Cast Iron Bridge at Coalbrookdale*. 1782. Aberdeen Art Gallery, Aberdeen, Scotland. *The earliest iron bridges, made from the superior grade of iron that was being produced in the new factories, were molded and cast to look like wooden bridges. The first iron bridge, located at Coalbrookdale, became a favorite subject for many artists. Architects did not begin to use iron in building construction until the early 1800s.*

further expansion. Free of internal tariffs or duties, goods moved with ease from one area of Britain to another, and canals and waterways offered cheap and convenient transportation. Britain's naval victories had resulted in the acquisition of colonies and trade rights that allowed its merchants access to raw materials and new overseas markets.

Three economic changes were necessary before these conditions could combine to produce industrialism: the substitution of machines for manual labor; the replacement of animal and human power with new sources of energy such as water and steam; and the introduction of new and large amounts of raw materials. By 1800 these changes had taken place.

An abundance of domestic iron ore and coal at home made it possible to launch new industries, and the changes in the iron and coal industries contributed to innovations in other areas. Better grades of iron, processed in more efficient furnaces, allowed manufacturers to produce stronger tools and building materials that soon began to replace wood (Figure 17.1). The demand for more coal led to new mining techniques, and a redesigned steam engine enabled miners to pump water out of the pits, thus opening unexplored deposits and making working conditions safer. Indeed, the steam engine, which James Watt patented in 1769, transformed the way power was generated.

The changes in the cotton cloth industry dramatically illustrate the impact of the Industrial Revolution in England. Local woolen producers, feeling threatened by the competition of cotton, persuaded Parliament to prohibit the importation of inexpensive cotton goods from India; but still the demand grew. The English industry tried to meet the mounting demand for cotton cloth at home and abroad through the putting-out system—a method of hand manufacture in which workers wove the fabric in

their homes—but this medieval technique proved hopelessly out-of-date. As a result, mechanics and entrepreneurs started tinkering with the manual looms and spinning machines in order to find ways to speed up manufacturing. The end result was the invention of the factory system: bringing together flying shuttles and power looms under one roof, and locating this building near a swiftly flowing stream that supplied the water for the steam engines that drove this massive equipment.

The laborers had to adjust their sense of time, their work habits, and their entire lives to the demands of the factory system. No longer could rural workers stay at home to work looms or spinning wheels at their own pace (although the domestic weaving industry did not cease to exist). Towns near the factory rapidly expanded and new ones sprang up in the countryside next to the mill. In both cases, employees were crowded into miserable living quarters that were usually assembled haphazardly with little thought given to even the basic amenities of human existence.

With the factories came the "working class," as they were known in England. A realigned class system—with the capitalists and workers at either extreme—transformed the social order, created new indicators of wealth and success, and established different patterns of class behavior. The earlier cooperation between the gentry and small farmers was replaced by increasingly strained relations between the factory owners and the working class.

Classical Economics: The Rationale for Industrialization

Although the process of industrialization did not produce anything resembling a school of philosophy, it did generate serious thinking about the kind of new economic system that was coming into being. Much of this thought could be interpreted as a rationale for industrialization and a justification for profit-seeking. The French Physiocrats and the Scotsman Adam Smith both advocated the abolition of mercantilism—the economy at the service of the state—and its replacement with a laissez-faire system—the economy at the service of the individual entrepreneur. In England, where Smith's views had the greatest influence, his ideas attracted a band of followers who carefully monitored the unfolding Industrial Revolution. What these observers wrote seemed to justify the economic changes that were transforming England from an agrarian country into an industrial power. Known as the Classical economists, this band of thinkers included Thomas Malthus and David Ricardo, along with Smith himself.

Smith's most significant contribution to Classical economics was his advocacy of a free-market system based on private property that would automatically regulate prices and profits to the benefit of all. He focused his *Wealth of Nations* (1776) on agriculture and commerce, while only glancing at manufacturing. As manufacturing started to loom larger in the English economy, however, businessmen read into his work a rationale for their activities. Smith was an optimist, a believer in the inevitability of progress—a man very much in the Enlightenment tradition. He argued that entrepreneurs acting mutually in enlightened self-interest would not only raise the standard of living for all but also get rich at the same time *if* the government left them alone. Such an argument was welcome news to the factory owners and other capitalists.

The ideas of Thomas Malthus (1766–1834) and David Ricardo (1772–1823) also tended to support the changes wrought by the Industrial Revolution. In his *Essay on the Principle of Population* (1788), Malthus forecast a world burdened with misery that would worsen if the human population continued to increase. Since the population grew at a geometric rate and the food supply advanced at an arithmetical rate, the number of human beings would soon far exceed the amount of food. Malthus's "law" of population led him to conclude that starvation could be prevented only by natural causes such as famines, plagues, and wars. Malthus's gloomy prediction persuaded most of the middle classes that laborers in the factories and mines were victims of their own thoughtless habits, including unrestrained sexuality, and could not be helped.

David Ricardo believed that he had identified a law that governed wages in an industrial society. In *Principles of Political Economy and Taxation* (1821) he maintained that wages for laborers would always hover around the subsistence level and workers would never be able to improve their standard of living beyond that level—his "iron law of wages." Tying Malthus's conclusion to his own, he argued that the working class was inevitably mired in poverty. Each new generation of workers would share the same plight—receiving barely enough remuneration to eke out a living. The theories of the Classical economists provided ammunition for the business classes as they sought to justify the methods of industrialization and the degradation it brought to workers.

POLITICAL REVOLUTIONS, 1760–1815

During the approximately fifty years between the Treaty of Paris (1763) and the Battle of Waterloo (1815), Europe saw monarchies fall and old societies swept away. By 1830 Europe was divided into two camps—a conservative eastern Europe and a progressive western Europe that included the former colonies in the New World. In western Europe economic liberalism was on the rise, and limited monarchies prevailed except in the former British and Spanish colonies, where republics had been established. In contrast, eastern Europe was dominated by reactionary regimes that feared the power of liberal and nationalistic ideas to move their masses to revolt. This twofold division of the West persisted well into the twentieth century (Time Line 17.1).

The American Revolution

Great Britain in the 1760s was suffering from an outmoded tax structure, and the nation's fiscal soundness had been strained by debts contracted in the Seven Years' War. The royal ministers, aware that the American colonists paid few taxes except local ones, tried numerous schemes to make the overseas lands share in the burden of empire. The colonists, calling the British government's new taxes on sugar, stamps, and tea unconstitutional, claimed immunity from imperial taxation because, they asserted, they were not represented in the British parliament.

Protests, demonstrations, and violence succeeded in nullifying the parliamentary taxes and also contributed to uniting the colonies in a common cause. The colonists came of age in 1774 with the convening in Philadelphia of a Continental Congress. Even though this convention possessed no legal authority, it spoke for the American people against the "foreign power" of Great Britain. In April 1775 conflict

TIME LINE 17.1   REVOLUTION, REACTION, AND CULTURAL RESPONSE

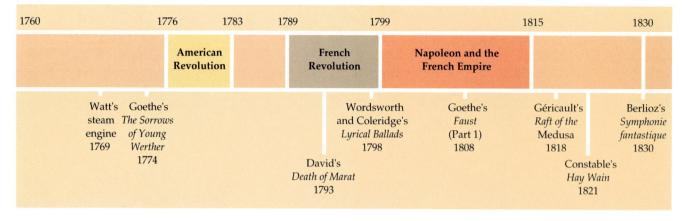

between British troops and colonists in Massachusetts triggered a war. The congress in Philadelphia proclaimed the American goals in the Declaration of Independence, signed on July 4, 1776: government by consent of the governed and the rights to life, liberty, and the pursuit of happiness. The struggle lasted until 1783 and resulted in the defeat of the British forces and independence for the colonies.

To realize their democratic goals, the Americans developed two new ideas: the constitutional convention and a written constitution. Both notions were activated by the Continental Congress, which in 1776 began to devise a plan for uniting the colonies—the Articles of Confederation. The Confederation era lasted only until 1788 because the new republic could not meet its fiscal needs, protect national rights abroad, or control the individual states. In 1787 a constitutional convention met in Philadelphia to draft a new charter. The central government could now assess and collect its own taxes, regulate commerce, and make and enforce laws through its own agencies. Fearing centralized power, the framers of the Constitution created three coordinate, although rival, branches of government—the legislative, the judiciary, and the executive—with specified powers delegated to each. The idea of a balance of powers is derived from the works of both the English political theorist John Locke and the French *philosophe* Montesquieu. They also limited the government's role in everyday life by accepting the superior claims of human rights.

The founders failed to extend rights to slaves, whose existence was barely noted, nor were women given the right to vote. Still, the Constitution made America the most democratic society of its day and the first successful democracy since Athens in the fifth century B.C. As an exemplary democracy,

America offered hope to the oppressed, and the successful struggle for independence provided a model for future revolution.

The French Revolution

Despite the importance of the American Revolution, the revolution in France overshadowed it. Because of its dramatic break with the past and its lasting worldwide effects, the French Revolution must be described as one of the major events of modern times.

At the time that Louis XVI took the throne in 1774, the French crown was confronted by a challenge from two sides: the aristocrats, who were resurgent after the death of Louis XIV, and an emerging bourgeoisie, who were clamoring for power. The affluent bourgeoisie tended to follow their own class interests. They aligned themselves with the nobles in supporting laissez-faire economics, but they joined the king in calling for an end to the feudal privileges of the aristocracy.

The peasant farmers endured burdensome taxes and continued to be subjected to feudal claims. Some peasants held free land and eked out a living on their small plots, but the majority were either tenant farmers or sharecroppers. In urban France, the lower middle class of small shopkeepers, salaried workers, and semiskilled artisans lived on the edge of starvation with scarcely any opportunity to escape their bleak existence. Below them existed the wage earners, the menial workers, and the marginal groups who drifted in and out of the criminal world. Oppressed by high taxes and harboring ill-disguised class hatred for those above them, the lower orders schemed to stay one jump ahead of the tax collector.

TABLE 17.1   SHIFTS IN THE FRENCH GOVERNMENT, 1789–1830

July 1789–September 1792	Limited Constitutional Kingdom
September 1792–August 1795	First Republic
August 1795–November 1799	Directory
November 1799–May 1804	Consulate
May 1804–June 1815	First Empire
June 1815–July 1830	Restored Bourbon Monarchy

In the 1780s France began to develop a huge national debt, fueled at first by its support of America in its revolution. As France sank deeper into debt, Louis XVI finally agreed to call the Estates-General, a representative body similar to the English Parliament, which had last met in the early 1600s. In 1789, when this body was convened, the third estate, representing the middle class, shunted aside the nobles and church leaders (the other two estates) and declared itself the National Assembly, the true representative of the nation. The Assembly then proceeded to end royal despotism and turn France into a limited, constitutional kingdom along the lines of England (Table 17.1).

The first phase of the revolution lasted from 1789 until September 1792. Dominated by the well-to-do middle classes, the Assembly embraced laissez faire, restricted the vote to property owners, overhauled the legal system, and declared the abolition of feudalism. It also introduced representative government and the idea of popular sovereignty. In framing the constitution of 1791, the Assembly attempted to embody the slogans of the revolution—liberty, equality, and fraternity—but class hatred made fraternity more an ideal than a reality. This first stage of the revolution failed because Louis XVI proved to be untrustworthy, and forces inside France were pressing its leaders for increasingly radical reforms. In 1792, the constitution of 1791 was suspended along with the monarchy, and the revolution entered its second and most violent phase.

Lasting from September 1792 until August 1795, the second phase was dominated by leaders from the lower bourgeois and working classes. These leaders executed the king, founded the French Republic, and briefly replaced Christianity with a state religion organized on rational ideals. Full voting rights were given to all males, including blacks and Jews, state education was opened to all, conquered people were allowed to decide their future through a vote, and the slave trade was abolished (Figure 17.2).

FIGURE 17.2   ANNE LOUIS GIRODET. *Jean-Baptiste Bellay, Deputy from Santo Domingo.* 1797. Oil on canvas, 63 × 45". Musée National du Chateau de Versailles, France. *The French Revolution fomented a slave uprising in the colony of Santo Domingo in 1791. Led by Toussaint L'Ouverture [TOO-san LOO-ver-tchur] (1743–1803), the revolt created the black republic of Haiti, which chose three delegates to the constitutional assembly called the Convention in Paris in 1794. In this portrait, Jean-Baptiste Bellay [buh-LAY]—one of Haiti's deputies—leans against a bust of Abbé Raynal [re-NAHL], the* philosophe *whose writings inspired L'Ouverture's struggle.*

Such far-reaching reforms alarmed many French people and nearly all Europeans. Soon the fledgling Republic faced civil war at home and invasions from abroad that set off another round of domestic political and financial crises. These events led to the Reign of Terror, the controversial policy whereby all suspected enemies of the revolution were executed. The Terror lasted for twelve months in 1793 and 1794, and its excesses overshadowed many of the Republic's accomplishments and discredited the idea of revolution among many of its early supporters. In August 1795 a more moderate government was instituted—a republic known as the Directory in which power was shared between two legislative houses and five directors.

FIGURE 17.3   ANTOINE-JEAN GROS. *Napoleon Crossing the Bridge at Arcole. 1796. Oil on canvas, 29½ × 23". Louvre. In this painting of Napoleon rallying his troops at the Battle of Arcole in northern Italy in 1796, the general is depicted as a courageous and charismatic leader of men. Painters helped to create the godlike mystique that surrounded the French military genius. Although Napoleon himself preferred ceremonial portraits by the Neoclassical artist David, other painters found him a captivating subject. Gros was a student of David, but he infused his works with such color, emotion, and drama that they inspired later Romantic painters.*

The Directory began inauspiciously and lasted for only four years. Although this government favored the commercial middle classes, giving the greatest political power to property owners and to the best educated, the Directory remained revolutionary in many ways, supporting state secondary schools as well as discouraging Christian attitudes and aristocratic privileges. But its leaders faced nearly insurmountable problems, such as growing counterrevolution, the collapse of the currency, and a breakdown in law and order. The directors appealed to the military for aid against their enemies, and in November 1799 General Napoleon Bonaparte staged a *coup d'etat* that abolished the Directory (Figure 17.3).

With the rise of Napoleon (1769–1821), events had come full circle, in effect returning France to a mon-

archy. Napoleon was a dictator and military genius who embodied the enlightened despotism of his century and at the same time anticipated modern totalitarianism. Above all, he was heir to the French Revolution.

The cost of Napoleonic rule was the loss of political liberty for the French. But in exchange, France between 1799 and 1815 enjoyed internal peace and a consolidation of most of the revolution's policies. Himself a product of France's new society, Napoleon kept careers open to talent, suppressed aristocratic privilege, rewarded wealthy property owners, and refashioned public education. He healed France's wounds from the revolutionary era by welcoming home noble emigrés, regicides (legislators who had voted to execute the king), priests, and wild-eyed radicals—provided that they were loyal to his regime. He restored relations with the papacy, though his efforts failed to achieve religious harmony. He also ended the civil war that had raged for more than a decade, and he stabilized the economy for the first time since 1791.

But Napoleon's most enduring legacy was the law code he personally helped to draft. Intended for universal application, the Napoleonic Code introduced rational legal principles and legitimized the idea of the lay state. The code rested on reforms of the revolutionary era, such as the abolition of serfdom, of the guilds, and of feudal property. Despite its reactionary ideas of paternal rule and the subservience of women, the code remains the basis of civil law both in France and in France's former colonies.

Napoleon's military conquests and diplomatic successes soon eclipsed his domestic achievements. He had already made his reputation as a brilliant field general before he seized power. Once he became emperor in 1804, Napoleon launched a series of wars that brought him a string of victories. When not winning battles, he pitted his enemies against one another, by exploiting the basic distrust among his foes so that the allied coalitions constantly fell apart. Specifically, he worked to keep Great Britain out of continental affairs while he crushed Prussia and Austria, who then sued for peace. Simultaneously, he annexed land for France or established satellite kingdoms ruled by members of his family or by his generals. As the self-proclaimed heir to the Age of Reason and the French Revolution, Napoleon reorganized his newly conquered territories along the lines of France. At first many local reformers welcomed the French, but they soon learned the high costs of occupation and began to resist their "liberators" (Map 17.1).

Napoleon's empire upset the European balance of power at a basic level, so that ultimately the other nations united to defeat him once he was proven vul-

MAP 17.1

Europe at the Height of Napoleon's Power, 1810–1811

nerable in battle by the terrible failure of his Russian campaign in 1812. Great Britain and the European states formed an alliance that brought Napoleon down in June 1815 at Waterloo (in modern Belgium). Exiled to an island in the South Atlantic, he died there in 1821, but Napoleon's spirit hovered over France and Europe for much of the nineteenth century.

REACTION, 1815–1830

After 1815 the victorious nations tried to restore Europe to its prerevolutionary status, but the forces of change had already altered the future of Western—and world—history. France had done more than simply conquer its enemies and occupy land. As heirs to the cosmopolitanism of the Enlightenment—the notion held by the *philosophes* that they were cit-

izens of the whole world—the French largely ignored the traditions of the peoples whom they conquered, believing as they did that the principles of their revolutionary society represented what was best for humanity.

Ultimately, however, the French were not as successful as they hoped to be in exporting their revolution. The European states and Great Britain not only defeated France but also devised strategies to contain radical change. France's enemies shared a conservative agenda that aimed to eliminate or at least to impede the advance of liberal ideas in Europe and elsewhere. At the Congress of Vienna in 1815 the victors restored the balance of power, halted or reduced reform programs, and inaugurated a period of reaction. France was stripped of most of its conquests and buffer states were installed on its borders.

Despite this redesign of the map, many Napoleonic reforms remained in force until 1830 and beyond. Even in France, where the allies restored the Bourbons, Louis XVIII (1815–1825) issued a charter that guaranteed a constitutional regime resembling the limited monarchy of 1791. Most western European states now had governments elected by their citizens and civil law based on the Napoleonic Code. By contrast, in central and eastern Europe the autocrats of Prussia, Russia, and Austria shared some authority with bodies of nobles, but these states remained basically untouched by democracy and representative government.

The fate of reform in Europe between 1815 and 1830 varied from modest changes in England to repression in Russia. In the immediate postwar period, attempts in Great Britain to reform Parliament or to institute free trade met with resistance from the government. But in the 1820s Great Britain began in a small way to dismantle the old regime. While Great Britain moved to modernize itself, France regressed toward absolutism as the restored Bourbons chipped away at the revolutionary heritage. By 1830 popular resistance to the crown mounted and the state became ungovernable. Finally, in the July Revolution of 1830 the people revolted and replaced Charles X with Louis Philippe, the Duke of Orleans (1830–1848), whose constitutional government put the middle class firmly in control.

In central Europe Austria masterminded events. Liberal feelings were kept under tight control inside and outside the country. Prussia, which had made important liberal reforms in the Napoleonic era, now seemed more interested in efficiency than in modernizing the state. After 1815 Prussia took a back seat to Austria in foreign affairs for several decades.

Russia became increasingly reactionary. When Czar Alexander I died in 1825, an uprising ensued with the aim of creating a constitutional monarchy, but the ill-conceived revolt failed. Nicholas I (1825–1855), frightened by the specter of revolution, escalated his predecessor's repressive policies. Until the 1860s, Russia's autocratic regime and Austria's domination of central Europe widened the gulf between eastern and western Europe.

REVOLUTIONS IN ART AND IDEAS: FROM NEOCLASSICISM TO ROMANTICISM

The makers of the French Revolution had at hand an artistic style that was perfectly suited to their purposes—the Neoclassical. In contrast to the frivolous Rococo, this style was high-minded, ethical, and se-

rious. Neoclassical artists and architects followed the ancient Greco-Roman ideals of balance, simplicity, and restraint, principles that were thought to embody the underlying order of the universe. Truth was seen as eternal, unchanging, the same for one and all. Art and literature created according to Classical principles were believed to be both morally uplifting and aesthetically satisfying.

In England, Classicism lingered on in the novels of Jane Austen. Untouched by the revolutions that dominated this age, Austen created fictional works that took England's deep countryside for their setting and dealt with the lives of the less wealthy gentry, an essentially middle-class world that appealed to her middle-class audience. Ignoring the fashionable Romanticism of the day, Austen adopted a literary style that linked her to the prevailing Neoclassicism of English letters in the eighteenth century, a style characterized by its precise and correct language, moral sense, and unquestioningly orthodox religious beliefs.

Advanced thinkers in France made the Neoclassical paintings of David a symbol of the new rational order they wanted to introduce into the world. The revolution intensified devotion to Classical ideals, and David became its official artist. Later, when the revolution lost its way and France began to see itself as a new Rome, Napoleon made David his court painter. After 1800, David transformed Neoclassicism into an imperial style that lingered on in France and the continent long after the French empire was exiled from Europe in 1815.

Even earlier, starting in about 1770, a new movement was emerging across Europe, one that was to have lasting effects on the Western consciousness. *Romanticism* was a whole way of thinking that came to dominate European arts and letters in the nineteenth century. Rejecting Neoclassicism as cold and artificial, the Romantics glorified unruly nature, uncontrolled feeling, and the mysteries of the human soul. They claimed that their ideals were more in tune with human nature than the order, reason, and harmony of Classicism. Certain ideas and elements of Romanticism have permeated our Western way of thinking and become articles of faith in the modern world.

Neoclassicism in Literature after 1789

During her brief life Jane Austen (1775–1817) wrote six novels that together rank as the finest body of fiction produced in this period. Austen approached novel writing in a Classical spirit, portraying her characters as inhabiting a serene environment reminiscent of the quiet domestic scenes of the seventeenth-century Dutch painter Vermeer (see Chapter 14). Calling herself a miniaturist, she concentrated her author's eye on a soon-to-be-swept-away world where the smallest important unit was the family and the most significant problems involved the adjustment of social relationships.

In the hands of a lesser writer, such a literary program might have failed by being too narrow, but Austen transcended her limited framework. She did this through clear writing, ironic understatement, and, above all, beautifully realized descriptions of the manners and little rituals of provincial life: the balls attended, the letters and conversations, the visits to relatives, and the unexpected social breakdowns, such as an elopement, a betrayed confidence, or a broken engagement. She was especially sensitive to the constraints her society imposed on women, depicting with great wit a world in which women were miseducated, confined to the domestic sphere, kept economically dependent on men, and socialized to be weak and sentimental. The best known of Austen's novels is *Pride and Prejudice* (1813), a gently satirical work whose plot revolves around the problems that arise when the Bennets— a shabby genteel family—try to find suitable husbands for five ready and eager daughters.

Neoclassical Painting and Architecture after 1789

Jacques-Louis David founded Neoclassicism in painting in the 1780s and remained its consummate exponent until his death in 1825. As official artist of the French revolution, he rendered contemporary events in the ancient manner. David's most successful painting from this period was his study of the revolution's famous martyr, Marat [muh-RAH], who was assassinated while seated in his bath (Figure 17.4). Himself an ardent supporter of the revolution, David meticulously planned this work in order to give universal meaning to a specific moment in French history. The setting is historically accurate because Marat suffered from a skin disorder and often conducted official business while seated in the bathtub. Once having established the scene, David suppresses every detail that does not contribute to the general impression of tragedy. As a result, the few details take on a highly charged quality. The figure of Marat resembles a piece of Classical sculpture against the stark background. His torso is twisted so that the bleeding wound and the peaceful face are fully visible. The pen and the inkwell remind the

FIGURE 17.4   JACQUES-LOUIS DAVID. *Death of Marat.* 1793. Oil on canvas, 65 × 50½". Musées Royaux des Beaux-Arts, Brussels. *David's presentation of figures in the nude in his Neoclassical history paintings was often denounced by literal-minded critics as unrealistic, but David defended this choice as consistent with "the customs of antiquity." The critics were silenced by David's depiction of the Marat murder scene, since in this case the nudity was true-to-life. In this painting David's Classical principles and the demands of realistic portrayal combined to produce a timeless image.*

viewer that Marat was killed while serving the revolution. In effect, David has portrayed Marat as a secular saint.

Barely escaping the revolution's most violent phase, David survived to become court painter to Napoleon, and modifications in the cause of political propaganda now appeared in his art. Napoleon, in order to enhance his image as a new Augustus, encouraged David to make his painting reflect the pomp and grandeur of the Napoleonic court. *The Coronation of Napoleon and Josephine* is typical of David's imperial paintings (Figure 17.5). This pictorial record of the investiture conveys the opulent splendor and theatrical ceremony that Napoleon craved as a way of validating his empire in the eyes of

FIGURE 17.5 JACQUES-LOUIS DAVID. *The Coronation of Napoleon and Josephine.* 1805–1808. Oil on canvas, 20′ × 30′6½″. Louvre. *Napoleon orchestrated his own coronation and then guided David in painting it. For instance, Napoleon's mother did not attend, probably because of her disapproval of her son's grandiose ambitions, but Napoleon insisted that David depict her seated prominently at the center of the festivities. David also shows the pope's hand raised in benediction, contrary to the report of eyewitnesses who described him sitting with both hands resting on his knees.*

Europe's older monarchs, who regarded him as an upstart. Napoleon's family members, who had been made kings, princes, princesses, and so on, are depicted in elaborate court dress. In addition, David's treatment of the coronation reveals the modern conception of political power. Instead of being crowned by the pope, Napoleon placed the crown on his own head. This painting shows Napoleon preparing to crown his empress, who is kneeling. Virtually ignored in this splendid moment for the Bonaparte family is the pope, who is seated at the right.

The only Neoclassical painter comparable to David is his pupil Jean-Auguste-Dominique Ingres [ANGR] (1780–1867). Ingres inherited the mantle of Neoclassicism from David, but he lacked his teacher's moral enthusiasm. As a result, Ingres's Classicism is almost cold-blooded and stark in its simple images. The finest expressions of Ingres's art are his portraits. With clean lines drawn with a sure and steady hand he created almost photographic images of his subjects. Of Ingres's numerous portraits, one

of the most exquisite is that of Madame Leblanc [luh-BLAH(N)], a member of the new social order of Napoleonic France (Figure 17.6). Ingres's portrait may not probe deeply into the subject's psychology, but he does convey the sitter's high social position, stressing her poise and alluding to her wealth through the rich details of the marble-topped table, the floral still life, and the dangling watch and chain. In his own way, Ingres gives this member of the new bourgeois aristocracy the same glamorous treatment that had been accorded prerevolutionary nobles in Rococo portraits.

FIGURE 17.6 JEAN-AUGUSTE-DOMINIQUE INGRES. *Madame Jacques Louis Leblanc.* 1823. Oil on canvas, 47 × 36½″. Metropolitan Museum of Art, New York. Wolfe Fund, 1918. *Ingres was the last great painter of portraits in a field that was to be taken over by the camera after 1840. Claiming that drawing was superior to painting, he was able to render intense likenesses, as in this portrait of Madame Leblanc. Ingres stands alone in his ability to convey a subject's physical presence.*

◀ **FIGURE 17.7** THOMAS JEFFERSON. Monticello. 1770–1784; remodeled 1796–1806. Charlottesville, Virginia. *The Palladio-inspired architecture of Monticello reflected Jefferson's ethical vision. Its portico in the plain style of a Roman temple mirrored his admiration for the Roman republic and its ideals of simplicity and order. Its overall devotion to mathematical principles and unobtrusive details were expressions of his commitment to disciplined living. Though built for one of America's elite, Monticello was conceived as a visual rebuke to the luxurious palaces of Europe's aristocrats.*

After 1789, the Neoclassical style in architecture spread to the European colonies, notably to the former British territories in North America. In the United States, the middle-class founders of the new republic made Neoclassicism synonymous with their own time, which is known as the Federal Period. They graced their capital, Washington, with the Classical architecture that symbolized devotion to republican and democratic sentiments.

The most profound influence on America's Classical heritage was exercised by Thomas Jefferson (1743–1826), the coauthor of the Declaration of Independence and the third president of the United States. Jefferson was a master architect along with his many other talents. Like other architects in this era, he was deeply indebted to the principles of the Italian architect Andrea Palladio (1508–1580), whose book on architecture he had read. Palladio's Villa Rotonda near Vicenza served as the model for Jefferson's home at Monticello near Charlottesville, Virginia (Figure 17.7). Like the Villa Rotonda (see Figure 12.20), Monticello is a country dwelling arranged around a domed central area, though it features only two symmetrical connecting wings. Executed in brick with wooden trim, Monticello has inspired so many imitations that it has come to symbolize the American dream of gracious living.

Just as Jefferson's plan for his personal residence influenced American domestic architecture, his design for Virginia's state capitol in Richmond has deeply influenced public architecture (Figure 17.8). From his plan for the Virginia statehouse arose the tradition of building public structures in the form of ancient temples. His model for the capitol building was the Maison Carrée (see Figure 5.12), a Roman

temple dating from the first century A.D. Though small by today's standards for public buildings, Jefferson's statehouse has a strong presence and is a marvel of refined elegance and simple charm. The most pleasing part of his original design is the central building with its perfectly proportioned features—columns, pediment, and windows. Even though two smaller wings were added later, they enhance rather than detract from Jefferson's symmetrical and harmonious plan.

Romanticism: Its Spirit and Expression

In contrast to Neoclassicism, Romanticism stood for everything that was unbounded and untamed. The Romantics' patron saint was Rousseau, whose emotionalism and love of nature had made him out of step with his own time. Like Rousseau, the Romantics preferred to be guided by emotion and intuition. Following these guides, they conjured up an image of the world that was deeply personal and alive with hidden meanings. Nature itself became God for many Romantics, who spiritualized nature so that divinity was expressed through bucolic scenes as well as terrifying natural forces. To characterize the latter face of nature they invented the term *Sublime* to convey the awesome and majestic power of earthquakes, floods, and storms.

Part of the Romantic reverence for nature stemmed from a desire to escape from the effects of the Industrial Revolution, which was altering the countryside for the worse (Figure 17.9). Not surprisingly, England, the first home of industrialization, became the center of a movement that exalted the preindustrial Middle Ages, creating a world of natural sentiment that existed only in imagination. The Romantics' rejection of the industrial world had many other consequences, including a preoccupation with the exotic East and the domains of the imagination, dreams, drugs, and nonrational mental states.

Another formative force in Romanticism was the French Revolution itself. Many early Romantics willingly saw in this awesome upheaval Europe's future. The revolutionary watchwords "liberty," "rights of man," "the individual," and "equality" became the basis of a moral and humanitarian viewpoint that could be applied beyond the orbit of the revolution. When Greece declared its independence from the feeble Ottoman Empire and fought for its freedom in the 1820s, for example, many Europeans, influenced by revolutionary principles, declared their solidarity with the rebels. Among them was the English

◀ **FIGURE 17.8** THOMAS JEFFERSON. State Capitol of Virginia. 1785–1796. Richmond, Virginia. *Jefferson described the Maison Carrée, the model for this statehouse, as "the most perfect and precious remain of antiquity in existence." Political considerations also influenced Jefferson's choice, for he identified this Roman temple as a symbol of Roman republican values. Like Monticello, Jefferson's statehouse design was an outgrowth of his ethical vision.*

FIGURE 17.9 PHILIP JACQUES DE LOUTHERBOURG. *Coalbrookdale by Night.* 1801. Oil on canvas, 26¾ × 42″. Science Museum, London. *At first glance, this painting seems to portray the world engulfed in a flaming inferno. Only gradually does the meaning of the scene—a depiction of one of England's new industrialized towns—emerge. As a terrifying symbol of industrialism, the painting helps to explain what Romantic art was rebelling against.*

Romantic poet Lord Byron, who died in Greece while aiding in the cause of Greek independence.

The French Revolution also sparked a strong negative reaction among some Romantics who criticized its seemingly random violence. They likewise deplored Napoleonic imperialism, which squeezed the life out of other cultures by conquering them and then imposing French customs. These conservative Romantics renounced the French Revolution's stress on abstract ideas and natural rights and focused their attention on history and the rights and traditions native to each country. They especially rebuked the revolution's international spirit and advocated instead a nationalistic point of view.

At first, Romantic nationalism was little more than a rejection of foreign influences and a reverence for those unique aspects of culture that are created by the common people—folk dancing, folk sayings, folk tales, folk music, and folk customs. This benign nationalism later developed into an aggressive attitude that insisted on the moral superiority of one people over all others and expressed unrelenting hostility toward outsiders. In its extreme form, militant nationalism encouraged the expulsion of "alien" groups who were not recognized as members of the national heritage. Aggressive nationalism lasted almost a century, from 1848 to 1945, climaxing in Nazi Germany, and still remains a potent force today.

The Romantics also generated a cult of nonconformity and held in great esteem outlaws, gypsies, and those who lived outside middle-class society. This hostility toward middle-class life has an ironic twist because those who professed it generally came from this class and sought its patronage. The unruly presence of Romanticism coincided with the rise to political dominance of the middle class. Out of the love-hate relationship between Romantics and the middle class emerged another familiar emblem of modern life, the anti-bourgeois bourgeois, that is, middle-class people who scorn their own social origins. From the dawn of the Romantic period until the present day, modern culture has been filled with middle-class rebels in revolt against their class.

France played a central role in Romanticism because of its culturally strategic position, and England also produced major figures in Romanticism, particularly in poetry and painting. Notwithstanding these achievements, the heart of Romanticism was German-speaking Europe. So great was the German cultural response that Romanticism is often called a German invention.

The Romantic Movement in Literature

Romanticism in literature was foreshadowed in the German literary movement known as **Sturm und Drang**, or Storm and Stress. This movement flourished briefly in the 1770s and early 1780s, arising as a revolt against Classical restraint and drawing inspiration from Rousseau's emotionalism. On a positive level, this literary movement idealized peasant life and the unconventional, liberated mind. The *Sturm und Drang* writers attacked organized religion because of its hypocrisy and followed Rousseau in finding God in nature. These middle-class authors objected to the formality and tedium of eighteenth-century life and letters and valued free expression in language, dress, behavior, and love. By the mid–1780s, the movement had settled down, drained of its rebelliousness. The most influential members became fully integrated into the German literary scene.

The *Sturm und Drang* movement's outstanding writer was Johann Wolfgang von Goethe [GUHR-tuh] (1749–1832), the greatest of German writers. In 1774, while still in his twenties, Goethe acquired a European-wide reputation with *The Sorrows of Young Werther*, a novel in which the young hero commits suicide because of disappointment in love. So successful was this novel that it led to Wertherism, the social phenomenon in which young men imitated the hero's emotionalism, sometimes even to the point of killing themselves. Werther is a complex character: passionate and excitable, given to inappropriate outbursts, moved by the innocence of children, attracted to social misfits, and overwhelmed by God's presence in nature. He embodies many of the characteristics central to Romanticism.

With the publication in England in 1798 of *Lyrical Ballads* by William Wordsworth (1770–1850) and Samuel Taylor Coleridge (1772–1834), a turning point in the history of literary style was reached, and Romanticism truly began. Rejecting what they considered to be the artificiality of the Neoclassicists, the two poets turned to more natural types of verse, Coleridge to ballad forms and Wordsworth to simple lyrics of plain folks, voiced in the common language of the "middle and lower classes of society." Henceforth many Romantic writers, both in poetry and prose, sought to reproduce the language of customary speech—a literary revolution that was the equivalent of the coming of democracy.

The task Wordsworth assigned himself in *Lyrical Ballads* was to compose verses about the pleasures of everyday existence. He responded to this challenge with poems filled with deep feeling, which were mainly about finding wisdom in simple things. A famous poem from this collection entitled "Lines Composed a Few Miles Above Tintern Abbey" shows Wordsworth's pantheism, or the belief that God lives in nature. In it, speaking to his sister Dorothy, he recalls the strong emotions he felt in his early life when he "bounded o'er the mountains, by the sides/of the deep rivers, and the lonely streams,/wherever nature led. . . . " Now he describes himself as subdued but still "a worshipper of Nature." Wordsworth's nature is a world of overgrown hedgerows, meadows, orchards, and peasant cottages. The beauty of the ordinary became Wordsworth's lifelong preoccupation; he is regarded as the English language's most stirring poet of nature.

Soon after the appearance of the *Lyrical Ballads*, Goethe published his verse play *Faust* (Part I, 1808). Goethe's Werther had been a social rebel, the prototype of the anti-bourgeois bourgeois. But his Faust was a universal rebel, unwilling to let any moral scruple stand in the way of his spiritual quest for the meaning of life. Faust's two distinguishing marks are his relentless pursuit of knowledge and his all-consuming restlessness. Having exhausted book learning, Faust hopes that experience will satisfy his spiritual hunger, and thus he turns to the Devil (Mephistopheles), who proposes to give Faust all of the exciting experiences that have so far been lacking in his life. If Faust finds any moment completely satisfying, then his immortal soul is forever condemned to hell. Under such conditions Faust signs the compact, in his blood, with Mephistopheles.

Mephistopheles helps Faust recover his youth and involves him in a series of adventures that include drunkenness, sexual excess, seduction, and murder. His mistress kills their illegitimate child and perishes in despair. *Faust,* Part I, concludes with Faust more dissatisfied than when he began and no nearer to his goal. Goethe later added Part II (1832) to his drama in which God redeems Faust because of his willingness to sacrifice his life for others, but lacking the emotional intensity of the first part, this second half failed to reach a large audience.

Goethe's *Faust,* Part I, however, proved irresistible. His drama became the most often performed German-language play in the world. It inspired numerous paintings and several works of music. The word **Faustian** came into usage to characterize one who is willing to sacrifice spiritual values for knowledge, experience, or mastery.

Another powerful voice in Romantic literature was the English poet George Gordon, Lord Byron (1788–1824). Better known on the Continent than his compatriots Wordsworth and Coleridge, Byron was called by Goethe the "herald of world literature." The personality of Byron has fascinated successive generations of Western artists and thinkers. At a time when the middle classes were ruled by a restrictive code of respectability, he created a model for rebellious youth with his flowing hair, open shirt collar, and love of ungovernable forces (Figure 17.10). His greatest Romantic creation was probably himself—the "Byronic hero," who was moody, passionate, absorbed in exploring and expressing his innermost self.

Yet the English treated Byron as a pariah and drove him into exile for his unconventional life. Perhaps in retaliation, Byron's most admired poem, *Don Juan* (1819–1824), presented the notorious seducer as a virtuous hero—a literary device intended to expose the hypocrisy of society. Like Goethe's *Faust,* Byron's *Don Juan* was a study in moral duality and reflected the author's fascination with subterranean drives in human nature.

English Romanticism also produced two of the most pervasive figures of Western culture—Frankenstein and his manufactured monster. Made familiar through countless films and cartoons, these two fictional characters first appeared in the novel *Frankenstein* (1818) by Mary Wollstonecraft Shelley (1797–1851). Shelley was well-connected to two of the most unconventional literary families of the day; she was the daughter of Mary Wollstonecraft, a founder of modern feminism (see Chapter 16), and she was the wife of Percy Bysshe Shelley (1792–1822), a free-thinking Romantic poet and close friend of Lord

FIGURE 17.10   RICHARD WESTALL. *George Gordon, Lord Byron.* 1813. Oil on canvas, 36 × 28″. National Portrait Gallery, London. *Westall's portrait of Lord Byron captures the brooding and dark good looks that made him the exemplar of the Romantic hero. Gazing intently into the distance while resting his chin on his hand, Byron seems lost in thought, like a melancholy Hamlet. His isolation is heightened by the overall darkness except for his face, hand, and shirt collar. It was this image of Byron—a person coiled tight like a spring—that caused one female admirer to describe him as "mad, bad, and dangerous to know."*

FIGURE 17.11   JOHN CONSTABLE. *The Hay Wain.* 1821. Oil on canvas, 51¼ × 73″. National Gallery, London. *Although the pastoral subject was alien to them at the time, French Romantic painters recognized in Constable a kindred spirit when* The Hay Wain *was exhibited at the Paris Salon of 1824. Evidently the scene's informality, the strong colors, and the natural lighting converted them, and a later French school of landscape painters was influenced by Constable.*

Romantic Painting

Romanticism in painting appeared first in England, perhaps as an antidote to the growing industrial squalor, manifesting itself as part of a cult of nature. The English cult of nature had two distinct aspects, the pastoral and the Sublime. Painters of pastoral scenes specialized in landscapes in which peasant life was equated with the divine order of things, thus forging a moral link between human beings and the natural environment. The painter John Constable was the chief exponent of this point of view. In contrast, painters of Sublime subjects focused on devastating natural or human-made calamities, reflecting a world order beyond mortal control or understanding. The leading exponent of the Sublime was the painter J. M. W. Turner.

The landscapes of John Constable (1776–1837) reveal his sense of God's universal presence in nature. A man of the people, he found God in ordinary things. Accordingly, he was led to paint natural scenes such as one might see on a country walk, a decision in which he was influenced by the Dutch landscape painters of the 1600s. He had an almost holy vision of art that was true to nature without using what he called tricks or crass emotional appeals.

While Constable's art was not fully appreciated by his contemporaries, a few works won acclaim and helped to redefine the way that the public looked at nature. Of these the most famous is *The Hay Wain* (Figure 17.11). Over the years this painting has been reproduced so often that it is sometimes dismissed as "calendar art," but when it first appeared it excited admiration at home and in Paris. The freshness of the simple images attracted viewers to the beauty of the scene. *The Hay Wain* added many features of everyday rural life to the repertoire of Romantic motifs, including a thatch-roofed cottage, a gently flowing stream, a dog running along a river bank, cows grazing in the background, and overhead the ever-changing English sky.

Constable loved to paint the Suffolk region, where his father's flour barges traveled down the river Stour. The site to which he was drawn again and again was Dedham Vale, the valley along the Stour

Byron. In Shelley's novel, Dr. Frankenstein, having thoughtlessly constructed a humanlike being with no prospect for personal happiness, is eventually hunted down and killed by his own despairing creature. Part of the Romantic reaction against Enlightenment rationalism, which began with Rousseau (see Chapter 16), Shelley's novel presented Frankenstein as a man driven by excessive and obsessive intellectual curiosity and the monster as a tragic symbol of science out of control. Written in the optimistic dawn of the industrialized age, when humanity seemed on the verge of taming the natural world, Shelley's *Frankenstein* is one of the earliest warnings that scientific research divorced from morality is an open invitation to personal and social disaster.

with its waterways and village church in the distance (Figure 17.12). Constable made this painting more than a mere country idyll by his handling of the play of natural light over the grass, trees, water, and distant village. The sky serves as the unique source of light and is the dominant object on the canvas. In his attempt to portray the out-of-doors in all of its lively color, Constable was an important influence on the nineteenth-century Impressionists.

As for the Sublime, Joseph Mallord William Turner (1775–1851) created a new type of subject, "the sublime catastrophe," in which he specialized from 1800 until about 1830. He was the most original artist of his age, prefiguring the Impressionists with his virtuoso use of color and anticipating modern

FIGURE 17.12   JOHN CONSTABLE. *Dedham Vale*. 1828. Oil on canvas, 57⅛ × 48". National Gallery of Scotland, Edinburgh. *Constable's paintings demonstrated the painter's identification of God with nature. But this spiritual dimension was less important than Constable's frequently expressed desire to achieve a feeling of spontaneity in his work. He often sketched on site and then transformed his impressions into a finished painting that preserved the feeling of immediacy. This method enabled Constable to develop a style that was solid and at the same time sensitive to the natural environment.*

FIGURE 17.13 JOSEPH MALLORD WILLIAM TURNER. *Snowstorm: Hannibal and His Army Crossing the Alps.* 1810–1812. Oil on canvas, 4′9½″ × 7′9½″. Tate Gallery, London. *Like so many Romantic painters, Turner borrowed subjects from literary sources. This scene of Hannibal crossing the Alps was based on an episode in a Gothic novel of the time. But Turner also had contemporary events in mind, since the titanic struggle between Hannibal and Rome mirrored the generation of warfare between Napoleon and England in the early 1800s.*

abstract painting in his depictions of wild nature. An example of Turner's sublime catastrophes is *Snowstorm: Hannibal and His Army Crossing the Alps* (Figure 17.13). Although inspired by an episode from Roman history, this painting is more about the fury of nature than it is about the Carthaginian general, Hannibal. The actual subject is the snowstorm, whose sweeping savagery threatens to annihilate everything, including soldiers and horses. No artist before Turner had handled paint in the way that he does here. He turns the sky, which occupies at least three-fourths of the canvas, into an abstract composition, a series of interpenetrating planes of differently colored light.

The Sublime appeared in German painting at about the same time that it developed in England. It was launched by Caspar David Friedrich (1774–1840), a painter who specialized in brooding landscapes, usually with a few human figures to give them a spiritual scale. A lifelong resident of Pomerania on northern Europe's Baltic coast, he drew artistic inspiration from his homeland's deserted beaches, dense forests, and chalky cliffs. What sets his landscapes apart from those of earlier artists on the same

subject is his desire to turn natural scenes into glimpses of the divine mystery. Avoiding traditional Christian subjects, Friedrich invented his own symbols for conveying God's presence in the world.

In *The Chalk Cliffs of Rugen* (Figure 17.14) the setting is the stark Baltic seacost as viewed from a cliff. Friedrich's intention is to convey how weak humans are when confronted by nature's power. By showing the figures from the back or the side—he never painted faces—Friedrich is encouraging the viewer to see what they see and to feel what they feel. What they are experiencing may be inferred from their gestures. The woman on the left is feeling a fascinated horror as she holds to a bush and points to the yawning abyss before her. The male figure in the middle (probably Friedrich himself) is transfixed with terror; having thrown down his hat and cane, he kneels, hardly daring to peer over the cliff's edge. Lost in meditation is the third figure, who boldly stands on a scrub tree and gazes into space. The three figures together represent a common Romantic theme and a favorite of Friedrich's—the wonderful moment in friendship when a shared spiritual intimacy occurs.

FIGURE 17.14 CASPAR DAVID FRIEDRICH. *The Chalk Cliffs of Rugen.* 1818. Oil on canvas, 90 × 70 cm. Museum Stiftung Oskar Reinhart, Winterthur, Switzerland. *In his seascapes Friedrich often included sailing ships approaching the land. These ships, as depicted here, became symbolic messengers, bringing tidings from some infinite realm to those human figures watching from shore. Friedrich thus reveals the underlying spiritual order of the world—a favorite theme of the Romantics.*

In Spain, Romanticism flourished in the anti-Classical paintings of Francisco Goya (1746–1828), a major figure in Spanish culture. Reflecting a nightmarish vision of the world, his art ranges from Rococo fantasies, to sensual portraits, to grim studies of human folly, to spiritual evil, and finally to scenes of utter hopelessness. Various reasons have been suggested for Goya's descent into despair, but certainly his dashed hopes for the regeneration of Spain's political and social order were central to his advancing pessimism, as was his slow decline into deafness.

In the 1790s Goya was serving as court painter to King Charles IV, and signs of the artist's political disaffection can be detected in his revealing portrait of the royal family (Figure 17.15). He depicts the queen (center) as a vain, foolish woman and the king (right, front) as a royal simpleton. History has judged Goya's interpretations to be accurate, for this was a corrupt and stupid court. Perhaps the lace-covered gowns, the glittering medals, and the general elegance of the ensemble allowed him to get away with such unflattering portraits and survive within this dangerous environment.

In 1797 Goya published a collection of etchings that set forth his savage indictment of the age's social evils and established him as an outstanding humanitarian artist. The title of this series was *Caprichos,* or *Caprices,* a Romantic genre that allowed artists to express their personal feelings on any subject. One of the eighty *caprichos, The Sleep of Reason* was intended as the series' frontispiece and is the key to Goya's artistic purpose (Figure 17.16). The inscription on the

FIGURE 17.15 FRANCISCO GOYA. *The Family of Charles IV.* 1800. Oil on canvas, 9'2" × 11'. Prado, Madrid. *Following a well-established Spanish tradition, Goya has painted himself into the canvas on the left, from which vantage point in the shadows he observes the royal family. Velásquez had followed this tradition 150 years earlier in* The Maids of Honor *(see Figure 14.10), which this painting echoes. Goya portrayed the ravaged face of the king's sister on the left as a reminder of the fleeting nature of human beauty.*

FIGURE 17.16 FRANCISCO GOYA. *The Sleep of Reason*. 1797. Etching and aquatint, 215 × 150 mm. Museum of Fine Arts, Boston. Gift of Mr. and Mrs. Burton S. Stern, Mr. and Mrs. Bernard Shapiro, and the M. and M. Karolik Fund. *Goya's artistic technique in the* Caprichos *series is aquatint, a process that uses acid on a metal plate to create subtle shades of light and dark. The absence of color in the resulting engravings heightens the moral message of these works.*

desk reads, ''The sleep of reason brings forth monsters,'' a statement that conveys the need for eternal vigilance against cruelty and superstition. The nocturnal creatures—bats, owls, and cats—symbolize the dark forces that continually threaten rationality.

Napoleon's conquest of Spain and the subsequent Spanish war of liberation form the background to Goya's masterpiece, *The Execution of the Third of May, 1808* (Figure 17.17). This protest against French imperialism is one of the world's most compelling depictions of the horrors of war. It shows Spanish captives being executed by a French firing squad. The French troops are a faceless line of disciplined automatons, and the Spanish soldiers a band of ill-

FIGURE 17.18 THÉODORE GÉRICAULT. *The Raft of the* Medusa. 1818. Oil on canvas, 16'1" × 23'6". Louvre. *The devastated humanity on the raft underscored the breakdown in civilization that the entire* Medusa *incident came to represent. The painting itself became a rallying point for the critics of the restored Bourbon monarchy, who saw in the portrayal of a crew cast adrift a metaphor for the French nation.*

assorted irregulars. The Spanish patriots are arranged in three groups: Those covered with blood and lying on the ground are already dead, those facing the firing squad will be dead in an instant, and those marching forward with faces covered are scheduled for the next round. The emotional center of this otherwise somber-hued painting is the white-shirted man bathed in brilliant light. With his arms outstretched, he becomes a Christ figure, symbolizing Goya's compassion for all victims who die for a "good cause."

◄ **FIGURE 17.17** FRANCISCO GOYA. *The Execution of the Third of May, 1808.* 1814–1815. Oil on canvas, 8'9" × 13'4". Prado, Madrid. *A comparison of this painting by Goya with David's portrait of the assassinated Marat (see Figure 17.4) shows the difference in tone between Romantic and Neoclassical art. David makes Marat's death a heroic sacrifice in spite of its tragic circumstances. In contrast, Goya's passionate portrayal of the Spanish martyrs shows that there is nothing heroic about their deaths; their cause may be just, but the manner of their death is pitiless and squalid.*

Romantic painting arrived in France in 1819 with the appearance of *The Raft of the* Medusa, a work by Théodore Géricault [zhay-rih-KOH] (1791–1824) that was based on an actual incident (Figure 17.18). The *Medusa*, a sailing ship, had foundered in the South Atlantic, and it was believed that all aboard were lost. Then after almost two months, a handful of survivors were rescued from a makeshift raft. From their story came shocking details of mutiny, crimes by officers, murder, cannibalism, and a government cover-up.

Géricault was attracted to this incident in which a few men outwitted death against all odds. Focusing on the precise moment of their rescue, he depicts these ordinary humans as noble heroes nearly overwhelmed by the terrible forces of nature. The nude and partially clad bodies in the foreground convey a powerful sense of dignity and suffering. From here, the figures surge upward toward the black youth who is hoisted aloft and waving a flag at the unseen rescue ship. Géricault wanted his painting to be as

452

FIGURE 17.19 EUGÈNE DELACROIX. *Greece Expiring on the Ruins of Missolonghi.*
1826. Oil on canvas, 6'11½" × 4'8¼". Musée des Beaux-Arts, Bordeaux. *Delacroix's
representation of Greece as a woman was part of the Romantic convention of using female
figures as national symbols. This trend climaxed in the writings of the French historian
Jules Michelet, who concluded in 1846 that "France is a woman herself."*

FIGURE 17.20 EUGÈNE DELACROIX. *Liberty Leading the People*. 1831. Oil on canvas,
8'6" × 10'8". Louvre. *Delacroix's canvas bears some meaningful resemblances to
Géricault's* Raft of the Medusa. *Each painting takes a contemporary event as its subject
and transforms it into a symbol of France. Moreover, Delacroix's placement of two dead
male figures, one partially nude and the other clothed, echoes similar figures in Géricault's
work. Delacroix's portrayal of the people triumphant thus seems to be an optimistic
response to Géricault's image of France adrift.*

realistic as possible—he interviewed survivors and
had a replica of the raft constructed—but at the same
time he imbued it with expression and pathos. The
result was a highly emotional work that embodied
the spirit of Romanticism.

Many of Géricault's ideas were taken up by Eugène Delacroix [del-uh-KWAH] (1798–1863), who
became the leader of a school of Romantic painting
that was in open rivalry with Ingres and the Neoclassicists. Like Géricault, Delacroix was a humanitarian who drew artistic inspiration from his violent
times. In the 1820s he identified with the Greeks in
their war of independence against the Turks, expressing his support in the allegorical painting

Greece Expiring on the Ruins of Missolonghi (Figure
17.19). Lord Byron had died at Missolonghi while
trying to bring warring Greek factions together, an
event the painting commemorates. Delacroix portrays Greece as a grieving woman kneeling on a
group of blasted stones from which a dead hand pro-
trudes. Behind her stands a turbaned Turk, the symbol of Greece's oppressors.

Delacroix's *Liberty Leading the People* was also inspired by a political incident, the July Revolution of
1830 (Figure 17.20). The painting combines realism
and allegory, depicting revolutionaries on the barricades led by an idealized, bare-breasted goddess
of Liberty. Surrounding Liberty are three central

FIGURE 17.21   EUGÈNE DELACROIX. *The Death of Sardanapalus.* 1828. Oil on canvas, 12'10¼" × 16'¼". Louvre. *Delacroix's opulent painting caused a scandal when it was exhibited in the Paris Salon of 1827, but it also raised Delacroix to a position of leadership in the Romantic school. Its subject reflected the interest in the exotic Orient, which was a strong feature of French Romanticism. The subject allowed Delacroix's genius to run wild, imbuing the scene with confusion and surging colors.*

figures who symbolize the various classes that constitute "the People": The man in the tall hat represents the middle classes, the chief beneficiaries of the revolution; the kneeling figure in the cap stands for the working-class rebels; and the boy brandishing the twin pistols is an image of the street urchin, among the lowest social groups.

The focal point of the painting is the tricolor, the revolutionary flag adopted in the revolution of 1789, outlawed from 1815 until 1830, and now restored as France's unifying symbol. The flag's red, white, and blue determine the harmony of color in the rest of this painting. Completed soon after the 1830 revolution, this work was purchased by the new king as a fitting tribute to the struggle that brought him to power. It was quickly hidden away, however, for the bourgeois establishment found the revolutionary heritage an embarrassment. Only later, with the creation of the Second Republic in 1848, did the French public see the painting.

Despite paying homage to radical forces, Delacroix was no true revolutionary. Even before painting *Liberty Leading the People,* Delacroix had been turning toward a more sensual art, an art that relied on gorgeous colors, as in *The Death of Sardanapalus* (Figure 17.21). Taking an anecdote from ancient history that had been dramatized by Lord Byron, he converted it into an image of Romantic destruction. In Delacroix's version, the doomed tyrant Sardanapalus, preparing to commit suicide, gazes unemotionally on the chaos caused by his order to kill everything—harem women, horses, and dogs—that he has ever loved. Much of the success of this haunting image depends on dramatic juxtapositions: passivity and passion, love and death, black and white, male and female. In paintings like this, Delacroix embodied the Romantic fascination with exotic, sensual, and violent subjects.

German Idealism

In philosophy the Romantic spirit led to idealism, a system of thought that flourished mainly in Germany and that espoused a spiritual view of life. From Kant through Hegel, the Germans constructed idealism as a philosophic alternative to conventional religion. In the 1790s Immanuel Kant [KANT] (1724–1804) began the revolution in thought when he distinguished the world of phenomena (appearance) from the world of noumena (spirit). In Kantian terms, the phenomenal world may be understood by science, but the noumenal world may be studied, if at all, only by intuitive means.

Kant's followers, nonetheless, tried the impossible when they began to map out the spiritual realm. Johann Gottlieb Fichte [FICK-tuh] (1762–1814) found reality in the World Spirit, a force having consciousness and seeking self-awareness. Friedrich Wilhelm Joseph von Schelling [SHEL-ing] (1775–1854) equated nature with the Absolute, his name for ultimate reality. He also was the first to espouse the romantic belief in the religion of art by claiming that artists reveal divine truths in inspired works. Schelling's teaching on art influenced the English poet Coleridge and through him English Romanticism in general.

The climax of idealism occurred with Georg Wilhelm Friedrich Hegel [HAY-guhl] (1770–1831) who explained human history as the record of the World Spirit seeking to know its true nature. Self-knowledge for the World Spirit arose only through a dialectical struggle. In the first stage, the Spirit developed a thesis that, in turn, produced an antithesis; in the second stage, a conflict then ensued between these two ideas that led to a synthesis, or a new thesis, which in turn gradually provoked new strife—a

third stage, and so on *ad infinitum.* Hegel's theory of history ignored individuals because humans in the mass became tools of the World Spirit in its quest for freedom. In this view, wars, riots, and revolts were merely evidence of spiritual growth. For this reason, Hegel characterized Napoleon and his wars as embodiments of the World Spirit.

Hegelianism had a tremendous impact on later Western thought. Revolutionaries like Karl Marx borrowed his dialectical approach to history. Conservatives, especially in Germany, used Hegel's thought as a justification for a strong centralized state, and nationalists everywhere drew inspiration from his thought. Other thinkers rejected his denial of human responsibility and founded existentialist philosophies that glorified the individual.

The Birth of Romantic Music

As the middle class gained political power between 1789 and 1830, they converted the musical scene into a marketplace. Replacing elite forms of patronage, the bourgeoisie now attended programs that required admission fees and paid performers. Salaries and the demand for performances freed musicians from the patronage system. With their newly won independence, they became eccentric and individualistic—attitudes that were encouraged by the Romantic cult of the artist. Music grew more accessible as democracy progressed, and new industrial techniques and production allowed more people to own inexpensive musical instruments.

The most gifted composer of this period, and one of the greatest musical geniuses of all time, was Ludwig van Beethoven [BAY-toe-vuhn] (1770–1827), a German who spent most of his life in Vienna. He personified the new breed of musician, supporting himself through concerts, lessons, and the sales of his music (Figure 17.22). His works represent both the culmination of Classical music and the introduction of Romantic music. Working with the standard Classical forms—the sonata, the symphony, and the string quartet—he created longer works, doubling and even tripling their length. He also wrote music that was increasingly expressive and that showed more warmth and variety of feeling. He made several other significant musical innovations, including the use of choral voices within the symphonic form and the introduction of *program music,* that is, music that portrays a particular setting or tells a story.

Beethoven's career may be divided into three phases, but his extreme individualism left his unique stamp on everything that he composed. In the first

FIGURE 17.22 FERDINAND GEORG WALDMÜLLER. *Ludwig van Beethoven.* 1823. Oil on canvas, 72 × 58 cm. Archiv Breitkopf and Härtel, Leipzig, Germany. Original destroyed in World War II. *Beethoven in his later years was the embodiment of the Romantic genius, disheveled in dress, singing to himself as he strolled Vienna's streets, mocked by street urchins; on one occasion, he was even arrested by the police as a tramp. In this 1823 portrait Waldmüller suggests Beethoven's unkempt appearance, but through the strong expression, fixed jaw, and broad forehead he also conveys the great composer's fierce determination and intelligence.*

phase, from the 1790s until 1803, he was under the shadow of Haydn, with whom he studied in Vienna. His First Symphony (1800) may be termed a Classical work, but in it he reveals a new spirit by lengthening the first and third movements and making the middle movement more lively than usual.

In the second phase, from 1803 until 1816, Beethoven's genius gave birth to Romantic music. He began to find his own voice, enriching and deepening the older forms. The Third Symphony (1803), which Beethoven called the "Eroica" ("Heroic"), is the most characteristic work from this second stage. The composer originally dedicated this symphony to Napoleon, whom he admired as a champion of democracy. But when the French ruler declared himself emperor in 1804, Beethoven angrily tore up the page and dedicated it instead "to the memory of a great man." In the Third Symphony, Beethoven substantially expands the musical material beyond the limits characteristic of earlier symphonies, making it longer and more complex. The music is grand, serious, and dignified, a truly heroic work.

In the third phase, from 1816 until 1827, Beethoven's music becomes freer and more contemplative, reaching its culmination in the Ninth Symphony (1822–1824). In the last movement of this work, Bee-

thoven included a choral finale in which he set to music the poem "Ode to Joy" by the German Romantic poet Friedrich von Schiller [SHIL-uhr] (1759–1805). Despite a life of personal adversities that included deafness from the age of thirty, Beethoven affirmed in this piece his faith in both humanity and God—"Millions, be you embraced! For the universe, this kiss!" The magnificent music and the idealistic text have led to the virtual canonization of this inspirational work.

Vienna also contributed another outstanding composer in Franz Schubert [SHOO-bert] (1797–1828), who was famous for the beauty of his melodies and the simple grace of his songs. He lived a rather bohemian life, supporting himself, like Beethoven, by giving lessons and concerts. But unlike Beethoven, Schubert wrote mainly for the living rooms of Vienna rather than for the concert hall and is most famous for perfecting the *art song*, called in German **lied** (plural, *lieder*). The emergence of this musical form in the Romantic period was tied to the revival of lyric poetry. Schubert composed the music for over six hundred *lieder*, with texts by Goethe, Shakespeare, and other poets. His efforts raised the song to the level of great art.

A final composer of significance in this first period

of Romanticism was the Frenchman Hector Berlioz [BAIR-lee-ohz] (1803–1869). His most famous work is the *Symphonie fantastique* (*Fantastic Symphony*) (1830), a superb example of program music. Subtitled "Episode of an Artist's Life," this symphonic work illustrates musically a story that Berlioz described in accompanying written notes. In the tale, which takes the form of an opium dream, an artist-hero hopelessly adores an unfaithful woman and eventually dies for her. Relatively conventional in form, the symphony is most original in its use of a recurring musical theme, called an **idée fixe**, or "fixed idea," that becomes an image of the hero's beloved. Because every section contains the *idée fixe* in a modified form, it unifies the symphony in an innovative way. The success of Berlioz's symphony helped to strengthen the fashion for program music in the Romantic period.

The Legacy of the Age of Revolution and Reaction

During this period of revolution and reaction the West turned away from the past, with its monarchical forms of governments, its hierarchical society dominated by aristocratic landowners, its glacial rate of change, and its patronage system ruled by social, ecclesiastical, and political elites. Three events in particular—the Industrial Revolution and the American and the French revolutions—have left an indelible stamp on the modern world. The Industrial Revolution, which continues today, has gradually made humanity master of the earth and its resources, while at the same time accelerating the pace of life and creating the two leading modern social groups, the middle class and the working class. The Industrial Revolution also spawned Classical economics, the school of economists who justifed the doctrine of laissez faire that is still held to be the best argument for capitalism and continuous industrial growth. It is this same doctrine that has altered the patronage system, subjecting the creative works of modern artists, writers, musicians, and humanists to the law of the marketplace.

The American Revolution produced the first successful modern democracy, one that today stands as a beacon of hope for those oppressed by authoritarian regimes. The French Revolution contributed the idea of an all-encompassing upheaval that would sweep away the past and create a new secular order characterized by social justice and fairness. Although viewed with skepticism by some, for multitudes of others the notion of such a revolution became a sustaining belief. From the French Revolution also arises the idea that race and religion should not be used to exclude people from the right to vote—a reflection of its emphasis on the "brotherhood of man." Another outgrowth of the French Revolution is the Napoleonic Code, the law code that is used in the French-speaking world today.

Both the French and the American revolutions contributed certain beliefs that have become basic statements of Western political life, such as the idea that constitutions should be written down and that basic human liberties should be identified. Indeed, the progressive expansion of natural and civil rights to embrace all of society is an outgrowth of these two revolutions.

Other enduring legacies of this late eighteenth- and early nineteenth-century period are the Neoclassical buildings in Washington, D.C., and in most of the state capitals of the United States, the body of music of the Romantic composers, and the paintings of the Neoclassical and early Romantic schools. An ambiguous legacy of this period has been nationalism, the belief in one's own country and its people. At its best, nationalism is a noble concept, for it encourages people to get in touch with their roots and preserve their collective identity and heritage. At its worst, it has led to cutthroat behavior, dividing the people of a country against each other and leading to the disintegration of nations. Both forms of nationalism remain potent forces in the world today.

On a more personal level, this period saw the development of the Romantic view of life, an attitude that stresses informality, identification with the common people, the importance of feeling and imagination, and enjoyment of simple pleasures. Perhaps more than any other legacy of this period, the Romantic outlook has helped to shape the way that most men and women live in today's world.

KEY CULTURAL TERMS

Romanticism   *program music*
Sublime   *art song* (lied)
Sturm und Drang   idée fixe
Faustian

SUGGESTIONS FOR FURTHER READING

PRIMARY SOURCES

AUSTEN, J. *Pride and Prejudice. Sense and Sensibility.* Introduction by D. Daiches. New York: Modern Library, 1950. Both novels deal with English provincial life. *Pride and Prejudice* (1813) focuses on the proud Mr. Darcy, who must be humbled before the "prejudiced" Elizabeth Bennet can take seriously his marriage proposal; *Sense and Sensibility* (1811) uses practical-mindedness ("sense") to expose the self-indulgence of the "picturesque" spirit ("sensibility"), an aspect of genteel taste in the late eighteenth century.

BYRON, G. G., LORD. *Don Juan.* Edited by T. G. Steffan, E. Steffan, and W. W. Pratt. New York: Penguin, 1973. One of Byron's most admired works, full of autobiographical references; dates from 1819–1824.

FICHTE, J. G. *Addresses to the German Nation.* Translated by R. F. Jones and G. H. Turnbull. Chicago: Open Court, 1923. The work that helped to launch German nationalism when first published in the early 1800s.

GOETHE, J. W. V. *Faust.* Part I. Translated and with an introduction by D. Luke. New York: Oxford University Press, 1987. A good modern English version of Goethe's drama of a man prepared to sacrifice his soul for the sake of knowledge based on feeling; originally published in 1808.

———. *The Sorrows of Young Werther.* Translated by E. Mayer and L. Bogan. Foreword by W. H. Auden. New York: Vintage, 1990. The 1774 Romantic novel that brought Goethe his earliest European-wide fame, translated by modern poets.

HEGEL, G. W. F. *Reason in History.* Translated and with an introduction by R. S. Hartman. New York: Liberal Arts Press, 1953. The best source for Hegel's theory that history moves through a dialectical process; first published in 1837.

KANT, I. *Critique of Pure Reason.* Introduction and glossary by W. Schwarz. Aalen, Germany: Scientia, 1982. A good recent version of Kant's difficult work that tried to establish what human reason can know apart from experience; dates from 1781.

MALTHUS, T. *On Population.* Edited and with an introduction by G. Himmelfarb. New York: Random House, 1960. One of the more recent editions of the influential essay, first published in 1788, that identified the modern dilemma of keeping population growth in equilibrium with food production.

RICARDO, D. *On the Principles of Political Economy and Taxation.* New York: Penguin, 1971. Ricardo's "iron law of wages"—that wages tend to hover around the subsistence level—became a central tenet of nineteenth-century laissez-faire theory.

SCHELLING, F. W. J. V. *Ideas for a Philosophy of Nature.* Translated by E. E. Harris. New York: Cambridge University Press, 1988. An excellent translation of Schelling's 1799 work that helped shape Romantic thinking by claiming to find God both in nature and in the human intellect.

SHELLEY, M. *Frankenstein.* With an introduction by D. Johnson. New York: Bantam, 1991. The original source of the Frankenstein legend, published in 1818 when Shelley was twenty-one years old; inspired by an evening of reading and discussing ghost stories.

WORDSWORTH, W. *Lyrical Ballads.* Edited by R. L. Braett and A. R. Jones. London: Routledge and Kegan Paul, 1988. A new edition of the original volume by Wordsworth and Coleridge that initiated the age of Romantic poetry in England; contains good introductory material.

SUGGESTIONS FOR LISTENING

BEETHOVEN, LUDWIG VAN (1770–1827).

Composing mainly in Classical forms, notably the symphony and the string quartet, Beethoven moved from a Classical style in the manner of Haydn and Mozart to a Romantic style that was his own. The First Symphony (1800) shows his Classical approach; the Third Symphony, the "Eroica" (1803), inaugurated his Romantic style with its intense emotionalism and rich thematic variations. Of special note is the Ninth Symphony (1822–1826), a semi-mystical work whose final section blends full orchestra with a massed chorus. The emotional nature of the Violin Sonata No. 9 ("Kreutzer Sonata") inspired the Russian writer Leo Tolstoy to use the piece as a catalyst for murder in his story "The Kreutzer Sonata." Beethoven's stylistic development can also be traced in his sixteen string quartets: The first six quartets, dating from 1800, reflect the grace of Haydn and Mozart, and the last five, Nos. 12 through 16 (1823–1826), are technically difficult to play, enormously long, and characterized by mood shifts from light to tragic and unusual harmonic juxtapositions. The familiar piano piece *Für* Elise is a fine example of the rondo form.

BERLIOZ, HECTOR (1803–1869).

Berlioz was typically Romantic in going beyond the forms of Classicism and stressing the emotional possibilities of his music. For example, his *Requiem* (1837) is less a religious work than a dramatic symphony for orchestra and voices; its inspiration was the tradition of patriotic festivals originated during the French Revolution. Similarly, his opera *Damnation of Faust* (1846) is not an opera in a conventional sense but a series of episodes based on Goethe's play, a form that allowed the composer to focus on those scenes that seemed full of theatrical potential. Finally, the *Symphonie fantastique* (1830) is more than a symphony; it has been called "a musical drama without words"—the prototype of Romantic program music.

SCHUBERT, FRANZ (1797–1828).

Though a prolific composer of symphonies, operas, and piano sonatas, Schubert is most famous for perfecting the art song, or *lied*. Two of his best-known songs, with texts by Goethe, are *Gretchen am Spinnrade* ("Gretchen at the Spinning Wheel," 1814) and *Erlkonig* ("The Erlking," 1815). One of Schubert's most frequently played songs is *Die Forelle* ("The Trout," 1821), in which the lively, fluid music suggests the energetic movements of a swimming fish.

THE TRIUMPH OF THE BOURGEOISIE
1830—1871

The revolutions of the late eighteenth century broke the monopoly on power that the aristocracy had held since the Early Middle Ages. The French and American revolutions offered the hope of political power to all disenfranchised groups, and the Industrial Revolution promised material gains to the impoverished. These expectations remained largely unfulfilled in Europe, however, as the nineteenth century unfolded. Benefits were reaped mainly by one group—the middle class, especially its wealthiest sector. Prosperous and successful, these businessmen, commercial property owners, and politicians dominated governments and enjoyed the fruits of the Industrial Revolution.

Left behind by the victory of the middle class was a new group created by industrialization—the proletariat, or working class. These urban workers remained dissatisfied and expressed their frustrations through political uprisings and social movements. The less prosperous segment of the middle class joined them in demanding universal suffrage and a fairer distribution of power and wealth. Against the liberalism of the bourgeoisie some of them set forth the ideals of socialism. But reform was limited at best, and successive waves of revolutionary uprisings failed to win significant improvements.

These dramatic changes were echoed in the cultural realm. From its brief peak in the 1820s, Romanticism began a long decline until it finally became

◀ ÉDOUARD MANET. *A Bar at the Folies Bergère.* 1882. Courtauld Institute Galleries, University of London (Courtauld Collection).

exhausted toward the end of the century. Embraced by the middle class, it gained respectability and lost much of its creative fire. By midcentury a new style was emerging that reflected changing political and social conditions. Known as Realism, it focused on ordinary people and attempted to depict in objective terms "the heroism of everyday life." At the same time, industrialization continued to spread, and people's ideas about themselves and the world were being challenged by everything from the theories of Charles Darwin to the invention of the camera (Time Line 18.1).

THE POLITICAL AND ECONOMIC SCENE: LIBERALISM AND NATIONALISM

Two powerful forces drove many events in Europe during the nineteenth century—liberalism and nationalism. The basic premise of liberalism was that the individual should be free from external control, a notion that resonated with the need of the bourgeoisie to liberate themselves from aristocratic society. The liberal political agenda included constitutionally guaranteed political and civil rights such as free speech, religious toleration, and voting rights for the propertied classes. Liberals themselves wanted to be left alone by the government, but they wanted the government to hold in check the aristocracy, the military, and organized religion. Perhaps most important, liberalism embraced the laissez-faire ideals in

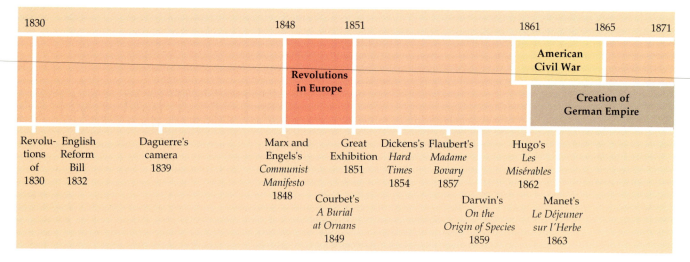

| 1830 | | 1848 | 1851 | | 1861 | 1865 | 1871 |

Revolutions in Europe

American Civil War

Creation of German Empire

Revolutions of 1830

English Reform Bill 1832

Daguerre's camera 1839

Marx and Engels's *Communist Manifesto* 1848

Great Exhibition 1851

Dickens's *Hard Times* 1854

Flaubert's *Madame Bovary* 1857

Hugo's *Les Misérables* 1862

Courbet's *A Burial at Ornans* 1849

Darwin's *On the Origin of Species* 1859

Manet's *Le Déjeuner sur l'Herbe* 1863

MAP 18.1

Europe after the Congress of Vienna, 1815

economics that allowed the wealthy middle class to maximize their profits in the business world.

Liberal ideals had been at the heart of the American and French revolutions in the eighteenth century, and now a new generation of liberals carried forward the goals embraced by their predecessors. The spread of liberalism across Europe was uneven, however. It was most successful in England, France, and Belgium; it failed to take root in Italy and central and eastern Europe; and Russia remained reactionary throughout this whole period.

The other driving force of this era, nationalism, emphasized cooperation among all of a country's people who shared a common language and heritage. Overlooking class divisions, nationalists advocated humanitarian values, stressing the concept that all members of a nation are brothers and sisters. As nationalism proliferated, these basic ideas were often expanded to include other notions, notably liberalism, republican principles, and even democratic beliefs. Nationalism became a driving force in central, southern, and eastern Europe, where the states of Germany and Italy, in particular, were still little more than "geographical expressions" (Map 18.1). After 1848 nationalism took on an increasingly militant aspect.

The Revolutions of 1830 and Their Aftermath

The repressive policies that had been imposed by the Congress of Vienna in 1815 were challenged in 1830 by a series of uprisings across Europe. The chain of revolutionary events started in July 1830 when the French overthrew their Bourbon ruler and put on the throne the so-called bourgeois monarch Louis Philippe (1830–1848), who pledged to uphold a liberal constitution (Figure 18.1). Liberal revolutions quickly followed elsewhere, including Belgium and areas of central and southern Europe.

In France, Louis Philippe established a liberal regime, but it increasingly became the tool of the newly rich middle class at the expense of the workers. Voting was limited to wealthy male property owners, and laws favored economic growth. Having gained political dominance and fulfilled their liberal agenda, the middle class intended to keep the benefits for themselves.

In central Europe, liberalism was stamped out. Local conservatives backed by Austrian troops quickly crushed the uprisings of 1830. Restored to power, they punished rebels, imposed martial law, reinstituted censorship, and took control of the school systems. Although liberals continued to hope for moderate reforms, conservatives kept their ideas

FIGURE 18.1 FRANÇOIS RUDE. *The Departure of the Volunteers. 1833–1836. Ca. 42 × 26'. Paris. Under the "citizen king" Louis Philippe, bourgeois leaders were nervous about the revolutionary events that had brought them to power. Nevertheless, this group sculpture depicting the people on the march was hailed by all social ranks as an acceptable image of France's revolutionary past, including the revolution of 1830. Designed for the Arch of Triumph in Paris, the work came to be known affectionately as* La Marseillaise, *the name of the French national anthem.*

in check through threats or direct suppression. Across central and eastern Europe, the one force emerging as a rallying point was nationalism, focusing as it did on ethnic identity and common cultural heritages.

The Revolutions of 1848

Accumulated   dissatisfactions   and   frustrations erupted in another series of uprisings across Europe

TABLE 18.1   MAJOR POLITICAL EVENTS OF THE
1815–1871 PERIOD

EVENT AND DATE	OUTCOME
Congress of Vienna, 1815	Inaugurates an era of repression
July Revolution in France, 1830	Ends the Bourbon dynasty and installs the bourgeois monarchy
First English Reform Bill, 1832	Extends voting rights to wealthy middle-class males
Revolution in France, 1848	Ends the bourgeois monarchy and installs the Second Republic with Louis-Napoleon as president
Revolutions in Europe, 1848–1851	Their failure leads to an era dominated by *Realpolitik*
Creation of Second French Empire, 1851	Louis-Napoleon becomes Napoleon III and leads empire until 1870
Creation of German Empire, 1862–1871	Engineered by Bismarck using a policy of "blood and iron"; unites German states around Prussia
American Civil War, 1861–1865	Preserves national union and abolishes slavery
Second English Reform Bill, 1867	Extends voting rights to working-class males
Franco-Prussian War, 1871	Destroys the Second French Empire, proclaims the German Empire, and leaves a legacy of French bitterness toward Germany

in 1848 (Table 18.1). Liberal ideals and nationalistic goals were driving forces behind these revolutions, but they were preceded by mounting political tension and popular unrest in France, the Italian peninsula, and the Austrian Empire. As in 1789, the 1848 revolutions were triggered by a number of economic crises—a decline in production, a rise in unemployment, and a fall in agricultural prices. Demonstrations and riots in February 1848 in Paris served as a signal for rebellions across Europe. The call to arms by liberals and reformers was answered by nationalists who wanted to overthrow foreign rulers, by middle-class eastern Europeans who demanded political power, and by factory and urban laborers who desired better living and working conditions.

In the spring of 1848 an axis of revolution ran from Paris through Berlin to Vienna. All along this line the bourgeoisie, intellectuals, workers, students, and nationalists toppled kings and ministers, including Louis Philippe of France and Count Metternich, the Austrian minister who embodied the most reactionary attitudes in Europe. Temporary governments, led by liberals and reformers, arose and drove out foreign troops and set up constitutional

monarchies or republics. Some provisional bodies enfranchised all property owners, while others created democracies with universal male suffrage. A few governments—influenced by a new movement known as socialism—addressed themselves to economic problems by passing laws to stimulate productivity, to improve working conditions, and to aid the poor with relief or employment programs.

Hope for lasting change faded rapidly in the fall of 1848 as the conservatives—the army, the aristocrats, and the church—rallied to defeat the frequently disorganized revolutionaries. By January 1849 many of the old rulers were back on their thrones, and the liberals' popular assemblies had been dispersed. Many liberals, social reformers, and nationalists had learned a hard lesson at the street barricades and within the hastily organized constitutional conventions. After 1848 the dominant wisdom demanded an unsentimental vision of politics and diplomacy backed by pragmatic use of force—what came to be known as *Realpolitik*, a German term that is a polite way of saying "power politics."

European Affairs in the Grip of *Realpolitik*

From 1850 to 1871 *Realpolitik* guided the European states as rulers faced the issues that had surfaced in the 1848 revolts. Rejecting the claims of liberals and workers, conservative regimes turned to strong and efficient armies, short, fierce wars, and ambiguously written agreements to resolve problems. Otto von Bismarck, the prime minister of Prussia and future architect of German unification, mocked the failure of the liberals to reform through parliamentary means and asserted that his country's fate would be settled not with speeches but with "blood and iron." Nationalists in Italy, thwarted by the presence of Austrian troops, learned that Italian unity could be achieved only by military force and clever diplomacy. The Russian czars, seldom supporters of any type of reform, were reinforced in their belief that if any change did come, it would begin at the top, not the bottom, of society.

Limited Reform in France and Great Britain   One of the most astute observers of the revolutions of 1848 was Louis-Napoleon Bonaparte, the nephew of the former French emperor. Louis-Napoleon jockeyed his way to power in France by appealing to the bourgeoisie and by making promises to the working classes. After being elected president of the Second French Republic in 1848, he proclaimed the Second French Empire and declared himself Emperor Napoleon III (1852–1870). A benign despot, he ruled over a sham representative

FIGURE 18.2 CHARLES BARRY AND A. W. N. PUGIN. The Houses of Parliament. 1836–1860. London. *In contrast to the revolutionary tradition on the Continent, Great Britain struggled to respond to changing political and social realities through debate and reform. To many observers in England and abroad, Parliament symbolized the success of liberalism and the representative legislative system. The Gothic spires of the Houses of Parliament rose in the mid–nineteenth century after the old buildings burned. Along with the independent clock tower known as "Big Ben" (a name applied originally only to the bell), they still stand today as the most recognizable image of modern London.*

government supported by a growing middle class made prosperous by the expanding industrial base. He took care of the poor through social services, however, and with a coordinated economic plan and subsidies kept up a high standard of living for most urban workers and farmers.

Across the channel, Great Britain was inching toward peaceful solutions to the political inequities wrought by industrialism and outdated electoral mechanisms (Figure 18.2). A reform bill had been pushed through the House of Commons in 1832 by the Whigs, a liberal coalition of landed and business interests, over the protests of the conservatives. This new law redrew the political map of England to reflect the massive shift in population resulting from industrialism, and it enfranchised thousands of new male voters by lowering the property qualifications for voting (although millions of British citizens were still denied the vote). In 1867 a second reform bill extended suffrage to working-class males and once

again rearranged the electoral map. With Queen Victoria (1837–1901) on the throne and political forces balanced evenly between liberals and conservatives, Great Britain reached its apex of economic power and prestige during this period.

Wars and Unification in Central Europe Among the German-speaking states, the small principalities tended to discard liberalism and embrace militant nationalism. Their concerns were overshadowed, however, by the power struggle between Prussia and Austria for control of central Europe. Although Austria was the more powerful state at midcentury, the government was distracted by unrest among its many ethnic minorities. The scales in the struggle were tipped in Prussia's favor when William I became king in 1861 and Bismarck was appointed his prime minister. Over the next few years Bismarck built the Prussian army into a fierce fighting machine while ignoring liberal protests and the Prussian assembly and its laws.

MAP 18.2

Europe in 1871

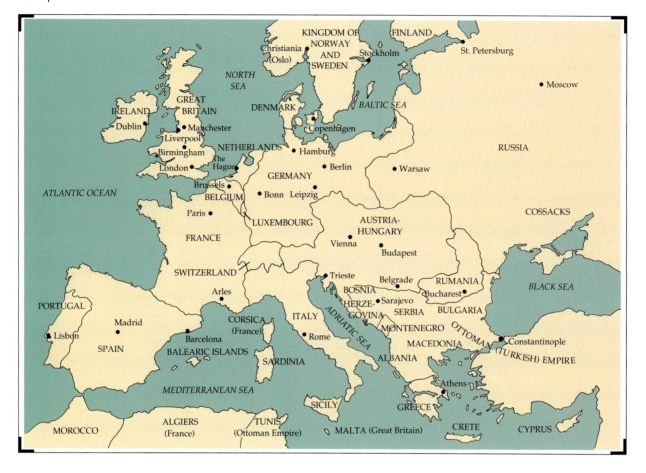

Nationalism replaced liberalism as the rallying cry of the Prussians, and Bismarck took advantage of this shift in attitudes to carry out his plans to unite the Germans around the Prussian state at the expense of Austria and France.

Bismarck achieved his goal by neutralizing potential enemies through deft diplomacy and fighting those who opposed him when diplomacy failed. By 1866 he had united the German states into the North German Confederation, a union that excluded Austria. In 1870 he engineered a diplomatic crisis that forced France to declare war on Prussia. Costly French defeats brought the ensuing Franco-Prussian War to an abrupt end later that year, toppled the Second Empire of Napoleon III, and resulted in France's humiliation in 1871 at Versailles, where the German Empire was proclaimed. The seeds of World War I were sown by this dramatic turn of events (Map 18.2).

Liberalism and nationalism were also at work in disruptions on the Italian peninsula, most of which was ruled by Austrian princes. In the 1830s, Italian liberals inspired by the revolutionary writings of Giuseppe Mazzini [maht-SEE-nee] (1805–1872) had banded together to form Young Italy, a nationalistic movement, and the independent Italian state of Piedmont-Sardinia emerged as the hope of liberals and Young Italy. One of the few Italian states ruled by a native son, Piedmont was a constitutional monarchy that honored its subjects' civil and political rights. Its economy was well balanced between farming and trade, and in the 1840s it began to be industrialized. Under Prime Minister Count Camillo Benso di Cavour [kuh-VOOR] (1810–1861) Piedmont raised the standard of living for many of its citizens, in particular the middle-class merchants and manufacturers. In the 1850s Cavour made Piedmont a player in European affairs and thus set the stage for a move against Austria.

Between 1859 and 1871 Piedmont expelled most of the Austrians and became the center of an emerging state. As part of his grand strategy to unite Italy, Cavour allied himself with the sometimes unreliable Napoleon III of France, whose support encouraged

FIGURE 18.3 JOSEPH MALLORD WILLIAM TURNER. *The Slave Ship (Slavers Throwing Overboard the Dead and Dying, Typhoon Coming On).* Ca. 1840. Oil on canvas, 35¾ × 48¼". The Museum of Fine Arts, Boston. Henry Lillie Pierce Fund. *Growing revulsion against slavery led Parliament to abolish it in the British colonies in the 1830s, but the slaves in the United States were not freed until 1863. Turner's terrifying image of natural calamity and human cruelty reflected the humanitarian values that had surfaced during the parliamentary and national debates about slavery. The ghoulish scene, painted in Turner's unique Romantic style, depicts the castaway bodies of the dead and dying, encircled by hungry fish, as they sink into the stormy sea.*

Cavour to annex parts of central and southern Italy. Further assistance came from the fiercely patriotic soldier Giuseppe Garibaldi [gahr-uh-BAHL-dee] (1807–1882), who, with his personal army of a thousand ''Red Shirts,'' invaded and liberated the Kingdom of the Two Sicilies from its Spanish Bourbon ruler. In 1860 the citizens of this now free region voted overwhelmingly to join Piedmont in a Kingdom of Italy, and soon thereafter the rest of the pieces of the Italian mosaic fell into place. In 1866 Austria yielded Venezia, its last Italian holding, to the new kingdom, and in 1870 Rome fell to nationalist troops and became Italy's capital.

Civil War in the United States

Paralleling the unification of Italy and Germany were the expansion and centralization of the United States, a vigorous and dynamic process that carried within it the seeds of conflict. The United States' economy was mixed and sharply divided between

regions. On one side stood the Northeast, the national leader in commerce, trade, and banking and the site of a growing factory system; on the other side was America's South, a land dominated by huge plantations raising cotton plants cultivated by thousands of black slaves. The unsettled western lands and the ever-changing western frontiers formed a third element.

After 1830 the economic issues that divided the northern and the southern states became intensified over the question of slavery (Figure 18.3). As settlers moved into the central parts of the country, the debate over the spread of slavery into these areas aggravated sectional interests. Tempers were temporarily cooled through a series of compromises over ownership of slaves in the new territories and states, but by the late 1850s these compromises had failed, and in 1861 the southern states seceded from the union and provoked a civil war.

Unlike Europe's contemporaneous wars, which were short and resulted in relatively few deaths, the American Civil War lasted four years with huge losses on both sides. The northern victory in 1865, engineered by President Abraham Lincoln (1861–1865), saved the union and guaranteed freedom for the slaves. But animosity between the American north and south continued to smolder during the war's aftermath, called Reconstruction (1865–1876). Relations between these two sections remained strained, especially over racial matters, for more than a century.

The Spread of Industrialism

Serving as a backdrop for all the political events of the nineteenth century was the growing industrialization of the Western world. Industrialism started to take root in France in the 1830s, and a short time later Belgium entered the industrial age. For the next forty years Belgium and France were the chief economic powers on the Continent. From France and Belgium industrialism spread, and by 1871 the factory and the railway systems radiated from Paris and Brussels to Vienna and Milan.

In the meantime, Great Britain passed into the second phase of the Industrial Revolution. England continued to build ships, to construct factories, and to lay rail lines; by 1850 all its major cities were linked (Figure 18.4). In 1846 Britain abolished tariffs on foreign wheat to usher in a free-trade era. The principles of free trade seemed to be justified by the results. Lower bread prices benefited workers and allowed employers to cut wages, and the fears that additional imports of grain would destroy the agrarian economy proved to be false because agriculture had to expand to meet the demands of a mushrooming urban population.

Prior to 1848 European mining and manufacturing were localized near ore deposits or clustered around urban areas, and railway construction was uncoordinated. But after 1848 rail lines expanded rapidly, and by 1870 a network of 65,000 miles cov-

FIGURE 18.4 W. P. FRITH. *The Railway Station*. Ca. 1862. Oil on canvas, 3′10″ × 8′5″. Royal Holloway College and Bedford New College, Surrey, England. *London was the hub of England's economy long before the Industrial Revolution, and with the coming of the railroads its position was enhanced. The massive new railway stations, often constructed of glass and iron, symbolized the changing business and leisure habits of life. In this painting of one of London's new rail stations, Frith's well-dressed middle-class citizens convey the excitement of travel as well as its novelty and uncertainty.*

FIGURE 18.5 JOSEPH NASH. Detail of *The Crystal Palace*. 1851. Color lithograph with watercolor. Ca. 21½ × 29⅝". Victoria and Albert Museum, London. *This detail from an 1851 lithograph illustrates the splendor and pageantry surrounding the moment when Queen Victoria opened the Great Exhibition of that year. After the fair closed, the Crystal Palace was disassembled, moved, and rebuilt in a suburb in south London, where it stood as an arts and entertainment center until it was destroyed by fire in 1936. Nevertheless, the "pre-fab" construction principles of the Crystal Palace foreshadowed modern building methods.*

ered Europe. Inventions in communications such as the telegraph brought Europeans closer together, and in 1866 engineers laid a transatlantic telegraph cable, making communication easier between Europe and America. The opening of new coal and iron deposits in Europe and the rise of imports in raw materials for textiles and other goods kept the machines of industry humming. British financiers, joined by continental bankers, made loans to fledgling companies for new factories, warehouses, ships, and railways, thereby generating more wealth for capitalists who had surplus funds to invest.

As Europe's economy grew, two marvels of the industrial age—the Crystal Palace in London and the Suez Canal in Egypt—captured the world's imagination. The iron and glass Crystal Palace housed the Great Exhibition of 1851—in effect, the first world's fair. In a structure that used the most recent building materials and employed some of the most advanced architectural methods, the newest inventions and the latest machine-made goods were put on display for everyone—rich and poor—to see. Although other nations displayed products and inventions, Britain's exhibits were the most impressive and proved that it was the world's leading industrial and agricultural power (Figure 18.5).

The second marvel to attract the world's attention was the digging of the Suez Canal to link the Gulf of Suez and the Red Sea with the Mediterranean Sea. Funded by a French company and opened in 1869, the canal shortened the distance between Europe and India, thus enabling steamships to ferry passengers and goods around the globe more quickly and comfortably (Figure 18.6).

The Crystal Palace and the Suez Canal and all of the other wonders of the age were made possible by

FIGURE 18.6 ANONYMOUS. *Suez Canal Opening.* 1869. Colored engraving. British Library, London. *Just as Great Britain showed the world what it could achieve through industry and agriculture, so France demonstrated its technological and engineering genius in digging the Suez Canal. The Suez Canal Company, headed by the French entrepreneur Ferdinand de Lesseps [duh-lay-SEPS] (1805–1894), began its work in 1859 and finally completed the canal ten years later after overcoming many financial and building problems.*

the labor of millions of workers—men, women, and children. On the Continent, the working and living conditions of this group were no better than the squalid circumstances found in Great Britain in the first stage of the Industrial Revolution. The negative side of industrialism, notably the rapid growth of cities that threw poor and ill-trained people into slums and ghettoes, cannot be easily dismissed. Denied access to economic and political power and exploited for their labor, these workers lived degraded lives in subsistence conditions. Individual laborers could improve their lot through thrift and hard work, but as a class their best hope was through collective organization. The slums became breeding grounds for class hatred and offered ready audiences for revolutionaries and socialists advocating revolt and social changes. What flashed across the continent in 1848 was partly caused by the mounting frustrations in these working-class areas. The city laborers failed to make many gains during those heady days, but they learned how to be more realistic in plotting future revolutions.

Even a large segment of the middle class remained cut off from economic and political power. In the United States, all white males were granted suffrage in the 1820s, and in England voting rights were granted to working-class males in the Reform Act of 1867. The revolutions of 1830 and 1848 widened the franchise for French, Italian, German, and Austrian men, although important government posts were always reserved for aristocrats. Except for American and British workers, wage earners and members of the lower middle class, as well as women everywhere, still could not vote in 1871. Universal suffrage was not yet a reality.

NINETEENTH-CENTURY THOUGHT: PHILOSOPHY, RELIGION, AND SCIENCE

At the heart of the debate over liberalism was the question, Which is primary, the individual or the group? Liberalism glorified the value of free expression for each human being, and capitalists used liberal arguments to justify their economic policies. But the corollary of these policies seemed to be poverty, degradation, and injustice for workers, and new voices began to be raised in support of other approaches that promised antidotes to the injustices of industrial capitalism. Primary among these were a variety of socialisms, a form of political and social organization in which material goods are owned and distributed by the community or government.

Liberalism Redefined

In the late eighteenth century English philosopher and social theorist Jeremy Bentham (1748–1832) had developed a variant of liberalism known as **Utilitarianism**. Bentham made "utility" his supreme moral principle, meaning that what gave pleasure to both the individual and society was right and what gave pain was wrong. Utility for society was always identified with "the greatest happiness for the greatest number"—a view that reflected Bentham's commitment to democracy. Accepting liberalism's laissez-faire ideal, yet tempering it with the principle of utility, Bentham pushed for a renovation of the repressive and outmoded governments of his time, including reform of the legal system, prisons, and education.

After 1830 Bentham's ideas were eloquently reinterpreted by bourgeois liberalism's strongest defender, the English philosopher John Stuart Mill (1806–1873). Mill was the son of James Mill, Jeremy Bentham's close friend and chief spokesman. James Mill introduced his son, who was a child prodigy, to Utilitarian theory, classical economics, and the ideas of the Enlightenment. His education made him an empiricist and rationalist on most political and social issues.

Growing to maturity in the second phase of the industrial age, Mill became increasingly fearful that the masses and a powerful state would ultimately destroy individual rights and human dignity. In his essay *On Liberty* (1859) Mill argued that the continued existence of the "civilized community" required the fullest freedom of speech, discussion, and behavior that was possible among all citizens, so long as no person was physically harmed. Mill's essay represents the high tide of English liberalism.

After having advocated laissez-faire economics in his 1848 edition of the *Principles of Political Economy*, in later editions he embraced a mild form of socialism. Condemning unbridled economic competition, he reasoned that though production was subject to economic laws, distribution was not, and thus humans should divide the benefits of industrialism along rational lines. Mill also campaigned for religious toleration and minority rights and became a staunch supporter of women's right to vote and own property.

Socialism

Liberalism provided support for bourgeois values, but **socialism** seemed to many to be the irresistible wave of the future. Socialism began as a reaction to industrialism and came to be its most severe critic, holding out a vision of what society might become if only certain fundamental reforms were made. Two main groups spoke for socialism in the 1800s: the utopian socialists and the Marxists. The utopians, who reached their peak before 1848, believed that the ills of industrial society could be overcome through cooperation between workers and capitalists. Conversely, the Marxists, who flourished after 1848, held the utopians in contempt as naive idealists and called for revolutions, violence, and the inevitable triumph of scientific socialism.

The principal utopian socialists—Robert Owen (1771–1858) (himself a wealthy industrialist), Comte de Saint-Simon [SAN-SEE-MOH(N)] (1760–1825), and Charles Fourier [FOOR-ee-ay] (1772–1837)—shared the belief that a more just society could be introduced using the discoveries about society made in communal associations that served as laboratories for their philosophical ideas. All three thinkers were concerned more about the consumption of the fruits of industrialism than they were about the creation of goods. To them, the workers were simply not receiving a fair share for their efforts and were being victimized by a ruthless, competitive system. To solve these problems, the utopian socialists proposed a number of alternatives, but their often impracticable schemes had little chance of succeeding in an age that was becoming more scientific and realistic.

The utopian socialists and their supporters quickly faded from view once Karl Marx (1818–1883) appeared on the scene. As a student at the University of Berlin Marx studied Hegel's dialectical explanation of historical change, but as an atheist he rejected Hegel's emphasis on Spirit. Since Marx's radical politics made a teaching post untenable in reactionary Prussia, he became editor of a Cologne newspaper. When the police shut down the paper, Marx sought refuge abroad. From Brussels he and Friedrich Engels (1820–1895), his lifelong friend and coauthor, were asked to develop a set of principles for a German workers' society. The resulting pamphlet, *The Communist Manifesto* (1848), became the bible of socialism. Both men played minor roles in the 1848 revolts, seeing in them the first steps of a proletarian revolution. Marx spent his last years in London, writing his major work, *Capital* (volume 1, 1867; volumes 2 and 3, completed by Engels, 1885–1894), and founding an international workers' association to implement his ideas.

Marx's approach to historical change differed radically from the utopian view. According to Marx, history moved in a dialectical pattern as the Hegelians had argued, but not in rhythm with abstract ideas or the World Spirit. Instead, Marx thought that

material reality conditioned historical development; the various stages of history, which were propelled by class conflicts, unfolded as one economic group replaced another. For example, the middle class, which had emerged out of the collapse of the feudal system, represented only a moment in history, destined as it was to bring forth its own gravedigger, the proletariat, or the urban working class. Moreover, the institutions and ideas of a society constituted a superstructure erected on the foundation of economic reality; governments, law, the arts, and the humanities merely reflected the values of a particular ruling class.

Marx forecast that the next and final stage of history would be a revolt by the proletariat, who would then install a classless society. Marx believed that the workers' revolution would be international in scope and that communist intellectuals would assist in bringing an end to bourgeois rule. Elaborating on his theories, Marx's followers created Marxism and, inspired by his ideal society, organized to abolish the capitalist system, although their impact prior to 1871 was minimal.

Religion and the Challenge of Science

The growing interest in objective, rational analysis was not confined to investigations of the workings of society. In a development that alarmed some Christians, a group of Protestant scholars in Germany began to study the Bible not as a divinely inspired book incapable of error but simply as a set of human writings susceptible to varied interpretations. In Germany this movement to treat the Bible like any other book was called *higher criticism*. Scholars began to try to identify the author or authors of each of the biblical books rather than rely on old accounts of their origins, to study each text in order to determine its sources rather than treat each book as a divine revelation, and, most importantly, to assess the accuracy of each account rather than accept it as God's final word. By 1871 orthodox Christians were engaged in intellectual battles with the higher critics, some of whom portrayed Jesus not as God's son but as a mythological figure or a human teacher.

While the higher critics chipped away at Christianity from within, science assaulted it from the outside. Geologists first discredited the biblical story of creation, and then biologists questioned the divine origin of human beings. The challenge from geology was led by the Englishman Charles Lyell [LIE-uhl] (1797–1875), whose fossil research showed that the earth was much older than Christians claimed. By treating each of God's six days of creation as symbolic of thousands of years of divine activity, Protestant Christians were able to weather this particular intellectual storm. Not so easily overcome, however, was biology's threat to biblical authority.

Following the Bible, the church was clear in its explanation of humanity's origin: Adam and Eve were the first parents, having been created by God after he had fashioned the rest of the animate world. Paralleling this divine account was a secular argument for evolution. Based on Greek thought, but without solid proofs, it remained a theory and nothing more for centuries. In 1859, however, the theory of *evolution* gained dramatic support when the Englishman Charles Darwin (1809–1882) published *On the Origin of Species*. Marshaling data to prove that evolution was a principle of biological growth rather than a mere hypothesis, Darwin showed that over the course of millennia modern plants and animals had evolved from simpler forms through a process of natural selection.

In 1871, in *Descent of Man*, Darwin applied his findings to human beings, portraying them as the outcome of millions of years of evolution. Outraged clergy attacked Darwin for his atheism, and equally zealous Darwinians heaped ridicule on the creationists for their credulity. Today, the theory of evolution is one of the cornerstones of biological science, despite some continuing criticism.

Other advances in science were helping to lay the groundwork for the modern world. In the 1850s French scientist Louis Pasteur [pass-TUHR] (1822–1895) proposed the germ theory of disease, the notion that many diseases are caused by microorganisms. This seminal idea led him to important discoveries and proposals for change. Claiming that germs were responsible for the spread of disease, he campaigned for improved sanitation and sterilization and thus paved the way for antiseptic surgery. He demonstrated that food spoilage could be prevented by killing microorganisms through heating, a discovery that resulted in the "pasteurization" of milk. His studies of rabies and anthrax led him to the first use of vaccines against these diseases. As the founder of bacteriology and an important figure in the development of modern medicine, Pasteur is the embodiment of Francis Bacon's seventeenth-century assertion, "knowledge is power."

In chemistry a fruitful way of thinking about atoms was finally formulated, moving beyond the simplistic notions that had been in vogue since fifth-century B.C. Greece. In about 1808 the Englishman John Dalton (1766–1844) invented an effective atomic theory and, in 1869, the Russian Dmitri Mendeleev [men-duh-LAY-uhf] (1834–1907) worked out a periodic table of elements, based on atomic weights, a system that, with modifications, is still in use. By 1871 other chemists had moved from regarding molecules as clusters of atoms to conceiving of them as structured into stable patterns. Nevertheless, without means and equipment for studying the actual atoms, atomism remained merely a useful theory until the twentieth century.

Advances in chemistry also led to changes in anesthetics and surgery. In the 1840s chemists introduced nitrous oxide, chloroform, and other compounds that could block pain in human beings. Use of these new pain killers in obstetrics increased after Queen Victoria was given chloroform to assist her in childbirth in 1853. These desensitizers revolutionized the treatment of many diseases and wounds and made modern surgery possible.

CULTURAL TRENDS: FROM ROMANTICISM TO REALISM

In its triumph, the middle class embraced both Neoclassical and Romantic styles in the arts. In Neoclassicism, the bourgeoisie found a devotion to order that appealed to their belief that the seemingly chaotic marketplace was actually regulated by economic laws. In Romanticism, they found escape from the sordid and ugly side of industrialism.

But both styles slowly grew routinized and pretentious under the patronage of the middle class. One reason for this development was the inevitable loss of creative energy that sets in when any style becomes established. Another reason was the conversion of the cultural arena into a marketplace. Lacking the deep learning that had guided many aristocratic patrons in the past, the new bourgeois audiences demanded art and literature that mirrored their less refined values. Catering to this need, artists and writers produced works that were spectacular, sentimental, and moralistic. Simply put, successful art did not offend respectable public taste.

Adding to this bourgeois influence was the growing ability of state institutions to control what was expressed in art and literature. The most powerful of these was France's Royal Academy of Painting and Sculpture, founded in 1648 for the purpose of honoring the nation's best painters. After 1830 its leaders became obsessed with rigid rules, thus creating what was called "official art." Those artists who could not obtain the academy's approval for exhibiting their works in the annual government-sponsored Salons, or art shows, were virtually condemned to poverty unless they had other means of

FIGURE 18.7 ÉDOUARD MANET. *A Bar at the Folies-Bergère.* 1882. Courtauld Institute Galleries, University of London (Courtauld Collection). *The Folies Bergère was the grandest of the glorified beer halls, or cafés-concerts, which sprang up in Paris after 1850, offering drinks and raucous stage entertainment. Catering initially to a lower middle class prospering from the period's booming economy, these cafés-concerts created a loud and vulgar environment. Soon these places became classless settings in which all strata of society could anonymously rub elbows: respectable couples with children, shop clerks, workers in their Sunday best, prostitutes, men of all classes on the town, and tourists wanting to see the "real" Paris.*

Manet was drawn to the spectacle of these cafés-concerts. In A Bar at the Folies-Bergère he captures the drama of the setting and its ghastly white light: the barmaid who gazes stoically, surrounded by bottles of wine and beer; the crush of customers of both sexes; the acrobat's green feet standing on the trapeze in the top left corner. He also manages to hint at prostitution, for which the Folies-Bergère was notorious, in the exchange between the top-hatted man (a wealthy patron) and the barmaid on the right. However, this work presents one obvious problem, the impossibly placed mirror (behind the barmaid), which means that the barmaid must be doing two things at once: standing before the top-hatted man and looking at the viewers.

financial support. Rejected artists soon identified the Royal Academy as a defender of the status quo and an enemy of innovation. No other western state had a national academy with as much power as France's Royal Academy, although in other European countries similar bodies tried to regulate both art and literature.

In reaction to the empty, overblown qualities of official art, a new style began to appear in the 1840s. Known as **Realism**, this style focused on the everyday lives of the middle and lower classes (Figure 18.7). The Realists depicted ordinary people without idealizing or romanticizing them, although a moral point of view was always implied. Condemning Neoclassicism as cold and Romanticism as exaggerated, the Realists sought to convey what they saw around them in a serious, accurate, and unsentimental way. Merchants, housewives, workers, peasants, and even prostitutes replaced kings, aristocrats, goddesses, saints, and heroes as the subjects of paintings and novels.

Many forces contributed to the rise of Realism. In diplomacy this was the era of Bismarck's *Realpolitik*, the hard-nosed style that replaced more cautious and civilized negotiation. In science Darwin demystified earthly existence by rejecting the biblical view of creation and concluding that the various species, including human beings, evolved from simpler organisms. The spread of democracy encouraged the Realists to take an interest in ordinary people, and the camera, invented in the 1830s, probably inspired the Realists in their goal of truthful accuracy. All these influences combined to make Realism a style intent on scientific objectivity in its depiction of the world as it is.

Literature

In literature the Romantic style continued to dominate both poetry and novels until midcentury, when it began to be displaced by Realism. The Romantic authors were concerned with the depth of their characters' emotions and had great faith in the power of the individual to transform his or her own life and the lives of others. The Realists, by contrast, tended to be determinists who preferred to let the facts speak for themselves. They rejected the bourgeois world as flawed by hypocrisy and materialism and denounced the machine age for its mechanization of human relationships. Realism in literature flourished between 1848 and 1871, chiefly in France, England, and Russia.

The Height of French Romanticism: Victor Hugo   In France the leading exponent of Romanticism was the poet, dramatist, and novelist Victor Hugo (1802–1885). His poetry established his fame, and the performance of his tragedy *Hernani* in February 1830 solidified his position as the leader of the Romantic movement. Enlivened with scenes of rousing action and by characters with limitless ambition, this play seemed with one stroke to sweep away the artificialities of Classicism. Its premiere created a huge scandal. When the bourgeois revolution erupted in July 1830, many French people believed that Hugo's *Hernani* had been a literary prophecy of the political upheaval.

Hugo became something of a national institution, noted as much for his humane values as his writing. Because of his opposition to the regime of Napoleon III, he was exiled from France for eighteen years, beginning in 1851. While in exile he published his most celebrated novel, the epic-length *Les Misérables* (*The Wretched*) (1862), which expresses his revulsion at the morally bankrupt society he believed France had become after Napoleon I.

The hero and moral center of the book is the pauper Jean Valjean, who is imprisoned for seventeen years for stealing a loaf of bread. He escapes and becomes a prosperous, respectable merchant, but the law is unrelenting in its pursuit of him, and he is forced into a life of hiding and subterfuge. Hugo makes Valjean a symbol of the rising masses' will to freedom, and his bourgeois readers were fascinated and horrified at the same time by Valjean's ultimate triumph.

Romanticism in the English Novel   In England, Romanticism found its most expressive voices in the novels of the Brontë sisters, Charlotte (1816–1855) and Emily (1818–1848). Reared in the Yorkshire countryside far from the mainstream of cultured life, they created two of the most beloved novels in the English language. Their circumscribed lives seemed to uphold the Romantic dictum that true artistic genius springs from the imagination alone.

Emily's *Wuthering Heights* (1847) creates a Romantic atmosphere through mysterious events, ghostly apparitions, and graveyard scenes, but it rises above the typical Gothic romance. The work is suffused by a mystical radiance that invests the characters and the natural world with spiritual meanings beyond the visible. A tale of love and redemption, the story focuses on a mismatched couple, the genteel Catherine and the outcast Heathcliff, who are nevertheless soulmates. In the uncouth, passionate Heathcliff, Brontë creates a Byronic hero who lives apart from conventional morality. Her portrayal of him as a man made vengeful by cruel circumstances has led some to label this the first sociorevolutionary novel.

Charlotte Brontë published *Jane Eyre* in the same year *Wuthering Heights* appeared. A dark and melancholy novel, the work tells the story of a governess's love for her brooding and mysterious employer. Her hopes for happiness are crushed by the discovery that the cause of his despair is his deranged wife, kept hidden in the attic. Narrated in the first person, the novel reveals the heroine's deep longings and passions as well as her ultimate willingness to sacrifice her feelings for moral values. Recognized at the time as a revolutionary work that dispensed with the conventions of sentimental novels, *Jane Eyre* was attacked by critics but welcomed by the reading public, who made it a best seller.

Realism in French and English Novels   Realism began in France in the 1830s with the novels of Honoré de Balzac [BAHL-zak] (1799–1850). Balzac foreshadowed the major traits of Realism in the nearly one hundred novels that make up the series he called *The Human Comedy*. Set in France in the Napoleonic era and the early industrial age, this voluminous series deals with the lives of over two thousand characters, both in Paris and in the provinces. Balzac condemns the hollowness of middle-class society, pointing out how industrialism has caused many people to value material things more than friendship and family, although there are virtuous and sympathetic characters as well.

France's outstanding Realist is Gustave Flaubert [floh-BAIR] (1821–1880), who advocated a novel free from conventional, accepted moral or philosophical views. His masterpiece is *Madame Bovary* (1857), which caused a scandal with its unvarnished tale of adultery. In contrast to Balzac's broad sweep, Flaubert focused on one small town and the daily comings and goings of a family, concentrating his greatest attention on a single person, the unhappy and misguided Emma Bovary. Objectively and clinically, he sets forth the inner turmoil of a frustrated middle-class woman trapped by her dull marriage and her social standing. By stressing objectivity and withholding judgment, Flaubert believed he was following in the footsteps of modern science. As a social critic he portrays with meticulous detail everyday life among the smug members of this small-town, bourgeois society. Notwithstanding the scandal it caused, *Madame Bovary* became an instant success and established the new style of Realism. For most readers, Emma Bovary became a poignant symbol of people whose unrealistic dreams and aspirations doom their lives to failure.

English novelists also wrote in the new Realist style. Like their French counterparts, they railed against the vulgarity, selfishness, and hypocrisy of the middle class, but unlike the French they chose mundane rather than sensational subjects, avoided sexual matters, and spoke out for social justice. England's most popular writer of Realist fiction was Charles Dickens (1812–1870), who favored stories dealing with the harsh realities of urban and industrial life. Forced to meet strict deadlines for his works, which first appeared as serialized magazine stories, Dickens poured out a torrent of words over a long literary career that began when he was in his twenties.

In his early works such as *Oliver Twist* (1837–1839) and *David Copperfield* (1849–1850) Dickens was optimistic, holding out hope for his characters and, by implication, for society in general. But in later novels like *Bleak House* and *Hard Times,* both published between 1851 and 1854, he was pessimistic about social reform or correcting the excesses of industrialism. Dickens's rich descriptions, convoluted plots with unexpected coincidences, and topical satire were much admired by Victorian readers, and his finely developed and very British characters, such as Mr. Pickwick, Oliver Twist, and Ebenezer Scrooge, have survived as a memorable gift to literature.

Realist fiction in England was also represented by important female writers. The two most successful were Elizabeth Gaskell (1810–1865) and Mary Ann Evans (1819–1880), better known by her pen name, George Eliot. Both wrote novels about the hardships imposed on the less fortunate by England's industrial economy. Gaskell's *North and South* (1855) underscores the widening gap between the rich, particularly in England's urban north, and the poor, concentrated in the rural south, within the context of the rise of the labor unions. Typically, her themes involve contrasts, contradictions, and conflicts, such as the helplessness of human beings in the face of impersonal forces and the simultaneous need to affirm the human spirit against the inequalities of the factory system. Similarly, in novels like *Middlemarch* (1872) George Eliot explores the ways human beings are trapped in social systems that shape and mold their lives, for good or ill. Eliot's outlook is less deterministic, however, stressing the possibility of individual fulfillment despite social constraints as well as the freedom to make moral choices.

The Russian Realists   During the Realist period, Russia for the first time produced writers whose works received international acclaim: Leo Tolstoy [TAHL-stoy] (1828–1910) and Feodor Dostoevsky [dahs-tuh-YEV-ske] (1821–1881). Like English and French Realists, these Russians depicted the grim face of early industrialism and dealt with social problems, notably the plight of the newly liberated serfs. Their realism is tempered by a typically Russian concern: Should Russia embrace Western values or should it follow its own traditions, relying on its Slavic and Oriental past? Significantly, Tolstoy and Dostoevsky transcend Western Realism by stressing religious and spiritual themes.

In his early works Tolstoy wrote with a clinical eye, free of moralizing. The novel *Anna Karenina* (1875–1877) describes the unhappy consequences of adultery in a sophisticated but unforgiving society. *War and Peace* (1865–1869), his greatest work, is a monumental survey of Russia during the Napoleonic era, portraying a huge cast of characters caught up in the surging tides of history. Although Tolstoy focuses on the upper class in this Russian epic, he places them in realistic situations without romanticizing them. In these early works he was a determinist, convinced that human beings were at the mercy of forces acting independently of their own will. But in 1876, after he had a religious conversion to a simple form of Christianity that stressed pacifism, plain living, and radical social reform, he repudiated all art that lacked a moral vision, including his own. Tolstoy devoted the rest of his life to this plain faith, following what he believed to be Jesus' teachings and working for a Christian anarchist society.

Feodor Dostoevsky was a powerful innovator who introduced literary devices that have become standard in Western letters. For example, *Crime and Punishment* (1866), long before the work of Sigmund Freud, analyzes the inner life of a severely disturbed personality. In *Notes from Underground* (1864) the unnamed narrator is hopelessly neurotic—the first appearance of a modern literary type, the anti-hero, the character who lacks the virtues conventionally associated with heroism, but who is not a villain.

In *The Brothers Karamazov* (1879–1880) Dostoevsky reaches the height of his powers. Like Flaubert in *Madame Bovary*, Dostoevsky sets his story in a small town and builds the narrative around a single family. Each of the Karamazov brothers personifies certain traits of human behavior, though none is a one-dimensional figure. Using the novel to address one of life's most vexing questions—If God exists, why is there suffering and evil in the world?—Dostoevsky offers no easy solution. Indeed, he reaches the radical conclusion that the question is insoluble, that suffering is an essential part of earthly existence and without it human beings could have no moral life.

Art and Architecture

Realism in art grew up alongside an inflated and overstated version of Romanticism that persisted well beyond midcentury. Even Neoclassicism was represented in the official art of France throughout this period. Both styles found favor with the wealthy bourgeoisie.

Neoclassicism and Romanticism after 1830   Jean-Auguste-Dominique Ingres, who had inherited the position of Neoclassical master painter from David, now held virtually complete power over French academic art until his death in 1867. He understood the mentality of the Salon crowds, and his works catered to their tastes. What particularly pleased this audience—composed almost exclusively of the wealthy, educated middle class—were chaste nudes on mythological or exotic themes, as in *The Turkish Bath* (Figure 18.8). The women's tactile flesh and the abandoned poses, though superbly realized, are depicted in a cold, Classical style and lack the immediacy of Ingres's great portraits.

Delacroix, Ingres's chief rival, remained a significant force in French culture with almost comparable artistic power. Delacroix perfected a Romantic style filled with gorgeous colors and fiery action. One of his finest works from this period is *The Abduction of Rebecca*, based on an incident in the novel *Ivanhoe* by the Scottish writer Sir Walter Scott (Figure 18.9). This

FIGURE 18.8 JEAN-AUGUSTE-DOMINIQUE INGRES. *The Turkish Bath.* Ca. 1852–1863. Oil on canvas, diameter, 42½". Louvre. *Paintings of harem scenes reflected interest in Oriental themes, a continuous thread in France's nineteenth-century bourgeois culture. In his rendering of a Turkish bath, Ingres used a harem setting in which to depict more than twenty nudes in various erotic and nonerotic poses. The nudes nevertheless are portrayed in his typical Classical manner, suggesting studio models rather than sensual human beings.*

FIGURE 18.9   EUGÈNE DELACROIX. *The Abduction of Rebecca*. 1846. Oil on canvas, 39½ × 32¼". Metropolitan Museum of Art, New York. Wolfe Fund, 1903. *Romantic themes abound in Delacroix's painting of the abduction of Rebecca, such as its medieval subject, its literary source, and its use of bold colors to accentuate the violence. In addition, the struggling horse was a favorite symbol of Romantic artists, representing the untamable energy of nature.*

literary subject inspired Delacroix to create a painting that is a feast for the eyes. In the foreground, the swooning Rebecca is kidnapped by knights and placed on the back of a spirited horse; in the background, flames pour through the openings in a burning castle and lick the sky. In this and later paintings Delacroix tried to work out the secret laws governing colors—especially the effects that they have on the viewer. The results in *The Abduction of Rebecca* are seductive hues and the almost total absence of black. Later, the Impressionists based some of their color theories on Delacroix's experiments.

Like Romantic painting, nineteenth-century architecture tended to be romantically nostalgic, intrigued by times and places far removed from the industrial present. Particularly appealing were medieval times, which were considered exotic and even ethically superior to the present. Patriotism also contributed to the trend among Romantic architects to adapt medieval building styles, notably the Gothic, to nineteenth-century conditions, since the Middle Ages were a time when the national character of many states was being formed.

In London, when the old Houses of Parliament burned to the ground in 1834, a decision had to be made about the style of their replacement. Since English rights and liberties traditionally dated from the Magna Carta in 1215, during the Middle Ages, a parliamentary commission chose a Gothic style for the new building (see Figure 18.2). Designed by Charles Barry (1795–1860) and A. W. N. Pugin (1812–1852), the Houses of Parliament show a true understanding of the essential features of the Gothic style, using pointed arches and picturesque towers. Despite these features, this building is not genuinely Gothic, for it adheres to Classical principles in the regularity of its decorations and its emphasis on the horizontal.

The Rise of Realism in Art Dissatisfied with the emotional, exotic, and escapist tendencies of Romanticism, a new breed of painters who wanted to depict the real-life events they saw around them brought their vision to public attention after 1848. In that year the jury of the Salon, influenced by the democratic sentiments unleashed by the 1848 revolutions, allowed a new kind of painting to be shown. The artist most identified with this event was Gustave Courbet [koor-BAY] (1819–1877), a painter renowned for his refusal to prettify his works in the name of an aesthetic theory. His provocative canvases outraged middle-class audiences and made him the guiding spirit of militant Realism. Until about 1900, most painters in one way or another followed in Courbet's footsteps. A man of the people, a largely self-taught painter, and a combative individ-

FIGURE 18.10 GUSTAVE COURBET. *A Burial at Ornans.* 1849. Oil on canvas, ca. 10 × 22'. Louvre. *Courbet's realistic burial scene reveals a modern, secular outlook. Previously in such scenes, artists had focused on religious values, either suggesting that death is a preparation for heaven or stressing that the body is mortal. Courbet does neither; instead he portrays the final rites as a community affair, making no distinctions between clerical participants and lay mourners. For him this funeral is simply a social ritual, nothing more.*

FIGURE 18.11 GUSTAVE COURBET. *Interior of My Studio: A Real Allegory Summing Up Seven Years of My Life as an Artist*. 1855. Oil on canvas, 11'9¾" × 19'6⅝". Louvre. *Romanticism and Realism are joined in this allegorical work. The subjects—the artist and artistic genius—were major preoccupations of the Romantic era, as was the use of allegory. But undeniably Realist is Courbet's mocking attitude toward academic art and society.*

ual, Courbet began to attract notice in 1849 by painting common people engaged in their day-to-day activities. Above all, he strove for an art that reflected the conditions of ordinary life.

In *A Burial at Ornans* Courbet shows a funeral party of provincials around an open grave in the stark countryside near his home (Figure 18.10). Exhibited in the Salon of 1850, this huge painting caused an outcry from critics because it depicted people of no importance or interest to the wealthy bourgeoisie, and the mourners' realistic portrayal offended what was considered good taste. Instead of idealizing or romanticizing the peasants, Courbet portrayed them as flesh and blood, showing the same degrees of public sorrow as their so-called social betters. In the middle of the nineteenth century such humane treatment of the ''lower orders'' smacked of socialism. Courbet relished the controversy, claiming that this work represented the burial of Romanticism.

Courbet's art was not readily accepted under France's Second Empire. Typical of his neglect was an episode in 1855 when the Salon jury refused to accept for exhibit the monumental work that is today

regarded as his masterpiece, *Interior of My Studio* (Figure 18.11). An intensely personal painting that visually summarizes his approach to art until this time, this work uses realistic contemporary figures to convey allegorical meaning. Its subtitle suggests Courbet's intent: *A Real Allegory Summing Up Seven Years of My Life as an Artist*. At the center of this canvas is the artist himself, in full light and painting a landscape while he is watched by a naked model and a small boy. The model and the fabric may be ironic references to the Salon's preference for nudes and still lifes. To the left of this central group, in shadow, are depicted those who have to work for a living, the usual subjects of Courbet's paintings, including peasants (the hunter and his dog) and a laborer. To the right, also in shadow, are grouped those for whom he paints, including his friends and mentors, each representing a specific idea. For example, the man reading a book is the poet Charles Baudelaire [bohd-LAIR], a personification of lyricism in art. As a total work, *Interior of My Studio* shows Courbet as the craftsman who mediates between the ordinary people pursuing everyday lives and the world of art and culture, bringing both to life in the process.

FIGURE 18.12 HONORÉ DAUMIER. *Le Ventre Législatif (The Legislative Belly).* 1834. Lithograph, 431 × 280 mm. Museum of Fine Arts, Boston. Bequest of William P. Babcock. *Daumier's career as a caricaturist was made possible by technological advances associated with the industrial era. After drawing a cartoon, he reproduced it for the mass market by the lithographic process, the first application of industrial methods to art. In early lithography the artist rendered an image on a flat stone surface and treated it so the nonimage areas would repel ink. Today's lithography makes use of zinc or aluminum surfaces instead of stone.*

Although Courbet is considered the principal founder of the Realist style in art, he had a worthy predecessor in Honoré Daumier [DOH-m'yay] (1808–1879), a painter of realistic scenes before Realism emerged as a recognized style. Daumier chronicled the life of Paris with a dispassionate, clinical eye. In thousands of satirical lithographs, from which he earned his living, and hundreds of paintings, he depicted its mean streets, corrupt law courts, squalid rented rooms, ignorant art connoisseurs, bored musicians, cowardly bourgeoisie, and countless other urban characters and scenes. His works not only conjure up Paris in the middle of the century, but also symbolize the city as a living hell where daily existence could be a form of punishment.

No one and nothing were safe from Daumier's gaze. For example, in *Le Ventre Législatif (The Legislative Belly)* he depicts the legislators of the bourgeois monarchy of Louis Philippe as fat politicians feeding at the public trough (Figure 18.12). His razor-sharp wit was reflected in the politicians' bloated stomachs, cruel frowns, whispered asides, and general air of smug self-satisfaction. For such satire Daumier was awarded a six-month prison term in 1832, but to his adoring audience he was a hero.

One of the most famous of Daumier's images is the painting entitled *The Third-Class Carriage* (Figure 18.13). In Paris third-class coach was the cheapest sort of rail travel, and the resulting accommodations were cramped and plain. In Daumier's scene the foreground is dominated by three figures—a mother and her sleeping child, an old woman, and a sleeping boy. Behind them are crowded other peasants and middle-class businessmen, the latter recognizable by their tall hats. Although caricature is hinted at in this work, the painting is a realistic portrayal of the growing democratization of society brought on by the railway.

In contrast to Daumier with his urban scenes, Jean-François Millet [mee-YAY] (1814–1875) painted the countryside near Barbizon, a French village south of Paris where an artists' colony was located

FIGURE 18.14 JEAN-FRANÇOIS MILLET. *The Sower.* 1850. Oil on canvas, 40 × 32½". Museum of Fine Arts, Boston. Gift of Quincy Adams Shaw through Quincy A. Shaw, Jr. and Mrs. Marian Shaw Haughton. *Like Daumier's peasant travelers, Millet's farmhand is depicted as a social type rather than as an individual. But Millet's Realist vision of peasant life is less forgiving than that of Daumier. He portrays the sower as little more than an animal and places him in a dark, nearly monochromatic landscape. Whereas Daumier's caricatures had provoked laughter or anger, Millet's painting produced fear.*

◄ **FIGURE 18.13** HONORÉ DAUMIER. *The Third-Class Carriage.* Ca. 1862. Oil on canvas, 25¾ × 35½". Metropolitan Museum of Art, New York. Bequest of Mrs. H. O. Havemeyer, 1929. *Close study of this oil painting reveals Daumier's genius for social observation: the mother's doting expression, the old woman's stoicism, and the melancholy profile of the top-hatted man in the shadows at the far left. None of the figures is individualized, however, for all represent social types. Despite the cramped quarters, Daumier stresses the isolation of individual travelers by the jumbled heads in the back and the staring eyes that do not see.*

in the 1840s. Millet and the Barbizon school were influenced by the English Romantic Constable, whose painting *The Hay Wain* had been admired in the Paris Salon of 1824 (see Figure 17.11). Unlike Constable, who treated human beings only incidentally in his landscapes, Millet made the rural folk and their labors his primary subject.

One of Millet's early Barbizon paintings was *The Sower,* which he exhibited in the Salon of 1850 (Figure 18.14). This work depicts a youth casting seeds into a freshly plowed field; dimly visible in the background are a flock of birds and two oxen with a plowman. Ordinarily such a pastoral scene would have been a romantic idyll symbolizing the dignity of human work, but in Millet's canvas the toil degrades the laborer. Millet forces attention on the solitary peasant, isolated from the world in a desolate landscape. The resulting image is that of a hulking presence, powerfully muscled and striding boldly

FIGURE 18.15 Jean-François Millet. *The Gleaners.* 1857. Oil on canvas, 33 × 44″. Louvre. *Millet's realistic scenes of peasants were inspired in part by the biblical quotation, "In the sweat of thy face shalt thou eat bread . . ." (Genesis 3:19). In* The Gleaners *he expresses this idea with controlled beauty, depicting the women with simple dignity despite their hard lot. The painting's earth tones reinforce the somber nature of the subject.*

across the canvas. Salon critics reacted by calling the picture "savage" and "violent."

In *The Gleaners* Millet showed another type of farm worker, the women laborers whose daily bread depended on scavenging the grain left over from the harvest (Figure 18.15). These women were part of a depressed class that had fallen hopelessly behind in France's rush into industrialism. Millet's portrayal of stoop labor outraged some bourgeois critics, who called him a "socialist." But from today's perspective, this painting is a sympathetic and truthful record of a way of life that was fast disappearing.

If the Parisian art world was disturbed by the paintings of Courbet and Millet, it was outraged by the work of Édouard Manet [mah-NAY] (1832–1883), a painter whose style is difficult to classify. He con-

tributed to the events which gradually discredited the Salon and the Academy, encouraging painters to express themselves as they pleased, and thus was a bridge between the Realists of the 1860s and the group that became known in the 1870s as the Impressionists. His notoriety arose in 1863 when Emperor Napoleon III authorized a *Salon des Refusés* (Salon of the Rejects) for the hundreds of artists excluded from the official exhibit. An audacious painting by Manet in this first of the counter-Salons made him the talk of Paris and the recognized leader of new painting.

Manet's "scandalous" painting is called *Le Déjeuner sur l'Herbe,* which is usually translated as *Luncheon on the Grass,* a title that the hostile audience attached to the work in place of its actual name, *Le Bain*

(The Bath) (Figure 18.16). The woodland scene—two properly dressed young men accompanied by a seated nude female and a second woman bathing in the background—offended public decency. It seemed to depict living French citizens in an erotic setting. In actuality, however, the subject had roots deep in art history. Two clothed males and two nude females had been the subject of a painting by the sixteenth-century Venetian painter Giorgione [jahr-JOH-nee], and the pose of the three central figures was borrowed from a work by the Renaissance master Raphael.

More important than these historical connections, however, are Manet's artistic theories and practices, which strained against the boundaries of Realism. Unlike the other Realists, whose moral or ideological feelings were reflected in the subjects they painted, Manet moved toward a dispassionate art in which the subject and the artist have no necessary connection. What had confused bourgeois critics and

FIGURE 18.16 ÉDOUARD MANET. *Le Déjeuner sur l'Herbe (Luncheon on the Grass).* 1863. Oil on canvas, 7' × 8'10". Louvre. *The bourgeoisie adopted many of the pleasures that had previously been the exclusive privilege of nobility. A leisure activity that particularly attracted the middle-class public was the public outing, and the holiday picnic was established as a suitable subject for painting by the mid–nineteenth century. One of the reasons for the furor surrounding Manet's painting was that he seemed to suggest that such picnics furnished opportunities for immoral behavior. To outraged bourgeois critics, Manet's picnic seemed a lewd joke.*

FIGURE 18.17 MATHEW BRADY. *President Abraham Lincoln and General George B. McClellan. 1861. Library of Congress. This hastily arranged photograph underscores the tension between the president and his general. The impression is confirmed by the men's isolation in the tent, their awkward composure, and their lack of sympathy for one another. Using the camera as a painter would wield a brush, Brady heightens the drama of the scene with light and dark contrasts, placing Lincoln (left) in the shadows and McClellan (right) more in the light. Brady's intuitive genius turned what could have been a routine double portrait into an incisive psychological study.*

audiences about *Le Déjeuner sur l'Herbe* was that they had tried to impose a little story onto what was simply the portrayal of four figures in a landscape with a still life (the picnic on the left). Manet's achievement was revolutionary, for he had discarded the intellectual themes of virtually all western art: reliance on anecdote, the Bible, Christian saints, politics, nostalgia, Greece and Rome, the Middle Ages, and sentimental topics. With his work, he opened the door to an art that had no other purpose than to depict what the artist chose to paint. In sum, Manet was the first truly modern painter.

Photography

One of the forces impelling painting toward a more realistic and detached style of expression was the invention of the camera. Two types of camera techniques were perfected in 1839. In France, Louis-Jacques-Mandé Daguerre [duh-GAIR] (1787–1851) discovered a chemical method for implanting images on silvered copper plates to produce photographs called daguerrotypes. In England, William Henry Fox Talbot (1800–1877) was pioneering the negative-positive process of photographic images, which he called "the pencil of nature." Not only did the camera undermine the reality of the painted image, but it quickly created a new art form, photography. From the beginning, many photographers began to experiment with the camera's artistic potential, though only recently has photography received wide acceptance as serious art.

Among these early photographers was the American Mathew Brady (about 1823–1896), who abandoned his spacious Broadway studio in New York to create a pictorial record of the American Civil War. Brady was able to transform banal scenes into haunting images of psychological insight, as in his photograph of President Abraham Lincoln visiting General George B. McClellan on the battlefield. Their meeting arose because Lincoln, disappointed in the progress of the war, wanted to have a personal word with his general. Brady's photograph subtly conveys the tension between the two men. Lincoln's grim face shows his moral determination, while McClellan stares quizzically at the Commander-in-Chief. A few days after this photograph was taken, McClellan was relieved of his command (Figure 18.17).

Music

Originating shortly after 1800, Romantic music reigned supreme from 1830 until 1871. Romantic works grew longer and more expressive as composers forged styles reflecting their individual feelings. To achieve unique voices, Romantic composers adopted varied techniques such as shifting rhythms, complex musical structures, discordant passages, and minor keys. In addition, with the spread of nationalistic feelings across Europe, especially after 1850, composers began to incorporate folk songs, national anthems, and indigenous dance rhythms into their music. Nonetheless, throughout this era Romantic composers stayed true to the established forms of Classical music composition—the opera, the sonata, and the symphony.

Although a Baroque creation, opera rose to splendid heights under Romanticism. Partly accountable for this striking development was that the bourgeois public, bedazzled by opera's spectacle and virtuoso singers, eagerly embraced this art form. Operatic composers sometimes wrote works specifically to show off the vocal wizardry of the performers. So prolific were these musicians that they wrote over half of the operas still performed today.

Romanticism had an important impact on opera. The orchestras for operas became larger, inspiring composers to write long, elaborate works requiring many performers. Composers also began to integrate the entire musical drama, creating orchestral music that accentuated the actions and thoughts of the characters on stage. Most importantly, the form of opera itself was transformed. At first composers imitated the form that they had inherited, writing operas in which a series of independent musical numbers, that is, *arias* (melodious songs), alternated with *recitatives* (text either declaimed in the rhythms of natural speech with slight musical variations or sung with fuller musical support). The Italian composer Verdi brought this type of opera to its peak, advancing beyond the mechanical aria-recitative alternation. But even as Verdi was being lionized for his operatic achievements, a new style of opera was arising in Germany in the works of Wagner, which were written not as independent musical sections, but as continuous musical scenes.

Giuseppe Verdi [VAYR-dee] (1813–1901), Italy's greatest composer of opera, followed the practice of the time and borrowed many of his plots from the works of Romantic writers. He was particularly attracted to complicated plots filled with passion and full-blooded emotionalism.

One of the operas that brought him international fame was *Rigoletto* (1851), based on a play by Victor Hugo. What makes this opera such a favorite with audiences are its strong characters, its beautiful melodies, and its dramatic unity—features that typify Verdi's mature works. A study in Romantic opposites, this work tells of a crippled court jester, Rigoletto, deformed physically but emotionally sensitive, coarse in public but a devoted parent in private. The jester's daughter Gilda is also a study in contrasts, torn between love for her father and attraction to a corrupt noble.

In *Rigoletto* Verdi continues to alternate arias with sung recitatives, but overall his music for the orchestra skillfully underscores the events taking place on stage. In addition, he employs musical passages to illustrate the characters' psychology, using convoluted orchestral backgrounds to accompany Ri-

goletto's monologues, for example, or shifts from simple to showy musical settings to demonstrate Gilda's conflicted nature. Other operas followed, enhancing Verdi's mounting celebrity: *La Traviata* in 1853, based on a play written by the French Romantic writer Alexandre Dumas [doo-MAH] the younger, and *Aida* in 1871, commissioned by Egypt's ruler and first performed in the Cairo opera house.

Romantic opera reached its climax in the works of Richard Wagner [VAHG-nuhr] (1813–1883), who sought a union of music and drama. A political revolutionary in his youth and a visionary thinker, Wagner was deeply impressed by the Romantic idea that the supreme expression of artistic genius occurred only when the arts were fused together. To this end he not only composed his own scores, but wrote the *librettos*, or texts, frequently conducted the music, and even planned the opera house in Bayreuth, Germany, where his later works were staged.

Wagner's major musical achievement was the monumental project entitled *The Ring of the Nibelung* (1853–1874), a cycle of four operas—or *music dramas*, as Wagner called them—that fulfilled his ideal of fusing music, verse, and staging. In these works the distinction between arias and recitatives was nearly erased, giving a continuously flowing melodic line. This unified sound was marked by the appearance of recurring themes associated with particular characters, things, or ideas, known as **leit-motifs**. Based on a popular Romantic source—medieval Norse myths—the *Ring* also reflected Wagner's belief that opera should be moral. In its totality the *Ring* cycle warns against overweening ambition, its plot relating a titanic struggle for world mastery in which both human beings and gods are destroyed because of their lust for power. Wagner may have been addressing this warning to the Faustian spirit that dominated capitalism in the industrial age—a message that went unheeded.

Another German, Johannes Brahms (1833–1897), dominated orchestral and chamber music after 1850 in much the same way that Wagner did opera. Unlike Wagner, Brahms was no musical innovator. A classical Romanticist, he took up the mantle vacated by Beethoven, and he admired the Baroque works of Bach. In Vienna, his adopted home, Brahms became the hero of the traditionalists who opposed the new music of Wagner. Neglecting the characteristic Romantic works of operas and program music, he won fame with his symphonies and chamber music. His individual sound is mellow, always harmonic, delighting equally in joy and melancholy.

Despite his conservative musicianship, Brahms's work incorporates many Romantic elements. Continuing the art-song tradition established by Schubert (see Chapter 17), he introduced folk melodies into his pieces. In his instrumental works he often aimed for the expressiveness of the human voice, the "singing" style preferred in Romanticism. He was also indebted to the Romantic style for the length of his symphonies, the use of rhythmic variations in all of his works, and, above all, the rich lyricism and songfulness of his music.

Despite the dominance of Classical musical forms, this period was the zenith of Romantic *lieder,* or art songs. The continuing popularity of *lieder* reflected bourgeois taste and power, since amateur performances of these songs were a staple of home entertainment for the well-to-do, especially in Germany and Austria. In the generation after Schubert, the best composer of *lieder* was the German Robert Schumann (1810–1856), a pianist who shifted to music journalism and composition when his right hand became crippled in 1832. Splendid fusions of words and music, his songs function as duets for voice and piano with the piano providing a rich environment in which the voice can come and go at will.

Schumann's *lieder* are often part of song cycles held together with unifying themes. One of his best known song cycles is *Dichterliebe* (*A Poet's Love*) (1840), set to verses by Heinrich Heine (1797–1856), Germany's preeminent lyric poet. This song cycle superbly illustrates the Romantic preoccupation with program music. For instance, the song *Im Wunderschönen Monat Mai* (*In the Marvelously Beautiful Month of May*) conveys the longing of Heine's text through ascending lines of melody and an unresolved climax. The passion in this song cycle was inspired by Schumann's marriage to Clara Wieck (1819–1896), a piano virtuoso and composer in her own right.

The Legacy of the Bourgeois Age

We in the modern world still live in the shadow of the bourgeois age. From this period come the political consequences caused by the unification of Germany in 1871, which upset the balance of power on the Continent, unleashed German militarism, and led to smoldering French resentment at Germany. The two world wars of the twentieth century had their seeds in these events. On the intellectual front this period gave birth to Marx's analysis of history, Darwin's theory of evolution, and Pasteur's work in immunology and microbiology. With liberalism in the ascendant, the middle-class values of hard work, thrift, ambition, and respectability became paramount, as did the notion that the individual should take precedence over the group.

On the artistic level this period introduced the camera and the art of photography, revived Gothic architecture, made Realism the reigning style, and inaugurated the high-tech tradition in art and architecture with London's Crystal Palace. Perhaps the most far-reaching development during this time was Manet's adoption of the artistic credo of "art for art's sake," a bold move followed by other artists in the post-1871 period.

KEY CULTURAL TERMS

Utilitarianism	*aria*
socialism	*recitative*
higher criticism	*libretto*
evolution	*music drama*
Realism	leitmotif

SUGGESTIONS FOR FURTHER READING

PRIMARY SOURCES

BALZAC, H. DE. *Cousin Bette.* Translated by M. A. Crawford. New York: Penguin, 1972. A representative novel from the *Human Comedy* series, Balzac's monumental commentary on French bourgeois society in the post-Napoleonic era.

———. *Père Goriot.* Translated by J. M. Sedgwick. New York: Dodd, Mead, 1954. Another of the best-known of Balzac's almost one hundred novels in the Human Comedy series.

BRONTË, C. *Jane Eyre*. Edited and with an introduction by M. Smith. London: Oxford University Press, 1973. A classic of Romanticism, this novel deals with a theme dear to the hearts of nineteenth-century women readers, the life and tribulations of a governess.

BRONTË, E. *Wuthering Heights*. Edited and with an introduction by I. Jack. New York: Oxford University Press, 1983. A classic of Romanticism, this novel recounts the doomed affair of the socially mismatched but passionate soulmates Heathcliff and Catherine.

DICKENS, C. *Hard Times*. London: Methuen, 1987. A depiction of life in the new industrialized cities, this grim tale of forced marriage and its consequences reveals what happens when practical, utilitarian thinking replaces human values.

———. *Oliver Twist*. London: Longman, 1984. Dickens's moving tale of the orphan Oliver and his experiences among London's poor in the sordid conditions of the 1830s.

DOSTOEVSKY, F. *Crime and Punishment*. Translated by S. Monas. New York: New American Library, 1980. A masterpiece of psychological insight, this gripping tale of murder explores the themes of suffering, guilt, redemption, and the limits of individual freedom.

———. *The Brothers Karamazov*. Translated by D. Magarshack. New York: Penguin, 1982. In his novel Dostoevsky deals with broad metaphysical and psychological themes, such as the right of human beings to reject the world made by God because it contains so much evil and suffering, as dramatized through the actions and personalities of the brothers and their father.

ELIOT, G. *Middlemarch*. New York: Penguin, 1965. This classic of Realist fiction explores the psychology and growth in self-understanding of the principal characters.

FLAUBERT, G. *Madame Bovary*. Translated by A. Russell. New York: Penguin, 1961. One of the first Realist novels, and possibly the finest, Flaubert's work details the heroine's futile attempts to find happiness in a stifling bourgeois environment.

GASKELL, E. C. *North and South*. New York: Dutton, 1975. A portrait of economic and social disparities in mid-nineteenth-century England.

HUGO, V. *Les Misérables*. Translated by L. Wraxall. New York: Heritage Press, 1938. A good English version of Hugo's epic-length novel of social injustice in early nineteenth-century France.

MARX, K., and ENGELS, F. *Basic Writings on Politics and Philosophy*. Edited by L. Feuer. Boston: Peter Smith, 1975. A representative selection of their prodigious writings, which challenged industrial capitalism in the mid–nineteenth century and provided the theoretical basis for socialism and communism.

MILL, J. S. *On Liberty*. New York: Norton, 1975. Mill's examination of the relationship between the individual and society.

———. *Utilitarianism*. Indianapolis, Ind.: Hackett, 1978. A defense of the belief that the proper goal of government is to provide the greatest happiness for the greatest number.

TOLSTOY, L. *War and Peace*. Translated by L. and A. Maude. London: Oxford University Press, 1984. Tolstoy's epic novel traces the impact of the Napoleonic wars on the lives of his Russian characters and explores such themes as the role of individual human beings in the flow of history.

SUGGESTIONS FOR LISTENING

BRAHMS, JOHANNES (1833–1897).
Brahms's four symphonies (1876, 1877, 1883, and 1885) demonstrate the disciplined style and majestic lyricism that made him the leader of the anti-Wagner school. Brahms also excelled in chamber music, a genre usually ignored by Romantic composers. His chamber works show him to be a worthy successor to Beethoven, especially in the Piano Quartet in G minor, Op. 25 (late 1850s), the Clarinet Quintet in B minor, Op. 115 (1891), and three string quartets, composed between 1873 and 1876.

SCHUMANN, ROBERT (1810–1856).
Continuing the art song tradition perfected by Schubert, Schumann composed song cycles such as *Dichterliebe* (*A Poet's Love*) (1840) and *Frauenliebe und -leben* (*A Woman's Love and Life*) (1840), both filled with heartfelt passion and set to verses by Romantic poets. Schumann also had much success with his works for solo piano, including the delightful *Kinderszenen* (*Scenes from Childhood*) (1839), which he called ''reminiscences of a grown-up for grown-ups.'' Unlike the *lieder* and piano music, Schumann's other works are often neglected today, such as his four symphonies (1841, 1845–1846, 1850, 1851), two choral offerings (*Das Paradies und die Peri* (*Paradise and the Peri*) (1843) and *Der Rose Pilgefahrt* (*The Pilgrimage of the Rose*) (1851), incidental music for the stage (Byron's *Manfred*), and assorted chamber works.

VERDI, GIUSEPPE (1813–1901).
Primarily a composer of opera, Verdi worked exclusively in the Romantic tradition, bringing to perfection the style of opera that alternated arias and recitatives. His operatic subjects are based mainly on works by Romantic authors, such as *Il Corsaro* (*The Corsair*) (1848), adapted from Lord Byron, and *La Traviata* (*The Lost One*) (1853), adapted from Alexandre Dumas the younger. Shakespeare, whom the Romantics revered as a consummate genius, inspired the librettos for *Otello* (1887) and *Falstaff* (1893). Like the Romantics generally, Verdi had strong nationalistic feelings that he expressed in, for example, *Les Vêpres Siciliennes* (*The Sicilian Vespers*) (1855) and *La Battaglia di Legnano* (*The Battle of Legnano*) (1849).

WAGNER, RICHARD (1813–1883).
Wagner created a new form, music drama, that fused all the arts—a development that reflected his theory that music should serve the theater. His early style may be heard in *Der Fliegende Holländer* (*The Flying Dutchman*) (1842), which alternates arias and recitatives in the traditional way. By 1850, in *Lohengrin,* he was moving toward a more comprehensive operatic style, using continuously flowing music and the technique of recurring themes, called *leitmotifs*. He reached his maturity with *Der Ring des Nibelungen* (*The Ring of the Nibelung*), written between 1853 and 1874; in this cycle of four operas he focuses on the orchestral web with the arias being simply one factor in the constantly shifting sounds. His works composed after 1853 pushed the limits of Classical tonality and became the starting point for modern music.

19

THE AGE OF
EARLY MODERNISM
1871–1914

Between 1871 and 1914, the European continent enjoyed an almost unprecedented period of tranquility, completely free of military conflict. Many people thought that Europe had entered the new age predicted by the optimistic Enlightenment thinkers—a halcyon period in which war was no longer used as an instrument of national policy. But hindsight allows us to see this period as an age of rampant nationalism, aggressive imperialism, and burgeoning militarism, culminating with the outbreak of World War I in 1914. The prolonged and violent nature of that global struggle put to rest forever the unclouded optimism of prewar Europe.

At the same time the phenomenon known as "modern life" was emerging—the comfortable existence shared by an ever-growing proportion of society. Modern life evolved as people shared in the fruits of the Second Industrial Revolution and in the benefits of citizenship in strong nation-states. And in the cultural realm the period witnessed the birth of *Modernism*, a movement that rejected both the Greco-Roman and the Judeo-Christian legacies and tried to forge a new perspective, a vision of life true to modern secular experience. Modernism lasted for about one hundred years, going through three distinct stages. During its first phase (1871–1914), which is treated in this chapter, artists, writers, and thinkers established the movement's principles. The

second phase, the zenith of Modernism (1914–1945), is the subject of Chapter 20; and the exhaustion and decline of the movement, the third phase (1945–1970), is covered in Chapter 21.

EUROPE'S RISE TO WORLD LEADERSHIP

The period between 1871 and 1914 was an age of stupendous change and stress stimulated by imperialism, nationalism, and militarism. Acting as a catalyst was the middle class, which controlled the states of central and western Europe (Figure 19.1). Less affected by these forces were the relatively unindustrialized countries of eastern Europe, still dominated by landed gentry, agrarian economies, and weak centralized governments.

Imperialism—the quest for colonies—began as a search for new markets and increased wealth. Success over less developed areas was virtually assured by the superiority of European technology, military might, and management skills. In short order, Europe became a world power encircling the globe with a network of interlocking political and economic interests. Ironically, the competitive spirit that world-power status produced divided Europe against itself, transforming most countries into massed armed camps. Combined with ever-growing feelings of nationalism, imperialistic and militaristic impulses created an atmosphere in which rival states seemed incapable of stopping the headlong rush to war.

◀ MARY CASSATT. *The Bath*. 1891. Soft-ground etching with aquatint and drypoint on paper. 12⅜ × 8⅞". National Museum of Women in the Arts, Washington, D.C.

FIGURE 19.1 CLAUDE MONET. *Rue Montorgueil, Decked Out With Flags, 1878.* 1878. Oil on canvas, 30 × 20½". Musée des Beaux Arts, Rouen, France. *This colorful depiction of a street festival by Monet, a founder of Impressionism, is a fitting symbol of the first stage of Modernism. Such public spectacles were now flourishing across Europe, as the masses rose from obscurity to high visibility in urban life. The French flags lining the streets, represented by Monet as bright spots of color, give evidence of the importance of nationalistic feelings during this period.*

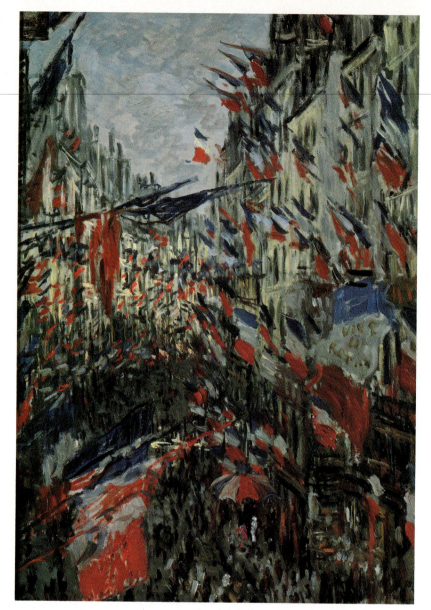

The Second Industrial Revolution and the Making of Modern Life

The Second Industrial Revolution differed in several major ways from its predecessor. For one thing, Great Britain, the world's industrial leader since 1760, now faced strong competition from Germany and the United States; factories even began to spring up in Russia and central and southern Europe. For another, science and research had a stronger influence than in the basically pragmatic first revolution. For example, scientific research into chemicals led to many new and improved industrial products, including fertilizers, synthetic dyes, soap, paper, and cheap steel. Finally, steam and water power gave way to newer forms of industrial energy. Electricity ran machines in factories, offices, and homes, and electric trains began to displace horse-drawn street-

cars in the cities. The internal combustion engine replaced the steam engine in ships and in the early 1900s gave birth to the automobile and the airplane. Oil began to be used as an energy source, though only later did it overcome coal's supremacy.

Technology, the practical offspring of science, was also busily reshaping the world. In communications, the wireless superseded the telegraph, the telephone made its debut, and national and international postal services were set up. Typewriters and tabulators made office and business practices more efficient. The rotary press enabled newspaper owners to print and sell thousands of copies of their papers per day to an increasingly literate public.

The Second Industrial Revolution affected almost every aspect of the economy. In transportation, more efficient steam engines meant lower transportation costs and cheaper products. Refrigeration techniques permitted perishable foods to be carried great distances without spoilage. Advertising became a significant source of revenue for publishers and at the same time a powerful force in the consumer economy. As a result of advertising, consumers were stimulated to buy household furnishings, ready-to-wear clothing, and prepared foods. Increased wealth meant more leisure, and new recreations cropped up, such as seaside resorts, music halls, movies, and bicycles—all contributing to the phenomenon known as modern life.

Industrialized cities with their promises of well-paying jobs, comfortable lives, and noisy entertainments were like magnets to the residents of small towns and farms, who flocked to the urban centers and cast off their rural ways. By 1900 nearly 30 per-

cent of the people in the West lived in cities (Figure 19.2).

As cities grew in industrialized countries, the standard of living improved, especially for the middle class. Much of this prosperity was attributable to a general decline in prices and to steady—albeit low—wages and salaries, thus benefiting consumers. The latter years of this period, from 1900 to the outbreak of World War I, constituted a golden age for the wealthy middle class, who led a leisured existence, pampered by hovering servants (Figure 19.3).

While the middle classes enjoyed unprecedented prosperity, misery mounted among urban workers despite the creation of state-funded social welfare programs. Urban slums grew more crowded and

FIGURE 19.2 CAMILLE PISSARRO. *The Great Bridge to Rouen.* 1896. Oil on canvas, 29³⁄₁₆ × 36½". Carnegie Museum of Art, Pittsburgh. Purchase. *Pissarro's painting captures the energy of Rouen and transforms this French river town into a symbol of the new industrial age. Contributing to the sense of vitality are the belching smokestack, the bridge crowded with hurrying people, and the dock workers busy with their machinery. The fast pace is underscored by the Impressionist technique of "broken color," giving an immediacy to the scene.*

FIGURE 19.3 CLEMENT FLOWER. *The Empire Promenade.* 1902. Radio Times Hulton Picture Gallery, London. *Early twentieth-century England was a time of elegant sophistication and glittering social gatherings for the upper classes. Evening performances at the theater were events where it was important to be seen with the right people, dressed in the latest fashions. This style of life was swept away by the Great War in 1914, though its memory survived as a reminder of a brilliant bygone age.*

living conditions worsened. The presence of squalor in the midst of plenty pricked the conscience of many citizens, who began to work for better housing and less dangerous working conditions for laborers. When these reforming efforts proved inadequate, the stage was set for the birth of labor unions and their best weapon, the strike.

One of the reforms directed to the working class did succeed in a spectacular fashion: the founding of secular public education. Inspired by the liberal belief that religion was a private matter, reformers wanted to take education out of the hands of the church. They argued that public schools, financed by taxes and supervised by state agencies, would prepare workers for jobs in industrialized society and create an informed citizenry—two basic needs of modern life. Although the pattern was uneven, every Western country made some effort to spread literacy to the masses. An unanticipated result of the establishment of public school systems was that age-old ties between children and parents were loosened. Families were still expected to foster social and moral values, but in certain areas of their lives children became wards of the state.

FIGURE 19.4 EYRE CROWE. *The Dinner Hour at Wigan.* 1874. Oil on canvas, 30 × 42¼". Manchester City Art Gallery, Manchester, England. *Social possibilities for English women opened up to some degree during this era. This painting depicts a factory scene in which the young female workers gain a brief respite from their tasks. A few talk together quietly, while others remain apart or finish a chore. They all seem dwarfed by the huge mill in the background, a towering symbol of industrial power.*

The position of women also changed dramatically. New employment opportunities opened up for them in teaching, nursing, business offices, and retailing. Since some of these jobs required special skills, colleges and degree programs were developed to teach them to women. Many young females still turned to domestic service, but new household appliances reduced the need for servants. Female labor in factories was now regulated by state laws, but the wives of small shopkeepers continued to work long hours in family businesses (Figure 19.4).

A small number of women reformers, primarily from the middle class, advocated more freedom for females, continuing a tradition that had begun on a limited scale prior to 1871. These reformers launched successful campaigns to revise property and divorce laws, giving women greater control over their wealth and their lives. In several countries they founded suffrage movements, using protests and marches to dramatize their situation. Following a vigorous, occasionally violent, campaign, women won the right to vote in Great Britain in 1918 and in the United States in 1920.

Response to Industrialism:
Politics and Crises

With the dawn of the age of Early Modernism, liberalism was in retreat in industrialized countries, its assumptions challenged from many quarters. Except in Britain and the United States, liberals were under siege in national legislatures both by socialists—who wanted more central planning and more state services for the workers—and by conservatives—who feared the masses and supported militant nationalism as a way to unify their societies. After 1900 political parties representing workers and trade unionists further threatened the liberals' hold on power. Although never actually ruling, these workingmen's parties were strong enough to pass laws aimed at correcting the worst social problems of industrialism.

Most embarrassing of all—to liberals, at any rate—events seemed to discredit liberal theory. Theoretically, under free trade the population ought to decline or at least remain stable, and the economy ought to operate harmoniously, but neither happened. Population was surging and industrial capitalism was plagued by repeated uncertainty. Many observers therefore concluded that the so-called laws of liberal economics did not work.

Domestic Policies in the Heavily Industrialized West
Whether they relied on liberal principles or not, Germany, France, Great Britain, and the United States all faced serious domestic crises during this period. Founded in 1871, the German Reich, or Empire, moved toward unity under the astute leadership of its first chancellor, Otto von Bismarck, and the new kaiser, or emperor, William I (1871–1888), former King of Prussia (Figure 19.5). Despite the illusion of parliamentary rule, foreign affairs and military policy were under the control of the chancellor, his ministers, and the kaiser. Many of the ruling elite were Prussian *Junkers*, owners of vast estates who clung to the old ways, and they set the tone of the imperial reich: conservative, militaristic, and nationalistic.

FIGURE 19.5 ANTON VON WERNER. *The Proclamation of the King of Prussia as German Emperor at Versailles.* 1871. Oil on canvas. National Portrait Gallery, London. *This painting commemorates the moment when the German Empire was proclaimed and King William of Prussia became its first emperor. Von Werner uses reflections from Versailles' famed Hall of Mirrors to make the stirring scene more theatrical, and added drama comes from the raised swords of the officers. The strong presence of the army was prophetic of the dominant role the military was destined to play in the German Empire.*

FIGURE 19.6 EDGAR DEGAS. *The Cotton Bureau in New Orleans.* 1873. Oil on canvas, 29⅛ × 36¼". Musée des Beaux-Arts, Pau, France. *By the third quarter of the nineteenth century the United States was offering challenges to English supremacy in world trade. The French painter Degas must have observed this scene—the interior of a cotton exchange in New Orleans—while visiting relatives in Louisiana. Whether consciously or not, Degas accurately depicted the social realities of this bourgeois work space: the capitalist idlers reading a newspaper, examining a cotton tuft, and lounging against a wall and, in contrast, the paid employees intent on their work.*

In France, the Third Republic was founded after the Second Empire's humiliating defeat by Germany in 1871. The government had made a remarkable recovery by 1875, although it remained hopelessly divided. The ceaseless struggle between republicans and monarchists was reflected in the regime's many prime ministers and coalition cabinets. Regardless of their politics, however, the republic's leaders initiated laws to correct the most glaring social injustices in order to counteract the rise of workers' political parties, the spread of socialism, and the threat of syndicalism—a movement whose central belief was that a general strike would bring down the capitalist state and lead to a more just form of government.

Yet the workers' complaints, as well as other groups' demands, never seemed to be adequately addressed, and the specter of Napoleon or some other "man on horseback" haunted the Third Republic throughout its days. The nation's liberal center gradually evaporated, creating bitter deadlocks between socialists and conservatives that no government could resolve.

In contrast to the relative failures of the German Reich and France's Third Republic, Great Britain was remarkably successful in solving its domestic problems during this period. Controlled by political parties that represented the upper and middle classes, the British government passed social legislation that improved the working and living conditions of many poor families and created opportunities for mobility through a state secondary-school system. As in Germany and France, these reform efforts did not prevent workers from forming their own political party. British workers joined with the Fabians, a group of intellectuals who believed in evolutionary socialism, to found the Labour party. Not until after World War I, however, did Britain see its first Labour government.

Across the Atlantic, the United States began to challenge British industrial supremacy. America's rapidly expanding economy allowed big business to dominate politics at all levels until the reform movements of the early 1900s (Figure 19.6). These movements, spurred by America's democratic tradition, temporarily derailed the power of the large business conglomerations called trusts.

Another major development in America at this time was an enormous increase in population from overseas. In the last decades of the nineteenth century, Europeans came to America in the largest migration of human population ever recorded. These newcomers—after painful adjustments, particularly in the crowded slums of the eastern cities—gradually entered the mainstream of American life. Largely from eastern and central Europe, they transformed the United States into a much richer ethnic society than it had been before, making powerful contributions to the culture both as groups and individuals.

Domestic Policies in Central and Eastern Europe The less industrialized states of central, southern, and eastern Europe faced problems even more difficult than those arising in Germany, France, and England. As the factory system made inroads into the region, these countries had no well-developed political and economic traditions for solving the resulting problems. Italy's response to industrialism was dictated by powerful regional interests that proved stronger than the unity the Italian kingdom had achieved at its founding in 1871. Led by weak prime ministers, the government allowed the northern areas to become industrialized, while the southern parts, including Sicily, remained in a semifeudal condition. As a result, the north, driven by an expanding middle class, moved far ahead of the agrarian south, with its vast estates worked by peasant labor.

In the Austro-Hungarian Empire the government's major problem was ethnic unrest, a direct outgrowth of the denial of political freedom to Slavic minorities, notably the Czechs and the Slovaks. In 1867 in the compromise that had created the Dual Monarchy, the Austrian Germans had given political parity to the Hungarians, allowing them free rein within their land. But nothing was done to address the simmering discontent among the Slavs. Even while the Dual Monarchy seethed with ethnic violence, however, its capital, Vienna, became a glittering symbol of Modernism. From *fin-de-siècle* ("end-of-the-century") Vienna came such familiar features of today's world as the cultural style called Expressionism and the psychology of Sigmund Freud.

Farther east, the Russian Empire slowly entered the industrial age, hampered by its vast size and its sluggish agrarian economy. Adding to Russia's woes were violent revolutionaries who despaired of any reform in this autocratic society. In 1881 an anarchist assassinated the liberal Czar Alexander II; his successor, Alexander III (1881–1894), was a tyrant who dismantled his predecessor's reforms. Under Nicholas II (1894–1917) the economy worsened and the imperial ministers grew more reactionary. Political parties were banned, and budding representative institutions ceased to exist. In 1905 Japan's defeat of Russia in the brief Russo-Japanese War (1904–1905), setting off a short-lived revolution led by underpaid factory workers and starving peasants. By promising relief the czar weathered the storm, but few of his pledges were fulfilled. Tensions mounted as the state violently repressed dissent, and the imperial court grew dangerously isolated.

Imperialism and International Relations

In 1871 most European nations believed that colonial matters were secondary to domestic issues and that internal law and order was the first priority. By 1914, these beliefs had been reversed. Domestic politics were no longer primary, and national interests tended to be calculated in terms of each state's role in the global economy and in foreign affairs.

The Scramble for Colonies Prior to 1875 the common wisdom was that a colony was a mixed blessing to a modern state. Although it was recognized that an overseas holding could be beneficial (by serving as a naval fueling station, for example), most authorities believed that a colony was a drain on the mother state's purse. Even Great Britain, the leading imperial power of the mid–nineteenth century, shared this ambivalence.

After 1875, however, Western thinking about colonies abruptly changed. Europe's industrialized states began to compete for colonies and for trade rights around the world. In order to maintain a high standard of living at home, they had to find new markets, underdeveloped areas in which to invest capital, and cheap sources of raw materials.

Given these needs, the continent of Africa was an imperialist's dream. The European states carved up

MAP 19.1

Imperialism in Africa: Colonial States, 1914

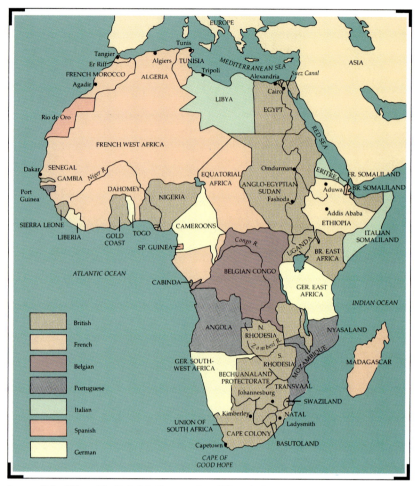

Source: Felix Gilbert, *The End of the European Era, 1890 to the Present.*
New York: Norton, 1970, p. 23.

this product-rich continent, redrawing its map and sharing the spoils. France and Britain got the lion's share, with Germany and Italy receiving the more barren, less commercially desirable areas (Map 19.1).

In the Far East, imperialists competed for colonies mainly in two areas: the islands of the South Pacific, and China. A special feature of this rivalry was that the Europeans were now joined by the United States (successor to Spain's empire after winning the Spanish-American War in 1899) and Japan (the leading power in the Far East after military victories over China in 1895 and Russia in 1905) (Map 19.2).

Imperialism fomented many crises, particularly in Africa, but no major conflict occurred. By 1900 many Europeans took it as self-evident that war was a thing of the past. The few struggles that did break out were brief and involved only a handful of states in out-of-the-way places. In this tranquil climate,

people began to believe that peace depended on the secret alliances constructed by the major powers. These diplomatic pacts, reinforced by strong armies and navies, had originated after the Franco-Prussian War. By the end of this period, Europe was divided into two armed camps—France, Great Britain, and Russia (called the Triple Entente) against Germany, Austria-Hungary, and Italy (known as the Triple Alliance) (Map 19.3).

The Outbreak of World War I   In July 1914, however, an incident took place for which diplomacy had no peaceful remedy: the assassination of the heir to the Austro-Hungarian throne, Archduke Francis Ferdinand. With this act the stage was set for a showdown among the states that had been at odds for decades. The Austrians were convinced that Serbia, a Balkan state and ally of Russia, was behind the murder of the

MAP 19.2

Imperialism in Asia: Colonial States, 1914

Source: Felix Gilbert, *The End of the European Era, 1890 to the Present.*
New York: Norton, 1970, pp. 24–25.

crown prince. They demanded a full apology and punishment of the guilty parties. Serbia's reply proved unsatisfactory, and Austria declared war.

Austria's action set in motion the mobilization plans required by the alliance system. Frantic efforts to restore peace failed. By August 4, 1914, Russia, France, and Britain were fighting Germany and Austria-Hungary while Italy watched from the sidelines. Modern life—symbolized by huge armies, military technology, and industrial might—had plunged Europe, and, later, much of the world, into the bloodiest war that civilization had yet witnessed.

EARLY MODERNISM

As previously noted, the dawn of the age of Modernism saw a widespread belief that the human race had turned a corner, that a golden era was about to begin. This sanguine outlook was fueled by the spread of self-government, new technology, and advances in science that held the promise of unlimited moral and material progress for humanity. As a result, there was everywhere a passion for novelty, a desire to cast off the dead hand of the past.

MAP 19.3
Europe on the Eve of World War I

Philosophy and Psychology

Toward the end of the nineteenth century, new directions in philosophy and psychology reshaped

At the same time, however, a mood of uncertainty began to creep into the Modernist vocabulary and undercut the optimism. A few artists and thinkers, for whom rebellion was a primary response to the world, had doubts about many traditional features of Western civilization, including its ethics, religion, customs, and most deeply held beliefs. They expressed their cultural doubts and fears in many ways, but chiefly through constant experimentation, through a desire to return to aesthetic fundamentals, and, especially among the painters, through a belief that the art process itself was more valuable than the completed work. As the pace of events accelerated in every area of life, a vigorous **avant-garde**, or vanguard of writers, artists, and intellectuals, pushed Western culture toward an elusive, uncertain future (Figure 19.7).

these intellectual disciplines and fostered the shift to Modernism. These German-inspired ideas undercut cherished Western beliefs that dated from the Enlightenment—ideas about human rationality, universal moral order, and personal freedom. The creators of these seminal innovations were the philosopher Friedrich Nietzsche and the psychologists Sigmund Freud and Carl Jung.

Friedrich Nietzsche [NEE-chuh] (1844–1900) was a prophet of Modernism who was notorious for his corrosive thought. He saw beyond the optimism of his times and correctly predicted the general disasters, both moral and material, that would afflict Western culture in the twentieth century. To him the philosophies of the past were all false because they were built on nonexistent absolute principles. Denying moral certainty, Nietzsche asserted that he was the philosopher of the "perhaps," deliberately cultivating ambiguity. Nietzsche vehemently rejected middle-class and Judeo-Christian ideals, identifying them with "herd" or "slave" values. For the same reason he heaped scorn on many of the "isms" of his day—liberalism, socialism, and Marxism—

FIGURE 19.7 UMBERTO BOCCIONI. *Unique Forms of Continuity in Space.* 1913. Bronze (cast 1931), 43⅞ × 34⅞ × 15¾". Collection, The Museum of Modern Art, New York. Acquired through the Lillie P. Bliss Bequest. *"No more masterpieces!" With this battle cry, the Futurists—an Italian-based literary and artistic movement that typified Early Modernism's rejection of the past—set out to create a new concept of art. The Futurists called for the destruction of existing art forms and of museums and libraries. The streamlined sculptures of Umberto Boccioni are the most striking works of this school. In this striding bronze figure, Boccioni distorts form and space to create an airstreamed image of speed, the new modern icon.*

claiming that they appealed to humanity's lowest common denominator and were thus destroying Western civilization.

Nevertheless, there were affirmative, positive aspects to Nietzsche's thought. He believed in a new morality that glorified human life, creativity, and personal heroism. He forecast the appearance of a few *Übermenschen,* or supermen, who had the "will to power," the primeval urge to live beyond the herd and its debased values. He praised these supermen for living "beyond good and evil," for refusing to be bound by society's rules and mores.

Virtually unknown when he died, Nietzsche became one of the giants of twentieth-century thought. His radical thinking—notably in affirming that civilization itself is nothing more than a human invention—has touched nearly every phase of modern thought, including religion, philosophy, literary criticism, and psychology. An extreme individualist, he was contemptuous of the strong German state, though the Nazis in the 1930s used his writings to justify their theory of Aryan supremacy. His glorification of individualism was also a powerful stimulus to many artists, writers, and musicians.

Rather than making a blanket condemnation of much of human morality and behavior, Sigmund Freud [FROID] (1856–1939) offered an approach to human psychology that could be used for further explorations into the study of the self. Part of the highly influential group of intellectuals and artists who flourished in Vienna around 1900, Freud was a neurologist who broke new ground, turned over established ideas, and invented a new way of thinking about human nature that profoundly affected Western society.

Freud's analysis of the human mind challenged the Enlightenment's belief that human beings are fully rational. Freud argued that the human personality was the product of an intense internal struggle between instinctual drives and social reality. According to Freud, each psyche, or self, is composed of an *id,* a *superego,* and an *ego.* The id is the source of primitive, instinctual drives and desires, notably sex and aggression. The superego corresponds to the will of society internalized as the conscience. The ego represents the conscious public face that emerges from the conflict between the inborn instincts and the conscience and acts as the balancing component that establishes inner resolutions. In Freud's view, a true, lasting equilibrium among the three components of the psyche could not be reached; the internal struggle was constant and inescapable. Those in whom the imbalance was pronounced would suffer varying degrees of mental illness, ranging from mild neurosis to extreme psychosis. Even though Freud's theory tends toward determinism, he held out hope for human freedom. For those prepared to accept their inescapable limitations, he believed that the truth about the human condition would liberate them from damaging habits of thought and enable them to function as morally free individuals.

Freud's greatest achievement was the founding of psychoanalysis, a type of therapy dedicated to the principle that once the roots of neurotic behavior are unraveled, a patient can lead a freer, healthier life. As part of treatment he devised the "free association" method whereby his patients were asked to

TIME LINE 19.1   EARLY MODERNISM

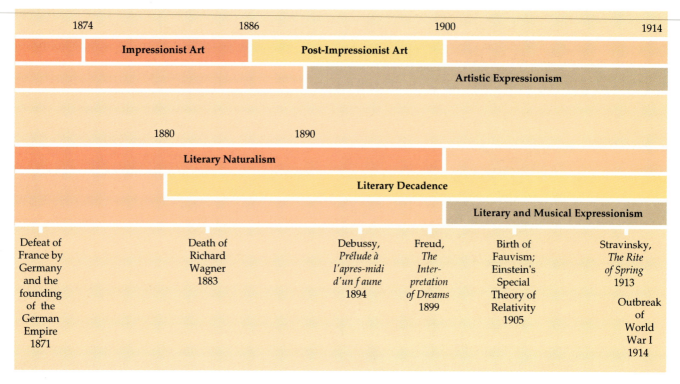

say, spontaneously and without inhibition, whatever came into their minds—memories, random observations, anything at all—and thus uncover traumas buried in their unconscious. He also studied his patients' dreams, which he thought were forms of wish fulfillment, a theory he set forth in *The Interpretation of Dreams* (1899). Discoveries made in his own self-analysis taught him to explore patients' early sexual histories and memories. In a related development, his psychoanalytic work led him to believe in infantile sexuality, the notion that children even at birth have erotic urges. Freud's theory of infantile sexuality caused shock waves in his era, but today it is an accepted principle of psychology.

A challenge was made to Freud's views by a former associate, the Swiss psychologist Carl Jung [YOONG] (1875–1961). Jung developed a theory of a universal, collective unconscious, shared by all humans, that exists in conjunction with each individual's own "personal" unconscious. Jung speculated that the secrets of the unconscious could be revealed by studying archetypes, ancient images that recur again and again in human experience and appear in dreams, myths, and folktales. His conception of archetypes opened a rich source of images and subjects for many Modernist artists and writers. Despite their differences, however, Freud and Jung agreed that the conscious mind is only a very small part of in-

dividual personality—a belief that is a cornerstone of Modernism.

Literature

Three overlapping and contradictory styles characterize the literature of Early Modernism: Naturalism, Decadence, and Expressionism. The first of these, *Naturalism*, was inspired by the methods of science and the insights of sociology to focus on such issues as working-class unrest and women's rights. Naturalistic writers strove for clinical objectivity and tended to see modern industrial society in a harsh light. *Decadent* writers rejected material values, scorned science, and were in flight from bourgeois society, which they identified with respectability and mediocrity.

Expressionism, the third of these styles, was built on the premise that bourgeois culture had robbed the traditional vocabulary of the arts of its capacity to express the truth and therefore new methods and forms of expression must be sought. To a greater or lesser degree, these three styles share a disdain for middle-class life and values (Time Line 19.1).

Naturalistic Literature   The founder and chief exponent of Naturalism was Émile Zola [ZOH-luh] (1840–

1902), the French writer whose fame rests on the *Rougon-Macquart* series (1870–1893), twenty novels depicting the history of a single family under France's Second Empire. The novels treat socially provocative themes such as prostitution (*Nana*, 1880) and the horrifying conditions in the coal-mining industry (*Germinal*, 1884). They offer a richly detailed portrait of French society in the mid–nineteenth century and also illustrate Zola's belief in biological determinism. Whether the novels' characters became prostitutes or virtuous housewives, family men or drunken suicides, Zola traces their ultimate fates to inborn dispositions. Nevertheless, Zola was no rigid fatalist. His novels convincingly portray people fervently trying to control their destinies in an uncaring universe.

Another outstanding Naturalist was the Norwegian dramatist Henrik Ibsen (1828–1906). An important playwright, Ibsen helped to establish the problem play as a staple of the modern theater and is its most eloquent practitioner. Ibsen lived mainly in Germany and Italy, writing plays about the middle-class Norwegian world he had fled, treating with frankness such previously taboo themes as venereal disease, suicide, and the decay of Christian values.

In *A Doll's House* (1879), Ibsen portrays a contemporary marriage, questioning the wife's subservient role. Perhaps because of its controversial ending—the wife leaves her husband, asserting that her duties to herself are more sacred than her duties to him—this play created a greater first impression than any other drama in the history of the theater. In Ibsen's play Nora is treated by her husband, Torvald, as a charming child whose sole purpose is to amuse him. When Nora borrows money to save Torvald's life, she deceives him about it because she knows how ''painful and humiliating'' it would be for him to know he owed her anything. But his reaction when he discovers it—condemning her bitterly and then forgiving her like a father—makes her realize she is living with a stranger. Faced with such lack of understanding, she deserts both husband and family, closing the door on bourgeois ''decency.'' Ibsen's play was an international success, and its liberated heroine became the symbol of the new woman of the late 1800s.

The major naturalistic writer from eastern Europe was the Russian Anton Chekhov [CHEK-ahf] (1860–1904), a physician turned playwright and short story writer, who found his subject in the suffocating life of Russia's small towns. He peopled his gently ironic plays with men and women in anguish over their ordinary lives, although his most arresting characters are those who endure disappointment without overt complaint. It is this latter quality that has made Chekhov's comedies, as these bittersweet plays are called, such favorites of both actors and audiences.

The Three Sisters (1901), a play that dramatizes the uneventful lives of a landowning family confined to the drab provinces, is characteristic of Chekhov's work. The characters conceal their depression behind false gaiety and self-deceit. His heroines, the three sisters, are bored, restless, and frustrated, not quite resigned to their mediocre existence. They talk constantly of a trip to Moscow, a journey longed for but never made. Today *The Three Sisters* and the rest of Chekhov's plays suggest the dying world of Russia's out-of-touch ruling class, who were about to be swept away by the Marxist revolution of 1917.

An important naturalistic writer in the United States was Kate Chopin (born Catherine O'Flaherty, 1851–1904), a short story writer and novelist whose fiction reflected the general trend in nineteenth-century American literature from romanticism and local color to realism and naturalism. A prevalent theme in Chopin's writings was a romantic awakening, usually by a female character; the setting for it was sketched out in *local color*, or regional details; and her method of tracking the action was naturalistic, that is, it based plot twists on biological and socioeconomic factors. A St. Louis native, Chopin focused her stories and novels on *Creole* and *Cajun* life in Louisiana, a world that caught her imagination during a twelve-year-long marriage to a Creole planter and merchant.

The Awakening (1899) was Kate Chopin's masterpiece and the novel that abruptly ended her literary career, as she was stunned into silence by a hostile public reaction. A tale of adulterous passion, this novel is an American Madame Bovary (see Chapter 18). The story of Edna Pontellier, the Kentucky-born wife of a Creole husband, *The Awakening* explores a woman's passionate nature and its relation to self, marriage, and society. Ruthlessly determined to go her own way, Edna rejects conventional morality, social duty, and personal obligations to her husband and children. Casting off the bonds of marriage and family, she establishes her own home, earns money with her painting, accepts one lover, and pursues another. Ultimately, however, Edna's bid for freedom fails. She drowns herself—brought down by tradition, prejudice, and other societal pressures. Chopin's ending has been criticized for its shift to commonplace morality, but the novel nevertheless is an early attempt to deal with the issue of woman's liberation. More than a simple naturalist, Chopin is hailed today as a precursor of Post-Modernism (see Chapter 21) with her keen interest in marginal people and feminist themes.

Decadence in Literature   The Decadent movement began in France with Joris-Karl Huysmans [we-SMAHNS] (1848–1907), a follower of Zola, who in 1884

FIGURE 19.8 AUBREY BEARDSLEY. *The Stomach Dance* from *Salome.* 1894. Pen drawing. Princeton University Library, Princeton, NJ. *The visual counterpart to Wilde's decadent style in literature was Art Nouveau, especially as practiced by Aubrey Beardsley. Typical of his work is this black-and-white illustration for Wilde's play-poem* Salomé; *in this print an evil musician plays for the dancing Salome before she commands the beheading of John the Baptist. Blending organic shapes and flowing lines with perverse themes, Beardsley's artificial style reveals Art Nouveau's affinity with an underworld of depravity.*

broke with the social-documentary style of Naturalism and wrote the perverse novel *À rebours* (*Against Nature*). Paris was astonished by this partly autobiographical work. In it Huysmans presents an exotic hero, Des Esseintes, bristling with vivid eccentricity and neurotic feelings and yet filled with inexpressible spiritual yearnings. Des Esseintes, hating modern life for its vulgarity and materialism, creates a completely encapsulated, silent world where he cultivates affected pleasures, particularly those that are out of fashion in respectable society. He collects plants whose very nature is to appear diseased. He stimulates his senses with unusual sounds, colors, and smells, orchestrating them to music so that he experiences a sensory overload. And, in a violent rejection of Classicism, he embraces the crude Latin works of late Rome.

In Great Britain Oscar Wilde (1854–1900) was the center of the 1890s Decadent movement, with its generally relaxed view of morals and cynically amused approach to life (Figure 19.8). Like Huysmans, Wilde's own outrageous manner can scarcely be separated from his literary achievements. Dressed in velvet and carrying a lily as he sauntered down London's main streets, Wilde gained notoriety as an *aesthete*—one unusually sensitive to the beautiful in art, music, and literature—even before he achieved fame as a dramatist of witty comedies of manners, such as *The Importance of Being Ernest* (1895). Wilde's only novel, *The Picture of Dorian Gray* (1894), features a hero immersed in exotic pleasures and secret vices, his youth preserved while his portrait ages horribly.

Today's most widely admired Decadent writer, the Frenchman Marcel Proust [PROOST] (1871–1922), made his appearance at the end of this period. Starting in 1913 and concluding in 1927, Proust published a series of seven autobiographical novels collectively entitled *A la recherche du temps perdu* (*Remembrance of Things Past*). In this massive undertaking he recreates the world of upper bourgeois society that he had known as a young man but had deserted in 1903. Withdrawn into a cork-lined retreat reminiscent of Des Esseintes's silent hideaway in *À rebours*, Proust resurrected in the pages of his novels the aristocratic salons, the vulgar bourgeois world, and the riffraff of mistresses, prostitutes, and rich homosexuals. Today Proust's novels may be read in contradictory ways, as the supreme expression of a life lived for art or as the exemplification of a life empty of spiritual meaning.

Expressionist Literature   Expressionism, the third of these styles, was the only one that did not originate in France, arising instead in Scandinavia in the works of the Swedish playwright August Strindberg and in central Europe in the fiction of Franz Kafka. Strindberg (1849–1912), having first achieved fame through Naturalistic drama, shifted to an Expressionist style in the 1890s. *The Dream Play* (first produced in 1907) is typical of his Expressionist dramas in employing generic figures with symbolic, all-purpose names ("Daughter," "Father," and so on), shadowy plots, and absurd fancies. In *The Dream Play* time and place became meaningless, as, for instance, when a lovesick soldier suddenly becomes old and shabby and his bouquet of flowers withers before the audience's eyes. Strindberg's innovative techniques were not meant to obscure his meaning but rather to initiate the public into new ways of seeing and understanding life.

The ultimate pioneer of Expressionism was Franz Kafka (1883–1924), whose strange, boldly symbolic stories invite the reader to question traditional concepts of reality. One of Kafka's most striking achievements is the short story *Metamorphosis* (1919), in which the hero awakens to discover that while asleep he has been transformed into a giant insect—a vivid image of an identity crisis and a gripping parable of what happens to a person who is suddenly perceived to be totally different from other people.

The Trial, a novel completed in 1914 and published in 1925, features a doomed main character with the generic name of Joseph K. An obscure minor government official, Joseph K. has his well-ordered world shattered when he is accused of a nameless crime. Unable to identify either his accusers or his misdeed and denied justice by the authorities, Joseph K. is finally executed by two bureaucrats in top hats. Kafka's faceless, powerless hero has become one of the most widely discussed figures of Modernism. In effect, Kafka has transformed his own alienation—as a German-speaking Jew from the Czech-speaking and Protestant section of predominantly Roman Catholic Austria—into a modern Everyman victimized by forces beyond human control (Figure 19.9).

The Advance of Science

The advance of science around the turn of the century was particularly strong in biology and chemistry. In biology, the Austrian monk Gregor Johann Mendel (1822–1884) had done groundbreaking research in 1865, but it was not until around 1900 that his discoveries were published, thus founding the new science of genetics. By applying mathematics to biological theory, Mendel proved the existence of dominant and recessive characters, and using the laws of probability he worked out the pattern for offspring over the generations. Mendelian laws were quickly applied to every kind of animal and plant.

In chemistry, the outstanding development was radiochemistry, the study of radioactive materials. The founder of this new discipline was Marie Sklodowska Curie (1867–1934), a Polish physicist and the first scientist to be awarded two Nobel prizes. Working with her French husband, Pierre Curie (1859–1906), in 1908 Madame Curie identified two new radioactive elements, polonium and radium. The isolation of radium stimulated research in atomic physics. Another contributor to radiochemistry was the German physicist Wilhelm Conrad Roentgen [RENT-guhn] (1845–1923) whose 1895 discovery of X rays led to their use in diagnostic medicine.

The discoveries in genetics and radiochemistry boosted the optimism and faith in progress that characterized this period, but developments in physics had the opposite effect, adding to the undercurrent of uncertainty and doubt that also existed. Three brilliant scientists—Max Planck, Niels Bohr, and Albert Einstein—launched a revolution that led other scientists to discard the previously accepted belief that Newton's laws of motion were universal and applied everywhere.

Max Planck (1858–1947) laid the foundation for modern physics in 1900 with research in quantum theory. His research called into question the wave theory of radiation, which dated from the 1700s. Working with hot objects, Planck observed that the radiative energy that emanated from a heat source did not issue in a smooth wave but in discrete bursts. He measured each burst of radiation and computed a mathematical formula for expressing the released energy, a unit that he called a *quantum*—a word meaning a specified amount, derived from the Latin *quantus*, or "how much." When Planck could not fit his quantum formula into wave-theory physics, he realized the revolutionary nature of his discovery. Planck's quantum theory became a primary building block in the speculation of the second of the trio, Danish physicist Niels Bohr.

Bohr (1885–1962) was the prime mover in solving the mystery of the structure of the atom. When he began his research, the ancient Greek idea of the indivisible atom had already been laid to rest. Scientists in the early 1900s had proved that each atom is a neutral body containing a positive nucleus with negatively charged particles called electrons. And one researcher had speculated that electrons orbit a nucleus in much the same way that the planets move around the sun—suggesting a correspondence with Newtonian theory.

Until Bohr's theory of atomic structure was set forth in 1912, however, no one could explain how these miniature solar systems actually worked. Bohr's solution was based on bold assumptions: that an electron could revolve about a nucleus only in certain privileged orbits and that when it was in these orbits it did not emit radiation. Moving from these assumptions, he concluded that an electron radiated only when it leaped from orbit to orbit. Using Planck's quantum theory, he called these leaps quantum jumps, referring to the amount of radiative energy released. Bohr's discovery had tremendous consequences, leading eventually to the development of nuclear energy for weaponry and electrical generation.

German-born Albert Einstein (1879–1955) also did important theoretical work in atomic physics, but his most significant research in the early twentieth century involved the relationship between time and space. Newton had maintained that there

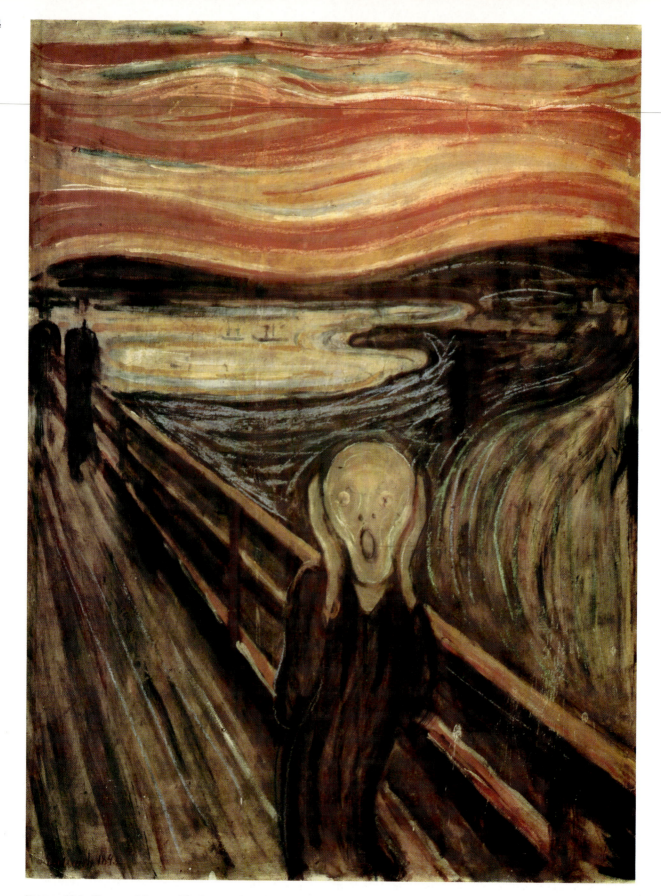

FIGURE 19.9 EDVARD MUNCH. *The Scream.* 1893. Oil on canvas, 36 × 29″. Nasjonalgalleriet, Oslo. *The Expressionists, whether writers, artists, or musicians, responded to the uncertainty of the modern world with images of despair, anxiety, and helplessness. The work of the Norwegian painter Edvard Munch provides a visual counterpart to the bleak and brooding plays of Strindberg and the terrifying stories of Kafka. Munch, whose paintings reflect a nightmarish vision of life as a tormented existence never free from pain, once said, ''I hear the scream in nature.''*

existed absolute rest and absolute velocity, absolute space and absolute time. Einstein asserted that the only absolute in the universe is the speed of light, which is the same for all observers. He concluded that all motion is relative and that concepts of absolute space and absolute time are meaningless. If two systems move with relatively uniform motion toward each other, there exist two different spaces and two different times. He called this finding the special theory of relativity. This theory replaces Newtonian absolute space with a grid of light beams that in effect determines the meaning of space in each situation. Einstein's special theory was the first step in a reformulation of scientific concepts of space and time.

The Modernist Revolution in Art

After 1871 a revolution began in the arts and architecture whose aim was to discredit Renaissance ideals and replace them with Modernist principles. Although there were many trends within this revolution, in painting and sculpture it generally meant a shift from an art that reflected the natural world to one rooted in the artist's inner vision, from an art based on representational or naturalistic images to one devoted to nonrepresentational or nonobjective forms, and from an art focused on content to one dedicated to the process of creation itself. By the time the revolution in painting and sculpture was complete, artists had given up realism and made **abstraction** their ideal. In architecture, the Modernist revolution was less radical, though architects slowly turned away from the forms of the Greco-Roman and Gothic styles and created functional buildings devoid of decoration.

Impressionism   The stylistic innovation in painting known as *Impressionism* began in the 1870s. In spite of owing much to Realism and even to Romanticism, this new style marked a genuine break with the realistic tradition that had dominated Western art since the fourteenth century. The Impressionists wanted to depict what they saw in nature, but they were inspired by the increasingly fast pace of modern life to portray fragmentary moments. They concentrated on the play of light over objects, people, and nature, breaking up seemingly solid surfaces, stressing vivid contrasts between colors in sunlight and shade, and depicting reflected light in all of its possibilities. Unlike earlier artists they did not want to observe the world from indoors. They abandoned the studio, painting in the open air and recording spontaneous impressions of their subjects instead of making outside sketches

and then moving indoors to complete the work from memory.

Some of the Impressionists' painting methods were affected or made possible by technological advances. For example, the shift from the studio to the open air was made possible in part by the advent of cheap rail travel, which permitted easy and quick access to the countryside or seashore, and second by newly discovered chemical dyes and oils that led to collapsible paint tubes, which enabled artists to finish their paintings on the spot.

Although Impressionism was both a reflection and an outgrowth of industrial society, it was at the same time indebted to the past. From Realism the Impressionist painters learned to find beauty in the everyday world. From the Barbizon painters (a group of French landscape painters active in the mid–nineteenth century) they took the practice of painting in the open air. From the Romantics they borrowed the techniques of "broken color"—splitting up complex colors into their basic hues—and of using subtle color shadings to create a shimmering surface effect.

Impressionism acquired its name not from supporters but from angry art lovers who felt threatened by the new painting. The term *Impressionism* was born in 1874, when a group of artists who had been meeting and working together for some time organized an exhibition of their paintings in order to draw public attention to their work. Reaction from the public and press was immediate, and derisive. Among the 165 paintings exhibited was one called *Impression: Sunrise,* by Claude Monet [moh-NAY] (1840–1926). Viewed through hostile eyes, Monet's painting of a rising sun over a misty, watery scene seemed messy, slapdash, and an affront to good taste. Borrowing Monet's title, art critics extended the term *Impressionism* to the entire exhibit. In response, Monet and his twenty-nine fellow artists in the exhibit adopted the name as a badge of their unity, despite individual differences. From then until 1886 Impressionism had all the zeal of a "church," as the painter Renoir put it. The Impressionists gave eight separate art shows. Monet was faithful to the Impressionist creed until his death, although many of the others moved on to new styles.

Argenteuil, a Seine river town west of Paris, was important in the development of this style. Monet lived there from 1871 to 1878, and two other Impressionists, Auguste Renoir and Alfred Sisley, spent time nearby. Originally a sleepy backwater, Argenteuil in these years was undergoing radical changes. Not only were factories being thrown up—twenty in the 1870s alone—but crowds of pleasure seekers found the town a convenient half-hour train ride from Paris. With few exceptions, Monet's

FIGURE 19.10 CLAUDE MONET. *Red Boats at Argenteuil.* 1875. Oil on canvas, 5' × 6'9". Louvre. *Monet's* Red Boats *illustrates the immediacy of Impressionism. With fresh eyes, the artist has transformed the substantial world of nature and its weighty human inhabitants into a constantly shifting, fragmented collection of daubs of broken color. As a result, everything in the painting, including the weathering boats, seems to be reduced to external appearances.*

FIGURE 19.11 CLAUDE MONET. *Water Lilies.* Ca. 1920. Oil on canvas, 16' × 5'15/16". Carnegie Museum of Art, Pittsburgh. Acquired through the generosity of Mrs. Alan M. Scaife. *Knowledgeable about the art market and determined to escape a life of poverty, Monet produced nonthreatening works that appealed to conservative middle-class collectors. For these patrons he painted natural scenes, such as water lilies, that evoked pleasant memories of simple rural values. Begun in 1899, the water lily series occupied him for the rest of his life. Setting up his easel in his splendid garden at Giverny and working at different times of the day, Monet captured the effect of changing sunlight on this beloved subject.*

Argenteuil canvases present a carefree world of river vistas, rocking sailboats, and idle gaiety. His *Red Boats at Argenteuil* is typical of this period (Figure 19.10). Streaks of broken color in the water simulate dancing light, and the varied red shadings applied to the hulls convey the sun's weathering effect on the wood. That these techniques succeed so well shows the harmony between his scientific eye and painterly hand. His studies of changing light and atmosphere, whether depicting haystacks, Rouen cathedral, or water lilies (Figure 19.11), demonstrate his lifelong devotion to Impressionism.

Unlike Monet, Auguste Renoir [REN-wahr] (1841–1919) did not remain faithful to the Impressionist movement. In the early 1880s personal and aesthetic motives led him to move away from Impressionism and exhibit in the official Salon (when

FIGURE 19.12 AUGUSTE RENOIR. *The Luncheon of the Boating Party.* 1881. Oil on canvas, 51 × 68". Phillips Collection, Washington, D.C. *Renoir's return to traditional values is reflected in this vivid painting. He uses the restaurant's terrace to establish conventional perspective, the left railing forming a diagonal line that runs into the distance. He balances the composition, weaving the young men and women into a harmonious ensemble, painting some standing and others sitting. He also employs colors effectively, using orange, blue, and black to offset the vast expanses of white in the tablecloth and the men's shirts and women's blouses.*

he could get his work accepted). In his modified style he shifted from a soft-focus image to a concentration on form, a move that brought quick support from art critics and wealthy patrons.

Painted around the time of his break with Impressionism, *The Luncheon of the Boating Party* demonstrates Renoir's splendid mastery of form (Figure 19.12). Its subject is a carefree summer outing on a restaurant terrace on an island in the Seine, the company being composed of the painter's friends, including fellow artists, a journalist, the cafe owner, and an actress. *The Boating Party* shows that Renoir had not given up—nor would he ever—his Impressionist ties, for his stress in this work on the fleeting, pleasure-filled moment was basic to the style, as was his use of broken color in a natural background. Nevertheless, what remained central to Renoir's creed were the foreground figures, treated clearly and with substance.

In contrast to Monet and Renoir, whose careers bloomed in poverty, Berthe Morisot [MAH-REE-ZOH] (1841–1895) was a member of the upper middle class. Her wealth and artistic connections—Fragonard was her grandfather and Manet her brother-in-law—allowed her to apply herself to painting and play an important role in the founding of the Impressionist school. In her work she focused on atmosphere and the play of light on the human form, although she never sacrificed her subjects to the cause of color alone. Her trademark became sensitive and warm scenes of middle-class mothers and daughters in gardens or close friends relaxing at the seashore (Figure 19.13).

A few Americans also made significant contributions to this style. The most important of them was Mary Cassatt [kuh-SAT] (1845–1926), a young woman who joined the Impressionist circle while

FIGURE 19.13 BERTHE MORISOT. *Girl in a Boat with Geese.* Ca. 1889. Oil on canvas, 25¾ × 21½". National Gallery of Art, Washington, D.C. Ailsa Mellon Bruce Collection. *A dedicated Impressionist, Morisot exhibited in most of the school's shows. Her canvases typically emphasize the flatness of the picture's plane, in contrast to the three-dimensionality of paintings like Renoir's* Luncheon of the Boating Party. *Lack of depth was a prime characteristic of the Modernist revolution in painting.*

FIGURE 19.14 MARY CASSATT. *The Bath.* 1891. Soft-ground etching with aquatint and drypoint on paper. 12⅜ × 8⅞". National Museum of Women in the Arts, Washington, D.C. Gift of Wallace and Wilhelmina Holladay. *This Cassatt print, in Japanese-inspired style, symbolizes the globalization of Western culture that was well under way in Early Modernism. The first of ten prints in a series, it is the only one that could be called a true imitation. It uses simple design, Japanese spatial pattern, flat areas of color, and a hint of Japanese facial features to create a Western version of a* ukiyo-e *print—except that it is made on a metal plate and not a woodblock. In the rest of this series Cassatt adopted a more Western style, notably adding a complete background, such as wallpaper and windows. Her interest in Japanese prints coincided with Gauguin's experiments (see Figure 19.17) with Tahitian-inspired art; both are forerunners of Post-Modernism.*

FIGURE 19.15 GEORGES SEURAT. *A Sunday Afternoon on the Island of La Grande Jatte.* 1884–1886. Oil on canvas, 6'9" × 10'1". Art Institute of Chicago. Helen Birch Bartlett Memorial Collection, 1926. *Unlike most Impressionists, Seurat worked slowly and methodically. In the case of* La Grande Jatte, *he spent years organizing the canvas and then painting the thousands of dots required by the Pointillist technique. Such painstaking attention to detail was necessary to achieve the harmonious effect his finished paintings demonstrate.*

studying painting in Paris. Cassatt was from a prosperous, well-connected Philadelphia family, and it is largely through her social ties that Impressionist painting was introduced to America. She suggested to her wealthy friends that this art was worth collecting, and some of the most notable Impressionist works in American museums are there because of her influence.

Cassatt, however, was not devoted exclusively to Impressionism. Like other artists of this era, she was fascinated by Japanese prints from French collections that were on exhibit in Paris in 1890, and she was the first to imitate all aspects, including color, of the **ukiyo-e** prints—the woodcuts which had developed in Japan in the 1600s—as in *The Bath*, or *The Tub* (about 1891; Figure 19.14). This genre scene depicting a mother and child was a typical subject in Cassatt's art.

Post-Impressionism   The rebellious, experimental spirit instilled by the Impressionists had freed art from the tyranny of a single style. Artists now moved in many directions, united only by a common desire to extend the boundaries of Impressionism. This ambition signified the triumph of the Modernist notion that art must constantly change in order to reflect new historical conditions—the opposite of the Classical ideal of eternal truths. Impressionism was succeeded by *Post-Impressionism* (1886–1900), whose four most important artists are Georges Seurat, Paul Cézanne, Paul Gauguin, and Vincent van Gogh.

Like the Impressionists, Georges Seurat [suh-RAH] (1859–1891) painted the ordinary pleasures of Parisian life in a sunlit atmosphere, but his way of doing so was formulaic and theoretical, markedly different from the approach of, say, Monet. After studying scientific color theory, Seurat developed a technique known as *Pointillism* (or Divisionism), which meant applying to the canvas thousands of tiny dots of pure color juxtaposed in such a way that, when viewed from the proper distance, they merged to form a natural, harmonious effect of color, light, and shade. His most famous Pointillist work is *A Sunday Afternoon on the Island of La Grande Jatte* (Figure 19.15), an affectionate, good-humored look at Parisians enjoying themselves. The technique may be novel and "scientific," but the composition is Classical and serene, with carefully placed and balanced figures and repeated curved shapes, visible in the umbrellas, hats, and other objects. Seurat's style led to a minor school of painters, but his influence was overshadowed by that of Cézanne.

Paul Cézanne [say-ZAN] (1839–1906), one of the pivotal figures in the history of Western art, was the prophet of abstraction in Post-Impressionism and a precursor of Cubism. With Édouard Manet, he is one of the founders of modern painting. He had exhibited with the original Impressionist group in 1874, but he had rejected the movement by 1878. He came to see the style as flawed because its depiction of nature lacked substance and weight, and he began a quest for a new way to portray nature so as to reveal its underlying solidity and order. After many experiments, Cézanne concluded that nature was composed of such geometric forms as cylinders, spheres, cubes, and cones. By trying to reveal this idea in his works, he opened up a new way of painting that has influenced art to the present day.

Cézanne's greatest works came after 1886, when he left Paris for his home in Aix-en-Provence in southern France in order to work in isolation. Among his favorite subjects was the nearby mountain, Mont Sainte-Victoire (Figure 19.16), which he painted many times. Like many of his later works, this painting points toward abstraction but never quite gives up representation. Amid the dense geometric forms in the picture's lower half, house shapes peek through daubs of green foliage, reminding the viewer that this is a realistic landscape. Later artists, like Kandin-sky and Malevich, took up Cézanne's challenge of telescoping the two-dimensional and the three-dimensional and created the first truly abstract paintings, the most visible signs of twentieth-century art (see Chapter 20).

The Post-Impressionist Paul Gauguin [GO-GAN] (1848–1903) began the movement known as *primitivism*—the term used to describe the West's fascination with non-Western culture as well as pre-Renaissance art. Gauguin's eccentric personal life also made him a legendary figure of Modernism. Rejecting the comforts of Parisian bourgeois life, he abandoned his career and his family and exiled himself to the French colony of Tahiti, living a decadent, bohemian existence.

Before moving to the South Pacific, Gauguin lived and painted among Breton peasants. He developed a personal style that favored flattened shapes and bright colors and avoided conventional perspective and modeling. He also became interested in non-Western, "primitive" religions, and many of his Tahitian works refer to indigenous beliefs and practices, as in *Manao Tupapau—The Spirit of the Dead Watching* (Figure 19.17). When exhibited in Paris, this painting created an uproar, for Western audiences were not accustomed to seeing dark-skinned nudes in art, and certainly not presented reclining on a bed as had been a custom for white-skinned subjects since the Renaissance (see Figure 16.6). Furthermore, the seated ghost at the left was a direct challenge to a secular world view. Today the shock caused by this and other paintings by Gauguin has subsided, and his role in art has been reevaluated.

FIGURE 19.16 PAUL CÉZANNE. *Mont Sainte-Victoire.* 1904–1906. Oil on canvas, 28⅞ × 36¼″. Philadelphia Museum of Art. George W. Elkins Collection. *Although Cézanne was the founder of the Post-Impressionist movement that culminated in abstraction, he had a conservative approach to art. He claimed that he wanted to create paintings that had the solidity of the art in the museums, especially the works of the seventeenth-century painter Nicolas Poussin. Hence Cézanne continued to rely on line and geometric arrangement as well as on color and light, simplifying his paintings into austere images of order and peaceful color.*

He is now honored for his introduction of other cultural traditions into Western art, which enriched its vocabulary, and for his expressive use of color.

With the Post-Impressionist Vincent van Gogh (1853–1890) the tradition of Expressionism begins to emerge in Western art, although he was not part of any of the various Expressionist schools of painters to be discussed later. "Expressionism" in his case meant that the work of art served as a vehicle for his private emotions to an unprecedented degree. Van Gogh sometimes allowed his moods to determine what colors to use and how to apply paint to canvas, a principle that led to a highly idiosyncratic style.

Van Gogh's life was filled with misfortune. Everything that this tormented Dutchman touched seemed to turn out badly except his painting, and even that had little recognition in his lifetime. In his early years he was rebuffed in his efforts to do missionary work among poverty-stricken Belgian coal miners. His attempts at friendship ended in failure, including a celebrated episode in the south of France with the painter Gauguin. Throughout his life overtures to women resulted in utter humiliation. In the end he became mentally unstable and committed suicide.

From his personal pain he created a memorably expressive style, however. Rejecting the smooth look

FIGURE 19.17 PAUL GAUGUIN. *Manao Tupapau—The Spirit of the Dead Watching.* 1892. Oil on burlap mounted on canvas, 28½ × 36⅜″. Albright-Knox Art Gallery, Buffalo. A. Conger Goodyear Collection, 1965. *Until recently, Gauguin's life was viewed as one of the supreme archetypes of Modernism: the artist who abandons family duty and middle-class morality in his quest for aesthetic and sexual freedom. But this version of Gauguin's experience has been revealed as a myth. According to the latest research, Tahiti was no hedonistic paradise; the islanders were severely puritanical about sex; and contacts with the West had transformed the local culture, beginning more than a century before the painter's arrival. Even Gauguin's years in the South Pacific were less than idyllic: He died a lingering death from syphilis, contracted from an island prostitute.*

FIGURE 19.18 VINCENT VAN GOGH. *Self-Portrait with a Gray Hat.* 1887. Oil on canvas, 17¼ × 14¾″. Vincent van Gogh Foundation/National Museum Vincent van Gogh, Amsterdam. *Van Gogh's self-absorption is reflected in the thirty-six self-portraits he painted during his eleven-year-long artistic career. Anguished and prone to mental breakdown, he must have found a measure of reassurance in recording the subtle changes in his own countenance. A constant in all of his likenesses is the haunted eyes, showing the inner torment from which he could never quite escape.*

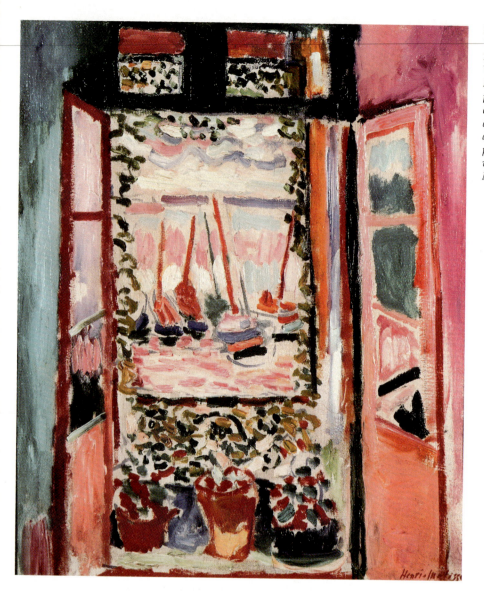

FIGURE 19.19 HENRI MATISSE. *Open Window, Collioure.* 1905. Oil on canvas, 21¾ × 18⅛". Courtesy Mrs. John Hay Whitney, New York. *Like van Gogh, Matisse resisted quiet surface effects, preferring the look of paint applied in thick daubs and strips of varying length. His dazzling optical art was created by his use and placement of vibrant colors. In this painting Matisse interprets the glorious view from his studio overlooking the Mediterranean.*

of traditional painting and stirred by the colorful canvases of the Impressionists, he sometimes applied raw pigments with his palette knife or fingers instead of with a brush. His slashing strokes and brilliant colors often mirrored his mental states, giving the viewer a glimpse into his volatile personality. For instance, his *Self-Portrait with a Gray Hat* is dominated by shades of blue, suggesting his profound melancholy (Figure 19.18). The anguish in his eyes is reinforced by the vortex of color framing the head and the deep facial lines. In a sense, van Gogh's works constitute his psychological signature, and his style is perhaps the most easily recognizable one in Western art.

Fauvism, Cubism, and Expressionism The preeminence of Paris as the fulcrum of Western culture was

enhanced by the arrival of Henri Matisse and Pablo Picasso in about 1900. These innovative and prolific artists emerged as the leaders of the pre–World War I generation, later dominating the art world of the twentieth century in much the same way as Ingres and Delacroix had in the nineteenth century.

Henri Matisse [ma-TEES] (1869–1954) rose to fame in 1905 as a leader of ***Fauvism***. The *Fauves*—French for "wild beasts," a name their detractors gave to them—were a group of loosely aligned painters who exhibited together. Matisse's work, like that of his colleagues, stemmed from the tradition of van Gogh, with color as its overriding concern. In *Open Window, Collioure* Matisse paints a kaleidoscope of colors—pinks, mauves, bluish greens, bright reds, oranges, and purples—that do not derive from the direct observation of nature but from the artist's belief that color harmonies can control the composition (Figure 19.19). The colors are "arbitrary" in the sense that they bear little reference to what one would actually see from the window, but they are far from arbitrary in their relation to one another—which is what interests Matisse.

Pablo Picasso [pi-KAHS-oh] (1881–1973), a talented young Spanish painter, was attracted to Paris's *avant-garde* art community about 1900. In 1907 he proved his genius with *Les Demoiselles d'Avignon* (*The Young Ladies of Avignon*), perhaps the most influential painting of the twentieth century. This revolutionary work moved painting close to abstraction— the realization of Cézanne's dream. An unfinished work, *Les Demoiselles* reflects the multiple influences operating on Picasso at the time—the primitivism of African masks, the geometric forms of Cézanne, and the ancient sculpture of pre-Roman Spain. Despite its radical methods, this painting still has a conventional composition: five figures with a still life in the foreground. Nevertheless, with this painting Picasso redirected objective art into channels that would ultimately move beyond abstraction and into the development of nonobjective painting—although not in the work of Picasso himself—thus overturning a standard founded in the Renaissance (Figure 19.20).

Les Demoiselles was the prelude to **Cubism**, one of the early twentieth-century styles leading Western art toward abstraction. With his French colleague Georges Braque [BRAHK] (1882–1963), Picasso developed Cubism. This style of painting, which went through different phases at the hands of different artists, basically fragments three-dimensional objects and reassembles them in a pattern that stresses their geometric structure and the relationships of these basic geometric forms. Braque and Picasso worked so closely together that their paintings could sometimes not be separately identified, even, it is said, by the artists themselves. An example of Picasso's Cubist style is *Pigeon with Baby Peas* (Figure

FIGURE 19.20   PABLO PICASSO. *Les Demoiselles d'Avignon. (The Young Ladies of Avignon.)* 1906–1907. Oil on canvas, 8′ × 7′8″. Collection, The Museum of Modern Art, New York. Acquired through the Lillie P. Bliss Bequest. *This painting's title derives from Picasso's native Barcelona, where Avignon Street ran through the red-light district. First intended as a moral work warning of the dangers of venereal disease (the figures still show provocative poses), the painting evolved over the months, changing as Picasso's horizons expanded. That he left the painting unfinished—like a scientist's record of a failed laboratory experiment— illustrates a leading trait of Modernism, the belief that truth is best expressed in the artistic process itself.*

FIGURE 19.21 PABLO PICASSO. *Pigeon with Baby Peas.* 1912. Oil on canvas, 25⅝ × 21¼". Musée d'Art Moderne de la Ville de Paris. Bequest of Dr. Maurice Girardin. *This painting's title, along with the undistorted word ''Cafe,'' suggest that Picasso's subject was his dinner. But content mattered little to him in this Cubist exercise with form. From now on in works by Picasso, as well as other artists, the battle between form and content became a central theme of Modernism.*

19.21). With Cubism, Picasso gave up Renaissance space completely, representing the subject from multiple angles simultaneously and shaping the figures into geometric designs. He also added a new feature to Cubism when he applied bits and pieces of other objects to the canvas, a technique called *collage* (French for "pasting"). Collage nudged Cubism closer to pure abstraction; the flat plane of the painting's surface was now simply a two-dimensional showcase for objects.

Although Paris remained the capital of Western art, other cities were also the scene of aesthetic experiment. Oslo, Munich, Vienna, and Dresden became artistic meccas, especially for Expressionist painters who followed the path opened by van Gogh and the *Fauves.*

In Munich, for example, Expressionism led to the formation of an international school of artists known as *Der Blaue Reiter* (The Blue Rider), named after a frequently used image. Rejecting the importance of artistic content and refusing to paint "safe" objects, this group of painters concentrated on basics such as color and line, which were meant to express inner feelings. Founded by the Russian exile Wassily Kandinsky [kan-DINT-skee] (1866–1944) in 1911, this school made the first breakthrough to abstract art— nonrepresentational or nonobjective paintings that defy any sense of reality or connection to nature and are, as the artist himself put it, "largely unconscious, spontaneous expressions of inner character, nonmaterial in nature." Kandinsky's "improvisations," as he labeled them, were free forms, possessing no objective content, consisting only of meandering lines and amorphous blobs of color (Figure 19.22). For all their seeming randomness, however, his paintings were planned to look that way. He consciously worked out the placement of the lines and the choices of color, leaving nothing to chance.

New Directions in Sculpture and Architecture Few sculptors of any consequence appeared in the 1871–1914 period and only one genius: Auguste Rodin [ROH-dan] (1840–1917). Rejecting the lifeless Classicism of the mid–nineteenth century, Rodin forged an eclectic style that blended Romantic subject matter, Renaissance simplicity, and Gothic angularity with the radical changes underway in painting. In the sculptural group *The Burghers of Calais* (Figure 19.23), he created a spiky Gothic effect using modern means, gouging, twisting, and otherwise torturing the surface of the

FIGURE 19.22 WASSILY KANDINSKY. *Improvisation 33 for "Orient."* 1913. Oil on canvas, 34¾ × 39¼". Stedelijk Museum, Amsterdam. *Kandinsky's radical Expressionism rested on the Romantic idea that serious art can function as a substitute for religion. In 1912 he published his aesthetic beliefs in the treatise* Concerning the Spiritual in Art, *a work that became a fundamental text for modern artists. He also linked the fluidity of painting with the lyricism of music, a connection suggested in this work by the meandering lines.*

FIGURE 19.23   AUGUSTE RODIN. *The Burghers of Calais.* 1884–1895. Bronze, 6'10½"
× 7'10" × 6'3". Rodin Museum, Philadelphia Museum of Art. Gift of Jules E.
Mastbaum. *The surface of Rodin's sculpture is Modernist, but its soul—the artistic
form—remains firmly rooted in the Classical ideals of the Renaissance. In this sculptural
group, which depicts six medieval citizens who were prepared to sacrifice their lives for
their city's freedom, he drew on the tradition of Michelangelo. First modeling the
individual figures in the nude, he then prepared clothed versions that he cast in bronze.
In their finished state, the sculptures are distinctively Michelangelesque, with powerful
muscularity, quiet dignity, and a general air of nobility under duress.*

human figures. The end result was both impressionistic (the play of light on the convoluted surfaces) and
expressionistic (the traces of Rodin's fingers on the
bronze medium, which so dramatically suggest the intensity of the artist's involvement).

Having lagged behind the other arts for most of
the century, architecture began to catch up in the

1880s. The United States led the way, notably in the
works of the Chicago School. The skyscraper, perfected by Chicago-based architects, became synonymous with Modernism and modern life. Unlike
Modernist painting and sculpture, the new architecture arose for practical reasons: dense populations
and soaring real estate values.

Using the aesthetic dictum that "form follows function," the Chicago School solved design problems without relying on past techniques and traditions. The author of this dictum, Louis Sullivan (1856–1924), produced a masterly example of the Chicago School's style in the Guaranty Building in Buffalo, New York, a structure whose steel frame is covered by a skin of stone and glass (Figure 19.24). Sullivan's imprint can be seen in the way he allows the building to speak for itself: The plan of the exterior skin reflects the internal steel skeleton in the thin, continuous piers between the windows that rise from the base to the rounded arches at the top. The effect of this organization is to turn the building's exterior into a grid, a visual expression of the structural frame underneath. Although Sullivan rejected the rich ornamentation of the nineteenth-century Gothic as well as the balanced decorations of Classicism, he nevertheless developed his own decorative scheme, which may be seen in the vertical and horizontal elements, for example, and the spaces (blocks) between the windows.

Sullivan defined the public building for the twentieth century, and his disciple Frank Lloyd Wright (1869–1959) did the same for domestic architecture around 1910. In the Victorian era architects had discovered that the middle-class demand for comfortable, spacious housing was an excellent source of income. This same class of patrons continued to demand well-built homes, and for them Wright created a new type of dwelling he called "organic," a term he coined to describe a building that was constructed of local woods and stone and therefore harmonized with the physical environment. Although unconventional in his own life, he was rather a romantic about his bourgeois patrons. To strengthen domestic

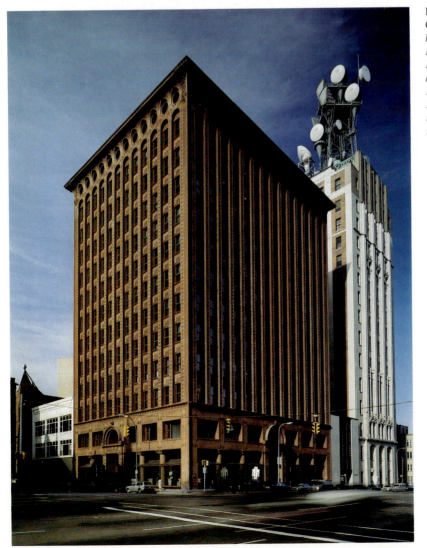

FIGURE 19.24 LOUIS SULLIVAN. Guaranty Building, Buffalo. 1895. *Purity became an identifying characteristic of Modernist style. It was apparent in Matisse's color experiments, Picasso's abstract Cubist forms, and even in the Expressionist's goal of unvarnished truth. In architecture, Louis Sullivan introduced the purity principal with his artistic credo that "form follows function."*

FIGURE 19.25 FRANK LLOYD WRIGHT. W. W. Willits House. 1902. Highland Park, Illinois. *Between 1900 and 1910 Wright introduced his "prairie houses," named for the* Ladies Home Journal *article (1901) in which their designs first appeared. The Willits house, built in an affluent Chicago suburb, is a fine example of this Midwestern American style that became a model for domestic buildings all over the United States. Laid out in a cruciform shape, this dwelling has a central chimney core. The style's strong focus on horizontal lines, resulting in shifting planes of light across the facade, may be compared with the multiple perspectives of Cubism, the parallel development in painting.*

values he planned houses that encouraged the inhabitants to identify with the natural surroundings; his structures also broke down the typical reliance on fixed interior walls in order to encourage fluid family relationships and a free flow of traffic. In time, Wright's style became standard for progressive architects throughout the United States, expressed in the exterior in strong horizontal lines, overhanging eaves, banks of windows, and an absence of decorative detail (Figure 19.25).

Music: From Impressionism to Jazz

Richard Wagner died in 1883, but in certain respects he is the commanding musical presence in Early Modernism. Most composers were either utilizing in their own way the harmonic advances he had made, working out the implications of these advances, or reacting to his influence by elaborately rejecting it.

For example, a musical style influenced by Wagner was Impressionism, which was in part inspired by his shimmering, constantly alternating chords. The Impressionist composers did not stay under his tutelage, however. Where Wagner was philosophical and literary, seeking to fuse all the arts, the Impressionists explored sound for its own sake. Like Impressionist painters, Impressionist composers thought that all moments—no matter how real—were fleeting and fragmentary, and their musical compositions illustrated this principle. Their music, without conventional thematic development or dramatic buildup and release, often sounds veiled or amorphous when compared with the music of, for example, Haydn.

Claude Debussy [deb-you-SEE] (1862–1918), a French composer, founded the Impressionist style. He created constantly shifting colors and moods through such musical methods as gliding chords and chromatic scales derived from non-Western sources that sound exotic to Western ears. Debussy's music represents the climax of the nineteenth-century interest in programmatic titles, large orchestras, rich chords, and relatively free rhythms and forms.

One of Debussy's programmatic works, *Prélude à l'après-midi d'un faune* (*Prelude to the Afternoon of a Faun*) (1894) is generally recognized as the first Impressionist orchestral masterpiece. This work is a sensuous confection of blurred sounds and elusive rhythms. To achieve its mood of reverie, Debussy used a meandering musical line played by a soulful solo flute, backed by muted strings and delicately voiced brasses and woodwinds.

Impressionist music produced a second major voice in France during this period: Maurice Ravel [ruh-VEL] (1875–1937), a composer loosely indebted to Debussy. Unlike Debussy, Ravel had a taste for the clear structure of Classical musical forms as well as established dance forms. Perhaps the most Impressionistic of Ravel's compositions is *Jeux d'eau* (*Fountains*) (1901), a programmatic work for piano marked by sounds evoking sparkling and splashing water. Even before the writing of *Jeux d'eau*, Ravel's Classical inclinations were evident in *Pavane pour une infante defunte* (*Pavane for a Dead Princess*) (1899), a work for piano with a melancholy quality; here, the music captured the stately rhythm of the Baroque **pavane**, an English court dance of Italian origin. Dance also inspired Ravel's work for piano entitled *Valses nobles et sentimentales* (*Waltzes Noble and Sentimental*) (1911), based on the waltzes of Schubert (see Chapter 17) and the Parisian ballrooms of the 1820s, and his work for orchestra called *La Valse* (*The Waltz*) (1920), a sardonic homage to the waltzes of nineteenth-century Vienna. Ravel's best known work, *La Valse* is in actuality an embittered metaphor in which the increasingly whirling, ever more discordant sounds of the music represent the forces that generated the catastrophe of World War I.

A trend in opposition to Wagner was Expressionism, which developed simultaneously with Expressionist art in Vienna. Drawing on the insights of Freudian psychology, musical Expressionism offered a distorted view of the world, focusing on anguish and pain. Its most striking feature was its embrace of *atonality*, a type of music without major or minor keys. To the listener, atonal music sounds discordant and even disturbing, because it offers no harmonious frame of reference. It is characterized by wide leaps from one tone to another, melody fragments, interrupted rhythms, and violent contrasts. Rejecting traditional forms, Expressionist composers made experimentation central to their musical vision.

The founder and leader of the Expressionist school was Arnold Schoenberg [SHUHN-buhrg] (1874–1951), who gave up a Wagnerian style around 1907 and moved toward atonality. At first Schoenberg employed traditional musical forms, as in the Second String Quartet (1908), although no string quartet had ever sounded like his dissonant creation. Scored without a designated key and filled with snatches of melody, this work offered the listener no recognizable frame of reference. Violinists were required on occasion to play the most extreme notes of which their instruments were capable.

Besides traditional forms, Schoenberg also established a favorite compositional method of Expressionism: setting a literary text to music and following its changes in character and feeling. An influential example of Expressionist music with text was *Pierrot lunaire* (*Moonstruck Pierrot*) (1912), based on poems by a Belgian writer and scored for chamber quintet and voice. Though Schoenberg downplayed the source text's importance, the music's violent shifts and prevailing discord clearly complement the alienated psychology and shocking language of the text. Instead of conventionally singing the text, the solo vocalist declaims or chants the text by combining speech and song.

Pierrot lunaire represents the extreme of Schoenberg's Expressionism prior to World War I. This work made him one of the two most highly respected composers of Early Modernism. Unwilling to rest on his laurels, he continued to experiment with innovative musical techniques (see Chapter 20).

The other outstanding twentieth-century musical genius active during this period was the Russian Igor Stravinsky [struh-VINT-skee] (1882–1971). Untouched by Wagnerism but attuned to the revolutionary events unfolding in the arts and in literature, Stravinsky acquired his great reputation at about the same time as Schoenberg. In 1913 Stravinsky wrote the music for *The Rite of Spring,* a ballet produced by Sergei Diaghilev [dee-AHG-uh-lef] (1872–1929) for the Russian Ballet in Paris. Stravinsky's music and the ballet's choreography tapped into the theme of primitivism in art that was currently the rage in the French capital. Stravinsky's jackhammer rhythms evoke a pagan ritual, using abrupt meter changes, a hypnotic beat, and furious *syncopation*, the musical technique of accenting a weak beat when a strong beat is expected. The "savage" music coupled with the erotic dancing created a scandal that made Stravinsky the leading *avant-garde* composer in the world. Despite his innovative rhythms, Stravinsky was no relentless experimenter. After World War I, Stravinsky, though touched by Modernism's influences, became the head of a Classical school that was centered in France and opposed the more extreme theories being introduced by Schoenberg through his work in Vienna.

As Western music moved away from ancient and medieval sources, a new tradition, jazz, rooted in

African-American tradition, began to emerge in the United States. The word "jazz," originally a slang term for sexual intercourse, reflects the music's origins in the New Orleans sexual underworld. Jazz combined West African and African-Caribbean rhythms with Western harmony, along with an improvisatory call-and-response style rooted both in African songs and in gospel songs of the urban Protestant revival in the 1850s. Jazz drew on two other African-American musical forms as well—ragtime, which was chiefly instrumental, and the blues, which originated as a vocal art.

Ragtime flourished from 1890 to 1920. The word "ragtime" is derived from the phrase "ragged time," the original name for this type of syncopated music perfected by black pianist and composer Scott Joplin (1868–1917) and based on a blend of African-American rhythms and Western harmony. The *blues* grew out of the rural African-American tradition of work songs and spirituals and evokes the pain to be found in life, love, poverty, and hard work. Blues and jazz are both powerfully expressive musical forms, considered specifically American contributions to world music.

The Legacy of Early Modernism

From the unsettled period of 1871–1914 come many of the trends that have made the twentieth century such an exciting—and dangerous—era. The legacy of militant nationalism has given birth to the two great world wars that devastated our century. Even today, nationalism remains a potent force, threatening to overturn state boundaries and governments. Imperialism, another legacy, has had radically contradictory consequences. On the one hand it has exported Western peoples, values, and technology around the globe, bringing a higher standard of living and greater expectations for the future. On the other hand it has disturbed if not destroyed older ways of life and led to a series of wars as colonial peoples have struggled to cast off the yoke of Western oppression. And militarism, a third legacy, has made rivalry among states a perpetual source of anxiety and destruction.

On the cultural scene, the era of Early Modernism set the stage for our century. The rise of the masses has led to a growing proletarization of culture. As a result, the middle classes have been subjected to a cultural assault from urban workers in much the same way that aristocrats were attacked and displaced by the middle classes. Technology has fueled the rise of mass culture. A second legacy of this era has been the *avant-garde*, whose leaders have systematically tried to destroy the last vestiges of Judeo-Christian and Greco-Roman tradition. And finally, Early Modernism established the emotional and aesthetic climate of this century—its addiction to experimentalism, its love-hate relationship with uncertainty and restlessness, its obsession with abstraction, its belief in the hidden depths of the human personality, and its willingness to think the unthinkable.

KEY CULTURAL TERMS

Modernism	*Post-Impressionism*
avant-garde	*Pointillism*
Naturalism	*primitivism*
Decadence	*Fauvism*
Expressionism	*Cubism*
local color	collage
Creole	*pavane*
Cajun	*atonality*
aesthete	*syncopation*
abstraction	*ragtime*
Impressionism	*blues*

SUGGESTIONS FOR FURTHER READING

PRIMARY SOURCES

CHEKHOV, A. P. *Plays.* Translated and edited by E. K. Bristow. New York: Norton, 1977. Excellent versions of Chekhov's most memorable plays: *The Sea Gull, Uncle Vanya, The Three Sisters,* and *The Cherry Orchard.*

CHOPIN, K. *The Awakening.* Edited by M. Culley. New York: Norton, 1976. The story of a sensual woman's coming of age that shocked the American public, whose outrage then silenced its author; with notes, excerpts from contemporary reviews, and essays in criticism. The novel was first published in 1899.

FREUD, S. *Civilization and Its Discontents*. Translated and edited by J. Strachey. New York: Norton, 1962. Freud's ideas about history and civilization, based on his psychological findings and theories; Strachey is the editor of the Standard Edition of Freud's complete works.

———. *The Interpretation of Dreams*. Translated and edited by J. Strachey. New York: Basic Books, 1955. Freud's seminal work about the role of the unconscious in human psychology and his new theory of psychoanalysis; considered by many his most important work.

HUYSMANS, J.-K. *Against Nature*. Translated by R. Baldick. New York: Penguin, 1966. A superb English version of this curious work, first published in 1884.

IBSEN, H. *A Doll's House*. Translated by C. Hampton. New York: S. French, 1972. An excellent English version of Ibsen's most often performed play, the story of a woman's awakening to the facts of her oppressive marriage.

JUNG, C. G. *Basic Writings*. Edited with an introduction by V. S. de Laszlo. New York: Modern Library, 1959. A good selection of the most important works of the Swiss psychiatrist who explored the importance of myths and symbols in human psychology.

———. *Memories, Dreams, Reflections*. Edited by A. Jaffé. New York: Vintage, 1963. Jung's highly readable autobiography in which he describes the origins of his theories.

KAFKA, F. *The Trial*. Translated by W. and E. Muir. New York: Schocken Books, 1968. A definitive edition of Kafka's nightmare novel in which the lead character is tried and convicted of a crime whose nature he cannot discover.

———. *The Metamorphosis, The Penal Colony, and Other Stories*. Translated by W. and E. Muir. New York: Schocken Books, 1988. This volume contains the best of Kafka's brilliant short prose works, all concerned with anxiety and alienation in a hostile and incomprehensible world.

NIETZSCHE, F. W. *The Portable Nietzsche*. Selected and translated by W. Kaufmann. New York: Penguin, 1976. A collection of the most important writings of the German philosopher, compiled by the American scholar who rescued Nietzsche from the charge of proto-Nazism into which his philosophy had fallen during the Nazi era.

PROUST, M. *Remembrance of Things Past*. Translated by C. K. Scott Moncrieff, T. Kilmartin, and A. Mayor. London: Chatto & Windus, 1981. Contains all seven volumes of Proust's monumental work, which portrays the early twentieth century as a transitional period with the old aristocracy in decline and the middle class on the rise.

WILDE, O. *The Portrait of Dorian Gray*. New York: Oxford University Press, 1981. Wilde's only novel recounts the story of a man whose portrait ages and decays while he remains young and handsome despite a dissolute life; the most enduring work of the Decadent school of late-nineteenth-century English literature.

ZOLA, E. *Germinal*. Translated and with an introduction by L. Tancock. New York: Penguin, 1954. A Realist novel that exposes the sordid conditions in the French mining industry.

SUGGESTIONS FOR LISTENING

DEBUSSY, CLAUDE (1862–1918).
Debussy's veiled, subtly shifting harmonies helped to found Impressionist music. Excellent examples of his style may be heard in the orchestral works *Prélude à l'après-midi d'un faune* (*Prelude to the Afternoon of a Faun*) (1894) and *Nocturnes* (1899); in the collections for piano called *Estampes* (*Prints*) (1913) and *Préludes* (1910–1913); and in the opera *Pelléas et Mélisande* (1902). Not all of his music was Impressionistic, however; for example, in the piano music called *Children's Corner* (1908) he blended Classical values with his typical harmonic structures.

RAVEL, MAURICE (1875–1937).
Working in the shadow of Debussy, Ravel was an Impressionist with Classical inclinations; where Debussy was rhapsodic, Ravel was restrained. The work for solo piano, *Jeux d'eau* (*Fountains*) (1901), shows Ravel's Impressionist style to perfection. His Classicism is most evident in compositions indebted to dance forms, including two works for solo piano, *Pavane pour une infante defunte* (*Pavane for a Dead Princess*) (1899) and *Valses nobles et sentimentales* (*Waltzes noble and sentimental*) (1911), and two works for orchestra, *La Valse* (*The Waltz*) (1920) and *Bolero* (1928).

SCHOENBERG, ARNOLD (1874–1951).
By the end of this period, in 1914, Schoenberg was recognized as the leader of Expressionist music, particularly with the atonal work *Pierrot lunaire* (*Moonstruck Pierrot*) (1912), scored for chamber quintet and voice. In earlier works, he was less radical, as in the Second String Quartet (1908), which fused Classical forms and fragmentary melodies. Only after 1923 did Schoenberg make a breakthrough to serial composition, the type of music with which he is most identified (see Chapter 20).

STRAVINSKY, IGOR (1882–1971).
Stravinsky, who along with Schoenberg has dominated twentieth-century music, also began writing music during this period, principally as a composer of ballet scores based on Russian folk tales and traditions. These were *The Fire Bird* (1910), *Petrushka* (1911), and *Le Sacre du Printemps* (*The Rite of Spring*) (1913). With *Le Sacre* he established his originality as a composer, especially in his innovative rhythms and his handling of folk themes.

JOPLIN, SCOTT (1868–1917).
Typical of Joplin's ragtime compositions with a syncopated beat are *Maple Leaf Rag* (1899), *Sugar Cane Rag* (1908), and *Magnetic Rag* (1914). He also wrote a ragtime opera *Treemonisha* (1911), a failure in his lifetime but a modest success in recent revivals.

20

THE AGE OF THE MASSES AND THE ZENITH OF MODERNISM

1914—1945

The years between 1914 and 1945 were dominated by wars, depression, and totalitarian movements. Below the surface of these chaotic events even more potent forces were at work, including the rise of the masses at the expense of the bourgeoisie and the debate over the rival ideologies of democracy, capitalism, socialism, and communism. Old ideas, one after the other, were challenged and overturned, leading scholars to describe this turbulent period as an era of illusions.

The events of the first half of the twentieth century are seen differently today than they were seen at the time. Historians are beginning to see World War I (1914–1918) and World War II (1939–1945) not as two separate conflicts but as a single struggle divided by a twenty-year peace. They believe that the Great Depression of the 1930s was not a signal that the capitalist system didn't work but was simply an episode of economic downturn. And they know that the making of the masses into a historically powerful force was the most significant event of this time and of greater consequence than the wars, the economic hardships, or the political upheavals. The rise of the masses heralded the onset of a new phase of culture in which ordinary men and women from the lower middle class and working class challenged bourgeois dominance in much the same way as the bourgeoisie had earlier threatened and eventually overcome the aristocracy.

◀ FRIDA KAHLO. *Self-Portrait with Thorn Necklace and Hummingbird.* 1940. Oil on canvas. 24½ × 17¾". Collection, Harry Ransom Humanities Research Center, University of Texas at Austin.

The appearance of the masses on the world stage was also instrumental in shaping cultural events. The needs of this public led to the birth of mass culture, resulting in fresh forms of popular expression. Mass culture triggered negative responses in most serious artists, writers, and musicians, who preferred the difficult and somewhat remote style of Modernism that had arisen after 1870 and who had been nurtured in an environment hostile to bourgeois, industrialized society. The leaders of Modernism, partly under pressure from the extreme popularity of mass culture, now fashioned works that grew more and more revolutionary in form, constantly testing the limits of the arts. The period between 1914 and 1945 saw both the rise of mass culture and the zenith of Modernism.

THE COLLAPSE OF OLD CERTAINTIES AND THE SEARCH FOR NEW VALUES

Before World War I, liberal values guided the expectations that most people had for their personal lives and their societies. During the period between the outbreak of World War I and the ending of World War II, however, the values of liberalism were sorely tried and in some cases overthrown. Wars, revolutions, and social upheavals often dominated both domestic and foreign affairs. Even the brief breathing spaces during the rare months of peace were fraught with tensions as some states prepared for new

FIGURE 20.1 PABLO PICASSO. *Guernica.* 1937. Oil on canvas, 11'5½" × 25'5¾".
Prado, Madrid. *Guernica is a vivid symbol of the violent twenty years between World
War I and World War II. Depicting the bombing of the unarmed town of Guernica by Nazi
planes during the Spanish Civil War, the painting transforms the local struggle into an
international battle between totalitarianism and human freedom—the issue that also
dominated the age's ideological debates.*

rounds of conflict. To those who clung to liberalism,
the world seemed to have gone mad (Figure 20.1).
Civility appeared outmoded because war now
seemed a more normal condition than peace, and
other key liberal ideas were assaulted by the period's
events. The ideal that government should represent
the desires of the people was rendered meaningless
in Russia, Italy, Germany, and Spain, where totalitarian forms of government were established. In
these states individual rights became secondary to
the needs of the total society or often simply to the
wishes of the ruling party. The doctrine of laissez
faire also fell into discredit during the Depression of
the 1930s, bringing capitalism itself into question
and leading to the rise of state-controlled economies.

When World War II ended in 1945, little vitality
remained in the liberal tradition among Europeans.
Europe—shattered by the war, its major cities devastated, its population diminished, its transportation
system destroyed, its economy in ruins—was at a
crossroads, uncertain whether to stay on the liberal
path or move in the direction of socialism.

Most Americans in 1945, however, still held to the
liberal vision. Not having been subjected to a land
war at home in either of the two worldwide conflicts,
Americans were less pessimistic than Europeans.
Moreover, Europe's devastation meant that the
United States was now the world's leading military,
industrial, and financial power.

World War I and Its Aftermath

In 1914 came the war that nobody expected. Despite
predictions to the contrary, it dragged on for four
years and took the lives of an estimated ten million
soldiers and civilians. On one side were Germany,
Austria-Hungary, Turkey, and Bulgaria—the Central Powers. The principal war aim of these countries
was to assert the power of their central European
region, which had been eclipsed by western Europe
for almost two hundred years. The most dramatic
cause of central Europe's new feeling of importance
was the unification of Germany in 1871, which made
the German Empire the most powerful industrial and
military state on the Continent. Austria-Hungary,
though little industrialized, wanted to spread its
imperial power into southeastern Europe, replacing
the Turkish influence and countering the Russians,
who had been trying to dominate this region.

Opposed to the Central Powers were the Allied
Powers of France, Russia, and Great Britain. In 1915
Italy, blaming its former friends Germany and
Austria-Hungary for starting the war, joined the
Allied Powers. The Allies refused to allow the Central Powers to revise the balance of power and, in
particular, were determined to keep Germany from
gaining new lands. Both sides, hopeful of swift victory, found themselves bogged down in seige war-

fare that led to huge losses on the battlefield and ap-palling hardships at home (Figure 20.2).

In the spring of 1917 the stalemate between the Allies and the Central Powers was upset by two dramatic events. First, the United States entered the war on the side of the exhausted Allies, promising fresh troops and supplies. Second, revolution broke out in Russia, interrupting its war effort and eventually causing the newly formed Communist regime to make peace with the Central Powers in early 1918. Freed from fighting the Russians in the east and determined to strike before American troops could reach Europe in great numbers, the Germans launched a massive attack on the western front, but the Allies, supported by thousands of American troops, foiled the Germans, forcing them to sue for peace in November 1918.

The armistice that ended the war was based in part on a plan outlined by the U.S. president, Woodrow Wilson (1913–1921). Wilson believed that his plan—calling for self-determination of nations, democratic governments, and an international agency to maintain the peace, known as the League of Nations—would keep Europe safe from war. The president's proposals were modified by the victorious Allies and became the basis for the 1919 Treaty of Versailles.

Despite the optimism surrounding its signing, the Versailles Treaty sowed the seeds of discord that contributed to World War II (Map 20.1). The German diplomats who signed the treaty were representatives of a hastily thrown together civilian govern-ment and not the officials and army officers who had suffered defeat. Later these defeated officials and officers rallied nationalist feelings by denouncing the treaty as a humiliation for their country, especially those provisions that were meant to keep Germany industrially and militarily weak and the requirement that Germany pay war claims—called reparations—to the victorious Allies.

Peace brought boom times to the economies of the victorious Allied Powers. Britain and France returned to business as usual, as political parties shifted in and out of office. The United States reverted to its prewar isolationism, turning its back on Europe. Between 1924 and 1929 the United States also exhibited the best and the worst of free enterprise—unprecedented prosperity and rampant greed.

The Central Powers also rebuilt their economies in the 1920s. After a shaky start, Germany survived near bankruptcy to become once again the leading industrial state on the Continent. Germany was now known as the Weimar Republic, after the city where its postwar constitution was drafted; Weimar had once been Goethe's home, and for many it symbolized a new era. Once again, Germany became a center for European culture, providing key leaders in *avant-garde* painting and literature. Conversely, Austria was reduced to a shadow of its former self, its imperial lands stripped away and reorganized into democratic nations and its Slavic population dispersed among several states. The Austro-Hungarian monarchy ceased to exist. Austria, lacking a sound economic base, never fully recovered from its defeat.

FIGURE 20.2 PAUL NASH. *"We Are Making a New World."* 1918. Oil on canvas, 28 × 36". Imperial War Museum, London. *Paul Nash, one of Britain's official artists during World War I, made the reality of the war's destructive power evident to civilians at home. In his battle scenes farmlands were turned into quagmires and forests into "no man's lands." The artist's choice of the title for this painting mocks the politicians' promises that tomorrow will be better.*

MAP 20.1

Europe after World War I

Territory lost by

Germany

Bulgaria

Russia

Austria-Hungary

As the 1920s drew to a close a warning signal sounded: the crash of the New York stock market in October 1929. After the market crash the buoyant atmosphere of the twenties lingered for a few months until the early 1930s. Then economic depression in the United States, now a central cog in the world's economy, brought down Europe's financial house.

The Great Depression of the 1930s

The Depression wiped out prosperity, and the order of the day became mass unemployment, street demonstrations, and near starvation conditions for many people. As a result, severe strains were placed on Europe and the United States, forcing governments to try various experiments in order to restore their economies. Great Britain and France were compelled to discard some cherished ideas, such as free trade and the gold standard, and move toward government-controlled economies and paper money systems. Under President Franklin Delano Roosevelt (1933–1945) and his New Deal program, the United States followed a policy of state intervention as the answer to its economic plight (Figure 20.3). Roosevelt started public projects—dams, roads, and conservation programs—"priming the pump," as he called it. He also sponsored programs to benefit working people, including social security and unemployment insurance. To prevent another panic, he introduced legislation regulating Wall Street and the banks. Depressed conditions, notably high unemployment, hung on until World War II, however.

Germany suffered the most of any country in Europe from the Great Depression. Domestic problems, brought on in part by bank failures and rising unemployment, led to a series of political crises that doomed the Weimar experiment in democracy and set the stage for the coming to power of the National Socialists, or Nazis, under Adolf Hitler.

While Europe suffered, Japan prospered. Since 1926 Japan had been ruled by Emperor Hirohito (1926–1989), who was worshiped as a god, although actual power was wielded by military leaders and businessmen. In the 1930s these groups pursued expansionist and militaristic policies, first taking over Manchuria and then making war on China. As storm clouds gathered over Europe in the late 1930s, Japan was able to take a free hand in southeast Asia.

The Rise of Totalitarianism

At the peace conference of 1919 democracy seemed triumphant. It was the form of government practiced by the winning Allies and the new states carved out of the defeated powers. By 1939, a mere twenty years later, most of the new democracies had become

FIGURE 20.3 WALKER EVANS. *Elizabeth Tengle in the Kitchen, Hale County, Alabama.* 1936. Photography Collection, Harry Ransom Humanities Research Center, the University of Texas at Austin. *Tenant farmers in the southern United States, who had been victimized by low cotton prices and high interest rates for decades, were reduced to subsistence levels or worse by the Great Depression. This photograph shows the misery of one of the farm women in her kitchen with little food, few utensils, and no labor-saving appliances. Walker Evans's shocking photographs, which accompanied James Agee's book* Let Us Now Praise Famous Men, *provided the supporters of Roosevelt's New Deal with visual documentation of the wretched living conditions of tenant families.*

totalitarian: those bearing the brunt of defeat (Germany and Austria-Hungary), those left out of the postwar settlements (Russia, Italy, and Spain), and those created by the peace treaties (Bulgaria and Rumania).

Totalitarianism on a massive scale is a twentieth-century phenomenon, but its roots reach back to the policies of Robespierre and the Committee of Public Safety during the French Revolution. Totalitarian governments control every aspect of the lives and thoughts of their citizens. The state becomes monolithic and inescapable, and nothing has authority except the wishes of those in power. Art, literature, the press—all exist only in the service of the state. "Truth" itself becomes a matter of what the state says it is. Between the wars, totalitarianism emerged in two forms: Russian communism and European fascism.

Russian Communism Russian communism was based on the writings of Karl Marx, whose theory was reinterpreted and put into practice by the revolutionary leader V. I. Lenin (1917–1924). Lenin accepted Marx's basic premise that economic conditions determine the course of history, and he also accepted Marx's conclusion that history leads inevitably to a communist society run by and for the workers. Lenin disagreed with Marx over the tactics needed to introduce a classless society, however. Marx thought that only a mass movement could effect revolutionary change, but Lenin was convinced that radical reform could only occur when a relatively small elite group seized power in the name of the people. Lenin spent the years after 1900 putting together a crack team of revolutionaries, awaiting the moment to strike.

That moment came in 1917. At the time, Russia was plagued by an incompetent ruler, an inefficient military staff, an economy no longer able to sustain the war effort, and a society torn by rising social and political discord. As the battles of World War I dragged on, desertions at the front spread and unrest in the cities mounted. In February a revolution broke out. Power changed hands several times before a small band of Marxist communists—the Bolsheviks—seized the government in October. Led by Lenin, the Bolsheviks began to restructure the economy and consolidate their hold over the political system. Under their plan, the state would control production and distribution while soviets—or councils—of workers, military personnel, and peasants would be set up at the local level to restructure the social and economic order, as directed by the Communist party under Lenin.

On Lenin's death in 1924 a power struggle ensued from which Joseph Stalin (1928–1953) emerged as the sole ruler of the Soviet Union, as the Russian empire was now called. Stalin proceeded to impose his will over the state with a vengeance. Through a series of five-year plans he kept the workers busy building up heavy industry, increasing farm production through state-owned farms, boosting factory output, and bringing electrical power to remote regions. He created a paper constitution that purported to guarantee voting and other civil rights, but it was a sham. No political party other than the Communist party was permitted, and elections were closely monitored to ensure support for prearranged voting results.

Stalin was ruthless to his opponents and critics, either having them murdered or imprisoning them in a vast network of forced-labor camps built in the wilderness of Siberia and known as the Gulag. The data on Stalin's victims is beyond human imagining. According to one scholarly estimate, more than ten million men, women, and children met unnatural deaths in the period of forced collectivization of agriculture, 1929–1936; an additional four million were murdered during the purges of 1936–1938, including 30,000 army officers and one million party members; the deaths in the Gulag numbered about one million a year from 1936 onward.

European Fascism European fascism, another form of totalitarianism, was based on the idea that the masses should participate directly in the state. The people's involvement should not be through a legislative or deliberative body such as a parliament, however, which fascists denounced as bourgeois and outmoded, but through a fusion of the population into a whole. Fascism sought to bind the masses together by appealing to nonrational, intuitive feelings about national destiny, bringing them in line with the "spirit" of the race. Like communists, fascists believed that the individual was insignificant and the nation-state was the supreme embodiment of the destiny of the people.

Because it claimed to speak for the soul of the masses, fascism in practice led to loss of personal freedom, as did communism for a similar reason. Fascism's ideals of economic stability and social peace could be achieved only through dictatorship, along with tight control over the press and education, a ruthless police force, and a swift and stern judicial system. Fascism was also inevitably aggressive because its idealistic nationalism readily deteriorated into hostility both to foreigners and to internal groups who did not share the majority's history, race, or politics. The movement's innate aggressiveness led to strong military establishments, which were used either to conquer new lands in Europe or to win colonial empires, or both. Fascism first appeared in Italy in the 1920s and then in Germany and Spain in the 1930s.

In Italy a floundering economy and mounting national frustration led more and more people to follow the Fascists, a group of revolutionary adventurers who took their name from the Latin word *fasces*, an ancient Roman symbol of authority. Led by Benito Mussolini [moo-suh-LEE-nee] (1922–1945), the Fascists dreamed of a revitalized Italy restored to its ancient glory. When no political party could get the country back on the road to recovery in the postwar years, Mussolini marched his Fascist troops into Rome and seized power in 1922. As the first right-wing totalitarian regime in Europe, the Fascists set examples for other similar movements. Mussolini achieved some success with his programs, and as the rest of Europe suffered through the Depression, his pragmatic policies gained admirers.

Germany in the 1930s was wracked by depression, unemployment, and political extremism. Amid this chaos, in 1933 the German voters turned to the National Socialist (Nazi) party. Within three years the Nazis had turned the economy around, restoring industrial productivity, eliminating unemployment, and winning the support of many business leaders and farmers.

The success of the National Socialists depended ultimately on their *Führer*, or "leader," Adolph Hitler (1933–1945). Hitler, a middle-class Austrian and a decorated veteran, had hammered together a strong mass movement built on anti-Semitism and anticommunism. He used his magnetic personality and hypnotic speaking style to attract devoted followers with promises to restore Germany to prewar glory through a planned economy, militarism, and imperial expansion. From the beginning, the Nazis' ruthless treatment of political enemies, of the Jews, and of any dissidents aroused fears, but most Europeans ignored these barbaric acts, preferring to focus on the regime's successes (Figure 20.4).

Spain, a country relatively untouched by industrialism and liberal politics in 1914, sat out World War I as a neutral. Industrial growth in the 1920s began to strain its agrarian economy and traditional institutions, however, and in the early 1930s a coalition of reformers overthrew the king and created a secular republic with a constitution guaranteeing civil rights. The landed aristocrats, the Roman Catholic Church, and some generals plotted to restore monarchical rule and the church's influence. In 1936 civil war broke out. General Francisco Franco (1939–1975) led the conservative forces to victory in 1939, defeating an alliance of republicans, socialists, anarchists, and communists. During hostilities, Hitler and Mussolini supplied Franco's fascist army with troops and

FIGURE 20.4   Nuremberg Nazi Party Rally. 1933. *Under the skillful orchestration of their propaganda chief, Joseph Goebbels, the National Socialists staged massive demonstrations whose goal was to overpower the emotions of participants and observers alike. In this anonymous photograph, Nazi party members and private army units pass in review. In the 1930s such demonstrations succeeded in uniting the German masses with the Nazi leader.*

equipment, while Stalin backed the losing faction. For the Germans and the Italians, Spain's civil war was a practice run for World War II. For example, the bombing of unarmed towns like Guernica foreshadowed the indiscriminate bombing and killing of civilians that characterized the later war.

World War II: Origins and Outcome

The origins of World War II lay in the Versailles Treaty, the Great Depression, and nationalistic feelings. Hardly was the ink dry on the Versailles Treaty before many Germans were denouncing it as a "dictated" peace. Especially infuriating to nationalistic Germans was the loss of lands to Poland and France.

The worldwide economic breakdown in the 1930s further fanned the fires of German resentment against the treaty, causing the lost territories to become burning political issues. Once the Nazis had secured their position, they turned their attention to recovering the former territories as well as annexing other areas with large German populations.

After less than a year in office, Hitler began a campaign to revise the Versailles Treaty while at the same time engaging in a propaganda crusade that focused on Germany's glorious past. His regime, he boasted, was the Third Reich, or empire, which would last for a thousand years—like the centuries-long Holy Roman Empire (1000–1806) rather than the short-lived German Empire (1871–1918). Hitler withdrew Germany from the League of Nations, to which it had been admitted in the 1920s, and renounced the provision of the Versailles Treaty that forbade Germany to rearm. In 1936 he marched troops into the Rhineland, the industrial heartland of Germany, which had been demilitarized by the treaty. When the world failed to respond to this challenge, Hitler concluded that Germany's former enemies were weak and proceeded to initiate a plan to conquer Europe.

In the next two years, Europe watched as Hitler took Austria and Czechoslovakia and began to threaten Poland. France and Great Britain followed a policy of appeasement, believing that if Hitler's demands were met, war could be averted, but they promised to come to Poland's aid if Germany attacked. World War II began on September 1, 1939, when Germany invaded Poland; France and Britain responded with declarations of war.

Within nine months the Nazis occupied most of western Europe. By the fall of 1940 Britain stood alone, taking the brunt of the German air raids. The British, under their wartime leader Winston Churchill, bravely held on. Hitler, unable to defeat England by air, now turned eastward and initiated a land invasion against the Soviet Union in June 1941, breaking a mutual nonaggression pact he had signed with Stalin in August 1939 (Figure 20.5). Shortly thereafter the Soviet Union and Great Britain became allies against Nazi Germany. Then in December 1941 Japan attacked American bases in the Pacific, and a few days later Germany and Italy joined Japan by declaring war on the United States.

The war in Europe lasted until May 1945, when the combined armies of the Allied powers—Britain, the Soviet Union, and the United States—forced the Axis power Germany to surrender. Italy, the second European Axis power, had negotiated an armistice with the Allies in September 1943 after anti-Fascists overthrew Mussolini and set up a republic. In the Pacific the war against the Asian Axis power, Japan, was brought to an abrupt end, in August 1945, by America's dropping atomic bombs on the Japanese cities of Hiroshima and Nagasaki. The more than 200,000 Japanese killed in these two raids climaxed the bloody six years of World War II, adding to its estimated thirty to fifty million deaths.

By 1945 the world had witnessed some of the most brutal examples of human behavior in history. Few were prepared for the shock of the Nazi death camps, however. Gradually it became known that the Nazis had rounded up the Jews of Germany and eastern Europe and transported them in cattle cars

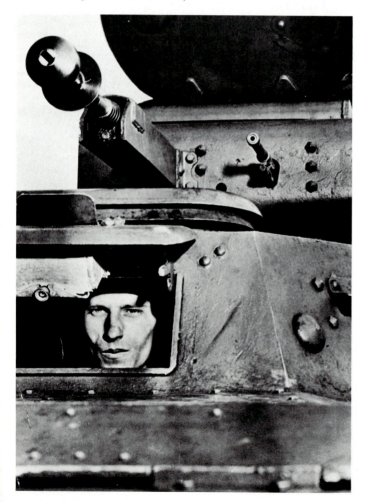

FIGURE 20.5 MARGARET BOURKE-WHITE. *Russian Tank Driver. 1941. Photojournalism, a popular form in which the photograph rather than the text dominates the story, reached new heights during World War II, particularly in illustrated magazines like* Life. *Margaret Bourke-White, one of the first women war journalists, was the only foreign correspondent-photographer present in the Soviet Union when the Germans invaded in June 1941. In this photograph she shows a Russian tank driver peering through his window with the cannon jutting out over his head—a vivid image of the integration of human beings into mechanized warfare.*

FIGURE 20.6 Nazi Death Camp in Belsen, Germany. 1945. *When the Nazis came to power in Germany in 1933 they secretly began to imprison their political enemies in concentration camps, where they were tortured or executed. By 1942 the Nazis had extended this secret policy across Europe to include foreign civilians, particularly Jews. Photographs such as this one revealed to the world the horrible atrocities committed by the Nazi regime.*

to the extermination camps, where they were killed in gas chambers. The Nazis referred to their plan to eliminate the Jewish people as the Final Solution, but the rest of the world called it the Holocaust. This genocidal policy involved the murder of six million Jews out of a population of nine million, along with millions of other people the Nazis deemed undesirable, such as gypsies and homosexuals (Figure 20.6).

In 1945, after six years of war waged across the globe, Germany and Japan lay in ruins. Italy escaped with less damage. France, partly occupied by the Germans for most of the war, was readmitted to the councils of the Allies. England, though victorious, emerged exhausted and in the shadow of her former allies, the United States and the Soviet Union. The old European order had passed away. The Soviet Union and the United States were now the two most powerful states in the world.

THE ZENITH OF MODERNISM

Modernism had originated in the latter part of the nineteenth century as a reflection of the fast-paced modern world whose foundations and boundaries seemed to be constantly shifting. The Modernist sensibility, with its underlying spirit of skepticism and experimentation, continued to guide artistic and literary expression in the twentieth century. But this style was limited in its appeal, and an ever-growing general public was isolated from *avant-garde* developments in art, music, and literature. If and when this wider audience bestirred themselves about high culture, they usually responded negatively to Modernist works, which they often considered incomprehensible, obscene, or decidedly provocative in some way. They turned instead to the increasingly available and affordable pleasures offered by *mass culture*.

Like Modernism, mass culture was a direct outgrowth of industrialized society. Its roots reached back to the late nineteenth century, when skilled workers began to enjoy a better standard of living than had previously been possible for members of the lower classes. This new generation of consumers demanded products and amusements that appealed to their tastes: inexpensive, energetic, and easily accessible.

In response to their desires, entrepreneurs using new technologies flooded the market with consumer goods and developed new entertainments. Unlike the folk culture or popular culture of earlier times, modern mass culture was also mass-produced culture. The untapped consumers' market led to the creation or expansion of new industries, in particular automobiles, household products, and domestic appliances. Most forms of mass culture—the radio, newspaper comic strips and cartoons, professional sports, picture magazines, recordings, movies, and musical comedies—had originated before World War I, but now, between the wars, they came into their own. The 1920s was the golden age of Broadway's musical comedies, and radio reached its peak in the years after 1935.

The spread of mass culture heightened the prestige of the United States as it became known as the source of the most vigorous and imaginative popular works. The outstanding symbol of America's dominance of popular culture is Walt Disney (1901–1966), the creator of the cartoon figures of Mickey Mouse (1928) and other characters. By 1945 in the more advanced societies, mass culture was playing an ever-growing role in the public and the private lives of most citizens. A handful of creative people began to incorporate elements of mass culture into their works, using jazz in "serious" music or film in theatrical performances, for example, but in the main most artists, writers, and musicians stood apart from mass culture. Their isolation reflected an almost sacred commitment to the Modernist ideals of experimentation, newness, and deliberate difficulty. And some Modernists, especially among the visual artists, imbued these ideals with spiritual meaning.

Experimentation in Literature

Modernist writers between 1914 and 1945 maintained Early Modernism's dedication to experimentation, a stance that reflected their despair over the instability of their era. By challenging the traditional norms and methods of literature through their carefully composed experimental works, the Modernists were convinced that they could impose an order on the seeming randomness and meaninglessness of human existence.

The Novel   Depiction of the narrator's subjective consciousness was a principal concern of the Modernist novelists, who otherwise differed markedly from one another. The most famous method that arose from this concern was *stream-of-consciousness* writing, a method in which the narrative consists of the unedited thoughts of one of the characters, through whose mind readers experience the story. Stream-of-consciousness fiction differs from a story told in the first person—the grammatical "I"—by one of the characters (for example, Dickens's *David Copperfield*) in that it is an attempt to emulate the actual experience of thinking and feeling, even to the point of sounding fragmented, random, and arbitrary.

The Irish author James Joyce and the English writer Virginia Woolf were important innovators with the stream-of-consciousness technique. In his novel *Ulysses*, James Joyce (1882–1941) uses this device as a way of making the novel's characters speak directly to readers. For instance, no narrator's voice intrudes in the novel's final forty-five pages, which are the scattered thoughts of the character Molly Bloom as she sinks into sleep. This long monologue is a single run-on sentence without any punctuation except for a final period.

Despite the experimental style of *Ulysses*, Joyce aspired to more than technical virtuosity in this monumental work. He planned it as a modern version of the *Odyssey*, contrasting Homer's twenty-four books of heroic exploits with an ordinary day in the lives of three Dubliners. Joyce's sexual language, while natural to his characters, offended bourgeois morals. *Ulysses*, first published in France in 1922, became the era's test case for artistic freedom, not appearing in America or England until the 1930s.

Rejecting traditional narrative techniques, Virginia Woolf (1882–1941) experimented with innovative ways to explore time, space, and reality. In her early novel *Jacob's Room* (1922), for example, she develops the title character through fragments of other people's comments about him. In *Mrs. Dalloway* (1925) she uses interior monologues to trace a woman's experiences over the course of a day in

London. Like her contemporaries Joyce and Freud, Woolf was interested in examining the realities that lie below surface consciousness. Many consider *To the Lighthouse* (1927) Woolf's finest novel. In it she uses stream-of-consciousness to strip the story of fixed realism and capture the differing senses of reality experienced by the characters—in much the same way as the Cubist painters aimed at representing multiple views. To this end she focuses on the characters' inner selves, creating diverse effects through interior monologues. For instance, one character's narrow, matter-of-fact mentality differs from his wife's emotional, free-ranging consciousness. A distinguished literary critic and the author of well-known feminist works such as *A Room of One's Own*, Woolf gathered around her the *avant-garde* writers, artists, and intellectuals known as the Bloomsbury Group and founded, with her husband Leonard, the Hogarth Press.

American writers also contributed experimental fiction to the Modernist revolution. By and large these Americans made their first contacts with Europe during World War I and stayed on until the Great Depression drove them home (Figure 20.7). Ernest Hemingway (1899–1961) was the first of the Americans living abroad to emerge as a major literary star. His severely disciplined prose style relied heavily on dialogue, and he often omitted details of setting and background. His writing owed a debt to popular culture: From the era's hardboiled detective fiction he borrowed a terse, world-weary voice to narrate his works, as in his 1926 novel, *The Sun Also Rises*. In this novel he portrays his fellow American exiles as a "lost generation" whose future was blighted by World War I—a Modernist message. In Hemingway's cynical vision, politics was of no importance; all that mattered were drinking bouts with male friends and casual sex with beautiful women.

William Faulkner (1897–1962) was another American who became one of the giants of twentieth-century literature. The stream-of-consciousness technique is central to his 1929 masterpiece, *The Sound and the Fury*. With a story line repeated several times but from different perspectives, this novel is especially audacious in its opening section, which narrates events through the eyes of a mentally defective character. More important than his use of such Modernist devices was his lifelong identification with his home state of Mississippi, where, after a brief sojourn in Europe, he began to explore themes about extended families bound together by sexual secrets. Faulkner's universe became the fictional county of Yoknapatawpha, which he peopled with decaying gentry, ambitious poor whites, and exploited blacks. His artistic power lay in his ability

FIGURE 20.7   PABLO PICASSO. *Gertrude Stein*. 1906. Oil on canvas, 39¼ × 32". Metropolitan Museum of Art, New York. Bequest of Gertrude Stein, 1946. *Talented Americans were introduced to Paris by American writer and expatriate Gertrude Stein, who made her studio a gathering place for the Parisian avant-garde. There she entertained Matisse and Picasso, composer Igor Stravinsky, writers Ernest Hemingway and F. Scott Fitzgerald, and many other brilliant exponents of Modernism. Stein was shocked at first by the starkness and brooding presence of Picasso's portrait of her, but she came to regard it as an accurate likeness, saying, "For me it is I, and it is the only reproduction of me which is always I."*

not only to relate these characters to their region but to turn them into universal symbols.

While experimentalism was a highly visible aspect of Modernist fiction, not all Modernist writers were preoccupied with innovative methods. Other writers were identified with the Modernists because of their pessimistic viewpoints or their explosive themes. The Modernism of the British writer D. H. Lawrence (1885–1930), for example, was expressed in novels of sexual liberation. Frustrated by the coldness of sexual relations in bourgeois culture, Lawrence, the son of a miner, concluded that the machine age emasculated men. As an antidote, he preached a religion of erotic passion. He set forth his doctrine of sexual freedom most clearly in the 1928 novel *Lady Chatterley's Lover*, issued privately and quickly banned for its explicit language and scenes. Not until the 1960s, and only after bitter court battles, was this novel allowed to circulate freely. In the novel the love-making episodes between Lady Chatterley, wed to an impotent aristocrat, and the lower-class gamekeeper Mellors were presented as models of sexual fulfillment with their mix of erotic candor and moral fervor.

Falling outside the Modernist classification is the English novelist and essayist George Orwell (1903–1950), who nevertheless is one of the major figures of the interwar period. Born Eric Blair to an established middle-class family, Orwell changed his name, rejected his background, lived and worked among the poor and downtrodden, and became a writer. He also became the conscience of his generation because he remained skeptical of all of the political ideologies of his day. In the allegorical novel *Animal Farm* (1945) he satirized Stalinist Russia. In the anti-utopian novel *1984* (1948) he made totalitarianism the enemy, especially as practiced in the Soviet Union, but he also warned of the dangers of repression in capitalist society. What made Orwell remarkable in this age torn by ideological excess was his claim to be merely an ordinary, decent man. It is perhaps for this reason that today Orwell is claimed by socialists, liberals, and conservatives alike.

Poetry   Modern poetry found its first great master in William Butler Yeats (1865–1939). His early poems are filled with Romantic mysticism, drawing on the myths of his native Ireland. By 1910 he had stripped his verses of Romantic allusions, and yet in his later works, he never gave up entirely his belief in the occult or the importance of myth. As Irish patriots grew more hostile to their country's continued submersion in the United Kingdom, climaxing in the Easter Rebellion of 1916, Yeats's poems took on a political cast. His best verses came in the 1920s, when his primary sources were Irish history and Greco-Roman myth. Perhaps his finest lyric is "Sailing to Byzantium," a poem that conjures up the Classical past in order to reaffirm ancient wisdom and redeem the tawdry industrialized world.

T. S. Eliot (1888–1965) was another founder of Modern poetry. Reared in St. Louis and educated at Harvard, Eliot moved to London in 1915, becoming an English citizen in 1927. He and Ezra Pound (1885–1972), another American exile, established a school of poetry that reflected the crisis of confidence that seized Europe's intellectuals after World War I. Like those of the late Roman poets, Eliot's verses relied heavily on literary references and quotations.

"The Waste Land," published in 1922, showed Eliot's difficult, eclectic style; in 403 irregular lines, he quotes from or imitates thirty-five separate authors, including several citations from Shakespeare and Dante, adapts snatches from popular songs, and uses phrases in six foreign languages. Form matches content because the "waste land" itself represents a sterile, godless region without a future, a symbol drawn from medieval legend but changed by Eliot into a symbol of the hollowness of modern life. In 1927 he moved beyond such atheistic pessimism, finding solace by being received in the Church of England—a step he celebrated in the poem "Ash Wednesday," published in 1930.

The black American poet Langston Hughes (1902–1967) also belongs with the outstanding Modernists. Hughes drew inspiration from many sources, including Africa, Europe, and Mexico, but the ultimate power of his poetry came from the American experience: jazz, spirituals, and his anguish as a black man in a white world. Hughes's emergence, like that of many black writers, occurred during a population shift that began in 1914 when thousands of blacks from the American South settled in northern cities like New York, Chicago, and Detroit in hopes of a better life.

At the same time that America's ethnographic map was being redrawn, a craze for Negro culture sprang up that was fueled by jazz and the *avant-garde* cult of primitivism. This craze sparked the Harlem Renaissance, a 1920s cultural revival in the predominantly black area of New York City called Harlem. Hughes was a major figure in this black literary movement. His earliest book of verses, *The Weary Blues* (1926), contains his most famous poem, "The Negro Speaks of Rivers." Dedicated to W. E. B. DuBois (1868–1963), the founder of the National Association for the Advancement of Colored People, Hughes's verse memorializes the deathless spirit of his race by linking black history to the rivers of the world.

Another outstanding figure of the Harlem Renaissance was Zora Neale Hurston (about 1901–1960), the most prolific African-American woman writer of her generation. Poet, novelist, and essayist, Hurston made her literary task the exploration of what it means to be black and female in a white- and male-dominated society. An excellent example of her handling of this theme is the short essay "How It Feels to Be Colored Me," published in 1928. A controversial work today because of its socially reactionary ideas, this essay presented two then current black stereotypes: the "happy Negro" who performed for white folks for money and sheer joy and the educated black person who, despite a veneer of learning, was still "uncivilized." Rejecting both stereotypes as diseased, Hurston's essay (like her other writings) envisioned a future, free of racism, in which African-Americans no longer had to struggle every minute for a healthy existence. As for herself, Hurston claimed, "I belong to no race nor time. I am the eternal feminine with its string of beads." Hurston's quest for self-understanding through autobiographical-rich writing was part of the Western tradition of confessional writing, originated by Rousseau in the Romantic era (see Chapter 16).

Drama   During the interwar years drama moved in new directions in both Europe and America. An Expressionist in aesthetics and a Marxist in politics, the German Bertolt Brecht [BREKT] (1898–1956) blended a discordant style learned from the Berlin streets with his hatred of bourgeois society into what he called

"*epic theater.*" Rebelling against traditional theater, which he thought merely reinforced class prejudices, he devised a radical theater centered on a technique called the "alienation effect," whose purpose was to make the bourgeois audience uncomfortable (Figure 20.8). Alienation effects could take any form, such as outlandish props, inappropriate accents, or ludicrous dialogue. By breaking the magic spell of the stage, Brecht's epic theater challenged the viewers' expectations and prepared them for his moral and political message. A victim of Nazi oppression, Brecht fled first to Scandinavia and then to America, where he lived for fifteen years before moving to East Berlin in 1952 to found a highly influential theater company.

A year before he officially embraced Marxism, Brecht teamed with the German-born composer Kurt

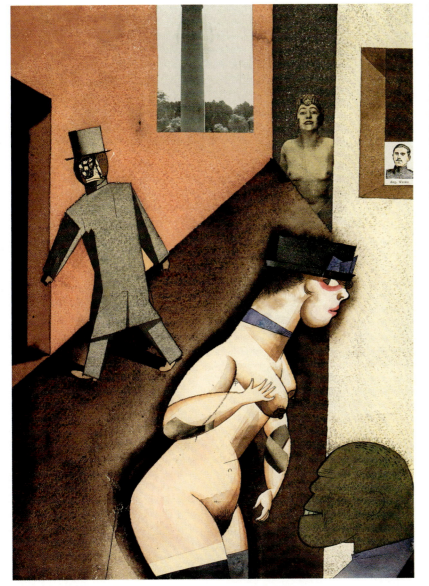

FIGURE 20.8   GEORGE GROSZ. *Life Model (Akt).* Ca. 1919. Watercolor, India ink, and collage, 42 × 29 cm. Thyssen-Bornemisza Foundation Collection, Lugano, Switzerland. *The works of German artist George Grosz provide a visual counterpart to the dramas of Brecht. Grosz portrays bourgeois society as morally bankrupt, as in this painting of a brothel scene that shows a prostitute as a willing victim. Brecht makes the same point in the drama* Mother Courage *by presenting a businesswoman heroine interested only in making money even though it means sacrificing her sons in war.*

Weill [WILE or VILE] (1900–1950) to create one of the best-known musicals in modern theater, *The Three-penny Opera* (1928). Loosely based on an eighteenth-century English opera, Brecht and Weill's Expressionist version was raucous, discordant, violent, and hostile to bourgeois values. The playwright, believing that bourgeois audiences wanted goodness to triumph over evil, made the hero a small-time hoodlum ("Mack the Knife") and then saved him at the last moment from a hanging that he richly deserved.

Besides such pathfinders as Brecht, this period also produced two major Modernist playwrights. The first of these was Jean Cocteau [kahk-TOE] (1889–1963), a French dramatist who helped to launch the French trend for modernizing the Greek classics. For example, Cocteau's *The Infernal Machine* (1934) updates Sophocles' *Oedipus.* In this modern retelling, the story is filled with Freudian overtones—Oedipus is portrayed as a "mother's boy"—and film clips are introduced for flashbacks. A second major Modernist was Eugene O'Neill (1888–1953), America's first dramatist to earn worldwide fame. Like Cocteau, O'Neill sometimes wrote new versions of Greek tragedies, as in *Mourning Becomes Electra* (1931), which was modeled on Aeschylus's *Oresteia.* But O'Neill's best plays are his tense family dramas in which generations battle one another, as in *Long Day's Journey into Night,* staged posthumously in 1956.

Philosophy and Science: The End of Certainty

During this period the Idealist philosophy that had dominated continental speculation since the early 1800s was replaced by two new schools of thought. First, in Austria and England Ludwig Wittgenstein developed ideas that helped establish the logical positivist school, which became known after World War II as the analytical school. Second, in Germany Martin Heidegger founded the existentialist school. Both schools tried to create new philosophies that were in harmony with Modernist developments.

◄ **FIGURE 20.9** ALBERTO GIACOMETTI. *Hands Holding the Void.* 1934. Plaster sculpture, original cast, ht. 61½".
Yale University Art Gallery, New Haven, Connecticut. Anonymous gift. *The uncertainty of the modern world—as demonstrated both by physics and by the economic and social realities of everyday life—is poignantly symbolized in Giacometti's sculpture. Despite the problems they faced, human beings could no longer expect answers to their questions from traditional sources, such as science and philosophy. Giacometti's melancholy figure clutching an invisible object evokes the anguish of this predicament.*

The Austrian Ludwig Wittgenstein [VIT-guhn-stine] (1889–1951) believed that the West was in a moral and intellectual decline that he attributed to faulty language, for which he surmised that current philosophical methods were to blame. Wittgenstein asserted that traditional philosophical speculation was senseless because, of necessity, it relied on language that could not rise above simple truisms.

Wittgenstein's solution to this intellectual impasse dethroned philosophy from the summit from which it had looked down on the rest of culture since the time of the Greeks and made philosophy simply the servant of science. He set forth his conclusion in his *Tractatus Logico-Philosophicus* in 1922. In this treatise he reasoned that, although language might be faulty, there still were tools for comprehending the world, namely mathematical computation and scientific empiricism. He proposed that thinkers give up the study of values and morals and assist scientists in a quest for truth. This conclusion led to *logical positivism*, a school of philosophy dedicated to defining terms and clarifying statements.

Wittgenstein later rejected the idea that language is a flawed instrument and substituted a theory of language as games, in the manner of children's play. Nevertheless, it was the point of view set forth in the *Tractatus* that made Wittgenstein so influential in the universities in England between 1930 and 1960 and in America after World War II.

While Wittgenstein was challenging philosophy's ancient role, Martin Heidegger [HI-deg-uhr] (1889–1976) was assaulting traditional philosophy from another angle by founding modern *existentialism*, although the result of Heidegger's massive criticism was to restore philosophy to its central position as the definer of values for culture. Heidegger's major work, *Being and Time*, was published in 1927. The focal point of his thinking was the peculiar nature of human existence (the source of the term "existentialism") as compared with other objects in the world. In his view human existence leads to anxiety, a condition that arises because of the consciousness that there is a future that includes choices and death. He noted that most people try to avoid facing their inevitable fate by immersing themselves in trivial activities. For a few, however, Heidegger thought that the existential moment offered an opportunity in which they could seize the initiative and make themselves into authentic human beings. "Authenticity" became the ultimate human goal: to confront death and to strive for genuine creativity—a typical German philosophical attitude shared with Goethe and Nietzsche.

Heidegger is among the twentieth century's foremost philosophers, but his politics have made him a controversial figure. He used his post as a German university professor to support the rise of Nazism in the 1930s. To hostile eyes, Heidegger's existential views—which acknowledged that individuals, powerless to reshape the world, could only accept it—seemed to support his political position. Indeed, some commentators have condemned existentialism for this reason.

Heidegger's best-known disciple, though one who rejected Nazism, was the French thinker Jean-Paul Sartre [SAHRTR] (1905–1980). Sartre's major philosophical work, *Being and Nothingness* (1943), was heavily indebted to his mentor's concepts. From Heidegger came his definition of existentialism as an attitude characterized by concern for human freedom, personal responsibility, and individual choices. Sartre used these ideas to frame his guiding rule: Because human beings are condemned to freedom, that is, not free *not* to choose, they must take responsibility for their actions and live "without excuses." After 1945 Sartre rejected existentialism as overly individualistic and thereafter tended to support Marxist collectivist action.

In the sciences, physics remained the field of dynamic activity. The breakthroughs made before World War I were now corroborated by new research that compelled scientists to discard the Newtonian model of the universe as a simple machine. They replaced it with a complex, sense-defying structure based on the discoveries of Albert Einstein and Werner Heisenberg (Figure 20.9).

Einstein was the leading scientist in the West, comparable to Newton in the eighteenth century. His special relativity theory, dating from 1905, was accepted by most physicists. By this theory the Newtonian concept of fixed dimensions to time and space was overthrown because, in Einstein's view, absolute space and time are meaningless categories since they vary with the situation. In 1915 he expanded this earlier finding into a general theory of relativity, a universal law based on complex equations that applied throughout the cosmos.

The heart of the general theory was that space is curved as a result of the acceleration of objects (planets, stars, moons, meteors, and so on) as they move through undulating trajectories. The earth's orbit about the sun is caused not by a gravitational "force" but by the curvature of space-time around the sun. In 1919 a team of scientists confirmed his theory by observing the curvature of space in the vicinity of the sun. They found that space curved to the degree that Einstein's theory had forecast. Since then his general theory has survived many tests of its validity and has opened new paths of theoretical speculation.

Despite his commanding role in twentieth-century science, Einstein ignored the other great breakthrough of modern physics, the establishment of quantum physics. Prior to 1914 the German physicist Max Planck had discovered the quantum nature of radiation in the subatomic realm. Ignoring the classical theory that energy is radiated continuously, he proved that energy is emitted in separate units that he called *quanta,* after the Latin for "how much" (as in *quantity*), and he symbolized these units by the letter *h*.

Working with Planck's *h* in 1927, which by now was accepted as a fundamental constant of nature, the German physicist Werner Heisenberg [HIZE-uhn-berg] (1901–1976) arrived at the uncertainty principle, a step that encompassed a decisive break with classical physics. Heisenberg showed that a scientist could identify an electronic particle's exact location or its path, but not both. This dilemma led to the conclusion that absolute certitude in subatomic science is impossible because scientists with their instruments inevitably interfere with the accuracy of their own work—the uncertainty principle. The incertitude involved in quantum theory caused Einstein to remark, "God does not play dice with the world." Nevertheless, quantum theory joined relativity theory as a founding principle of modern physics.

A practical result of the revolution in physics was the opening of the nuclear age in August 1945. The American physicist J. Robert Oppenheimer [AHP-uhn-hi-muhr] (1904–1967), having made basic contributions to quantum theory, was the logical choice to head the team that built the first atomic bomb. Oppenheimer's other role as a member of the panel that advised that the atomic bombs be dropped on Japan raised ethical questions that divided the scientific community then and continues to do so.

Art, Architecture, and Film

The art, architecture, and film of the interwar period were driven by the same forces that were transforming literature and philosophy. Modernism reached its zenith in painting and architecture, and the movies became established as the world's most popular form of mass culture (Time Line 20.1).

Painting   Painting dominated the visual arts in the interwar period. Painters launched new art movements every two or three years, although certain prevailing themes and interests could be discerned underneath the shifting styles: abstraction, primitivism and fantasy, and Expressionism. This era's most explosive art was produced within these stylistic categories. Picasso and Matisse, the two giants of twentieth-century art, continued to exercise their influence, yet they too worked within these three categories, all of which had arisen in the Post-Impressionist period.

ABSTRACTION   The history of modern painting has been rewritten in the last twenty-five years to accommodate the contributions of Soviet painters to abstract art. No one questions the primary role played by Picasso and Braque in Cubist paintings prior to World War I, but Soviet painters, beginning in 1917, moved beyond

FIGURE 20.10   KASIMIR MALEVICH. *Suprematist Composition, Black Trapezium and Red Square*. After 1915. Oil on canvas, 101.5 × 62 cm. Stedelijk Museum, Amsterdam. *Malevich's geometric style reflected his belief that abstract images had a spiritual quality comparable to religious icons. In other words, an abstract form could become a meditation device. His belief was typical of thinking among the German and Russian avant-garde in the early 1900s. In the interwar period the principle of the spirituality of abstract art became widely accepted by Modernist painters throughout Europe and, after World War II, by Abstract Expressionist artists in America.*

TIME LINE 20.1   HIGH MODERNISM, 1914–1945

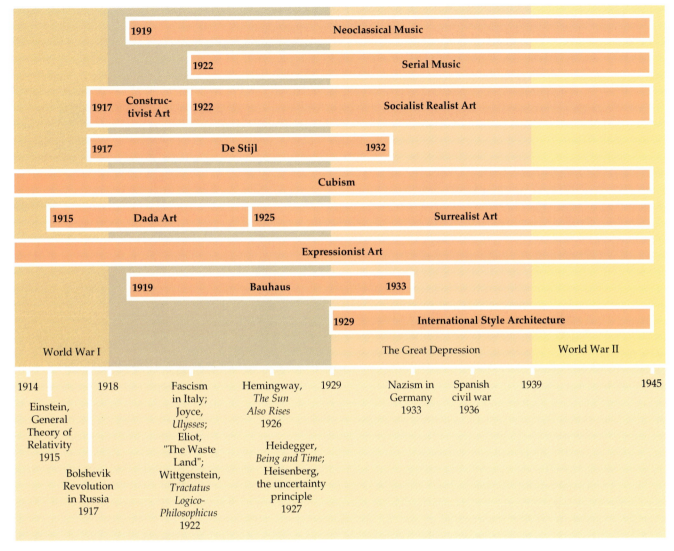

Cubism and toward full abstraction, thus staking out claims as early founders of modern abstract art. The most influential of these Soviet artists was Kasimir Malevich [muhl-YAVE-yich] (1878–1935).

Influenced by the Cubists and the Futurists—an Italian school of artists who depicted forms in surging, violent motion—Malevich was already working in an abstract style when World War I began in 1914. Four years later he was painting completely nonobjective canvases. Believing that art should convey ethical and philosophical values, he created a style of painting devoted to purity, in which he made line, color, and shape the only purposes in his art. He called this style *Suprematism*, named for his belief that the feelings are "supreme" over every other element of life—"feelings," that is, expressed in a purely rational way.

Searching for a way to visualize emotions on can-

vas, Malevich adopted geometric shapes as nonobjective symbols, as in *Suprematist Composition, Black Trapezium and Red Square* (Figure 20.10). In this painting design has triumphed over representation. There are only geometric shapes of different sizes, dominated by the trapezium and the square, along with lines of varying length. The choice of the geometric shapes reflects their role as basic elements of composition with no relation to nature. The qualities shown in Malevich's painting—flatness, coolness, and severe rationality—remain central to one branch of abstract art today.

Malevich's Suprematism helped to shape *Constructivism*, the first art style launched by Lenin's regime in 1917 and the last modern art movement in Russia. Malevich's philosophical views, which were rooted in Christian mysticism, ran counter to the materialism of the Marxist government, however, and

PM 21

◀ **FIGURE 20.11** PIET MONDRIAN. *Composition in Red, Yellow, and Blue.* 1921. Oil on canvas, 80 × 50 cm. Collection Haags Gemeentemuseum, The Hague. *Allied with those artists who identified abstract forms with spiritual values, Mondrian originated "the grid" as the ideal way to approach the canvas, allowing the verticals and horizontals to establish the painting area. Mondrian's devotion to "the grid," along with his spare use of color, gave rise to many of the dominant trends in art after World War II: two-dimensional images, geometric shapes, and "all over" paintings without a specific up or down.*

the flowering of abstraction in the Soviet Union was abruptly snuffed out in 1922. In that year Lenin pronounced it a decadent form of bourgeois expression, and its leaders were imprisoned or exiled. In place of Constructivism the Soviet leaders proclaimed the doctrine of *Socialist Realism*, which demanded the use of traditional techniques and styles and the glorification of the communist ideal. This type of realistic art also had greater appeal to the Soviet masses, who had been alienated by the abstract style of Constructivism.

A movement similar to Suprematism and Constructivism, called **De Stijl** (The Style), originated in the Netherlands during this period, lasting from 1917 to 1932. *De Stijl* artists shared the belief that art should have spiritual values and that if artists were to revamp society along rational lines, from town planning to eating utensils, a more harmonious vision of life would result.

The *De Stijl* movement was led by the painter Piet Mondrian [MAHN-dree-ahn] (1872–1944), who after 1919 worked successively in Paris, London, and New York. He developed an elaborate theory to give a metaphysical meaning to his abstract paintings. A member of the Theosophists—a mystical cult that flourished around 1900—he adapted some of their beliefs to arrive at a grid format for his later paintings, notably using the Theosophists' stress on cosmic duality in which the vertical represented the male and the horizontal the female. His paintings took the form of a rectangle divided by heavy black lines against a white background. Into this highly charged field he introduced rectangular patches of the primary colors, blue, yellow, and red, which in his mystic vision stood as symbols of the sky, the sun, and dynamic union, respectively (Figure 20.11).

Despite the pioneering work of Suprematism and the *De Stijl* school, Cubism remained the leading art movement of this period, and Pablo Picasso was still the reigning Cubist. Picasso's protean genius revealed itself in multiple styles after 1920, but he continually reverted to his Cubist roots, as in *The Three Musicians* (Figure 20.12). Like the rest of his works, this painting is based on a realistic source, in this case a group of masked musicians playing their in-

struments. The forms appear flattened, as if they were shapes that had been cut out and then pasted to the pictorial surface—the ideal of flatness so prized by Modern art.

The most famous work of Picasso's long career also dates from this period: the protest canvas *Guernica*, painted in a modified Cubist style. Picasso named this painting for an unarmed town that had been bombed by the Nazi air force (in the service of Franco) during the Spanish Civil War. Picasso used every element in the work to register his rage against this senseless destruction of human life (see Figure 20.1). The black, white, and grey tones conjure up newspaper images, suggesting the casual way that newspapers report daily disasters. An all-seeing eye looks down on a scene of horror made visible to the world through the modern media—as symbolized by the electric bulb that acts as a retina in the cosmic eye. Images of death and destruction—the mother

FIGURE 20.12 PABLO PICASSO. *The Three Musicians.* 1921. Oil on canvas, 6'8" × 6'2". Philadelphia Museum of Art. The A. E. Gallatin Collection. *This Cubist painting captures the energy of a musical performance. Here and there among the flattened shapes can be seen hints of musical instruments being fingered by disembodied hands. Only a little imagination is needed to bring this masked trio to life. The brilliant colors coupled with the broken and resynthesized forms evoke the jagged rhythms the musicians must have been playing.*

cradling a child's body, the stabbed horse, the enraged bull, the fallen man, and the screaming woman—are made even more terrifying by their angular forms. In retrospect, *Guernica* was a watershed painting both topically and stylistically. The blending of Cubism with social protest was new—as was Franco's type of unbridled warfare. *Guernica* forecast even more horrifying events to come.

The American painter Georgia O'Keeffe (1887–1986) refused to follow European painters down the path to pure abstraction. Instead she pursued a distinctively American type of abstraction, using American subjects drawn from nature, which she pared to their pure form and color; at the same time, she kept representation of the natural world as a primary goal of her art. A native of Wisconsin, she found a spiritual home in the American Southwest—Texas and especially New Mexico—whose sundrenched, stark landscapes inspired some of her most famous images. Sensitive to light, color, texture, and atmosphere, she registered in her paintings the previously hidden beauties of this desert world, as in *Cow's Skull with Calico Roses* (Figure 20.13). As early as the Renaissance, painters had occasionally used death's heads as *memento mori* (reminders of death), but no artist before O'Keeffe had thought of presenting a cow's skull as an art subject. The already abstract form of the cow's skull, stripped bare of flesh, became even more abstract as she simplified it and presented it close up with two roses nearby. The result is an image of shocking beauty.

PRIMITIVISM AND FANTASY   The Modernists' admiration for Primitivism led to **Dada**, the most unusual art movement of the twentieth century. Named for a nonsense word chosen for its ridiculous sound, Dada flourished in Zurich and Paris between 1915 and 1925, chiefly as unruly pranks by disaffected artists who wanted to "hurl gobs of spit in the faces of the bourgeoisie." They staged exhibits in public lavatories, planned meetings in cemeteries, and arranged lectures where the speaker was drowned out by a bell. Slowly it became evident that these outrageous acts conveyed the message that World War I had made all values meaningless. These artists could no longer support the spiritual claims and traditional beliefs of Western humanism. The Dada group embraced anti-art as the only ethical position possible for an artist in the modern era.

The most influential exponent of Dada was the French artist Marcel Duchamp [dew-SHAHN] (1887–1968), who abandoned Cubism in about 1915. His best-known Dada piece is the "definitely incomplete" work called *The Bride Stripped Bare by Her Bachelors, Even*, a mixture of oil, wire, and lead foil on two glass panels made between 1915 and 1923, sometimes called *The Large Glass* (Figure 20.14). Although it is certainly enigmatic, and in the eyes of many viewers it looked like a giant swindle, much is clear about *The Large Glass*. It has an erotic theme, as indicated by the bride's "apartment" in the upper half, the bachelors' "chamber" below, and the thin tubes filled with oil linking the two segments. Duchamp's point seems to be similar to that of the novelist D. H. Lawrence: Sex in the machine age has become boring and mechanized.

FIGURE 20.13   GEORGIA O'KEEFFE. *Cow's Skull with Calico Roses.* 1931. Oil on canvas. 36⁵/₁₆ × 24¹/₈". The Art Institute of Chicago. Gift of Georgia O'Keeffe. *The simplified forms— the skull and the rose—link this painting to the period's trend to abstraction, but their placement so as to suggest the image of a "face" devouring a rose implies a connection with another development of this period, Surrealism, a style which delighted in realistic images with double meanings (see Figure 20.15). Whether intentional or not, O'Keeffe's overlapping of stylistic boundaries was typical of the fluid artistic scene in the years between the two world wars.*

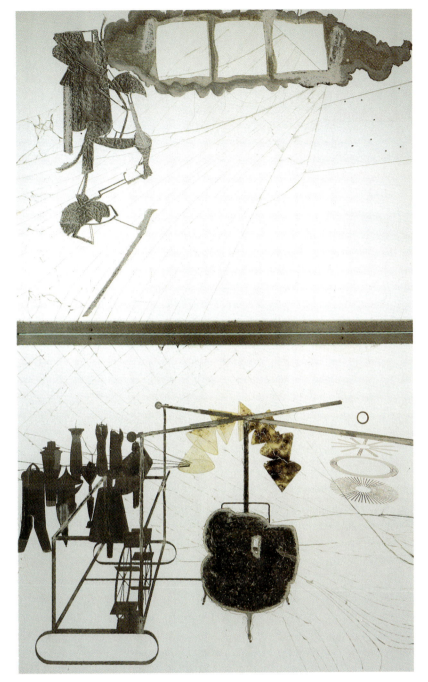

FIGURE 20.14 MARCEL DUCHAMP. *The Bride Stripped Bare by Her Bachelors, Even (or, The Large Glass).* 1915–1923. Oil and lead wire on glass, 9'1¼" × 5'9⅛". Philadelphia Museum of Art. Bequest of Katherine M. Dreier. *Shortly after this legendary assemblage was built, the glass shattered. Duchamp repaired the work, replacing the glass with heavier panes and installing a reinforced frame. But effects of the accident are still apparent. Duchamp claimed to be delighted by these chance additions to his original design. In making this claim, he was the forerunner of the Modernist idea that chance should play a guiding role in art. After World War II many artists began to incorporate random effects into their works.*

Dada led to *Surrealism*, an art movement that began in the 1920s. Unlike Dada, Surrealism was basically a pictorial art. Inspired by Freud's teaching that the human mind conceals hidden depths, the Surrealists wanted to create a vision of reality that also included the truths harbored in the unconscious. They portrayed dream imagery, fantasies, and hallucinations in a direct fashion that made their paintings more startling than Dada. Among the leading Surrealists were Salvador Dali and Paul Klee.

The Spanish painter Salvador Dali [DAH-lee] (1904–1989) concentrated on subjects that surfaced from his lively imagination and often contained thinly disguised sexual symbols. Probably his most famous work is the poetically named painting *The Persistence of Memory*, which depicts soft, melting watches in a desert-like setting (Figure 20.15). Sexual themes may be read in the limp images of watches—perhaps a reference to sexual impotence. Regardless of its meaning, the painting gives a strange twist to ordinary things, evoking the sense of a half-remembered dream—the goal of Surrealist art. Despite obvious painterly skills, Dali cultivated a controversial, even scandalous personal image. His escapades earned him the public's ridicule, and the Surrealists even disowned him. From today's vantage point, however, Dali is admired for two reasons: for having created some of Modernism's most fantastic images and for being a link with the Pop artists of the 1960s.

The Swiss painter Paul Klee [KLAY] (1879–1940) may be grouped with the Surrealists, but he was too changeable to be restricted to a single style. He is best known for an innocent approach to art, which

FIGURE 20.15 SALVADOR DALI. *The Persistence of Memory.* 1931. Oil on canvas, 9½ × 13". Collection, The Museum of Modern Art, New York. Given anonymously. *Dali liked to paint images that were actually optical illusions. In this painting, the watch depicted on the right is draped over an amorphous shape that, on inspection, appears to be that of a man. Dali's use of such optical effects reflected his often-stated belief that life itself is irrational.*

FIGURE 20.16 PAUL KLEE. *Arab Song.* 1932. Gouache on unprimed burlap, 35⅞ × 25½". Phillips Collection, Washington, D.C. *Klee's enigmatic art is difficult to classify. Because he preferred small images, he is sometimes classified as a minor artist. And unlike most European artists of his generation, who made spiritual claims for art, Klee had modest, earthbound goals for his whimsical works. Yet Klee's playful images remain in the mind long after the stark abstract designs of Malevich and Mondrian have faded.*

was triggered by his fondness for children's uninhibited scrawls. The childlike wonder portrayed in his whimsical works has made him a favorite with collectors and viewers. A professor from 1920 until 1930 at the Bauhaus, Germany's leading art institute between the wars, Klee created poetic images, rich in color and gentle wit, as in *Arab Song* (Figure 20.16). The draperies, painted on burlap, evoke an Arabic mood with their twin references to tents and to a veiled woman. The leaf and bud, floating in space, contribute an unexpected, lyrical note. Other traits of Klee's style may be seen in *Arab Song*'s small scale, radiant colors, and playfulness.

The Mexican painter Frida Kahlo [KAH-low] (1907–1954), famed for her bizarre self-portraits (Figure 20.17), might be classified with the Surrealists, though she is usually linked with the Mexican Muralists, the politically-motivated artists who flourished between the two world wars and who painted mural (wall) cycles in public buildings to dramatize their socialist vision and solidarity with Mexico's native peoples. Most of her life she was involved in a tempestuous marriage to Diego Rivera (1886–1957), a leading Mexican Muralist, but she was much more than the wife of a famous painter. Kahlo was an important artist in her own right, creating works which reflected her physical (polio at age six, serious accident at 18) and spiritual suffering. Today she is known as an artist who turned private anguish into art with universal resonance.

EXPRESSIONISM The chief Expressionist painters in this era were Henri Matisse, a founder of Fauvism before World War I, and Max Beckmann, the heir to German Expressionism. In the 1930s Matisse's art was distinguished by its decorative quality, a tendency since his Fauvist days. *Large Reclining Nude* shows his new style, which is characterized by a fresh approach to the human figure: enlarged, simplified, though clearly recognizable (Figure 20.18). The nude figure is depicted completely flat, without modeling or shading, so that it looks as if it has been cut out and glued to the gridded surface. Matisse has also abandoned the highly saturated colors of Fauvism and replaced them with cooler tones, in this case a cotton-candy pink. Nevertheless, he stayed true to the Expressionist principle of distortion, as demonstrated by the nude figure's elongated body and dangling limbs.

Matisse has been rebuked for concentrating on pretty subjects while the world slipped into anarchy. No such charge can be made against the German painter Max Beckmann (1884–1950), whose Expressionist paintings register horror at the era's turbulent events. *The Temptation of St. Anthony* is typical of his paintings, being concerned with both personal

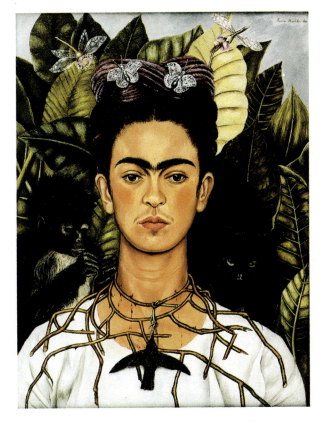

FIGURE 20.17 FRIDA KAHLO. *Self-Portrait with Thorn Necklace and Hummingbird.* 1940. Oil on canvas. 24½ × 17¾". Collection, Harry Ransom Humanities Research Center, University of Texas at Austin. *Kahlo's self-portrait grew out of her ongoing love affair with death and suffering. Whereas Renaissance artists occasionally portrayed themselves in Christ's image as the Suffering Savior (see Figure 13.9), Kahlo reveals a Modernist sensibility in this likeness, which draws on multicultural sources, including Christianity and her Mexican heritage. The painting itself resembles a religious icon with its strict frontality and lack of depth. The web of thorns, which makes her neck bleed, refers both to Christ's crown of thorns worn on the day of the crucifixion and to the Aztec prophetic ritual that required self-mortification with maguey thorns. The dead hummingbird and the butterflies are Aztec symbols of the souls of dead warriors, and the cat is a more generalized symbol of death. Only the monkey (one of two who were pets and who figure in eight of her self-portraits) stands free from this sense of impending doom.*

and spiritual issues (Figure 20.19). The structure of the painting—divided into three panels like a medieval altarpiece—suggests that it has religious meaning. In the central panel Beckmann depicts an artist, bound at the wrists and ankles and musing before a nude model, perhaps a symbol of Beckmann himself, whose art the Nazis condemned as degenerate. The side panels, with themes of temptation and cruelty, reinforce the connection between the artist-sufferer and a medieval saint. In the same year this painting was completed, pressure from the Nazis forced Beckmann to seek refuge in Amsterdam, where he managed to survive World War II.

Architecture In the 1920s and 1930s, architects continued their search for a pure style, free of decoration and totally functional. Their search resembled a mystical quest, stemming from the belief that new architecture could solve social problems by creating a new physical environment—a recurrent theme in European Modernism.

This visionary conception of architecture was best expressed in Germany's Bauhaus, an educational institution whose aim was to bring about social reform through a new visual environment, especially in the design of everyday objects. To this end, the school brought together artists, craftspeople, and architects. During its brief lifetime, which lasted from its founding in 1919 until 1933 when it was closed by the Nazis, the Bauhaus, under Walter Gropius [GROH-pee-uhs] (1883–1969), was the center of abstract art in Germany. The Bauhaus affected later culture in two ways. First, it developed a spartan type of interior decoration characterized by all-white rooms and wooden floors, streamlined furniture, and lighting supplied by banks of windows by day and recessed lamps at night. Second, it introduced the *International Style* in architecture, which is sleek, geometrical, and devoid of ornament.

The International Style's most distinguished representative in the period between the wars was the Swiss architect Charles-Edouard Jeanneret, better known as Le Corbusier [luh-kahr-BEW-zee-ay] (1887–1965). Le Corbusier's artistic credo was expressed in the dictum, ''a house is a machine for living.'' In pursuit of this ideal, he pioneered building methods like prefabricated housing and reinforced concrete as ways to eliminate ordinary walls. His Sa-

FIGURE 20.18 HENRI MATISSE. *Large Reclining Nude.* 1935. Oil on canvas, 66 × 92 cm. Baltimore Museum of Art. The Cone Collection. Large Reclining Nude *established the archetypal images—a still life and a model in an interior—that Matisse painted for the rest of his life. It was also the first expression of his later style, which was characterized by the human figure being simply another element in an overall design.*

Figure 20.19 Max Beckmann. *The Temptation of St. Anthony.* 1937. Oil on canvas, triptych, center panel, 6'6¾" × 5'7"; side panels each 7'1" × 3'3⅜". Bayerische Staatsgalerie Moderner Kunst, Munich. *Beckmann often adopted Christian symbols as his paintings became more overtly spiritual in their content. In paintings like* Temptation *he identified twentieth-century artists with medieval saints, drawing the parallel that both had to go against the common wisdom of their times in order to reach seemingly impossible goals.*

voye House became the prototype of private houses for the wealthy after World War II (Figure 20.20). The Savoye House was painted white and raised on columns; its ground floor had a curved wall; and its windows were slits. A painter before becoming an architect, Le Corbusier designed architecture that combined Cubism's abstractness (the raised box) with Constructivism's purity (whiteness).

Film   Motion pictures—the movies—were immediately popular when they were introduced early in the twentieth century, and by the mid–1920s they had become the most popular mass entertainment, drawing larger audiences than the theater, vaudeville, and the music halls. The American film director D. W. Griffith (1875–1948) showed in such pioneering works as *The Birth of a Nation* (1915) and *Intolerance* (1916) that it was possible to make movies that were serious, sustained works of art. His technical innovations, such as crosscutting and the close-up, made more complex film narratives possible, but such attempts to develop the medium were rare. Although other directors quickly appropriated Griffith's techniques, few went beyond them, and the movies remained resolutely lowbrow. The present-day distinction between "movies" (the widest possible audience) and "film" (appealing to

more educated, intellectual audiences) had not yet arisen.

One of the era's most inventive directors was the Russian Sergei Eisenstein [IZE-uhn-stine] (1898–1948), who introduced directorial techniques that had an enormous influence on the rise of art films. In *The Battleship Potemkin* (1925) he pioneered the montage technique, which consisted of highly elaborate editing patterns and rhythms. He developed the montage because he believed that the key element in films was the way the scenes were arranged, how they faded out and faded in, and how they looked in juxtaposition to one another. By focusing on the material of the film itself instead of highlighting the plot or the characters' psychology, Eisenstein showed his allegiance to the artistic aspect of movie making.

The United States (which eventually meant Hollywood, California) had dominated the motion picture industry since World War I, and the industry underwent important changes during the interwar years. Sound movies became technically feasible in the late 1920s, and in the early 1930s three-color cinematography processes were developed. Both these technical developments became basic to the movies throughout the world, but other experiments, such

FIGURE 20.20 LE CORBUSIER. Savoye House. 1929–1931. Poissy, near Paris. *Le Corbusier wanted to make a break with previous styles of architecture and create a new style in tune with the machine age. His design for the Savoye House realizes this ambition completely through its severe geometrical form, its absence of decoration except for architectural details, and its sparkling white walls. When finished, the Savoye House had the streamlined look associated with industrial machinery, an achievement much admired in the 1930s.*

as wide-screen and three-dimensional photography, were less successful. Another important development in this period was the descent on Hollywood of many German filmmakers in flight from the Nazis. In the Hollywood of the 1930s these exiles helped to create some of the outstanding achievements in world cinema.

A sign of the excellence of Hollywood movies in these years is Orson Welles's *Citizen Kane* (1941), often called America's best film. An American, Welles (1915–1985) had learned from the German exiles and their Expressionist methods. From them he borrowed such devices as theatrical lighting and multiple narrative voices. Welles's own commanding presence in the lead role also contributed to making this an unforgettable movie. But one of the hallmarks of the movie—its dark look, which underscores the brooding theme of unbridled lust for power—was in actuality a money-saving device to disguise the absence of studio sets. Is *Citizen Kane* a "film" or a "movie"? It is a measure of Welles's success that it is triumphantly both: The frequency of its showing both on television and in theaters attests to its popularity, yet it has probably been discussed and analyzed in film journals and books as much as any film ever made.

Music: Atonality, Neoclassicism, and American Idiom

During the 1920s and 1930s Western music was fragmented into two rival camps as a result of developments that had begun in the period before World War I. On one side was the Austro-German school headed by Arnold Schoenberg, who had introduced

atonality before 1914 and in the 1920s pioneered serial music. On the other side was the French school led by Igor Stravinsky, who had experimented with primitive rhythms and harsh dissonances in the early 1900s but after World War I adopted a stern Neoclassical style.

Having abandoned tonality in 1909, Schoenberg in the 1920s introduced **serial music**, a method of composing with a **twelve-tone scale**—twelve tones that are related not to a tonal center in a major or minor key but only to each other. Lacking harmonious structure, serial music sounded dissonant and random and tended to create anxiety in listeners. As a result, serial music appealed to cult rather than mass audiences. Lack of a huge responsive public did not halt Schoenberg's pursuit of atonality. His serial system culminated in *Variations for Orchestra* (1928), a composition that uses the Classical form of theme with variations. In 1933 he emigrated to America, where his devotion to atonality mellowed. Some of Schoenberg's later works mix twelve-tone writing with tonality.

Stravinsky, in exile from the Soviet Union after 1917, was now living in Paris, where he became the dominant figure of *Neoclassicism* in music, borrowing features from seventeenth- and eighteenth-century music (Figure 20.21). In his Neoclassical works, he abandoned many of the techniques that had become common to music since the Baroque period, such as Romantic emotionalism and programmatic composition as well as Impressionism's use of dense orchestral sounds. Austere and cool, his Neoclassical compositions used simple instrumental combinations and sounded harmonious. Stravinsky's works from this period made him the outstanding composer of the twentieth century.

Stravinsky originated Neoclassicism in 1919 with the ballet *Pulcinella* and brought the style to a close in 1951 with the opera *The Rake's Progress*. Between these two major works is one of his most admired compositions, the *Symphony of Psalms*, dating from 1930. *Pulcinella* and *The Rake's Progress* owe much to the music and comic operas of the Classical composers Pergolesi and Mozart, respectively, and the *Symphony of Psalms* follows a Baroque model in its small orchestra and musical structure. Despite borrowing forms and ideas, Stravinsky made them his own, introducing occasional dissonances and continuing to experiment with complex rhythmic patterns.

American music, meanwhile, was discovering its own idiom. Charles Ives (1874–1954) focused on American melodies, including folk songs, hymns, marches, patriotic songs, ragtime tunes, and music of his beloved New England. Working without models, Ives experimented with tonality and rhythm in similar ways to the European *avant-garde*. Typical of his work is the *Concord Sonata* for piano (1909–1915). Another American composer, Aaron Copland (1900–1990), had achieved some success by imitating European styles, but in the 1930s he began to develop a distinctive American style. His ballet scores *Billy the Kid* (1938), *Rodeo* (1942), and *Appalachian Spring* (1944) draw on hymns, ballads, folk tunes, and popular songs of the period. His delightful melodies, brilliant sound, jazzy experimentation, and upbeat rhythms ensured the popularity of these pieces.

A major American composer who cared less about developing a purely American idiom and more about exploring music's frontiers was George Antheil [an-TILE] (1900–1959). Living in Europe from 1922 to 1933, Antheil became part of the intellectual *avant-garde* who were intrigued by the machine-oriented culture of the Age of the Masses. In worshipping the machine, these artists and musicians followed in the steps of the Futurists, the Italian group who had raised "speed" into an artistic principle before World War I (see Figure 19.7). As part of the 1920s European scene, Antheil was led to incorporate industrial sounds—the music of the masses—into his compositions. Hence, his *Ballet mécanique* (*Mechanical Ballet*) (1924; revised 1952) included scoring for unusual "instruments" (electric bells, small wood propeller, large wood propeller, metal propeller, siren, and sixteen player pianos) as well as more traditional instruments (piano and three xylophones). Antheil claimed this as his goal in composing this iconoclastic work: "It is the rhythm of machinery, presented as beautifully as an artist knows how . . . It is the life, the manufacturing, the industry of today."

During this period jazz began to reach larger au-

FIGURE 20.21 PABLO PICASSO. *Stravinsky*. 1920. Pencil on gray paper, 24⅜" × 19⅛". Musée Picasso, Paris. *Picasso's pencil sketch of Stravinsky is a perceptive character study. Long before Stravinsky became almost unapproachable, Picasso portrayed him as an aloof, self-absorbed young man. Stravinsky's cold demeanor is obvious in the tense posture, the harsh stare, and the clasped hands and crossed legs. Picasso's sketch also hints at Stravinsky's genius by exaggerating the size of his hands, perhaps to emphasize their role in the composer's creative life.*

diences, in part because of the development of the radio and phonograph. Many jazz greats created their reputations in these years. The fame of the finest jazz composer, Duke Ellington (born Edward Kennedy Ellington, 1899–1974), dated from 1927 at Harlem's Cotton Club. Ellington's songs balanced superb orchestration with improvisation and ranged from popular melodies, like *Sophisticated Lady* (1932), to major suites, like *Such Sweet Thunder*, based on Shakespeare. Jazz's premiere female vocalist also appeared now, Billie Holiday (1915–1959), whose bittersweet style was marked by innovative phrasing.

Two jazz performers whose careers extended well beyond this period are Louis Armstrong (1900–1971) and Ella Fitzgerald (1918–). Armstrong, better known as "Satchmo," became a goodwill ambassador for the United States with his loud and relaxed New Orleans-style trumpet playing. Ella Fitzgerald, a vocalist noted for her bell-like voice and elegant phrasing, became the peerless interpreter of jazz standards as well as pop tunes. In the next period, jazz fragmented into a host of styles and was a vital ingredient in the explosive birth of rock-and-roll, the popular music form originating in the 1950s that has since dominated popular music.

The Legacy of the Age of the Masses and Modernism

The Age of the Masses has transformed material civilization in the West in both good and bad ways. It has given us the most destructive wars of history, the greatest economic depression since the fourteenth century, the most absolute forms of government since the late Roman Empire, the first modern attempt to eliminate an entire people, and a weapon capable of destroying the planet. At the same time, it has brought a better standard of living to most people in the West and given millions of Westerners their first taste of democracy.

This age has also had a contradictory impact on cultural developments. On the one hand, it saw the growth of a worldwide mass culture, led by American ingenuity, which began to dominate public and private life for most people. On the other hand, it inspired a revolt by Modernist artists, writers, and musicians to create works free of mass culture's influence. Their Modernist creations were experimental, perplexing, and often committed to what they defined as spiritual values. A few Modernists refused to become mass culture's adversaries, and these moderating voices pointed toward a healthier relationship between mass culture and the elitist tradition after World War II.

Besides the polarization between mass and high culture, this period left other cultural legacies. During this time films became accepted as a serious art form, and they remain the greatest legacy of mass culture to the twentieth century. It was also during this period that America emerged as a significant cultural force in the West, partly because of the tide of intellectuals flowing from Europe, partly because of America's growing political, economic, and military power, and partly because of excellent native schools of writers, musicians, and artists. And finally, a questioning mood became the normative way of looking at the world, replacing the certainty of previous centuries.

The Modernists had pioneered a questioning spirit around 1900, and in this period the revolution in physics seemed to reinforce it. Einstein's conclusion that space and time are interchangeable was echoed by artists, writers, and musicians who focused on form to define content in their work. And Heisenberg's uncertainty principle seemed to reverberate everywhere—from Wittgenstein's toying with language, to the highly personal narrative voices that dominated the novel, to the constantly shrinking set of basic beliefs that characterized the period's religious thought, and ultimately to the widespread belief that Western civilization had lost its course.

KEY CULTURAL TERMS

mass culture
stream-of-consciousness
epic theater
logical positivism
existentialism
Suprematism
Constructivism
Socialist Realism

De Stijl
Dada
Surrealism
International Style
serial music
twelve-tone scale
Neoclassicism

SUGGESTIONS FOR FURTHER READING

PRIMARY SOURCES

BRECHT, B. *The Threepenny Opera.* English version by D. Vesey and English lyrics by E. Bentley. New York: Limited Editions Club, 1982. An excellent adaptation of Brecht's biting drama about the underworld in Victorian England; Bentley's lyrics capture the slangy flavor of the German play first staged in 1928.

COCTEAU, J. *The Infernal Machine and Other Plays.* Norfolk, Conn.: New Directions, 1964. Cocteau fuses Classicism with experimental methods in his Modernist plays; he updates the Oedipus legend, for example, by introducing Freudian ideas and using film clips to present flashbacks.

ELIOT, T. S. *Collected Poems, 1909–1962.* New York: Harcourt, Brace & World, 1963. Eliot's early portrayal of his times as an exhausted era abandoned by God made him a pillar of Modernism.

FAULKNER, W. *The Sound and the Fury*. New York: Modern Library, 1946. The most admired novel from the Yoknapatawpha series, Faulkner's monumental study of post-Civil War Mississippi society.

HEIDEGGER, M. *Being and Time*. Translated by J. Macquarrie and E. Robinson. New York: Harper, 1962. First published in 1927, this work helped launch the existentialist movement by portraying the universe as a meaningless place and human existence as a never-ending quest for authenticity.

HEMINGWAY, E. *The Sun Also Rises*. New York: Scribner, 1970. Hemingway's semiautobiographical first novel, set in France and Spain in 1925.

HUGHES, L. *Selected Poems of Langston Hughes*. London: Pluto, 1986. Poetry by one of the twentieth century's outstanding black writers.

JOYCE, J. *Ulysses*. New York: Penguin, 1986. This classic of Modernism uses a tapestry of narrative styles to portray a day in the lives of three middle-class citizens of Dublin.

LAWRENCE, D. H. *Lady Chatterley's Lover*. New York: Modern Library, 1983. A controversial work that poses sex as a panacea for the ills of contemporary industrialized life.

O'NEILL, E. *Three Plays: Desire Under the Elms, Strange Interlude, Mourning Becomes Electra*. New York: Vintage, 1961. O'Neill's trilogy of plays based on Aeschylus's *Oresteia* and involving a contemporary New England family.

ORWELL, G. *Animal Farm; Burmese Days; A Clergyman's Daughter; Coming Up for Air; Keep the Aspidistra Flying; Nineteen Eighty-four*. New York: Octopus/Heinemann, 1980. This volume contains Orwell's most significant writings, most of which convey the author's hatred of tyranny and his skepticism about the future of humanity.

SARTRE, J.-P. *Being and Nothingness: An Essay in Phenomenological Ontology*. Translated and with an introduction by H. E. Barnes. Abridged. New York: Citadel Press, 1956. Sartre sets forth his existentialist philosophy, focusing on such key ideas as individual freedom and personal responsibility.

WALKER, A., ed. *I Love Myself When I Am Laughing . . . And Then Again When I Am Looking Mean and Impressive: A Zora Neale Hurston Reader*. Introduction by M. H. Washington. Old Westbury, N.Y.: The Feminist Press, 1979. A judicious collection of Hurston's writings, including excerpts from novels (*Their Eyes Were Watching God*, 1936) and autobiography (*Dust Tracks on a Road*, 1942), essays ("How It Feels to Be Colored Me," 1928), essays ("Crazy for Democracy," 1945), and short stories ("The Gilded Six-bits," 1933); with an admiring "afterword" by the celebrated writer Alice Walker.

WOOLF, V. *To the Lighthouse*. London: Hogarth Press, 1974. A typical Woolf novel in its stream-of-consciousness technique and its exquisitely detailed observations of contemporary thinking.

WITTGENSTEIN, L. *Tractatus Logico-philosophicus*. Translated by D. F. Pears and B. F. McGuiness, with an introduction by B. Russell. London: Routledge and Kegan Paul, 1974. An excellent English-language version of the treatise that led to logical positivism in philosophy.

YEATS, W. B. *The Collected Poems of W. B. Yeats*. Edited by R. J. Finneran. New York: Collier Books, 1989. One of Modernism's leading voices, Yeats wrote poetry devoted to such themes as Celtic myth, the tragic violence of Irish history, and the mystical nature of human existence.

SUGGESTIONS FOR LISTENING

ANTHEIL, GEORGE (1900–1959).
An American composer who worked in both experimental and traditional forms, Antheil lived in Europe in the 1920s and 1930s. His best known experimental work is *Ballet mécanique (Mechanical Ballet)* (1924; revised 1952), scored for airplane propellers and other industrial noises. Recognizing that his mechanical aesthetic was at a dead end with this work, Antheil spent the rest of his career searching for a personal style: from Neoclassicism (1925–1927), as in the lyrical *Piano Concerto* (1926); to Americana experiments (1927–1942), as in the opera *Transatlantic* (1927–1928), a political farce about an American presidential election; to neoromanticism, as in *Symphony Number 4* (1942) and *Symphony Number 5* (1947–1948), which blend melodic and rhythmic experiments with Classical forms.

COPLAND, AARON (1900–1990).
Copland's most popular works incorporate folk melodies and pay homage to the American way of life. Copland used cowboy songs in the ballet scores *Billy the Kid* (1938) and *Rodeo* (1942); he incorporated variations on the Shaker hymn *The Gift to Be Simple* in *Appalachian Spring* (1944), originally a ballet score that was later rearranged as a suite for symphony orchestra. His faith in the future of democracy is expressed most fully in the short, often-performed work, *Fanfare for the Common Man*.

ELLINGTON, EDWARD KENNEDY ("DUKE") (1899–1974).
Ellington's jazz style blended careful orchestration with ample opportunity for improvisation. Many of his songs have become standards in the popular music repertory, such as *Creole Love Call* (1928), *Mood Indigo* (1934), *Don't Get Around Much Anymore* (1940), and *Sophisticated Lady* (1932). Less well known are his serious compositions, like *Such Sweet Thunder* and *In the Beginning God* (1965), a religious work.

IVES, CHARLES (1909–1951).
America's first great composer, Ives experimented with atonality, clashing rhythms, and dissonant harmony long before these became a standard part of twentieth-century music. He frequently drew on American themes, as in the *Concord Sonata* for piano (1909–1915) and the orchestral *Three Places in New England* (1903–1914, first performed in 1931), works that evoked the landscape of his native region. A good example of one of his atonal works is *The Unanswered Question* (1908), a small work for trumpet, four flutes, and strings.

SCHOENBERG, ARNOLD (1874–1951).
During this period Schoenberg, the leader of the school of atonality, originated serialism as a method of composing, as may be heard in *Variations for Orchestra* (1928), the unfinished opera *Moses and Aaron* (1932), and *Violin Concerto* (1936).

STRAVINSKY, IGOR (1882–1971).
Schoenberg's rival Stravinsky became the leader of Neoclassicism in music with the ballet *Pulcinella* (1919) and continued this musical style in such works as the *Symphony of Psalms* (1930), the opera-oratoria *Oedipus Rex (Oedipus the King)* (1927), the *Symphony in C* (1940), and the opera *The Rake's Progress* (1951).

21

THE AGE OF ANXIETY AND BEYOND

1945—

Fear of nuclear war had a profound and chilling effect on attitudes and events after 1945. It led to a massive buildup of weapons by the United States and the Soviet Union, since the conventional wisdom was that the specter of mutually assured destruction—MAD—was the best deterrent to war. The arms race in turn contributed to out-of-control national budgets devoted to military spending at the expense of needed domestic programs. Anxiety about nuclear war led many people to work for disarmament, but for others it produced a sense of absurdity and a mood of despair. Against the backdrop of these realities, the cultural style known as Late Modernism captured the feelings of anguish experienced by many artists, writers, and intellectuals.

Starting in about 1970, however, some of the gloom lifted as threats of nuclear war showed signs of subsiding and international tensions relaxed. In the arts, a more upbeat style referred to as Post-Modernism began to emerge. Characterized by a cautious optimism and an interest in reinterpreting past styles, Post-Modernism reflects a search for more positive ways of responding to the world.

Dramatic events in recent years have further altered the shape of the modern world and influenced its direction for the future. Changes in the political and economic structures of the Soviet Union and the countries of eastern Europe, a broadening of inter-

national influence beyond the traditional Western powers, and pressing environmental concerns have all contributed to the emergence of a global perspective on world events. The growth of a global culture is reflected in Post-Modernism, which is democratic and embraces diversity. At this point, the trend for the future seems to be toward a world civilization that recognizes common human concerns and honors the creative impulse in all people (Time Line 21.1).

FROM A EUROPEAN TO A WORLD CIVILIZATION

The end of World War II, instead of bringing peace, brought the Cold War, an era of international tensions and conflicting ideologies. World relations were governed by a bipolar balance of power. The United States stood for free enterprise and individual freedom and the Union of Soviet Socialist Republics (USSR) symbolized state planning and collectivist values. The American bloc came to include western Europe, the British Commonwealth, and the states defeated in World War II—Japan, West Germany, and Italy—and the Soviet bloc embraced virtually all of eastern Europe and, after 1949 when the Communists took power, China.

The chance that the Cold War could become a hot war seemed to increase daily for two reasons. First, the superpowers extended their confrontations to the Third World, rushing in to fill the vacuum as the West's colonial empires fell and were replaced by

◄ ROMARE BEARDEN. *The Prevalence of Ritual: Baptism.* 1964. Collage on board, 9 × 12". The Hirshhorn Museum and Sculpture Garden, Smithsonian Institution, Washington, D.C.

TIME LINE 21.1   CULTURAL STYLES, 1945–PRESENT

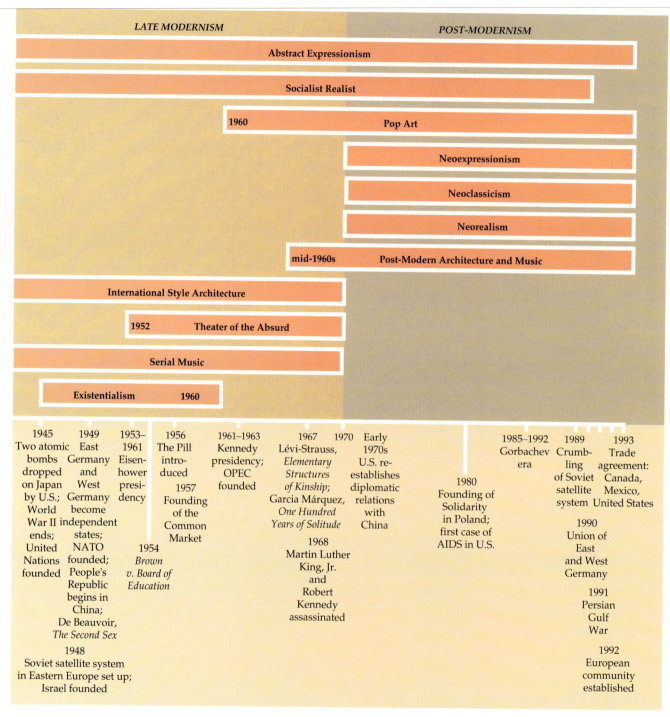

LATE MODERNISM   POST-MODERNISM

Abstract Expressionism

Socialist Realist

1960   Pop Art

Neoexpressionism

Neoclassicism

Neorealism

mid-1960s   Post-Modern Architecture and Music

International Style Architecture

1952   Theater of the Absurd

Serial Music

Existentialism   1960

1945	1949	1953–	1956	1961–1963	1967	1970	Early		1985–1992	1989	1993

1945
Two atomic
bombs
dropped
on Japan
by U.S.;
World
War II
ends;
United
Nations
founded

1949
East
Germany
and
West
Germany
become
independent
states;
NATO
founded;
People's
Republic
begins in
China;
De Beauvoir,
The Second Sex

1953–
1961
Eisen-
hower
presi-
dency

1954
*Brown
v. Board of
Education*

1956
The Pill
intro-
duced

1957
Founding
of the
Common
Market

1961–1963
Kennedy
presidency;
OPEC
founded

1967
Lévi-Strauss,
*Elementary
Structures
of Kinship;*
Garcia Márquez,
*One Hundred
Years of Solitude*

1968
Martin Luther
King, Jr.
and
Robert
Kennedy
assassinated

1970
Early
1970s
U.S. re-
establishes
diplomatic
relations
with
China

1980
Founding of
Solidarity
in Poland;
first case of
AIDS in U.S.

1985–1992
Gorbachev
era

1989
Crumb-
ling
of Soviet
satellite
system

1993
Trade
agreement:
Canada,
Mexico,
United States

1990
Union of
East
and West
Germany

1991
Persian
Gulf
War

1992
European
community
established

1948
Soviet satellite system
in Eastern Europe set up;
Israel founded

struggling independent states. Second, the development of ballistic missiles capable of hurtling nuclear weapons across intercontinental distances raised the possibility of sudden strikes and mass destruction without warning.

Other dramatic changes intensified the postwar period's growing mood of uncertainty. These included an international population explosion that raised the specter of food shortages and famines, new technological breakthroughs that seemed to entail employment crises, and mounting environmental calamities that threatened the earth's ecosystem. By the 1970s these issues were being recognized as world problems and not simply Western dilemmas, and thus they contributed to the rise of a global culture (Figure 21.1).

FIGURE 21.1 ANSELM KIEFER. *The High Priestess/The Land Between the Rivers.*
*1985–1989. 5 × 8 × 1 meters. Astrop Collection, Oslo. Courtesy Anthony D'Offay
Gallery, London. Kiefer's monumental work stands as a judgment on five thousand years
of history that began in Mesopotamia, the land between the Tigris and Euphrates rivers
and the cradle of civilization. Weighing several tons, the twin bookcases contain some two
hundred books made of lead. They are angled to suggest the two rivers, and, more
specifically, the accumulated wisdom of world culture. The books are linked by copper
threads, Kiefer's image of destructive technology, which he identifies with a pagan
goddess—the high priestess of the work's title. Though the books embrace all human
knowledge, their pages are stuffed with odds and ends of dried peas, human hair, and
photographs of polluted earth, sky, and water, and thus they are symbols of civilization in
ruins. A powerful representative of the Age of Anxiety, Kiefer is a Late Modernist in his
pessimism and a Post-Modernist in his global thinking.*

The Era of the Superpowers, 1945–1970

Between 1945 and 1970, the West was divided into two patterns of civilization. For the American bloc of states, democracy was the rule, social welfare expanded without becoming comprehensive, and the economies were booming. For the Soviet bloc countries, collectivist regimes prevailed, social welfare was comprehensive, and the economies either stagnated or grew slowly. The two systems emerged as seemingly inevitable consequences of World War II.

Postwar Recovery and the New World Order   The chief Allied powers—the United States, led by Franklin D. Roosevelt; Great Britain, led by Winston Churchill; and the Soviet Union, led by Joseph Stalin—began to plan for the postwar era well before World

War II ended. They agreed to occupy Germany and Japan, giving those nations representative forms of government and drastically curbing their military systems. They also joined with forty-eight other countries in 1945 to found the United Nations, a peace-keeping and human rights organization set up to deal with international disputes and problems (Figure 21.2). Finally, the Allies laid the groundwork for worldwide economic recovery by establishing a transnational monetary fund to help nations devastated by the war.

When peace came in September 1945, the victorious Allies began to rethink their options and to tailor their recovery plans to address conditions on a continent whose cities, factories, and railroads were in ruins. In order to restore this ravaged society, they had to cooperate, and, most importantly, they had to find visionary leaders who could inspire the people, whose hopes for orderly lives had been wrecked by

FIGURE 21.2 WALLACE K. HARRISON INTERNATIONAL COMMITTEE OF ARCHITECTS. United Nations Headquarters. 1949–1951. New York. *The decision to locate the United Nations in New York made that city the unofficial capital of the world, and the choice of a "glass box" skyscraper for the United Nations Secretariat, on the left, helped to ensure that the International style would be the reigning style of architecture in the postwar period. Although this type of structure had been used in Europe before the war, the U.N. Secretariat was the first instance of it in New York.*

war. The most troubling problem was that the key to the full recovery of Europe was a rejuvenated Germany—the state that provoked the war.

Convinced that Germany should be demilitarized and denazified, the Allies split the country into four occupied zones—British, French, American, and Soviet. In 1949 Britain, France, and the United States united their zones into the Federal Republic of Germany (West Germany), and the USSR set up its sector as the German Democratic Republic (East Germany). East and West Germany gradually became separate and distinct societies. By 1969 West Germany, led by moderates devoted to capitalism, was transformed into Europe's chief industrial power, and East Germany, under a collectivist regime, lagged far behind. This contrast mirrored changes that were occurring within the American and Soviet blocs.

Even more spectacular than West Germany's rise from the ashes of defeat was Japan's postwar success. The American victors imposed on Japan a democratic constitution that kept the emperor as a figurehead, introduced a parliamentary system, gave the vote to women, workers, and farmers, and virtually eliminated the military. Between 1950 and 1973, under this renovated system, Japan's domestic product grew at the amazing average of more than 10 percent a year, surpassing that of any other industrialized nation.

While West Germany and Japan were undergoing their economic miracles, Great Britain and France were moving along a more rocky path to recovery. By the early 1950s both countries were enjoying a moderate economic boom, although each was beset

with continuing labor unrest. To deal with worker discontent, left-wing governments in both states nationalized major industries and founded national health-care systems, although periodically conservative leaders came along and returned some businesses to private hands.

France and West Germany were the first to recognize that in the age of the superpowers the era of the small state was over. In order to guarantee peace and economic stability, they had to join economic forces, and in 1957 France and West Germany became the nucleus for a free-trade zone that also included Belgium, the Netherlands, Luxembourg, and Italy. Called the European Economic Community, or the Common Market, this organization became the driving force in Europe's prosperity over the next decade.

Part of the reason for the formation of the Common Market was that the Soviet Union, as it established its superpower status, threatened to dominate Europe. When World War II ended, Soviet troops remained in neighboring countries in eastern Europe as an occupying force, ostensibly to provide a military shield for the U.S.S.R. By 1948 the Soviets had converted these countries into Communist satellites, their industrial and agricultural systems tied to the Soviet economy. Thus, the Soviet Union loomed more as a menace than an ally to western Europe.

The architect of the Soviet Union's rise to superpower status was Joseph Stalin, who from 1945 until his death in 1953 rebuilt the U.S.S.R.'s war-shattered economy. A tyrant and a devout communist, he was determined to keep the collectivist system free of the taint of capitalism and the Western idea of freedom.

He demanded extreme sacrifices from Soviet citizenry as they were forced to keep up with the pace set by the advanced industrialized states.

Stalin's successors, Nikita Khrushchev (1956–1964) and Leonid Brezhnev (1964–1982), were more moderate, but both continued the policies of censorship and repression. Without detracting from the primary goal of building a nuclear arsenal, they also tried to broaden their priorities to include greater availability of consumer goods and the elimination of chronic food shortages, but with little success.

The United States, the other superpower, took up the torch of free world leadership in 1945, claiming to have earned this status because of crucial contributions to Allied victory. It further believed that the war had been a moral crusade for human freedom and thus had given the country a blank check to protect the rights of people everywhere. Armed with these beliefs, the United States abandoned its old isolationist foreign policy and took on the role of the world's watchdog.

Between 1945 and 1970 the United States was probably the wealthiest and most powerful state that ever existed. Its heyday was under President Dwight Eisenhower (1953–1961), a former general who had served as Supreme Commander of the Allied forces in Europe during the war. He was succeeded by John F. Kennedy (1961–1963), a charismatic and popular figure whose assassination stunned a country unused to political violence.

American domestic life in this era was marked by a radical shift in mood from the 1950s to the 1960s. The 1950s was a decade of complacency and blandness symbolized by the "man in the gray flannel suit." The 1960s, in contrast, was a turbulent decade around the world, of which the American experience was only a part. A cultural event in itself, the 1960s was one of the most unruly periods in modern history, involving radical protests by millions of people against the War in Vietnam, racism, and old ways of thinking. Hippies cultivated a bohemian lifestyle and contributed to the emergence of a "counterculture" that rejected mainstream values. These protests showed that many Americans, along with much of the world's population, distrusted authority and were skeptical of traditional beliefs.

Of the domestic problems faced by the United States at this time, racial prejudice was the most pressing because it was so embedded in the country's history. In 1954 the Supreme Court declared segregation in public schools—"separate but equal" facilities—unconstitutional. In the next year, Rosa Parks (1913–   ), a black Alabaman, refused to move to the back of a bus as required by state law and was jailed. The social protest that erupted around the jailing of Parks marked a watershed in race relations in America. Rejecting a historically passive role, black citizens began to use civil disobedience as a weapon in their crusade to win equal rights.

Nevertheless, the civil rights movement did not begin on a national scale until the Kennedy presidency. After some foot dragging, the federal government threw its weight behind the movement to bring about changes in education, living conditions, and voting rights. What Kennedy started, President Lyndon Johnson (1963–1969) tried to complete with his War on Poverty and Great Society plans. In 1968 the civil rights struggle temporarily lost direction and momentum when its leader, Martin Luther King, Jr., was assassinated, but fresh faces arose in America's black community who have continued the struggle against racism.

The Cold War The hopes for peace and cooperation among the victorious powers disappeared after 1945 as the Soviet Union and the United States squared off and defined their respective spheres of influence. By 1949 an "iron curtain," to use Winston Churchill's phrase, had descended in Europe, dividing the West (France, England, Belgium, the Netherlands, Luxembourg, Italy, West Germany, and, later, Austria) from the East (Poland, Hungary, Rumania, Bulgaria, Czechoslovakia, East Germany, and Russia) (Map 21.1).

Events soon caused the Cold War to heat up. In 1949 fear of a Russian invasion led the western democracies to form a military alliance called the North Atlantic Treaty Organization (NATO) with the United States as its leader. The eastern bloc countered with the Warsaw Pact, an alliance headed by the Soviet Union. A race to stockpile weapons ensued, dividing the industrial world into armed camps. By 1955 a balance of terror seemed to have been reached because both the United States and the USSR now possessed the atomic bomb and the even more deadly hydrogen bomb. Nevertheless, the urge for more weapons continued to mount.

Although the East-West conflict originated in Europe, the contest spread to other regions of the world, where it threatened to become a three-sided struggle. In 1949 Chinese Communists defeated General Chiang Kai-shek [je-AHNG KYE-SHEK] (1928–1949) and his Kuomintang party and commenced to build a socialist system under the leadership of Mao Zedong [MAU (D)ZE-DUHNG] (1949–1976) (Figure 21.3).

The triumph of Communism in China shifted the struggle between the superpowers to the Far East, where a limited type of warfare now emerged in Korea—divided after World War II into two independent states reflecting the influence of the United

MAP 21.1
Europe in 1955

ICELAND

*ATLANTIC
OCEAN*

NORWAY

SWEDEN

FINLAND

*NORTH
SEA*

*BALTIC
SEA*

SOVIET UNION

IRELAND

UNITED
KINGDOM

DENMARK

NETHERLANDS

EAST
GERMANY

POLAND

BELGIUM

LUXEMBOURG

WEST
GERMANY

CZECHOSLOVAKIA

FRANCE

AUSTRIA

HUNGARY

SWITZERLAND

RUMANIA

*BLACK
SEA*

YUGOSLAVIA

PORTUGAL

ITALY

BULGARIA

SPAIN

ALBANIA

*MEDITERRANEAN
SEA*

GREECE

TURKEY

ALGERIA

Original NATO Alliance

Communist Bloc (Members of Warsaw Pact)

States and the Soviet Union. In 1950 Soviet-dominated North Korea invaded South Korea to reunite the two states. Alarmed at this expansion of Communism, the United States, under the auspices of the United Nations, sent troops in support of the South Koreans. Later in the year, China sent soldiers to help the North Koreans. After months of bloody fighting, a stalemate resulted along the old borders, which were guaranteed in 1953 by an armistice. The Korean War ended in a draw, but it established one of the guiding principles of the nuclear age—that wars would be fought with conventional weapons rather than with nuclear arms.

The early 1960s witnessed worsening relations between the United States and the Soviet Union over the Berlin Wall and the Cuban missile crisis. The Berlin Wall was built in 1961 by East Germany, with the permission of the Soviet Union, to prevent its citizens from going to West Berlin. Conceived as a way of saving Communism, this armed boundary only intensified divisions between the two Europes. Then in 1962 the Soviet plan to base missiles in Cuba

brought the superpowers to the brink of war, but in the end both states backed away from armed conflict.

The severest strain on the superpower system was the Vietnam War, which erupted in the early 1960s. Originating as a civil war, it became a Cold War contest when the United States joined South Vietnam to repel the troops invading from the Communist north. For American soldiers the war was doubly difficult to wage because it was fought in unfamiliar jungle terrain using conventional arms against a guerrilla army and because it became so violently unpopular at home. At the peak of the war in May 1970, protests spread across the United States, culminating in incidents at universities in Ohio and Mississippi, when six students were killed in clashes with public authorities (Figure 21.4).

The Vietnam War proved to be a turning point in world affairs. The United States withdrew from South Vietnam in 1973, thereby allowing its eventual conquest by North Vietnam. Certain conclusions were quickly drawn from this setback to American

FIGURE 21.3 ANDY WARHOL. *Mao*. 1973. Acrylic and silkscreen on canvas, 14′6⅞″ × 11′4½″. The Art Institute of Chicago. Mr. and Mrs. Frank G. Logan Purchase Prize and Wilson L. Mead Funds. *A feature of totalitarian societies in this century has been the personality cult, the practice of giving a political leader heroic dimensions. In Communist China the cult of Mao Zedong established Mao as a secular god. American pop artist Andy Warhol turned Mao's official photograph into a pop culture icon, suggesting that there is no difference between propaganda in a totalitarian state and media stardom in a free society.*

might. First, because the Vietnam War weakened the United States internally by dividing the citizens about the war and its goals, it cast doubt on the country's superpower status and made the leaders reluctant to exercise military power abroad except in the Western Hemisphere, an area historically subject to American intervention. Second, the Vietnam War illustrated a new principle of foreign relations—namely, that even superpowers could not conquer minor states by conventional forces alone. Taken together, these post–Vietnam era principles suggested that the international influence of the United States was in decline and opened the door to new forms of global cooperation in the 1970s.

Emergence of the Third World After 1945 Europe's overseas territories began to struggle for freedom and self-government, and by 1964 most of the empires had

FIGURE 21.4 The National Guard at Kent State, Ohio. 1970. *This photograph bears a striking resemblance to Goya's* Execution of the Third of May, 1808 *(see Figure 17.17), a painting that protested the killing of Spanish civilians by French soldiers. In the tense days after the Kent State deaths, this photograph served a similar function in American society as many people began to think of the dead students as martyrs to the anti–Vietnam War cause.*

been replaced by independent countries. Independence for the former colonies came at different times and in diverse ways. In the Far East, the United States led the way in 1946 when it let go of its former colony, the Philippines. Great Britain, the West's largest imperial power, followed in 1947 by agreeing to divide India into a Hindu-dominated state—India—and a separate Muslim state—Pakistan. A year later the British withdrew from Burma, thus ensuring its free status. The Dutch gave up the East Indies, which in 1950 became Indonesia. France tried to hold on to Indochina, having reclaimed it from Japan, but in 1954 the French were driven out by a bloody uprising, and the former colony was divided into two separate countries, North and South Vietnam. In 1975 these two countries were finally unified as a single state at the conclusion of the Vietnam War.

In the Middle East, the small, mainly Arab states were freed by France and Britain, who had dominated them since 1919. After 1945 the region was kept in turmoil because its rich oil fields were needed by the industrialized states, its geopolitical position in the eastern Mediterranean attracted the superpowers, and Islamic fundamentalism gave birth to militant Arab nationalism. But the founding of Israel as a Jewish state following World War II and the Holocaust contributed the most to an unstable Middle East. Israel's founding in 1948—pushing the British out—resulted in the expulsion of more than a half million Arabs from Palestine, and the fate of these refugees has kept the region in turmoil. With the refugee problem unresolved, Israel, backed by the United States, has had to fight constantly against its Arab neighbors to remain an independent nation. Further instability in the region has been caused by a change in the balance of power—the decline of Iran and the rise of Iraq as an aggressive state.

In Africa nearly all of the colonies became free, but the transition was usually painful and often costly. In 1962 France concluded a bloody war in Algeria, releasing its ties to this once prized possession. Having learned her lesson, France freed most of her colonies in West Africa during the 1960s. In East Africa, the British, at the same time, withdrew slowly, leaving behind bureaucracies that could serve the new states. Rhodesia became Zimbabwe in 1980, achieving independence under black majority rule.

Toward a New Global Order, 1970–1994

The year 1970 marked a turning point in history, not only for Western civilization but also for the world. The balance of political power began to shift from the bipolar, superpower model to a multipolar system embracing the superpowers along with Japan, China, and western Europe. This reshuffling of global influence began when the superpowers moved toward *detente*, a French term meaning a waning of hostility. By the early 1970s *detente* produced several arms limitations treaties between the Soviet Union and the United States and thus created a favorable climate for a reappraisal of Cold War attitudes. *Detente* soon led to a reduction of ideological battles in Europe and around the world. In addition, the industrialized nations began to experience energy shortages that showed how dependent they were on the oil-producing states—countries that heretofore had exerted little influence on world events.

National Issues and International Realignment   The general rise in the standard of living for most citizens in western Europe and the United States suffered a sharp setback with the Arab oil embargo of the early 1970s. In 1960 the oil-rich states of the Middle East had founded the Organization of Petroleum Exporting Countries (OPEC), a cartel that initiated an energy-price revolution whose consequences are still being felt. As a result, most western nations went into a recession that resulted in both rising unemployment and inflation—two economic events that most experts believed could not occur at the same time. The Soviet Union was also experiencing economic problems as it became increasingly clear that the regimented system was no longer able to produce both arms and consumer goods.

Politically, the 1970s were a time of drift in the United States. President Richard Nixon (1969–1974) began to wind down the Vietnam War in 1970, thus defusing domestic discontent. When South Vietnam fell to the Communists in 1975, most American units were already back home. He also made a historic opening to China, a step that eventually led to a realignment of the world's powers. But Nixon disgraced himself through the Watergate scandal of 1973–1974, which turned on the question of his knowledge of illegal wiretaps and attempted obstruction of justice. As a result, several high government officials were imprisoned, and he resigned from the presidency—a first in American history.

The 1980s brought dramatic changes both nationally and internationally. The United States experienced an economic turnaround under President Ronald Reagan (1981–1989), whose advisers prescribed a dose of ''Reaganomics,'' or laissez-faire policies, to treat inflation and recession. The economy responded with the longest run of uninterrupted prosperity since World War II. The nation paid dearly for its prosperity, however, with increased military spending, an astronomical national debt, and, in foreign trade, a shift from creditor to

FIGURE 21.5 Fall of the Berlin Wall. 1989. *Given the Soviet Union's previous use of force in Eastern Europe, no one had predicted that the collapse of the Communist states would be so quick and bloodless. The most symbolic event of this extraordinary period has been the dismantling of the wall that separated East Berlin from West Berlin.*

debtor status. And for those trapped in poverty, homelessness, and urban violence, reduced government spending under Reagan and his successor, George Bush, turned the American dream into a nightmare.

Reagan also launched a massive military spending campaign to strengthen the American presence around the world. This was partly in response to two events that had clouded the international scene—a Soviet invasion of Afghanistan in 1979 in support of local Communist leaders and the founding in 1980 of Solidarity in Poland, a labor movement that used strikes to push for economic reform. When Solidarity brought the country to the edge of revolution, the government, supported by the Soviet Union, ruthlessly suppressed the movement. In a hostile international atmosphere, Cold War sentiments revived, ongoing disarmament talks between the superpowers broke down, and an intensified arms race seemed imminent.

All this changed in 1985 with the appearance of Mikhail Gorbachev [gore-bah-CHOF] (1985–1991) as leader of the Soviet Union. Using a moderate approach, partly because the Soviet economy was in shambles, he introduced a new era of *detente* and helped to bring the Cold War to a peaceful close. His

overtures to the United States resulted in limited arms reductions and, more importantly, opened up lines of communication between the two superpowers.

At home, Gorbachev made changes in the state bureaucracy and the Communist party designed to raise the standard of living. His plans—restructuring the economy's production and distribution system (*perestroika*) and allowing public criticism of the Communist party (*glasnost*)—dramatically altered the course of history in the Soviet Union, eastern Europe, and the world. In the Soviet Union, Gorbachev's reforms contributed to the breakup of the centralized structure of the U.S.S.R., as some member states—Latvia, Estonia, and Lithuania, for example—declared their independence while other member states gained more local control of their affairs. From the wreckage of the Soviet system, following more than 70 years of communism, a desperately weakened Russia reemerged, shorn of its vast empire yet still managing to hold on to some ethnic republics through a ramshackle commonwealth arrangement.

After 1989 Gorbachev's policies toward the satellite states, whether intentional or not, destroyed the Communist bloc in eastern Europe (Figure 21.5).

Newly independent, these former Communist states, including Russia itself, appear torn between maintaining their social welfare programs and worker protection legislation and moving rapidly toward democratic governments and market economies. Despite such strains, all of these countries are now redesigning their production and distribution systems, dismantling secret police units, and rewriting their constitutions to ensure civil rights, a multiparty political system, and freedom of expression and thought.

Friendly ties between the superpowers and other changes in international affairs are products of the new world order. Earlier, during the Cold War, it was clear that neither world power had the will to eliminate the other, and, today, it is equally clear that neither has the wealth and resources to dominate the world. The superpowers must now accept a multipolar arrangement that includes China and Japan, both rising in international influence, as well as the growing economic might of the other new economic powers in the Pacific Rim, such as South Korea, Taiwan, Singapore, and Thailand. Likewise, the superpowers now face the challenge of western Europe, organized into a free trade zone in 1992 and soon to be made more interdependent by a single currency—potentially the most powerful economic region of the world. In the emerging global economic order of the Post-Modern world, all countries, including those in Africa, the Middle East, eastern Europe, and Latin America, seem to recognize that if they are to share in the wealth and goods of the planet, they must develop market economics and become competitive.

The Persian Gulf Crisis and Its Impact   Despite the promising developments of 1989, a new crisis arose in 1990. The world was shocked when Iraq, under the leadership of Saddam Hussein [hoo-SAYN] (1979–   ), invaded and annexed Kuwait, its small, wealthy neighbor on the Persian Gulf, and appeared ready to move on into Saudi Arabia. Concerned about both the already precarious balance of power in the Middle East and the world's oil supply, U.S. President Bush (1989–1993) declared the aggression unacceptable. Under the auspices of the United Nations, the United States put together a broad diplomatic and military coalition of nearly fifty countries dedicated to freeing Kuwait and keeping oil flowing from the Middle East. In a historic first, the Soviet Union joined in condemning its former ally Iraq in the United Nations. By mid-January 1991, the United States and its allies had gathered a military force of about 500,000 troops in Saudi Arabia, where they faced about the same number of Iraqi soldiers—the largest massing of troops since World War II. Following an all-out air campaign against Iraq and a brief

ground assault, the allied coalition achieved its major war aim with the liberation of Kuwait (Figure 21.6).

The Persian Gulf crisis brought into clearer focus the broader trends underway in the world since 1970. It dramatically validated the perception that the Cold War is over; at the same time, it reasserted the image of the United States as a superpower and signaled a decline in the Soviet Union. The crisis also underscored the nature of the global economy and its dependence on oil.

In the aftermath of the Gulf War, it quickly became evident that the defining issue of the 1990s is not the threat of all-out war but the almost universal problem of sluggish economies. Oil is now flowing from the Middle East, but around the world, economies are experiencing the most serious downturn since the 1930s. There are many reasons for this crisis. Germany, the bellwether of Europe, is suffering from the effects of the 1991 unification of its prosperous western half with its bankrupt eastern half. The former Iron Curtain countries, struggling to convert to free market systems, make the situation more desperate with their massive need for foreign capital. Divided internally between budding capitalists and nostalgic communists and led by the reform-minded but erratic Boris Yeltsin (1992–   ), Russia seems adrift, unable to put its own economic house in order.

Outside Europe the economic prospect is equally bleak. The United States has now begun a slow recovery from the late 1980s depression that brought down President Bush and helped to elect William Clinton (1993–   ) as his successor. Japan began an economic slump in the 1990s, its post–World War II boom finally at an end. Beyond the industrialized world, the Third World is languishing, its economies overburdened by debt and millions of its people migrating to more prosperous lands, notably western Europe, Canada, and the United States. These migrations have almost overwhelmed already economically troubled western Europe, inspired murderous racial attacks on foreigners, and spawned anti-alien political movements in a dozen countries.

Problems with a Global Dimension   A positive result of the nuclear age was that it taught the West and the rest of the world to think globally. As the threat of nuclear war has subsided since 1970, other menacing problems have surfaced that transcend national borders and affect all people all over the planet. The urgency of these issues makes them seem more relevant to people's lives than events that occur on a local or national level. Of the international problems facing the world, the two most pressing are the population explosion and the deteriorating environment, neither of which appears to have a simple solution.

FIGURE 21.6 Kuwaitis Celebrate Their Country's Liberation, March 1991. *Parading in front of the U.S. embassy in Kuwait City, these Kuwaiti citizens celebrate their country's liberation from Iraq. They wave small Kuwaiti flags and a large American flag emblazoned with a picture of the late Hollywood star Marilyn Monroe. The juxtaposition of Monroe's face and the stars and stripes is a vivid reminder of the way American political power and American mass culture are intertwined in many minds. This image, flashed around the world by satellite and news wire services, also exemplifies how this "TV war" was presented to the global village.*

The world's population is in danger of becoming an unbearable burden on the globe's limited resources. In the 1980s there were devastating famines in Ethiopia and elsewhere (Figure 21.7). In 1990 the earth's population was estimated to be 5.23 billion and projected to reach 6.2 billion by 2000. Many international groups have called for ways to limit the birth rate, ranging from abortion to contraceptives. But because all birth control proposals affect moral and religious beliefs, they have touched off heated debates and, in the case of abortion, have led to violence. The abortion question is further complicated by being in conflict with the women's movement, for there seems to be no way to reconcile the claims of a fetus with a woman's right to control her own body.

The environmental problem turns on the issue of preserving the natural world for future generations.

Even though assaults on the planet's ecosystem occurred earlier, the period of greatest destruction to the earth began after 1945, especially with the advent of nuclear power, of a huge rise in the earth's population, and of the growing industrialization of the world. Today few parts of the globe are free from diseases caused by industrial pollution and waste from factories. Two glaring examples of environmental disasters are the Chernobyl nuclear power plant fire in the Soviet Union in 1986 and the mammoth oil spill in Alaska in 1989. There are many other environmental hazards, such as acid rain, which threatens the world's flora and fauna; the warming of the earth, which might melt the polar ice caps; the depletion of the ozone layer, which would destroy the planet's protective shield; and the poisoning of rivers and oceans, which would eliminate fish and pollute much of humanity's water supply.

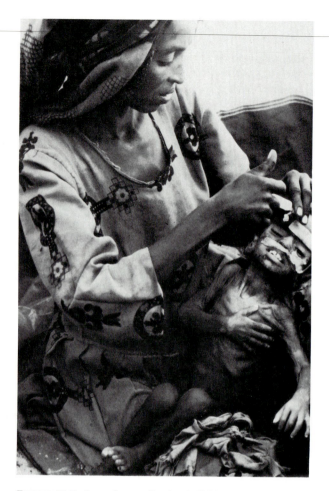

FIGURE 21.7 JOHN ISAAC. Famine in Ethiopia. 1984. *In the early 1980s the nightly television news brought images of famine and death in Ethiopia into living rooms around the world, just as it had earlier brought images of the War in Vietnam. The Ethiopians were the victims of drought and other natural disasters, of civil war, and of short-sighted economic policies that had replaced local agriculture with export crops. Although food was sent by international relief agencies, partisan soldiers often prevented it from reaching the people. The agony of Ethiopia taught the world that solving environmental problems also means dealing with tough political and economic issues.*

THE END OF MODERNISM AND THE BIRTH OF POST-MODERNISM

In 1947 the British-American author W. H. Auden published a poem entitled "The Age of Anxiety" that expresses the melancholy spirit of his times. He describes a period caught between a frantic quest for certainty and a recognition of the futility of that search. Responding to the unparalleled violence of World War II, Auden's anxious age is characterized by a sense of death and destruction, fueled by memories of the Holocaust in Europe and the two atomic bombs dropped on Japan. As relations between the Soviet Union and the United States deteriorated and made World War III seem inevitable, melancholy could and often did turn into despair. In this gloomy setting Modernism entered its final phase.

Late Modernism, flourishing from 1945 until 1970, expressed the vision of a group of artists, writers, and thinkers who seemed almost overwhelmed by this despairing age. Existentialism—with its advice to forget the past and the future and to live passionately for the present—appeared to be the only thinking that made sense. Paradoxically, diminished faith in humanity kept the Modernists at their creative tasks and prevented them from falling into hopeless silence.

Like earlier Modernists, Late Modernists thought of themselves as an elite. They were committed to saving what they considered worth saving in Western culture while destroying all in the past that was irrelevant, ignoring mass culture, and borrowing insights from depth psychology and non-Western sources. Armed with a sense of mission, they stripped their works down to the most basic components, abandoning strict rationality and making randomness the rule. They threw subject matter out the window and pressed experimentation to the extreme, reducing painting to lines and colors, sculpture to textures and shapes, and music to random collections of sound. Like earlier Modernists, they then invested these works with spiritual or metaphysical purposes by claiming that abstract paintings and sculptures were meditation devices and that music that mixed noise and harmony echoed the natural world.

In the early 1970s Late Modernism was challenged by a new movement that became known as *Post-Modernism.* Having grown to maturity after World War II and feeling that Late Modernism's anxiety was outdated, the Post-Modernists turned from existentialism to *structuralism,* a type of thinking that affirmed the uniformity of the human mind in all places and times. Unlike the Late Modernists, this new generation embraced mass culture and preferred a more playful approach to creativity (Figure 21.8). Because the United States is a microcosm of global society, its artists and scholars have played a key role in establishing the culture of Post-Modernism.

The Post-Modernists' cultural vision caused them to look in two directions at the same time—forward to an emerging global civilization that was many-voiced and democratic and backward to the roots of the Western tradition. This vision embraced the works of women, minority group members, and representatives of the Third World at the same time that it reexamined both Classical and pre-Classical civilizations. Only time will tell if Post-Modernism is merely a period of fragmentation prior to regrouping or the beginning of a cultural revolution.

Philosophical, Political, and Social Thought

Existentialism, born between the two world wars, dominated Western thought from 1945 until the 1960s, when it was eclipsed by structuralism and other intellectual movements, notably feminism and black consciousness. Unlike existentialism, with its focus on freedom and choice, structuralism asserts that human freedom is limited. Structuralists maintain that innate mental patterns cause human beings to interact with nature and each other in recurring ways, regardless of the historical period or the social setting. It follows that civilization (as represented in governments, social relations, and language, for example) and ideas (such as freedom, health, and beauty) arise from deep-seated modes of thought instead of from the environment or progressive enlightenment. Structuralists reason that not only is all knowledge conditioned by the mind but civilization itself reflects the mind's inborn nature. By defining and analyzing the substrata of culture, they attempt to garner some understanding of the elemental nature of the human mind.

The two leading structuralists are Noam Chomsky [CHAHM-skee] (1928–), an American linguist, and Claude Lévi-Strauss [lay-vee-SHTRAUS] (1908–), a French anthropologist. Chomsky's *Syntactic Structures* (1957) prompted a revolution in linguistics, the scientific study of languages. He argues that below the surface form of sentences (that is, the grammar) lies a deeper linguistic structure that is intuitively grasped by the mind and is common to all languages. Similarly, Lévi-Strauss made war on empirical thinking with his 1967 study, *The Elementary Structures of Kinship*. He claimed that beneath the varied relations among clans in different societies exist certain kinship archetypes with such common themes as the incest taboo and marriage patterns. Chomsky and Lévi-Strauss imply the existence of common universal structures running through all minds and all societies that can be expressed as a general code. This conclusion gives a strong psychoanalytic cast to structuralist thought, because it leads researchers to focus on the subconscious mind.

Following Chomsky and Lévi-Strauss, other scholars have studied subsurface patterns in such

FIGURE 21.8   KEITH HARING. *Andy Mouse 2*. 1986. Silkscreen print, 38 × 38″. Courtesy George C. Mulder, New York. *Post-Modernist Keith Haring embraced the emblems and vocabulary of mass culture as Andy Warhol had done earlier. In this silkscreen print he pays homage to Warhol and celebrates his lifelong love affair with mass culture. Haring emblazoned Mickey Mouse's face on a cartoon dollar bill held aloft by two jubilant figures—presumably, Warhol and himself. The dancing figures, surrounded with radiant lines, were Haring's trademark.*

disciplines as history, child development, and literature. No thinker has yet unified the various structuralisms into a coherent theory of mind. It is an intriguing coincidence, however, that the trend of thought that points to a universally shared mind-set parallels the rise of a global culture under Post-Modernism.

The revival of feminist thought has been another significant development in philosophy since World War II. The French thinker and novelist Simone de Beauvoir [duh-boh-VWAHR] (1908–1986) sparked this revival, following the dry spell that set in after many Western women won the right to vote in the 1920s. In her 1949 treatise *The Second Sex*, de Beauvoir argued that women were treated as "the Other," an anthropological term meaning that men accord women a different and lower existence than themselves. Drawing on personal anecdote and existentialist thought, she advised women who wanted independence to avoid marriage and, like men, create their own immortality (Figure 21.9).

De Beauvoir's message was heard around the world, but it was especially in the United States that women heeded her. America's outstanding feminist

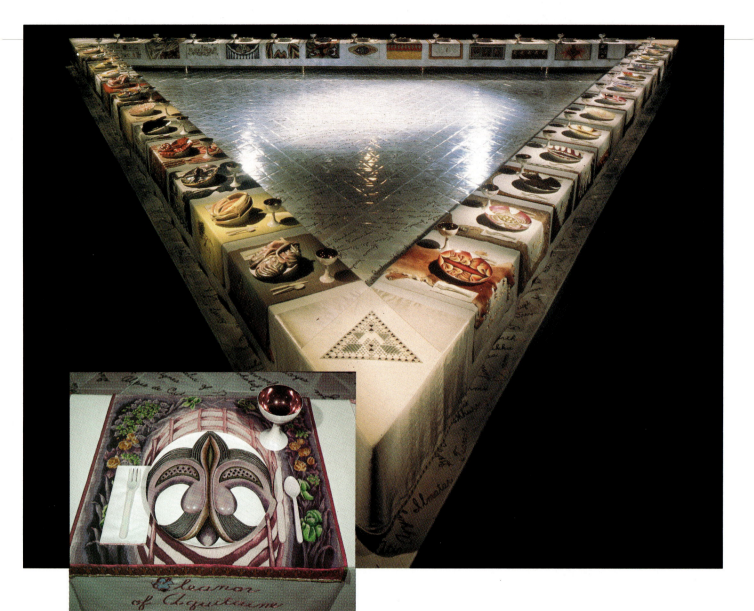

FIGURE 21.9 JUDY CHICAGO. *The Dinner Party.* 1979. Installation view. Multimedia, china painting on porcelain, needlework, 48 × 48 × 48' installed. © Judy Chicago. *The rebirth of feminism led some women artists to adopt explicit feminist themes in their art, as in the works of Judy Chicago (born Gerowitz, 1939–). Chicago abandoned Abstract Expressionism in the late 1960s at about the same time she changed her name, thereafter devoting her art to the feminist cause.* The Dinner Party, *her most ambitious project to date, is dedicated to leading historical and mythological women of Western civilization. In this work she arranges a triangular-shaped dining table with thirty-nine places decorated in individual styles, honoring such famous women as Sappho and Eleanor of Aquitaine (inset).*

in the 1960s was Betty Friedan (1921–). She awakened the dormant women's movement with *The Feminine Mystique* (1963), arguing that society conspired to idealize women and thus discourage them from competing with men. In 1966 she founded the National Organization for Women (NOW), a pressure group that has attracted millions of members. According to its founding manifesto, NOW supports "equal partnership with men" and is committed to "integrating women into the power, privileges, and responsibilities of the public arena." Friedan did not always agree with the more radical feminists of the 1970s, and in 1982 she showed that she was still a moderate in *The Second Stage*, a book that advocated men's liberation as a condition for women's equality.

Like feminism, the black consciousness movement has flourished since 1945 (Figure 21.10). The

FIGURE 21.10 ROMARE BEARDEN. *The Prevalence of Ritual: Baptism.* 1964. Collage on board, 9 × 12". The Hirshhorn Museum and Sculpture Garden, Smithsonian Institution, Washington, D.C. *Romare Bearden (1914–1988), the United States' most honored post–World War II black painter, blended Modernism with elements from his cultural heritage. In the 1960s he developed a style reminiscent of Cubism that used collage and flattened, angular figures and that drew on his personal experiences, as in this painting of a baptismal scene—an allusion to the important role played by churches in the black American tradition. Bearden places the person to be baptized in the center of the composition, a large hand over his head. The references to African masks suggest that this ritual unites an ancient way of life with the present.*

earliest significant theorist of black identity was Frantz Fanon [FAY-NON] (1925–1961), a psychiatrist from French Martinique who practiced medicine among the Arabs of Algeria. An eyewitness to French oppression, Fanon became convinced that the West had doomed itself by abandoning its own moral ideals. By the late 1950s Fanon began to justify black revolution against white society on the basis of existential choice and Marxism. In 1961 in *The Wretched of the Earth* he issued an angry call to arms, urging nonwhites to build a separate culture. Some black leaders in America welcomed Fanon's message in the 1960s, as did Third World thinkers who turned their backs on Western ideologies in the 1970s.

America in the 1960s produced a radical black voice in Malcolm X (1925–1965), the pseudonym of Malcolm Little. A fiery personality, he made sharp ideological shifts, moving from advocacy of black separatism to a call for an interracial civil war and, after his conversion to orthodox Islam, to support of racial harmony. Assassinated allegedly by former colleagues, he remains today a prophetic voice for many African-Americans who want a clearer sense of their history, culture, and accomplishments in a predominantly white society.

In the turbulent 1960s Malcolm X's voice was overpowered by that of Martin Luther King, Jr. (1929–1968), a visionary who dreamed of a world free from racial discord. Probably the most famous black figure in Western history, King was an advocate of civil disobedience—based on Christian teachings, the writings of the New England philosopher and abolitionist Henry David Thoreau, and the example of India's liberator, Gandhi. An inspirational leader and a superb orator, King galvanized blacks, along with many whites, into the Southern Christian Leadership Conference, a mass movement to end segregation in American life, notably in schools and universities. Though King was assassinated before his dream was fully realized, his vision of an integrated society lived on, and he left a cadre of able leaders.

Science and Technology

Although important developments occurred in biology and physics during the postwar period and after, for most people more important were the spectacular advances in applied science. Ordinary life and manners have been irretrievably altered by an unending stream of inventions and discoveries, notably the birth control pill, communication satellites, and the computer. The invention of a safe birth control pill in 1956 triggered a sexual revolution that slowed down only in the 1980s with the advent of AIDS (acquired immune deficiency syndrome) and a dramatic rise in the incidence of other sexually transmissible diseases. The introduction of communication satellites, a by-product of the United States space program of the 1960s, has made a global culture possible. Multinational corporations are linked by these satellites, and individuals all over the world watch televised events at the same time thanks to satellite communication.

Perhaps most important, the computer has revolutionized life on every level, making previously unimaginable quantities of data immediately accessible, simplifying complex tasks, and contributing to "cocooning," a mode of living in which people center their lives in their private homes surrounded by electronic devices and venture out into the public domain for amusement and social contact less and less.

Breakthroughs in medicine also changed the nature of human life for millions. In the 1950s polio was eradicated through vaccines developed by the American physicians Jonas Salk (1914–   ) and Albert Sabin (1906–1993). Innovative surgical methods, radiation treatment, and chemotherapy drastically reduced cancer mortality. Organ transplants and the use of artificial organs have prolonged life for many otherwise without hope, although these practices have embroiled the medical profession in ethical controversy because of charges that only a few or the wealthy benefit from these costly procedures. Likewise, new methods in human reproduction, such as test-tube fertilization and surrogate parenting, while helping a few, have also raised moral dilemmas and led to court cases.

The Literature of Late Modernism: Fiction, Poetry, and Drama

France's leading postwar thinkers, Jean-Paul Sartre and Albert Camus, were among Late Modernism's outstanding voices. In a trio of novels called *Roads to Freedom*, published between 1945 and 1950, Sartre interwove Marxist collectivist beliefs with existentialism's focus on the individual. While accepting the existentialist view that life is cruel and must be confronted, he portrayed his characters as cooperating for a new and better world, presumably one in which they would be able to live in harmony. Sartre also wrote a series of plays on current issues that are infrequently performed today. His most successful drama, and perhaps his most enduring literary work, was *No Exit*, which showed how three characters turned their lives into living hells because of their unfortunate choices in desperate situations.

Like Sartre, the Algerian-born writer and thinker Albert Camus [KAH-MEW] (1913–1960) wrote novels, plays, and philosophical works that mirrored his political thinking and personal values. His finest literary work was *The Fall* (1956), a novel published at the height of his reputation as one of the West's main moral voices. In 1957 he was awarded the Nobel Prize in literature, an honor that Sartre declined in 1964. Written as a single rambling monologue, *The Fall* portrays an anguished, self-doubting central character who accuses himself of moral fraud. When admirers recognized Camus himself in the narrator's voice, they were shocked because they were unwilling to accept this harsh self-judgment. Whether this self-mocking confession heralded Camus's move toward God—as some critics have maintained—can never be known, for an auto accident prematurely ended his life.

Existentialism's rejection of bourgeois values and its affirmation of identity through action appealed to black writers in the United States. As outsiders in a white-dominated society, these writers identified with the French thinkers' call to rebellion. The first black author to adopt an existential perspective was Richard Wright (1908–1960), whose outlook was shaped by his birth on a Mississippi plantation. His works, such as his novel *Native Son* (1940) and his autobiography *Black Boy* (1945), were filled with too much rage at racism to be accepted by white literary critics in the 1940s. His later years were spent in Paris, where he further developed his interest in existentialism.

The most successful black American author of this time was James Baldwin (1924–1987), who began to write during a self-imposed exile in France (1948–1957), where he had fled from racial discrimination.

In a series of novels and essays, he explored the consequences of growing up black in a predominantly white world. In the novel *Go Tell It on the Mountain* (1953), he drew on his Christian beliefs to mute his anger against the injustices that he believed blacks daily endured. This novel, which held out hope for an integrated society, established the literary theme that he pursued until Martin Luther King, Jr.'s assassination caused his vision to darken. In later novels, such as *No Name in the Street* (1972), he regretfully accepted violence as the only path to racial justice for black Americans.

In postwar fiction existentialism sometimes took second place to a realistic literary style that concentrated on exposing society's failings. Three major writers who blended existential despair with Realism's moral outrage were Norman Mailer (1923–), Doris Lessing (1919–), and Alexander Solzhenitsyn [sol-zhuh-NEET-suhn] (1918–). Their goal was to uncover the hypocrisy of their age.

Mailer, an American, drew on his experience as a soldier in World War II to capture the horror of modern war in his first and finest novel, *The Naked and the Dead* (1948). This work portrays a handful of enlisted men, a microcosm of America, as victims of their leaders' bad choices. He describes their officers as pursuing fantasies of glory, inspired by a notion that the world is godless and without lasting values. In the late 1960s Mailer began to write journalism, eventually achieving so much fame that today his essays overshadow his novels. His best journalism is the book-length essay *The Armies of the Night* (1968), an account of the October 1967 peace march on Washington, D.C., in which he participated. This book won Mailer a Pulitzer Prize.

Doris Lessing, a British writer, used Realism to show the contradictions at work in her homeland, Rhodesia (modern Zimbabwe), between blacks and whites, British and Dutch, British and colonials, capitalists and Marxists, and, always, women and men. In the *Children of Violence* series (1950–1969), consisting of five novels, she presents the story of the rise of black freedom fighters and the diminishing of white control in what was then a British colony. This disintegrating world serves as a backdrop to the existential struggle for self-knowledge and independence by the main character, Martha Quest. In her best-known novel, *The Golden Notebook* (1962), Lessing addresses, among other issues, the socialization process that stifles women's creativity. Her concerns, however, are not just female identity but the moral and intellectual fragmentation and confusion she sees in the modern world. In recent years she has turned to science fiction to address these issues.

The Russian Solzhenitsyn writes realistic novels that praise the Russian people while damning Marxism, which he regards as a "Western heresy," opposed to Orthodox Christianity. His short novel *One Day in the Life of Ivan Denisovich* (1962) reflects his own rage at being unjustly imprisoned under Stalin. This novel, published during Khrushchev's de-Stalinization drive, offers an indelible image of the tedium, harassment, and cruelty of life in a forced labor camp. And yet Ivan Denisovich remains a Soviet John Doe, dedicated to Marxism, his work, and his comrades (Figure 21.11).

When Solzhenitsyn's later books, which were banned in the Soviet Union until its fading years, revealed his hatred for communism, he was deported in 1974. Choosing exile in the United States, he settled in a Vermont hideaway from which he expressed moral disgust with the West for its atheistic materialism and softness toward the Soviet system. His values—Christian fundamentalism and Slavophilism, or advocacy of Russia's cultural supremacy—resemble those of Russia's great nineteenth-century pre-existentialist novelist, Dostoevsky. Believing that communism was finally dead, he returned to Russia in the spring of 1994.

Many Late Modernist poets used a private language to such a degree that their verses were often unintelligible to ordinary people. A few who used more conventional verse styles, however, earned a large readership. Of this latter group the Welsh poet Dylan Thomas (1914–1953) was the most famous and remains so today. Thomas's poems mirror the obscurity favored by the times, but what makes his works so memorable is their glorious sound. With their strong emotional content, jaunty rhythms, and melodious words, they are perfect to read aloud.

Better known than Thomas's poems, though, is his verse play *Under Milk Wood* (1954), arguably the best-loved poetic work of Late Modernism. Unlike the poems, this verse play is direct and imbued with simple emotions. Originally a play for radio, it presents a typical day in a Welsh village, a world he knew well, having grown up in such a place. His portrait of the colorful speech and intertwined lives of the eccentric villagers has moved millions of listeners, evoking for them bittersweet memories of their own youth.

A Late Modernist poet who is able to be experimental and yet win a large audience for his verses is the American writer Allen Ginsberg (1926–), the most significant poet produced by the Beat Generation of the 1950s. Like Dylan Thomas, he has an ear for colloquial speech, and his ability to construct new forms to convey iconoclastic views is unequaled by any other poet of his time. His outstanding poem tialism's bleak vision and determined to find new ways to express that outlook, a group of dramatists emerged called the *"theater of the absurd."* The absurdists shifted the focus of their plays away from the study of the characters' psychology to stress poetic language and abandoned realistic plots in order to concentrate on outrageous situations. A typical absurdist play mixed tragedy with comedy, as if the playwright thought that the pain of existence could be tolerated only if blended with humor.

Samuel Beckett (1906–1989), an Irish writer who lived in Paris, is the best-known dramatist of absurdist theater. His *Waiting for Godot* (1952) is a play in which almost nothing "happens" in the conventional sense of that word. Combining elements of tragedy and farce, *Waiting for Godot* broke new ground with its repetitive structure (the second act is almost a replica of the first); its lack of scenery (the stage is bare except for a single tree); and its meager action (the characters engage in futile exchanges based on British music hall routines). What plot there is also reinforces the idea of futility, as the characters wait for the mysterious Godot, who never appears.

In later years Beckett's works began to explore the dramatic possibilities of silence, as in the one-act drama *Not I* (1973). In this play, a voice—seen only as a mouth illuminated in a spotlight—tries to, but cannot, stop talking. Beckett's plays portray human consciousness as a curse; yet at the same time his works affirm the human spirit's survival in the face of despair.

The Literature of Post-Modernism

Post-Modernist literature is notable for the rise of new literary voices in Latin America and in central and eastern Europe, a shift that was part of the general decline of the dominance of the Paris–New York cultural axis and the rise of a more broadly based civilization. For the first time, Latin American authors put the Spanish-American novel on the international map. Most of these writers were distinguished by left-wing political opinions and devotion to a literary style called *"magic realism,"* which mixed realistic and supernatural elements. The ground had been prepared for the magic realists by the Argentinian author Jorge Luis Borges [BOR-hays] (1899–1986), whose brief, enigmatic stories gave this movement its stress on fantasy and linguistic experimentation.

The outstanding representative of the magic realist school is Gabriel Garcia Márquez [gahr-SEE-uh MAHR-kays] (1928–) of Colombia, who received

FIGURE 21.11 VITALY KOMAR AND ALEKSANDER MELAMID. *Stroke (About March 3, 1953).* 1982–1983. Oil on canvas, 6′ × 3′11″. Collection Evander D. Schley. Courtesy Ronald Feldman Fine Arts, New York. *The two Russian emigré painters Komar and Melamid—who work as a team—have devoted their artistic efforts to trying to understand the Russian Revolution and the reign of Stalin. In* Stroke *they depict the lonely death of Stalin and the discovery of his body by a member of his inner circle. The artists subtly criticize both Stalin and the Soviet system in the way the official stares unmoved at the dead tyrant. Komar and Melamid show their Post-Modernist tendencies in their use of elements from earlier styles of art, such as the theatrical lighting and unusual perspective typical of Caravaggio.*

is "Howl" (1956), a work of homage to rebel youth and illicit drugs and sex. Overcoming censorship, this poem of Ginsberg's opposed capitalist, heterosexual, bourgeois society and became the anthem of the Beat Generation.

During Late Modernism the most radical changes in literature took place in drama. Sharing existenthe 1982 Nobel Prize for literature—the first Latin American novelist to be so honored. His *One Hundred Years of Solitude* (1967) is among the most highly acclaimed novels of the postwar era. Inspired by William Faulkner's fictional county of Yoknapatawpha, Mississippi, Garcia Márquez invented the town of Macondo to serve as a symbol of his Colombian birthplace. Through the eyes of an omniscient narrator—probably an unnamed peasant—who sees Macondo as moving toward a predestined doom, he produced a hallucinatory novel that blends details from Latin American history with magical events, such as a character's ascent into heaven.

While Latin America's authors were enjoying international renown for the first time, the writers of central and eastern Europe—the other new center of Post-Modernism—were simply renewing an old tradition. From the early 1800s until communist regimes were installed in this century, the finest writers of central and eastern Europe had often been honored in the West. The revival of the literature of this region was heralded by the 1950s cultural thaw initiated by Soviet leader Khrushchev, but this thaw proved premature as controversial writers were either silenced or forced to seek refuge in the West.

Exile was the choice of the novelist Milan Kundera [KOON-dee-rah] (1929–) of Czechoslovakia, who moved to France after his first novel, *The Joke* (1969), put him in disfavor with Czech authorities. Kundera's style has affinities with magic realism, notably the blending of fantasy with national history, but unlike the authors of Latin America, he uses fantasy to emphasize moral themes, never for its own sake. He is also more optimistic than the magic realists, hinting that the power of love can lead its devotees to a different and better life. Indeed, Kundera tends to identify sexual freedom with political freedom.

The equation of sexual and political freedom is certainly the message of Kundera's finest novel to date, *The Unbearable Lightness of Being* (1984). He made the center of this work two historic events—the coming of Communism to Czechoslovakia in 1948 and its reimposition after the 1968 uprising. He describes the obsessive and ultimately destructive behavior of his main characters as they try to define their sexual natures in the repressive Czech state. Although his novel shows how insignificant human existence is in the face of political repression, he refuses to despair. That his characters struggle for sexual fulfillment, even when faced by overpowering odds, is his way of affirming the strength of human nature. Ultimately, Kundera endorsed the belief of humanism that the human spirit can be diminished but never broken.

A similar belief is apparent in the work of the American writer Alice Walker (1944–). In her poetry, essays, and fiction she brings a positive tone to her exploration of the African-American experience. Her most engaging novel to date is *The Color Purple* (1982), the story of a black woman abused by black men and victimized by white society. The literary device she uses to express this woman's anguish is an old one, a story told through an exchange of letters. What is unique is that in some letters the suffering woman simply pours out her heart to God—an unexpected but moving twist in the skeptical atmosphere of the postwar world. *The Color Purple* also drew on Walker's feminist consciousness, showing that the heroine's survival depended on her solidarity with other black women.

Maxine Hong Kingston (1940–) has enriched Post-Modernism by putting Chinese-Americans into American literature through her autobiographical books, a novel, short stories, and articles. Her avowed aim as a writer has been to "claim America," meaning to show that the Chinese have the right to belong through their labor in building the country and supporting themselves. In staking out this claim, she was influenced by the poet William Carlos Williams (1883–1963), a Modernist who envisioned an American culture distinct from Europe and fashioned from indigenous materials and forms. Not only does Kingston's writing celebrate Chinese strength and achievement but it also serves to avenge wrongs—by calling exploitation, racism, and ignorance by their true names.

The daughter of Chinese immigrants whose language was Say Yup, a dialect of Cantonese, Kingston has used her own life as a paradigm of the Chinese-American experience. Drawing on childhood stories told in the immigrant community, she wrote two works that summarize her Chinese heritage: *The Woman Warrior: Memoirs of a Girlhood Among Ghosts* (1976), dealing with matriarchal influence, and *China Men* (1980), telling of the patriarchal side. The many literary prizes given both these works will help ensure Kingston's success in the goal of claiming America for the Chinese.

Late Modernism and the Arts

In the postwar art world, leadership shifted from Paris to New York. The end of Parisian dominance had been predicted since the swift fall of France to the Nazis in 1940, and the economic and military superiority of the United States at the war's end ensured that America's largest city would be the new hub of Western culture. New York's cultural leaders

FIGURE 21.12 JACKSON POLLOCK. *Blue Poles.* 1952. Oil, enamel, and aluminum paint, 210.4 × 486.8 cm. Collection, Australian National Gallery, Canberra. *This painting is virtually unique among Pollock's drip canvases by having a recognizable image, the blue poles. He achieved this effect by first swirling paint onto the canvas and then applying a stick covered in blue pigment onto its surface. His refusal to use traditional methods reflects both his belief that rational approaches to art are flawed and his faith that subconscious feelings, when released, reveal hidden truths—an attitude typical of the Abstract Expressionists.*

were divided in 1945, however. On one side stood those who wanted to build on the native school of American art, which was realistic and provincial, while on the other side was a group ready to take up the mantle of leadership of the West's *avant-garde.* The chief institutional ally of this latter group, which soon dominated the field, was the Museum of Modern Art (MOMA) in New York City, founded principally by the Rockefeller family in 1929.

In determining the direction of Modern art, the New York artists had to contend with the domination of painting by Picasso, whose restless experimentation seemed to define art's leading edge; the prevalence of psychological theories that encouraged artists to experiment with spontaneous gestures and to seek insights from primitive peoples and from religious experience; and the cardinal need for constant newness. Although these had all been elements in Modernism since 1900, what made the postwar scene different was that the need to dispel illusions was greater and the level of despair higher, based on the destructive war, the Holocaust, and the postwar arms race.

Painting Shortly after 1945 an energetic style of painting arose that dominated Late Modernism and still plays a major role: *Abstract Expressionism*, sometimes called Action Painting. Like earlier Modernists, the Abstract Expressionists made spiritual claims for their work, identifying their spontaneous methods as liberating the human spirit. One of the founders of Abstract Expressionism was the American Jackson Pollock (1912–1956), who launched this style with his "drip paintings," created between 1947 and 1950. Influenced by Jungian therapy to experiment with spontaneous gestures, Pollock nailed his canvases to the floor of his studio and dripped loops of house paint onto them from buckets with holes punched in their bottoms (Figure 21.12). The drip canvases led to a new way of looking at art in terms of randomness, spontaneity, "all overness," and stress on the actual physical process of painting. Pollock's tendency to move around the canvas during its execution also introduced the idea of the artist interacting with the artwork.

The first generation of Abstract Expressionists was attracted by the movement's energy, rawness, and seriousness. An outstanding recruit to the new

FIGURE 21.13 MARK ROTHKO. *Ochre and Red on Red.* 1954. Oil on canvas, 7'8⅝" × 5'3¾". Phillips Collection, Washington, D.C. *In his paintings Rothko aims to create secular icons for a nonreligious age, a spiritual theory inherited from the Russian Constructivist tradition. Accordingly, he banishes all references to nature from his art and focuses on fields of color floating in space—timeless, universal images.*

art was Mark Rothko [RAHTH-koh] (1903–1970), a Russian émigré who painted in a style very different from Pollock's. A mystic, Rothko envisioned eliminating pigment and canvas and suspending clouds of shimmering colors in the air. After 1950 he settled for creating huge paintings that focused on no more than two or three fields of color (Figure 21.13).

By the mid-1950s a new generation of Abstract Expressionists emerged, the most important of whom were Helen Frankenthaler [FRANG-kuhn-thahl-uhr] (1928–), Jasper Johns (1930–), and Robert Rauschenberg [RAU-shun-buhrg] (1925–). Following in Pollock's footsteps, Frankenthaler adopted a method of spilling pigment onto canvas from coffee cans. By guiding the paint's flowing trajectory, she stained the canvas into exquisite, amorphous shapes that, though completely flat, seem to suggest a third dimension (Figure 21.14).

Johns and Rauschenberg found Abstract Expressionism too confining and overly serious, however. Although he did not abandon Expressionism, Johns added ordinary objects to his works, as in *Target with Plaster Casts* (1955) (Figure 21.15). In this work he paints a banal image below a row of wooden boxes enclosing molds of body parts. A basic feature of his art is the contrast between the precisely rendered human organs (above) and the painterly target (below). Johns's fascination with such tensions paved the way for the self-contradicting style of Post-Modernism. Similarly, Rauschenberg abandoned pure painting to become an **assemblage** artist, mixing found objects with junk and adding a dash of paint. In *Monogram,* he encircles a stuffed goat with a rubber tire and splashes the whole thing with color, thus turning ready-made objects into an abstract image (Figure 21.16).

◀ **FIGURE 21.14**   HELEN FRANKENTHALER. *Jacob's Ladder.* 1957. Oil on unprimed canvas, 9'5⅜" × 5'9⅞". Collection, The Museum of Modern Art, New York. Gift of Hyman N. Glickstein. *Frankenthaler's staining method—pouring paint onto a canvas—illustrates the tension between spontaneity and control typical of Abstract Expressionism. On the one hand, this technique leads naturally to surprises because of the unpredictable flow of the paint. On the other hand, the artist exercises control over the process, ranging from choosing the colors and thickness of the paint to manipulating the canvas during the staining. In effect, she becomes both a participant in and the creator of the final work of art.*

Johns and Rauschenberg, with their playful attack on serious art, opened the door to the ***Pop Art*** movement. Rejecting the Modernist belief that spiritual values may be expressed in nonrealistic works, the Pop artists frankly admitted that they had no spiritual, metaphysical, or philosophic purpose—they simply created two-dimensional images. Even though a kind of Pop Art developed in London in the 1950s, it was not until a new generation of New York artists began to explore commercial images in the early 1960s that the movement took off.

The most highly visible Pop artist was Andy Warhol (1927–1987), a former commercial artist who was fascinated by the vulgarity and energy of popular culture. Warhol's deadpan treatment of mass culture icons became legendary, whether they were Campbell's Soup cans, Coca Cola bottles, or Marilyn Monroe (Figure 21.17). By treating these icons in series, much in the same way as advertisers blanket the media with multiple images, he conveyed the ideas of repetitiveness, banality, and boredom. An artist who courted fame, Warhol recognized America's obsession with celebrity in his often-quoted line, "In the future everyone will be famous for fifteen minutes."

FIGURE 21.15   JASPER JOHNS. *Target with Plaster Casts.* 1955. Encaustic on canvas with plaster cast objects, 51 × 44 × 3½". Courtesy Leo Castelli Gallery, New York. *Johns was a key figure in the transitional generation of painters between the Abstract Expressionists and the Pop Artists. He rebelled against the pure abstraction of the older movement, yet he shied away from embracing mass culture images as directly as did the younger school of painters. His* Target with Plaster Casts *is typical of his playful, witty style. In this work he makes a visual play on words, juxtaposing a bull's-eye with plaster casts of body parts, each of which has been a "target," that is, a subject, for artists to represent throughout history.*

FIGURE 21.16 ROBERT RAUSCHENBERG. *Monogram.* 1959. Multimedia construction, 4 × 6 × 6'. Moderna Museet, Stockholm. *In his glorification of junk, Rauschenberg helped to open the door to Post-Modernism. In works such as* **Monogram** *he showed that anything, no matter how forlorn, even a stuffed goat and a discarded automobile tire, could be used to make art. Such irreverence reflected a democratic vision in which no object is seen as having greater artistic merit than any other.*

FIGURE 21.17 ANDY WARHOL. *Marilyn Monroe.* 1962. Oil, acrylic, and silkscreen enamel on canvas, 20 × 16". Collection, Jasper Johns. Courtesy Leo Castelli Gallery, New York. *Warhol's portrait of Marilyn Monroe, America's most famous postwar sex symbol, was typical of his style, which placed little value on originality. Working from a photograph supplied by her Hollywood studio, he merely used his brushes and paint to heighten the image that studio hairdressers and cosmetologists had already perfected. In effect, Warhol's art was a gilding of the lily. His commercial approach to portraiture made him the most celebrated society artist of his generation.*

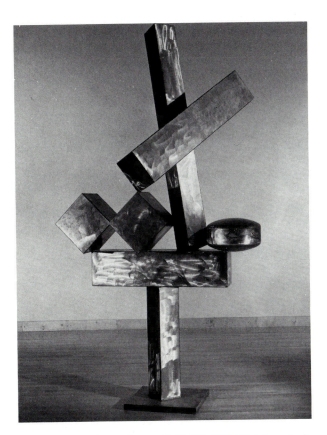

Sculpture Styles in sculpture were similar to those in painting. Abstract Expressionist painting had its equivalent in the works of several American sculptors, notably David Smith (1906–1965) and Louise Nevelson (1899–1988), a Russian émigrée. Smith's point of departure, however, differed from that of the painters in that he drew inspiration from the symbols of primitive cultures, as in *Cubi XIX*, a geometric work that, according to the artist, represents an altar with a sacrificial figure (Figure 21.18). If the viewer is unaware of this intended meaning, however, this stainless steel work has the inaccessible look of a Pollock drip canvas. In contrast, the wooden sculptures of Louise Nevelson are not about representation at all but are simple compositions fashioned from old furniture and wooden odds and ends (Figure 21.19). The use of found objects allowed Nevelson to realize the Abstract Expressionist's goal of spontaneous art devoid of references to the artist's life.

Pop Art was an influence in the works of George Segal (1924–). Segal's ghostly sculptures are made by applying a plaster mixture to his living subjects to produce generic figures, as in his dual portrait of Robert and Ethel Scull, leading patrons of the Pop Art movement (Figure 21.20). Segal himself rejects the Pop Art label—pointing out that his sculptures have expressionistic surfaces, like Rodin's works (see Chapter 19)—but his method reduces the body to a cartoon form and thus relates it to popular culture.

FIGURE 21.18   DAVID SMITH. *Cubi XIX*. 1964. Stainless steel, 9'5⅛ × 21¾ × 20¾". Tate Gallery, London. *Smith's ability as a sculptor of enormous and rather destructive energies shines through in the monumental* Cubi *series, the last artworks he made before his accidental death. A machinist by training, Smith liked to work with industrial metals, welding and bending them into geometric units to meet his expressive needs. His desire to shape mechanical images into expressive forms related him to the Abstract Expressionist movement in painting.*

FIGURE 21.19   LOUISE NEVELSON. *Sky Cathedral*. 1958. Assemblage: wood construction, painted black, 11'3½" × 10'1¼" × 18". The Museum of Modern Art, New York. Gift of Mr. and Mrs. Ben Mildwoff. *Though a Modernist, Nevelson anticipated Post-Modernism by combining genres, as in this free-standing wall that integrates architecture, sculpture, and painting. Typical of her art of this time, she divided the wall into a grid, stuffed found objects into the wall's compartments, and painted the finished work black. In the Post-Modern period Nevelson's decorative walls have had more influence on architects, such as Venturi, than on sculptors, who have tended to favor realistic styles.*

FIGURE 21.20 GEORGE SEGAL. *Robert and Ethel Scull.* 1965. Plaster, canvas, wood, and cloth, 8 × 6 × 6'. Private Collection. Courtesy Sidney Janis Gallery, New York. *Segal distances himself from fellow Pop artists by looking at the world through existential eyes. Where Warhol glamorizes his celebrity subjects, Segal portrays his wealthy patrons, the Sculls, as beset by anxiety. He conveys their anguish through fixed facial expressions and heavy limbs, while keeping their appearances generalized. His modeling technique, which requires subjects not to move any muscles until the plaster dries, reinforces the melancholy image.*

FIGURE 21.21 LUDWIG MIËS VAN DER ▶ ROHE AND PHILIP JOHNSON. *Seagram Building.* 1954–1958. New York City. *Miës's decision to use bronze-tinted windows as virtually the only decorative feature of the Seagram Building's simple geometrical design had a profound impact on his contemporaries. Following his lead, other architects made the high-rise skeleton-frame building with tinted windows the most recognizable symbol of Late Modernism.*

Architecture In Late Modernist architecture the most influential architect was the German-born Ludwig Miës van der Rohe [mees-van-duh-ROH] (1886–1969). The last head of the Bauhaus, Germany's premier design school before World War II, Miës closed its doors in 1933 and moved to the United States in 1938. In the 1950s he captured the world's attention with a glass skyscraper, New York's Seagram Building (Figure 21.21). Based on the artistic creed "less is more," this building's design is simple, a bronze skeletal frame on which are hung tinted windows. The implementation of his ideals of simplicity and restraint also led him to geometrize the building, planning its structural relationships according to mathematical ratios. So successful was Miës van der Rohe's "glass box" building that today skyscrapers built according to similar designs dominate the skylines of cities around the world.

Post-Modernism and the Arts

The arts began to change around 1970 as artists and architects struggled to move beyond Late Modernism, which seemed to have dissolved into weak minimalist schools. In Post-Modernism, the shock of the new gave way to the shock of the old. Seeking a way out of Late Modernism's chaotic pessimism and its focus on abstraction that seemed to have led to a dead end, Post-Modern artists were more optimistic and revived earlier styles, although always with added layers of meaning, nuance, or irony. Realism made a triumphant return to art, flourishing as *Neorealism*, a style based on photographic clarity of detail; as *Neoexpressionism*, a style that offers social criticism and focuses on nontraditional painting methods; and as *Neoclassicism* (not to be confused

FIGURE 21.22 PHILIP PEARLSTEIN. *Female on Eames Chair, Male on Swivel Stool.* 1981. Watercolor, 60 × 40". Collection of Eleanor and Leonard Bellinson. Courtesy Donald Morris Gallery, Birmingham, Mich. *Pearlstein's refusal to glamorize his nude subjects is part of a democratizing tendency in Post-Modernism. Just as some Post-Modernist authors borrow freely from mass-circulation genres such as Sherlock Holmes and science fiction, so Pearlstein focuses attention on bodily features like sagging breasts and bulging veins that had been overlooked by realistic painters.*

with the Neoclassicism of the late eighteenth century), which had been dormant since the early twentieth century and pronounced dead by the Late Modernists. Neoclassicism is the most striking style within Post-Modernism, in both painting and architecture, perhaps because it looks so fresh to modern eyes. In addition to these various forms of realism, Modernist abstraction remains a significant facet of Post-Modernism. In their openness to artistic possibilities and their refusal to adopt a uniform style, the Post-Modernists resembled the Post-Impressionists of the late nineteenth century.

Painting   An outstanding Neorealist painter is the American Philip Pearlstein (1924–   ), who specializes in nonidealized nudes. Starting in the 1960s he made his chief subject human bodies beyond their prime, perhaps as a way of reflecting the melancholy of the age. His nudes are rendered in stark close-up, the bodies at rest like hanging meat, and with cropped heads and limbs as in a photograph (Figure 21.22). His works seem to parody the "centerfold sexuality" that accompanied the sexual revolution brought on in part by the birth control pill.

Whereas Neorealism tends to neutrality or moral subtlety, Neoexpressionism uses realism to create paintings that are overtly socially critical. The outstanding Neoexpressionist and the most highly regarded painter among the Post-Modernists is the German artist Anselm Kiefer [KEE-fuhr] (1945–   ). Kiefer's works have blazed new trails with nontraditional painting materials, including dirt, tar, and copper threads. Existential anguish is alive in his works, which tend to focus on apocalyptic images of a blasted earth—a chilling reference to the threat of nuclear destruction (Figure 21.23). Post-Modern optimism may nevertheless be read in his borrowings from Mesopotamia and Egypt, which affirm the continuity of Western culture from its earliest stages to the present. In his use of personal references and historical allusions, Kiefer is perhaps the contemporary artist closest to the German Expressionists of the early twentieth century.

The British painter Sue Coe (1951–   ), who now lives and works in America, is another important Neoexpressionist whose art serves social and political causes. Daughter of a working-class London family, she is a counter-culturalist who came of age in the stormy sixties. Committed to feminist and overtly political art, she does not espouse any specific ideology but simply confronts injustice wherever she sees it. She once described her creed in these words: "If you remove your armies from other people's countries, I won't paint war." In a broad sense, she wants her art to be a tool for change, to bear witness to the vices of capitalist and urban society, as in *Modern Man Followed by the Ghosts of His Meat* (Figure 21.24), one of the works in her indictment of the meat industry and its shocking treatment of animals. While the message constantly threatens to overpower the art, Coe's paintings are meant to move viewers to share the artist's concerns and thus work for reform.

A painter who uses Neoclassicism to make a subtle commentary on modern life is the American Stone Roberts (1951–   ). In *The Conversation* he blends Classical features of Renaissance space, Ba-

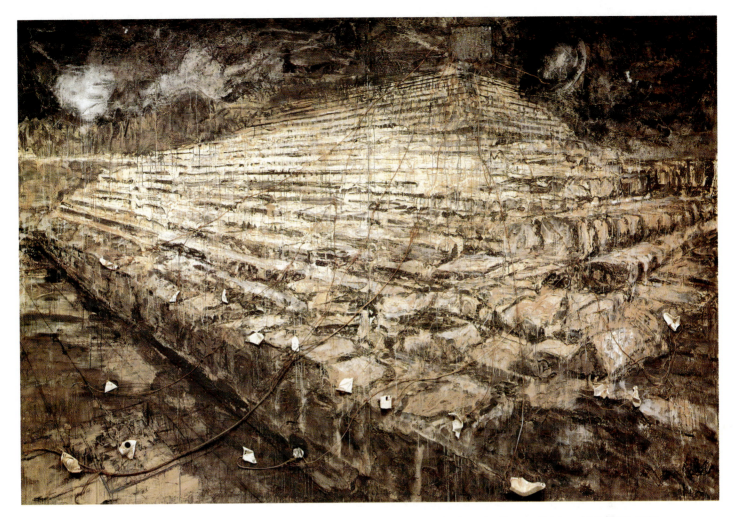

FIGURE 21.23 ANSELM KIEFER. *Osiris and Isis*. 1985–1987. Diptych, mixed media on canvas, 12′6″ × 18′4½″ × 6½″. The San Francisco Museum of Modern Art. Courtesy Marian Goodman Gallery, New York. *Kiefer drew on an ancient Egyptian myth to give shape to his fears of modern technology. He represents Isis, the goddess who restored her husband-brother Osiris to life, as an electronic keyboard at the top of a pyramid. He adds actual copper wires to connect the circuit board to broken bits of ceramics, his symbol of Osiris's fragmented body. In Kiefer's Post-Modern imagination, technology has become a deity with the capacity to destroy or create.*

roque lighting, and Dutch genre precision (Figure 21.25). A representation of a bittersweet moment in middle-class life, it evokes the feeling of a social gathering when guests are reluctant to depart. The darkening background reinforces the air of melancholy and hints that this way of life is passing.

Modernist abstraction continues to have a powerful impact on Post-Modernism. The most brilliant current disciple of abstraction is Frank Stella (1936–   ), a painter who has produced an immense and varied body of work. A minimalist in the 1950s, painting black-striped canvases, he became a forerunner of Neoexpressionism in the 1970s, using gaudy color and decorative effects. He has remained true to abstract ideals, as in *Norisring*, one of the *Shard* series that uses the scraps left over from other works (Figure 21.26). Fully abstract and nonrepresentational, this work is nevertheless Post-Modernist since it combines the genres of painting and sculpture—an ambition of many Post-Modernists.

modern man followed by the ghosts of his meat......

FIGURE 21.25 STONE ROBERTS. *The Conversation.* 1985. Oil on canvas, 6′ × 7′6″. Private Collection. Courtesy Robert Schoelkopf Gallery, New York. *In* The Conversation *Roberts brings Classicism up-to-date by applying its features and principles to a contemporary American context. He fills the setting with Classical references, including fluted columns, a Greek-style marble fireplace, a rounded arch, and vases after Greek models. The figures are grave and self-contained, and the symmetry of the fireplace and columns reflects the Classical ideal of harmony.*

◀ **FIGURE 21.24**   SUE COE. *Modern Man Followed by the Ghosts of His Meat. Copyright © Sue Coe 1990. Gallerie St. Etienne, New York. This is one of the works in the protest booklet* Meat: Animals and Industry *by Sue Coe and her sister Mandy, inspired by visits to slaughterhouses and factory farms. This work is in the vein of an editorial cartoon inspired by a Dickens novel. Coe prefers to work with graphic arts (''handmade, mechanically reproduced images''), as they engage the viewer more directly and allow the artist to reach a larger audience than more traditional means do.*

FIGURE 21.26   FRANK STELLA. *Norisring (XVI, 3X).* 1983. Mixed media on etched aluminum, 6'7" × 5'7" × 1'3". Private Collection. Courtesy M. Knoedler & Co., New York. *Largely because of his lively intelligence, Stella has stayed on the cutting edge of Post-Modernism. He has kept abstraction alive almost singlehandedly at a time when realist styles are dominant. His 1960s innovation, the shaped canvas, allowed him to replace the rectilinear canvas with an abstract form. By the early 1980s he had transformed the shaped canvas into a blend of sculpture and painting, as in the* Shard *series.*

FIGURE 21.28 ROBERT VENTURI. Guild House. 1965.
Philadelphia. *Venturi's aesthetic aim is to transform the
ordinary into the extraordinary. He followed this democratic ideal
in Guild House, where he took a "dumb and ordinary" (his term)
concept and tried to give it a monumental look. Whether he
succeeds in achieving his goal is a matter of taste. Nevertheless,
his ironic intelligence and his perverse delight in mass culture
have made him a guiding spirit of Post-Modernism.*

of its starkness, he attempts to create buildings that
express the energy and ever-changing quality of contemporary life. Fascinated by mass culture, he is inspired by popular styles of architecture, such as Las
Vegas casinos and motels in the form of Indian te-
pees—a kitsch style sometimes called "vernacular." A
work that enshrines his love of the ordinary is his
Guild House, a retirement home in a lower-middle-
class section of Philadelphia (Figure 21.28). Faceless
and seemingly artless, this building is indebted to popular culture for its aesthetic appeal—for instance, the
wire sculpture on the roof looks like a television an-
tenna, and the recessed entrance and sign evoke memories of old-time movie houses. Venturi's playful assault on Modernism opened the door to the diversity
of Post-Modernism.

One of the strains in Post-Modernism is called
high tech, a style that revives industrial techniques
whose roots stretch back to the Crystal Palace (see
Figure 18.5) and the Eiffel Tower. Richard Rogers
(1933–) of England and Renzo Piano (1937–) of
Italy launched this revival with the Pompidou Center in Paris, which boldly displays its factory-made
metal parts and transparent walls (Figure 21.29).
Commissioned by France to restore Paris's cultural
position over New York, the Pompidou Center has
spawned many imitations as well as a style of interior decoration.

The most controversial building in Post-Modern
architecture is the thirty-seven-story, pink granite
headquarters building of American Telephone and
Telegraph, executed in a Neoclassical style (Figure
21.30). Designed by Philip C. Johnson (1906–), an
American disciple of Miës van der Rohe, this building was a slap in the face to the Modernist ideal because it used Classical forms. The AT&T Building

FIGURE 21.27 JOHN DE ANDREA. *Seated Man and Woman.*
1981. Polyvinyl, polychromed in oil, life-size. Courtesy ACA
Galleries, New York. *Unlike Pearlstein, who uses nudity to
register his disgust, De Andrea designs his polyvinyl nudes to
celebrate the glossy lives of the upper middle class. The bodies of
his nude subjects convey what today's consumer culture urges
everyone to be: healthy, sleek, athletic, and sexy.*

Sculpture Like painters, Post-Modernist sculptors began to work with realistic forms. For example, serving
as complements to the Neorealist paintings of Philip
Pearlstein are the sculptures of the American John De
Andrea (1941–). Typically, De Andrea uses traditional poses, as in *Seated Man and Woman* (Figure
21.27), a work inspired by Rodin. But De Andrea's human figures are fully contemporary, suggestive of two
young upwardly mobile professionals ("yuppies")
who have taken off their clothes. Whether or not his
works are satirical, he manages to capture in sculptural
form the erotic quality considered so desirable by
modern advertising, movies, and mass media.

Architecture The chief exponent of Post-Modern architecture is the American Robert Venturi (1925–),
whose ideas are summarized in his book *Complexity
and Contradiction in Architecture* (1966). Rejecting Modernist architecture, which he thinks inhuman because

FIGURE 21.29 RICHARD ROGERS AND RENZO PIANO. The
Georges Pompidou Center for Art and Culture. 1971–1977.
Paris. *Designed in a gaudy industrial style and erected in the
heart of a quiet section of Paris called Beaubourg, the Pompidou
Center was controversial from the start, as it was planned to be.
Its showy appearance sharply contrasted with the historic styles of
neighboring structures—a contrast that has become a guiding
ideal of Post-Modernist architects. The furor that greeted the
Pompidou Center on its opening has occurred in other places
where city governments have placed colorful and brash high-tech
temples amid their more traditional buildings.*

has a base, a middle, and a top, corresponding to the foot, shaft, and capital of a Greek column—the basic element of Greco-Roman building style. As a final blow to Modernist purity, Johnson topped his building with a split pediment crown, causing a hostile critic to compare it to an eighteenth-century Chippendale highboy. Notwithstanding the furor surrounding its creation, this building heralded the resurgence of Neoclassicism in the Post-Modernist age.

Late Modern and Post-Modern Music

The major musical styles that were dominant prior to World War II persisted in Late Modernism. New York was the world's musical capital, and styles were still polarized into tonal and atonal camps, led by Stravinsky and Schoenberg, respectively. After Schoenberg's death in 1951, however, Stravinsky abandoned tonality and adopted his rival's serial method. Stravinsky's conversion made serialism the most respected type of atonal music, though other approaches to atonality sprang up, notably in the United States. Under Late Modernism, this dissonant style became the musical equivalent of the spontaneous canvases painted by Pollock and the Abstract Expressionist school.

Despite embracing the dissonance and abstraction of serialism, Stravinsky filled his Late Modernist works with energy and feeling, the touchstones of his musical style. Two of his finest serial works were *Agon* (1957), a score for a ballet with no other plot than a competition among the dancers, and *Requiem Canticles* (1968), a religious service for the dead marked by austere solemnity.

Dissonance also characterizes the music of Krzysztof Penderecki [pen-duhr-ETS-ke] (1933–   ), a member of the "Polish School" who is anything but a doctrinaire Modernist. Committed to an older musical ideal, he believes that music, above all things, must speak to the human heart. Nevertheless, he has been a constant innovator, seeking especially to create new sounds through the unconventional use of stringed instruments and the human voice. Marked by Classical restraint, his compositions are clearly structured works permeated by fluctuating clouds of sounds, as in *Threnody for the Victims of Hiroshima* (1960), scored for 52 stringed instruments. (A "threnody" is a "song of lamentation.") Reflective of the melancholy mood of Late Modernism, this work conjures up the eerie nine minutes, in 1945 at Hiroshima, between the dropping of the atomic bomb and its detonation. Penderecki achieves unearthly effects

FIGURE 21.30   PHILIP C. JOHNSON AND JOHN BURGEE. *American Telephone and Telegraph Headquarters.* 1979–1984. New York. *Although Classical rules were followed in the planning of Johnson and Burgee's AT&T Headquarters, it was built using Modernist methods. Like Modernist structures, the building has a steel frame to which exterior panels are clipped. Despite its Modernist soul, the physical presence of this Post-Modernist building conveys the gravity and harmony customarily associated with Classical architecture.*

through the use of *glissando* (the blending of one tone into the next in scalelike passages) in an extremely high register and by the string players' bowing their instruments in abnormal ways.

The most influential Late Modernist was John Cage (1912–1992), whose unusual, even playful, approach to music opened the door to Post-Modernism. Briefly Schoenberg's student, Cage gained most of his controversial notions—in particular, his goal of integrating noise into music—from the enigmatic teachings of Zen Buddhism. A work that demonstrates this goal is called *4'33"* (*Four Minutes and Thirty-three Seconds*). The title describes the time period that the performer is to sit immobile before a piano keyboard so that the music, in effect, becomes the concert hall sounds during the silence. Cage's spirited experiments made him the darling of the *avant-garde*. Along with assemblage artists, choreographers, and sculptors, he helped to break down the divisions among the art forms—an anticipation of a Post-Modernist development.

In the 1960s innovative composers appeared who rejected atonality for its overintellectuality and its apparent devotion to harsh sounds. In place of atonality, these composers founded a Post-Modern style devoted to making music more emotionally appealing, though they remained committed to experimental methods. Among the most notable composers working within this style is the American Philip Glass (1937–   ), who has made it his mission to return exuberance to music. He has pursued this goal while working in a minimalist tradition, although he draws on varied sources, including classical Indian music, African drumming, and rock-and-roll. Much of Glass's music is written for *synthesizer,* a machine with a simple keyboard that can duplicate the sounds of up to twelve instruments simultaneously. He composes with simple tonal harmonies, pulsating rhythms, unadorned scales, and, above all, lilting arpeggios, the cascading sounds produced by playing the notes of a chord in rapid sequences. A Glass piece is instantly recognizable for its repetitiveness and obsessive quality.

A composer of chamber works, film scores, and dance pieces, Glass has gained the widest celebrity

for his operas. His first opera, *Einstein on the Beach* (1976), produced in collaboration with the equally controversial American director Robert Wilson (1941–), was staged at New York's Metropolitan Opera, a rarity for a living composer in this century. In their kaleidoscopic work, Glass and Wilson redefined the operatic form, staging a production lasting four and one-half hours without intermission and with Glass's driving music set to Wilson's texts with no recognizable plot, no formal arias, and no massed choruses. So successful was this venture that Glass followed it with operas based on other remarkable figures, *Satyagraha* (1978) dealing with the life of Gandhi, India's liberator, and *Akhnaten* (1984) focusing on the Egyptian pharaoh who is sometimes called the first monotheist.

Another powerful presence in Post-Modern music is Laurie Anderson (1947–), who is the queen of **performance art**—a democratic type of mixed media art born in the 1960s that ignores artistic boundaries, happily mixing high art (such as music, painting, and theater) and popular art (such as rock 'n roll, film, and fads) to create a unique, non-reproducible, artistic experience. Anderson's performance art consists of sing-and-tell story-songs about mundane events of daily life, which somehow take on unearthly significance. These monologues are often tinged with humor and are delivered in a singsong voice backed up by mixed media images, strange props, and varied electronic media, including electronic musical instruments, photo projection, manipulated video, and devices that alter the sound of her voice (Figure 21.31). Central to the performance is her stage persona, rather like Dorothy in *The Wizard of Oz*, in which she gazes with wide-eyed wonder on the modern technological world. A gifted violinist, she intends her music to play only a supporting role in her art, though her recordings [for example, *Strange Angels* (1990), based on a work called *Empty Places* (1989)] have found eager listeners. Anderson's ongoing popularity is a testament to her ability to stay ahead of the ever-shifting *zeitgeist*.

Mass Culture

In the postwar era American mass culture began to serve as the common denominator of an emerging world civilization. Because of its democratic and energetic qualities, sexual content, and commitment to free expression, this culture has attracted people around the globe. Scenes of American life—conveyed through television, movies, and advertising—have mesmerized millions, who imitate these images

FIGURE 21.31 EBET ROBERTS. Laurie Anderson performing at the Brooklyn Academy of Music, October, 1989. Empty Places Tour. *Laurie Anderson, whose works virtually define performance art, is pictured here in the midst of a performance at the Brooklyn Academy of Music. The self-consciously theatrical costume and punk hairstyle are typical of her stage persona; the background, with its alienating effects created by electronic means, suggests the technological world that is the principal concern of her art.*

as far as they are able. The popularity of the clothing (jeans, T-shirt, and running shoes), the food (hamburgers, fries, and cola), and the music (rock-and-roll) of the American teenager has influenced behavior even in eastern Europe, Russia, and the Third World.

The information boom has been the explosive force Americanizing the world and transforming it into a global village, with television providing the means of transformation. As the earth has shrunk, more electronic gear—the videocassette recorder, the compact-disc player, the digital recorder, the camcorder, the computer—has reduced the individual's world even more, turning each home into a communications center.

The rise of a worldwide mass culture has produced an insatiable demand for popular entertainment. It has led to the replacement of old types of amusements with new forms, such as the rock concert and the rock video, along with the creation of innovative means of media coverage, including cable television with MTV and all-sports channels (Map 21.2). This demand has given birth to extravagantly popular figures—like Elvis Presley (1935–1977), America's first postwar music idol, Michael Jackson (1958–), America's superstar of the mid-1980s, and Madonna (1959–), America's queen of popular songs in the early 1990s—who are role models for teenagers and young adults across the world. Except for the Beatles, the British rock quartet that was the most popular rock group of the 1960s, few superstars are non-American. Only time will tell if Post-Modernist mass culture can produce a civilization that is truly pluralistic and global.

MAP 21.2

The Global Village: Countries with CNN and MTV

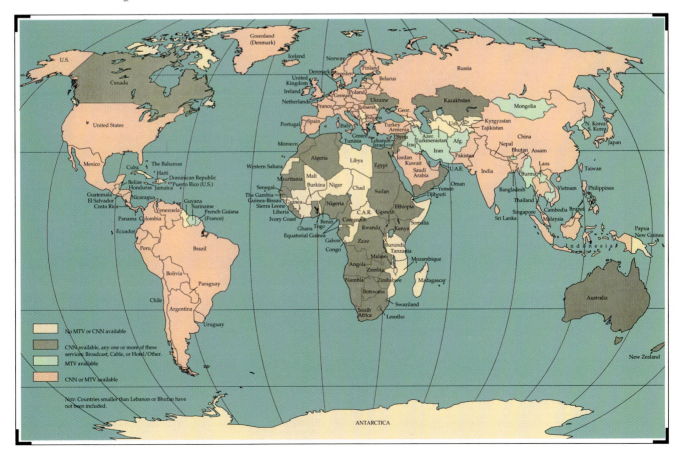

A Summing Up

We stand on the threshhold of a new era. The division of the world into rival armed camps after World War II seems to be at an end, and many voices have proclaimed the death of the Cold War. Winds of freedom are blowing everywhere. After forty-five divided years, Germany is reunited. *Glasnost* has opened up the societies of the satellite countries of the Soviet system, and the former Soviet Union is caught in turbulent events whose outcome is unpredictable. South Africa, where a white minority has always denied rights to the black majority, shows signs of a change to a more just society.

Future shifts in economic power among the world's great states promise more changes in the old political order. In 1992 western Europe became the world's largest free trade zone, only to be overtaken, in 1993, by a new economic union of Canada, Mexico, and the United States. The unification of Germany is having incalculable ramifications on global events. And growing debt among the Third World states makes them perennial trouble spots because of their vulnerability to internal unrest and external aggression.

A new world order may already be seen, struggling to be born, in our Post-Modernist era. It is global and democratic and embraces the contributions, tastes, and ideas of many groups of people, men and women, people of all races, and people of all countries. It is also open-ended, freely borrowing from high culture and mass culture. Nevertheless, the driving force for the emerging global culture in the foreseeable future is Western civilization, largely because of its immense capacity to adapt and bend and yet ultimately to survive—something Western artists, writers, and peoples have been doing since the first cities were founded in Sumer and Egypt five thousand years ago.

KEY CULTURAL TERMS

Late Modernism	*Pop Art*
Post-Modernism	*Neorealism*
structuralism	*Neoexpressionism*
theater of the absurd	*Neoclassicism*
magic realism	*high tech*
Abstract Expressionism	*glissando*
assemblage art	*synthesizer*

SUGGESTIONS FOR FURTHER READING

PRIMARY SOURCES

The Autobiography of Malcolm X. With the assistance of A. Haley. Secaucus, N.J.: Castle Books, 1967. In his own words Malcolm X describes his rise from obscurity to become a powerful figure posing radical solutions to racial problems.

BALDWIN, J. *Go Tell It On the Mountain.* New York: Grossett and Dunlap, 1953. A novel representative of Baldwin's early optimism about reconciliation of the black and white races.

———. *No Name in the Street.* New York: Dial Press, 1972. A novel representative of Baldwin's bitterness after the murder of Martin Luther King, Jr.

BECKETT, S. *Waiting for Godot.* Edited and with an introduction by H. Bloom. New York: Chelsea House Publishers, 1987. The central image of Beckett's absurdist play—pointless waiting—has become a metaphor for the disappointed hopes of Late Modernism.

CAMUS, A. *The Fall.* Translated by J. O'Brien. New York: Knopf, 1957. Camus's most autobiographical novel, dealing with self-deceit and spiritual yearning.

CHOMSKY, N. *Syntactic Structures.* The Hague: Mouton, 1957. The work that revolutionized linguistics by claiming that there is a structure that lies hidden beneath the surface of language.

DE BEAUVOIR, S. *The Second Sex.* Translated and edited by H. M. Parshley. New York: Vintage, 1974. One of the books that helped launch the feminist revival by arguing that women must abandon "femininity" and create their own immortality just as men do.

FANON, F. *The Wretched of the Earth.* Translated by C. Farrington. New York: Grove Press, 1968. Fanon's ground-breaking study of racism and colonial liberation; a classic of modern revolutionary theory.

FRIEDAN, B. *The Feminine Mystique.* New York: Norton, 1963. Denouncing men for conspiring to keep women in second place, this work was a milestone in the rebirth of feminism in the United States.

GARCIA MÁRQUEZ, G. *One Hundred Years of Solitude.* New York: Cambridge University Press, 1990. A classic of Post-Modernism that mixes magical happenings with realistic events in the mythical Colombian town of Macondo.

GINSBERG, A. *Collected Poems, 1947–1980.* New York: Harper & Row, 1984. A Late Modernist, Ginsberg writes poetry that reflects his openness to diversity and his passion for freedom.

KING, M. L., JR. *A Testament of Hope: The Essential Writings of Martin Luther King, Jr.* New York: Harper & Row, 1986. A good introduction to the thought of the most powerful black American in history.

KINGSTON, M. H. *The Woman Warrior: Memoirs of a Girlhood Among Ghosts.* New York: Knopf, 1976. A novel dealing with the confusion of growing up Chinese-American in California; the ''ghosts'' of the subtitle refer to both the pale-faced Americans of the author's childhood and the spirits of Chinese ancestors and legendary female avengers brought to life by immigrant tales.

———. *China Men.* New York: Knopf, 1980. Kingston's autobiographical work, dealing with her patriarchal heritage, and which complements *The Woman Warrior,* which focuses on matriarchal influences.

KUNDERA, M. *The Unbearable Lightness of Being.* Translated by M. H. Heim. New York: Harper & Row, 1984. A novel that explores the anguish of life under Communism in eastern Europe.

LESSING, D. *Children of Violence.* (Includes *Martha Quest, A Proper Marriage, A Ripple from the Storm, Landlocked.*) New York: Simon and Schuster, 1964–1966. *The Four-gated City.* New York: Knopf, 1969. Together, these five books make up the *Children of Violence* series. Covering the period between the 1930s and 1960s, this series is Lessing's literary meditation on the transformation of her colonial homeland, Rhodesia, into the black state of Zimbabwe. Martha Quest, the focal point of this quintet of novels, is the author's surrogate witness to these turbulent events.

LÉVI-STRAUSS, C. *The Elementary Structures of Kinship.* Translated by J. H. Bell and others. Boston: Beacon Press, 1969. A classic of social anthropology, this work established that there are only a few basic patterns of kinship relationships in all societies.

MAILER, N. *The Naked and the Dead.* New York: Rinehart, 1948. Mailer's novel of World War II, his first and best work.

SARTRE, J.-P. *The Age of Reason* and *The Reprieve.* Translated by E. Sutton. *Troubled Sleep.* Translated by G. Hopkins. New York: Knopf, 1947, 1947, and 1950. Sartre's trilogy of novels, called *The Roads to Freedom,* demonstrates existentialism in action.

———. *No Exit and Three Other Plays.* Translated by L. Abel and S. Gilbert. New York: Vintage, 1976. *No Exit* is Sartre's most famous drama illustrating his idea that ''Hell is other people'' because they strive to define us and see us as objects; also includes *Dirty Hands, The Respectful Prostitute,* and *The Flies.*

SOLZHENITSYN, A. *One Day in the Life of Ivan Denisovich.* Translated by R. Parker. New York: Dutton, 1963. Published with permission of the Soviet authorities, this novel revealed the existence of Stalin's slave labor camps.

THOMAS, D. *The Collected Poems of Dylan Thomas.* New York: New Directions, 1953. The finest lyric poet of the Late Modern period, Thomas wrote on such themes as sex, love, and death.

———. *Under Milk Wood, A Play for Voices.* New York: New Directions, 1954. A verse play set in a mythical Welsh village that comes to symbolize a lost world in an urbanized age.

WALKER, A. *The Color Purple.* New York: Harcourt Brace Jovanovich, 1982. An uplifting novel that describes the central black female character's rise from degradation to modest dignity. The heroine's use in her letters of awkward but poignantly moving black English underscores the difficulty and the ultimate heroism of her victory.

WRIGHT, R. *Native Son.* New York: Grossett and Dunlap, 1940. Wright's most celebrated novel, the powerful story of the violent consequences of racism in the life of the black hero.

———. *Black Boy: A Record of Childhood and Youth.* New York: Harper, 1945. Wright's description of his rise from share-cropper status to international renown.

SUGGESTIONS FOR LISTENING

ANDERSON, LAURIE (1947–   ).
The premier performance artist of our time, Anderson has come a long way since 1973's *Duets on Ice,* when, dressed in a kilt and skating on ice, she played duets with herself on the violin (it had been altered to play a prerecorded solo) on Manhattan street corners, the duration of the piece dependent on the melting ice. Today her performances are memorialized through records such as *Mister Heartbreak* (1984); *Sharkey's Day* (1984), based on a Bauhaus work by Oskar Schlemmer; and *Strange Angels* (1989), taken from the performance piece entitled *Empty Places.* Her most popular work to date—almost 900,000 copies sold—is *O Superman* (1980), a single record which was later incorporated into the epic-length *United States* I–IV (1983).

CAGE, JOHN (1912–1992).
Since the late 1950s Cage's music came to be characterized by wholly random methods that he called *aleatory* (from the Latin *alea* for dice), as represented by 4'33" (*Four Minutes and Thirty-three Seconds*) (1952), *Variations IV* (1963), and *Aria with Fonatana Mix* (1958).

GLASS, PHILIP (1937–   ).
Glass's pulsating rhythms and cascading sounds have made him a popular and successful figure in Post-Modern music. He is best known for his operas, including *Einstein on the Beach* (1976), *Satyagraha* (1978), and *Akhnaten* (1984), and for his film scores, such as *Koyaanisqatsi* (1983) and *Mishima* (1985).

PENDERECKI, KRZYSTOF (1933–   ).
Penderecki, an eclectic composer, draws inspiration from diverse sources, including Stravinsky and Classical and church music. Reflective of the turbulence of contemporary Poland, his music centers on themes of martyrdom, injustice, and persecution. The first work that made him an international musical star was *Threnody for the Victims of Hiroshima* (1960), a piece for orchestra that uses stringed instruments and human voices in unusual ways. Perhaps his masterpiece is the more traditional oratorio *Passion and Death of Our Lord Jesus Christ According to St. Luke,* more commonly called ''The St. Luke Passion'' (1966), which incorporates Gregorian chant, folk music, nonverbal choral sounds, and modified serialism. He also has had success with operas, as in the simultaneously dissonant and lyrical *Paradise Lost* (1978), based on Milton's epic poem (see Chapter 14).

STRAVINSKY, IGOR (1882–1971).
After 1951 Stravinsky replaced his Neoclassical style with the techniques of serial music, as in the song *In Memoriam Dylan Thomas* (1954), the ballet *Agon* (1954–1957), and the orchestral works *Movements* (1959) and *Orchestral Variations* (1964).

APPENDIX

Writing for the Humanities: Research Papers and Essay Examinations

The most important part of a man's education is the ability to discuss poetry intelligently.
—PROTAGORAS, FIFTH CENTURY B.C.

I would have the ideal courtier accomplished in those studies that are called the humanities.
—CASTIGLIONE, SIXTEENTH CENTURY A.D.

The idea of ''writing for the humanities'' has a long history, extending back over twenty-five centuries to ancient Greece. There, in fifth-century-B.C. Athens, the Sophists invented what we today call a ''liberal education.'' These philosophers, who could be termed the first humanists, taught literature, the arts, music, and philosophy, along with what we call political science, anthropology, psychology, and history, to young Athenians, particularly those who hoped to play a leading role in politics. Not only did the Sophists demand that their students master a specific body of knowledge, but they also took care to instruct them in putting the humanistic disciplines into practice. They believed that individuals who had honed their analytical skills in the study of the humanities would be able to make wise judgments in private and public matters and to contribute to the community's political affairs.

The Sophists' educational ideal—training for good citizenship—was later adopted by the Romans, who transmitted it to the medieval West where it became a guiding principle of university education down to the present. Today, college humanities professors give writing assignments because of their belief in the liberal education ideal as well as because

of their conviction that writing, despite the spread of mass media technology, remains an essential tool of private and public communication and the hallmark of the truly educated person.

AN INTEGRATIVE APPROACH TO WRITING ABOUT THE HUMANITIES

In your study of the humanities, you will probably be given writing assignments that reflect the integrative approach of *The Western Humanities* (see the Introduction). This means that your papers and examinations will not be limited to a single humanistic discipline. Instead, you will be expected to draw information from all of the humanities as well as other disciplines that help illuminate the historical setting, such as political science, economics, and psychology. For example, if you were assigned a term paper on some aspect of nineteenth-century Europe, you would have to consider the civilization as a whole, both its material and cultural developments, and at the same time bring into clearer focus such specific factors as the impact of the ruling middle class on stylistic changes in the arts and literature or the influence of the rise of nationalism on cultural developments. This integrative approach to writing reinforces the message of the textbook—that the humanities are best understood when studied holistically in their historical setting.

GENERAL RULES FOR WRITING

Typically, writing assignments for a college-level humanities course are out-of-class research or term papers and in-class essay examinations. Regardless of the writing format, keep in mind three general rules. First, think of writing as an exercise in persuasion. Assume the teacher is unfamiliar with the topic, and write to demonstrate your mastery of the material. Second, follow basic principles of good grammar and punctuation. Some teachers will penalize you for mistakes in grammar and punctuation. Even if this is not the case, instructors cannot help but be skeptical of your learning if your writing is riddled with errors. Third, accept criticism and learn from past mistakes. Few individuals are born with a gift for writing; most have to struggle to reach a writing level that is personally satisfying. Even many authors, including famous ones, still find the writing process itself deeply frustrating. Like swimming, writing cannot be learned by talking about it; it is a skill you acquire through experience. Writing well requires patience, practice, and the willingness to learn from mistakes.

RESEARCH AND TERM PAPERS

Learning to write well starts with good work habits. Establish a quiet and comfortable work space, such as a table at a library, a desk in a dormitory room, a computer station, or a desk in an empty classroom. A typewriter or computer is useful, as is access to references, such as dictionaries and biographical books. Develop an orderly schedule of study; plan ahead so things are not left until the last minute. Balancing work and play is a prelude to writing well, since you need brief respites from intense study to rest and refresh your mind. If you arm yourself with good work habits, you will be ready to face the challenge of writing a research or term paper.

Steps in Writing a Paper

The first step in writing a research or term paper is to pick a topic. Choose a topic that is interdisciplinary, involving at least two humanistic fields of study, like the arts and literature of a specific historical period. Make sure your topic is manageable, neither too narrowly nor too broadly focused for your paper's length. Above all, select a topic that sparks some intellectual interest in you. Otherwise, your finished paper, even if it is carefully researched, may turn out to be uninspired and pedestrian. If you cannot find something that appeals to you on a list of suggested topics, consult with your instructor about a new subject satisfactory to both of you. As part of choosing a topic, you should also decide what approach to use in your paper, such as analytical, impressionistic, overview, or other. These approaches are described in detail in the next section.

The next step is to establish a basic bibliography. Scan your school library's holdings, either through the card catalogue system or by computer, to identify books and articles relevant to your topic. Once you have accumulated a bibliography of perhaps twenty to thirty sources, check the library stacks for additional books with appropriate call numbers that you may have overlooked in your search thus far. Then survey all these sources, treating them as background reading. At this preparatory level, take some notes on file cards and draw up a fuller list of secondary and, if needed, primary sources, such as diaries or documents, from the bibliographies in the books you are examining. After completing this survey, you are ready to make an outline.

The outline—whether for a five-page paper or a major research project—is mandatory. The outline is a memory device that serves several functions: It forces you to stick to the main topics, keep an accurate perspective, incorporate relevant information, follow the framing narrative, and proceed in an orderly fashion from the opening to the conclusion. Rework your outline until it includes all relevant points and ideas. Think of it as the framework on which you raise your final piece of writing, molded into a coherent shape.

With the outline set, you are ready to make a first draft of your paper. One approach is to expand each section of the outline into a paragraph, incorporating your ideas, the facts, your examples, and your references into a narrative. Be sure to relate each paragraph to both the preceding and the succeeding paragraphs, keeping in mind the overall organization of the paper. Each paragraph should begin with a topic sentence, include examples and references to support the topic, and conclude with a summary sentence or an idea that leads into the next paragraph. Strive to remain invisible in the narrative except where a personal observation might be helpful, and try to write in the active rather than the passive voice. At times you will have to search for the word or phrase that best expresses your thought, perhaps with the help of a dictionary or a thesaurus.

The next step is to edit and re-edit your work until it sounds right. When you reread a first draft, it usually sounds like a first draft, tentative and filled with half-finished thoughts. A good test of your first draft is to read it aloud, either to yourself or to a fellow student. You will be more likely to notice gaps in logic, infelicitous words or phrases, and obvious errors in fact when you hear them out loud. At this point your good work habits will pay off, because you should now have time to polish and improve the text. Don't forget to proof the papers for misspelled words, typographical errors, and misstatements. Attention to literary style and correctness makes the difference between a satisfactory and an excellent paper.

Especially critical in writing a research paper is the citation of sources, or footnotes. Instructors have their varying policies about the use of footnotes, but the following rules apply in most situations. Short quotations (that is, a phrase or one or two sentences) may be cited in the text if the proper recognition is given. Sources for longer quotations (that is, three or more sentences) should be placed in a footnote. A full bibliography listing all books consulted, whether cited directly in the paper or not, should be included at the end of the paper. Regardless of the style you use, make sure the citation forms for footnotes are consistent throughout the paper. You should purchase a writing and style manual; often the instructor will tell you which one to buy. Three of the most frequently used manuals are the following:

Bailey, E. P., and P. A. Powell. *Writing Research Papers.* 2d ed. New York: Holt, Rinehart and Winston, 1986.

Gibaldi, J., and W. S. Achtert. *MLA Handbook for Writers of Research Papers.* 3d ed. New York: Modern Language Association of America, 1988.

Turabian, K. *Student's Guide to Writing College Papers.* 3d ed. Chicago: University of Chicago Press, 1976.

Types of Term Papers Assigned in the Humanities

In your humanities course you may be assigned any one of various types of research or term papers, reflecting the breadth of the disciplines that are covered under the humanities rubric. The most common types are the impressionistic paper, the analytical paper, the historical overview, and the integrative paper. Each type requires a different approach, even though the basic writing techniques described above are valid for all.

The Impressionistic Paper   In this type of paper you offer a personal, though informed, reaction to some aspect of culture, such as the Gothic style or Post-Modernist art and architecture. Despite its focus on subjective feelings, the impressionistic paper nevertheless has to be documented with specific information, such as key historical events, biographical data, and details about particular works of art, literature, and music.

The Analytical Paper   Here, you compare and contrast two creative works. More strictly scholarly than an impressionistic paper, the analytical research paper usually requires that you study both the original works and the leading secondary sources that provide critical commentaries. Using this approach, you might examine two works within the same historical period, such as Aeschylus's tragedy *Agamemnon* and Sophocles' tragedy *Oedipus Rex*; or works across historical periods, such as Aeschylus's tragedy *Agamemnon* and Shakespeare's tragedy *Hamlet*; or works across genres, such as Aeschylus's tragedy *Agamemnon* and Verdi's opera *Rigoletto*.

The Historical Overview   In this type of paper you survey a specific time period in order to establish or explain a particular outcome, such as the prevailing world view, or the leading cultural characteristics, or the impact of a particular social class. For example, if your topic were the role of aristocratic courts on the arts of the Italian Renaissance, you would have to survey fifteenth- and sixteenth-century Italian history and culture as well as the history of specific courts, such as that of the Medici in Florence and the Sforza in Milan.

The Integrative Paper   This type of paper offers a versatile approach, since it allows for a combination of many topics. For example, if you wanted to write on Freudian theory and its application to culture, you would have to research the principles of Freudian theory and discuss Freudian interpretations of specific examples of art and literature. Or, if your topic were the Classical ideal of restraint in the late eighteenth century, you would have to research the period's music, art, literature, economic theory, and political theory.

ESSAY EXAMINATIONS

Besides research papers, you will also have to write essay tests in most college-level humanities courses. The purpose of such tests is to allow you to demonstrate how well you comprehend the course lectures and readings. To succeed on essay tests, you must learn to take notes efficiently during class and while reading out-of-class assignments and to analyze the assigned material in study sessions.

The following steps will help you write better essays on examinations:

1. Before the exam, master the assigned material through sound and productive work habits. This means keeping up with daily assignments, rereading and studying lecture notes, and reviewing study materials over a four- to five-day period prior to the test.

2. During the exam, read the entire test carefully before beginning to write. This will ensure that you understand all the questions and allow you to set a time frame for completing each section of the exam. If you are unsure about the meaning of a question, do not hesitate to ask the instructor for a clarification.

3. If there are choices, answer those questions first that seem the easiest. This rule simply reflects common sense; it is always best to lead with your strength.

4. Briefly outline the answer to each question. The outline should include an introduction, a section for each part of the question, and a conclusion. If time permits, it is also helpful to include the major points you want to cover, specific examples or illustrations, and ideas for topic sentences and conclusions of paragraphs. The outline will help you stick to the main topics and finish the exam on time. It can also trigger more ideas while you are writing it.

5. Follow sound writing rules in composing each essay. Begin each paragraph with a topic sentence; then give examples from a wide range of sources in the humanities to support the opening statement; and conclude with a paragraph that pulls the main arguments together. Take nothing for granted. Be concise but specific. Unless they are asked for, keep your own opinions to a bare minimum.

6. Review the exam. Prior to turning in the exam to the monitor, review your test to correct errors, give added examples, and clarify arguments, where needed. Always allow time to proofread an essay exam.

If you score poorly on the first essay exam in a course, consult with the instructor about how to improve your performance. But remember that improvement is seldom instantaneous and good writing is achieved only after practice. Old habits die hard; the only way to do better on papers and essay exams is to keep on writing.

GLOSSARY

Italicized words within definitions are defined in their own glossary entries.

Abstract Expressionism Also known as Action Painting, a nonrepresentational artistic style that flourished after World War II and was typified by randomness, spontaneity, and an attempt by the artist to interact emotionally with the work as it was created.

abstraction In Modern art, nonrepresentational or nonobjective forms in sculpture and painting that emphasize shapes, lines, and colors independent of the natural world.

a capella [ah kuh-PEL-uh] From the Italian, "in chapel style"; music sung without instrumental accompaniment.

aesthete One who pursues and is devoted to the beautiful in art, music, and literature.

aisles The side passages in a church on either side of the central *nave*.

Alexandrianism [al-ig-ZAN-dree-an-ism] A literary style developed in the Hellenistic period, typically formal, artificial, and imitative of earlier Greek writing.

ambulatory [AM-bue-la-tor-e] A passageway for walking found in many religious structures, such as outdoors in a cloister or indoors around the *apse* or *choir* of a church.

Anglicanism The doctrines and practices of the Church of England, which was established in the early sixteenth century under Henry VIII.

anthropomorphism [an-thro-po-MOR-fizm] The attributing of humanlike characteristics and traits to nonhuman things or powers, such as a deity.

apocalypse [uh-PAHK-uh-lips] In Jewish and early Christian thought, the expectation and hope of the coming of God and his final judgment; also closely identified with the last book of the New Testament, Revelation, in which many events are foretold, often in highly symbolic and imaginative terms.

apse In architecture, a large projection, usually rounded or semicircular, found in a *basilica*, usually in the east end; in Christian basilicas the altar stood in this space.

arabesque [air-uh-BESK] Literally, "Arabian-like"; decorative lines, patterns, and designs, often floral, in Islamic works of art.

arcade A series of arches supported by *piers* or columns, usually serving as a passageway along a street or between buildings.

Archaic style The style in Greek sculpture, dating from the seventh century to 480 B.C., that was characterized by heavy Egyptian influence; dominated by the *kouros* and *kore* sculptural forms.

architrave [AHR-kuh-trayv] The part of the *entablature* that rests on the *capital* or column in Classical *post-beam-triangle* construction.

aria [AH-ree-uh] In music, an elaborate melody sung as a solo or sometimes a duet, usually in an *opera* or an *oratorio*, with an orchestral accompaniment.

art song (lied) In music, a lyric song with melody performed by a singer and instrumental accompaniment usually provided by piano; made popular by Schubert in the nineteenth century.

ashlar [ASH-luhr] A massive hewn or squared stone used in constructing a fortress, palace, or large building.

assemblage art An art form in which the artist mixes and/or assembles "found objects," such as scraps of paper, cloth, or junk, into a three-dimensional work and then adds paint or other decorations to it.

ataraxia [at-uh-RAK-see-uh] Greek, "calmness"; in *Hellenistic* philosophy, the state of desiring nothing.

atonality [ay-toe-NAL-uh-tee] In music, the absence of a key note or tonal center and the use of the tones of the chromatic scale impartially.

atrium [AY-tree-uhm] In Roman architecture, an open courtyard at the front of a house; in Christian *Romanesque* churches, an open court, usually colonnaded, in front of the main doors of the structure.

attic The topmost section or crown of an arch.

aulos In music, a reed woodwind instrument similar to the oboe, usually played in pairs by one player as the double aulos; used in Greek music.

autarky [AW-tar-kee] Greek, "self-sufficient"; in *Hellenistic* thought, the state of being isolated and free from the demands of society.

avant-garde [a-vahn-GARD] French, "advanced guard"; writers, artists, and intellectuals who push their works and ideas ahead of more traditional groups and movements.

baldacchino [ball-duh-KEE-no] An ornamental structure in the shape of a canopy, supported by four columns, built over a church altar, and usually decorated with statues and other ornaments.

balustrade In architecture, a rail and the row of posts that support it, as along the edge of a staircase or around a dome.

baptistery A small, often octagonal structure, separated from the main church, where baptisms were performed.

bard A tribal poet-singer who composes and recites works, often of the *epic poetry* genre.

Baroque [buh-ROKE] The prevailing seventeenth-century artistic and cultural style, characterized by an emphasis on grandeur, opulence, expansiveness, and complexity.

barrel vault A ceiling or *vault* made of sets of arches placed side by side and joined together.

basilica [buh-SILL-ih-kuh] A rectangular structure that included an *apse* at one or both ends; originally a Roman building used for public purposes, later taken over by the Christians for worship. The floor plan became the basis of nearly all early Christian churches.

bay A four-cornered unit of architectural space, often used to identify a section of the *nave* in a *Romanesque* or *Gothic* church.

bel canto [bell KAHN-toe] Italian, "beautiful singing"; a style of singing characteristic of seventeenth-century Italian *opera* stressing ease, purity, and evenness of tone along with precise vocal technique.

blind arcade A decorative architectural design that gives the appearance of an open *arcade* or window but is filled in with some type of building material such as stone or brick.

blues A type of music that emerged around 1900 from the rural African-American culture, was originally based on work songs and religious spirituals, and expressed feelings of loneliness and hopelessness.

Byzantine style [BIZ-uhn-teen] In painting, decoration, and architecture, a style blending Greco-Roman and Oriental components into a highly stylized art form that glorified Christianity, notably in domed churches adorned with *mosaics* and polished marble; associated with the culture of the Eastern Roman Empire from about 500 until 1453.

Cajun A descendant of French pioneers, chiefly in Louisiana, who in 1755 chose to leave Acadia (modern Nova Scotia) rather than live under the British Crown.

calligraphy Penmanship or handwriting, usually done with flowing lines, used as a decoration or as an enhancement of a written work; found in Islamic and Christian writings.

Calvinism The theological beliefs and rituals set forth in and derived from John Calvin's writings, placing emphasis on the power of God and the weakness of human beings.

campanile From the Latin "campana," bell; a bell tower, especially one near but not attached to a church; an Italian invention.

canon A set of principles or rules that are accepted as true and authoritative for the various arts or fields of study; in architecture, it refers to the standards of proportion; in painting, the prescribed ways of painting certain objects; in sculpture, the ideal proportions of the human body; in literature, the authentic lists of an author's works; in religion, the approved and authoritative writings that are accepted as divinely inspired, as for Jews and Christians the *Scriptures*; and in religious and in other contexts, certain prescribed rituals or official rules and laws. In music, a **canon** is a composition in which a melody sung by one voice is repeated exactly by successive voices as they enter.

canzone [kan-ZOH-nee] Latin, "chant"; a type of love poem popular in southern France during the twelfth and thirteenth centuries.

capital In architecture, the upper or crowning part of a column, on which the *entablature* rests.

cathedral The church of a bishop that houses a *cathedra*, or throne, symbolizing the seat of power in his administrative district, known as a diocese.

cella [SELL-uh] The inner sanctum or walled room of a *Classical* temple where sacred statues were housed.

chanson [shahn-SAWN] French, "song"; a fourteenth- to sixteenth-century French song for one or more voices, often with instrumental accompaniment. Similar to a *madrigal*.

chanson de geste [shahn-SAWN duh zhest] A poem of brave deeds in the *epic* form developed in France during the eleventh century, usually to be sung.

chiaroscuro [key-ahr-uh-SKOOR-oh] In painting, the use of dark and light contrast to create the effect of modeling of a figure or object.

chivalric code The rules of conduct, probably idealized, that governed the social roles and duties of aristocrats in the Middle Ages.

choir In architecture, that part of a *Gothic* church in which the service was sung by singers or clergy, located in the east end beyond the *transept*; also, the group of trained singers who sat in the choir area.

chorus In Greek drama, a group of performers who sang and danced in both tragedies and comedies, often commenting on the action; in later times, a group of singers who performed with or without instrumental accompaniment.

Christian humanism An intellectual movement in sixteenth-century northern Europe that sought to use the ideals of the *Classical* world, the tools of ancient learning, and the morals of the Christian *Scriptures* to rid the church of worldliness and scandal.

chthonian deities [THOE-nee-uhn] In Greek religion, earth gods and goddesses who lived underground and were usually associated with peasants and their religious beliefs.

civilization The way humans live in a complex political, economic, and social structure, usually in an urban environment, with some development in technology, literature, and art.

Classic, or **Classical** Having the forms, values, or standards embodied in the art and literature of Greek and Roman *civilization*; in music, an eighteenth-century style characterized by simplicity, proportion, and an emphasis on structure.

Classicism A set of aesthetic principles found in Greek and Roman art and literature emphasizing the search for perfection or ideal forms.

clerestory windows [KLEER-stor-ee] A row of windows set along the upper part of a wall, especially in a church.

collage [koh-LAHZH] From the French *coller*, "to glue"; a type of art, introduced by Picasso, in which

bits and pieces of materials such as paper or cloth are glued to a painted surface.

comedy of manners A humorous play that focuses on the way people in a particular social group or class interact with one another, especially regarding fashions and manners.

concerto [kuhn-CHER-toe] In music, a composition for one or more soloists and *orchestra*, usually in a symphonic form with three contrasting movements.

consort A set of musical instruments in the same family, ranging from bass to soprano; also, a group of musicians who entertain by singing or playing instruments.

Constructivism A movement in nonobjective art, originating in the Soviet Union and flourishing from 1917 to 1922 and concerned with planes and volumes as expressed in modern industrial materials such as glass and plastic.

contrapposto [kon-truh-POH-stoh] In sculpture and painting, the placement of the human figure so the weight is more on one leg than the other and the shoulders and chest are turned in the opposite direction from the hips and legs.

Corinthian The third Greek architectural order, in which temple columns are slender and *fluted*, sit on a base, and have *capitals* shaped like inverted bells and decorated with carvings representing the leaves of the acanthus bush; this style was popular in *Hellenistic* times and widely adopted by the Romans.

cornice In architecture, the crowning, projecting part of the *entablature*.

Counter-Reformation A late-sixteenth-century movement in the Catholic church aimed at reestablishing its basic beliefs, reforming its organizational structure, and reasserting itself as the authoritative voice of Christianity.

covenant In Judaism and Christianity, a solemn and binding agreement or contract between God and his followers.

Creole An ambiguous term, sometimes referring to descendants of French and Spanish settlers of the southern United States, especially Louisiana; used by Kate Chopin in her short stories and novels in this sense. In other contexts, *Creole* can refer either to blacks born in the Western hemisphere (as distinguished from blacks born in Africa) or to residents of the American Gulf States of mixed black, Spanish, and Portuguese ancestry.

cruciform [KROO-suh-form] Cross-shaped; used to describe the standard floor plan of a church.

Cubism A style of painting introduced by Picasso and Braque in which objects are broken up into fragments and patterns of geometric structures and depicted on the flat canvas as if from several points of view.

culture The sum of human endeavors, including the basic political, economic, and social institutions and the values, beliefs, and arts of those who share them.

cuneiform [kue-NEE-uh-form] Wedge-shaped characters used in writing on tablets found in Mesopotamia and other ancient *civilizations*.

Cynicism A *Hellenistic* philosophy that denounced society and its institutions as artificial and called on the individual to strive for *autarky*.

Dada [DAH-dah] An early-twentieth-century artistic movement, named after a nonsense word, that was rooted in a love of play, encouraged deliberately irrational acts, and exhibited contempt for all traditions.

Decadence A late-nineteenth-century literary style concerned with morbid and artificial subjects and themes.

deductive reasoning The process of reasoning from the general to the particular, that is, beginning with an accepted premise or first statement and, by steps of logical reasoning or inference, reaching a conclusion that necessarily follows from the premise.

Deism [DEE-iz-uhm] A religion based on the idea that the universe was created by God and then left to run according to *natural laws*, without divine interference; formulated and practiced in the eighteenth century.

De Stijl [duh STILE] Dutch, "the style"; an artistic movement associated with a group of early-twentieth-century Dutch painters who used rectangular forms and primary colors in their works and who believed that art should have spiritual values and a social purpose.

devotio moderna [de-VO-tee-oh mo-DER-nuh] The "new devotion" of late medieval Christianity that emphasized piety and discipline as practiced by lay religious communities located primarily in northern Europe.

Diaspora [dye-AS-puhr-uh] From the Greek, "to scatter"; the dispersion of the Jews from their homeland in ancient Palestine, a process that began with the Babylonian Captivity in the sixth century B.C. and continued over the centuries.

Doric The simplest and oldest of the Greek architectural orders, in which temple columns have undecorated *capitals* and rest directly on the *stylobate*.

Early Renaissance style A style inspired by *Classical* rather than *Gothic* models that arose among Florentine architects, sculptors, and painters in the late fourteenth and early fifteenth century.

empiricism The process of collecting data, making observations, carrying out experiments based on the collected data and observations, and reaching a conclusion.

Enlightenment The eighteenth-century philosophical and cultural movement marked by the application of reason to human problems and affairs, a questioning of traditional beliefs and ideas, and an optimistic faith in unlimited progress for humanity, particularly through education.

entablature [en-TAB-luh-choor] In architecture, the

part of the temple above the columns and below the roof, which, in *Classical* temples, included the *architrave*, *frieze*, and *pediment*.

entasis [EN-ta-sis] In architecture, convex curving or enlarging of the central part of a column to correct the optical illusion that the column is too thin.

epic poetry Narrative poetry, usually told or written in an elevated style, that recounts the life of a hero.

epic theater A type of theater, invented by Brecht, in which major social issues are dramatized with outlandish props and jarring dialogue and effects, all designed to alienate middle-class audiences and force them to think seriously about the problems raised in the plays.

Epicureanism [ep-i-kyoo-REE-uh-niz-uhm] A *Hellenistic* philosophy, founded by Epicurus and later expounded by the Roman Lucretius, that made its highest goals the development of the mind and an existence free from the demands of everyday life.

eschatology [es-kuh-TAHL-uh-jee] The concern with final events or the end of the world, a belief popular in Jewish and early Christian communities and linked to the concept of the coming of a *Messiah*.

evangelists From the Greek *evangelion*, a term generally used for those who preach the Christian religion; more specifically, the four evangelists, Matthew, Mark, Luke, and John, who wrote about Jesus Christ soon after his death in the first four books of the New Testament.

evolution The theory, set forth in the nineteenth century by Charles Darwin, that plants and animals, including humans, evolved over millions of years from simpler forms through a process of natural selection.

existentialism [eg-zi-STEN-shuh-liz-uhm] A twentieth-century philosophy focusing on the precarious nature of human existence, with its uncertainty, anxiety, and ultimate death, as well as on individual freedom and responsibility and the possibilities for human creativity and authenticity.

Expressionism A late-nineteenth-century literary and artistic movement characterized by the expression of highly personal feelings rather than of objective reality.

fan vault A decorative pattern of *vault* ribs that arch or radiate out from a central point on the ceiling; popular in English *Perpendicular* architecture.

Faustian [FAU-stee-uhn] Resembling the character Faust in Goethe's most famous work, in being spiritually tormented, insatiable for knowledge and experience, or willing to pay any price, including personal and spiritual integrity, to gain a desired end.

Fauvism [FOH-viz-uhm] From the French *fauve*, "wild beast"; an early-twentieth-century art movement led by Matisse and favoring exotic colors and disjointed shapes.

fête galante [fet gah-LAHNN] In *Rococco* painting, the theme or scene of aristocrats being entertained or simply enjoying their leisure and other worldly pleasures.

Flamboyant style [flam-BOY-uhnt] A Late French *Gothic* architectural style of elaborate decorations and ornamentation that produce a flamelike effect.

Florid Baroque style A variation of the *Baroque* style specifically identified with the Catholic church's patronage of the arts and used to glorify its beliefs.

fluting Decorative vertical grooves carved in a column.

flying buttress An external masonry support, found primarily in *Gothic* churches, that carries the thrust of the ceiling or *vault* away from the upper walls of the building to an external vertical column.

forum In Rome and many Roman towns, the public place, located in the center of the town, where people gathered to socialize, transact business, and administer the government.

Fourth Century style The sculptural style characteristic of the last phase of the *Hellenic* period, when new interpretations of beauty and movement were adopted.

French Baroque style A secular variation of the *Baroque* style that was identified with French kings and artists, was rooted in *Classical* ideals, and was used mainly to emphasize the power and grandeur of the monarchy.

fresco A painting done on wet or dry plaster that becomes part of the plastered wall.

friars Members of a thirteenth-century mendicant (begging) monastic order.

frieze [FREEZ] A band of painted designs or sculpted figures placed on walls; also, the central portion of a temple's *entablature* just above the *architrave*.

gallery In architecture, a long, narrow passageway or corridor, usually found in churches and located above the *aisles*, and often with openings that permit viewing from above into the *nave*.

gargoyle [GAHR-goil] In architecture, a water spout in the form of a grotesque animal or human, carved from stone, placed on the edge of a roof.

genre [ZHON-ruh] From the French, "a kind, a type, or a class"; a category of artistic, musical, or literary composition, characterized by a particular style, form, or content.

genre subject In art, a scene or person from everyday life, depicted realistically and without religious or symbolic significance.

geocentrism The belief that the earth is the center of the universe and that the sun, planets, and stars revolve around it.

glissando [gle-SAHN-doe] (plural, **glissandi**) In music, the blending of one tone into the next in scalelike passages that may be ascending or descending in character.

goliards [GOAL-yuhrds] Medieval roaming poets or scholars who traveled about reciting poems on topics ranging from moral lessons to the pains of love.

Gospels The first four books of the New Testament (Matthew, Mark, Luke, and John) that record the life and sayings of Jesus Christ; the word itself, from Old English, means good news or good tales.

Gothic style A style of architecture, usually associated with churches, that originated in northern France and whose three phases—Early, High, and Late—lasted from the twelfth to the sixteenth centuries. Emerging from the *Romanesque* style, Gothic is identified by pointed arches, *ribbed vaults*, *stained glass* windows, *flying buttresses*, and carvings on the exterior.

Greek cross A cross in which all the arms are of equal length; the shape used as a floor plan in many Greek or Eastern Orthodox churches.

Gregorian chant A style of *monophonic* church music sung in unison and without instrumental accompaniment and used in the *liturgy*; named for Pope Gregory I (590–604).

groined vault, or cross vault A ceiling or *vault* created when two *barrel vaults*, set at right angles, intersect.

heliocentrism The belief that the sun is the center of the universe and that the earth and other planets revolve around it.

Hellenic [hell-LENN-ik] Relating to the time period in Greek civilization from 480 to 323 B.C., when the most influential Greek artists, playwrights, and philosophers, such as Praxiteles, Sophocles, and Plato, created their greatest works; associated with the *Classical* style.

Hellenistic [hell-uh-NIS-tik] Relating to the time period from about 323 to 31 B.C., when Greek and Oriental or Middle Eastern cultures and institutions intermingled to create a heterogeneous and cosmopolitan *civilization*.

hieroglyphs [HI-uhr-uh-glifs] Pictorial characters used in Egyptian writing, which is known as hieroglyphics.

High Classical style The style in Greek sculpture associated with the ideal physical form and perfected during the zenith of the Athenian Empire, about 450–400 B.C.

higher criticism A rational approach to Bible study, developed in German Protestant circles in the nineteenth century, that treated the biblical *Scriptures* as literature and subjected them to close scrutiny, testing their literary history, authorship, and meaning.

High Renaissance The period from about 1495 to 1520, often associated with the patronage of the popes in Rome, when the most influential artists and writers of the *Renaissance*, including Michelangelo, Raphael, Leonardo da Vinci, and Machiavelli, were producing their greatest works.

high tech In architecture, a style that uses obvious industrial design elements with exposed parts serving as decorations.

Homeric epithet A recurring nickname, such as "Ox-eyed Hera," used in Homer's *Iliad* or *Odyssey*.

hubris [HYOO-bris] In Greek thought, human pride or arrogance that leads an individual to challenge the gods, usually provoking divine retribution.

humanism An attitude that is concerned with humanity, its achievements, and its potential; also, the study of the *humanities*; in the *Renaissance*, identified with *studia humanitatis*.

humanities In the nineteenth century, the study of Greek and Roman languages and literature; later set off from the sciences and expanded to include the works of all Western peoples in the arts, literature, music, philosophy, and sometimes history and religion; in *Post-Modernism* extended to a global dimension.

hymn From the Greek and Latin, "ode of praise of gods or heroes"; a song of praise or thanksgiving to God or the gods, performed both with and without instrumental accompaniment.

idealism In Plato's philosophy, the theory that reality and ultimate truth are to be found not in the material world but in the spiritual realm.

idée fixe [ee-DAY FIX] French, "fixed idea"; in music, a recurring musical theme that is associated with a person or concept.

ideogram [ID-e-uh-gram] A picture drawn to represent an idea or a concept.

idyll A relatively short poem that focuses on events and themes of everyday life, such as family, love, and religion; popular in the *Hellenistic* Age and a standard form that has been periodically revived in Western literature throughout the centuries.

illuminated manuscript A richly decorated book, painted with brilliant colors and gold leaf, usually of sacred writings; popular in the West in the Middle Ages.

illusionism The use of painting techniques in *Florid Baroque* art to create the appearance that decorated areas are part of the surrounding architecture, usually employed in ceiling decorations.

impasto [ihm-PAHS-toe] In painting, the application of thick layers of pigment.

Impressionism In painting, a style introduced in the 1870s, marked by an attempt to catch spontaneous impressions, often involving the play of sunlight on ordinary events and scenes observed outdoors; in music, a style of composition designed to create a vague and dreamy mood through gliding melodies and shimmering tone colors.

impressionistic In art, relating to the representation of a scene using the simplest details in order to create an illusion of reality by evoking subjective impressions rather than aiming for a totally realistic effect; characterized by images that are insubstantial and barely sketched in.

inductive reasoning The process of reasoning from particulars to the general or from single parts to the whole and/or final conclusion.

International style In twentieth-century architecture,

a style and method of construction that capitalized on modern materials, such as ferro-concrete, glass, and steel, and that produced the popular "glass box" skyscrapers and variously shaped private houses.

Ionic The Greek architectural order, developed in Ionia, in which columns are slender, sit on a base, and have *capitals* decorated with scrolls.

Italo-Byzantine style [ih-TAL-o-BIZ-uhn-teen] The style of Italian *Gothic* painting that reflected the influence of *Byzantine* paintings, *mosaics*, and icons.

Jesuits [JEZH-oo-its] Members of the Society of Jesus, the best organized and most effective monastic order founded during the *Counter-Reformation* to combat Protestantism and spread Roman Catholicism around the world.

key In music, a tonal system consisting of seven tones in fixed relationship to a tonic, or keynote. Since the Renaissance, key has been the structural foundation of the bulk of Western music, down to the *Modernist* period.

keystone The central stone at the top of an arch that locks the other stones in place.

koine [KOI-nay] A colloquial Greek language spoken in the *Hellenistic* world that helped tie together that *civilization*.

kore [KOH-ray] An *Archaic* Greek standing statue of a young draped female.

kouros [KOO-rus] An *Archaic* Greek standing statue of a young naked male.

Late Gothic style A style characterized in architecture by ornate decoration and tall cathedral windows and spires and in painting and sculpture by increased refinement of details and a trend toward naturalism; popular in the fourteenth and fifteenth centuries in central and western Europe.

Late Mannerism The last stage of the *Mannerist* movement, characterized by exaggeration and distortion, especially in painting.

Late Modernism The last stage of *Modernism*, characterized by an increasing sense of existential despair, an attraction to non-Western cultures, and extreme experimentalism.

lay A short lyric or narrative poem meant to be sung to the accompaniment of an instrument such as a harp; based on Celtic legends but usually set in feudal times and focused on courtly love themes, especially adulterous passion. The oldest surviving lays are those of the twelfth century poet Marie de France.

leitmotif [LITE-mo-teef] In music, and especially in Wagner's *operas*, the use of recurring themes associated with particular characters, objects, or ideas.

liberalism In political thought, a set of beliefs advocating certain personal, economic, and natural rights based on assumptions about the perfectibility and autonomy of human beings and the notion of progress, as first expressed in the writings of John Locke.

libretto [lih-BRET-oh] In Italian, "little book"; the text or words of an *opera, oratorio,* or musical work of a similar dramatic nature involving a written text.

liturgical drama Religious dramas, popular between the twelfth and sixteenth centuries, based on biblical stories with musical accompaniment that were staged in the area in front of the church, performed at first in Latin but later in the *vernacular languages;* the mystery plays ("mystery" is derived from the Latin for "action") are the most famous type of liturgical drama.

liturgy A rite or ritual, such as prayers or ceremonies, practiced by a religious group in public worship.

local color In literature, the use of detail peculiar to a particular region and environment to add interest and authenticity to a narrative, including description of the locale, customs, speech, and music. Local color was an especially popular development in American literature in the late nineteenth century.

logical positivism A school of modern philosophy that seeks truth by defining terms and clarifying statements and asserts that metaphysical theories are meaningless.

logos [LOWG-os] In *Stoicism,* the name for the supreme being or for reason—the controlling principle of the universe—believed to be present both in nature and in each human being.

lute In music, a wooden instrument, plucked or bowed, consisting of a sound box with an elaborately carved sound hole and a neck across which the (often twelve) strings pass. Introduced during the High Middle Ages, the lute enjoyed a height of popularity in Europe from the seventeenth to eighteenth centuries.

Lutheranism The doctrine, liturgy, and institutional structure of the church founded in the sixteenth century by Martin Luther, who stressed the authority of the Bible, the faith of the individual, and the worshiper's direct communication with God as the bases of his new religion.

lyre In music, a hand-held stringed instrument, with or without a sound box, used by ancient Egyptians, Assyrians, and Greeks. In Greek culture, the lyre was played to accompany song and recitation.

lyric poetry In Greece, verses sung and accompanied by the lyre, a stringed instrument; today, intensely personal poetry.

machiavellianism [mahk-ih-uh-VEL-ih-uhn-iz-uhm] The view that politics should be separated from morals and dedicated to the achievement of desired ends through any means necessary ("the end justifies the means"); derived from the political writings of Machiavelli.

madrigal [MAD-rih-guhl] A *polyphonic* song performed without accompaniment and based on a secular text, often a love lyric; especially popular in the sixteenth century.

maenad [MEE-nad]   A woman who worshiped Dionysus, often in a state of frenzy.

magic realism   A literary and artistic style identified with Latin American *Post-Modernism* that mixes realistic and supernatural elements to create imaginary or fantastic scenes.

Mannerism   A cultural movement between 1520 and 1600 that grew out of a rebellion against the *Renaissance* artistic norms of symmetry and balance; characterized in art by distortion and incongruity and in thought and literature by the belief that human nature is depraved.

Mass   In religion, the ritual celebrating the Eucharist, or Holy Communion, primarily in the Roman Catholic Church. The Mass has two parts, the Ordinary and the Proper; the former remains the same throughout the church year, whereas the latter changes for each date and service. The Mass Ordinary is composed of the Kyrie, Gloria, Credo, Sanctus, and Agnus Dei; the Mass Proper includes the Introit, Gradual, Alleluia or Tract, Sequence, Offertory, and Communion. In music, a musical setting of certain parts of the Mass, especially the Kyrie, Gloria, Credo, Sanctus, Benedictus, and Agnus Dei. The first complete Mass Ordinary was composed by Guillaume de Machaut [mah-SHOH] (about 1300–1377) in the fourteenth century.

mass culture   The tastes, values, and interests of the classes that dominate modern industrialized society, especially the consumer-oriented American middle class.

medallion   In Roman architecture, a circular decoration often found on triumphal arches enclosing a scene or portrait; in more general architectural use, a tablet or panel in a wall or window containing a figure or an ornament.

Messiah   A Hebrew word meaning "the anointed one," or one chosen by God to be his representative on earth; in Judaism, a savior who will come bringing peace and justice; in Christianity, Jesus Christ (*Christ* is derived from a Greek word meaning "the anointed one").

metope [MET-uh-pee]   In architecture, a panel, often decorated, between two *triglyphs* on the *entablature* of a *Doric* Greek temple.

minaret   In Islamic architecture, a tall, slender tower with a pointed top, from which the daily calls to prayer are delivered; located near a *mosque*.

miniature   A small painting, usually of a religious nature, found in *illuminated manuscripts;* also, a small portrait.

minstrel   A professional entertainer of the twelfth to seventeenth centuries, especially a secular musician; also called *jongleur*.

Modernism   A late-nineteenth- and twentieth-century cultural, artistic, and literary movement that rejected much of the past and focused on the current, the secular, and the revolutionary in search of new forms of expression; the dominant style of the twentieth century until 1970.

modes   A series of musical scales devised by the Greeks and believed by them to create certain emotional or ethical effects on the listener.

monophony [muh-NOF-uh-nee]   A style of music in which there is only a single line of melody; the *Gregorian chants* are the most famous examples of monophonic music.

monotheism   From the Greek "monos," single, alone, and the Greek "theos," god; the belief that there is only one God.

mood   In music, the emotional impact of a composition on the feelings of a listener.

mosaic   An art form or decoration, usually on a wall or floor, created by inlaying small pieces of glass, shell, or stone in cement or plaster to create pictures or patterns.

mosque   A Muslim place of worship, often distinguished by a dome-shaped central building placed in an open space surrounded by a wall.

motet   A multivoiced song with words of a sacred or secular text, usually sung without accompanying instruments; developed in the thirteenth century.

mural   A wall painting, usually quite large, used to decorate a private or public structure.

muse   In Greek religion, any one of the nine sister goddesses who preside over the creative arts and sciences.

music drama   An *opera* in which the action and music are continuous, not broken up into separate *arias* and *recitatives*, and the music is determined by its dramatic appropriateness, producing a work in which music, words, and staging are fused together; the term was coined by Wagner.

narthex   The porch or vestibule of a church, usually enclosed, through which worshipers walk before entering the *nave*.

Naturalism   In literature, a late-nineteenth-century movement inspired by the methods of science and the insights of sociology, concerned with an objective depiction of the ugly side of industrial society.

natural law   In *Stoicism* and later in other philosophies, a body of laws or principles that are believed to be derived from nature and binding on human society and that constitute a higher form of justice than civil or judicial law.

nave   The central longitudinal area of a church, extending from the entrance to the *apse* and flanked by *aisles*.

Neoclassical style   In the late eighteenth century, an artistic and literary movement that emerged as a reaction to the *Rococo* style and that sought inspiration from ancient *Classicism*. In the twentieth century, between 1919 and 1951, *Neoclassicism* in music was a style that rejected the emotionalism favored by Romantic composers as well as the dense orchestral sounds of the Impressionists; instead, it borrowed features from seventeenth- and eighteenth-century music and practiced the ideals of balance, clarity of texture, and nonprogrammatic works. Also, since 1970, **Neoclassicism** is a highly visible submovement in *Post-Modernism*, particularly prominent in painting and architecture, that restates the principles of *Classical* art—balance, harmony, idealism.

Neoexpressionism   A submovement in *Post-Modernism*, associated primarily with painting, that offers social criticism and is concerned with the expression of the artist's feelings.

Neorealism   A submovement in *Post-Modernism* that is based on a photographic sense of detail and harks back to many of the qualities of nineteenth-century *Realism.*

Neolithic   Literally, "new stone"; used to define the New Stone Age, when human *cultures* evolved into agrarian systems and settled communities; dating from about 10,000 or 8000 B.C. to about 3000 B.C.

Neo-Platonism   A philosophy based on Plato's ideas that was developed during the Roman period in an attempt to reconcile the dichotomy between Plato's concept of an eternal World of Ideas and the ever-changing physical world; in the fifteenth-century *Renaissance,* it served as a philosophical guide for Italian humanists who sought to reconcile late medieval Christian beliefs with *Classical* thinking.

New Comedy   The style of comedy favored by *Hellenistic* playwrights, concentrating on gentle satirical themes—in particular, romantic plots with stock characters and predictable endings.

Nominalism [NAHM-uh-nuhl-iz-uhm]   In medieval thought, the school that held that objects were separate unto themselves but could, for convenience, be treated in a collective sense because they shared certain characteristics; opposed to *Realism.*

octave   In music, usually the eight-tone interval between a note and a second note of the same name, as in C to C.

oculus [AHK-yuh-lus]   The circular opening at the top of a dome; derived from the Latin word for eye.

Old Comedy   The style of comedy established by Aristophanes in the fifth century B.C., distinguished by a strong element of political and social satire.

oligarchy   From the Greek "oligos," few; a state ruled by the few, especially by a small faction of persons or families.

Olympian deities   In Greek religion, sky gods and goddesses who lived on mountaintops and were worshiped mainly by the Greek aristocracy.

opera   A drama or play set to music and consisting of vocal pieces with *orchestral* accompaniment; acting, scenery, and sometimes *choruses* and dancing are used to heighten the dramatic values of opera.

oratorio   A choral work based on religious events or *scripture* employing singers, *choruses,* and *orchestra* but without scenery or staging and performed usually in a church or concert hall.

orchestra   In Greek theaters, the circular area where the *chorus* performed in front of the audience; in music, a group of instrumentalists, including string players, who play together.

organum [OR-guh-nuhm]   In the ninth through the thirteenth centuries, a simple and early form of *polyphonic* music consisting of a main melody sung along with a *Gregorian chant;* by the thirteenth century it had developed into a complex multivoiced song.

Paleolithic   Literally, "old stone"; used to define the Old Stone Age, when crude stones and tools were used; dating from about 2,000,000 B.C. to about 10,000 B.C.

pantheism   The doctrine of or belief in multitudes of deities found in nature.

pantomime   In Roman times, enormous dramatic productions featuring instrumental music and dances, favored by the masses; later, a type of dramatic or dancing performance in which the story is told with expressive or even exaggerated bodily and facial movements.

pastoral   A type of *Hellenistic* poetry that idealized rural customs and farming, especially the simple life of shepherds, and deprecated urban living.

pavane [puh-VAHN]   A sixteenth- and seventeenth-century English court dance of Italian origin; the dance is performed by couples to stately music. Ravel based *Pavane for a Dead Princess* (1899) on this Baroque dance form.

pediment   In *Classical*-style architecture, the triangular-shaped area or gable at the end of the building formed by the sloping roof and the *cornice.*

pendentive [pen-DEN-tiv]   In architecture, a triangular, concave-shaped section of *vaulting* between the rim of a dome and the pair of arches that support it; used in Byzantine and Islamic architecture.

Performance Art   A democratic type of mixed media art born in the 1960s, that ignores artistic boundaries, mixing high art (such as music, painting, and theater) and popular art (such as rock 'n roll, film, and fads), to create a unique, non-reproducible, artistic experience. Associated with the work of Laurie Anderson.

peristyle [PAIR-uh-stile]   A colonnade around an open courtyard or a building.

Perpendicular style   The highly decorative style of *Late Gothic* architecture that developed in England at the same time as the *Late Gothic* on the European continent.

perspective   A technique or formula for creating the illusion or appearance of depth and distance on a two-dimensional surface. **Atmospheric perspective** is achieved in many ways: by diminishing color intensity, by omitting detail, and by blurring the lines of an object. **Linear perspective,** based on mathematical calculations, is achieved by having parallel lines or lines of projection appearing to converge at a single point, known as the *vanishing point*, on the horizon of the flat surface and by diminishing distant objects in size according to scale to make them appear to recede from the viewer.

philosophes [FIL-uh-sawfs] A group of European thinkers and writers who popularized the ideas of the *Enlightenment* through essays, novels, plays, and other works, hoping to change the climate of opinion and bring about social and political reform.

phonogram A symbol used to represent a syllable, word, or sound.

Physiocrats [FIZ-ih-uh-kratz] A group of writers, primarily French, who dealt with economic issues during the *Enlightenment*, in particular calling for improved agricultural productivity and questioning the state's role in economic affairs.

pianoforte [pee-an-o-FOR-tay] A piano; derived from the Italian for "soft/loud," terms used to describe the two types of sound emitted by a stringed instrument whose wires are struck with felt-covered hammers operated from a keyboard.

pictogram A carefully drawn, often stylized, picture that represents a particular object.

pier In architecture, a vertical masonry structure that may support a *vault*, an arch, or a roof; in *Gothic* churches, piers were often clustered together to form massive supports.

Pietà [pee-ay-TAH] A painting or sculpture depicting the mourning Virgin and the dead Christ.

pilaster [pih-LAS-tuhr] In architecture, a vertical, rectangular decorative device projecting from a wall that gives the appearance of a column with a base and *capital*; sometimes called an applied column.

Platonism The collective beliefs and arguments presented in Plato's writings stressing especially that actual things are copies of ideas.

podium In architecture, a low wall serving as a foundation; a platform.

Pointillism [PWANT-il-iz-uhm] Also known as Divisionism, a style of painting, perfected by Seurat, in which tiny dots of paint are applied to the canvas in such a way that when they are viewed from a distance they merge and blend to form recognizable objects with natural effects of color, light, and shade.

polyphony [puh-LIF-uh-nee] A style of musical composition in which two or more voices or melodic lines are woven together.

polytheism [PAHL-e-the-iz-uhm] The doctrine of or belief in more than one deity.

Pop Art An artistic style popular between 1960 and 1970 in which commonplace commercial objects drawn from *mass culture*, such as soup cans, fast foods, and comic strips, became the subjects of art.

portico In architecture, a covered entrance to a building, usually with a separate roof supported by columns.

post-and-lintel construction A basic architectural form in which upright posts, or columns, support a horizontal lintel, or beam.

post-beam-triangle construction The generic name given to Greek architecture that includes the post, or column; the beam, or lintel; and the triangular-shaped area, or *pediment*.

Post-Impressionism A late-nineteenth-century artistic movement that extended the boundaries of *Impressionism* in new directions to focus on structure, composition, fantasy, and subjective expression.

Post-Modernism An artistic, cultural, and intellectual movement, originating in about 1970, that is more optimistic than *Modernism*, embraces an open-ended and democratic global civilization, freely adapts elements of high culture and *mass culture*, and manifests itself chiefly through revivals of earlier styles, giving rise to *Neoclassicism*, *Neoexpressionism*, and *Neorealism*.

Praxitelean curve [prak-sit-i-LEE-an] The graceful line of the sculpted body in the *contrapposto* stance, perfected by the *Fourth Century style* sculptor Praxiteles.

primitivism In painting, the "primitives" are those painters of the Netherlandish and Italian schools who flourished before 1500, thus all Netherlandish painters between the van Eycks and Dürer and all Italian painters between Giotto and Raphael; more generally, the term reflects modern artists' fascination with non-Western art forms, as Gauguin's Tahitian-inspired paintings. In literature, primitivism has complex meanings; on the one hand, it refers to the notion of a golden age, a world of lost innocence, which appeared in both ancient pagan and Christian writings; on the other hand, it is a modern term used to denote two species of cultural relativism, which either finds peoples isolated from civilization to be superior to those living in civilized and urban settings, as in the cult of the Noble Savage (Rousseau), or respects native peoples and their cultures within their own settings, yet accepts that natives can be as cruel as Europeans (expressed by Montaigne).

program music Instrumental music that depicts a narrative, portrays a setting, or suggests a sequence of events; often based on other sources, such as a poem or a play.

Protestant Baroque style A variation of the *Baroque* style identified with Dutch and English architects and painters who wanted to reduce Baroque grandeur and exuberance to a more human scale.

Puritanism The beliefs and practices of the Puritans, a small but influential religious group devoted to the teachings of John Calvin; they stressed strict rules of personal and public behavior and practiced their beliefs in England and the New World during the seventeenth century.

putti [POOH-tee] Italian, plural of *putto*; in painting

and sculpture, figures of babies, children, or sometimes angels.

ragtime A type of instrumental music, popularized by African-Americans in the late nineteenth and early twentieth centuries, with a strongly syncopated rhythm and a lively melody.

Rayonnant [ray-yo-NAHNN] A decorative style in French architecture associated with the *High Gothic* period, in which walls were replaced by sheets of *stained glass* framed by elegant stone *traceries.*

Realism In medieval philosophy, the school that asserted that objects contained common or universal qualities that were not always apparent to the human senses but that were more real or true than the objects' physical attributes; opposed to *Nominalism.* In art and literature, a mid- to late-nineteenth-century style that focused on the everyday lives of the middle and lower classes, portraying their world in a serious, accurate, and unsentimental way; opposed to *Romanticism.*

recitative [ress-uh-tuh-TEEV] In music, a rhythmically free but often stylized declamation, midway between singing and ordinary speech, that serves as a transition between *arias* or as a narrative device in an *opera.*

Reformation The sixteenth-century religious movement that looked back to the ideals of early Christianity, called for moral and structural changes in the church, and led ultimately to the founding of the various Protestant churches.

regalia [Plural in form, often used with a singular verb.] The emblems and symbols of royalty, as the crown and scepter.

relief In sculpture, figures or forms that are carved so they project from the flat surface of a stone or metal background. **High relief** projects sharply from the surface; **low relief** or **bas relief** is more shallow.

Renaissance [ren-uh-SAHNS] From the French for "rebirth"; the artistic, cultural, and intellectual movement marked by a revival of *Classical* and *humanistic* values that began in Italy in the mid–fourteenth century and had spread across Europe by the mid–sixteenth century.

revenge tragedy A type of play popular in sixteenth-century England, probably rooted in Roman tragedies and concerned with the need for a family to seek revenge for the murder of a relative.

ribbed vault A masonry roof with a framework of arches or ribs that reinforce and decorate the *vault* ceiling.

rocaille [roh-KYE] In *Rococo* design, the stucco ornaments shaped like leaves, flowers, and ribbons that decorate walls and ceilings.

Rococo style [ruh-KOH-koh] An artistic and cultural style that grew out of the *Baroque* style but that was more intimate and personal and that emphasized the frivolous and superficial side of aristocratic life.

romance A story derived from legends associated with Troy or Celtic culture but often set in feudal times and centered on themes of licit and illicit love between noble lords and ladies.

Romanesque style [roh-muhn-ESK] A style of architecture, usually associated with churches built in the eleventh and twelfth centuries, that was inspired by Roman architecture such as the *basilica* and was thus Roman-like. Romanesque buildings were massive, with round arches and *barrel* or *groined vaulted* ceilings, and had less exterior decoration than *Gothic* churches.

Romanticism An intellectual, artistic, and literary movement that began in the late eighteenth century as a reaction to *Neoclassicism* and that stressed the emotional, mysterious, and imaginative side of human behavior and the unruly side of nature.

rose window A large circular window, made of *stained glass* and held together with lead and carved stones set in patterns, or *tracery*, and located over an entrance in a *Gothic* cathedral.

sarcophagus [sahr-KAHF-uh-guhs] From the Greek meaning "flesh-eating stone"; a marble or stone coffin or tomb, usually decorated with carvings, used first by Romans and later by Christians for burial of the dead.

satire From the Latin, "medley"—a cooking term; a literary *genre* that originated in ancient Rome and that was characterized by two basic forms: (a) tolerant and amused observation of the human scene, modeled on Horace's style, and (b) bitter and sarcastic denunciation of all behavior and thought outside a civilized norm, modeled on Juvenal's style. In modern times, a literary work that holds up human vices and follies to ridicule or scorn.

satyr-play [SAT-uhr] A comic play, often featuring sexual themes, performed at the Greek drama festivals along with the *tragedies.*

scenographic [see-nuh-GRAF-ik] In Renaissance architecture, a building style that envisioned buildings as composed of separate units; in the painting of stage scenery, the art of *perspective* representation.

scherzo [SKER-tso] From the Italian for "joke"; a quick and lively instrumental composition or movement found in *sonatas* and *symphonies.*

scholasticism In medieval times, the body or collection of knowledge that tried to harmonize Aristotle's writings with Christian doctrine; also, a way of thinking and establishing sets of arguments.

Scientific Revolution The seventeenth-century intellectual movement, based originally on discoveries in astronomy and physics, that challenged and overturned medieval views about the order of the universe and the theories used to explain motion.

scripture The sacred writings of any religion, as the Bible in Judaism and Christianity.

serial music A type of musical composition based on a *twelve-tone scale* arranged any way the composer chooses; the absence of a tonal center in serial music leads to *atonality.*

Severe style The first sculptural style of the *Classical* period in Greece, which retained stylistic elements from the *Archaic* style.

sfumato [sfoo-MAH-toh] In painting, the blending of one tone into another to blur the outline of a form and give the canvas a smokelike appearance; a technique perfected by Leonardo da Vinci.

shaft graves Deep pit burial sites; the dead are usually placed at the bottom of the shafts.

skene [SKEE-nee] A small building behind the *orchestra* in a Greek theater, used as a prop and as a storehouse for theatrical materials.

Skepticism A *Hellenistic* philosophy that questioned whether anything could be known for certain, argued that all beliefs were relative, and concluded that *autarky* could be achieved only by recognizing that inquiry was fruitless.

social contract In political thought, an agreement or contract between the people and their rulers defining the rights and duties of each so that a civil society might be created.

socialism An economic and political system in which goods and property are owned collectively or by the state; the socialist movement began as a reaction to the excesses of the factory system in the nineteenth century and ultimately called for either reforming or abolishing industrial capitalism.

Socialist Realism A Marxist artistic theory that calls for the use of literature, music, and the arts in the service of the ideals and goals of socialism and/or communism, with an emphasis in painting on the realistic portrayal of objects.

sonata [soh-NAH-tah] In music, an instrumental composition, usually in three or four movements.

sonata form A musical form or structure consisting of three (or sometimes four) sections that vary in key, tempo, and mood.

stained glass An art form characterized by many small pieces of tinted glass bound together by strips of lead, usually to produce a pictorial scene of a religious theme; developed by *Romanesque* artists and a central feature of *Gothic* churches.

stele [STEE-lee] A carved or inscribed vertical stone pillar or slab, often used for commemorative purposes.

Stoicism [STO-ih-sihz-uhm] The most popular and influential *Hellenistic* philosophy, advocating a restrained way of life, a toleration for others, a resignation to disappointments, and a resolution to carry out one's responsibilities; Stoicism appealed to many Romans and had an impact on early Christian thought.

stream-of-consciousness A writing technique used by some modern authors in which the narration consists of a character's continuous interior monologue of thoughts and feelings.

structuralism In *Post-Modernism,* an approach to knowledge based on the belief that human behavior and institutions can be explained by reference to a few underlying structures that themselves are reflections of hidden patterns in the human mind.

studia humanitatis [STOO-dee-ah hu-man-ih-TAH-tis] (**humanistic studies**) The Latin term given by Renaissance scholars to new intellectual pursuits that were based on recently discovered ancient texts, including moral philosophy, history, grammar, rhetoric, and poetry. This new learning stood in sharp contrast to medieval *scholasticism.*

Sturm und Drang [STOORM-oont-drahng] German, ''Storm and Stress''; a German literary movement of the 1770s that focused on themes of action, emotionalism, and the individual's revolt against the conventions of society.

style galant [STEEL gah-LAHNN] In *Rococo* music, a style of music developed by French composers and characterized by graceful and simple melodies.

stylobate [STY-luh-bate] In Greek temples, the upper step of the base that forms a platform on which the columns stand.

Sublime [suh-BLIME] In *Romanticism,* the term used to describe nature as a terrifying and awesome force full of violence and power.

Suprematism [suh-PREM-uh-tiz-uhm] A variation of abstract art, originating in Russia in the early twentieth century, characterized by the use of geometric shapes as the basic elements of the composition.

Surrealism [suh-REE-uhl-iz-uhm] An early-twentieth-century movement in art, literature, and theater, in which incongruous juxtapositions and fantastic images produce an irrational and dreamlike effect.

symbolic realism In art, a style that is realistic and true to life but uses the portrayed object or person to represent or symbolize something else.

symphony A long and complex *sonata,* usually written in three or four movements, for large *orchestras;* the first movement is traditionally fast, the second slow, and the third (and optional fourth) movement fast.

syncopation [sin-ko-PAY-shun] In music, the technique of accenting the weak beat when a strong beat is expected.

syncretism [SIN-kruh-tiz-uhm] The combining of different forms of religious beliefs or practices.

synthesizer [SIN-thuh-size-uhr] An electronic apparatus with a keyboard capable of duplicating the sounds of many musical instruments, popular among *Post-Modernist* composers and musicians.

tabula rasa [TAB-yuh-luh RAH-zuh] ''Erased tablet,'' the Latin term John Locke used to describe the mind at birth, empty of inborn ideas and ready to receive sense impressions, which Locke believed were the sole source of knowledge.

tempo In music, the relative speed at which a composition is to be played, indicated by a suggestive word or phrase or by a precise number such as a metronome marking. (A metronome is a finely calibrated device used to determine the exact tempo for a musical work.)

terza rima [TER-tsuh REE-muh]   A three-line stanza with an interlocking rhyme scheme (aba bcb cdc ded, and so on), used by Dante in his *Divine Comedy*.

theater of the absurd   A type of theater that has come to reflect the despair, anxieties, and absurdities of modern life and in which the characters seldom make sense, the plot is nearly nonexistent, bizarre and fantastic events occur on stage, and tragedy and comedy are mixed in unconventional ways; associated with *Late Modernism*.

theocracy   From the Greek "theos," god; a state governed by a god regarded as the ruling power or by priests or officials claiming divine sanction.

theology   The application of philosophy to the study of religious truth, focusing especially on the nature of the deity and the origin and teachings of an organized religious community.

tracery   Ornamental architectural work with lines that branch out to form designs, often found as stone carvings in *rose windows*.

tragedy   A serious and deeply moral drama, typically involving a noble protagonist and describing a conflict between seemingly irreconcilable values or forces; in Greece, tragedies were performed at the festivals associated with the worship of Dionysus.

transept   In church architecture, the crossing arm that bisects the *nave* near the *apse* and gives the characteristic *cruciform* shape to the floor plan.

triglyph [TRY-glif]   In Greek architecture, a three-grooved rectangular panel on the frieze of a *Doric* temple; triglyphs alternated with *metopes*.

triptych [TRIP-tik]   In painting, a set of three hinged or folding panels depicting a religious story, mainly used as an altarpiece.

trope [TROHP]   In *Gregorian chants*, a new phrase or melody inserted into an existing chant to make it more musically appealing; also called a turn; in literature, a figure of speech.

troubador [TROO-buh-door]   A composer and/or singer, usually an aristocrat, who performed secular love songs at the feudal courts in southern France.

twelve-tone scale   In music, a fixed scale or series in which there is an arbitrary arrangement of the twelve tones (counting every half-tone) of an *octave*; devised by Arnold Schoenberg.

tympanum [TIM-puh-num]   In medieval architecture, the arch over a doorway set above the lintel, usually decorated with carvings depicting biblical themes; in *Classical*-style architecture, the recessed face of a *pediment*.

ukiyo-e   A type of colorful Japanese print, incised on woodblocks, that is characterized by simple design, plain background, and flat areas of color. Developed in seventeenth-century Japan; admired by late–nineteenth-century Parisian artists, who assimilated it to a Western style that is most notable in the prints of Mary Cassatt.

Utilitarianism [yoo-til-uh-TARE-e-uh-niz-uhm]   The doctrine set forth in the social theory of Jeremy Bentham in the nineteenth century that the final goal of society and humans was "the greatest good for the greatest number."

vanishing point   In linear *perspective*, the point on the horizon at which the receding parallel lines appear to converge and then vanish.

vault   A ceiling or roof made from a series of arches placed next to each other.

vernacular language [vuhr-NAK-yuh-luhr]   The language or dialect of a region, usually spoken by the general population as opposed to the wealthy or educated elite.

vernacular literature   Literature written in the language of the populace, such as English, French, or Italian, as opposed to the language of the educated elite, usually Latin.

via antiqua [VEE-uh ahn-TEE-kwah]   The "old way," the term used in late medieval thought by the opponents of St. Thomas Aquinas to describe his *via media*, which they considered outdated.

via media [VEE-uh MAY-dee-ah]   The "middle way" that St. Thomas Aquinas sought in reconciling Aristotle's works to Christian beliefs.

via moderna [VEE-uh moh-DEHR-nah]   The "new way," the term used in late medieval thought by those thinkers who opposed the school of Aquinas.

virtuoso [vehr-choo-O-so]   An aristocratic person who experimented in science, usually as an amateur, in the seventeenth century, giving science respectability and a wider audience; later, in music, a person with great technical skill.

voussoir [voo-SWAR]   A carved, wedge-shaped stone or block in an arch.

word painting   In music, the illustration of an idea, a meaning, or a feeling associated with a word, as, for example, using a discordant melody when the word "pain" is sung. This technique is especially identified with the sixteenth-century *madrigal*; also called word illustration, or madrigalism.

ziggurat [ZIG-oo-rat]   A Mesopotamian stepped pyramid, usually built with external staircases and a shrine at the top.

INDEX

Page numbers in *italics* indicate pronunciation guides; page numbers in **boldface** indicate illustrations. For readers using the two-volume set of *The Western Humanities*, page numbers 1–327 refer to material in Volume I: *Beginnings Through the Renaissance* and 273–591 refer to material in Volume II: *The Renaissance to the Present*.

Chapter One   1.2, Ampliaciones y Reproducciones MAS, Barcelona; 1.3, Archiv für Kunst und Geschichte, Berlin; 1.4, From *The Sumerians* by Samuel Kramer. ©1963 University of Chicago Press; 1.6, Erich Lessing/Archiv für Kunst und Geschichte, Berlin; 1.7, Scala/Art Resource, New York; 1.8, Hirmer Fotoarchiv, Munich; 1.9, Hirmer Fotoarchiv, Munich; 1.10, PHOTRI Inc.; 1.11, From *People of the Earth* by Brian Fagan. Reprinted by permission of Harper Collins publishers; 1.12, ©Tim Schermerhorn; 1.13, Erich Lessing/Magnum; 1.14, Archiv für Kunst und Geschichte, Berlin; 1.17, Bildarchiv Preussischer Kulturbesitz, Berlin; 1.18, C. M. Dixon, Canterbury; 1.19, Hirmer Fotoarchiv, Munich; 1.21 © Lee Boltin.

Chapter Two   2.1, Hirmer Fotoarchiv, Munich; 2.2, The Ancient Art and Architecture Collection, London; 2.3, Scala/Art Resource, New York; 2.4, Erich Lessing/Magnum; 2.5, Hirmer Fotoarchiv, Munich; 2.6, Hirmer Fotoarchiv, Munich; 2.7, Hirmer Fotoarchiv, Munich; 2.8, Erich Lessing/Magnum; 2.12, SEF/Art Resource, New York; 2.13, Art Resource, New York; 2.15, C. M. Dixon, Canterbury; 2.16, Hirmer Fotoarchiv, Munich; 2.17, C. M. Dixon, Canterbury; 2.18, Hirmer Fotoarchiv, Munich; 2.19, Hirmer Fotoarchiv, Munich.

Chapter Three   3.1, Photo Nimatallah/Art Resource, New York; 3.2, Marburg/Art Resource, New York; 3.3, Hirmer Fotoarchiv, Munich; 3.5, Hirmer Fotoarchiv, Munich; 3.6, Erich Lessing/Magnum; 3.7, Photo Nimatallah/Art Resource, New York; 3.8, The Ancient Art and Architecture Collection, London; 3.12, The Granger Collection, New York; 3.13, C. M. Dixon, Canterbury; 3.14, The Ancient Art and Architecture Collection, London; 3.15, Scala/Art Resource, New York; 3.16, Hirmer Fotoarchiv, Munich; 3.17, Hirmer Fotoarchiv, Munich; 3.18, Hirmer Fotoarchiv, Munich; 3.19, Marburg/Art Resource, New York; 3.20 Erich Lessing/Archiv für Kunst und Geschichte, Berlin; 3.21, Hirmer Fotoarchiv, Munich; 3.22, From *Greek Architecture* by Roland Martin. ©1980 Electa/Rizzoli New York. Drawing by Pepi Merisio; 3.24, Photo Nimatallah/Art Resource, New York; 3.25, Hirmer Fotoarchiv, Munich.

Chapter Four   4.3, From *Greek Society* by Frank Frost. ©1987, DC Heath and Company; 4.7, Alinari/Art Resource, New York; 4.9, Hirmer Fotoarchiv, Munich; 4.10, C. M. Dixon, Canterbury; 4.11, Marburg/Art Resource, New York; 4.12 Erich Lessing/Magnum; 4.14, Archiv für Kunst und Geschichte, Berlin; 4.15, The Bridgeman Art Library, London; 4.16, Photo Nimatallah/Art Resource, New York; 4.17, Hirmer Fotoarchiv, Munich; 4.18, Archiv für Kunst und Geschichte, Berlin.

Chapter Five   5.1, Scala/Art Resource, New York; 5.2, Alinari/Art Resource, New York; 5.3, Alinari/Art Resource, New York; 5.4, Alinari/Art Resource, New York; 5.5, Leonard von Matt, Buochs, Switzerland; 5.6, Hirmer Fotoarchiv, Munich; 5.7, Fototeca Unione, Rome; 5.8, Scala/Art Resource, New York; 5.9, Archiv für Kunst und Geschichte, Berlin; 5.10 The Ancient Art and Architecture Collection, London; 5.12, Giraudon/Art Resource, New York; 5.13, Alinari/Art Resource, New York; 5.14, Leonard von Matt, Buochs, Switzerland; 5.15, Fototeca Unione, Rome; 5.16, Scala/Art Resource, New York; 5.17, Scala/Art Resource, New York; 5.18, The Bettman Archive; 5.19, Fototeca Unione, Rome; 5.20 Lionel Isy-Schwart/The Image Bank; 5.21, C. M. Dixon, Canterbury; 5.23, Archiv für Kunst und Geschichte, Berlin; 5.24, Alinari/Art Resource, New York; 5.25, The Ancient Art and Architecture Collection, London; 5.26, Scala/Art Resource, New York; 5.27, Scala/Art Resource, New York; 5.28, Scala/Art Resource, New York; 5.29, Archiv für Kunst und Geschichte, Berlin; 5.30 Erich Lessing/Magnum.

Chapter Six   6.2, The Bettman Archive; 6.3, Erich Lessing/Magnum; 6.4, ©Richard Nowitz; 6.7, ©Paul W. Lapp; 6.8, Zev Radovan, Jerusalem; 6.9, Zev Radovan, Jerusalem; 6.10 ©Carl Purcell; 6.11, Scala/Art Resource, New York; 6.12, Hirmer Fotoarchiv, Munich; 6.13, Scala/Art Resource, New York; 6.14, Erich Lessing/Magnum.

Chapter Seven   7.1, Hirmer Fotoarchiv, Munich; 7.2, Scala/Art Resource, New York; 7.3, Erich Lessing/Archiv für Kunst und Geschichte; 7.4, C. M. Dixon, Canterbury; 7.5, Scala/Art Resource, New York; 7.7, From *Roman Imperial Architecture* by J. B. Ward-Perkins. The Pelican History of Art, 1981. ©J. B. Ward-Perkins, 1970, 1981; 7.8, ©E. Michael Fisher; 7.9, -Archiv für Kunst und Geschichte, Berlin; 7.10 From *Drawings of Great Buildings* by W. Blaser and O. Hannaford. Reprinted with the permission of Birkhäuser Verlag, Basel; 7.11, Archiv für Kunst und Geschichte, Berlin; 7.12, Alinari/Art Resource, New York; 7.13, Scala/Art Resource, New York; 7.14, ©1991 ARS New York/SPADEM; 7.15, Gabinetto Fotografico Nazionale, Rome; 7.16, C. M. Dixon, Canterbury; 7.17, German Archaeological Institute, Rome; 7.18, Alinari/Art Resource, New York; 7.20 Erich Lessing/Magnum; 7.21, Hirmer Fotoarchiv, Munich.

Chapter Eight   8.1, C. M. Dixon, Canterbury; 8.2, Archiv für Kunst und Geschichte, Berlin; 8.3, Centre d'Etudes Gabriel Millet, Ecole Pratique des Hautes Etudes, Paris; 8.4, Costa Manos/Magnum; 8.5, Erich Lessing/Magnum; 8.6, Scala/Art Resource, New York; 8.7, Scala/Art Resource, New York; 8.8, Archiv für Kunst und Geschichte, Berlin; 8.9, Foto Hinz, Allschwil, Switzerland; 8.10 Werner Forman Archives, London; 8.11, Ampliaciones y Reproducciones MAS, Barcelona; 8.13, C. M. Dixon, Canterbury; 8.14, The Ancient Art and Architecture Collection, London; 8.15, Courtesy Uitgeverij Het Spectrum BV 1974; 8.16, Courtesy Marian Moffett; 8.18, Rheinisches Bildarchiv/Museen der Stadt Koln; 8.21, Marburg/Art Resource, New York.

Chapter Nine   9.1, Archiv für Kunst und Geschichte, Berlin; 9.2, Hirmer Fotoarchiv, Munich; 9.4, The Bridgeman Art Library, London; 9.5, The Bettmann Archive; 9.6, Scala/Art Resource, New York; 9.7, Giraudon/Art Resource, New York; 9.8, Giraudon/Art Resource, New York; 9.9, From *Drawings of Great Buildings* by W. Blaser and O. Hannaford. Reprinted with the permission of Birkhäuser Verlag, Basel; 9.10 Giraudon/Art Resource, New York; 9.11, Courtesy Lawrence Wodehouse; 9.12, ©1991 ARS New York/SPADEM; 9.13, Hirmer Fotoarchiv, Munich; 9.16, Hirmer Fotoarchiv, Munich; 9.17, From *Gardner's Art Through the Ages*, sixth edition, by Horst de la Croix and Richard G. Tansey, ©1975 by Harcourt Brace Jovanovich, Inc. reprinted by permission of the publisher; 9.18, From *Drawings of Great Buildings* by W. Blaser and O. Hannaford. Reprinted with the permission of Birkhäuser Verlag, Basel; 9.19, Hirmer Fotoarchiv, Munich; 9.20 The Ancient Art and Architecture Collection, London; 9.21, The Ancient Art and Architecture Collection, London; 9.22, Hirmer Fotoarchiv, Munich; 9.23, Hirmer Fotoarchiv, Munich; 9.24, ©1991 ARS New York/SPADEM; 9.25, Giraudon/Art Resource, New York; 9.26, From *Drawings of Great Buildings* by W. Blaser and O. Hannaford. Reprinted with the permission of Birkhäuser Verlag, Basel; 9.27, Hirmer Fotoarchiv, Munich; 9.28, Hirmer Fotoarchiv, Munich.

Chapter Ten   10.1, Giraudon/Art Resource, New York; 10.2, Ampliaciones y Reproducciones MAS, Barcelona; 10.3, Giraudon/Art Resource, New York; 10.5, Archiv für Kunst und Geschichte, Berlin; 10.7, ©1991 ARS New York/SPADEM; 10.8, Scala/Art Resource, New York; 10.9, Scala/Art Resource, New York; 10.10 Scala/Art Resource, New York; 10.11, The Ancient Art and Architecture Collection, London; 10.12, Scala/Art Resource, New York; 10.13, Scala/Art Resource, New York; 10.14, Kavaler/Art Resource, New York; 10.15,

Archiv für Kunst und Geschichte, Berlin; 10.16, Art Resource, New York; 10.17, Archiv für Kunst und Geschichte, Berlin; 10.18, Scala/Art Resource, New York; 10.19, Scala/Art Resource, New York; 10.20 The Bridgeman Art Library, London.

Chapter Eleven 11.1, Scala/Art Resource, New York; 11.3, Scala/Art Resource, New York; 11.4, Scala/Art Resource, New York; 11.5, Photo Nimatallah/Art Resource, New York; 11.6, From *Renaissance Architecture* by Peter Murray. ©1971 Electa/Rizzoli International Publications. Drawing by Pepi Merisio; 11.7, Bill Chaitkin/Architectural Association, London; 11.8, Scala/Art Resource, New York; 11.9, Alinari/Art Resource, New York; 11.10 Photo Nimatallah/Art Resource, New York; 11.11, Scala/Art Resource, New York; 11.12, Alinari/Art Resource, New York; 11.13, Alinari/Art Resource, New York; 11.14, Alinari/Art Resource, New York; 11.15, Archiv für Kunst und Geschichte, Berlin; 11.16, Scala/Art Resource, New York; 11.17, Erich Lessing/Archiv für Kunst und Geschichte, Berlin; 11.18, Scala/Art Resource, New York; 11.19, The Bridgeman Art Library, London; 11.20 Giraudon/Art Resource, New York.

Chapter Twelve 12.1, Giraudon/Art Resource, New York; 12.2, Archiv für Kunst und Geschichte, Berlin; 12.3, Foto Hinz, Allschwil, Switzerland; 12.4, Scala/Art Resource, New York; 12.5, Scala/Art Resource, New York; 12.6, Archiv für Kunst und Geschichte, Berlin; 12.7, ©Nippon Television Network Corporation, Tokyo; 12.8, From *Italian Renaissance Painting* by James Beck. ©1981. Reprinted by permission of HarperCollins publishers, New York; 12.9, ©Nippon Television Network Corporation, Tokyo; 12.10 Archiv für Kunst und Geschichte, Berlin; 12.11, Scala/Art Resource, New York; 12.12, Archiv für Kunst und Geschichte, Berlin; 12.13, Scala/Art Resource, New York; 12.14, The Bridgeman Art Library, London, 12.15, Alinari/Art Resource, New York; 12.16, The Bridgeman Art Library, London; 12.17, Archiv für Kunst und Geschichte, Berlin; 12.18, SEF/Art Resource, New York; 12.19, Fototeca Unione, Rome; 12.20 Alinari/Art Resource, New York; 12.21, From *Gardner's Art Through the Ages*, sixth edition, by Horst de la Croix and Richard G. Tansey, ©1975 by Harcourt Brace Jovanovich, Inc. Reprinted by permission of the publisher.

Chapter Thirteen 13.6, Ampliaciones y Reproducciones MAS, Barcelona; 13.7, Erich Lessing/Archiv für Kunst und Geschichte, Berlin; 13.8, Conjectural Reconstruction of the Globe Playhouse by C. Walter Hodges. From *Introducing Shakespeare* by G. B. Harrison (Penguin Books, third edition, 1966). ©G. B. Harrison, 1939, 1945, 1966; 13.9, Artothek, Peissenberg, Germany; 13.11, The Bridgeman Art Library, London; 13.14, The Bridgeman Art Library, London; 13.17, Scala/Art Resource, New York.

Chapter Fourteen 14.1, Archiv für Kunst und Geschichte, Berlin; 14.2, Erich Lessing/Magnum; 14.3, From *Gardner's Art Through the Ages*, sixth edition, by Horst de la Croix and Richard G. Tansey, ©1975 by Harcourt Brace Jovanovich, Inc. Reprinted by permission of the publisher; 14.4, Alinari/Art Resource, New York; 14.5, Scala/Art Resource, New York; 14.6, The Bridgeman Art Library, London; 14.7, Scala/Art Resource, New York; 14.8, Scala/Art Resource, New York; 14.9, Scala/Art Resource, New York; 14.10, Scala/Art Resource, New York; 14.11, Giraudon/Art Resource, New York; 14.12, ©Lawrence Burr; 14.13, Erich Lessing/Archiv für Kunst und Geschichte, Berlin; 14.14, The Bridgeman Art Library, London; 14.15, Artothek, Peissenberg, Germany; 14.16, Scala/Art Resource, New York; 14.17, The Bridgeman Art Library, London; 14.18, The Bridgeman Art Library, London; 14.20, Courtesy of the British Tourist Authority; 14.21, Ampliaciones y Reproducciones MAS, Barcelona.

Chapter Fifteen 15.4, Scala/Art Resource, New York; 15.5, Giraudon/Art Resource, New York.

Chapter Sixteen 16.1, Scala/Art Resource, New York; 16.3, Courtesy German Information Center, New York; 16.4, Scala/Art Resource, New York; 16.5, Archiv für Kunst und Geschichte, Berlin; 16.6, Scala/Art Resource, New York; 16.7, Archiv für Kunst und Geschichte, Berlin; 16.9, Photo Bulloz, Paris; 16.10 Erich Lessing/Magnum; 16.12, Giraudon/Art Resource, New York; 16.14, English Heritage Photo Library, London; 16.15, English Heritage Photo Library, London; 16.16, ©1991, ARS New York/SPADEM.

Chapter Seventeen 17.2, Lauros-Giraudon/Art Resource, New York; 17.3, Scala/Art Resource, New York; 17.4, Giraudon/Art Resource, New York; 17.5, The Bridgeman Art Library, London; 17.7, Thomas Jefferson Memorial Foundation, Inc.; 17.8, Virginia Division of Tourism; 17.13, The Bridgeman Art Library, London; 17.15, Giraudon/Art Resource, New York; 17.17, Scala/Art Resource, New York; 17.18, Scala/Art Resource, New York; 17.19, Giraudon/Art Resource, New York; 17.20 Scala/Art Resource, New York; 17.21 Archiv für Kunst und Geschichte, Berlin; 17.22, Archiv für Kunst und Geschichte, Berlin.

Chapter Eighteen 18.1, Giraudon/Art Resource, New York; 18.2, Courtesy National Buildings Record, London; 18.4, The Bridgeman Art Library, London; 18.6, The Granger Collection, New York; 18.8, The Bridgeman Art Library, London; 18.10 Archiv für Kunst und Geschichte, Berlin; 18.11, Archiv für Kunst und Geschichte, Berlin; 18.15, Scala/Art Resource, New York; 18.16, Giraudon/Art Resource, New York.

Chapter Nineteen 19.1, The Bridgeman Art Library, London; 19.3, The Bettmann Archive/Hulton Picture Library; 19.5, The Granger Collection; 19.6, Giraudon/Art Resource, New York; 19.9, Courtesy Oslo Kommunes Kunstsamlinger/Munchforlaget A/S; 19.10 Lauros-Giraudon/Art Resource, New York; 19.19, ©1991 Succession H. Matisse/ARS New York; 19.20 ©1991 ARS New York/SPADEM; 19.21, ©1991 ARS New York/SPADEM; 19.22, ©1991 ARS New York/ADAGP; 19.24, ©Thomas Payne; 19.25, Hedrich-Blessing/Chicago Historical Society.

Chapter Twenty 20.1, Archiv für Kunst und Geschichte, Berlin. ©1991 ARS New York/SPADEM; 20.4, AP/Wide World Photos; 20.5, Margaret Bourke-White, Life Magazine ©1950 Time Warner Inc.; 20.6, AP/Wide World Photos; 20.7, ©1991 ARS New York/SPADEM; 20.8, ©Estate of George Grosz/VAGA, New York 1991; 20.9, ©1991 ARS New York/ADAGP; 20.11, ©Estate of Piet Mondrian/VAGA, New York 1991; 20.12, ©1991 ARS new York/SPADEM; 20.15, ©1991 Demart Pro Arte/ARS New York; 20.18, ©1991 Succession H. Matisse/ARS New York; 20.19, Artothek, Peissenberg, Germany. ©Estate of Max Beckmann/VAGA, New York 1991; 20.20, ©1991 ARS New York/SPADEM; 20.21, Archiv für Kunst und Geschichte, Berlin. ©1991 ARS New York/SPADEM.

Chapter Twenty-One 21.2, United Nations Photo Library; 21.3, ©1991 The Estate and Foundation of Andy Warhol/ARS New York; 21.4, John A. Darnell, Life Magazine ©1970 Time Warner Inc.; 21.5, Patrick Piel/Gamma-Liaison; 21.6, AP/Wide World Photos; 21.7, United Nations Photo Library; 21.8, ©1991 The Estate of Keith Haring; 21.12, ©1991 Pollock-Krasner Foundation/ARS New York; 21.13, ©1991 Kate Rothko-Prizel and Christopher Rothko/ARS New York; 21.14, ©Helen Frankenthaler; 21.15, ©Jasper Johns/VAGA New York 1991; 21.16, ©Robert Rauschenberg/VAGA, New York 1991; 21.17, ©1991 The Estate and Foundation of Andy Warhol/ARS New York; 21.18, ©The Tate Gallery, Millbank, London; 21.20, ©George Segal/VAGA, New York ____; 21.21, Ezra Stoller/Esto; 21.26, ©1991 Frank Stella/ARS New York; 21.28, William Watkins/Courtesy Vent____; 21.29, PHOTRI Inc./Ken Kaminsky; 21.30, Courtesy John Burgee Associates; 21.31, ©Ebet Roberts, with ____ New York.